DUTCH PURITANISM

DUTCH PURITANISM

A History of English and Scottish Churches of the Netherlands in the Sixteenth and Seventeenth Centuries

BY

KEITH L. SPRUNGER

WIPF & STOCK · Eugene, Oregon

Wipf and Stock Publishers
199 W 8th Ave, Suite 3
Eugene, OR 97401

Dutch Puritanism
A History of English and Scottish Churches of the Netherlands
in the Sixteenth and Seventeenth Centuries
By Sprunger, Keith L.
Copyright©1982 by Sprunger, Keith L.
ISBN 13: 978-1-5326-0932-9
Publication date 10/14/2016
Previously published by E. J. Brill, 1982

*To
David, Mary
and Philip*

CONTENTS

Preface... IX
Abbreviations... XII

PART ONE

SIXTEENTH-CENTURY BEGINNINGS

I. Britain and the Netherlands: Ancient and Familiar Neighbours....................................... 3
II. English Religion in the Sixteenth-Century Netherlands... 13

PART TWO

THE CHURCH BUILDING AGE (1600-1660)

III. The Amsterdam Separatists and Anabaptists........... 43
IV. The English Reformed Church at Amsterdam 1607 to 1660.. 91
V. Churches at Leiden, The Hague, and Delft to 1660...... 123
VI. Churches at Rotterdam, Brielle, and Dort to 1660...... 162
VII. The Churches in Zeeland: Middelburg, Flushing, and Veere to 1660....................................... 187
VIII. The Utrecht and Arnhem Churches to 1660............ 212
IX. The Merchant Adventurers............................ 233
X. Churches on the Military Frontier in Brabant, Gelderland and Overijssel................................ 262
XI. The English Synod, Printing and Other Puritan Enterprises... 285
XII. Developments in Theology and Church Government..... 319
XIII. Relations between the Dutch and British Churches...... 354
XIV. Times of Wars and Revolution 1640-1670.............. 378

PART THREE

FROM THE RESTORATION TO THE GLORIOUS REVOLUTION (1660-1700)

XV. After the Restoration: Churches at Amsterdam, Haarlem, Leiden, The Hague, Delft 1660-1700.............. 397

XVI. The Post-Restoration Churches at Rotterdam, Dort, Middelburg, Flushing, Veere, and Utrecht 1660-1700.... 427
XVII. Epilogue: The Puritan Mind in England, The Netherlands, and America 457
Bibliography... 462
  I. Manuscripts... 462
 II. Primary Sources 465
III. Secondary Works... 466
Index of Persons 471
Index of Subjects and Places... 480

PREFACE

The history of the English and Scottish churches of the Netherlands in the sixteenth and seventeenth centuries reaches out in many directions. During the period of 1550 to 1700 numerous Netherlands British churches were closely interrelated with events in England, Scotland, and America. Six of the churches were founded in the sixteenth century, and during the seventeenth century another thirty-four emerged, counting officially established churches, garrison churches, and Separatist congregations (at least forty English-language churches in all). Hundreds of English and Scottish ministers (I worked with a file of over 350 ministers) served the Netherlands English-Scottish churches or otherwise resided or traveled in the Low Countries from 1550 to 1700. These churches were almost uniformly Puritan in theology and practice, or if Scottish, Presbyterian and Covenanter. A large portion of the preachers in the pulpit were Puritans or Covenanter Scots, many of them in forced exile. During the Puritan Revolution, however, the tide reversed, and as the Puritans went home, Anglicans became the exiles of the 1640s and 1650s. After the Restoration, the Puritans came back.

This study attempts, first of all, to give an overall history of the English-language churches functioning in the Dutch Netherlands 1550-1700. Second, the emphasis is on the connection of the overseas churches to the Puritan and Covenanter movements of England, Scotland, and America. International Puritanism had three interconnected centers: England, America, and the Netherlands. The Dutch side of the story is best approached through the history of the various congregations of the Netherlands, in which the Puritans made their headquarters. Puritanism was a wide movement of English Calvinist dissent against established Anglican religion, including Presbyterians, Separatists and non-Separatists, Congregationalists, and Baptists; and in its broadest sense Puritanism also encompasses the origins of English Anabaptism and Quakerism. Although the Spanish Netherlands functioned in a similar role to English Catholics, they are not included in this history.

There have been many books on aspects of English religion in the Netherlands, especially on the Separatists of Amsterdam and Leiden. Like all scholars of Dutch Puritanism, I am much indebted to the Separatist studies of Henry M. Dexter, Champlin Burrage, B. R. White, and Leland Carlson; and to Raymond P. Stearns, my advisor in graduate school days, and Alice Clare Carter for their work on the non-

Separatist English churches. Building on their work, my goal has been to write a general history of all the churches, Separatist and non-Separatist, Puritan and Anglican, and to show the relationship of each to the larger picture of English-Scottish religion in the Low Countries.

The research and writing has been mostly pleasure. The work began on my first sabbatical from Bethel College in 1969-70, which was spent in Amsterdam and London. I returned to England and the Netherlands in the summer of 1973 and for my second sabbatical in 1976-77. Perhaps much of the writing could have been done in Kansas, but it has been immensely more pleasurable to be on the scene in England and the Netherlands. Grants from the Social Science Research Council and the American Philosophical Society in 1969-70 and a fellowship from the American Council of Learned Societies in 1976-77 are gratefully acknowledged. I also received assistance from the Bethel College faculty development fund.

A traveling scholar (in search of Puritan history) is daily dependent on the expert assistance of librarians and archivists, and I thank each one who helped to make my work possible. In England: The British Museum (now the British Library), the Public Record Office, the Bodleian Library and the libraries of Merton College and Regents Park, Oxford; Dr. Williams's Library; St. Bride's Printing Library; Lambeth Palace Library; Registry Office, Somerset House. In Scotland: The Scottish Record Office; New College Library, Edinburgh; the National Library of Scotland. In the Netherlands: Koninklijke Bibliotheek of The Hague, the university libraries of Amsterdam, Leiden, and Utrecht; the Algemeen Rijksarchief, The Hague; the library and archives of the Nederlandse Hervormde Kerk, 100 Javastraat, The Hague; the Archief and Library Ver. Doopsgezinde Gemeente, Amsterdam; the Rijksarchieven of Gelderland, Zeeland, Utrecht, and Noord-Brabant; the Gemeente Archieven of Amsterdam, Arnhem, Bergen op Zoom, Breda, Brielle, Delft, Dordrecht, Gorinchem, Haarlem, The Hague, 's-Hertogenbosch, Leiden, Nijmegen, Rotterdam, Utrecht, and Vlissingen. The archives of Hamburg, Zutphen, Zwolle, and Gouda gave me help by correspondence. I express special thanks to John Russell and James Morrison for access to the archives of the Scots Church of Rotterdam and to Ds. C. Hamoen for use of the records at the church of Heusden. And not least of all, thanks to Martha Stucky and the staff of the Bethel College Library and to Robert Kreider, David Haury, and the staff of the Mennonite Library and Archives at Bethel College.

Many friends and scholars were helpful along the way. I can only mention a few: Dr. Simon Hart of the Gemeente Archief of Amsterdam for his vast knowledge of Amsterdam history and introduction into the notary archives; fellow scholars of British-Dutch church history, Michael Moody and Ian Cranna, for clues and suggestions; Rosalie Neufeld for expert typing. I also wish to express my thanks to Professor Heiko A. Oberman for his helpful suggestions and for including this book in the series *Studies in the History of Christian Thought*. Most of all I am grateful to my wife Aldine and my children, David, Mary, and Philip, who joined me for periodic treks to England and Holland, always sustaining interest and all good will towards the Puritans, in whose steps we trod.

Bethel College
North Newton, Kansas   Keith L. Sprunger

ABBREVIATIONS

A.H.R.	*American Historical Review.*
A.R.A.	Algemeen Rijksarchief, The Hague.
B.L.	*Biografisch lexicon voor de geschiedenis van het Nederlandse Potestantisme.* Vol. 1. Kampen: J. H. Kok, 1978.
B.M.	British Museum, London.
Bod.	Bodleian Library, Oxford.
B.P.	Boswell Papers, Add. MSS. 6394, 6395, B.M.
Brook, *Puritans*	Benjamin Brook. *The Lives of the Puritans.* 3 vols. London, 1813.
Browne, *Congregationalism*	John Browne. *History of Congregationalism and Memorials of the Churches in Norfolk and Suffolk.* London, 1877.
Burrage, *E.E.D.*	Champlin Burrage. *The Early English Dissenters in the Light of Recent Research.* 2 vols. Cambridge: Cambridge Univ. Press, 1912
B.W.P.G.N.	*Biographisch woordenboek van protestantsche godgeleerden in Nederland.* 5 vols. The Hague: Nijhoff, 1919-56.
Calamy, *N.M.*	Edmund Calamy. *The Nonconformist's Memorial.* 2nd ed. 3 vols. London, 1802-03.
Cal.S.P.D.	*Calendar of State Papers Domestic.*
Carleton, *Letters*	Sir Dudley Carleton. *The Letters from and to Sir Dudley Carleton.* London, 1757.
C.R.	Consistory Register.
Davids, *Annals*	T. W. Davids. *Annals of Evangelical Nonconformity in the County of Essex.* London, 1863.
Dexter, *Congregationalism*	Henry Martyn Dexter. *The Congregationalism of the Last Three Hundred Years.* 2 vols. New York: Harper & Brothers, 1880.
Dexter and Dexter, *England and Holland*	Henry Martyn Dexter and Morton Dexter. *The England and Holland of the Pilgrims.* Boston: Houghton Mifflin, 1905.
D.N.B.	*Dictionary of National Biography.*
D.W.L.	Doctor Williams's Library, London.
E.H.R.	*English Historical Review.*
E.R.C.	English Reformed Church.
Franeker Univ. Album	*Album Studiosorum Academiae Franekerensis, 1585-1811, 1816-1864.* Franeker, 1968.
Fuller, *C.H.*	Thomas Fuller. *The Church History of Britain.* 3rd ed. 3 vols. London, 1842.
Ferguson, *Scots Brigade*	James Ferguson. *Papers Illustrating the History of the Scots Brigade.* 3 vols. Edinburgh, 1899-1901.
F.E.S.	*Fasti Ecclesiae Scoticanae.* Ed. H. Scott. 8 vols. Edinburgh, 1915-50.
G.A.	Gemeente Archief (municipal archive).
Hanbury, *Memorials*	Benjamin Hanbury. *Historical Memorials relating to the Independents, or Congregationalists.* 3 vols. London, 1839-44.
H.M.C.	Historical Manuscripts Commission.
Hoop Scheffer, "De Brownisten te Amsterdam"	J. G. de Hoop Scheffer. "De Brownisten te Amsterdam gedurende den eersten tijd na hunne vestiging," *Verslagen en Mededeelingen van de Koninklijk Academie van Wetenschappen afd. Letterkunde* (1881).
Hoop Scheffer, *Free Churchmen*	J. G. de Hoop Scheffer. *History of the Free Churchmen Called Brownists, Pilgrim Fathers and Baptists in the Dutch Republic.* Ed. William E. Griffis. Ithaca, N.Y., 1922.
Hessels, *E.L.B.A.*	J. H. Hessels. *Ecclesiae Londino-Batavae Archivum.* 3 vols. Cambridge, 1887.

Knuttel, *Acta Synoden Zuid-Holland*	W. P. C. Knuttel. *Acta der particuliere synoden van Zuid-Holland 1621-1700*. 6 vols. The Hague, 1908-16.
Leiden Univ. *Album*	*Album Studiosorum Academiae Lugduno Batavae, MDLXXV-MDCCLXXV.* The Hague, 1875.
Mather, *Magnalia*	Cotton Mather. *Magnalia Christi Americana*. Ed. Thomas Robbins. 2 vols. New York: Russell and Russell, 1967.
Matthews, *Cal. R.*	A. G. Matthews. *Calamy Revised*. Oxford, 1934.
Matthews, *W.R.*	A. G. Matthews. *Walker Revised*. Oxford, 1948.
N.A.K.	*Nederlands Archief voor Kerkgeschiedenis.*
N.H.A.	Nederlandse Hervormde Kerk Archief, 100 Javastraat. The Hague.
N.H.K.	Nederlandse Hervormde Kerk.
N.N.B.W.	*Nieuw Nederlandsch Biografisch Woordenboek*. 10 vols. Leiden, 1911-37.
Not. Archive	Notarial Archive.
P.C. *Acts*	*Acts of the Privy Council* (1613-1631). London, 1921-64.
R.A.	Rijksarchief.
Reitsma and Van Veen	J. Reitsma and S. D. van Veen. *Acta der provinciale en particuliere synoden, gehouden in de noordelijke Nederlanden gedurende de jaren 1572-1620*. 8 vols. Groningen, 1892-99.
Res.	Resolutiën, Resolutions.
Steven	William Steven. *The History of the Scottish Church, Rotterdam.* Edinburgh, 1833.
Thurloe, *S.P.*	John Thurloe. *A Collection of the State Papers*. 7 vols. London, 1742.
T.C.H.S.	*Transactions* of the Congregational Historical Society.
Utrecht Univ. *Album*	*Album Studiosorum Academiae Rheno-Trajectinae MDCXXXVI-MDCCCLXXXVI.* Utrecht, 1886.
Venn and Venn	John Venn and J. A. Venn. *Alumni Cantabrigienses*. Cambridge, 1922-54.
Walker, *Creeds*	Williston Walker. *The Creeds and Platforms of Congregationalism*. 1893; rpt. Boston: The Pilgrim Press, 1960.
Winwood, *Memorials*	Ralph Winwood. *Memorials of Affairs of State*. 3 vols. London, 1725.
Wood, *Ath. Oxon.*	Anthony A. Wood. *Athenae Oxonienses*. 4 vols. London, 1813-20.

ERRATA AND ADDENDA

P. 50, line 19. Vloonburg

P. 76, Section on Anabaptism. For more information on English Anabaptism in Holland, see the following articles:

> Keith Sprunger and Mary Sprunger, "The Church in the Bakehouse: John Smyth's English Anabaptist Congregation at Amsterdam, 1609–1660," *Mennonite Quarterly Review*, 85 (April 2011), 219–58.

> Keith Sprunger, "The Meeting of Dutch Anabaptists and English Brownists: Reported by P. J. Twisck," in *The Contentious Triangle: Church, State, and University*, ed. Rodney L. Petersen and Calvin Augustine Pater (Kirksville: Thomas Jefferson Press, 1999), 221–231.

P. 76, note 162. S. P. 84, vol. 154, fol. 44

P. 141, section on Leiden Printers. For more on the Pilgrim Press, see chapter by Keith Sprunger, "The Godly Ministry by Brewster and Brewer, 170–77, in *The Pilgrim Press*, (a revised edition of the 1920 book by Harris and Jones), ed. by R. Breugelmans (Nieuwkoop: De Graaf Publishers, 1987).

P. 237, line 5. Forbes at Delft kept up the Antwerp–Middelburg tradition . . .

P. 268, line 10. I John 2:21.

PART ONE

SIXTEENTH-CENTURY BEGINNINGS

CHAPTER ONE

BRITAIN AND THE NETHERLANDS: "ANCIENT AND FAMILIAR NEIGHBOURS"

The histories of Britain and the Netherlands overlap at many points. The waters separating England from the Continent, although a barrier, could serve just as well as a bridge for frequent intercourse. Ships and people went back and forth; by the reign of Elizabeth, England had closer links with the Netherlands than with any other country.[1] They were allies in the same struggle against Spain; they were embued with a common Protestant spirit; they traded with each other. The townspeople of Flushing in 1572, fearing the Spanish and the French, hailed the English as "their ancient friends and neighbours." Elizabeth used a similar phrase in a declaration of 1585, in which she called the Dutch "most ancient and familiar neighbours."[2] Although not perpetually friendly, the relationship was strong.

The British were a traveling and colonizing people. The English-Scottish migration to America is a famous story, but their movement eastward to the Continent played a nearly equal role in British history. The migration to the Continent, at least up to about 1650, very likely equaled or exceeded the American immigration: "A man had to decide whether to go to New England or to Holland, and some thousands chose the latter refuge."[3] The English community in the northern and southern Netherlands was larger than "all the people of English extraction scattered over the rest of the continent."[4] A similar community of Dutchmen resided in England in several populous centers, largely as a result of a sixteenth-century Protestant migration to escape from the Spanish furies. The chief places of Dutch concentration were at London, Norwich, Canterbury, Colchester, Yarmouth, Southampton, Maidstone, and Sandwich.[5] Opening the doors to the distressed Dutch

---

[1] J. R. Jones, *Britain and Europe in the Seventeenth Century* (New York: W. W. Norton, 1966), p. 38.

[2] Charles Wilson, *Queen Elizabeth and the Revolt of the Netherlands* (Berkeley: Univ. of California Press, 1970), p. 29; Jones, *Britain and Europe*, p. 38.

[3] Carl Bridenbaugh, *Vexed and Troubled Englishmen, 1590-1642* (New York: Oxford Univ. Press, 1968), pp. 395, 466.

[4] John W. Stoye, *English Travellers Abroad, 1604-1667: Their Influence in English Society and Politics* (London: Jonathan Cape, 1952), p. 240.

[5] F. Dekker, *Voortrekkers van Oud-Nederland in Engeland, Frankrijk, Achter-Indië, Formosa en Perzie* (The Hague: Boucher, 1947), chapter 1; J. F. Bense, *The Anglo-Dutch Relations from the Earliest Times to the Death of William the Third* (The Hague: Nijhoff, 1924), pp. 101-07.

refugees, thought Thomas Fuller, was "the honest paying of a due debt" for the hospitality given earlier to the Marian exiles on the Continent.[6] The Flemish refugees also brought with them to England the art of the "New Drapery," which soon produced great economic gains for the English cloth industry. The traffic between the two countries went both ways.[7]

Immigration to the Low Countries was no peculiar thing. The entire Netherlands, in a sense, was a nation of strangers. Although the Netherlands, as the economic center of northern Europe, naturally drew an international population, its cosmopolitan complexion came also from the tolerant policy, after the United Provinces gained their independence from Spain, of allowing intellectual and religious dissenters to come in. "No part of Europe so hanted with all sorts of Forreners," exclaimed English traveler James Howell in 1622. Seven or eight languages were in daily use in the business centers.[8] Mingling in the Dutch cities were southern Netherlanders, English Brownists, Jews, merchants from all over Europe, sailors and foreign artisans seeking employment, authors of indiscreet books, unorthodox philosophers like Descartes and Pierre Bayle. At Amsterdam, the chief city of the Netherlands, strangers were the rule. Of sailors marrying at Amsterdam, over half were not native Dutch at all, but German, Norwegian, Swedish, Danish, and English.[9] Throughout the Eighty Years War, the majority of soldiers serving the Dutch were foreign, and the East India and West India companies depended on men recruited abroad.[10] Sir William Boswell, ambassador to the Netherlands, in 1635 "upon most credible informacion" estimated that one-fifth or more of sailors on Dutch ships were English and Scots.[11] Once arrived in the Netherlands, the refugee of conscience was fairly safe from harassment. "Hardly any Alliance, Treaties, or Interests, have ever been able to divert or remove them." The seventeenth-century French ambassador never regained a single French fugitive by extradition, and the English government fared almost as bad in recovering

---

[6] Fuller, *C. H.*, II, 405.

[7] Charles Wilson, *England's Apprenticeship, 1603-1763* (New York: St. Martin's, 1966), p. 75; John J. Murray, "The Cultural Impact of the Flemish Low Countries on Sixteenth- and Seventeenth-Century England," *A. H. R.*, 62 (July 1957), 837-54.

[8] James Howell, *Epistolae Ho-Elianae. Familiar Letters Domestic and Forren*, 2nd ed. (London, 1650), II, 26; Paul Zumthor, *Daily Life in Rembrandt's Holland*, trans. S. W. Taylor (New York: Macmillan, 1963), pp. 261-65.

[9] Simon Hart, "The Dutch and North America in the First Half of the Seventeenth Century. Some Aspects," *Mededelingen van de Nederlandse Vereniging voor Zeegeschiedenis*, 20 (Mar. 1970), 7.

[10] Charles R. Boxer, *The Dutch Seaborne Empire: 1660-1800* (New York: Alfred A. Knopf, 1970), pp. 89-90.

[11] S. P. 84, vol. 149, fol. 114.

fugitives.[12] When the going got rough at home, the door was nearly always open in the Netherlands.

Dutch toleration paid off handsomely in expanding commerce and population. "No sort of people was denyed admission there."[13] Dutch Calvinist religion proved to be particularly congenial to economic development.[14] So much so, that cynical Englishmen accused the Dutch of having no values but profit, allowing such disorder of opinion "and what not" as a means of increasing trade. "They admit persons of all countries and opinions amongst them, knowing well that this liberty draws people, numbers of people increase trade, and that trade brings money."[15] From an orthodox viewpoint, tolerance was the debasing of pure religion, but in profits and prosperity the Dutch method worked. Sir William Temple (English ambassador 1668-70) granted that "Religion may possibly do more good in other places, But it does less hurt here."[16]

Numerically, the English-Scottish community in the Netherlands, although one of the smaller foreign groups, was in the tens of thousands. The English ambassador in 1624 reckoned them as a major factor in relations between the two countries: "the number of your majesties subjects, both English and Scottish as well soldiers as inhabitants, being great in these provinces."[17] The largest segment of the British was soldiers serving in the pay of the States General in the war against Spain. Beginning in 1585, England provided between 5,000 and 6,000 troops and this number prevailed well into the seventeenth century.[18] By 1621, four English regiments and two Scottish regiments were 13,000 men if at full strength. A force of six regiments, about one hundred companies, was the rule up into the 1640s.[19]

Another clue to the size of the English-Scottish community comes from the English churches in the Dutch cities. At Leiden 200 British households petitioned for a church in 1609; at Flushing 128 English households petitioned in 1619; at Utrecht 120 English households peti-

---

[12] William Temple, *Observations upon the United Provinces of the Netherlands*, ed. George Clark (Oxford: Clarendon Press, 1972), p. 113; Zumthor, *Rembrandt's Holland*, p. 263; K. H. Haley, *The Dutch in the Seventeenth Century* (New York: Harcourt, Brace, Jovanovich, 1972), p. 169.

[12] Roger Coke, *A Discourse of Trade* (London, 1670), p. 53.

[14] John Northleigh, *Topographical Descriptions: With Historico-Political, and Medico-Physical Observations* (London, 1702), p. 109; Jelle C. Riemersma, *Religious Factors in Early Dutch Capitalism, 1550-1650* (The Hague: Mouton, 1967), pp. 83-84.

[15] John Reresby, *The Memoirs and Travels of Sir John Reresby* (London, 1813), pp. 156-57; Gerardt Brandt, *Historie der Reformatie* (Amsterdam, 1671), I, 811.

[16] Temple, *Observations*, p. 107.

[17] S. P. 84, vol. 117, fol. 132.

[18] Wilson, *Elizabeth and the Revolt*, p. 86.

[19] S. P. 84, vol. 104, fols. 189-90.

tioned in 1622, at Delft 70 families in 1636.[20] At Amsterdam the English Reformed church in 1607 had 68 members and by 1623 the membership had increased to 450, and it was only one of six English churches in the city.[21] Nearly every town with any significant trade with Britain had a colony of British residents and other British monuments: an *Engelse kerk* or *Schotse kerk, Engelse huis, Engelse kaai*, or even, as at Harlingen, the brothel at "the sign of the King of England."[22]

The records of early English immigration to the Netherlands are scanty, but some clues remain through passport records preserved at Yarmouth for the years 1637-39. These reveal that between Michaelmas, 1637 and Michaelmas, 1638 a total of 337 passengers sailed to the Netherlands for reasons of travel, trade, manufacturing, and military service. Although carefully hiding their true intentions, some of the Yarmouth passengers were religious refugees.[23] Many were skilled workers, taking their crafts abroad. "Multitudes" have gone over, complained Roger Coke, so that, he grandly judged, Rotterdam, Middelburg, and Flushing by his time, the 1670s, "are about ¼ *English*, and of *English* extraction." Obviously an exaggeration, but Coke was an economist making a point: Free trade and free emigration pays off in profits for the Dutch, "which at this day is as much advantageous to the *Dutch*, and prejudiced to us."[24]

The English and Scots resided in all of the chief towns, with large concentrations at Amsterdam, Rotterdam, The Hague, Leiden, Utrecht, Delft, Dort, Veere, Middelburg, Brielle, and Flushing. The latter two were the cautionary towns under English governance 1585-1616, "by reason whereof many of his Majesty's subjectes have long lived in these townes, and have planted themselves and their familyes."[25]

In most cases, the English and Scots were hospitably entertained with liberty to shape their own lives. Their economic skills and military service made them a valued part of Dutch cosmopolitan society. Puritan religious and intellectual deviations caused little commotion, the Dutch

---

[20] See below, chapters on Leiden, Flushing, Utrecht, Delft.

[21] Alice C. Carter, *The English Reformed Church in Amsterdam in the Seventeenth Century* (Amsterdam: Scheltema & Holkema, 1964), p. 116.

[22] W. B. S. Boeles, *Frieslands Hoogeschool en het Rijks Athenaeum te Franeker* (Leeuwarden: H. Kuipers, 1878-79), I, 481.

[23] As for example, Paul Amyraut and Julius Hering, ejected ministers, Charles B. Jewson, *Transcript of Three Registers of Passengers from Great Yarmouth to Holland and New England, 1637-1639*, Norfolk Record Society, 25 (1954), 5, 25, 48; Stoye, *English Travellers*, pp. 240-41.

[24] Coke, *Discourse*, pp. 52-53; Margaret James, *Social Problems and Policy during the Puritan Revolution* (New York, Barnes & Noble, 1966), p. 368.

[25] P. C. *Acts*, 1615-16, pp. 541-42.

"not troubling their heads so much with other points of Religion."[26] Among the Dutch amenities provided for the British settlers was financial provision for churches; these offered not only food for the British soul but also served as the central focus of English-Scottish life in the different cities. The *Engelse* or *Schotse Kerk* was the one British institution uniformly found in all the scattered British communities. The British church was a political, economic, social, and religious institution.

Although the Netherlands settlements of English-Scottish people rivaled in size the settlements in the New World, their history and development differ. The American was likely to be a permanent settler, whereas the settler in the Netherlands was probably transient, serving in the army or trade for a few years with the intention of someday returning "home." The tolerant Dutch environment encouraged mingling and assimilation, so that the British families that remained for a generation became more Dutch than British. After only thirteen years, the Pilgrim Fathers in 1620 could see it coming, "How likely we were to lose our language, and our name of English."[27] Although only a small percentage stayed long enough to be transformed into Dutchmen, the Dutch sojourn seldom failed to leave its mark.

Apart from casual travelers, the British community drew primarily four kinds of settlers: merchants and workers (economic men), students, soldiers, and religious refugees. Economically, England and the Netherlands were interrelated by trade. In the early seventeenth century, the Dutch were the world economic power and the English a "junior partner." As late as 1670, the volume of Dutch-owned shipping "considerably exceeded" that of England, Spain, Portugal, France, Scotland, and Germany combined. The products of her workshops commanded wide markets, and her ships carried the trade of all western Europe. The Dutch were "the main source of British imports, the principal market, finishing depot and retail centre for British exports"; however, across the years, British dependence gradually diminished.[28] The primary English cloth trade to the Continent was in the hands of the Merchant Adventurers. In addition to the great economic men who made their fortunes in the Netherlands, there was also a steady stream of little people who hoped to find some modest prosperity on the other side, among them the artisans of 1631 who "by reasons of deadness of trade and change of

---

[26] Thomas Edwards, *Reasons against the Independent Government of Particular Congregations* (London, 1641), p. 38.

[27] Winslow in Edward Arbor, ed., *The Story of the Pilgrim Fathers, 1606-1623 A.D.* (London: Ward and Downey, 1897), p. 263.

[28] Wilson, *England's Apprenticeship*, pp. 39-42, 271. *The Cambridge Economic History of Europe* (Cambridge: Cambridge Univ. Press, 1967), IV, 210.

fashion have travelled for work and found the same at Amsterdam."[29] After the Restoration, ambassador George Downing reported that craftsmen and tradesmen *"come daily from England hither"* and *"also bring with them their families,* and who *pretend* the reason thereof to be *for the liberty of their consciences."*[30]

To the south and east, on the military frontiers, soldiers and their families were the bulk of the settlers, drawn as mercenaries fighting in the wars. "Pay day, O pay day, O sweete pay day, come away, make hast."[31] For sweet pay, British soldiers fought on both sides.[32] "God hath stirred up this action to be a school to breed up soldiers to defend the freedom of England," declared Thomas Wilford, "a most fit school and nursery to nourish soldiers."[33] A great part of the Dutch field army fighting the Spanish, and several of the most famous officers, were English and Scottish. Down to the English Revolution, the Netherlands was the training camp, "school and nursery," for English officers.[34] Along with military skills, the troops were also indoctrinated in Puritan religion, which was prevalent among the Dutch chaplains.

Students to the Netherlands went as first choice to Leiden University, founded in 1575, and occasionally to Franeker University, founded in 1585. Between 1575 and 1675, about 950 English-speaking students matriculated at Leiden.[35] Franeker, although less attractive to English students because of its geographical location, always had its group of the *Engelse natie,* some of them drawn there specifically to study with William Ames, professor of theology, 1622-1633. Although only a few English and Scottish students, about two or three a year, actually matriculated at Franeker, the number of drifting students was considerably larger. When Doctor Ames transferred from Franeker to a pastorate at Rotterdam in 1633, he was expected to carry along to Rotterdam ten or twenty English students.[36] Utrecht University, founded in 1636, attracted nonconformist English and Scottish students in large numbers, especially after 1660. The Dutch universities were prominent academic centers in their own

---

[29] Carter, *English Reformed Church,* p. 117.

[30] T. H. Lister, *Life and Administration of Edward, First Earl of Clarendon* (London, 1837-38), III, 218; James, *Social Problems,* pp. 60, 368.

[31] Thomas Raymond, *Autobiography,* ed. G. Davies, Camden Society, 3rd ser., 28 (1917), 39.

[32] For example, Sir Roger Williams, in his *The Actions of the Low Countries,* ed. D. W. Davies (Ithaca: Cornell Univ. Press, 1964).

[33] Wilson, *Elizabeth and the Revolt,* p. 91.

[34] John W. Fortescue, *A History of the British Army* (London: Macmillan, 1899), I, 134, 168-69.

[35] Stoye, *English Travellers,* p. 295.

[36] Boeles, *Frieslands Hoogeschool,* I, 26; Keith L. Sprunger, *The Learned Doctor William Ames* (Urbana: Univ. of Illinois Press, 1972), p. 237.

right; and with their Calvinist theology, they were attractive for sons of Puritan-minded families in England. At Utrecht, Professor Gisbertus Voetius was a great Puritan inspiration and friend of English and Scots.[37]

Wherever they went, the British settlers established churches. The churches, of which there were "25 or 30" by 1630,[38] preserved English and Scottish identity and culture. In some cities, the English were split into two, three, or even more congregations as at Amsterdam, Rotterdam, and Leiden. Most of these churches were Puritan-inclined, "Seminaries of disorderly preachers." Although the members of the congregations were merchants, artisans, soldiers, and students who had come over for their own business, mostly respectable people, the ministers serving the churches were nonconformist Puritans, fugitives sometimes. As Sir Dudley Carleton pointed out in 1637, "The difficulty of haveing men of learning and sober life together and conformable to our Church, to supply those poor places in the Low Countreys appeared to me allwayes to be the cheif reason and occasion, that inconformable men were there used."[39] In the case of the Separatists, entire congregations migrated as a group. The Dutch toleration policies made the Netherlands the "hiding place" for English Puritans.[40] Many chapters of the Puritan story happened in the Low Countries.

The relationship of the English and Scottish churches to the Continent is part of a larger story of Christian connections between Britain and Europe: Boniface preaching and converting in Friesland, Willabrod crossing over to become bishop of Utrecht, the Marian exiles at Frankfurt, Erasmus at Oxford. Owen Chadwick in an essay on the English church and Europe observed that "the history of the Reformation in England is to a large extent a history of continental influences upon English minds."[41] When the religious situation became repressive at home, exile to a more hospitable place was one answer—shifting the nucleus of religious dissent abroad. The establishment of religion in exile happened several times, as with the Marian exiles, the Catholic exiles, and to a certain extent, the Puritans in the early seventeenth century. Running away? Of course, but thereby the dissenting movements were preserved and nurtured. Historian Thomas Fuller found a most convenient text for the exiles in the Saviour's precept: "But when they

---

[37] "Schotten en Britten te Utrecht," *Maandblad van "Oud-Utrecht,"* 27 (Jan. 1954), 124.
[38] S. P. 16, vol. 224, no. 57.
[39] B. P., I, 250-51.
[40] William Bridge, *The True Souldiers Convoy* (Rotterdam, 1640), p. 69.
[41] In C. R. Dodwell, ed., *The English Church and the Continent* (London: Faith Press, 1959), p. 60.

persecute you in this city, flee into another."[42] English religion has a significant history not only in England proper but at outposts at Amsterdam, Rotterdam, Leiden, Utrecht, and in America. "Therefore thus sayeth the Lorde," reported Robert Browne from Middelburg, "I feede not my flocke at Paules Crosse in London, or *Saint Maries in Cambridge*, or in your Englishe Parishes."[43]

The effect of this scattering of English religion was a radicalizing one. The ministers who led the foreign congregations were themselves many times of extremist views, and their Puritan nonconformity rubbed off on the rank and file of the congregation. The continental example of simplified, Reformed theology and practice made a strong impression. The Marian exiles at Frankfurt "abrogated many things formerly used by them in the church of England," so laying some of the foundations for Puritanism. Their Church of England liturgy, they learned from Calvin, contained "foolish things."[44] In the Netherlands, English refugees formulated many of the tenets of Separatism and English Anabaptism, and some of them learned free will from Arminius. If the radical innovations from Holland and other distant places had been quarantined across the water, the story would be much shorter; but in the constant travel to and fro, ideas were blown about, infecting Britain and nourishing its nonconformist spirits. Even in 1702, a powerful argument for establishing Anglican churches in the Netherlands was to prevent Puritan infiltration by nipping it in the bud: "Hitherto those bred in Holland have returned for the most part with great prejudices against the Church, because they could receive instruction from none but Enemies or those who were themselves ignorant of the doctrine & worship of the Church of England."[45]

Those coastal parts of England having most contact with the Netherlands or other Reformed areas were most likely to be saturated with foreign doctrines. For this reason, the Bishop of Norwich complained in 1530 that erroneous religious beliefs most infected "merchants and such that hath their abiding not far from the sea."[46] Not only was this the case in sixteenth- and seventeenth-century East Anglia and London, but in nearly all trading cities. At York the most obstinate Puritans were merchants with extensive foreign connections in the Netherlands and Prussia; the situation was the same at Newcastle on Tyne, where mer-

---

[42] Fuller, *C. H.*, II, 405.
[43] Robert Browne, *The Writings of Robert Harrison and Robert Browne*, ed. Albert Peel and Leland H. Carlson (London: George Allen and Unwin, 1953), p. 208.
[44] Fuller, *C. H.*, II, 407, 411.
[45] Finch Papers, Add. MS. 29,588, fol. 348 (B. M.).
[46] A. C. Dickens, *The English Reformation* (New York: Schocken Books, 1969), p. 69.

chants traded with Amsterdam and the Baltic cities. "It is not possible to discount the effect of these foreign influences on Newcastle," wrote Roger Howell.[47] The Archbishop of Canterbury in dealing with commotions at Yarmouth laid the blame on "continual intercourse with those of Amsterdam."[48] If the Netherlands could have been cut off as a sanctuary for Puritanism, or if the foreign innovations in religion could have been kept away, the history of Puritanism and English religion as a whole would have been much different. The Netherlands served "as a refuge of such ministers of both nations as could not conforme," and by merely existing as a place where Puritans could go, it became a symbol that inspired more nonconformists to hold forth in the face of repression. In line with his duties the English ambassador in 1628 warned Bishop Laud concerning Holland, that "It is noe wayes fit it should serve for a nursery to non conformists."[49] The efforts to repress Puritan dissenters were never successful. What the northern provinces were to radical English Prot-estantism, so were the southern Spanish provinces to English Catholicism. "For this Country is full of English priests & Jesuits & nuns, ... colledges & cloisters of Jesuits & nuns," wrote Edward Misselden in 1635 from Antwerp.[50] He feared equally the Puritan extremists of the north and the seduction of the Catholics of the south.

More English and Scots had knowledge about the Netherlands than of any other foreign place, being so "near our own country, as to be known to most persons, either by sight or relation."[51] English travelers found much to marvel at: the great trade and prosperity, the religious toleration, the equalitarianism—"the truth is, gentlemen have there the least respect in any place." Travelers also praised the Dutch system of inland boat transport, "of which one goes off every hour from one great town to another, affording an easy, certain, and commodious way of travelling through most of the Low Countries."[52] Like England, Holland was a sea-faring country, "plucked as it were out of the very Jawes of *Neptune.*"[53] The interests of the two countries often coincided and their prosperity proceeded together. "In generall, good men on both sides are

---

[47] Ronald A. Marchant, *The Puritans and the Church Courts in the Diocese of York, 1560-1642* (London: Longmans, 1960), p. 75; Roger Howell, Jr., *Newcastle Upon Tyne and the Puritan Revolution* (Oxford: Oxford Univ. Press, 1967), pp. 71-72.
[48] Browne, *Congregationalism*, p. 78.
[49] S. P. 16, vol. 90, no. 84.
[50] S. P. 84, vol. 149, fol. 164.
[51] Reresby, *Memoirs*, p. 144.
[52] Ibid., pp. 155-57, 143; John Ray, *Travels through the Low-Countries, Germany, Italy and France*, 2nd ed. (London, 1738), I, 21-22; Fynes Moryson, *An Itinerary written by Fynes Moryson Gent.* (London, 1617), pt. II, 56, pt. III, 93.
[53] Howell, *Epistolae*, II, 8-9.

to wish the continuance of Peace between *England* and these Provinces," wrote Fynes Moryson in 1595, "by which both Common-wealths haue long had, may still haue vnspeakable benefit." He looked to a good future. "Happie be the makers, cursed the breakers of our peace."[54] Although the two nations were often at cross purposes and even at war (three Anglo-Dutch wars in the seventeenth century), none of these made an irreparable break.

[54] Moryson, *Itinerary*, pt. II, 292.

CHAPTER TWO

ENGLISH RELIGION IN THE SIXTEENTH-CENTURY NETHERLANDS

English involvement with the Continent in the Tudor period had religious as well as political and military results. As a part of the Protestant movement, England was drawn into the Protestant ferment of Zurich, Frankfort, and Geneva, those "perfect" schools of Christ. England and Scotland participated in many of the hazardous affairs of Reformation and Counter-Reformation. British religion, moreover, had the practical duty of following abroad the stream of merchants and soldiers going over to the Continent. They required spiritual sustenance in the English language. Whereas pre-Reformation foreign chaplaincies had been mostly drowsy places out of the mainstream, the religious controversies of the sixteenth century galvanized English religion and pulled the foreign outposts into the Reformation action.

Apart from the chaplains traditionally maintained by merchants companies, the earliest sixteenth-century English congregations on the Continent were among the Marian exiles. Numbering nearly 800, the English Protestant refugees settled in eight communities, Emden, Basle, Wesel, Zurich, Strasbourg, Frankfort, Geneva, and Aarau, each with its own congregation.[1] The Marian exiles preserved a nucleus of English Protestantism during the period of Catholic restoration, but even more significantly, the exiles, rather than merely holding the faith, innovated and debated English religion. They broke new ground. At Frankfort arguments over the use of the Prayer Book presaged by a few years the soon-to-appear struggles between Anglican and Puritan in England; and at Geneva, the refugee scholars produced the famous "Geneva Bible."[2] Even though short-lived, these Marian congregations left a mark on English religious history. After 1558, with the accession of Queen Elizabeth, Protestantism's "English Deborah," the exiles returned home and the Marian congregations disappeared nearly as quickly as they had blossomed. The establishment of long-lived, permanent English congregations on the Continent dates from Elizabethan economic and

---

[1] Frederick A. Norwood, *Strangers and Exiles: A History of Religious Refugees* (Nashville: Abingdon Press, 1969), I, 342: Christina H. Garrett, *The Marian Exiles* (1938; rpt. Cambridge: Cambridge Univ. Press, 1966), p. 47.

[2] Norwood, *Strangers*, I, 339; Ronald J. Vander Molen, "Anglican against Puritan: Ideological Origins during the Marian Exile," *Church History*, 42 (Mar. 1973), 45-57.

military involvement. Religion, for the most part, followed trade and the flag.

The Merchant Adventurers at Antwerp and Middelburg

In the Low Countries, the Merchant Adventurers were the traders in English woolen cloth. At different times the staple had been located at Calais, Bruges, and Middelburg; during the sixteenth-century the staple port of the Merchant Adventurers was at Antwerp. A bustling economic city, Antwerp boasted a traffic of hundreds of ships a day. The English community of merchants shared in this brilliant prosperity and enjoyed at Antwerp the greatest days in their history. The English merchants came for the purpose of growing rich; meanwhile Antwerp also served as a haven for English religious dissenters. William Tyndale, Miles Coverdale, John Frith, William Roy, George Joye, John Lambert, John Bale, and in the 1550s, some of the Marian exiles lived at Antwerp.[3]

The religious life of the Merchants Adventurers was influenced as much by the dissenting currents coming over to Antwerp as by orthodox Church of England religion. The merchants in their various market towns had chapels with English chaplains, their maintenance being provided by a share of the fines collected for violations of the company statutes.[4] "Before the second quarter of the sixteenth century the religious life of the Merchant Adventurers in the Low Countries apparently followed nothing other than the quiet path of orthodoxy;" but after the Reformation, the story changed.[5] Their chaplains included John Lambert (or Nicholson, burned as a sacramentarian heretic at Smithfield in 1538); John Rogers (burned as a Protestant at Smithfield in 1555); Bernard Gilpin, Puritan "Apostle of the North," and also during the 1560s William Cole, one of the scholars of the Geneva Bible.[6] When English Protestants took refuge at Antwerp, the Adventurers gave them financial aid. "All the English at Antwerp are heretics," complained the Spanish officials in 1566.[7] Bishops of the Church of England also complained about Antwerp, that the Merchant Adventurers aided the dissident Puritan wing, rather than peacefully adhering to official orthodoxy.

---

[3] Oskar de Smedt, *De Engelse Natie te Antwerpen in de 16ᵉ eeuw (1496-1582)*, 2 vols. (Antwerp: De Sikkel, 1950-54), II, 605-40, 655; A. G. Dickens, *The English Reformation* (New York: Schocken, 1969), pp. 68-82.

[4] Jürgen Wiegandt, *Die Merchants Adventurers' Company auf dem Kontinent zur Zeit der Tudors und Stuarts* (Kiel: Kommissionsverlag Walter G. Mühlau, 1972), pp. 42-3, 153.

[5] Smedt, *Engelse Natie*, II, 601.

[6] Ibid., pp. 627-28, 658-59; Patrick Collinson, *The Elizabethan Puritan Movement* (Berkeley: Univ. of California Press, 1967), pp. 50, 67.

[7] Smedt, *Engelse Natie*, II, 661.

During the reign of Queen Elizabeth, 1558-1603, the merchant chapels were models of Reformed English churchmanship, not only at Antwerp but at other overseas market ports. In 1564 Bishop Grindal of London connived at their Calvinism and advised their chaplain, William Cole, to water down the Prayer Book to fit the Protestant environment at Antwerp. Use the Prayer Book, Grindal ordered, but only selectively, "as much and as little thereof as to your discretion by the advice of the seniors shall be thought good." Leave plenty of time for the sermon. "Neither need you use any surplice." Such instruction seemed to suit the Antwerp merchants very well. "No predelection here for 'the face of an English church'!" noted Patrick Collinson.[8]

The English Adventurers church, largely a private affair existing on suffrance of Catholic officials, took on a more formal organization in the late 1570s. The church met in the English House on Wool Street. In 1575 the Spanish governor tolerated their Protestantism without giving it encouragement, saying "that he woulde not enter to searche any Englishe man's consience, but woulde suffer the Companie to serve God in their howse secretlie."[9] To zealous Protestants, this smacked too much of holding the light under a bushel. After the "Spanish Fury" of 1576, the English community had withdrawn to Bruges for a short time; but in 1577 they returned to Antwerp.[10] After the Protestantizing of the city in May of 1579, Archduke Matthias, governor of the Low Countries, granted an order of freedom of religion for the Merchants and assigned them a public place of worship in the Italian Chapel near the church of St. Francis. In 1580 the English received use of the choir of the Franciscan church itself.[11] At the same time, the Antwerp merchants were working to transform their chapel into a disciplined, orderly church. They solicited in England for a regular preacher and talked of having a fixed discipline. In their reforming work, the merchants had the support of powerful men: William Davison, the Queen's ambassador in the Low Countries, Henry Killigrew, and even Sir Francis Walsingham. On May 8, 1578, Walsingham informed Davison of talk heard among London merchants about a design at Antwerp to alter the worship service in an extreme Protestant direction. Davison himself was reported as the principal "furtherer" of the design. Walsingham warned that the merchants were moving too fast.[12]

---

[8] Collinson, *Eliz. Puritan Movement*, pp. 67, 366.
[9] Smedt, *Engelse Natie*, II, 669.
[10] Ibid., II, 670.
[11] B. P., I, 104-07; Smedt, *Engelse Natie*, II, 678-79.
[12] A. F. Scott Pearson, *Thomas Cartwright and Elizabethan Puritanism, 1535-1603* (1925; rpt. Gloucester, Mass.: Peter Smith, 1966), p. 175.

In spite of cautious advice, the Antwerp church moved at a great rate of speed. With the help of Davison and Laurence Tomson, Walsingham's secretary, the search for a preacher led to Walter Travers, an outspoken Puritan. Travers served the Antwerp church from 1578-80. After his return to England, he was succeeded by Thomas Cartwright, the most famous Puritan of all. Cartwright was minister 1580-85.[13] The choosing of Travers and Cartwright advertized the Puritan sympathies of the Merchant Adventurers, and Travers and Cartwright, by going overseas, declared their extreme displeasure with official English religion. The High Commission in 1590 accused Cartwright that his "departing this realm" served "the more to testify his dislike and contempt." Cartwright and Travers were respectively the very "head" and "neck" of the presbyterian party in England, said historian Thomas Fuller. Under such preaching, Antwerp swiftly became an important religious center with connections into all parts of the Puritan movement in England.[14]

Travers's first act at Antwerp was to be ordained in the Reformed manner by a "synod" of twelve Dutch and French ministers of the Antwerp area—"the presbytery of a foreign nation," Thomas Fuller called them. This took place on May 8, 1578. Travers had never been ordained at home. On May 12, 1578, after preaching to his new congregation, "he was acknowledged and received most effectionately by the whole church."[15] After years of informal services, these events of 1578 constituted the founding of a settled English Presbyterian church at Antwerp. Two years later, Travers returned to England. Cartwright's residence in the Low Countries went back to at least 1577, when he was reported to be functioning as a "factor" (merchant) of the Merchant Adventurers at Middelburg in Zeeland, one of the smaller Adventurer settlements.[16] That he was ever a full time merchant is doubtful, but he may have been functioning informally as preacher or spiritual counsellor to the merchants. When the Antwerp position opened, Cartwright transferred there, serving first as *locum tenens* in Travers's absence. After Travers officially resigned the office on December 17, 1580, Cartwright was official minister; "the space of five years I preached at Antwerpe and Middelborough."[17]

---

[13] Ibid., pp. 171-233; S. J. Knox, *Walter Travers: Paragon of Elizabethan Puritanism* (London: Methuen, 1962), pp. 42-43. William Charke of London was first offered the position but declined it.
[14] Fuller, *C. H.*, III, 26, 105.
[15] Ibid., III, 126; Knox, *Travers*, p. 44.
[16] Pearson, *Cartwright*, p. 168.
[17] Knox, *Travers*, p. 50; Pearson, *Cartwright*, pp. 186-87.

The church records of the Merchant Adventurers, which could tell much of the story, are lost, except for a few extracts made in 1633 for Sir William Boswell, at that time English ambassador at The Hague. Included in the Boswell Papers, the extracts are entitled "Extracts out of ye Registre book of ye English Congregacion at Antwerpe A.D. 1579. 80. 81. 82." Boswell and his agents tried to get possession of the church register book in 1633, but they succeeded only in taking a few extracts. The elders would not hand over the book, but Boswell was told at the time that the church register concerned "such matters as conteyned divers ecclesiasticale censures together with examinations done" and the like.[18] Boswell's research of 1633, partisan though it was, is essential for a summary of the early history of the church.

From the Travers-Cartwright period, for well over fifty years, the Merchant Adventurers maintained a Reformed, Presbyterian-style church. When Ambassador Boswell investigated the church in 1633, he gave much attention to its form and discipline, and he found "the Disciplyne thereof presbyterian, and that the Company fell into this Fashion at the first graunt of Free Exercise of Religion vnto them, and hath soe continued from tyme to tyme, and from place to place of theyr Residence."[19] As a "Reformed" church, the English claimed fellowship with the Dutch church, as evidenced by Travers's ordination by a body of Dutch and French ministers. The English likewise gave "reference upon occasion to the Canons of the Synods of the Reformed Dutch Churches, as the Rules of theyr proceedinges and judgments in Causes of their Ecclesiastical Cognisance."[20] The "Extracts" of the church book contain a list of national synods of the *Ecclesia Belgica* (1568, 1571, 1574, 1578, 1581, 1586, 1618). When Cartwright was summoned before the High Commission in 1590, several of the charges against him detailed his leadership in setting up the Antwerp church in the form of a Reformed church "as a man discontented with the form of government ecclesiastical here by law established."[21] In some important respects, however, the Antwerp church did not become fully Presbyterian, most notably by omitting membership in any of the neighboring classes or synods. According to Boswell's findings, the church was "never classically subordinat unto them for Appeales or otherwise, nor holding other Correspondence then voluntary with them."[22] Financially, the church was also independent, not state supported in the usual Reformed man-

---

[18] B. P., I, 101, 106-07; S. P. 16, vol. 234, no. 8.
[19] S. P. 16, vol. 234, no. 8.
[20] Ibid.; S. P. 84, vol. 144, fols. 139-40.
[21] Fuller, *C. H.*, III, 105.
[22] S. P. 16, vol. 234, no. 8; H. M. C., *De L'Isle and Dudley MSS*, III, 374.

ner. "When I was at Antwerp," wrote Travers, "I reaped no benefit of my ministry by law, receiving only a benevolence and voluntary contribution."[23]

At the coming of Travers the church organized itself internally along Presbyterian lines with elders and deacons. The church book in 1579 records their electing "more" officers to replace earlier ones.[24] Although Travers laid the foundations, Cartwright was equally committed to having a Reformed church. The High Commission in their suit of 1590 charged him with establishing and promoting among the English merchants "a certain consistory, seminary, presbytery, or eldership ecclesiastical, consisting of himself, being bishop or pastor (and so president) thereof, of a doctor, of certain ancients, seniors, or elders, for government ecclesiastical, and of deacons for distributing to the poor." Further, charged the High Commission, this consistory had carried on functions of ordination and censure.[25] Among the elders were the greatest men of the city, including Ambassador Davison, George Gilpin, Secretary of the Company at Antwerp and later diplomatic agent for Queen Elizabeth to the States General, also Hugh Ratcliffe, Leonard Elliott, Nicholas Stockbridge, and Thomas Hill.[26] Such powerful support from men Puritanically inclined gave the church firm foundations. In the 1630s, Edward Misselden, Anglican deputy of the Adventurers, and Ambassador Boswell attempted to revive the custom of having the governor and the ambassador in the eldership. Their intention, however, was to subvert the church by gaining supervision over its affairs, thus to "bring in the discipline of England." Misselden hoped to arrange it that he "might be the head of the church heer as his Majesty is in England."[27]

Within the church the two Puritan preachers carried through many reforms desired by the Puritan wing of the Church of England. According to Boswell's report of 1633, in "the partes and Order of Divyne Service" no consistent course was followed throughout the years except that all innovations were nonconformist to the Church of England. "Theyr severall Ministers neyther Officiating according to theyr mother English, nor keeping the Canons of the Reformed Belgiq Churches, though shadowing themselues under theyr Coulours and name."[28] Once under the Reformed shadow, the merchants defended their church against all pressures from London by referring to their foundation and tradition.

---

[23] Knox, *Travers*, p. 46.
[24] B. P., I, 106.
[25] Fuller, *C. H.*, III, 106.
[26] B. P., I, 106.
[27] S. P. 84, vol. 144, fol. 140.
[28] S. P. 16, vol. 234, no. 8.

Any alteration, the merchants feared, would be "a great disobedyence" and "a dangerous aberracon." They said: "For our church buissines ... that being left as it hath bene ever practized, since it was first established at Antwerp by the procurement and authority of Queene Elizabethes Ambassador who was one of the first elders of our church there."[29]

"Neither English nor Reformed Belgic," in Boswell's phrase, summarizes accurately the worship pattern at Antwerp. In 1578, Walsingham advised Davison and Travers to make some use of the Prayer Book, such as having a reader for lessons from the Confession and Psalm before the sermon.[30] The Prayer Book, however, was a peripheral part of worship at Antwerp, sometimes used a little, sometimes not at all. To Travers and Cartwright, a little of the Prayer Book was not necessarily to be despised; Cartwright claimed that every Sunday for five years he "read the praier out of the booke." The High Commission believed otherwise and accused him, "that he the said Thomas Cartwright ... used not the form of Liturgy, or Book of Common-Prayer."[31] Certainly, the use of the book was minimal. The sermon was the center. Cartwright's position was that "as the fire stirred give the more heat, so the Word, as it were, blown by preaching, flameth more in the hearers, than when it is read."[32] His successor in the pulpit, Dudley Fenner, while at Middelburg wrote books on the vital relationship of preaching and sacraments, *The Groundes of Religion* (1587) and *The Whole Doctrine of the Sacrament* (1588). Preaching, said Fenner, was "of such necessitie, as if it be omitted, it destroyeth the Sacrament."[33]

Just a few months after Travers was installed at Antwerp, a crisis arose when the Adventurers's governor, Nicholas Loddington, abruptly interrupted one Sunday's service with a complaint that the Prayer Book was being omitted. Having come prepared, he tried to take over the service by reading the service from his own book. He further announced the discontinuence of church services in the English House for the time being. Loddington's zealous orthodoxy did not receive the expected backing from Davison and Walsingham. They rebuked him into silence—"So it seems the pills your honour gave him had a very effectual operation."[34]

Given the great freedom at Antwerp and Middelburg, Travers and Cartwright, after watering down the Prayer Book, led the church into

---

[29] Ibid.; S. P. 84, vol. 144, fol. 240.
[30] Knox, *Travers*, p. 48.
[31] Thomas Cartwright, *A Brief Apologie (n.p., 1596); Fuller, C. H.*, III, 106.
[32] Horton Davies, *The Worship of the English Puritans* (Westminster: Dacre Press, 1948), p. 186.
[33] E. Brooks Holifield, *The Covenant Sealed* (New Haven: Yale Univ. Press, 1974), pp. 36-37.
[34] Knox, *Travers*, pp. 46-47; Pearson, *Cartwright*, pp. 180-81.

developing its own forms. An alternative Puritan worship book was published by Robert Waldegrave at London in 1584 or 1585, entitled *A Book of the Forme of Common Prayer*; and, when its reprinting was prohibited at home by the Star Chamber, the book was printed at Middelburg by Richard Schilders in 1586, 1587, and 1602, with the inscription *cum privilego*. "More than likely" this Puritan book was the work of Cartwright, both "for the Waldegrave Liturgy and for the subsequent editions of it which were printed at Middelburgh."[35] Travers and Fenner may also have had a hand in it.

The worship book called for ten steps in the order of worship: call to worship, confession of sins, prayer for pardon, metrical psalm, Scripture reading, sermon, baptism and banns, long prayer and Lord's Prayer, metrical psalm, and the blessing.[36] If the Antwerp-Middelburg church followed along this line of worship service in the Travers and Cartwright years, as seems likely, obviously the English settlers tolerated considerable liturgy—no charismatic, free-wheeling eruption of the spirit. For a long time thereafter, the Middelburg prayer book was much favored by English Puritan preachers in the Netherlands. "It was a book allowed of by all the godly English," said minister Hugh Goodyear of Leiden in 1633.[37]

The Antwerp church developed the tools for discipline and admonition. The elders, it was reported in England, wielded "the censures and keys of the church,—as public admonition, suspension from the supper, and from execution of offices ecclesiastical, and the censures of excommunication."[38] The church book for 1579 and 1580 contains several references to discipline being administered to members, one of them being "denounced in the church" though not specifically by name.[39] The various innovations at Antwerp, however, did not lead to any formalized written covenant or constitution. "I cannot certainly say," reported Boswell, "that this company ... have ever had any Regular Constitucons and entyre frame of a Church."[40] In spite of large reforms and nearly discarding the Prayer Book, Cartwright always viewed the Merchant Adventurers church as a part of the Church of England, "in ecclesiae Anglicanae, quae in transmarinis partibus haeret," at least a part of the English church as it ought to be.[41]

---

[35] Davies, *Worship of the English Puritans*, pp. 124-25.
[36] Ibid.
[37] B. P., I, 80.
[38] Fuller, *C. H.*, III, 106.
[39] B. P., I, 106v.
[40] S. P. 16, vol. 234, no. 8.
[41] Pearson, *Cartwright*, p. 187.

One of the most controversial aspects of the Antwerp church was the ordination of ministers. The Antwerp church, beginning with Travers, functioned as an overseas Puritan ordination center for Englishmen who could not be ordained in England or who scorned episcopal ordination. The bishops objected to such ordinations, both because of the deficiency of presbyterian ordination and because of the encouragement given to disgruntled English dissenters who jumped across to Antwerp for ordination. In later times, Travers was challenged to defend his foreign ordination by Bishop Whitgift, who judged it quite inadequate. Cartwright was often charged with having renounced at Antwerp his episcopal ordination and receiving a new presbyterian laying on of hand, but this has never been proved. Cartwright himself before the Star Chamber denied having any new ordination at Antwerp, or anywhere else, nor does any record of it survive in the Low Countries. Nonetheless, the Antwerp church did stand available for some who came over as a place of alternative ordinations—untouched by the hands of bishops. The Star Chamber accused Cartwright of running nearly a Puritan ordination factory.[42] In a later hostile account, Peter Heylyn repeated the old charges and summarized the story: "They drew over many of the English Nation ... Some of which following the example of *Cartwright* himself, renounced the Orders which they had from the hands of the Bishops, and took a new Vocation from these Presbyters; as, *Fennor, Arton*, etc., and others there admitted to the rank of Ministers, which never were ordained in *England*; as Hart, Guisin, etc., not to say any thing of such as were elected to be Elders or Deacons in those Forreign Consistories, that they might serve the Churches in the same capacity at their coming home."[43] These stories were exaggerated, and the list of names supposedly ordained is not accurate. Some ordinations, however did occur, like Travers and in 1581 the Puritan Robert Wright, the later lecturer at Ipswich. Having scruples about episcopal ordination at home, Wright came to Antwerp and was examined, elected, ordained by Cartwright and an assembly of ministers from the French and Dutch churches, and then admitted to preach along side Cartwright.[44] After returning home to England, both Travers and Wright, uncontaminated by Episcopal touch, continued to preach and never submitted to any bishop's ordination.

In 1582 the Merchant Adventurers moved their principal Dutch market to Middelburg, and Cartwright and the Church also moved. If anything, the Puritanism of the church increased at Middelburg, due perhaps to the competition of the Brownists. Remaining at Middelburg

---

[42] Fuller, *C. H.*, III, 106; Pearson, *Cartwright*, pp. 176-78.
[43] Peter Heylyn, *Aerius Redivivus* (London, 1670), Bk. VII, 290.
[44] B. P., I, 107; Collinson, *Eliz. Puritan Movement*, p. 344.

until 1621, the merchant place of worship, for the majority of the time, was the Gasthuis kerk.[45] Cartwright and his people encountered at Middelburg a new problem—the Brownists. They had arrived earlier in 1582, or possibly late in 1581. Robert Browne and Robert Harrison with a few of their Separatist followers had fled from Norwich to Middelburg and set up a Separatist church.[46] Browne commenced to write and publish radical Separatist books, including the *Treatise of Reformation without Tarying for Anie* and *A Booke which sheweth* (both in 1582). Still at Antwerp, Cartwright received copies of these books, which he condemned as absurd: "so farre from approvinge the same, that he dothe utterly mislike the epistle, touchinge the reformation withoute attentinge the magistrate, and some other points of the doctrine therein contained, wherein he saithe Mr Browne hath absurdly erred."[47] Middelburg from about 1582 to 1585 had two English churches, the presbyterian Merchant Adventurers church and the Separatist or Brownist church.

Cartwright's tenure at Middelburg, although few particular details survive, was certainly troubled by the presence of the Brownists. His opinion of them never improved, even when they came into his own family. His sister-in-law, Alice Stubbe, went over to the Brownists in England about 1590.[48] The Brownist church would have no religious fellowship with Cartwright's church; and although Cartwright himself had no desire for Brownist fellowship, he resented being snubbed. In these circumstances, Cartwright wrote several letters and essays against Brownism which defended the Church of England (especially his own Reformed version of it) as a true church. Championing the Church of England was a new role for Cartwright, but in this situation, it was necessary. If it can be granted that the ordinary assemblies in England be true church of Christ, explained Cartwright, "the way will bee paued and plained for mutuall intercourse between vs." The fact was, Cartwright assured, that the English churches are "God churches;" they are the "Lordes confederates."[49] With faint praise, Cartwright used the analogy of a man's body; "for if any man shuld haue both his hands & his armes cut off, his eyes put out &c. yet as long as the head standeth and other vitall parts, he is to be accompted a man, although a maymed man." The church in England may be maimed, but still "it hath the due

---

[45] "Naamlyst der predikanten," no. 32, archive of the English church (R. A. Zeeland).

[46] The first reference to Browne's being at Middelburg is Aug. 22, 1582. Cartwright is still reported as "at Antwerp" on Sept. 2, 1582; Pearson, *Cartwright*, pp. 212, 215.

[47] Pearson, *Cartwright*, p. 215.

[48] Thomas Cartwright, *Cartwrightiana*, ed. Albert Peel and Leland H. Carlson (London: George Allen and Unwin, 1951), pp. 63-75.

[49] Ibid., pp. 50, 52.

and right of the church of god." He told Alice Stubbe, "There be I confesse in the Church of *England* divers things not suiting well with the sincerity of the gospell."[50] Such blemished, however, never justified Brownism.

While living at Middelburg, Cartwright was beginning his work on the refutation of the Rhemist New Testament, which had been published in 1582 at Rheims. This anti-Catholic project proved to be the largest scholarly endeavor of his entire career. The Rhemist New Testament, a product of the Douai English Catholics, had to be reckoned with seriously. Cartwright took on the writing of an answer at the urging of Walsingham, other Puritan friends, and the members of the Dedham Classis, with whom he kept contact. In 1586, after Cartwright had returned to England, Archbishop Whitgift stopped the project, which by then was nearly ready for publication. Whitgift, who had earlier denounced Cartwright's religion as resting on "rotten pillars," feared to have the Church of England defended from the Romanists by such "friends" as Cartwright. As suspected, many of the refutations of Catholic practices could apply nearly as well to English episcopal religion—"distastful passages (shooting at Rome, but glancing at Canterbury)"—and *The Confutation* was not published for a generation.[51] A portion was printed at Edinburgh in 1602; and finally in 1618 the full study appeared at Leiden by the secret "Pilgrim Press." A major work of scholarship, Thomas Fuller praised it as a book "so complete, that the Rhemists durst never return the least answer thereunto."[52]

Cartwright's ministerial duties at Antwerp and Middelburg were light, allowing ample time for study and writing. While minister to the merchants, Cartwright received offers of professorships at Leiden University and at St. Andrews in Scotland, but declined both. Travers also received and declined a call to St. Andrews.[53] The Antwerp-Middelburg years were significant to Cartwright for scholarly work and for the practical experience of pastoring a living, practicing Presbyterian church. In 1585, Cartwright resigned from the Middelburg church to return home. He gave his reason for resigning as ill health.[54]

Until 1621, the Adventurers at Middelburg were served by a succession of able Puritan-minded ministers: Dudley Fenner (d. 1587); Francis Johnson (1590-92); Matthew Holmes (1596-97); Henry Jacob (the late 1590s); Hugh Broughton (about 1605-1611); Lawrence Potts (1601-15)

---

[50] Ibid., pp. 54, 74.
[51] Pearson, *Cartwright*, pp. 89, 200-01, 209-10; Fuller, *C. H.*, III, 70.
[52] Pearson, *Cartwright*, pp. 204-05; Fuller, *C. H.*, III, 70.
[53] Pearson, *Cartwright*, pp. 190-98; Knox, *Travers*, pp. 51-52.
[54] Pearson, *Cartwright*, pp. 228-29.

and John Forbes (1610-1634).[55] Forbes moved with the Merchant Adventurers to Delft in 1621. In nearly every case, these ministers had been forced overseas because of deprivation or harassment. The merchants gave them shelter and employment and listened to their Puritan sermons. Broughton greatly praised the Adventurers for preserving Puritan religion: "Merchants have been a great help to hold the Gospel, maintaining our best learned abroad, to restore the truth."[56]

The most difficult years for the church came when Francis Johnson gained the pastorate, 1590-92. A fiery Puritan, former Fellow of Christ's College, Cambridge, Johnson was readily available for employment, because of being recently expelled from the university for nonconformity. During the past years he had also spent six months in jail for refusing the ex officio oath and preaching against the Church of England. "The Church of God ought to be governed by elders," he taught.[57] Although Johnson later became famous as a preacher of the Separatists, in 1590 he had not yet slipped across the line into Separatism. The willingness of the Middelburg merchants to entertain a man like Johnson reflects bravado and a desire for theological excitement—which Johnson soon produced. Financially, he was well provided for, a "certain maintenance" of £200 per annum, indicating that the church had put its finances on a more

---

[55] Fenner died at Middelburg in 1587, having served approximately 1585-87; he was identified in 1587 as "Preacher of the word of God, in Midlebrugh" in his *Groundes of Religion*; his *Song of Songs*, 1587, was dedicated to the Merchant Adventurers. Holmes wrote letters from Middelburg dated Oct. 30, Nov. 13, Dec. 20, 1596; see H. M. C., *Salisbury MSS*, VI, 460, 477-78, 531. Henry Jacob's tenure at Middelburg is more vague. Tradition (unsubstantiated) places him at Middelburg in 1599. He was in England 1603-05 and again in Holland about 1610-16. He signed the preface to his *Divine Beginning* at Leiden, Dec. 20, 1610, and the preface of *Declaration and Plainer Opening* at Middelburg, Sept. 4, 1611. By 1616 he had returned to London to establish a church. While at Leiden in 1610 he boarded with William Ames and Robert Parker; all three were in conversation with John Robinson. The remainder of Jacob's Dutch career is unknown. He published books at Middelburg in 1598, 1599, 1600, 1604, 1609, 1612, 1613; see Pearson, *Cartwright*, p. 229 and Hoop Scheffer, *Free Churchmen*, p. 73. Jacob's book publishing record with Schilders is similar to Fenner and Broughton and suggests an association with the Merchant Adventurers. Hugh Broughton "for a while was Preacher to the English at Middleburgh" (John Lightfoot's Preface in Broughton's *Works*). Broughton was at Middelburg on several occasions; writings were signed at Middelburg in 1597 and 1604, see *Works*, p. 575 and Harley MS. 787, fol. 94v; he dedicated a book to the Merchant Adventurers, his *Require of Agreement*, in *Works*, p. 614. In 1605 he was in Amsterdam but then left the city; most likely he was Merchant Adventurer preacher from 1605 to 1611, when he returned to England and died. In his "Petition to the Lord Chancellours" he wrote that Bancroft worked against him "when I was preaching at Middelboroug," *Works*, p. 784. Lawrence Potts returned to London about 1615 after 14 years of service (i.e. 1601) in Middelburg; see Dorothy W. Whitney, "London Puritanism," *Church History*, 32 (1963), 307; and Middelburg C.R., 1624, fol. 22.

[56] Hugh Broughton, *Works* (London, 1662), pp. 614-15.

[57] H. C. Porter, *Reformation and Reaction in Tudor Cambridge* (Cambridge: Cambridge Univ. Press, 1958), pp. 141, 157-63.

regular basis than when Travers and Cartwright had depended upon voluntary offerings.[58]

Two events are known from the period of Johnson's ministry, his seizing of Separatist books (April, 1591) and his attempt to introduce a written covenant into the church (October, 1591). Johnson in 1591 was a vehement anti-Separatist Puritan. He hated Separatism, which had roots at Middelburg, and worked to counteract its influence. The Browne-Harrison church by this time had disbanded, although there may have been a few scattered Separatists remaining; the Separatists of England, however, continued to print books in various Dutch cities. Johnson collaborated with Sir Robert Sidney, English governor at Flushing, in rooting out the Separatist books, "to intercept them at the press, and see them burnt." Around December of 1590, Barrow's and Greenwood's *A Plaine Refutation of M. G. Giffords Reprochful Booke* was in press at Dort, also Barrow's *Brief Discoverie of the False Church*. Working with Sidney, Johnson discovered the press and arranged to have the entire printing of the *Plaine Refutation* "openly burnt, himself standing by until they were all consumed to ashes"—except for two souvenir copies. The books were seized on April 20 and shortly thereafter destroyed by burning; 1000 copies of the *Plaine Refutation* were burnt and also some copies of the *Brief Discoverie*.[59] "But Marke the Sequell," says William Bradford. After studying the despised book, Johnson was convicted of his own error and underwent a gradual "conversion" to Separatism.[60] Meanwhile he continued to serve the Merchant Adventurer church.

The other event of Johnson's Middelburg ministry came a few months later. Although the church people were "shadowing themselves" under the colors of the Belgic Reformed church, Johnson apparently found them deficient in organization and mission. In October of 1591, a few months after the book burning, he drew up "Articles" or constitution for the church and urged the congregation to sign them:

> Francis Johnson his articles, which he vrged to be vnderwritten by the Englishe Marchants in Middleboroughe

---

[58] Burrage, *E.E.D.*, I, 140. Johnson can first be dated at Middelburg in April, 1591 but likely arrived a little earlier, probably 1590. The last known reference to Johnson in Middelburg is May 2, 1592, but perhaps before this time he may even have removed. See Acta Kerkeraad Middelburg, quoted in Hoop Scheffer, "De Brownisten te Amsterdam," p. 243.

[59] William Bradford, "A Dialogue or a sume of a Conference," *Publications* of the Colonial Society of Massachusetts, 22 (1920), 121-22; see also letters of Robert Sidney and notes by Leland H. Carlson in *The Writings of Henry Barrow, 1590-1591* (London: George Allen and Unwin, 1966), pp. 370-77. Sidney announced the seizure of the books on April 21, 1591, as having happened "last day." The books were burned somewhat later. In addition to Johnson's 2 copies, Sidney also saved about 6 copies of each of the books.

[60] Bradford, "Dialogue," pp. 121-22.

Wee whose names are vnderwritten, doe beleeve and acknowledge the truthe of the doctrine and faythe of our Lorde Jesus Christe, which is revealed vnto vs in the Canon of the Scriptures of the olde and newe Testament.

Wee doe acknowledge, that God in his ordinarie meanes for the bringinge vs vnto and keepinge of vs in this faythe of Christe, and an holie Obedience thereof, hath sett in his Churche teachinge and rulinge Elders, Deacons, and Helpers: And that this his Ordinance is to continue vnto the ende of the worlde as well vnder Christian princes, as vnder heathen Magistrates.

Wee doe willinglie ioyne together to live as the Churche of Christe, watchinge one over another, and submittinge our selves vnto them, to whom the Lorde Iesus committeth the oversight of his Churche, guidinge and censuringe vs accordinge to the rule of the worde of God.

To this ende wee doe promisse henceforthe to keepe what soever Christe our Lorde hath commaunded vs, as it shall please him by his holie spiritt out of his worde to give knowledge thereof and abilitie there vnto.[61]

These articles constitute virtually a church covenant, and if adopted, would have put the congregation on a covenantal basis. Johnson further urged (1) that any existing members who would not subscribe to the articles "and everie poynte of them" should be dropped from membership—"he may not be receaved as a member in this *Church*," and (2) that any faithful member, having subscribed, was never to join any church "in *Englande* or els where" except for one keeping a similar discipline. The Brownists had covenants, but for a Reformed, non-Separating church to reorganize around the covenant was a novelty indeed. Johnson was too innovative and his plan lost out after Thomas Ferrers, the deputy of the company, "withstoode" him; and others, no doubt, found the prospect of writing covenants and dropping members too Brownistic.[62] Johnson's ministry from the start was divisive.

His motivation for urging the covenant may have come from his reading of Separatist books, which he had in his possession since April. His congregation, however, had not yet detected him as a secret Brownist. Sidney of Flushing on October 13, 1591, wrote to Burghley that "there hat bin a iarre of late and is indeed yet between the Deputy of the English Marchants at Midleborrow and the Minister of them there, about the orders of theyr church." Sidney saw no great principle at stake; the particulars "they are tedius."[63] Possibly the covenant proposal may also have been a ploy on Johnson's part to undercut lingering Separatist

---

[61] Add. MS. 28,571, fol. 169 (B. M.). On the order of chronology of the books and the covenant, see B. R. White, *The English Separatist Tradition* (Oxford: Oxford Univ. Press, 1971), pp. 92-93; Burrage, *E.E.D.*, I, 137-40.

[62] Add. MS. 28,571, fol. 169.

[63] S. P. 84, vol. 43, fol. 100v.

sentiments among the English community of Middelburg. During 1592 Johnson openly began to reveal Separatist sympathies.

The combination of the two controversies, the covenant episode and the Brownist entanglement, produced ruin for Johnson's career at Middelburg. The congregation split into factions, and for a while the church ceased to function at all. Not surprisingly, the local Dutch Reformed ministers became uneasy at these scandals, especially at Johnson's views on church government. Johnson, either by order of his own elders or possibly by action of the consistory of the Dutch Reformed church of the city, was urged "to keep silent, hoping all will be settled ere long."[64] The result was the temporary halting of church services. Mention is made in Dutch consistory records in March of 1592 of "secret preaching" in the English church, but the record is unclear about who was preaching secretly and why. On march 28, 1592, the Dutch consistory urged "both parties of the English Church to submit their matter of dispute to the judgment of the Classis of Walcheren."[65] By April of 1592, Johnson had been silenced and was out of the pulpit. A letter of April 1, 1592, from the Dutch consistory at Middelburg to the Dutch church at London, the Austin Friars church, reported that the English church suffered from a serious quarrel that had destroyed all edification and caused the church to close. The consistory appealed to the Austin Friars people to approach the Merchant Adventurers in London to have them send over another minister to Middelburg, someone "agreeable with us in church government."[66] Writing several years later, 1607, Thomas Potts of the neighboring town of Flushing referred back to some previous "schism at Middelburg caused by the opinion of one or few." Potts almost certainly was referring to the Johnson schism of 1592, which, he thought, "in all likelihood" would have been prevented if the church had been joined to the local Dutch classis and subject to "the over ruling judgment of many."[67]

Whether dismissed by the elders or voluntarily withdrawing from a hot situation, Johnson left Middelburg in 1592; and according to Separatist tradition, his travel was for the reason of conferring with Henry Barrow and John Greenwood at London. "After which Conferrence; hee was soe satisfyed and Confeirmed in the truth as hee Neuer Returned to his place any more at Middleburrow." By September of 1592, Johnson had joined

---

[64] Acta Kerkeraad Middelburg, May 2, 1592, quoted in Hoop Scheffer, *Free Churchmen*, p. 46. The original kerkeraad records were destroyed during World War II.
[65] Ibid. (May 2, 1592, referring to action of Mar. 21, 1592).
[66] Hessels, *E.L.B.A.*, III, 937.
[67] H. M. C., *De L'Isle and Dudley MSS*, III, 374.
[68] Bradford, "Dialogue," p. 122.

Greenwood's Separatist congregation at London; and they elected him pastor.[68]

Under Johnson's successors, Holmes, Jacob, and Broughton, worship was restored, but the peaceful years have left fewer records than the tumultuous ones. Matthew Holmes, having been "compelled by the rigour of the bishops to come into Zeeland," in 1596 complained about the pestilential climate and his foul health. He returned to London as quickly as possible.[69] Not all of the ministers serving in the Low Countries could so easily return home and find employment. For some who had fled, like John Forbes, a foreign church was all that could be had and the Netherlands was their necessary refuge.

Middelburg in Elizabethan times served the Puritan cause in still another way by its printing shops. Puritans relied upon the print shop of Richard Schilders of Middelburg for production of many books unprintable in England. A Calvinist refugee from Engheim, Schilders had escaped to London and learned printing. In 1579 he crossed back to the Netherlands, and settled in Middelburg as municipal printer and "printer to the States of Zealand" (1583-1634). His sympathies were clearly Puritan, for during this time he published many English books by Puritan authors. The Brownists used his services to print books by Browne and Harrison; and several of the ministers of the Merchant Adventurers' church published books there, including Cartwright's *Brief Apologie*; Travers's *Defence of the Ecclesiastical Discipline*; nine books by Fenner; four by Jacob; two each by Broughton and Forbes; and three printings of the Puritan worship book, *Booke of the Forme of Common Prayers*.[70]

A short distance north from Middelburg is Veere (formerly Campveere), where the Scottish merchants had their own staple port, also with a church. During the sixteenth century no register book was kept and little can be recovered apart from the fact that the post of minister was very often vacant. Not until 1614 was the Veere church established on a regular basis with its own minister.[71]

The merchant church of Antwerp and Middelburg holds a significant place in sixteenth-century Puritanism. Its successful experiment with Presbyterian worship gave an inspirational example to English nonconformists, holding forth that there was a better way than the prelatical

---

[69] H. M. C., *Salisbury MSS*, VI, 460, 477-78, 531. Holmes had been former chaplain to the Earl of Essex.

[70] J. Dover Wilson, "Richard Schilders and the English Puritans," *Transactions* of the Bibliographical Society, 11 (1909-11), 65-134; J. G. C. A. Briels, *Zuidnederlandse boekdrukkers en boekverkopers in de Republiek der Verenigde Nederlanden omstreeks 1571-1630* (Nieuwkoop: B. de Graaf, 1974), pp. 435-38.

[71] John Davidson and Alexander Gray, *The Scottish Staple at Veere* (London: Longmans, Green, and Co., 1909), pp. 270-74.

Church of England. In England the planting of "Presbytery under the Wing of Episcopacie"[72] was a slow and hazardous affair, but at Antwerp and Middelburg the work could be done openly and resplendently. The church under the Puritan preaching of Travers and Cartwright pleased the merchants very well. One merchant sent back a report grandly comparing Cartwright's church to that of Christ and the disciples.[73]

The Separatists at Middelburg

The other English church at Middelburg was the Separatist congregation headed by Robert Browne and Robert Harrison. Extreme Puritans, they had given up on the Church of England and in 1581 separated themselves into an independent congregation at Norwich. Browne was pastor and Harrison was teacher. Although only a small group, Browne witnessed boldly and drew crowds of up to one hundred people—until he landed in prison in 1581 (the first of 32 imprisonments).[74] Convinced of a coming Brownist disaster, the powers of church and state repressed the new congregation and "used them cruelly," thus beginning a long, sad story for the Separatists.

Terrorized by the persecution, some of the nonconformists fled into exile in the Netherlands. Individuals of various persuasions had gone over to the Low Countries one by one in previous years—Travers and Cartwright among them—but Browne's group was the first Puritan company to emigrate as a church. Puritan historian Daniel Neal drew the lesson: "Men who act upon principles will not easily be beaten from them with the artillery of canons, injunctions, subscriptions, fines, imprisonments, &c. much less will they esteem a church that fights with such weapons."[75] The bishops and magistrates, however, were taking what they considered to be necessary steps for the safety of the kingdom. Groaning under "great trouble and bondage," the little group set out, "fullie perswaded that the Lord did call them out of England." Apparently he called them to the Netherlands, for shortly thereafter, in late 1581 or early 1582, they arrived in Middelburg.[76]

---

[72] Peter Heylyn, *Aerius Redivivus*, Bk. VII, 300.

[73] On the importance of the Merchant Adventurers for Puritanism, see Dickens, *English Reformation*, p. 69; Collinson, *Eliz. Puritan Movement*, pp. 234, 295.

[74] Dwight C. Smith, "Robert Browne, Independent," *Church History*, 6 (Dec. 1937), 299-302; Champlin Burrage, *The True Story of Robert Browne (1550?-1633) Father of Congregationalism* (Oxford: Oxford Univ. Press, 1906), pp. 14-16.

[75] Daniel Neal, *The History of the Puritans* (Rpt. Westmead, Farnborough, Hants: Gregg International Publishers, 1970), I, 301.

[76] Burrage hits upon "about January, 1581/2." (*E.E.D.*, I, 101). On or about August 2, 1581, Browne was in prison in England, but he is definitely reported in Middelburg on August 22, 1582 (S. P. 83, vol. 16, no. 117), by which time he had already published several treatises at the press of Schilders.

Browne and Harrison arrived before Cartwright and the Merchant Adventurers transferred their church from Antwerp.[77] Browne made no brotherly pretense of fellowship with any outpost of the Church of England—"bablinge Prayers and toying worshippe ... and a thousande moe abominations," he charged. "They are not Jerusalem."[78] His was to be the pure covenanted church of believers. As a completely voluntary group, small and self-supporting, the Brownists struggled from the start for mere physical survival. The church met in Browne's house and numbered no more than "some thirty or fourty persons, which ar in very poore estate, and for the moste parte visited with sickenes, not well aggreinge with the aire in those parts."[79] Some of Browne's group had been left behind, like "Father Tolwine," who, being "resolved to haue gone after him thither," was delayed in disposing of his property. Eventually he joined the Amsterdam Separatists.[80] Some histories state that the Brownists received municipal subsidies and had the use of a public church, but this is merely a pious tradition.[81] The Brownists or Separatists never received a burgomasters' subsidy or church building in any Dutch city. Browne at Middelburg had no church building but called his flock together in his house, "where (as it is said) he exerciseth a ministery in a corner."[82]

At first the Brownists received a good welcome from the Dutch population since they were refugees for the sake of religion and conscience. "Many of the towne understaninge englishe, doe oftentimes repaire to there praiers and assemblies, which ar kepte in Brownes house which he hathe hired in the towne."[83] Free at last, in spite of material privations, the Brownists could preach and pray without interference, and publish books. The Middelburg years were a highly productive period theologically for Browne and Harrison. Within the year of 1582, Browne had published three works, the famous *Treatise of Reformation without Tarying for Anie*; *A Treatise vppon the 23 of Matthewe*; and *A Booke which sheweth the life and manners of all true Christians*. Harrison in 1583 published *A Little Treatise vpon the first Verse of the 122. Psalme*. All of these were printed by

---

[77] Cartwright was still reported at Antwerp on September 2, 1582, S. P. 83, vol. 17, no. 3.

[78] Browne, *A Treatise vpon the 23. of Matthewe* (1582) in *The Writings of Robert Harrison and Robert Browne*, ed. Albert Peel and Leland H. Carlson (London: George Allen and Unwin, 1953), pp. 205-06.

[79] S. P. 83, vol. 17, no. 3. Stephen Offwood in *Heady and Rash Censures* (n.p.), p. 10, refers to 50-60 persons.

[80] Christopher Lawne, et al., *The Prophane Schisme of the Brownists or Separatists* (n.p., 1612), pp. 18-19.

[81] *Naamlyst der predikanten*, p. 2 (Middelburg, R. A., no. 32); Steven, p. 316.

[82] S. P. 83, vol. 16, no. 117.

[83] Ibid.

Richard Schilders. Harrison, "stretching his purse," provided the financing for the books and the printings were large, over 1000 copies, some being sold openly at Middelburg and "many sent into England."[84] The message was blunt: Reformation without delay. "Yea we must prese vnto his kingdome not tarying for anie." Wherever unholy polution defiles a church, "there is not the Lords Zions"—"they are not the Lordes Church." At Norwich, Browne's group had separated from the polluted Church of England and reconstituted themselves on the basis of the covenant, "to ioine them selues to the Lord, in one couenant & felloweshipp together."[85] Theirs was to be a church with covenant, discipline, and purity.

However, hard times were at hand and fellowship waned. The church had many unhappy days at Middelburg as they attempted to practice their discipline and purity. Inner quarrels led to a ruinous split between Browne and Harrison. Each had his own following. Browne has given his side of the story in *A Trve and Short Declaration* (about 1583), and according to him, "tales & slanders," also "whisperings, backbitings & murmurings" tore the congregation apart. There was also some controversy about Mrs. Browne's pride, which offended some of the members.[86] Each faction attempted to discipline the other, and at least three times Browne was deposed as pastor and then restored. A part of the brethren began to look back to England, and Harrison gave them encouragement "because he Taught them that Thei might Lawfully Returne INTO ENGLAND AND there haue their dwellinge ... Because thei Were Wearied of the hardnes of that contrie." Browne, however, warned the Harrison faction that "England was as AEgipt" and they "did sinn which had a ffull purpos to dwel stil in England."[87] After a few feeble reconciliations, the break became irreparable. Harrison, from his side, saw Browne as the troublemaker; Brown "hath cast vs off."[88] All in all, the Middelburg experiment in building a superior kind of church on Separatist foundations produced much bad publicity and little good result. Browne finally gave up on Middelburg and with a few of his steadiest supporters (four or five families) sailed to Scotland next door to

---

[84] Browne's three treatises are usually found bound together although surviving copies have the three parts rearranged in various ways, Wilson, "Schilders," pp. 78-80; S. P. 83, vol. 17, no. 3; Leona Rostenberg, *The Minority Press & the English Crown* (Nieuwkoop: B. de Graaf, 1971), p. 191.

[85] Browne, *Reformation without tarying for anie*, in *Writings*, pp. 155, 169; *Trve and Short Declaration*, in *Writings*, p. 422.

[86] Browne, *Writings*, pp. 425, 427. George Johnson in his *Discourse of Some Troubles* (Amsterdam, 1603), p. 7, refers to the pride Mr. Browne's wife.

[87] Browne, *Writings*, p. 428.

[88] Harrison's letter to London, *Writings*, p. 149.

"AEgipt," arriving at Edinburgh January 9, 1584.[89] Browne in later years conformed and returned to the Church of England. Harrison and his remnant were left behind to fare as they could.

After Browne's *Treatise of Reformation without Tarying*, the English government issued a prompt decree against the book and two men were hanged for selling it.[90] This kind of cruelty the Brownists expected. More painful was the rough treatment received from fellow Puritans, who had not separated. Cartwright withstood their doctrines and scolded them for separating not only from the prelatical Church of England but even from Puritan assemblies like his own, "from whome you haue thought good to sunder your selues."[91] In an exchange of letters in 1584 and 1585 (Harrison to Cartwright, but not surviving; Cartwright to Harrison, printed in 1585; and Browne to Cartwright, printed about 1585)[92] Harrison, Browne, and Cartwright argued out their controverted points: Is the Church of England a true church? Given the corruption in the church, is separation absolutely necessary? What is a true minister? In his answer to Cartwright, Browne identified the heart of their dispute as this, "Whether the ordinarie assemblies of the professors in Englande be the churches of Christ."[93] Cartwright's position was *yes*; so long as there be in every congregation one true Christian, all those Churches of England are "vnto vs the churches of God."[94] Browne went completely to the other side, that any "open and manifest offence is incurable" and breaks the covenant. "I maruaile howe his penne could droppe downe such poyson, and he not smell the stinck thereof as he wrote it."[95] The relationship between the Brownist and the merchant church was not amiable.

Except for Francis Johnson, all the Merchant Adventurer preachers were anti-Separatist. The Separatist cause rose mightlily when Francis Johnson was converted to their side, but thereafter the lines hardened and the Separatists were able to claim no further conversions among prominent Puritans in the Netherlands. The Merchant Adventurer preachers wrote frequently against the Separatists. Henry Jacob in 1599 wrote against Johnson in *A Defence of the Churches and Ministry of Englande* (published by Schilders). Although Jacob did exhibit certain "congregational" ideas about the covenant and the nature of the church while in the Netherlands, and more openly after returning to England, he remain-

---

[89] Burrage, *Robert Browne*, p. 28.
[90] Dexter, *Congregationalism*, I, 210.
[91] Burrage, *Robert Browne*, p. 17.
[92] Cartwright's letter is in *Cartwrightiana*, pp. 49-58; Browne's letter is in *Writings*, pp. 430-506.
[93] Browne, *Writings*, p. 435.
[94] Cartwright, *Cartwrightiana*, p. 51.
[95] Browne, *Writings*, pp. 437-38.

ed a stout critic of Separatism. Hugh Broughton in *Certayne Questions* (1605) called the Separatist church at Amsterdam "not a church, but a synagogue of Satan." Little wonder that the converted Separatist Francis Johnson complained of bloody treatment from former colleagues; "onelie let the reader note here againe, that not the Prelates alone, but you also (the forward preachers and professors) have wittinglie and willinglie your hand in our blood."[96]

The Middelburg Separatists, the better people knew them, lost public good will. On their arrival, the Dutch ministers were "not ill affected unto Browne and his followers."[97] Although the Brownists fared a little better at the hands of the Dutch Church than their Separatist brethren at Amsterdam, who were mercilously harassed, the mood at Middelburg also turned cool. The Brownist church was short-lived at Middelburg, but thereafter the Dutch churchmen made every effort to prevent a recurrence. In 1602 the Classis of Walcheren, which encompassed the city of Middelburg, sent for advice to the Dutch consistory of Amsterdam about how to handle a suspected Brownist situation.[98] The classis also prepared an anti-Brownist gravamen for the forthcoming Synod of Zeeland: "Whether it is advisable to respond in writing against fiery, ambitious spirits, whether Brownists or other sectaries, because they might use these writings for their own purposes and put them into print, to the stirring up of our church members, even to the slander of our own religion and church government and to the reinforcement of their own errors." The Classis, in another gravamen to the synod, thought it wise that English ministers, of whatever background, coming into churches in the Netherlands, "deliver a testimony of their faith and life from the place where they have come to the classis under which they will serve."[99]

The Separatist church at Middelburg had a short history, and the records of its existence and demise are obscure. Browne removed to Scotland (1584) and Harrison, the remaining leader, died at Middelburg some time in the 1580s (probably about 1585).[100] By 1592, when Francis Johnson was in the midst of his conversion to Separatism, no Netherlands Separatist church existed to offer him help. He found it necessary to go directly to London to confer with Barrow. There is no clear record of a functioning Brownist church at Middelburg after 1585.

---

[96] Jacob, *Defence*, p. 7; Broughton, *Certayne Questions*, p. 7; Johnson, *An Answer to Maister H. Jacob* (n.p. 1600), p. 177.
[97] S. P. 83, vol. 117, no. 3.
[98] Acta Kerkeraad Amsterdam, July 25, 1602, III, 82v (G. A. Amsterdam).
[99] Acta Classis Walcheren, July 11, 1602, in Hoop Scheffer, "De Brownisten te Amsterdam," p. 257; Acta Synod Zeeland, 1602, Reitsma and Van Veen, V, 53-54.
[100] Burrage, *E.E.D.*, I, 111, 115.

Nevertheless, the discussion about Brownism in the Walcheren Classis and the Zeeland Synod of 1602 indicates some late Brownist activity, either active or suspected. Some hostile reports charged that the Middelburg Brownists dispersed through apostacy. Christopher Lawne included a charge that at Middelburg "not one of them aliue in Browne's time continued faithfull, but became apostates." George Johnson had the same story. A Separatist tradition, however, spoke of faithfulness unto death; Harrison, at least, they said, "died at Middleburgh in this faith that we professe."[101] Whether from apostacy, schism, or merely natural attrition, the Middelburg Separatists disappeared. The center of Separatist activity moved to Amsterdam.

The Army Chaplains at Flushing and Brielle

Another movement of English and Scottish religion into the Netherlands came by way of the English and Scottish armies. Thousands of British soldiers served in the Eighty Years War against Spain. In the early stages of the Dutch revolt, they served as mercenaries for pay and fought in most of the battles, often at the forefront. "But the chief praise next unto God ought to be given to the English ensigns and armed men," said Sir Roger Williams after the second seige of Goes in 1572.[102] As mercenaries following their trade, they fought for either side for pay, although more ordinarily for the Dutch Protestants than for the Spanish Catholics. William fought on both sides of the war.[103] Beginning with the first fifty English casualties in 1572, Fortescue estimated them to be the "first of fifty thousand or twice fifty thousand who were to lay their bones in Holland during the next seventy years."[104]

English military involvement became formalized with the Treaty of Nonsuch in 1585, whereby the English Queen committed a force of 5,000 foot and 1,000 cavalry. Not as a gift, however. They came on conditions calculated to secure the investment. The Dutch were required to turn over to the English the towns of Vlissingen (Flushing) and Brielle (The Brill) to be garrisoned with English troops and to be held as English fortresses. The two "cautionary" towns stayed in English hands until 1616. From the time of the treaty onward, the English population in the Low

---

[101] Lawne, *Prophane Schisme*, p. 63; Johnson, *Discourse*, p. 9; Henry Ainsworth, *Counterpoyson* (n.p., 1608), p. 41.

[102] Roger Williams, *The Actions of the Low Countries* (1618), ed. D. W. Davies (Ithaca: Cornell Univ. Press, 1964), p. 75, and introduction by Davies.

[103] Charles Wilson, *Queen Elizabeth and the Revolt of the Netherlands* (Berkeley; Univ. of California Press, 1970), p. 67; John W. Fortescue, *A History of the British Army* (London: Macmillan, 1899), I, 160; Williams, *Actions*, p. 112, introduction, pp. x, xi.

[104] Fortescue, *Army*, I, 141.

Countries multiplied greatly, not only by the treaty soldiers but by additional volunteers recruited by the Dutch government to serve "in the States pay." With the flag went religion, and by the terms of the treaty the Dutch promised to provide places of worship for English religion.[105]

Robert Dudley, the Earl of Leicester, led the English expedition of 1585, and with him went a supply of chaplains to serve the spiritual needs. In the cautionary towns and wherever the English took up their positions, chaplains and chapels were provided, if not permanently at least on occasion. The States General gave funds, supplemented by local and provincial money, for church buildings at Brielle and Flushing. The sum of 8,000 florins for a church was promised by the States General in 1586 to Flushing.[106] Brielle also received an allotment from the States General. These "churches" were preaching places, not organized congregations, and during the military season, the chaplain would ordinarily follow the troops out into the field, leaving the garrison pulpit empty or to be filled by substitutes. The military chaplain was valued as a tool of discipline and good order; he was a great service both to Christianity and the Queen's government, "religion being a greater bond of obedience in the soldier."[107]

The most active of the army churches was at Flushing, which had a sizeable English garrison. When Fynes Moryson visited the town in 1592, he reported seeing ten English companies of 150 men each, under the governance of Sir Robert Sidney, keeping this "strong Toun" for the Queen. "The City is little and of a round forme," he noted, "but very strong."[108] The promised English church was finished only about 1592, having been much delayed because the money came in so slowly. An unpleasant quarrel over funds for the church, involving the Flushing magistrates, the States of Zeeland, and the States General, greatly hampered the project for six years.[109] Meanwhile the English preachers had to make do with some temporary quarters. By the time of Moryson's visit, he reported that the church was now "common to the English and Dutch at diuers houres." The city magistrates, because of overcrowding in the Groote Kerk, had assigned the Dutch congregation and English

---

[105] Wilson, *Elizabeth and the Netherlands*, p. 86; the treaty is printed in Jean DuMont, *Corps universel diplomatique der droit des gens* (Amsterdam, 1728), vol. 5, pt. 1, pp. 454-55.

[106] H. G. van Grol, "Iets van de oudste geschiedenis der Engelsche Kerk te Vlissingen," Bijlage, *Jaarverslagen betreffende het archiefwezen en de oudheidkundige verzameling der Gemeente Vlissingen* (1913), p. 2.

[107] Edward Conway to Robert Cecil, 1597, H. M. C., *Salisbury MSS*, VII, 286-87.

[108] Fynes Moryson, *An Itinerary written by Fynes Moryson Gent.* (London, 1617), pt. I, 50-51; James Howell in 1619 reported that formerly there had been 900 English soldiers, *Epistolae Ho-Elianae. Familiar Letters Domestic and Forren*, 2nd ed. (London, 1650), II, 17.

[109] Van Grol, "Engelsche Kerk te Vlissingen," pp. 4-7.

congregation to a shared use of the building. The new church building was known in Flushing history as the Kleine Kerk or Engelsche Kerk.[110]

The quality of chaplains recruited for the Netherlands and other overseas service was not very high, compared, at least, to the strong personalities associated with the Merchant Adventurers and Brownists. However, some of the sixteenth-century chaplains did stand out, notably Thomas Potts, the long-term preacher at Flushing (1605-16). He was a Puritan of powerful gifts. "Trewly he mooves very much and the soldiours are more attentife than ever I sawe them to any man," reported Sir William Browne, Deputy Governor of Flushing. "You shall find him an honest, zealous and learned man."[111] Potts was preceded by a Mr. Fitts and assisted until 1607 by Daniel de Dieu, a Dutch minister who could preach in English—"good Mr. Dannyell and honest Mr. Fitts."[112]

The zealous Potts was not content to run a haphazard religious assembly. In 1607 he petitioned governor Robert Sidney (Lord Sidney and Viscount Lisle) for permission to formally organize the garrison church "that we may have Elders to assist the Minister or Ministers in governing, according to the godly order of these churches." Potts also thought "it meetest that some of the Captains bear that office ... because of their authority." The policy of "ordaining some assistants," Potts believed, went back to the time of Sir Philip Sidney (1586) "and confirmed by the Earl of Leicester in her late Majesty's name." With such an organization it would be possible to administer discipline and keep the unworthy from the communion table, which as minister alone he found a difficult task. "If the title of Elder seems harsh," suggested Potts, "we might use the name of Churchwardens." Potts also requested that the church be joined to the Classis of Walcheren "for the better correspondence between our church and this of Zeeland."[113]

Obviously an energetic and forceful fellow, Potts served at Flushing until the garrison disbanded in 1616; and his brother, Lawrence Potts, was preacher at the Merchant Adventurers church at nearby Middelburg.[114] Not all of Potts's projects came to fruition; his proposal for membership in the classis did not succeed. After a while his zeal became tiresome to Browne, the Deputy Governor, who, after earlier praising him as "zealous and learned" (1605), was next calling him an "extreme Puritan" and "too vehement in many poincts" (1607).[115] Sir John

---

[110] Moryson, *Itinerary*, I, 50-51; Van Grol, "Engelsche Kerk te Vlissingen," p. 9.
[111] H. M. C., *De L'Isle and Dudley MSS*, III, 173.
[112] Ibid., III, 372-4; V, 338-39; *B.W.P.G.N.*, II, 492-95.
[113] De L'Isle and Dudley MSS, III, 372-4.
[114] Ibid., III, 374; IV, 23-24. Potts of Middelburg is identified as Lawrence Potts in *Church History*, 32 (1963), 307.
[115] *De L'Isle and Dudley MSS*, III, 442.

Throckmorton, a later Deputy Governor at Flushing, on the other hand, upheld his Puritanical ways: "Albeit he may a little dissent from the Canons of our Church established now in England, he is an honest man."[116] When the English garrison withdrew in 1616, and Flushing returned to Dutch authority, Potts petitioned the States of Zeeland to continue as English preacher of the city. He called himself preacher "of the English nation and garrison within Flushing." The States, however, declined: "It was not found good to continue an English church in Flushing."[117].

At Brielle the States General also provided funds for an English church building, in this case for restoring an unused building rather than building anew. The English received use of St. Jacob's Church (the Oude Mannenhuis Kerk) in the Noordeinde, at that time standing vacant.[118] The Brielle church was much less active than the Flushing church, and rather removed from the mainstream of English religion. For several years after 1585, the English had trouble supplying a minister for Brielle. Till 1589 the Dutch church of the city complained of inadequate ministry for the English community, no English chaplain being competent to baptize children and marry English couples. Then in 1590 came the happy news that "a good minister had come," able "to do all the services of the church."[119] The minister was Michael Seroyen, who served from 1590 to about 1616 or a little later (by 1620 the records refer to widow Seroyen). Unlike Potts at Flushing, Seroyen, who was probably of Dutch background, meddled little in Dutch-English Puritan affairs and devoted himself solely to baptizing, marrying, and preaching uncontroversial sermons. In 1603 Seroyen found time to take up the additional position of doctor and medicine maker.[120] After the departure of the garrison in 1616, the church faded out for a time.

Other towns where English soldiers were garrisoned also had their own English ministry. At The Hague, the English had use of the Sacrament Chapel in 1585.[121] Utrecht had an English military chapel beginning in 1586.[122] Leiden had an English chapel in 1587.[123] Bergen-op-Zoom, at

---

[116] H. M. C., *Downshire MSS*, III, 123 (1611).

[117] Van Grol, "Engelsche Kerk te Vlissingen," p. 10; *Notulen* van Staten van Zeeland (1616), p. 208 (R. A. Zeeland). Potts received a call to Amsterdam in 1617.

[118] Cornelis Veltenaar, *Het kerkelijk leven der gereformeerden in Den Briel tot 1816* (Amsterdam: A. H. Kruyt, 1915), pp. 99-100.

[119] H. de Jager, "Engelsche predikanten te Brielle," *De Navorscher*, 43 (1893), 595-97.

[120] H. de Jager, *De Brielsche Vroedschap in de jaren 1618-1794* (Rijswijk, 1904), p. 222.

[121] Fred. Oudschans Dentz, *History of the English Church at the Hague, 1586-1929* (Delft: W. D. Meinema, 1929), p. 16.

[122] C. H. D. Grimes, *The Early Story of the English Church at Utrecht* (Chambéry: Imprimeries Réunies, 1930), p. 9.

[123] Gerechtsdagboek, A, April 4, 1587, fol. 541 (G. A. Leiden).

the request of Leicester, established an English chapel in the St. Margaret's cloister. English merchants had long traded at Bergen-op-Zoom; and, in fact, Lutheranism had strongly infiltrated the English merchants here as at Antwerp. In 1592, Sir Francis Vere succeeded in bringing in Richard Hyts as garrison preacher. He was a native of Suffolk; and at Vere's request, the Classis of Tholen and Bergen-op-Zoom examined and approved him for service.[124] The garrison churches at Flushing, Leiden, and Brielle all died out by 1616 or earlier, but Flushing and Leiden were re-established during the seventeenth century as regular English Reformed churches. The English garrison churches at Bergen-op-Zoom, Utrecht, and The Hague continued on permanently, in spite of some interruptions, across the seventeenth century. Scottish soldiers joined the war in the Netherlands as early as the English and eventually the Scots Brigade consisted of three regiments, enrolled in 1586, 1603, and 1628. Andrew Hunter of Carnbee, Fifeshire was one of the early chaplains listed on the payroll of the Scots regiment.[125]

The Earl of Leicester gave a general oversight to the establishing of garrison churches in the late 1580s. Working cordially with the extreme Calvinists in the Netherlands—being the "champion of the Calvinist-Reformed"[126]—he pulled English religion in the Low Countries further toward the Puritan side. The chaplains he took with him were men of Puritan spirit (Humphrey Fen, John Knewstub, and for a short time Thomas Cartwright).[127] Religious zest quickened the more pious warriors of Leicester's army, who saw their anti-Spanish war in Holland as being for the defense of England and "the whole state of religion."[128] Leicester's political ambitions eventually overpowered his religion; nevertheless, his role in setting directions for English religion in the Low Countries was formative. He befriended Cartwright and brought him back to Holland. When Cartwright had returned to England in 1585, he appealed to Leicester as patron. When no particular position at that moment could be secured in England, Leicester took Cartwright back with the army to the Low Countries and then, in 1586, sent him to England as Master of the hospital at Warwick.[129] Sir William Boswell in his resear-

---

[124] J. van der Baan, "Engelsche gemeente te Bergen-op-Zoom," *Navorscher*, 32 (1882), 77; Korneel Slootmans, *Bergen op Zoom een stad als een huis* (n.p., 1966), p. 134.

[125] Andrew L. Drummond, *The Kirk and the Continent* (Edinburgh: St. Andrew Press, 1956), p. 78; Ferguson, *Scots Brigade*, I, 57. He entered service in the Netherlands in 1590, according to Steven, p. 338.

[126] L. Knappert, *Geschiedenis der Nederlandsche Hervormde Kerk gedurende de 16ᵉ en 17ᵉ eeuw* (Amsterdam: Meulenhoff, 1911), p. 51.

[127] Collinson, *Eliz. Puritan Movement*, p. 386.

[128] Wilson, *Elizabeth and the Netherlands*, p. 90; J. A. van Dorsten and R. C. Strong, *Leicester's Triumph* (Leiden: Leiden Univ. Press, 1964), pp. 75-76.

[129] Pearson, *Cartwright*, pp. 228-33.

ches attributed Cartwright's success in Puritanizing the church at Middelburg to "his power with the E. of Leycester (whose Chaplaine it seems he was.)"[130]

Leicester's policies in the cautionary towns encouraged a Puritan, Reformed form of worship, which the merchants and chaplains found edifying. The setting up of elders in the church of Flushing was a policy "confirmed by the Earl of Leicester," and everywhere Leicester was understood to commend Reformed, rather than Anglican, worship.[131] He served as patron and promoter of the Dutch National Synod of 1586, meeting at The Hague, which greatly favored the extreme Calvinist party. Pro-Laudian Anglicans later charged that the 1586 synod had things "sett downe more like our nonconformist way than in any other of the Synods."[132] Anglicans viewed Leicester's religious influence as baneful to the Church of England. Puritan preachers in the Netherlands appealed to Leicester's governorship as ordaining "that the English Churches in these Low Countries should conform themselves to the government here practised in the Dutch churches."[133] The *Booke of the Forme of Common Prayers*, published by Schilders at Middelburg in 1586, 1587, and 1602, corresponds with Leicester's tenure in the Netherlands and likely received his blessing. The book appeared with the official sounding words *cum privilegio*. What kind of *privilegium* and from whom it came was later a question. One assumption was "that the cum Privilegio seems to be Lesters."[134] All the later Puritan-Anglican controversies in the Netherlands harked back to the Leicester years: "And without question that was the beginning of all English Churches in the Low Countreys."[135]

The sixteenth-century Netherlands increasingly overlapped with English history. The English army, once committed to the field, continued to serve in the wars against Spain for nearly one hundred years, making the Netherlands, as predicted in 1585, "a school to build up soldiers ... a most fit school and nursery to nourish soldiers."[136] During the sixteenth century, several thousand soldiers were schooled in that nursery, and many more in the seventeenth century. Along with the

---

[130] S. P. 16, vol. 234, no. 8.
[131] Thomas Potts in 1607, *De L'Isle and Dudley MSS*, III, 374.
[132] B. P., I, 86; J. Reitsma and J. Lindeboom, *Geschiedenis van de hervorming en de Hervormde Kerk der Nederlanden*, 5th ed. (The Hague: Nijhoff, 1949), pp. 155-57.
[133] De L'Isle and Dudley MSS, III, 374; B. P., I, 35-38.
[134] B. P., I, 80, 86 (Stephen Goffe). Several, but not all, of Schilder's English books were published *cum privilegio*.
[135] Ibid., I, 86.
[136] Wilson, *Elizabeth and the Netherlands*, p. 91.

military arts, the Netherlands also turned into a school of English religion of the Puritan kind, not to the liking of bishops but according to Cartwright and Travers, Browne and Harrison. The most innovative movements of late sixteenth-century English religion found refuge and strength in the Netherlands.

PART TWO

THE CHURCH BUILDING AGE (1600-1660)

CHAPTER THREE

THE AMSTERDAM SEPARATISTS AND ANABAPTISTS

By land and sea all routes led to Amsterdam, "the greatest city in all the *Low-Countries*, and one of the richest and best traded empories of the whole world."[1] In the sixteenth century it was only one of several prosperous Dutch cities, but in the seventeenth century Amsterdam emerged as the unrivaled "empress city"[2] of the Netherlands. Her population leaped forward from about 14,000 at the beginning of the sixteenth century, to 50,000 in 1600 and over 200,000 by 1700. Many travelers spread news about the unparalleled prosperity of the city.[3] "One of the greatest Marts of *Europe*," exclaimed James Howell in 1619; "a vast, rich, populous, and beautiful City, equal to most in Christendom," thought William Mountague.[4] Although the climate and terrain were inhospitable, requiring that the entire city be built on long piles driven deep into the ooze, its location at the confluence of the Amstel River and Zuider Zee was strategically magnificent and beneficial for commercial enterprise. The IJ, the Amsterdam harbor, bristled with spars and sails from the huge fleets. "An infinite number of ships not to be numbered lie here," reported Sir William Brereton. During his visit in 1634, he was told five hundred ships a week went forth—"a most flourishing city."[5]

Immigrants to Amsterdam crowded in from the near and far corners of Europe. Wealth, power, and opportunity beckoned. To the city came the south Netherlanders fleeing from the Spanish, also Germans, Danes, Norwegians, and Frenchmen; here and there were colonies of English, Jews, Greeks, even Persians and Armenians. A cosmopolitan city, "Amsterdam had a heterogeneous character that is not surpassed by present day New York."[6] Sir William Temple, English ambassador to the

---

[1] John Ray, *Travels through the Low-Countries, Germany, Italy and France*, 2nd ed. (London, 1738), I, 34.

[2] Joost van den Vondel, "Op Amstelredam" (1631), in *Volledige dichtwerken en oorspronkelijk proza*, ed. Albert Verwey (Amsterdam: H. J. W. Becht, 1937), p. 935.

[3] Simon Hart, "The Dutch and North America in the First Half of the Seventeenth Century. Some Aspects," *Mededelingen van de Nederlandse Vereniging voor Zeegeschiedenis*, 20 (Mar. 1970), 7; Violet Barbour, *Capitalism in Amsterdam in the Seventeenth Century* (1950; rpt. Ann Arbor: Univ. of Michigan Press, 1966), p. 17.

[4] James Howell, *Epistolae Ho-Elianae. Familiar Letters Domestic and Forren*, 2nd ed. (London, 1650), II, 11; William Mountague, *The Delights of Holland* (London, 1696), p. 116.

[5] William Brereton, *Travels in Holland the United Provinces England Scotland and Ireland*, ed. Edward Hawkins, Chetham Society, 1 (1844), 65.

[6] D. G. Carasso, "Amsterdam—die grote Stad," *Ons Amsterdam*, 25 (Mar. 1973), 70.

Netherlands 1668-70, listed the factors that in his judgment made the Low Countries, and chiefly Amsterdam, the magnet of European immigration: The military strength of the cities, the constitution of the government which respected individual life and property, the banks of Amsterdam ("no place so secure as this" for money), and finally, the general acceptance and ease of liberty, including freedom of religion and opinions of all kinds. Holland was "the great ark of the refugees," said Pierre Bayle.[7]

Amsterdam, like other Dutch cities, concerned itself little with the political and religious opinions of the immigrants. It was an open city. Although the Dutch Reformed preachers frequently urged stricter policies, the city magistrates, Reformed to a man, "connived" at admitting dissenting groups, whether Jews, Roman Catholics, Mennonites, or English Brownists—so long as they discreetly behaved themselves, and fed the economic greatness of the city.[8] All the sects lived side by side, "there be well near as many Religions as there be houses," reported an English visitor, and "one Neighbour knowes not, nor cares not much, what Religion the other is of."[9] For the immigrant of conscience, Amsterdam offered considerable security from revengeful governments by virtue of the *asylum Amstaedamense*. Amsterdam seldom, if ever, surrendered religious or political fugitives for punishment to their home government, especially if the stranger took out citizenship in the city, notwithstanding various seventeenth-century English-Dutch treaties calling for surrender of fugitive rebels from one country to the other.[10]

The English and Scottish community in early seventeenth-century Amsterdam was small compared to the German, French, and Scandanavian settlers; but it was visible and growing. The status of citizen or *poorter* of Amsterdam was available for eight guilders (after 1622, fourteen guilders), and some English and Scots enrolled as citizens. Most of the English inhabitants of Amsterdam, however, never were required to enroll as citizens; consequently the *poorter* books can not be considered a very good indicator of total English or Scottish population.[11] The church

---

[7] William Temple, *Observations upon the United Provinces of the Netherlands*, ed. George Clark (Oxford: Clarendon Press, 1972), pp. 111-12; Frederick A. Norwood, *Strangers and Exiles* (Nashville: Abingdon Press, 1969), II, 57.

[8] Brereton, *Travels*, pp. 67-68.

[9] Howell, *Epistolae*, II, 11.

[10] Eduard van Zurck, *Codex Batavus*, 2nd ed. (Delft, 1727), pp. 40, 275; Paul Zumthor, *Daily Life in Rembrandt's Holland*, trans. S. W. Taylor (New York: Macmillan, 1963), pp. 261-65.

[11] On English and Scottish citizenship, see J. G. van Dillen, *Bronnen tot de geschiedenis van het bedrijfsleven en het gildewezen van Amsterdam*, R.G.P. (The Hague, 1929, 1933), I, table III, p. xxxiv; tables IV, V, p. xxxv; Barbour, *Capitalism in Amsterdam*, p. 16.

records tell much more, because for the immigrant, the comforts of English religion were a greater necessity than civic enrollment. The English Reformed Church had a membership of 450 by 1623, and the various Separatist churches counted together, were about equal in size. The Reverend John Paget in 1618 reported between 300 and 400 Separatists in Amsterdam.[12] Although the Separatists came for religious reasons, of necessity they practiced their trades to make a living. The non-Separatists, although often devout, were more clearly economic people. Some of the early seventeenth-century English immigrants rose to positions of wealth and prominence, like the merchant John Webster and John Jordan, the brandywine distiller.[13] Although the legal English cloth trade belonged to the Merchant Adventurers, stationed at Middelburg and later at Delft, Rotterdam, and Dort, the city of Amsterdam had its share of the trade through the English "interlopers" who carried on a prosperous, albeit illicit, business. The Amsterdam magistrates, in fact, preferred to rely on the interlopers, "who live here in great numbers and carry on much trade," rather than bringing in the monopolistic Merchant Adventurers Company and losing the interlopers. Edward Misselden, deputy of the Merchant Adventurers, in 1631 estimated that the Amsterdam interlopers carried on as great a trade as the Adventurers themselves.[14]

The English left many landmarks in the city. There were no fewer than five streets or passage ways called the "Engelschegang." There was also a Bruinistengang, several English taverns (the Engelse Roos, the Engelse Laars, the English Howse), and just across from the Mint Tower, the five "Engelse Huizen" of John Jordan. The famous "English houses" survived until 1876, when they were demolished.[15] The English Brownists had a long-established church, the Bruinisten Kerk, functioning until 1701; and the Engelse Kerk in the Begijnhof, founded in 1607, is still alive and active.

The Separatist Churches

The first of the English churches of Amsterdam was the Separatist church, transported from London to Amsterdam in the 1590s, about ten

---

[12] Alice C. Carter, *The English Reformed Church in Amsterdam in the Seventeenth Century* (Amsterdam: Scheltema & Holkema, 1964), p. 116; John Paget, *An Arrow against the Separation of the Brownist* (Amsterdam, 1618), "To the Christian Reader."

[13] I. H. van Eeghen, "John Jordan, de Engelsman," *Amstelodamum*, 55 (Feb. 1968), 7-12; Simon Hart, "Nogmaals John Jordan," *Amstelodamum*, 57 (Mar. 1970), 68-69.

[14] S.P. 84, vol. 144, fols. 107-08; Van Dillen, *Bronnen*, II, 261 (1617) and p. xxi.

[15] *Amstelodamum Jaarboek*, 4 (1906), J. C. Breen; *Amstelodamum*, 55 (1968), 236; *Ons Amsterdam*, 13 (Feb. 1961), 50-51.

years after the demise of Browne's church at Middelburg. A new Separatist congregation under the leadership of John Greenwood and Henry Barrow took shape at London in the late 1580s; and although there was no direct or visible tie between Browne and the Greenwood-Barrow group, their ideas were much in agreement, thus giving the Separatist movement a new impetus. Although the London dissenters separated from the Church of England, like the Brownists, they declined to bear the name of Brownist. "We are no Brownists, we hold not our faith in respect of any mortal men," they insisted; but all the same, the name of "Brownist" stuck.[16] Their congregation, "being pretty numerous" was gathered and officially organized in September of 1592 with Francis Johnson, newly returned from Middelburg, as pastor, Greenwood as teacher, and several elders and deacons.[17] Separatists, however, no matter how zealous and well-intentioned, had no good future in London, only promise of repression, imprisonment, and possible death. Barrow, Greenwood, and John Penry were executed in 1593—as Puritans saw it, "a sacrifice to the resentments of an angry prelate"—and over fifty more were lying in jails.[18] Perishing under this "barbarous crueltie," the Separatists began withdrawing to the Netherlands. "Forsweare our own Contrey & depart, or els bee slayne therein," they reasoned.[19] Many departed as speedily as possible although pastor Francis Johnson and a few others were detained at prison or remained behind. The first immigrants arrived at Amsterdam in late June and early July, 1593.

The first sign in the Netherlands of the Separatists was July 15, 1593, when the Dutch Reformed ministers of the Amsterdam consistory discussed "that here at the house of Israel Johnson (Janszoon) some preaching was done by an English preacher, and on the coming Sunday was again to take place." The English preacher was not identified. Johnson was an English merchant of Amsterdam with Separatist connections; and although the Dutch consistory had not yet identified Johnson's visitors as Brownists, they frowned on this unauthorized religious gathering. In some way they had been warned of "disreputable preaching," and they took a stand that it was "a matter of importance which should not be permitted to go further with their silence." The consistory sent

---

[16] B. R. White, *The English Separatist Tradition* (Oxford: Oxford Univ. Press, 1971), pp. 67-70, 72.

[17] Burrage, *E.E.D.*, I, 142; Daniel Neal, *History of the Puritans* (London: William Baynes, 1822), I, 428.

[18] White, *Separatist Tradition*, pp. 94-95; Neal, *Puritans*, I, 437.

[19] Preface to Confession of 1596, in Walker, *Creeds*, pp. 49-50; F. J. Powicke, *Henry Barrow Separatist (1550?-1593) and the Exiled Church of Amsterdam (1593-1622)* (London: James Clark, 1900), pp. 221-23.

Jacob Arminius and a colleague to warn Johnson against further preaching services at his house and to learn what the intentions of the English were.[20] The Separatists always believed that their prejudicial welcome resulted from letters sent from English authorities over to Amsterdam.[21]

The identity of Israel Johnson's English visitors comes to light in a notarial document of July 19, 1593, four days later. Johnson, "English merchant in Amsterdam," Jan Suderlandt, Scottish merchant, and Peter Allen, Andrew Fluet, and John Stuart, merchants from England, gave a statement on behalf of eleven Englishmen, whom "they have been dealing with for three weeks and know them well." The eleven were Willem Mainestone, Stanhal Mercer, John Lushe, Henry Tayler, David Grove, George Cleyten, William Witcomb, Samuel Witcomb, Thomas Dicker, Nicolas Cook, and Robert Bayley. Their intention, the English asserted, was to travel further and to "make their residence in the province of Overijsel."[22] All or most were Separatist people. Several of them (Stanshal Mercer, George Cleyton, and Robert Bayley, for example) can be identified as active Separatists.[23] Israel Johnson declared that they had been trading for three weeks, which would put the arrival of some of the London group about June 28, 1593 (N.S.). The notarized paper declaring that they were people of good, respectable intent likely was a response to the agitation of the Dutch ministers, who had insisted on interrogating them.

The information of their going on to Overijssel further associates them with the London Separatists. On September 2, 1593, the Amsterdam consistory had reports of Englishmen, "schismatics called Barrowists" (Baroisten), at Kampen, which is in the province of Overijssel. These were probably Israel Johnson's eleven. When the Amsterdammers learned that these "Barrowists" had been "honorably received by the Kampen magistrates," the exasperated *predikanten* assigned Arminius speedily to warn the Dutch consistory at Kampen of the schismatic danger. Arminius and Taffinus, the two Dutch preachers who took the lead in anti-Separatist action, both before and after the Separatists went to Kampen, explained their hostility on grounds of maintaining good order. "We considered it to be our duty, not only to warn them against making any attempts here without the leave of the Magistrates, but

---

[20] Acta Kerkeraad Amsterdam, II, 114 (G. A. Amsterdam); Carl Bangs, *Arminius: A Study in the Dutch Reformation* (Nashville: Abingdon Press, 1971), pp. 156-57. Israel Johnson is identified as a Separatist in George Johnson, *A Discourse of Some Troubles and Excommunications in the Banished English Church at Amsterdam* (Amsterdam, 1603), p. 32.

[21] Hanbury, *Memorials*, I, 83-84.

[22] Not. Archive 44 (Lieven Heijling), fol. 149 (G. A. Amsterdam).

[23] Burrage, *E.E.D.*, II, 134-36; Johnson, *Discourse*, pp. 32, 152, 212.

likewise to give the Magistrates notice of their meetings: This we did, not out of any unkind feeling towards them, but because we were afraid of falling under the just displeasure of the Magistrates if we kept silence.'' They sent letters to London for information and gathered what information they could find locally.[24]

The reason why the English chose Kampen over Amsterdam in 1593 is understandable in light of the harassment by the Dutch ministers, who took care to make Amsterdam unhospitable to these "disreputable" people. Kampen, on the contrary, at that very time was advertising for immigrants "of whatever nation" and promising all rights of citizenship without cost.[25] The Kampen residence, however, proved temporary and by October, 1595, the English settlers had moved to Naarden, a trading town closer to Amsterdam. The French or Walloon church at Amsterdam in October of 1595 was complaining about one of their members, Jean de l'Ecluse, who had separated and gone over to "de Engelsche van Naerden,"—"les Anglois de Nerden." Ecluse, a native of Rouen, had formerly lived in London, where he had been a member of the French Church. At different times he was a printer and a schoolmaster.[26] Various other reports make general mention of the Separatists living in Kampen and Naarden before returning to Amsterdam in 1596. John Payne's *Royall Exchange* (1597) rebuked "my countreymen of another kynd and company, removing from Campion to Narden, and from thence to Amsterdam," and both George Johnson and Francis Johnson in their books refer to incidents when the church was at Naarden. George Johnson recalled that Stanshal Mercer, one of Israel Johnson's visitors, was debarred from being chosen elder "while the church was at Narden."[27]

Although free at last from English persecutions, the Separatists found the Kampen-Naarden years (1593-96) to be painful times, much exacerbated by the lack of strong leadership. Pastor Francis Johnson was still detained in England and Greenwood, the elected teacher, had been martyred in 1593. Some of the elders had remained in England, so here was a flock separated from its shepherd and limping along with one deacon and half an eldership.[28] There is no evidence that Henry Ainsworth, who was

---

[24] Acta Kerkeraad Amsterdam, II, 118v; *The Works of James Arminius*, ed. James Nichols (London: Longman, 1825-75), I, 162-63.

[25] Hoop Scheffer, "De Brownisten te Amsterdam," p. 221.

[26] Acta Kerkeraad, II, 181 (Oct. 12, 1595); Hoop Scheffer, "De Brownisten te Amsterdam," p. 222. On Ecluse, see Hoop Scheffer and Arminius, *Works*, I, 163.

[27] John Payne, *Royall Exchange* (Haarlem, 1597), p. 48; Johnson, *Discourse*, p. 151; Dexter, *Congregationalism*, I, 268.

[28] Elder Daniel Studley was detained in England but elder George Knyviton immigrated; deacon Christopher Bowman also immigrated with the church; Johnson, *Discourse*, p. 151; White, *Separatist Tradition*, p. 98.

to play such a large role in Amsterdam Separatism, had yet joined them. Their one resident preacher, until Francis Johnson could join them in 1597, was William Smyth, former Church of England minister from Wiltshire, a comrade from the London prisons but not one to make a great mark on the movement.[29] Perhaps Ecluse, who had been with the church since 1595, also did some of the ministerial work since he had long aspired "to the office of the ministerie." John Paget scolded: "Among you he is allowed to preach and Prophesie."[30] At Naarden, the congregation in its poverty wrangled over some poor relief provided by the city magistrates, and deacon Christopher Bowman was tarred by the disgruntled members as "Judas the Purse-bearer in Narden."[31] "Now miserably rent, divided, and scattered here and there," the Separatist band was further decimated by Anabaptist inroads; "divers of them fell into the heresies of the Anabaptists" and had to be excommunicated. Other crises followed, so that the confusion reached the point where half the congregation was excommunicating the other half. "You have brused the tender reedes, quenched the smoking flaxe," warned John Payne, you who have a church "without Pastor and sacraments for these 3. yeres."[32] A generous estimate puts the church at no more than forty to sixty persons by 1596.[33]

They went back to Amsterdam. By the summer of 1596 the English, now labelled as Brownists (*bruynisten*), were meeting at the house of Jean de l'Ecluse. At this news (June 6 and 13, 1596), the Dutch Reformed consistory sent stern complaints to Ecluse and informed the city magistrates in hopes of quenching the Brownist revival in the city. The burgomasters, however, while giving scoothing words to the preachers, followed their usual policy of toleration and took no anti-Brownist action.[34] An upward turn came finally in 1597, when pastor Francis Johnson and the remaining Separatist leaders from London, including Daniel Studley and George Johnson, were able to rejoin the flock in Holland.[35] The election of Henry Ainsworth as teacher, perhaps a little

---

[29] *Writings of John Greenwood and Henry Barrow, 1591-1593*, ed. Leland H. Carlson (London: George Allen and Unwin, 1970), pp. 360-61 (Examination of William Smyth).

[30] Paget, *Arrow*, p. 120.

[31] Christopher Lawne, et al., *The Prophane Schisme of the Brownists or Separatists* (n.p., 1612), pp. 26-27.

[32] Payne, *Royall Exchange*, p. 48; White, *Separatist Tradition*, p. 100; Burrage, *E.E.D.*, I, 156.

[33] White, *Separatist Tradition*, p. 100; Dexter and Dexter, *England and Holland*, p. 423.

[34] Acta Kerkeraad, II, 197-98; on Amsterdam policy towards religious dissenters, see George L. Smith, *Religion and Trade in New Netherlands* (Ithaca: Cornell Univ. Press, 1973), pp. 72-73.

[35] Four of the Separatists, Francis Johnson, George Johnson, John Clerke, and Daniel Studley had been sent from London to a short exile to the Magdalen Islands in the Gulf of

before Johnson's arrival, also helped to bring the church up to strength of leadership once more. Daniel Studley, George Knyviton, and Matthew Slade were elders; Christopher Bowman was deacon. Hereafter, the Amsterdam Separatist church, which called itself the Ancient Church, began a period of growth and modest prosperity, if not tranquillity. Their numbers rose to three or four hundred.[36]

Like the Brownists at Middelburg in the 1580s, the London Separatists were responsible for providing their own building for worship. Officially recognized English Reformed churches received subsidies and church buildings; but the Separatists, although tolerated, had to pay their own way. For the first ten years Johnson's congregation worshipped in temporary quarters and private homes. In 1596, they met at the house of Ecluse, who lived on the Lange Houtstraat in an alley.[37] When Francis Johnson arrived, he lived in a "great house" with "sundry roomes" near the Regulierspoort, which likely also served as a community center for the Separatists, including worship.[38] In 1607, they built their first church building, located like Ecluse's house, on the Lange Houtstraat. This general area in which the Separatists clustered was called the Vloomburg. Although enclosed within the city walls since 1593, it was a relatively out-of-the-way area of storage sheds and lumber businesses frequented by Jews and sectaries. When James Howell visited Amsterdam in 1619, he lodged at Ecluse's house, where English travelers often stayed; "tis not far from the *Synagog* of Jews." Howell observed their long-bearded rabbi, and the Jews falling down to kiss his foot. Round about he found a hodgepodge of all religions and sects, "well near as many Religions as there be houses."[39]

That first church building suffered a freak accident during construction because of high wind and had to be rebuilt, which caused pastor John Paget of the rival English Reformed Church to rejoice: "The beforesayde Brownists preaching house being half reddy God send his strong [wind] most furious from heaven (psal. 45) and cast the house one-

---

St. Lawrence (April 8-Sept. 5, 1597). They crossed over to Amsterdam soon after their return to London; see David B. Quinn, "The First Pilgrims," *William and Mary Quarterly*, 23 (1966), 359-90, and Johnson, *Discourse*, pp. 109-13.

[36] William Bradford in his "Dialogue or the sume of a Conference," refers to "about three hundred comunicants" in 1608, when the Pilgrim Fathers were in Amsterdam (see *Publications* of the Colonial Society of Massachusetts, 22 (1920), 139); Paget in his *Arrow* records "three or four hundred of the Brownists," in "To the Christian Reader" (1618); Dexter, *Congregationalism*, I, 278.

[37] R.A. 2164, fol. 95v (G. A. Amsterdam); A. M. Vaz Dias, "Een verzoek om de Joden in Amsterdam een bepaalde woonplaats aan te wijzen," *Amstelodamum Jaarboek*, 35 (1938), 188-89.

[38] Johnson, *Discourse*, pp. 113, 180.

[39] Vaz Dias, "Verzoek om de Joden," p. 188; Howell, *Epistolae*, II, 9-11.

ly and no other flat downe unto the ground which ... was a signe and a teaching that they doe not buyld upon the Rocke the true and richt foundation."[40] Only a temporary setback, and the building was finished. The cost was financed by voluntary contributions of the congregation and by money raised abroad. It served both as "dwelling and preaching house." The legal ownership of the building and land was later a matter of contention when the congregation split. The new church was "32 feet wide and laying on the Vloomburg in the Lange Houtstraat outside St. Anthony Poort, named the English church."[41]

The building continued to serve as the English Separatist church up to 1662, when it burned down.[42] Bitter controversy arose when the congregation divided in 1610, a part remaining with Johnson and the seceding group going off with Ainsworth. Temporarily Ainsworth's group moved two houses down the street into a place, rather embarrassingly, that had once served for Jewish worship—an "idol-temple of the Jews" (taunted John Paget, whose congregation was meeting in a former Catholic church).[43] In 1613, Ainsworth's group brought legal suit for possession of the building and won. As a result, Francis Blackwell, one of Johnson's elders, gave over title for a settlement of 5,530 guilders.[44] Throughout their history, the Ancient Church had three church buildings: the Lange Houtstraat church until 1662; then after a fire, which destroyed the original building, a place on the Groenburgwal, 1662-68; and finally in 1668 a church on the Barndesteeg which served until the dissolution of the congregation in 1701, "a pretty handsome and convenient Church."[45]

Although tolerated by the civil authorities in Amsterdam, the Separatists found themselves under constant unfriendly scrutiny from the Dutch Reformed Church—they "did looke awry att them."[46] All notices in church records about the "Brownists" (as the Dutch preachers insisted on calling them) are hostile. The Synod of South Holland in 1596, in one of the earliest synodical references, began complaining about "Englishmen named Brownists"; and classis and synod references

---

[40] Baptismal Register, 1607, no. 81, fol. 2 (G. A. Amsterdam).

[41] R.A. 2164, fol. 95v; Baptismal Register, fol. 1.

[42] H. J. M. Roetemeijer, "De Bruinisten in Amsterdam, op- en neergang van een kerk," *Ons Amsterdam*, 21 (July 1969), 198; H. de la Fontaine Verwey, "Van kerk tot dievenhol, de geschiedenis van de Bruinistenkerk," *Amstelodamum*, 36 (1949), 150-56; Verwey, "De Bruinistenkerk," *Amstelodamum*, 37 (1950), 106-07.

[43] Paget, *Arrow*, p. 26

[44] R.A. 2164, fol, 95v.

[45] Roetemeijer, "De Bruinisten," p. 198.

[46] Bradford, "Dialogue," p. 131.

thereafter became frequent in areas where Separatists lived or were suspected.[47]

The Separatists proclaimed their faith and complete orthodoxy in a series of confessions. The original 1589 confession (*A True Description out of the Word of God, of the Visible Church*) was printed at Dort and again verbatim at Amsterdam in 1602, and occasionally thereafter. Another statement of faith, *A True Confession*, in forty-five articles, appeared at Amsterdam in 1596 and in Latin as *Confessio Fidei Anglorum Quorundam in Belgia Exulantium*, with preface dated 1598, also seemingly at Amsterdam. Further printings appeared in English, Dutch, and Latin. The *Confessio* was addressed to Christian scholars at Leiden University, St. Andrews, Heidelberg, and Geneva, the "reverend and learned men."[48] By moving from the English language into Latin, the Separatists were aiming for a wider audience in the established Reformed churches. In doctrine, except for separation, the English were in agreement with Reformed theology, but no amount of pamphlet arguments could overcome the barriers thrown up by the Dutch preachers.[49] The *Confessio* did spark a correspondence with Franciscus Junius, professor of theology at Leiden, but the result was quite the reverse of what the English had hoped for. Instead of approving their extreme zeal, Junius admonished them to keep silent and cease their commotion against the Church of England.[50] As the Separatists saw the situation, theirs was a friendly gesture, reaching out for brotherhood: "We being thus established in Christ, acknowledged the reformed Churches ... to be true Churches, & our brethren in the Lord." "And how do they accept of vs?" asked Ainsworth.[51]

The Dutch ministers were openly friendly to the non-Separating Puritan wing of the Church of England, and such Puritans found good welcome in the Netherlands. Not the Separatists. John Paget explained why the Dutch Reformed Church remained frozen and aloof. "When they saw many of your exceptions against the Church of England to be such as did also necessarily lead vnto separation from them, as well as from England, had they not reason to avoyd and beware of the new Disciples of such a separation, as being an vnlawfull assemblie established in Schisme and not in Christe?"[52] Puritans like Paget used their influence to disparage the Separatists before the Dutch church; and

---

[47] Reitsma and Van Veen, III, 71-72 (art. 28).
[48] The confessions are printed in Walker, *Creeds*, pp. 28-74.
[49] R. B. Evenhuis, *Oak dat was Amsterdam* (Amsterdam: W. Ten Have, 1965-74), II, 225.
[50] Dexter, *Congregationalism*, I, 301-05. C. de Jonge, "Franciscus Junius (1545-1602) en de Engelse Separatisten te Amsterdam," *N.A.K.*, 59 (1978), 133-59.
[51] Quoted by John Paget, *Arrow*, p. 45.
[52] Ibid., p. 55.

although the original Brownists had been graciously received at Middelburg, the Amsterdam church was hostile from the start, having been thoroughly prejudiced through letters to expect the worst from the Separatists.[53]

A new round of anti-Brownist agitation began in 1599. The Synod of North Holland, at the instigation of the Amsterdam church, issued warnings against Brownists and recommended that any Brownist disorders be referred to the civil magistrates.[54] A few months later a Separatist delegation from Johnson's church appeared before the Amsterdam consistory with grievance that the Dutch church had received as members persons who were excommunicates from the Separatist church. It was a stormy session. The scribe had begun the entry for the meeting with the words: "The deputies of the English church living here appeared ..." but on second thought, the word church (*kerk*) was fully and deliberately blotted out. A week later, at the next consistory meeting, the Dutch dismissed the English complaints because "we do not acknowledge their gathering as being a church." Quite a slap—not a *kerk*, only a *vergadering*. When Johnson remonstrated, they declined any serious response, answering, "they would do it if they saw it needfull, or if they found anything that was worthie of answere."[55] In 1606, during some law suits involving the Brownists, the magistrates also scorned Johnson's congregation by belittling their deputies: "that they held them not as a Church, but as a Sect." After all of this, Ainsworth asked, "Whether the separation be most on vs, or on them."[56]

Not surprisingly in such unfriendly circumstances, the Separatists turned cold toward the Dutch Reformed Church. A new confrontation came in April of 1601 when Johnson's church addressed ten questions to the Dutch church in a Latin document presented to the Amsterdam consistory. The document had existed since 1599. The meeting, like the earlier ones, was heated and ended with Petrus Plancius lecturing the English messengers: "Your words contain grave accusations, if true, and great calumnies if they are false. And they are false—as we will teach you, God helping us, in His time." One gain for the Brownists, however, was that the consistory register this time elevated them to being a church—"of the English church (*kerke*) within Amsterdam."[57]

The content of that Latin document is preserved in the minutes of the North Holland Synod (1601) where the Amsterdammers referred the

---

[53] Evenhuis, *Amsterdam*, II, 225.
[54] Reitsma and Van Veen, I, 276 (1599, art. 26).
[55] Acta Kerkeraad, III, 53 (Feb. 10, 17, 1600); Lawne, *Prophane Schisme*, p. 21.
[56] Paget, *Arrow*, pp. 45-46; Lawne, *Prophane Schisme*, p. 21.
[57] Acta Kerkeraad, III, 67r (April 5, 1601).

matter. The Separatists criticized the Dutch church on ten counts: (1) The church at Amsterdam is confused and lacks good order because it never meets together as one congregation; the ministers do not uphold the Lord's Day; the attendance of the members can not be checked; and excommunication and other public action can not be properly done; (2) They baptize children of non-members; (3) They use prayers in public worship other than the Lord's Prayer; (4) They do not observe the command of Christ in Matthew 18:15-17 about discipline and "Tell it to the Church"; (5) They worship in buildings which formerly were devoted to anti-Christ; (6) They do not support their ministers in the manner that Christ commands (I Corinthians 9:14) but follow the example of the Papists; (7) Their elders are elected annually, not for life; (8) They hold marriages in the church, as if it were an ecclesiastical service whereas it belongs to civil authority only; (9) They use a new church punishment of suspension which Christ did not ordain; and (10) They commemorate special days as being Christ's birth, resurrection, and ascension.[58] This document was not new; it had been first prepared for Matthew Slade when he left the Separatists for the Dutch Reformed Church to convince him of his error. Probably it was not originally designed for publication to the Dutch, who nevertheless learned of it, and found it highly offensive. Arminius and Taffinus had a copy of the ten articles which they sent to Junius in March 1599.[59]

Several versions (beginning in 1602) list an eleventh point: that the Dutch church received into membership people who were excommunicated (presumably from the Separatists). The Synod, after receiving the ten-article document from the consistory, regarded the points as not well founded and labelled the Separatists as "schismatics or schism-makers" (*schismatices ofte schuermakers*), also as "holders of conventicles." They scolded them for their talk of excommunication, which, some feared, implied a total Separatist excommunication of the Dutch Reformed Church. The Synod contemptuously sent notice to the city magistrates apprising them of the situation.[60]

Amidst all this hurling of epithets, it should be stressed that the two churches, the large Dutch Reformed and the tiny refugee Separatist church, had not completely written each other off. Theologically they had

---

[58] Reitsma and Van Veen, I, 306-08 (1601, art. 38); Dexter and Dexter, *England and Holland*, pp. 434-45.

[59] Arminius, *Works*, I, 159-65; For the eleventh article: *Certayne Letters* (1602); Francis Johnson, *An Inquirie and Answer of Thomas White his Discoverie of Brownisme* (n.p., 1606), pp. 78-80; Joseph Hall, *A Common Apologie of the Chvrch of England* (London, 1610), p. 131; Gerardt Brandt, *Historie der Reformatie* (Amsterdam, 1671), I, 843-45. On the 10th and 11th articles, see De Jonge, "Junius en de Separatisten," pp. 148-49.

[60] Reitsma and Van Veen, I, 307-08.

much in common; and no English Separatist theologian in Amsterdam ever went on record as absolutely refusing all communion with the Dutch church. "We hold here to be many true churches, Dutch & French; which yet have their corruptions, from which we desire they were purged," said Henry Ainsworth. Francis Johnson and John Canne, rather reluctantly, agreed.[61] George Johnson with a splintered group from the main Separatist congregation even went so far as to apply for membership in the Dutch Reformed consistory in 1603 but nothing came of it. Johnson was referred to at the time as "teacher of some of the English nation."[62]

Throughout the controversy, the church authorities were more fiery against dissenters than the magistrates, who exhibited a benign spirit against religious dissenters; the Dutch preachers probably would have expelled them. Business before religion was the rule at the *stadhuis*. When the Separatists began erecting their church buildings on the Lange Houtstraat in 1607, the Dutch consistory sent protests to the magistrates; but, as usual, they took no action. At this point the violent wind, reported by John Paget, hit the Separatists, "and their house onely and no other"—and knocked them flat.[63]

Rebukes, sneers, even an occasional hurricane, they could survive; and under Francis Johnson's leadership the church at Amsterdam took shape, growing both in numbers and confidence. Amsterdam served as the place of practical churchmanship for the Separatists as they placed in operation the various theories which had been so severely repressed at home. Their church from its beginning in London had been gathered by means of a covenant among the believers; subscribing to it became the means of membership. The Confession of 1596 in article 33 explained the covenant:

> That beeing come forth of this antichristian estate vnto the freedom and true profession of Christ, besides the instructing and well guyding of their own Families, they are willingly to ioyne together in christian communion and orderly couenant, and by confession of Faith and obedience of Christ, to vnite themselues into peculiar Congregations, wherein, as members of one body whereof Christ is the only head, they are to worship and serue God according to his word, remembering to keep holy the Lords day.[64]

---

[61] In Ainsworth and Broughton, *Certayne Questions* (n.p., 1605), p. 37; John Canne, *A Necessitie of Separation* (n.p., 1634), p. 188; Francis Johnson, *A Christian Plea* (n.p., 1617), p. 245.
[62] Acta Kerkeraad, III, 98 (June 26, 1603).
[63] Ibid., III, 154, 155v (Nov. 30, 1606, Jan. 4, 1607); Baptismal Register, E.R.C. (Feb.-Mar. 1607), fol. 1. See also Smith, *Religion and Trade*, p. 86.
[64] In Walker, *Creeds*, p. 69; White, *Separatist Tradition*, p. 84. On Browne's Separatist covenant at Middelburg, see chap. 2.

At that early period, it may not have been an explicit written church covenant, but at least the believer gave words like these: "that he wold walke with the rest of that congregacion soe longe as they did walke in the waye of the Lord and as farr as might be warraunted by the Word of God."[65]

The act of covenanting was serious business. The coming together of the believers was the foundation of the church and accepting the covenant meant adherence to the gathered church (the positive commitment) as well as renunciation of worldly pursuits (the negative commitment). George Johnson's history of the church, looking back to the pure age of the church under persecution in London, noted two conditions of membership: personal confession of faith and testimony of Christian walk. Seemingly, the negative commitment, based on hatred of the Church of England, played an increasingly large part in Separatist membership and group identity. If the new members "confesse the English church to be a false Church, promise to separate frome it, and walke with them, it is inough," complained George Johnson, who thought Francis Johnson's congregation was letting down standards.[66] The ex-Separatist Christopher Lawne also stressed the prevalence of the negative commitment; "Whosoeuer will come & acknowledge that England is a falce and Antichristian Church, they doe receive them, whereby they have many not only ignorant of religion, but of lewd disposition." When Lawne and his faction were excommunicated from the church, they flaunted their departure by a public announcement; we "openly renounce our couenant and profession of separation."[67]

No doubt, the ideal of gathering a pure church from amidst the dross was the most exhilarating of Separatist doctrines. Francis Johnson exhorted his group to press on, for they were reaching the goal; "they were by the mercie of God the purest Church, and the freest from corruptions, and set in more excellent order, than any Church that he knew this day in the world."[68] Henry Ainsworth in his debate with John Paget put the doctrine of separating into a syllogism:

> That separation which is onely from syn, and communion therewith, is of God, & is all good mens dutie:
> But our separation is onely from syn, and communion with syn: wherein we were intangled in your mother church:
> Therefore our separation is of God, etc.[69]

---

[65] *Writings of Greenwood and Barrow, 1591-93*, p. 306.
[66] Johnson, *Discourse*, p. 78.
[67] Christopher Lawne, *Brownisme tvrned the In-side out-ward* (London, 1613), p. 20; Lawne, *Prophane Schisme*, p. 2.
[68] Lawne, *Prophane Schisme*, p. 4.
[69] Quoted in Paget, *Arrow*, p. A3v.

In specifics, their separation from the Church had been a fleeing (1) from human liturgy, (2) from the mixture of unseparated congregations, (3) from the form and order of a popish diocesan church, and (4) from a ministry depending upon popish precedents.[70]

The Separatist attitude to the Dutch Reformed Church was ambiguous, and although certainly critical, was not totally rejecting of it. The Dutch preachers, however, interpreted the Separatist rhetoric "to be such as did also necessarily lead vnto separation from them," and such an implication could have easily been drawn. Ainsworth's church was remarkably severe, even to the point of disciplining some members who married Dutch spouses or had children baptized in the Dutch Reformed Church.[71] Ainsworth acknowledged that they "in deed mislike the faults that are in this Dutch Church about baptisme, & wil not suffer our members that hav ioined in covenant with vs, to run into those iniquities, or partake with them," but he denied that they excommunicated on those grounds. Others, like Stephen Offwood, claimed to know cases of such excommunications. However, neither the Johnsonian or Ainsworthian Separatists intended to go so far as to cut off the Dutch Reformed Church totally, and officially put it off limits. Ainsworth was hurt and puzzled that they were so rigidly excluded by the Dutch preachers and thought the estrangement to be more the fault of the Dutch church rather than of his own.[72]

The Amsterdam Separatists in their purified church developed a worship service spotlessly cleansed of the Prayer Book. Horton Davies lists the two important contributions of Separatism to English worship as the concrete examples of simplified worship to other Puritans and the opposition to any set forms of worship.[73] Separation from sin, insisted Henry Ainsworth, meant first of all separation from the Anglican Prayer Book, a mere human liturgy taken over from a "mass book"—"a read and dead service" instead of spiritual worship. The Separatists were chary of any set forms smacking of the despised liturgy, and one of the fiery issues between Separatists and non-Separatist Puritans was the Lord's Prayer—was that "read and dead?" If used as the Spirit leads, Ainsworth granted the value of the Lord's Prayer, but if used "by rote, as is the fashion of many, that I approve not."[74] One of Johnson's ten

---

[70] Ibid.

[71] Ibid., p. 55.

[72] Ainsworth and Broughton, *Certayne Questions*, p. 12; Paget, *Arrow*, p. 45; cf. Stephen Offwood, *An Advertisement*, pt. 2, "Heady and Rash Censures" (Amsterdam?, 1632), pp. 7-8.

[73] Horton Davies, *The Worship of the English Puritans* (Westminster: Dacre Press, 1948), p. 97.

[74] In Paget, *Arrow*, p. 4v.

critiques of the Dutch Reformed Church, in the Latin writing of 1601, was read prayers, "reading out of a book certain prayers which were invented and established by men."[75]

There was much preaching and praying, and, eventually, under Ainsworth's inspiration, singing as well. Ainsworth, an accomplished Hebrew scholar, gave the Separatists a book of Psalms, versed for singing, *The Book of Psalmes: Englished both in Prose and Meeter* (1612). The English worship services at Amsterdam were composed of the following parts: (1) prayer and giving of thanks by the pastor, (2) Scripture reading with brief explanation, (3) expounding of Scripture and preaching, (4) sacraments, (5) singing of psalms, (6) the collection.[76] The sacraments were administered simply and without ritual or book. The Ancient Church followed a freer and more fervent style than the Puritan worship used by Cartwright at Antwerp and Middelburg in the 1580s, where a worship book had been used in part. Some members of John Smyth's church at Amsterdam, a fellow-Separatist congregation, told of Sunday services from 8:00 to 12:00 noon, and afternoon exercises from 2:00 to 5:00 or 6:00 p.m. At the Ancient Church an "ancient widow," a deaconess, sat in a special place with a little birch rod and kept order among the children.[77]

That deaconess's little birch rod was, however, only the smallest part of discipline. The ministers and elders administered strong discipline to the congregation, for this was a part of being a separated church. Before Johnson's arrival at Amsterdam, there had been the famous scandal of half the congregation excommunicating the other half. Thereafter, the pace was more moderate but still severe. Rebukes, public confessions, and finally excommunication were the tools of discipline. According to Thomas Dawes's report, on Sundays "if any of ye maides or servants have comitted any faults in ye past weeke ye priest being informed there of seekes to reforme her & publisheth her fault. Now some wer found fault'd for celebrating a wedding all night & he told them though it were the Dutch fashion to celebrate them nightly—they did not approve of it."[78]

Any outside distraction which weakened the inner bond of the covenant was dealt with, whether it was marrying outside of the church, hearing sermons from other preachers, or anything else. Such deeds could require the offenders to give "publique confession of their fault, & to

---

[75] Gerardt Brandt, *Historie der Reformatie*, I, 844.
[76] Davies, *Puritan Worship*, pp. 166, 244.
[77] White, *Separatist Tradition*, p. 80; Davies, *Puritan Worship*, pp. 124-25; Dexter, *Congregationalism*, I, 317, 334.
[78] Add. MS. 29,492, fol. 11v (1623, B.M.).

repent openly for the same," even excommunication if perceived to be a forsaking of the covenant. If the outside sermons were Church of England, listening to them was condemned as "apostasy."[79] Christopher Lawne and Robert Bulward mockingly published their documents of excommunication from the Ancient Church. Their faults were "railing, slandering, abusing, and despising" the church government and the entire church.[80] Because excommunication, in the best sense, was intended to be redemptive, a way of rehabilitating a fallen member, the Separatists sharply complained when the Dutch or another of the English churches undercut the discipline process by taking the excommunicates in.[81] All English churches in the Netherlands, Separatist and non-Separatist, were disciplining churches; but their discipline often failed of its intended effect because of the suspended member's ability to find a less severe church, English or Dutch, willing to admit him.

Separatist life in Amsterdam was seldom placid. Amsterdam had collected together in the Johnson brothers and the rest of their company some of the hardiest and most single-minded souls of the times. Ordinary, peaceful timid folk were not the sort to rush into the hazards of Separatism and immigration. Separatists were ideological people who had staked everything on religion, and for them compromise was a thing of the past. Their extremism of religious belief, when coupled with strong personality, explains much of the continual controversy in the Separatist church. For the 300 or 400 who made the step, the Ancient Church was their covenanted fellowship, giving them an urgent sense of ownership and participation. Robert Parker, a critic from the rival English Reformed Church, himself a refugee from the High Commission, judged them leniently: "I thinke no other, but that manie of them loue the Lord," even in the midst of their error.[82] Their inner controversies, so public and shrill, brought the entire Separatist church into notoriety, and made respectable people, who abhorred excommunications, lawsuits, and noisy polemics, dissociate themselves with all speed. At the heart of the Separatist faith was a democratic, participatory tendency, but usually minimized by ministers and elders. The Separatist church at Amsterdam is a particularly clear example of the covenanted group taking itself and each individual member seriously—with consequent eruptions of

---

[79] Paget, *Arrow*, pp. 3, 30; White, *Separatist Tradition*, p. 99. Johnson in the *Discourse*, pp. 53-54, reports on the case of Richard Matley, who was prevented by church discipline from marrying a wife of the Dutch Reformed Church.
[80] Lawne, *Prophane Schisme*, pp. 6, 20-21.
[81] Brandt, *Historie der Reformatie*, I, 845.
[82] Lawne, *Prophane Schisme*, p. 69.

excessive spirit and conviction. No archbishop here to impose decorum and "the beauty of holiness."

An English visitor to the Separatists in late 1623, after Ainsworth's death, scoffed at the disorder in the church: "Were also at ye Brownists Church where one appointed as heere stands up & chooses his text & comments on it & if any one thinkes he saide either to little or to much or from the matter belonging to the text any one that will standeth up & delivers his mind, and so others find fault with him & fall to Arguing so that it is another Westminster hall rather then a place of divine service."[83] Johnson and elder Studley attempted to control the church in an authoritarian way, but the very nature of voluntary Separatism undercut the possibility of achieving an effective authoritarian regime. The membership felt too much a sense of participation and ownership to accept a non-participatory status; moreover, the rival English churches of the city provided an escape route if the mood of the Ancient Church became too oppressive. Consequently, there was a dash of Westminster Hall—debates and individualistic self-assertion—but in strong tension with the principle of discipline. The democratic, radically individualistic tendency was one of the major contributions of Amsterdam Separatism to English church life, although, as George Johnson's *Discourse* shows, the individualistic side was often beaten down. Participating in the Separatist covenant raised expectations of heavenly fellowship; all the greater was the bitterness of unfulfillment. Members who departed from the church went with a shout or whirlwind, sometimes writing a book or making an angry exposé—their revenge for ruined dreams.

The Separatist preachers did not encourage democracy. Quite the reverse; and as the years passed, Johnson and his circle in the church denounced full participatory church life as unbiblical. The Confession of Faith (*The True Confession* of 1596 and 1602) promised to the individual congregation power over its own affairs: "That as every christian Congregation hath powre and commandement to elect and ordeine their own ministerie.... So have they also powre and commandement when anie such defalt, either in their lyfe, Doctrine, or administration breaketh out, as by the rule of the word debarreth them from, or depriveth them of their ministerie, by due order to depose them from the ministerie they exercised; yea if the case so require, and they remayne obstinate and impenitent, orderly to cut them off by excommunication." Also, "Congregations bee thus distinct and severall bodyes, every one as a compact Citie in it self...."[84] From the outside, the Separatists were accused of

---

[83] Thomas Dawes, Add. MS. 29,492, fol. 11.
[84] Walker, *Creeds*, pp. 66 (art. 23) and 71 (art. 38).

being ultra democrats, holding that "the power of Christ, that is, authority to preach, to administer the sacraments, and to exercise the censures of the Church, belongeth to the whole Church, yea, to every one of them, and not to the principall members therof."[85] Johnson and Ainsworth, however, denied any intention of "popular government." "We hold it not, we approve it not." Likewise Elder Studley, Johnson's right hand man, a perpetual officer, denounced "popular government, the verie baine to all good order in church, and comon weale."[86] Such declarations, not surprisingly, came from men on the top, who already were in charge. They do not reflect the aspirations of the congregation as a whole. One of the lively debates in Amsterdam concerned the meaning of the words "Tell the church" (Matthew 18:17). Did the *church* mean "men, women and children in their own persons" or did it mean merely the "Christian eldership"? At Johnson's insistence, the Ancient Church declared in favor of the latter and denounced the congregational approach as "error." A similar agitation for English lay people to participate fully in congregational life and government appeared in the non-Separatist Amsterdam English Reformed Church.[87]

Although the Ancient Church of Johnson and Ainsworth was the first and most prominent English church in Amsterdam, it was not the only one. Henoch Clapham headed a little group of near-Separatist Puritans (in several cases, ex-Separatists) in the late 1590s. His book, *Theologicall Axioms or Conclusions* (1597) refers on the title page to "that poore English Congregation in Amstelredam: To whome H.C. For the present, administreth the Ghospel." The records of this church, which was very short-lived, are lost. Clapham was a legally ordained minister of the Church of England, having served in Lancashire before emigrating in 1593. The Bishop of Chester convicted him of Barrowism. Thereafter he lived in the Netherlands (Amsterdam and probably Middelburg) and Scotland and moved back and forth several times.[88] At Middelburg he may well have served as army chaplain or as a temporary preacher to the Merchant Adventurers. While in the Low Countries he was once again

---

[85] Henry Ainsworth, *Covnterpoyson* (n.p., 1608), p. 174. He was refuting the charges of Richard Bernard.

[86] *Covnterpoyson*, p. 177; Richard Clyfton, *An Advertisement concerning a Book Lately Published by Christopher Lawne and others* (n.p., 1612), pp. 112, 122.

[87] Francis Johnson, *A Short Treatise concerning the exposition of those words of Christ, Tell the Church, &c. Mat. 18.17*, also "Note of Some Things Called into Question" (n.p., 1611); Dexter, *Congregationalism*, I, 325-26. On the English Reformed Church, see chapter 4.

[88] Henoch Clapham, *Theologicall Axioms or Conclusions: Pvblikly Controverted, Discvssed, and Conclvded by that poore English Congregation in Amstelredam: To whome H. C. for the present, administreth the Ghospel* (n.p., 1597), "Epistle"; Burrage, *E.E.D.*, I, 194-200. The record of his conviction for Barrowism is in STAC 5/M 11/13 (P.R.O.); my thanks to Michael Moody for this reference.

accused by "our Englische teachers at Midleburgh" of being both a Brownist and Anabaptist, but in his *Theologicall Axioms* he strongly repudiated both sects. Nevertheless, he had several connections with Brownists and gave much suspicion of having been very close to them. His little congregation was composed chiefly of ex-Separatist cast-offs from Johnson's church (he referred to his "faithful brethren" Abraham Crottendine, Cristopher Symkins, Thomas Farrar, and others) and at Amsterdam he lodged at the house of Israel Johnson, a known Separatist sympathizer.[89] John Smyth and Henry Ainsworth lumped Clapham in with past Separatist dissenters; Smyth called Clapham a fearful "Apostate," like unto Richard Bernard and Thomas White.[90]

Clapham's "poore English congregation" was sharply distinct from Francis Johnson's Ancient Church; and in his Amsterdam writings he came out full blast against Separatism: "Our English Brownisme is but flat Donatisme."[91] The *Theologicall Axioms* lists twelve non-Separatist doctrines of the church. In one of his letters he gave a good word for the Church of England; although not approving her constitution, yet he granted that there were believers within her who "are visible members of Christ Jesus." He gave advice about hearing Church of England ministers; "I dare not condempne any one for hearing of some that preach in the Church of England (men honest, well qualified, going forwards in the faith, etc.)." Regarding Johnson's church, he disassociated himself, saying he "dare not medle. Theire judgements in diverse things are so hard and theire practizes in many things so unmercifull and preposterous."[92] Nothing more is specifically known about Clapham's little non-Separatist church except for its twelve axioms and slight references to it in his books and letters of 1597 and 1598, where a few names are listed. By 1600 he was back in England.[93]

Another briefly-existent English church was led by Thomas White. His people came from the "West parts of England," and then as a separated church immigrated to Amsterdam, "professing the same faith with vs," said Francis Johnson. Twelve or thirteen persons were in White's Separatist Amsterdam church. After associating with Johnson's church temporarily, White's people "ioined themselues here as a body

---

[89] Clapham, *The Syn against the Holy Ghoste* (Amsterdam, 1598), dedication: Harley MS. 7581, fol. 57, item 4. On the Separatist background of his members, see their names in Johnson, *Discourse*, especially pp. 32, 41.

[90] Smyth, *Paralleles, Censures, Observations* (n.p., 1609), p. 5; Ainsworth, *Covnterpoyson*, p. 41.

[91] Clapham, *Bibliotheca Theologica* (Amsterdam, 1597).

[92] Clapham letter (about 1597), Harley MS. 7581, fol. 57 *Writings of Greenwood and Barrow, 1591-93*, pp. 332-33.

[93] Clapham, *Antidoton* (London, 1600), p. 6.

together, to walk in the same faith and way as we do; reputing and calling themselves a Church, distinct from vs." By 1605, White and his group had disbanded, much disillusioned, and White, having returned to the Church of England, wrote an angry anti-Separatist book, *A Discoverie of Brownism* (1605).[94] As an insider, at last come to his senses, White told Separatist dirty stories of adulteries, thefts, cozenages, "in such abundance," and he tantilizingly hinted at "brokerage of whores, and other filthinesse, too too bad." Johnson wrote him a rejoinder, *An Inquirie and Answer of Thomas White* (1606), and several Separatists brought suit for slander against White in Amsterdam courts but won no redress.[95]

Although Johnson's Ancient Church survived at Amsterdam in one form or another until 1701, it suffered many schisms and inner turmoils, which in the usual course, became public quarrels. One of these early crises occurred when Matthew Slade, an elder of the church, left his office and was banished from the church. He had been appointed assistant master (conrector) of the Latin School in the Koestraat (1598), but was excommunicated by his own church. In 1602 he became rector of the school. He married the stepdaughter of Petrus Plancius. After being excommunicated (about 1598) for attendance at Dutch Reformed worship, and for defending Dutch practices, he became "a great enemy to the Brownists."[96] It was Slade's withdrawal from Separatism and his acceptance by the Dutch Reformed Church that prompted Johnson's ten point critique of the Dutch church in 1601, taken so bitterly by consistory and synod. Johnson's eleventh point, that the Dutch received as members those who were under excommunication from other churches, fits the Slade situation exactly.[97] John Paget recalled that Slade had defended the Dutch practice of baptism of infants whose parents were not members of the particular church and how the Brownists "had excommunicate *Mr. Slade*, for defending the practice of the Dutch herein."[98]

While the Slade affair simmered (1598), the church was further tested by a ferocious argument between brothers Francis and George Johnson (1597-1603). The controversy had begun back in England, when George objected to Francis's marriage, while in the Clink, to Mrs. Thomasine

---

[94] Johnson, *Inquirie and Answer*, preface, pp. 52-53; Burrage, *E.E.D.*, I, 186-87. The church existed perhaps 1603-05.

[95] Lawne, *Prophane Schisme*, pp. 27-29; Thomas White, *A Discoverie of Brownisme* (London, 1605), p. 7.

[96] Hoop Scheffer, "De Brownisten te Amsterdam," p. 252; C. P. Burger, "Een Metselaar-Latinist, *Het Boek*, 20 (1931), 305-10. See also the Hoop Scheffer MSS extracts, E.R.C. no. 14 (G. A. Amsterdam). Slade was excommunicated sometime between Oct. 12, 1598 (OS), and Mar. 3, 1598/99 (NS).

[97] Brandt, *Historie der Reformatie*, I, 845; Hoop Scheffer, "De Brownisten," pp. 252-56.

[98] Paget, *An Answer to the unjust complaints of William Best* (Amsterdam, 1635), pp. 40-41.

Boys, a fashionable widow. Eventually George wrote a book with his side of the story, *A Discourse of Some Troubles and Excommunications in the Banished English Church at Amsterdam* (1603), in which he referred to the new Mrs. Johnson's reputation as a "bouncing girle," proud and vain. "Many of the Saints are greeved." The controversy over her immodest clothes (busks, whalebone petticoats, great sleeves, lace) and "toyish" hats dragged from London to Amsterdam and much troubled the church for a good while. After many meetings, the congregation finally concluded that her hat was not toyish in nature, and pastor Johnson—ever the M.A. and Fellow of Christ's—proved himself still a master dialectician:

> What is not in the nature thereof toyish that used by any is not toyish:
> The hat in the nature thereof is not toyish;
> Ergo, being used by her it was not toyish.

The upshot of it all was that Francis Johnson's majority in 1598 or 1599 excommunicated George—he was impious, heathenish, hideous and had "crackbrainednes," they said. Their father, who came over to soothe the situation, was also excommunicated (1602).[99] George wrote his book in 1603. Apparently, George took a few of the stricter sort of the congregation with him and, as the Dutch consistory records show in 1603, became "teacher of some the English nation." Thereafter, still a Separatist, George returned to England and died in a Durham prison.[100]

Another tragic event in the church's history occurred in 1610 when Johnson and Ainsworth split, causing a permanent division in the congregation. The main part remained with Johnson, including Richard Clifton, a minister, who had come over with John Robinson, but a small group of thirty or so went with Ainsworth. The Ainsworthians included John Beauchamp, Thomas Bischop, Giles Thorp, Henry May, John Hales, John Peyne, William Schephard, Abraham Pulbery, John Crumford, and Richard Bennet.[101] Their final break took place on December 16, 1610. The elders remained with Johnson, except for Ecluse, who joined Ainsworth; Johnson also kept the Lange Houtstraat building. The most divisive issue had been the nature of church government and the meaning of Matthew 18:17, "Tell it to the Church." Johnson took an authoritarian position so that minister and elders were running the church without consultation: When Christ said, "Tell the Church," he

---

[99] Apart from Johnson's *Discourse* (see especially pp. 56, 94-98, 125), the story is told in Dexter, *Congregationalism*, I, 272-96. The best account is a modern critical edition of the *Discourse* with introduction and notes by Michael E. Moody, Diss. Claremont, 1979.

[100] Acta Kerkeraad Amsterdam, III, 98; Broughton and Ainsworth, *Certayne Questions* (1605, where he is reported dead), p. 14; Johnson, *Inquirie and Answer*, p. 61.

[101] R.A. 2164, fol. 95v.

meant "Tell the Congregation of Elders." Ainsworth supported the more traditional Separatist practice of congregational participation and decision-making, in conjunction with elders.[102] According to Matthew Slade's version, the two "have ben at great Variance about their own Discipline and Separation, which Johnson in some points disclaimed, and desired to be more conform to the reformed churches. Ainsworth withstood him; and after much debate, being separated one from another, each having his adherants, have written one against the other."[103] The church split was enlivened with excommunications and lawsuits. In 1613 Ainsworth's church won the building in a lawsuit, and Johnson's group thereafter withdrew from Amsterdam and migrated to Emden, Germany (1613-17).[104]

The succession of schisms and secessions (Slade, George Johnson, Thomas White, Ainsworth, Christopher Lawne, Offwood) produced a large blast of polemical exposés and counter-exposés. George Johnson's story of discontent, *A Discourse of Some Troubles*, spares very few of his old brethren; he disclosed many "blacke spots" or offenses: thirteen against his brother Francis, seven for Ainsworth, twelve for Studley, twenty-two against the elders as a whole, and ten for the entire congregation. So, said Christopher Lawne, although Separatism claims to be a white art, in actuality it is revealed to be a "very *blacke Art*."[105] Lawne was excommunicated in 1612 and thereafter went over to the English Reformed Church. Lawne's *Prophane Schisme of the Brownists* (1612), one of the harshest of the turncoat books, was fantastic and titilatingly lurid—Separatist elders molesting naked girls, whippings, naked virgins hanging from ceilings, incest, embezzlements, and tyrannies. Lawne labelled elder Studley as a "Matchievellian" guilty of "lasciuious" actions on young maids; and one of Ainsworth's members was known about town as "Mansfield the stripper" because of mistreatment of servant girls.[106] Stephen Offwood left the Church in 1616 but waited until 1632 to publish his book, *An Advertisement to John Delecluse, and Henry May*; if he had known all, "I would never have ioyned with them."[107] The high Anglican Stephen Goffe urged going up to Amsterdam to view the Brownists and "to see the sport."[108]

---

[102] Johnson, *Short Treatise*; White, *Separatist Tradition*, pp. 152-53; Dexter, *Congregationalism*, I, 325-31.
[103] S.P. 84, vol. 82, fol. 34v (Jan. 17, 1618).
[104] R.A. 2164, fol. 95v; Edward Arber, *The Story of the Pilgrim Fathers, 1606-1623 A.D.* (London: Ward and Downey, 1897), p. 117.
[105] Johnson, *Discourse*, pp. 180-98; Lawne, *Prophane Schisme*, p. 31.
[106] Lawne, *Prophane Schisme*, pp. 15-16, 32-41.
[107] Offwood, *Advertisement*, pt. 2, p. 36.
[108] B.P., I, 169 (Jan. 7, 1634).

By 1610 Amsterdam had at least five English churches, four of them Separatist. The Separatist churches were headed by Johnson, Ainsworth, John Smyth, and Thomas Helwys. The fifth was the non-Separatist English Reformed Church (1607), pastored by John Paget. A sixth church, John Robinson's, was briefly in Amsterdam but moved to Leiden in 1609. Starting in 1607, a new wave of Separatist immigration from England had led to the founding of several of the new churches. These Separatists came from the Scrooby, Bawtry, Gainsborough neighborhood of the Nottinghamshire, Lincolnshire, Yorkshire area, where they had attempted to form covenanted churches. John Smyth gathered a church at Gainsborough and John Robinson one at Scrooby. Another Church of England minister, Richard Bernhard of Worksop, briefly associated with them, and formed a small inner covenanted group within his parish; but then he took fright and loudly dissociated himself. He wrote a book, *Christian Advertisements and Counsels of Peace. Also Disuasions from the Separatists schisme* (1608). Like every other English place, Nottinghamshire and vicinity proved inhospitable to the Separatists. "Hunted and persecuted on every side, so as their former afflictions were but as fleabitings in comparison of these which now came upon them," the Separatists of the north in 1607 began to move to Amsterdam, "wher they heard was freedome of Religion for all men."[109]

Smyth's people went over first, some time after February 25, 1606/07. Although fellow Separatists with Johnson, Smyth did not unite with the Ancient Church but rather began another church, "the Second English Church at Amsterdam."[110] Smyth's Second Church, which in fact was Amsterdam's third, after Johnson's and the English Reformed, eventually evolved into an Anabaptist church. The church of Helwys split off from Smyth in 1610. John Robinson's Scrooby Church arrived in 1608. The Robinson group remained distinct from both Johnson and Smyth, largely for fear of being involved in the controversies among the older churches, "seeing how Mr. John Smith and his companie had allready fallen in to contention with the church that was ther before them," namely Johnson's. "Also that the flames of contention were like to breake out in that anciente church it selfe." In 1609 Robinson's Pilgrim Father

---

[109] William Bradford, *Bradford's History of Plymouth Plantation, 1606-1646*, ed. William T. Davis (1908; rpt. New York: Barnes & Noble, 1946), p. 32; Ronald A. Marchant, *The Puritans and the Church Courts in the Diocese of York, 1560-1642* (London: Longmans, 1960), pp. 141-66.

[110] Smyth's *Differences of the Churches of the Separation* (1608) refers to the "Second English Church at Amsterdam" on the title page; see also Johannes Bakker, *John Smyth, de stichter van het Baptisme* (Wageningen: H. Veenman & Zonen, 1964), p. 59; Marchant, *Puritans and the Church Courts*, p. 156.

church moved on to Leiden,[111] reducing the number of English churches; but when the Ancient Church in 1610 had its Johnson-Ainsworth schism, the number of English churches was once again four, and then five, counting the split in Smyth's Anabaptist church led by Thomas Helwys.

From the outside looking in, the world of Amsterdam Separatism was a whirl of motion and scandal: Johnson was accused by Ainsworth; Ainsworth was accused by Johnson: Smyth ("drunken with the dregges of error, and strange phantasies") was rejected by both Johnson and Ainsworth; Robinson held Johnson as apostate; Johnson thought Robinson even more apostate.[112] John Paget marvelled at it all; "of those who separate from the Church of God, there are many sorts" and "sundry sects."[113] The constant spectacle of excommunications and schisms gave Separatism its ill repute at Amsterdam. Hugh Peter told them: "You are hardly thought on because you haue excommunicated so many honest men."[114]

Johnson died at Amsterdam and was buried January 10, 1618, shortly after returning from Emden.[115] His death ended the distinct congregation of the "Franciscans." Some of his people attempted immigration to Virginia with elder Francis Blackwell and lost their lives at sea.[116] Matthew Slade, his former elder from the 1590s, gave Johnson final credit for having moderated his former rigidity, especially in his last book, published only a few days before his death, *A Christian Plea* (1617), "wherein he disclaimed most of his former singularities and refuted them." Slade and Johnson had a brief reconciliation near the end.[117] After the 1610 schism, Ainsworth became the leading spokesman for the Amsterdam Separatists, both as pastor and controversialist. "Mr. Henry Ainsworth, who appeared whilst he lived, a bright Star in Christs right hand ... like a faithful Shepherd, who never fled from the flock over which the holy Ghost had made him overseer, but like a valiant souldier of Jesus Christ riding upon the white horse of his Word, under the conduct of Christ our Captain." He carried the Ancient Church onward until his death, caused by "stone callicke" in 1622.[118]

---

[111] Bradford, *Plymouth Plantation*, pp. 38-39; Dexter and Dexter, *England and Holland*, pp. 449-69.
[112] Lawne, *Prophane Schisme*, pp. 63-64.
[113] Paget, *Arrow*, "To the Christian Reader."
[114] Offwood, *Advertisement*, pt. 2, p. 15.
[115] S.P. 84, vol. 81, fol. 143.
[116] Bradford, *Plymouth Plantation*, pp. 59-63.
[117] S.P. 84, vol. 82, fol. 34v.
[118] Thomas Wall (1657) in preface to Francis Johnson, *A Seasonable Treatise for This Age* (London: 1657); Offwood, *Advertisement*, p. 43.

After Ainsworth, the church lacked strong leadership and drifted along for several years. Jean de L'Ecluse, Giles Thorpe, and Henry May were elders in the 1620s, but they had no ordained minister; John Paget accused them in 1635 of being for many years "without Sacraments, and had neither Lords Supper nor Baptisme administred in their Church, their children for many yeares, remayning unbaptized, and sundry dying unbaptised." One report from 1623 reveals a church with some kind of leadership, a "priest," but few numbers. "Of this sect their is not above 80."[119] For the period of the 1620s, Champlin Burrage called the Ancient Church by the name of "l'Ecluse's church" because of his prominent role. Perhaps Ecluse, who liked to preach, was their only minister. During the Ecluse years, schism again hit the church; this time a faction was headed up by merchant, Sabine Staresmore, a former member of Henry Jacob's Independent church at London. When Ecluse's church excommunicated Staresmore, although Robinson admitted him at Leiden, he started his own.[120]

New life came to the Ancient Church about 1630 when John Canne, former pastor of Hubbard's church in London, arrived as pastor and succeeded temporarily in uniting the various dissident factions.[121] He preached a notable sermon, "The Way to Peace" (April 15, 1632) subtitled, as preached "at the Reconciliation of certain Brethren, between whom there had been former Differences."[122] Canne's church had possession of the 1607 Lange Houtstraat building. A partial list of membership can be reconstructed from a notarial document of 1636, when the church borrowed 3000 florins at $6^1/_4$ percent, using the church building "op Vloonburcg in Lange Houtstraat" as its collateral. The following names were signatories: John Canne, Jeffery Silleman, John Payne, John Dickens, Richard Jordan, Bethuel Blos, Henry Moot, George Corye, Ezeckiel Cockey, John Thomas, William Harger, Elias Arnold, Experience Sillimans, Robert Knight, John Wiat, John Hancock, Joseph Thorp, David Moot, Daniel Wild, Richard Quidler, Richard Horten, William Ley, Markus Lucar, Thomas Adams de jonge, Thomas Baker, Nathaniel Thorp, and Jan Ainsworth, "all members of

---

[119] Paget, *Answer*, p. 134; Add. MS. 29,492, fol. 11.

[120] Burrage, *E.E.D.*, I, 171-77; a notary document of Jan. 23, 1625, refers to Sabijn Staresmore, "English merchant now in Amsterdam," Not. Archive 351B, fol. 37. T. A. in his *Christian Reprofe against Contention* (n.p., 1631), refers to the schisme and gives an anti-Staresmore account. See Stephen Forster, *Notes from the Caroline Underground* (Hamden: Archon Books, 1978), pp. 21-23; 86-88.

[121] Canne may be placed in Amsterdam in 1632 on the basis of the printed sermon, "The Way to Peace," and by other reports in 1633 (B.P., I, 135). Conjecture, however, places Canne in Amsterdam as early as 1630; see below, no. 126.

[122] Burrage, *E.E.D.*, I, 178.

the Engelse Gemeente."[123] Canne, a printer as well as a preacher, brought visibility to the Separatist cause through his active writing and printing projects. He wrote and published *A Necessitie of Separation from the Church of England* in 1634 and *A Stay against Straying* in 1639.

By the 1630s, only two English churches remained in Amsterdam from the cluster of six in early century, Canne's Ancient Church and Paget's English Reformed Church. Canne's reconciling did not hold permanently, and the church came apart on several occasions. In 1633 a split divided the brotherhood once again; "some go along with Iohn D'ecluse, some with Mr Kan," and "they would all bee heads." In 1634 Sir William Brereton again reported two factions, one with John Canne, and "one Greenwood, an old man, a tradesman, who sells stockings in Exchange ... is the leader of another company." The Separatist break went unhealed throughout the 1630s, half of the congregation having censured and deposed Canne, the other half remaining with him. These newly erected churches of Separatists, observed John Paget, sometimes had only six or seven members—"incurable contentions."[124]

All reports indicate that the church of the 1640s and 1650s was a mere skeleton of its earlier vigorous form. Only one church, pastored by Canne, is reported. Robert Baillie, writing in 1645, mentioned Canne's ministry at Amsterdam, a church, hobbling along without a full corps of officers, "even yet they live without an Eldership." Behold, "their *spunk* was dying, and their little smoke, both at *Amsterdam* and *Leyden*, was well-neer vanished."[125] Canne remained at his post at least until 1647, and then, "after 17 years Banishment," returned to England where he ministered at various places, first as an Independent and then as a Fifth Monarchist. After the Restoration, Canne returned to Amsterdam, but whether as minister or not is unknown, and died there about 1667.[126]

---

[123] Not. Archive 848 (Joz. Steyns), 1636, end of Jan. or beginning of Feb.

[124] B.P., I, 135 (1633); Brereton, *Travels* (1634), pp. 64-65. As late as 1638 there are references to the continuing Separatist division, in S.P. 84, vol. 154, fol. 113v, which refers to Canne as preacher to *one* of the Brownist groups, and Paget in his *Defence of Chvrch-Government*, pp. 37-38, 158-59 (printed in 1641 but completed about 1638 when Paget died).

[125] Robert Baillie, *Dissvasive from the Errours of the Time* (London: 1645), pp. 15, 54; Paget, *Defence*, p. 152.

[126] Canne referred to the "17 years Banishment" in the Postscript to his *The Time of the End* (1657). When Canne left Amsterdam, i.e. the end of his banishment, is uncertain; he can be placed at Amsterdam in 1643, 1644, 1645, but in a letter of October 1647 he was back at London. He was, however, involved in a lawsuit in Amsterdam with Edmund Blake again in 1649; see I. H. van Eeghen, *De Amsterdamse boekhandel, 1680-1725* (Amsterdam, 1960-67), IV, 137. The 17-year banishment, consequently, could be dated 1630-47, 1631-48, 1632-49. See Champlin Burrage, "Was John Canne a Baptist?" *Transactions* of the Baptist Historical Society, 3 (1913), 224-25, 242; John F. Wilson, "Another Look at John Canne," *Church History*, 33 (Mar. 1964), 34-37.

Amsterdam for several decades, especially during the Johnson-Ainsworth period, was the mainspring of the Separatist movement. Nearly all of the educated leadership of the movement, at Johnson's insistence,[127] was drawn over to the Netherlands (Francis Johnson, M.A., Fellow of Christ's College; George Johnson, M.A. of Christ's College; William Smith, ordained minister; John Smyth, M.A., Fellow of Christ's College; John Robinson, M.A., Fellow of Corpus Christi; Thomas White, Richard Clifton, and William Gilgate, former ministers of the Church of England). Thomas Settle was one of the few educated Separatists to remain behind to minister in England. Consequently, Amsterdam became the Separatist headquarters, where books were written and printed, the doctrines announced, and the purest church life practiced. The remnant left behind in England looked to Amsterdam for leadership and inspiration. Francis Johnson carried the nickname "Bishop of *Brownisme*" because he "exerciseth authoritie ouer some assemblies in *England* and elsewhere."[128] Constant traffic back and forth in books and people—"wandering stars"—kept the Separatist network well tied in with Amsterdam, so that the Archbishop of Canterbury was complaining in 1626 of "continual intercourse" between Norwich Separatists and those of Amsterdam and also of "sundry schismatical books" imported from there.[129]

In the early years the Ancient Church at Amsterdam, as the only English church of the city, encompassed many substantial citizens and prosperous merchants; but across the seventeenth century the Separatists steadily dropped in social respectability and in the economic quality of its members. The better sort were drawn over to the English Reformed Church established in 1607, and this left the Separatist assembly increasingly a circle of "buttonmakers and weavers"—people "seemingly but Ordinary." A declining church, "after the death of *Ainsworth*, the *Brownists* at *Amsterdam* came to a small unconsiderable handful" and continued downhill.[130] The church disbanded in 1701.

Separatist Printers at Amsterdam

Amsterdam served for years as the Separatist print shop. "I suppose it is not unknown unto you," complained Archbishop Bancroft in 1606,

---

[127] Johnson, *Discourse*, pp. 88-89.

[128] Henoch Clapham, *A Chronological Discourse* (London, 1609), p. 12v.

[129] Browne, *Congregationalism*, p. 78; George Johnson, *Discourse*, p. 32, refers to the "wandering stars."

[130] Paul S. Seaver, *The Puritan Lectureship: The Politics of Religious Dissent 1560-1662* (Standford: Stanford Univ. Press, 1970), p. 325; Thomas Bowrey, *Papers* (1698), Hakluyt Society, 2nd ser., no. 58 (1925), p. 37; Baillie, *Dissvasive* (1645), p. 54.

how certain schismatic persons "have planted themselves in divers towns of the *Low Countries,* where they have liberty, without Impeachment or Contradiction, to publish in Print *many dangerous Books* and *Pamphlets in English.*"[131] Wherever established in the Low Countries, whether at Middelburg, Leiden, or Amsterdam, the Separatists founded a press or found a printer willing to serve them.[132] Giles Thorpe, an elder of the Ancient Church, was in charge of the Amsterdam press between 1604-22, but Separatist printing at Amsterdam well antedated 1604. Books by Francis Johnson, George Johnson, and the church's letters to Junius, *Certayne Letters*, came from some unidentified press available to the Separatists prior to Thorp's establishment.[133] Two other church officials besides Thorp, Jean de l'Ecluse, a former printer from Rouen, and Francis Blackwell, had printing experience. Hugh Broughton referred to Blackwell as Ainsworth's early printer or publisher; "you print for him."[134] Blackwell and Thorp in 1609 sold "an entire print shop," consisting of two presses and type, by which time the Separatists had apparently secured better equipment.[135] The Thorp Separatist press was not a commercial, money-making press; its work was propaganda. Between 1604 and 1622, Thorp printed at least forty books, the majority being Separatist books but also many other useful nonconformist books from Hugh Broughton, David Calderwood, Paul Baynes, and William Ames.[136]

Thorp died about 1622 or 1623, but the press carried on. Richard Plater's name or initials appear on three of the later books (1625, 1626, 1627). Plater, originally a Separatist, joined the English Reformed Church in 1621, after renouncing his Brownism.[137] Sabine Staresmore was another of the printers of the Separatist press. Although not a full time professional printer, he had several books to his printing credit. In 1634 Staresmore was reputed to be "the only English printer in the

---

[131] Winwood, *Memorials*, III, 195.

[132] J. Dover Wilson, "Richard Schilders and the English Puritans," *Transactions* of the Bibliographical Society, 9 (1909-11), 65-134; Leona Rostenberg, *The Minority Press & the English Crown* (Nieuwkoop: B. de Graff, 1971), pp. 183, 193.

[133] Francis Johnson, *An Answer to Maister H. Jacob* (1600), George Johnson, *Discourse* (1603), and the *Certayne Letters* (1602), "are the product of the same press," according to A. F. Johnson, "The Exiled English Church at Amsterdam and its Press," *The Library*, 5th ser., 5 (1951), 219.

[134] Hugh Broughton, "Admonition to Blackwell," in *The Works*, ed. John Lightfoot (London, 1662), p. 772; on Ecluse, Hoop Scheffer, *Free Churchmen*, pp. 187, 191.

[135] Not. Archive 265, fol. 18 (van Banchem); Barendt Otsen owed Blackwell 550 guilders for the purchase "van een geheele druckerye."

[136] Johnson, "Exiled English Church," p. 220.

[137] Ibid., pp. 230-31; E.R.C. Amsterdam, C.R., Aug. 18, 1621.

towne."[138] During the late 1630s, especially after 1637, pastor John Canne took the lead in the printing enterprise. His *Necessitie of Separation* of 1634, which he "caused to be printed," was done on the old Separatist printing press. "Canne a minister hath a printing house and he hath printed manie english Bookes," reported an informer in 1638. "He has a press in his house for printing."[139] Canne used a distinctive printers device with the motto "Richt-Right" or "Right-Right" (thus the nickname, Richt-Right Press) and a headpiece with the motto, "cor unum via una." Canne's Richt-Right Press, a continuation of the Thorp Press, was active 1637-42 or perhaps a little longer.[140] The printing work, proclaimed Canne, was a Christian outreach: For the "building vp of Sion," for the "publick good, that the glorious light of Christs wayes and truth might be known vnto the people of this nation" (England). Except possibly for some ill-fated Bible printing deals, Canne was not in printing as a money making business, "and therefore I neuer had scarse any thing for what was published, but cheiflie endeauored the spreading of what was don to the world ... I neuer got penny by the work in my life."[141] In printing Thomas Goodwin's *Aggravation of Sin and Sinning against Knowledge and Mercy* in 1639, Canne's edition carried notice, "printed for the Benefit of the English Churches in the Netherlands." Both in preaching and printing Canne was too much a zealous evangelist to take much care for providing of material things. "I have ten children, nine of which are in house with me," he wrote to a creditor in 1647, and his "outward condition was neuer lower then at the present."[142]

Many Puritans resorted to Amsterdam for their printing needs. John Paget made a survey of the Amsterdam printers available for Puritan printing in the 1630s; "Mr. Canne, preacher to the Brownists maintaines a presse and prints English bookes, but I think he is not for your use," he wrote to David Calderwood of Edinburgh in 1637. "There is an other printer a Dutchman that prints English very correctly with a good letter. He is inclined to Arminianisme, yet I conceave he deals very truely & faithfully for the worke that he is entrusted withall." The Dutch printer he referred to was Jan Fredericksz Stam, printer at Amsterdam from

---

[138] Paget in his *Answer* (1635) refers to "Sa. St." (Staresmore) as a printer who worked with Canne on bringing out John Davenport's *A Just Complaint against an Unjust Doer* (1634); he was also the printer of William Ames' *Fresh Suit* (1633), S.P. 16, vol. 246, no. 56. See Foster, *Caroline Underground*, pp. 21-23, 88-89. Foster believes that Staresmore may have been in charge of the entire press 1623-34.

[139] S.P. 16, vol. 387, no. 79; S.P. 84, vol. 153, fol. 293.

[140] C. E. Sayle, *Early English Printed Books in the University Library Cambridge* (Cambridge: Cambridge Univ. Press, 1900-07), III, nos. 6365-73; Johnson, "Exiled English Church," p. 231; Wilson, "Canne," pp. 40-42.

[141] Burrage, "Canne," pp. 226, 230.

[142] Ibid., p. 230.

1628 to 1657.[143] Stam was married to the widow of Joris Veseler, another Amsterdam printer, who earlier had taken on some Puritan printing, including Paget's *Arrow against the Separation* (1618). Between 1628 and 1639, Stam printed no fewer than nineteen English books, apart from Bibles. Among his authors were Alexander Leighton, Henry Burton, William Prynne, and John Bastwick. "He printeth much english."[144]

In addition to printing Puritan polemical books, which made no one a profit, the Amsterdam printers operated a profitable English Bible printing business. During the seventeenth century, thousands of English language Bibles were printed at Amsterdam and smuggled into England, where monopoly kept prices high. One printer alone, Joseph Athias, boasted in 1687 that he over the years "had printed more than ten times a hundred thousands Bibles in the English and Scottish languages."[145] J. F. Stam was an active Bible printer. In 1633 he did a Geneva edition for merchant Thomas Crafford with the imprint, "Imprinted at Amsterdam, for Thomas Crafoorth. By John Fredericksz Stam, dwelling by the South-Church at the signe of the Hope. 1633."[146] In 1638 Stam had a large order of 7,000 English Bibles in process, including Bibles in quarto, in folio, and in duodecimo, all with notes, "and manie marchantes bye great quantities of them ... and so bring them over." Again in 1642 he printed 12,000 English Bibles in duodecimo and in 1644 he contracted for 6,000 more Bibles in duodecimo.[147] Canne also tried the Bible trade in the 1640s, "smal bibles" (24°) in 1644 and 1649. His Bible printing was not very good and merchant Edmund Blake in 1644 sued Canne rather than take delivery of some Bibles as contracted. Blake charged Canne with total incompetency after finding over 6,000 errors in his Bibles, so "that they are not fit to be imported into England and ought to be burned." They were not burned, however, and Canne peddled them elsewhere, and some reached England. While printing Bibles, Canne had underway a scholarly project of writing a set of marginal notes to go with the authorized King James version. They first appeared in 1642 and were

---

[143] Wodrow MS., Folio XLII, fol. 253 (Nat. Lib. of Scotland).

[144] S.P. 16, vol. 387, no. 79; A. F. Johnson, "J. F. Stam, Amsterdam, and English Bibles," *The Library*, 5th ser., 9 (1954), 185. Jan Theunisz, Anabaptist bookseller, did publishing of English books by Hugh Broughton, see H. F. Wijnman, "Jan Theunisz alias Joannes Antonides (1569-1637)," *Amstelodamum Jaarboek*, 25 (1928), 29-123.

[145] I. H. van Eeghen, "De befaamde drukkerij op de Herengracht over Plantage (1685-1755)," *Amstelodamum Jaarboek*, 58 (1966), 83; Van Eeghen, *Amst. boekhandel*, IV, 101-02, 135-38.

[146] Johnson, "Stam," p. 190. Johnson had identified 8 or 9 English editions of the Bible done by Stam.

[147] Van Eeghen, *Amst. boekhandel*, IV, 101; S.P. 16, vol. 387, no. 79.

reprinted frequently thereafter. After the restoration of 1660, when Canne returned to Amsterdam, he again printed Bibles.[148]

Several other Amsterdam printers and books dealers had Separatist connections. Steven Swart (1641-83), Dutch printer of English Bibles, a member of the English Reformed Church, married Abigail May, daughter of elder Henry May of Ainsworth's church. Joseph Bruyningh, Amsterdam bookseller, was Henry May's brother-in-law, through his sister Susanna Bruyningh, who was married to May.[149] The Puritan printing enterprise required not only printers in the print shop but also publishers and financial patrons. Such men served as the "procurer" or "setter forth" of books. Stephen Offwood, the excommunicated Separatist, was one of these. After excommunication, he first went to the Dutch Reformed Church and next to the English Reformed Church of Paget; his wife and children, however, remained Separatists. According to Sir William Boswell, he "procured the printing of all the blew books" of the early 1630s. Several notable Puritan books appeared with the notice, "Published by S.O." Because Offwood operated a boarding house for English travelers, Boswell sneered at him as "an ignorant victualler."[150]

Another book patron was Thomas Crafford, a young merchant from Reading, who took his meals at Offwood's victullary. Among his projects were the Bible of 1633 by Stam ("Imprinted at Amsterdam for Thomas Crafoorth") and a printing of *A Guide unto Sion* in 1639 by Canne, also with Crafford's name on the title page. Boswell regarded Crafford in 1639 as the "principall setter forth" of venomous books. Although not chiefly a printer, Crafford was known to be "practiced and knowledgeable in printing." Crafford, however, had a bad reputation among the merchant community for having once gone bankrupt.[151] Many of his book dealings were with another merchant, Thomas Stafford from Selby, also of unsavory reputation, an excommunicate from the Separatists for cheating. He was married to Susanna Offwood, probably Stephen Offwood's daughter. The two merchants often worked together,

---

[148] Burrage, "Canne," p. 232; Wilson, "Canne," pp. 37, 47; Van Eeghen, *Amst. boekhandel*, IV, 137. John Wingfield, Humphrey Hodges, and William Taylor bought some of the 1644 "smal bibles." Not. Archive 2157, fols. 20-25 (1663).

[149] Van Eeghen, *Amst. boekhandel*, IV, 135-36, 138.

[150] S.P. 84, vol. 147, fol. 174; B.P., I, 135-36, 139. He joined the English Reformed Church on April 18, 1629. Among his published books were William Ames, *Fresh Suit against Human Ceremonies* (1633) and John Forbes, *Four Sermons* (1635), both with the notation "Published by S. O." Staresmore, however, was the printer of the *Fresh Suit.*

[151] B.P., I, 139; S.P. 84, vol. 155, fols. 79, 145; M. M. Kleerkooper and W. P. van Stockum, Jr., *De boekhandel te Amsterdam voornamelijk in de 17ᵉ eeuw* (The Hague: Nijhoff, 1914-16), pp. 1244-46.

but Stafford was also in the Bible business on his own in 1640 with a Geneva edition printed with his name: "And are to be sold at his house, at the signe of the Flight of Brabant, upon Milk-market, over against the Deventer Wood-market."[152]

In 1639 Crafford and Stafford joined efforts and contracted with William Christiaensz of Leiden for 1250 Bibles; in 1642 and 1644 Crafford contracted with J. F. Stam for buying and transporting Bibles into England.[153] The two Bible merchants fell out with each other in 1642 when Crafford libelled Stafford and was sentenced to six weeks in jail on bread rations. After another altercation with a Dutchman in 1649, Crafford was banished from the city for being a "rebellious libeller and dirty vagabond."[154] Men of greater reputation were also investing heavily in the book trade. Hugo Fitts, solid member of the English Reformed Church, bought 6,000 Bibles from Stam and Crafford in 1644. "One Mr. Beauchamp" of a prominent English family of the same church was another merchant who bought Bibles from Stam.[155] The English book and Bible trade of Amsterdam was sustained by merchant entrepreneurs who bought by the hundreds and thousands and shipped them across.[156]

The Amsterdam printing presses produced a great harvest on behalf of the Puritan cause. The Thorp-Canne press in the years up to 1635 sent forth over 90 books, probably many more; and thereafter Canne, using the "Richt Right" imprint, produced many volumes (eight books in a six-month period of 1637-38 alone). The Dutch printers Veseler, Stam, and Johannes Jansson were active printers of English books.[157] The English government mounted a strong campaign to silence the printing presses, but because the Netherlands had no central censorship policy like England's, control was always difficult, even in the rare cases where the Dutch authorities wished to oblige. The English ambassadors at The Hague had the assignment to stop the offending printers, and some help came from certain Dutch Reformed ministers who despised Brownism.

---

[152] T. H. Darlow and H. F. Moule, eds. *Historical Catalogue of the Printed Editions of Holy Scripture in the Library of the British and Foreign Bible Society* (London: The Bible House, 1903-11), I, no. 424. On Stafford's excommunication, see Not. Archive 1058, fols. 56-57.

[153] Kleerkooper and van Stockum, *Boekhandel*, pp. 1244-46; Van Eeghen, *Amst. boekhandel*, IV, 101. A. F. Johnson, "Willem Christiaans, Leyden, and His English Books," *The Library*, 5th ser., 10 (1955), 123. Perhaps the Stafford Bible of 1640 ("the Flight of Brabant") was a product of the 1639 Christiaensz deal.

[154] Van Eeghen, *Amst. boekhandel*, IV, 101.

[155] Ibid., IV, 101; S.P. 16, vol. 387, no. 79. Fitts was deacon of the English Reformed Church in 1651. Richard Beauchamp, the "Mr. Beauchamp" likely referred to, was deacon in 1631 and elder in 1633, 1642, 1648, 1652, 1656, 1660. The Beauchamp family were ex-Separatists.

[156] S.P. 16, vol. 387, no. 79.

[157] Johnson, "Stam," pp. 185-87; S.P. 16, vol. 387, no. 79.

In 1606, the Bishop of London complained about the Brownist books smuggled over from Amsterdam, and various Dutch preachers and the magistrates promised "to hinder the books," but without discernible success.[158] In 1619, the Pilgrim Press at Leiden was closed down; but somehow the equipment and print were spirited away to Amsterdam and combined with the Separatist press, so that the work went on as splendidly as ever.[159]

Canne as printer was under constant scrutiny, and in 1638 the English ambassador demanded that his house be searched and his books seized—so to stop his traffic in libellous books. Boswell instigated action under the rarely-enforced States General press law of 1621.[160] Thereupon Canne was harassed, arrested, fined (300 guilders on July 3, 1638, and summoned again January 27, 1639); his books were to be confiscated. The books, the magistrates said, were prejudicial against the king of Great Britain.[161] Throughout these proceedings, Canne still kept his printing press, and more Puritan polemics leaped forth. An Amsterdam minister, Johannes le Maire, hoping to ingratiate himself with Laud, collaborated closely with the Archbishop and kept the magistrates riled up against Canne, "master preacher of the Brownists att Amsterdam." When the officials "sought to take him, for to punish him for an example," Canne proved wily and "fearing a just punishment makes him selfe out of the waye, and is not to be found."[162] The Separatist book printers, in spite of severe warnings and occasional arrests, kept the presses going. "The Brownist libellers, and other such malicious spirits, resemble a smitten hydra, which having his head chopped off, springs forth with several more heads"—attacking the Brownists was like attacking the hydra.[163]

Anabaptism

Some of the Amsterdam Separatists became Anabaptists. Pastor John Paget, of the English Reformed Church, warned that Separatism, hateful

---

[158] Acta Kerkeraad Amsterdam, III, 146v (June 8, 1606); Hessels, *E.L.B.A.*, III, pp. 1179, 1186-87. The Dutch records refer to the "Bishop of London"; however, the Dutch may actually have meant Archbishop Bancroft, who made a 1606 complaint about printing (see above no. 131).

[159] D. Plooij, *The Pilgrim Fathers from a Dutch Point of View* (New York: New York Univ. Press, 1932), pp. 57-81; Johnson, "Exiled English Church," p. 230.

[160] S.P. 84, vol. 153, fol. 188; S.P. 84, vol. 153, fols. 293-96.

[161] S.P. 84, vol. 154, fols. 113-14, 148-53; S.P. 84, vol. 155, fols. 12-14. On Canne's printing and the press laws, see chapter 11.

[162] S.P. 84, vol. 138, fol. 44 (Oct. 1, 1638). Le Maire was preacher in the Reformed Church of Amsterdam 1601-42. He had traveled in England and his daughter was married to Thomas Turner, dean of Canterbury and Rochester (see Matthews, *W.R.*, p. 60; Evenhuis, *Amsterdam*, I, 194).

[163] Le Maire to Laud, S.P. 84, vol. 155, fol. 14 (Jan. 29, 1639).

in itself, was also "the way to Anabaptism."¹⁶⁴ The Johnsonian and Ainsworthian Separatists dissociated themselves absolutely from Anabaptism of any kind, but no precautions could prevent at least a small migration back and forth between the Separatists and Anabaptists. Although Separatists were very orthodox on the main creedal doctrines of Protestantism, except for "the doctrine of their separation," Paget accused the small company of Separatists of producing more Anabaptists and Arians "in one yeare then ten thousand members of the Reformed Dutch Church in this citie, have done in ten yeares or more."¹⁶⁵ Anabaptists were Separatists who built the church upon the basis of believer's baptism. The Netherlands, home of Menno Simons, was one of their chief centers; Amsterdam had several Anabaptist or Mennonite congregations.¹⁶⁶

Very little distinct Anabaptist belief had surfaced in sixteenth-century England itself, and the term "Anabaptist" was to Englishmen an epithet of contempt used broadly in polemical language to besmirch an opponent of radical religious views. Francis Johnson in the heat of battle accused his brother George, among many other things, of "Anabaptistry." When used so loosely and abusively, "Anabaptist" referred to any separatist radicalism going beyond mainstream Puritanism. "The very name of Anabaptist," said Isaac Backus of New England, "was used as a weapon to fight against reformation."¹⁶⁷ Anglicans agreed with Puritans in taunting the Separatists as being the road to Anabaptism. "There is no remedy: Eyther you must goe forward to Anabaptisme, or come back to vs," charged Joseph Hall (the future Bishop of Exeter). "If wee bee a true Church, you must returne; if wee bee not, ... you must rebaptize."¹⁶⁸ King James pronounced an equally dire situation, that Puritans led to Separatism and Separatism led finally to Anabaptism.¹⁶⁹

Just as the non-separating Puritans condemned the extreme Separatists, the Separatists roundly scourged the still more extreme Anabaptists. Johnson, Ainsworth, and Robinson absolutely denied the logic of Paget and Hall—that Separatism led to Anabaptism. Separatists

---

¹⁶⁴ Sermon of 1609, C.R., I, 43.

¹⁶⁵ Paget, *Arrow*, "To the Christian Reader"; Lawne, *Prophane Schisme*, p. 56.

¹⁶⁶ On Dutch Anabaptism, see C. Henry Smith, *The Story of the Mennonites*, 3rd ed. (Newton, Kansas: Mennonite Publication Office, 1950), pp. 161-236; Cornelius Krahn, *Dutch Anabaptism: Origin, Spread, Life and Thought* (The Hague: Nijhoff, 1968).

¹⁶⁷ Johnson, *Discourse*, p. 56; Ernest A. Payne, "Contacts between Mennonites and Baptists," *Foundations*, 4 (Jan. 1961), 5.

¹⁶⁸ Hall, *Common Apologie*, p. 31. Robert Baillie, while acknowledging the tie, argued that Anabaptism gave rise to Brownism, in *Anabaptism, the Trve Fovntaine of Independency, Brownisme, Familisme* (London, 1647), p. 54.

¹⁶⁹ David H. Willson, *King James VI and I* (Oxford: Oxford Univ. Press), p. 402.

had nothing in common with the Amsterdam Anabaptists, assured Robinson, nothing except for walking the same streets of the city.[170] In Amsterdam, in spite of Robinson's disclaimers, Anabaptism did infiltrate the Puritan movement, producing at first an English Anabaptist underground and finally a distinct English Anabaptist congregation.

From the earliest years in the Netherlands, the Ancient Church was troubled by Anabaptist inroads. Writing in 1606, Francis Johnson recalled the early Anabaptist threat of the 1590s, "about thirteen yeares synce" (i.e. about 1593) and "a while after ... Divers of them fell into the heresies of the Anabaptists (which are too common in these countreys) and so persisting were excommunicated by the rest." This Anabaptist schism might well refer to the Kampen-Naarden years (1593-96). The Anabaptists of the 1590s (the "Johnsonian Anabaptists")[171] did not establish a durable congregation. However, a few of their names are known; they included Leonard Pedder, Henry Martin, and Thomas Mitchell. All three of these had been participants in the Ancient Church at London but later dabbled in Anabaptist doctrines. George Johnson's *Discourse* mentioned at least two further cases of Anabaptism in the Ancient Church (Robert Jackson's wife and Thomas Odal).[172] Anabaptism in English religion, of course, preceded the Amsterdam period, with some Anabaptist stirrings in cities like London and Norwich. Accused "Anabaptists" were executed in England by Henry VIII and Elizabeth,[173] but these sixteenth-century English Anabaptists proved in several cases to have been Dutch immigrants residing in England rather than native English converts. "Their number in *England* till of late was not great; and the most of these were not *English* but *Dutch* strangers," said Robert Baillie in 1647.[174]

These early English Anabaptists have left scant records except for hostile references in the writings of their enemies. Henoch Clapham and John Payne, English settlers of the 1590s in Holland, treated Anabaptism as a serious threat. Henoch Clapham, non-Separatist minister in Amsterdam, gave several reports about English Anabaptism in the area. In a letter he wrote about a Thomas Mickl of Amsterdam (probably Thomas Mitchell), who gave Clapham "some suspicion of

---

[170] John Robinson, *An Answer to a Censorious Epistle* (1610), in Hanbury, *Memorials*, I, 200.

[171] Burrage's phrase, *E.E.D.*, I, 156, 222; Johnson, *Inquirie and Answer*, p. 63.

[172] Lawne, *Prophane Schisme*, p. 56; *Writings of Greenwood and Barrow, 1591-93*, p. 358 (on Pedder); pp. 305, 371 (on Thomas Mitchell). Johnson, *Discourse*, pp. 56, 194; Odal (Odell) joined the Dutch Mennonites by baptism in 1615.

[173] Irvin B. Horst, *The Radical Brethren: Anabaptism and the English Reformation to 1558* (Nieuwkoop: B. de Graaf, 1972), pp. 60-66.

[174] Robert Baillie, *Anabaptism*, p. 17.

Anabaptistree." "Truly, I have much disliked that, and have partly therefore rebuked him, although he is but a straunger unto our Congregacion." At the time of writing (about 1597), Mickl had returned or recently been to England.[175] In his *Theologicall Axioms* of 1597, Clapham refers to Anabaptism as a well-known danger among English people. He lumped together Anabaptism (also Catabaptism and German Polybaptism), Manicheanism, and Arianism as evil movements. Four of his theological axioms, which had been publicly "controverted, discussed and concluded" in his little church at Amsterdam, were tailored to refute Anabaptism: The first axiom, that Christ had come in "our nature," the third axiom, that natural man has no free will, the seventh axiom, that infants are to be baptized as within the covenant, and the ninth axiom, that the Christian magistrate, being a member of Christ's church, may bear the sword.[176] In his next book, *Bibliotheca Theologica* (also 1597), he defended himself against "thunderclaps from our english Donatists, Anabaptists, Arrians, and Sectes of all sortes." "They haue made an insurrection since my publishinge off the XII Theologicall Axioms."[177] Clapham even reported one case of self-baptism, 1600 or earlier, pre-John Smyth, "and so, one baptizeth himselfe (as Abraham first circumcised himselfe ...) and then he baptizeth other." In the margin Clapham inscribed: "I knew one such, and sundry can witnes it."[178]

John Payne's *Royall Exchange*, printed at Haarlem in 1597, contains many warnings against English Anabaptists in the Netherlands and England, and he singled out for admonition "the Anabaptist T. M.," prisoner at Norwich. Payne's Anabaptist T. M. (1597) sounds very much like Clapham's Anabaptist Thomas Mickl or Mitchell (also about 1597). Payne, a seaman and merchant, had contempt for the Johnsonian Separatists, but on this occasion he gave special urgency to unmasking the Anabaptists. "I wyshe you beware of the dangerouse opinions of suche Englyshe Anabaptists bred here." He listed their eight erroneous doctrines. "Gentlemen warned of the opinions of the Anabaptists" (the English and Dutch here): (1) that "Christ toke not his pure fleshe of the Virgin Mary;" (2) that the Godhead was subject to passions and death; (3) that infants of the faithful ought not to be baptized; (4) that souls sleep in the grave with the body till the resurrection; (5) that magistrates ought not to put malefactors to death; (6) that "they condemne all warrs and

---

[175] Harley MS. 7581, fol. 57, item 4; Mitchell perhaps returned to Amsterdam. A Thomas Michiels, turner from Cambridge, married at Amsterdam in 1606, see Hoop Scheffer, *Free Churchmen*, p. 188.
[176] Clapham, *Theologicall Axioms*, pp. Aiii, B, Biiii, Ciii.
[177] Clapham, *Bibliotheca Theologica*, "The Proeme."
[178] Clapham, *Antidoton*, p. 33; Burrage, *E.E.D.*, I, 223.

Subiects in armure in the feyld;" (7) that they deny predestination and the Lord's Day; and (8) that they favour the opinions of free will and the merit of works.[179] This Anabaptist list of doctrines overlaps considerably with Clapham's axioms; Payne's list neatly captures the basic Anabaptist program, especially in the areas of believer's baptism, nonresistance, free will, and pacifism, and sets Anabaptists apart from the main group of Separatists, whose major deviations were schism and bad manners.

The doctrine that Christ did not receive his fleshly body from the Virgin Mary, but merely passed through her, taught by Melchior Hoffman and accepted in modified form by Menno Simons and Dirk Philips, was a particularly evil doctrine in the eyes of Puritan theologians. The doctrine of Menno and Dirk was that Christ, conceived through the Holy Spirit, "was born *out of* Mary and not *from* Mary" (*uit* but not *van*).[180] This Hoffmanite doctrine, however, was not universal among Dutch or English Anabaptists, in spite of the accusations. Although the word "Anabaptist" was used loosely in the sixteenth and seventeenth centuries, the reports of Clapham and Payne reveal commited Anabaptists among the English, who believed and practiced adult baptism, nonresistance, and free will.

The next, and most visible, visitation of English Anabaptism came when John Smyth in 1608 led his English Separatist congregation, "the Second English Church at Amsterdam" into open Anabaptism.[181] Smyth's group on arriving at Amsterdam in 1607 never united with Johnson's older, more established congregation. Smyth raised critical questions about the Ancient Church on the using of Bible translations in worship but at first not the matter of baptism.[182] "Truely," said Smyth on arriving in the Netherlands, "wee being Now Come into a place of libertie are in Great danger if wee look not well to our wayes, for wee are

---

[179] John Payne, *Royall Exchange*, pp. 22, 45-48. The name of John Payne, not necessarily this author, shows up in several Separatist documents of the early seventeenth century.

[180] William E. Keeney, *The Development of Dutch Anabaptist Thought and Practice from 1539-1564* (Nieuwkoop: B. de Graaf, 1968), pp. 89-100; Lawne, *Prophane Schisme*, p. 56. For another Puritan view, see William Ames, *Conscience with the Power and Cases Thereof* (n.p., 1639), bk. IV, 11-12, also Keith L. Sprunger, "William Ames, a Seventeenth-Century Puritan, Looks at the Anabaptists," *Mennonite Quarterly Review*, 39 (Jan. 1965), 72-74.

[181] Bakker, *John Smyth*, p. 72; Burrage, *E.E.D.*, I, 237-39; Walter Burgess, *John Smith, the Se-Baptist, Thomas Helwys and the First Baptist Church in England* (London: James Clark, 1911), p. 149. Smyth's book, *The Character of the Beast*, dated March 24, 1608/09, contains Anabaptist views. Henoch Clapham, *Errovr on the Right Hand* (London, 1608), refers to an English Anabaptist congregation in the Netherlands (1608), "certaine *English* people of vs, that came out from the *Brownistes*," p. 18.

[182] Henry Ainsworth, *A Defence of the Holy Scriptures, Worship, and Ministerie* (Amsterdam, 1609), pp. 1-2.

like men sett upon the Iyce and therefore may ezely slyde and fall."[183] Within little more than a year, late 1608, Smyth slid into Anabaptism. Convinced that all existing churches had become apostate, he rebaptized himself and then rebaptized his followers. This event transformed one of the Separatist congregations into an Anabaptist church, the first historical English Anabaptist congregation. However, the English Anabaptists in turn further fragmented when Smyth repented of his se-baptism, because it implied a contempt for all surrounding churches, and sought union with the Waterlander Mennonites of Amsterdam, whom he now acknowledged as a true church. As Smyth began his Mennonite conversion, a secession of about ten members in 1610, including Thomas Helwys, John Murton, William Pigott, and Thomas Seamer, gave rise to a second English Anabaptist congregation, this one bitterly opposed to amalgamation with the Mennonites.[184] The Helwys congregation returned to England in 1612. Smyth and Helwys were the founders of the English General Baptists.

Smyth's espousal of Anabaptism cut him off from his former Separatist brethren, who charged him with "Inconstancy, and vnstable Judgment and being soe suddainly carryed away with thinges." Francis Johnson mixed the Anabaptists in with the Papists for misunderstanding and perverting the Bible "by insisting vpon the letter of the Scripture." The Papists err in insisting on "This is my body," and "the Anabaptistes pressing the letter, have erred in like maner about other wordes of Christ recorded by the same Evangelist, where it is saide, Teach all nations, and baptize them: Sweare not at all: Resist not evil, &c."[185] The Smyth-Helwys conversions were the only major English Amsterdam group to go over to Anabaptism *en masse*, but Anabaptism continued to draw individuals and families. Lawne's *Prophane Schism* (1612) carried a warning about the multiplication of English Anabaptists:

> Master *Smith* an Anabaptist of one sort, and master *Helwise* of another, and master *Busher* of another. *Iohn Hancock* will haue a separation by himselfe. The ground of master *Neuils* errors was also separation; though now hee bee further runne backward then euer he was forward; to speake nothing of *Pedder, Henrie Martin*, with the rest of those *Anabaptists*.[186]

The Smyth, Helwys, and Busher "sorts" of Anabaptists represented distinct groups at Amsterdam, the former two of them organized

---

[183] Bradford, "Dialogue," p. 137.
[184] Bakker, *John Smyth*, pp. 78-87; Burrage, *E.E.D.*, I, 237-41. Helwys's group revealed their secession in a letter of March 12, 1609/10; it may have happened earlier.
[185] Bradford, "Dialogue," p. 137; Johnson, *Short Treatise*, sig. A2.
[186] Lawne, *Prophane Schisme*, p. 56.

congregations. Pedder and Martin, apparently remnants of the Anabaptism of the 1590s, may still have been active by 1612 or were at least bitter memories. Leonard Busher, resident of the Low Countries and author of *Religions Peace: or a Plea for Liberty of Conscience* (1614), was an early promoter of religious toleration. In 1642, residing then at Delft, he wrote to the Amsterdam Mennonites for assistance in his old age.[187] Thomas Leamer, an English merchant of Amsterdam, had some Anabaptist tenets, and after associating with both Separatists and Smyth's Anabaptists, went off on his own into a unique heresy called "Arian chiliasm."[188] In addition to the two English Anabaptist congregations, some Englishmen as individuals applied directly to the Dutch Mennonites for membership.

The English Anabaptists drew up several confessions of faith. Smyth and his followers prepared a statement, "Corde credimus, & ore confitemur" (20 articles) and Helwys's group drew up a counter confession, "Synopsis fidei, verae Christianae Ecclesiae Anglicanae, Amsterodamiae" (19 articles). In 1610 Smyth and his church (forty-two in all) subscribed to a "A short confession of fayth" in thirty-eight articles, a translation of the Dutch Mennonite confession of faith by Lubbert Gerritsz and Hans de Ries. There is still another Smyth confession of faith of 100 articles, "Propositions and conclusions concerning true christian religion, conteyning a confession of faith of certaine English people, livinge at Amsterdam," printed after his death, 1612 or later, in the same volume as *The Last Booke of John Smith* (n.p., n.d.). The Helwys group in 1611 put forth a new confession of their own, "A Declaration of Faith of English People Remaining at Amsterdam in Holland" (n.p., 1611).[189] The Smyth Anabaptists adhered to the basic doctrines of the Dutch Anabaptists, namely believers' baptism, free will, nonresistance, and the general atonement. On the Hoffmanite doctrine of the incarnation of Christ, Smyth was vague. His posthumous English confession said: "The Word became flesh wonderfully by the power of God in the womb of the Virgin Mary; He was the seed of David according to the flesh." The Dutch version of the confession, however, added the words, "Godt Hem een licham bereyt hebbende" (God having prepared him a body). Smyth declined to be drawn into controversy on this doctrine,

---

[187] Burrage, *E.E.D.*, I, 276-80; W. T. Whitley, "Leonard Busher, Dutchman," *Transactions* of the Baptist Historical Society, 1 (April 1909), 107-13.

[188] Evenhuis, *Amsterdam*, II, 237-38; Lawne, *Prophane Schisme*, pp. 55-56.

[189] For the Anabaptist confessions, see Burrage, *E.E.D.*, I, 244-45, II, 178-200, Benjamin Evans, *The Early English Baptists* (London: J. Heaton, 1862-64), I, 253-72, and Burgess, *John Smyth*, pp. 239-69. Smyth's last confession (100 article confession) is found in a Dutch translation in the Doopsgezind Collection of the G. A. Amsterdam, no. 1365, having 102 articles.

because "the Scriptures do not lead us (as far as I conceive) to the searching of that point, whereof Christ's natural flesh was made." Some of the Smythites did accept the Hoffmanite teaching, as did Leonard Busher.[190]

Fragment of the Smyth records survive as notes in the archives of the Amsterdam Mennonite Church. Starting in 1610, Smyth began his applications to the Waterlanders, a branch of early Mennonites, to be admitted to their larger fellowship (while at this time Helwys and his followers withdrew).[191] A group of thirty-two English Anabaptists presented a petition in early 1610 to be received into the Mennonite "true church of Christ"; and a later petition, probably also 1610, contained forty-two names, including new petitioners and all but one of the original thirty-two. These lists present a helpful glimpse into the numbers of English Anabaptists. Because children were not included on the petitions, the size of the Anabaptist colony was certainly considerably greater than the forty two. Obstacles arose against a speedy union, and Smyth was dead before the English were finally admitted in 1615.

The English place of worship was in the old East India Company Bakehouse (bakery), in the area along the Amstel in the neighborhood of the Blauwe Brug and the present-day Rembrandtsplein. After the East India Company gave up the bakery, it came into possession of Jan Munter, a member of the Waterlander Mennonites, who served as a contact between Smyth's isolated congregation and the established Dutch Anabaptists of the city. The bakery provided both meeting hall and dwelling place for the English.[192] In recent times, a tiny alley, the Engelse Pelgrimsteeg, led to the old Bakehouse area.

Finally, on January 20, 1615, about thirty English persons from the Bakehouse, both men and women, appeared before the Mennonite council to transact the final arrangements. The English petitioners affirmed once again their commitment to the Mennonite faith, except for a handful, about four, who confessed reservations about the Mennonite stand regarding government and the oath. These four were held back, and the remainder on the next day, January 21, were received into the Mennonite brotherhood without a new baptism. Smyth's baptizing was

---

[190] Bakker, *John Smyth*, p. 76; Burgess, *John Smyth*, pp. 178-81. The article on the incarnation is no. 31 in the printed English version (reprinted in Burgess, p. 244) and no. 28 in the Dutch (Bakker, pp. 165-66; or Evans, I, 261, which has an English translation based on the Dutch MSS version). On Busher's view of incarnation, W. H. Burgess, "James Toppe and the Tiverton Anabaptists," *Transactions* of the Baptist Historical Society, 3 (1913), 204.

[191] Bakker, *John Smyth*, pp. 76-85; the documents are preserved in the Doopsgezind Collection of the G.A.

[192] Hoop Scheffer, *Free Churchmen*, pp. 143-45.

accepted as valid. The church book left space of half a page for the names of the new members; but unfortunately for historians, the scribe never found time to actually inscribe them. The page is half blank. Four additional Englishmen not listed on the petitions on that same day joined by baptism (Swithune Grindall, Thomas Odell, Anthoni Thomassen, and Thomas Huybersten).[193]

After 1615 until about 1640, the English met in the Bakehouse for services. Some of their church activities were recorded in the Waterlander Registers. The bakery congregation was an English-language outpost of the larger church on the Singel, and the English were subject to discipline and governance from the Dutch. The chief minister was Thomas Pygott (*Thomas de engelsman*), installed in 1620 "into the full ministry." He died about 1639.[194] Another prominent spiritual leader of the congregation was John Druw, a layman, who sponsored and recommended many of the English converts to membership. After Pygott's death, the English assembly in the bakery faded out as a separate body, the victim of acculturation and assimilation. In 1640 the Mennonite Church chose seven men to the ministry (to the *dienst des woordts*), one of whom was the Englishman Joseph Druw. He alone of the seven accepted the assignment; but several months later he sought release after experiencing language problems in Dutch, "because he was accustomed to the English language."[195] Naming an Englishman to the Dutch ministry was apparently a last step in the amalgamation of the two congregations.

An examination of the Waterlander church register indicates that a little trickle of English converts continued to join the bakery Anabaptists or the parent church but in no great numbers. From 1615 to 1640 between fifty-five and sixty-five English people, in addition to the original petitioners (about thirty), were admitted as members to the Mennonites, either at the bakery or at the Dutch meetinghouse. In the 1640s, fifteen or twenty more Englishmen joined the Dutch Mennonites. This makes a total of about one hundred fifteen persons recorded as joining. The number is somewhat uncertain because some names, when transcribed by a Dutch recorder, are not conclusively identifiable as English or non-English. Generally, the English converts are labeled as "van de Engelschen" ("of the English") or as being "int backhuys" ("in the bakehouse"). Such modest English additions as did occur, however, were hardly large enough to sustain the English as a distinct religious community. Between 1615 and 1620, while the original con-

---

[193] Wybrantsz Memoriael (A), fol. 12v-13r; Wybrantsz Memoriael (B), Jan. 20, 1615.
[194] Wybrantsz Memoriael (A), June 8, 1620; Hoop Scheffer, *Free Churchmen*, p. 167.
[195] Wybrantsz Memoriael (A), July 8, 1640, Dec. 8, 1640. Joseph Dreuw of Amsterdam was a student at Leiden in 1637; Leiden Univ. *Album*, col. 284.

gregation was consolidating itself, the largest numbers were added. Thereafter, for the next ten years, the English group as recorded in the Waterlander register seems static. Then again in the 1630s there was another cluster of additions to membership, including new family names not evident before, probably people coming over from England. A few of the Laudian exiles were Anabaptists.

If the applicants for membership had already received believer's baptism, they were admitted without further baptism. In 1615 two English women and one man, all previously baptized by John Smyth, were received without a new baptism; and in 1616 an additional Englishman came in on the same terms (no names were recorded). In 1630, Janneke Morton, at one time baptized by Smyth, was admitted to the fellowship. She was probably the wife of John Murton (Morton), returned to Amsterdam after the death of her husband in England. Michael Wallis was received in 1638 without baptism "because he had been baptized in his old age in England." Although Smyth's baptisms of his followers were accepted as true baptisms, his own baptism of himself, his se-baptism, was not considered adequate; and had he lived until 1615, when the union took place, the Mennonites would have demanded from him a new, lawful baptism.[196]

English additions to Anabaptist membership came considerably from the original founding families of 1610 to 1615, from their children and other relatives; but through the years other family names not present on the original lists of 1610 appeared. To the original English Anabaptists were added names like these, as candidates for membership or for marriage within the fellowship, either in the bakery or in the Mennonite Church: Matthew Auckland (marriage, 1615), Egmont Jaspersen and Jan Lenartsen (baptized, 1617), Edward Willemsen (marriage, 1618), Robert Pandert, alias Cramer (baptized, 1619), Garbrant Jansen, Scottish merchant (baptized, 1623), Thomas Withacker (baptized, 1634), Anna Wyat (baptized, 1635), Michael Wallis (received without baptism, 1638), Gràtieuse Willem and Lysbet Jelis (baptized, 1639), Jan Overtoom and Johan Blauwer (baptized in 1640). These are all identified in the records as Englishmen, or Scots in one case. Where occupations were noted, they were modest craftsmen or laborers.

From what groups did the Anabaptist converts come? Although the original Smyth group migrated to Anabaptism from Brownist Separatism, there is no sign of further major defections from the Separatists toward the more radical Anabaptists. However, several

---

[196] Ibid., fol. 17v, 20r, 55v, 63v; Cornelius J. Dyck, "Hans de Ries: Theologian and Churchman, a Study in Second Generation Dutch Anabaptism," Diss. Divinity School, Chicago, 1962, p. 166.

isolated converts did come from the Separatists. In 1617 Jan Lenartsen was baptized by the English, "who comes from the Brownists."[197] Considerably later, in 1639, Wyat, the husband of Anne Wyat, and Gratieuse Willem were baptized, "both having come from the Brownists.[198] Many of the new members were children of previous members, thus generated from within, not by evangelism. A few were noted as coming over from England, and several of the members of the 1630s who fell into this category were already Anabaptists before coming over. In the first years, 1615 and 1617, four English members from Utrecht were received by the Waterlanders: Joseph, a leather-stockingmaker, and his wife, also another "woman from Utrecht," and an unnamed artisan, a maker of wooden shoes.[199]

During the 1640s, after the Bakehouse congregation had ceased its separate existence, some English people continued to choose the Anabaptist way. Even without the advantages of an English-language assembly, nearly every year a handful of Englishmen joined the Amsterdam Waterlanders. Little was heard of the Bakehouse at this later date except as a dwelling for a few of the immigrants. During the first half of the seventeenth century, the Anabaptist movement in England itself had increased, a fact revealed by the regular notation of Englishmen coming over from England with adult baptism. In 1643, Richard Cortingey and his wife, Phebe Josephs, were received as members, Phebe without baptism because she had been "in haer oudtheyt gedoopt." In 1644, Joan Slo, Anna Kade, and James Oxford were admitted without rebaptism; "these 3 English were already baptized in England." Joan and Anna "understood no Dutch." In 1645, another new member was Joan Arsse(n), "an English woman baptized in England, living in the Bakehouse." In 1648, Eduart Davits joined without baptism because he in his mature years had been baptized by the English. New converts, of course, required baptism; Richard Horton in 1649, living at the Engelse Roos on the Achterburgwal, was baptized, and two years later his wife, Helena, was also baptized.[200]

One significant name among the English converts was Richard Overton, who applied for baptism in 1615 by presenting his own written confession of faith.[201] Quite likely, this Amsterdam Richard Overton was the later famous Leveller.[202] If the Amsterdam Overton and the London

---

[197] Wybrantsz Memoriael (A), Jan. 29, 1617.
[198] Ibid., Pentecost, 1639.
[199] Ibid., Sept. 2, 1615, Jan. 29, 1617, Sept. 6, 1617.
[200] Wybrantsz Memoriael (B), fols. 11v, 15r, 16r, 24r, 25v, 31r.
[201] No. 1353, Doopsgezind Collection.
[202] Evans, *Early English Baptists*, I, 256; H. N. Brailsford, *The Levellers and the English Revolution* (Stanford: Stanford Univ. Press, 1961), pp. 49-50.

Overton were one and the same, he provided a link between Amsterdam Anabaptism and radical English politics. Holland gave refuge to political extremists as well as to religious extremists. The name Overton (or Overtoom) continued to reappear in the records of the church, especially in the late 1630s. In 1639, Thomas, the son of Jan Overtoom, "Engelsche," was baptized by the Waterlanders; and in 1640, Jan Overtoom, "de jonge van de Engelsche," received baptism.[203] Two routes led into Anabaptism, one via the English congregation in the bakery and the other directly to the Dutch brotherhood.

Additional signs of early English Anabaptist sentiment were recorded in the records of the English Reformed Church of Amsterdam. In spite of the vigilance of Paget and the elders, Anabaptism lurked on the edges. They condemned both Brownist Separatism and Anabaptism; and if any members attended their assemblies or mouthed their doctrines, discipline was certain. One member of the church, Bartholomew Barwell, complained in 1609 that Mr. Paget spent too much time preaching that Brownism was the way to Anabaptism.[204] Paget's analysis was the usual hypothesis of respectable men, that the road down from the established churches led first to Brownism, then straight on to Anabaptism. On this the bishops and the non-separating Puritans agreed.

The English Reformed consistory register contained occasional references to members straying off into Anabaptism, usually recorded as "declining to the Anabaptists." The number of such reprobates, nevertheless, remained small. One of these was Lucy Setwell, excommunicated for Anabaptism in 1617 and another was Ellen Joens, who in 1619 was disciplined for her anabaptist views, namely, belief "that Infants are not to be baptysed and denying orygynall syne" and, worse yet, "persisting in these & other errors ... almost the space of foure years." In June she was reported for her views to the congregation with request that the brethren pray for her and exhort her from her errors. Six months later, in December of 1619, no amendment being evident, the consistory proceeded against her by excommunication.[205]

In 1621, two further cases of Anabaptism reared themselves. A poor man, Adam Dickson by name, was disciplined and forbidden to come to the Lord's Table because of contentions with his wife. In the consistory's judgment the discipline would bring him back to a more godly walk. Unfortunately, Dickson, while under suspension and seeking some spiritual companionship, "absented himself from the church & went unto the Anabaptists, for which cause he was further requested to abstayne from

---
[203] Wybrantsz Memoriael (A), Dec. 11, 1639; May 28, 1640.
[204] C.R., I, 43.
[205] Ibid., fols. 87, 98, 101.

the communion."[206] His declining to the Anabaptists was not permanent. While this case tarried, Richard Jones (probably the husband or other relative of Ellen Joens) came under scrutiny because "of his sinne in forsaking the church and declining to the anabaptists, not onely in denying the baptisme of infants, but also mayntaining that children had no originall sin, & that those which are regenerate are as able to keep the law as Adam was in his innocency." The elders and preachers labored with him for two years, but finally excommunicated him (October 5, 1622), "signifying that he hath these two last yeares forsaken this church and declyned to the Anabaptists; obstinately going on his errors being from time to time admonished by us."[207] In the 1640s two further cases of Anabaptism in the English Reformed Church appeared. Anthony Finch and his wife were suspended in 1648 for joining the Anabaptists, and Mrs. Burr required counseling from the minister "about her scrupples in reference to Baptisme of Infants."[208]

Anabaptist churches provided a shelter for members uncomfortable in the Reformed churches or the Brownist churches. Mr. Dickson, noted above, when temporarily expelled from his own congregation, resorted to the Anabaptists for worship. He was only "a poore man," Dickson complained, and he bitterly reproached his consistory, which had cast him out, with "false dealing" towards him.[209] Another backslider to the Anabaptists was Mrs. Goldstrey, an unfortunate widow with many children, and of unpleasant personality. After the congregation had thought themselves rid of her by demitting her from the church to return to England, she later reappeared seeking readmission to the church. Where had she been these last years? Then the truth came out—she "did acknowledge her sin in declining vnto Anabaptistry." Apparently, she had found something attractive in their fellowship, and so she had never returned to England at all.[210] The decliners to the Anabaptists for the most part were fringe members of the English church, people merely tolerated, rather than solid, respected members.

One member of the English Reformed Church, John Jordan, in his business activities became intimately acquainted with the English Anabaptists in the Bakehouse. Previously, since 1610, the bakery had belonged to Jan Munter, the Mennonite merchant; and perhaps through him Smyth's assembly had moved into close relationship with the

---

[206] C.R., II, 1-2.
[207] Ibid., fols. 3, 7, 20, 23.
[208] C.R., III, 185, 192.
[209] C.R., II, 1.
[210] On the Goldstreys, see Carter, *English Reformed Church*, pp. 125-27; C.R., II, 91; III, 71.

Mennonites. For many years John Jordan (sometimes Jan Jurriaensz), until his death in 1638, was one of the most prominent English merchants of the city. In the 1620s he was a deacon of the English Reformed Church. After Munter's death, Jordan in 1620 bought the Bakehouse from Munter's widow, and thus inherited the Anabaptists as neighbors. Jordan acquired considerable land along the Amstel, outside the old Regulierspoort, where he lived and set up a distillery. Although Jordan as landlord and neighbor failed to proselytize as effectively as Munter had done, he nevertheless felt friendly toward the English. In his will of 1635 he stipulated a bequest of 600 florins for the poor of the English community living in the Bakehouse, together with larger bequests for his own church (five houses) and 2,000 florins for the poor of Wolverhampton, his home town. A change of heart followed, perhaps because of business reverses; and in 1636 he cancelled the bequests to the Bakehouse English and the Wolverhampton poor.[211]

The English church under John Paget aggressively wooed the wayward stragglers back into the church, and carefully guarded the gate to keep the faithful in. Instead of losing members to the more radical Brownists and Anabaptists, Paget had success in winning radicals back. In 1615 a circle of repentant Separatists came humbly to the church, and in 1621 another group of fifteen confessed their error and were received, having acknowledged "that we have heretofore gone astray."[212] Through the years some went out to the Brownists or declined to the Anabaptists, but the larger movement was inward toward mainstream religion and away from the extreme religionists. Neither Brownism nor Anabaptism had sufficient drawing power to offset the movement away from radicalism toward the center.

The oft-repeated assertion that Separatism led downward to Anabaptism, or conversely that Anabaptism was the mother of Separatism, was only a half truth. Although the main recruits to Anabaptism (Smyth, Helwys, Pedder) did arrive by way of Separatism, the transmutation was not a general rule, in spite of various analyses such as Robert Baillie's ice-snow-water analogy. Because some Brownists became Anabaptists, and vice versa, Baillie thought the connection was proved. "The dissolution of Ice, Snow, or any other vapour into water, argues strongly for their originall from that Element," said Baillie, but that hardly proved much about the nature of Anabaptism.[213] Most Separatists did not become Anabaptists. In the free air of Amsterdam, the way was open but

---

[211] I. H. van Eeghen, "John Jordan, de Engelsman," pp. 7-12.
[212] C.R., I, Oct. 14, 1615; II, Aug. 18, 1621.
[213] Baillie, *Dissvasive* (1645), p. 13; Baillie, *Anabaptism*, p. 54.

only a few traveled the route down to Anabaptism; and the independent existence of the English Anabaptist congregation could not be maintained after mid-century. The weakening spirit of English Anabaptism at Amsterdam, and perhaps of English Anabaptism in general, arose from the competition of a vigorous Puritan movement, both Separatist and non-Separatist, that interposed itself between the radical Anabaptists and the official prelatical church. The absolutely irrepressible radicals went into Separatism more often than into Anabaptism, and the more moderate reformists composed the Puritan wing of the Church of England.

CHAPTER FOUR

THE ENGLISH REFORMED CHURCH AT AMSTERDAM
1607 TO 1660

The first half of the seventeenth century was the church-building age for English religion in the Netherlands. The scattered sixteenth-century congregations, primarily the garrison churches at Flushing and Brielle and the Separatists, were superseded by the establishment of officially-sponsored English Reformed Churches at Amsterdam, Leiden, Rotterdam, The Hague, Flushing, Middelburg, Utrecht, wherever a sizable settlement of English and Scots took root. Eventually there were about thirty congregations. These churches, officially recognized by the Dutch church and state, were viewed as the English-language wing of the Dutch Reformed Church, each a *gereformeerde gemeente* and thus on an entirely different foundation from the Separatists. The rationale for officially sponsoring English churches was to provide spiritual benefit for a friendly and economically important immigrant people. A second motive at Amsterdam was to undercut the Separatists, who were a nuisance. For the newly arrived English or Scot, the language barrier shut them off from Dutch religion, as Ralph Thoresby discovered when he attended Dutch church at Schiedam "but could not understand any thing; was not so careful of my thoughts, words, and deeds, as I ought to have been."[1] The English Church was a welcome sight to the new settlers.

The founding of the English Reformed Church at Amsterdam in 1607, the first *Engelse gereformeerde kerk* in the Netherlands, was an attempt to provide a respectable church for the English people of the city. For over ten years the Separatists had maintained a monopoly on English religion, and there was no place for reputable English people to worship in their own language. The move to establish the English church was largely an anti-Brownist strategy supported by the Dutch Reformed Church and the leading English citizens of the city. The fundamental decisions were made at the Dutch Reformed consistory and at meetings of the burgomasters.

The chief promoter of the new English church was rector Matthew Slade of the Latin School, excommunicated ex-Separatist of the Ancient Church, now an esteemed scholar and citizen. He presented to the Dutch

---

[1] Ralph Thoresby, *The Diary of Ralph Thoresby*, ed. Joseph Hunter (London, 1830), I, 20 (1678).

Reformed consistory on May 5, 1605, a written complaint against the Separatists, in which the consistory concurred; and thereafter the proposal to establish a new English church speeded along. The French church, which also had old grievances against the Separatists because of Jean de l'Ecluse, helped with preliminary planning. According to Slade: "Here in this city are a considerable number of English people, who do not understand the Dutch language, and therefore they earnestly request help in establishing an English Reformed church conformable in doctrine and church government with other Reformed churches in the Netherlands." Slade, however, who had become Dutch Reformed, never was a member of the new English church. A request from the church in 1611 to transfer Slade so he could serve as an elder was refused. By September of 1605 the magistrates had approved the plan for an English church and allotted a salary equal to the French preacher's salary.[2]

The search for a non-Separatist, orthodox minister was the next step. Hugh Broughton, residing at Amsterdam in 1605, was the first choice, but he declined and left the city. Other prospects were Thomas White, the ex-Brownist who was doing some preaching at Brielle, and Henry Grey of Hedon, near Hull; but for over a year, no preacher was appointed.[3] Finally in January of 1607 a successful call went to John Paget, chaplain to Sir Horace Vere and Sir John Ogle. Paget preached his first Amsterdam sermon on Febrary 5, 1607, on the text, "Create in me a cleane heart, O God" (Psalm 51:10) and was established in office by John Douglas, a Scottish chaplain. Like nearly every available English preacher residing in the Netherlands, Paget was a Puritan refugee, ejected from Nantwich, Cheshire because of his outspoken preaching. The magistrates and Dutch churchmen checked thoroughly into his background, lest he harbor signs of Brownism or other extremism, and found him orthodox and honest. The Dutch consistory, however, insisted that Paget would have to subscribe to the Reformed Belgic creed, catechism, and accept membership in the Amsterdam Classis. The English Reformed Church had its own consistory, making it an independent Reformed congregation parallel with the Dutch Amsterdam church but linked organically into the classical and synodical apparatus. From the Dutch perspective, Paget was the ideal choice because of his anti-

---

[2] Acta Kerkeraad Amsterdam, III, 128v, 129v; Alice C. Carter, *The English Reformed Church in Amsterdam in the Seventeenth Century* (Amsterdam: Scheltema & Holkema, 1964), p. 20. On Slade, Hoop Scheffer, *Free Churchmen*, pp. 56-57; C. P. Burger, "Een Metselaar-Latinist," *Het Boek*, 20 (1931), 305-10; Acta Kerkeraad, III, 265 (Oct. 20, 1611). Allis Slade, Matthew's first wife, was one of the church's 1607 charter members (C.R., I, 3). The archive of the English Reformed Church is in the G. A. Amsterdam.

[3] Acta Kerkeraad, III, 134-35, 136, 141, 147, 149, 158v; Hessels, *E.L.B.A.*, III, 1193 (no. 1669).

Separatism and his full commitment to the Dutch Reformed system. "When I lived in England," said Paget, "I testifyed against the evilles which I conceyved to be in the order of that Church"; but having fled from the Anglican corruptions to Amsterdam, he "reioyced to find those things that I had desired before and this without variablenes." Historian R. B. Evenhuis has commended Paget for being "zealous in his own congregation and in the classis for the pure reformed doctrine." Paget put on public record that as a parish priest back in England he had not much used the Prayer Book, since the church had two ministers, the other handling the necessary duties of the Book—"So that it was not imposed on me."[4]

The church was assigned to the Beguine Chapel, located in the "round Baginehoff," which has continued to be the church home of the English Reformed Church to the present time. Paget served as minister until 1637, when he was named emeritus minister. Other seventeenth-century ministers were: Thomas Potts (co-pastor with Paget 1617-31), Johannes Rulice (1636-39), Julius Hering (1637-45), Thomas Paget (1639-46), Richard Maden (1647-68), William Price (1648-59), Richard Woodward (1660-99), Alexander Hodge (1669-89), and Adriaan Oostrum (1691-92).[5] The church also had a reader, a coster or custodian, and at some times a deaconess and a schoolmaster. The original membership list of 1607 had sixty-eight persons.[6]

Members, both English and Scottish, were gathered from the British residents of the area, primarily from persons who wished to avoid the Separatist churches, some of them in the meanwhile having joined the Dutch Reformed Church. "Many yea and the greatest part of our Church at the first gathering were such as in their persons were then members of the Dutch Church, and were from them translated vnto vs with testimony of their sound faith and godly conversation."[7] The English Reformed church was the center of a cluster of English institutions. The church opened a school in 1608, which functioned 1608-09 and 1624-51, and in 1651 an orphan house, which absorbed the former

---

[4] Paget came over about 1605 and subscribed to the Dutch confession of faith Jan. 18, 1605. C.R., I, 1-2; Acta Kerkeraad, III, 156v, 158v; Paget, *An Arrow against the Separation of the Brownists* (Amsterdam, 1618), p. 34; Carter, *English Reformed Church*, pp. 23-25; Hoop Scheffer, *Free Churchmen*, p. 100; R. B. Evenhuis, *Ook dat was Amsterdam* (Amsterdam: W. Ten Have, 1965-74), I, 205.

[5] Carter, *English Reformed Church*, p. 218. Others who preached, but without a regular appointment, were John Forbes (1609), Robert Dury (1609), Randall Dodd (1611), Hugh Peter (1628-29), Thomas Hooker (1631), John Davenport (1634), Casper Stresso (1636), Patrick Forbes (1637), John Forbes of Corse (1644), Robert Mercer (1656-59).

[6] C.R., I, 3-5.

[7] Paget, *Arrow*, p. 124.

school and continued well into the eighteenth century. The church also accumulated property, most notably John Jordan's five "English Houses" by the Mint Tower and some endowments.[8] Its membership included the major English and Scottish merchants of the city and other prominent people. Even pastor John Paget became financially prosperous, owning two houses and becoming an investor in the West India Company. Undoubtedly, it was the one socially respectable English church of Amsterdam. Paget called it the "English Orthodoxicall church."[9]

Throughout the seventeenth century, the church had close connections with the Dutch church and state, which provided much stability for the English. The first entry in the Consistory Register proudly recounted the presence of important civic and ecclesiastical officials at the opening of the church, "publiquely erected by the consent of the honourable the Senate of the forenamed city: which their love and bountye towards us of the English nation the Lord repay unto them a thousand folde...." Three Dutch ministers assisted in all early matters of ordination and inauguration, giving "their right hands of fellowship in the middes of our people."[10]

Paget immediately took session in the Amsterdam Classis. To formalize the English-Dutch church relationship, the Dutch Reformed consistory in 1608 drew up a set of "Articles" (unfortunately lost but mentioned in part in the English records), which laid down conditions about classis membership and church membership. These "Articles between the Dutch Church and us" sparked some discussion at the English Church about a possibility of a future English classis if additional English Reformed churches would be established in the area, in which case the English proposed "that then we might be exempted from the Dutch classis and stand under the English." Paget renewed the topic of an English classis in 1611 and 1612, by which time an English Reformed church had also been planted at Leiden and others were taking shape, but the Dutch did not approve.[11] By the 1620s, when an English Classis

---

[8] Carter, *English Reformed Church*, pp. 125-38.

[9] Ibid., p. 25; Carter, "John Paget and the English Reformed Church in Amsterdam," *Tijdschrift voor Geschiedenis*, 70 (1957), 350; for Paget's investments, Not. Archive 719, Apr. 19, 1625 (Pieter Carelesz). Of the English people who paid the largest taxes, assessed on wealth (e.g. the tweehonderdste penning of 1631), the most affluent were English Reformed Church members (John Webster, William Watson, Henry Whitaker); see J. G. and P. Frederiks, *Kohier van den tweehonderdsten penning voor Amsterdam en onderhoorige plaatsen over 1631* (Amsterdam, 1890). Paget used the phrase "English Orthodoxicall Church" in membership registers, nos. 85, 86.

[10] C.R., I, 1; Paget, *Arrow*, p. 116.

[11] C.R., I, 36 (Aug. 20, 1608); Acta Classis Amsterdam, II, 73v, Acta Kerkeraad Amsterdam, III, 162, 191v, IV, 9-10 (G. A. Amsterdam).

was at last organized, Paget had changed his mind and insisted on remaining with the Dutch Classis. Amsterdam had three major foreign Reformed churches, the French, the English, and the German. The French church had its own consistory and belonged to a French classis or synod; the English church had its own consistory but not its own national classis (except for a brief experiment 1621-33 which the Amsterdam church did not join); the German church had neither its own consistory nor classis.[12]

At every step during the Paget years, the English church relied on the Dutch Reformed Church and the magistrates for guidance; Paget depended on this broader institutional support. When the English wished to give a ministerial call to Robert Parker, exiled Puritan preacher, as second minister in 1612, the Dutch churchmen discouraged the call and the magistrates completely vetoed Parker on grounds of expense and also of desiring "to maintain unity with neighboring princes" (obviously James I).[13] Paget acquiesced in the ruling and in due time he secured Thomas Potts of Flushing. When the congregation was still very small, Paget requested that a few Dutch Reformed laymen, who knew the English language, be lent to the English church to fill leadership positions as elders and deacons.[14] There was frequently a faction within the church which desired a more independent existence, but the church generally was quite docile in accepting tutelage from the Dutch. Paget himself was a positive defender of classical and magisterial prerogative: "There be many ecclesiasticall actions, which are done by the appoyntment of the Magistrate, as the holding of an ecclesiasticall Synod: the observation of solemne and religious fasts not by the appoyntment of the Church but by the Magistrate: yea the ordinary worship of God in preaching the word and other services here are and ought to be commanded by the Magistrates."[15]

The great vitality of the early seventeenth-century Separatists put the English Reformed Church in a defensive position. Paget visualized his church as a kind of fortress of truth surrounded by cunning foes—Johnson, Ainsworth, Smyth, Robinson, and Clifton. Many of the policies of the church flowed from this fortress philosophy. Paget's intense anti-Separatism did much to agitate his own peace of mind, and he produced a stream of militant sermons, books, and strategies to police his flock and ward off the wolves. The English Reformed Church was to be "that Orthodox Church here, which like a beautifull armie and ter-

---

[12] Evenhuis, *Amsterdam*, I, 274.
[13] Acta Kerkeraad, IV, 89.
[14] Ibid., IV, 141 (May 7, 1615).
[15] Paget, *Arrow*, p. 312.

rible, is vnder tents, and lyeth in the field (and that with happie and good successe) against that Schisme."[16]

In *An Arrow against the Separation of the Brownists* (1618) Paget listed four evil stages of Separatism: (1) "First, the mindes of many are troubled and distracted hereby; even of such as do not separate, but have some liking thereof." (2) Some who stop short of joining the Separatists are nevertheless tempted away from their lawful church, "living alone and hearing the word of God in no Church, as some do; how great is their miserie also?" (3) Those who become Separatist members "in effect excommunicate themselves from all other Churches of Christ." (4) Separatism gives rise to much Anabaptism and Arianism.[17] When Paget's church was established in close neighborhood with the Ancient Church, the Separatists charged Paget with ill will in setting up a competing church. "And you coming after gathered a people, and erected a ministerie in this Citie by vs, never communicating your purpose or proceedings with vs." According to Ainsworth, such action was the ultimate separation. Paget defended the course taken in establishing the church, because "I saw by your writings what evil counsailours you were ... and therfore thought it not meete to communicate our proceedings with you." He counted as his allies the learned ministers of the English, Scottish, Dutch, and French nations. "The hand of God was with vs."[18] Times have changed, and today the Begijnhof church is bedecked with several plaques and monuments to the early Separatists, and the center point in the chancel is a John Robinson window, contributed by American admirers of the Pilgrim Fathers.[19] Paget, however, would not have approved such hospitality.

Although not Separatist in any regard, the English Reformed Church was a Puritan-minded congregation with many contacts in England and Scotland. Paget habitually stressed the essence of the church as Reformed rather than Anglican. Members of the congregation took great offense at suggestion that "there is no difference betwixt vs and the Church of England." Paget, who refused to denounce the Church of England absolutely as a false church, portrayed their relationship as no more than

---

[16] Christopher Lawne, et al., *The Prophane Schisme of the Brownists or Separatists* (n.p., 1612), p. 69, quoting Robert Parker.

[17] Paget, *Arrow*, "To the Christian Reader."

[18] Ibid., pp. 37, 43.

[19] The *Record*, monthly newssheet of the English Reformed Church, Sept. 1967, p. 7, states: "While the 'Pilgrim Fathers' therefore, have no direct link with our Congregation, they must have had associations with it, as in the case of Matthew Slade. Several members of the 'Brownists' came into the membership of our Congregation ... It is therefore entirely appropriate that the Pilgrim Fathers should be commemorated—as they are—in our Church...."

fraternal in doctrines of faith and salvation. The Begijnhof people worshiped in Anglican churches when visiting in England, but "our Church is a distinct body from the Church of England" and we "testify against the corruptions therof." During the Separatist controversies, Paget was compelled to defend the purity of his own ministry because of his episcopal ordination many years before. "Whether you do administer here, by vertue of that calling which you had of the Bishops of England or have you renounced it?" Ainsworth taunted. "I pray your self to say, whether you stil have or approve of that ministerie which the Bishop gave you?" Bitter stinging words, and Paget pleaded that by his present Reformed calling at Amsterdam "his former calling ceasseth, though with out renunciation: So it is with me." Ainsworth claimed not to comprehend the fine distinction between Paget's non-Separating, "non-renouncing" Puritanism and the establishment Church of England. Those that cling to the "bosome of the Church of England," Ainsworth warned, "they suck the brests of your church."[20]

The English Reformed Church, free from all episcopal supervision, worshiped on the simplified Reformed model. They listened to Puritan preaching from ministers who had been silenced in England. Whenever a new minister was needed, the church sought a nonconformist Puritan from England. In seeking an associate for Paget, the elders went on record in 1632 "that an english minister should bee procrured from England, whear many silenced and distressed ministers ar which is judged to bee more for edefieng of this congregation, and the glory of God,"[21] The choice of ministers was consistently nonconformist; John Paget, ejected from Nantwich, Cheshire; Thomas Potts, vehement Puritan chaplain, some reports say ejected from England; Julius Hering, silenced at Shrewsbury; Thomas Paget, driven out from Blackley, Lancashire. The only pre-Civil War exception was Johannes Rulice, a German who spoke English, recommended by the Austin Friars church at London. In later century the English Reformed Church had William Price, Presbyterian member of the Westminster Assembly, and Alexander Hodge, deprived at Exeter.[22] At different times the congregation tried unsuccessfully to call such famous Puritans as Robert Parker, Thomas Hooker, and John Davenport.

As a Reformed church operating within the arena of Dutch Reformed religion, the English were required to follow a set procedure in

---

[20] Paget quoting Ainsworth, *Arrow*, pp. 1v, 3, 4v, 9, 15.
[21] C.R., III, 34.
[22] On Potts, see John Quick, "Icones Sacrae Anglicanae," I, 251-52; on Hering and Thomas Paget, J. S. Morrill, *Cheshire 1630-1660* (London: Oxford Univ. Press, 1974), p. 19.

ministerial recruitment. Whenever a pastoral position at the church fell open, the English would inform the magistrates, asking leave to have a new election. Any candidate chosen would have to be cleared once more with the magistrates and with the Amsterdam Classis before becoming an official call. The classis and the Amsterdam government, which paid the bills, called the tune. They determined who would be called, or at least in a negative sense, who would be vetoed. By the end of the seventeenth century "Burgomasters and Classis could virtually dictate their choice."[23]

The church was a discipline-minded church, quite exceeding the usual Dutch Reformed practice. The consistory register is well filled with records of discipline of members for card playing, Sabbath-breaking, whoring, fighting, and other moral backsliding. Within the English community the church served as a resource for counseling and reconciliation. James Russel and his wife Barbara, "being in strife one with another, she complaining of the strokes he gave her, and he of her evil and provoking speeches, and both of them being ready to leave and forsake one an other; by much perswasion they were at length reconciled, both of them confessing their faults and promised to live peaceably and christianly together." Two women, having raised commotions, "were both admonished to forgive one another ... which they promised to do."[24] The elders also functioned as a kind of church court by hearing grievances, calling witnesses, and where deemed necessary, by administering punishments. The church tried to be somewhat selective about admitting members and insisted on witnesses and testimonies. The elders barred the open sinner from the Lord's Table, "his ticket denyed him"; and before the communion services the eldership and ministers carried out a house to house visitation. Tickets for the Lord's Table were distributed and only those with tickets were served. Those not present and accounted for by ticket were thereafter checked into.[25] The style of the Lord's Table was definitely Reformed, far from the Prayer Book. Sir William Brereton told of receiving the bread and wine seated at a long table.[26]

In the matter of discipline for Sabbath observance, the English church was severe, and tried to serve as an example for higher standards of observance. Paget had strong convictions on Sabbath keeping but found the doctrine unpopular to uphold. He rebuked William Best, twice a deacon of the church, for Sabbath breaking and for allowing his wife, a

---

[23] Carter, *English Reformed Church*, p. 46.
[24] C.R., I, 95, II, 25; Carter, *English Reformed Church*, pp. 157-68.
[25] C.R., II, 28.
[26] William Brereton, *Travels in Holland the United Provinces England Scotland and Ireland*, ed. Edward Hawkins, Chetham Society, I (1844), 63.

member of the Dutch church, to keep a shop which sold fruit on Sundays. Best refused to accept the rebuke and he argued that Sunday selling was necessary for the benefit of the sick and for merchandising in perishable goods. Besides, said Best, the Dutch preachers had never troubled him or his wife on the matter.[27] On another item of discipline, business ethics and debt repayment, the English church was unanimous with the Dutch church. The economic issue of most concern to the Dutch church was debt payment and bankruptcy, very significant ethical doctrines in a commercial society. The churches administered spiritual discipline against delinquent debtors by barring bankrupts and sometimes their wives from the Lord's Table until restitution was made or some arrangements, at least, with the creditors. The English elders recorded in their consistory register the bankruptcy articles from the provincial synod of 1618 and administered the policy accordingly—no admittance to the Lord's Table for bankrupts until restitution. In 1686 the church, which had become more lenient in many practices, banned bankrupts from all church offices; no bankrupt who had not made full restitution "shall ever come in the nomination for an office." The system of English discipline stemmed from a vision of moral governance on the grand scale, moral, social, and economic. A blot on one member became a stain on the entire congregation. The elders severely admonished members against deeds which "might have brought a great scandal upon the church."[28]

In membership increase, the church prospered (68 members in 1607; 412 in 1623; 466 in 1649).[29] Within, the church underwent serious trials under the leadership of Paget. Factions attempted to pull the church in one direction or another. Brownists and Anabaptists, although luring some members away, were held in check, and the consistory disciplined any members who backslid to either of these alien religions.[30] Also, Paget supervised the printing of a spate of anti-Brownist books, including his own *Arrow against the Separation*, and he had a hand in Christopher Lawne's *Prophane Schism* (1612) and Lawne's *Brownism turned the In-side out-ward* (1613)—"disguised pamphletes that come out of your congregation." Ainsworth charged: "How you take a speciall delyte and think it for your vantage, to upbrayd mens differences, to rake into particular mens synns and infirmities."[31] In fact, Paget's anti-Separatist work was

---

[27] William Best, *The Chvrches Plea for Her Right* (Amsterdam, 1635), p. 5; Carter, *English Reformed Church*, pp. 30, 122-23.

[28] Articles XI, XII, 1618, see Reitsma and Van Veen, II, 23-24 (Synod of North Holland); C.R., I, 97, III, 85, 300; Carter, *English Reformed Church*, pp. 170-75.

[29] Membership registers, nos. 84-99, archives of E.R.C.

[30] C.R., I, 64; Paget often sought advice from the Classis about how to handle the Brownist problem, e.g. Acta Classis, II, 44, 75.

[31] Paget, *Arrow*, p. 331; William Best, *The Chvrches Plea*, p. 10.

remarkably successful, so much so that few Englishmen were dropping away to Separatism and some of those already in Separatism were won back. In 1615, Jacob Johnson, Edward Clyfton, and Mary Clyfton (names from famous Separatist families) renounced their Separatism and accepted read prayers, "not binding them hereby to approve of any particular errours or abuses in the booke of common prayer." In 1621 an additional fifteen ex-Separatists joined as a group, including Thomas Adams and Richard Plater, the printer. One of the conditions for membership for ex-Separatists was that they acknowledge the Begijnhof church and the Church of England as true churches.[32] Other Separatists joined as individuals (Christopher Lawne, Samuel Whitaker and wife Deliverance, who was daughter of Robert Penry, John Fowler, Robert Bulward, Stephen Offwood, John Osborne, and members of the Cockey and Shuttleworth families). By the 1630s "the more vigorous and energetic part of his congregation consisted of ex-Separatists."[33]

The most severe pressure for a change of direction in the church came from "Congregationalist"-minded Puritans of the Ames-Hooker-Davenport camp, drawing support from both the ex-Separatists and other reformist members. In the early years after 1607, only a few scattered members urged a broader policy of democratic church government and covenants; but by the 1630s a sizable group was actively working on behalf of Congregational doctrines—not Separatism, they said—to be adapted into the old framework. At every point Paget stood absolutely for the traditional Reformed way, but the commotion came near to splitting the church.

Some democratic practices had been a part of the church from the earliest foundation. The first elders and deacons were chosen in 1607 "by the most voyces of the whole congregation." However, this practice of congregational elections was lost through the years as the consistory became a self-perpetuating body having its own elections and announcing the results to the congregation. The consistory, composed of the most prestigious men of the congregation, made the serious decisions and carried on the business of the church.[34] Because Paget, the spokesman of the Reformed polity, was thoroughly associated with the status quo, the dissatisfied members centered their attacks on him. At different times, congregational factions asked for more discipline, wider discussion and decision-making, more stringent standards for membership, and, eventually, a new minister. Thomas Adams, one of the inevitable agitators,

---

[32] C.R., I, 84, II, 5; Acta Classis, II, 44.
[33] Carter, *English Reformed Church*, pp. 53-59.
[34] C.R., I, 6; John Trasy, Add. MS. 24,660, fol. 1v; Carter, *English Reformed Church*, pp. 28-29.

ex-Separatist, complained that the church "had the name of a reformed church and he wished it might so be but he did not see how our practise agreed with reformation and thought he had the word of God for it." Paget and the elders did not take Adams very seriously, and as a rule they distrusted anything smacking of congregational rule, "unlese we wold bring in the popular order and government of the Brownists among us," obviously "contrary to the order and pracktise of these reformed churches."[35]

Covenant-making, an essential part of Separatism and later of the non-Separating Congregationalists, soon became an issue in the church. Because the Ancient Church of Johnson and Ainsworth had a congregational covenant, Paget was under some compulsion to prove that his own church had a similar deep commitment to righteousness. His vision, however, as explicated in debate with Ainsworth, was an implied covenant by which members in the course of joining were assumed to be promising "to separate from knowen evils, and to serue the Lord in the Gospel of his Son, so far as it is revealed vnto you." To Ainsworth such covenant talk was only "generals"—where were the "particulars"?[36] Most likely, the Separatist presence in Amsterdam pushed Paget into using some of the covenant language as a counterweight to Johnson and Ainsworth. The elders sometimes waved the "covenant" commitment in front of negligent members. In 1624 Abraham Finch, a troublesome member, was excommunicated "for breaking his covenant made with this congregation, for forsaking the publique assemblies, refusing the worship of God, for profaning the Sabbath, despising admonition," and Patience Atley in 1637 they exhorted "to cary her self accordinge to the covenant made with God, and this church."[37]

The English Church, moreover, at one point in its early history adopted a written covenant and entered it in the Consistory Register:

> A forme of the Couenant which every one makes with the Church, when he is first admitted and receiued to be a member of it.
> 1. He is to Couenant & promise 1. that he will ordinarily frequent the publike assembly for hearing of the word, when it is preached, & receiueing the sacrement when it is administred,
> 2. That he will endeauor to liue peaceably & inoffensiuely with his fellow-members of the same congregacon; as becomes the gospell & the members of Christ,
> 3. That he doth receiue & imbrace, the religion which is professed in these

---

[35] C.R., II, 86, III, 43.
[36] Quoted by Paget, *Arrow*, p. 121.
[37] C.R., II, 43, III, 74.

reformed Churches; & will renounce all errors contrary thereunto so farre forth, as they are or shalbe manifested vnto him,

4. That he will submitt himselfe, to the gouerment & discipline of this Church; & to all the orders & constitutions of the same; while he liues as a member of it,
5. That if any complaint, be made against him; wheruppon he is sent for by the Eldership to answer to it, that he will come to Consistorie, & eyther giue them satisfaction, or submit himselfe to the Censure, which his fault shall deserue,
6. That if he haue occasion to complaine of any member in this Congregacon; he will bring his complaint to the Consistory in an orderly way, that is, after he hath dealt priuately with the party, both by himselfe, & with some other, & cannot receiue satisfaction in that priuate way,
7. That when he doth bring any complaint; to the Consistorie, it be attested by twoe witnesses,
8. That if he knowe any member of this Congregacon, that walkes inordinately & offensiuely; he doe priuately admonish him of his fault, & then take some other with him, that may testify the same, & if that doe not prevaile with him vnto a reformation, that then he make it knowen to the Consistorie; that they may take further, order with him.[38]

The covenant, written into the back of the consistory register along with other items of the 1630-31 period, is undated and was not entered into the regular deliberations of the eldership. It seemingly comes from the period when Thomas Hooker was at Amsterdam, and its existence reveals the intensity of feeling among a faction of members for having a church covenant, even though in actual fact the elders and ministers did not make extensive use of it.

For the Netherlands as a whole, the Congregational faction was centered in the English Classis or Synod (both names were used) founded in 1621 under the presidency of John Forbes. In spite of an earlier interest in such an organization, Paget declined to participate when he saw that the Forbes people had taken it over. The Dutch classis gave Paget and Potts permission to attend once, on condition that they not join, and Potts actually did attend English Synod sessions once. Paget was soon a public enemy of the synod Puritans.[39] Within the congregation, Paget's detractors sought a second minister of Congregational sympathies to offset his rigid Presbyterianism. They hoped to bring more vitality into the pulpit. In 1628 a deputation petitioned for the hiring of Hugh Peter, "to ease the ministers and to have a man ready yf one of the present pastors

---

[38] C.R., III, 335.
[39] Acta Classis, III, 38v (Apr. 3, 1623).

dye." (Potts lived till 1631; Paget till 1638). Paget "did not consent unto it." Some of the congregation supported Dr. William Ames of the University of Franeker, but Paget vetoed him as well; "I thought him not fit ... he denyed the authority of Synods and Classis." Others favored Thomas Weld, temporarily in the Netherlands in 1631.[40] The anti-Paget crisis came to a head over the candidacy of Thomas Hooker in 1631.

Thomas Hooker, powerful Puritan preacher of St. Mary's, Chelmsford and later the "light of the western Churches" in America, went into hiding in 1630 to escape the High Commission. With his career ruined, he was required to look abroad; and while underground somewhere in England, he received two calls for overseas service, one from Massachusetts, and the other an unofficial invitation from interested persons to become co-pastor of the English Reformed Church at Amsterdam, on whose behalf Stephen Offwood, "an Inne Keeper dwelling neer the old church at Amsterdam, wrote a Letter to Mr. Hooker." He agreed to go to Amsterdam if he would be given an official call from the church. "He would but come first to Rotterdam expecting the call from hence." In June of 1631, he arrived in the Netherlands and stopped first at Rotterdam.[41] Hooker's sojourn in the Low Countries lasted at least twenty months; perhaps a little longer. The last known reference to his presence there is January 7/17, 1633; and by March 20/30, 1633, he had departed from the land.[42] Hooker did not know, or at least dismissed too lightly, the bitter factionalism troubling the church. Offwood represented only one faction, and Hooker's identification with the radical Offwood group marked him as unacceptable to Paget and his adherents. Paget had no patience for the new "Congregational" Puritans like Hooker who were coming over in the 1620s and 1630s. Nevertheless, Hooker's name appealed greatly to the elders, swayed by Offwood's promotional work, and on July 2, 1631, the elders sent to him "in the name of the consistory desiring his presence to exercise his gift amongst us." This was Hooker's call, and he came, and he preached "to the good lijking of the church."[43]

---

[40] On Peter, C.R., III, 2, 11 (Nov. 1, 1628 and Apr. 23, 1631); on Weld, C.R., III, 24 (Nov. 23, 1631); on Ames, Paget, *An Answer to the unjust complaints of William Best* (Amsterdam, 1635), pp. 27-28.

[41] B.P., I, 139; C.R., III, 13, which reads, "in Junij 1631 Mr. Thomas Hooker preacher came into theis countries." See George Williams, et al., *Thomas Hooker: Writings in England and Holland, 1626-1633*, in Harvard Theological Studies, no. 28 (Cambridge: Harvard Univ. Press, 1975), pp. 1-35 ("The Life of Thomas Hooker in England and Holland, 1586-1633"); also Keith L. Sprunger, "The Dutch Career of Thomas Hooker," *The New England Quarterly*, 46 (Mar., 1973), 17-44.

[42] B.P., I, 68, 114.

[43] C.R., III, 13.

Hooker was off to a good start, and his preaching was immensely successful. Although he spent most of his time until late October in Amsterdam, the formalities of his appointment were not yet final. The crucial steps of approval by the magistrates, who paid the salary, and approval by the classis had not occurred, making the election procedures somewhat irregular. Although enjoying his preaching gifts, the church officials dallied in completing the official arrangements. For a time, Hooker left for The Hague to receive treatment for a sickness (in one undated letter from Rotterdam he mentioned suffering from the ague), but the elders brought him back with a money gift "for his former payns taken, and wythall to desier his returne heather if wee might have a more perfeckt triall of his gift which hee promised and also did performe to the full content of consistory and congregation." Paget, however, was not fully content. Hooker's theology was at variance from Paget's at several points, most notably on relations with the Brownists, on the baptism of children, and on the degree of congregational autonomy. None of these opinions of Hooker disqualified him in the eyes of the elders. "Heerupon the consistory concluded to proseed to his elecktion and to that end sent 2 elders unto Mr. Hooker to signify so much unto him." The official machinery was now at work; and Paget, rather than relinquishing his grievances without a fight, announced that he must interrogate Hooker.[44] Paget had twenty questions, and in no way could the consistory dissuade him from propounding them to the newly elected Hooker. Carefully designed to embarrass Hooker, the various questions lifted out the irregularities in his theology; and once Paget had the answers in writing, Hooker was in a most exposed position because several of them did not square well with either Paget or the Dutch Reformed churches.

Two versions of the twenty questions and answers, nearly identical, survive, one in the register of the English Reformed Church and the other in the papers of Sir William Boswell, English ambassador to the Netherlands, 1632-50.[45] Among the twenty questions, three troublesome topics stand forth: (1) on relations with the Brownists, Hooker, although opposed to Brownism, granted that "it is not a sin to hear them occasionally"; (2) on the baptism of children, Hooker expressed doubt about the Reformed practice of baptizing children whose parents were not members of the church; (3) on the powers of the individual congregation,

---

[44] Mather, *Magnalia*, I, 340; C.R., III, 13.

[45] The document of the twenty questions has been printed several times, see Carter, *English Reformed Church*, pp. 189-200; Stearns, *Congregationalism in the Dutch Netherlands* (Chicago: American Society of Church History, 1940), pp. 105-13; Williams, *Hooker*, pp. 271-91.

especially when choosing a minister, Hooker wrote that the congregation had full authority without recourse to the classis. These were not very prudent statements in the circumstances; and after writing his answers, Hooker decided to retire from the scene, signifying "he would suddenly depart this citty." The consistory, more and more angry with Paget, quickly deputed four elders to remonstrate with Hooker not to leave them, "and with much ado prevaled with hime" to stay a while longer.[46]

October and November of 1631 were tense months in the English Reformed Church as the Hooker affair superseded every other matter. A clear majority of the congregation, at least those who were willing to express themselves, wanted Hooker as minister, and they wanted him very much. The entire body of elders and deacons except Paget supported Hooker.[47] In the consistory Paget may have been a minority of one, but he had another recourse, an appeal to the classis to overrule his own church. Members of the consistory themselves, however, were coming to the regretful conclusion that Hooker would not be acceptable to the Dutch church at this time because of his slighting view of classes and synods; and unofficial conversations with key Dutch ministers like Jacobus Trigland revealed that Hooker's opinions as extracted by Paget "would bee a bar agaynst him."[48]

In these unfavorable circumstances, the elders and deacons of the English church decided to halt their proceedings and not to propose Hooker's name to the classis. Although this action sounded final, the implication is that the English officers were not giving up entirely on Hooker but deferring action until the mood would be more favorable. As the consistory register puts it, "to desist and not to proseed unto the classes about Mr. Hookers elecktion for that tyme at least, until Mr. Hookers judgment by farther communication might bee brought to alowe the authority of the classes." A tactical delay, "for that tyme at least"; and when Hooker was informed that his election was off, he departed from the city the next morning, but not permanently.[49]

The consistory meeting (October 5) must have been a long one, for the most heated business yet remained. The Hooker supporters viewed Paget as the chief villain. There was a "noyse that was amongst the peopell," complained Paget, "as if hee had done Mr. Hooker great iniury"; and this report he could not endure. Consequently, Paget announced that he would bring the topic to the next day's meeting of the Amsterdam Classis, of which he was a member, to find out once and for all if he had

---

[46] C.R., III, 19.
[47] The other exception was George Hewett, a member of the congregation.
[48] C.R., III, 19.
[49] C.R., III, 19.

done well in putting the twenty questions to Hooker, and further, to inquire if Hooker "weare fytt to be a minister to our congregation or no." The consistory expressed disapproval, even shock, at Paget's errand, for their purpose concerning Hooker was to desist "for that tyme," not to hazard an unfavorable and absolute judgment that might close the door to all further maneuvers. The consistory ordered Paget "by no means to proseed unto that classes," and in every way disassociated themselves from his solitary resolve. Still he would go. Following after him to the classis session were two elders delegated to counteract Paget's "business" in whatever way possible.[50]

In his various actions, Paget followed every punctilio of Reformed church practice, never neglecting any opportunity to invoke the authority of the Amsterdam Classis or the Synod of North Holland, where he anticipated full support. Throughout the episode he retained a serene confidence in the justness of his cause, and his account of the happening makes the Classis and Synod the doers of the deed against Hooker rather than any harshness on his part.

Why did Paget withstand Hooker so furiously? According to Paget's own story, it was a matter of conscience and truth; he acted, he told the classis, because "he had no full confidence" in Hooker. Perhaps so. Paget, above all, was consistent in his opposition to all Congregational-minded ministers.[51] Still there were also the personal, human factors: the aging Paget resentful of the younger, charismatic Hooker. Cotton Mather assumed as much by his statement that "the old man being secretly willing that Mr. Hooker should not accept of this invitation, he contrived many ways to render him suspected unto the *classis*."[52] During the fall of 1631 while Hooker preached at Amsterdam, he preached once about a wooden horse, which some of the congregation took to be an invidious allusion to Paget. When the elders quizzed Hooker about the incident, however, he "declared not to meane Mr. Pagett in the least."[53]

The Amsterdam Classis session of October 6 took up the matter of a "certain preacher" at the English church. The consistory still had some inkling of salvaging the Hooker candidacy by naming him lecturer or teacher so that he might minister to the English "although not as minister yeat as a leckturer."[54] However, the lectureship plan for Hooker came to nothing. To prove his case, Paget submitted to the classis a copy of the twenty questions and answers translated into Latin. In particular, the

---

[50] C.R., III, 19.
[51] Acta Classis, IV, 9.
[52] Mather, *Magnalia*, I, 339.
[53] C.R., III, 12.
[54] C.R., III, 19.

classis took unfriendly note of Hooker's responses to the following points of the document:

1. Whether it be lawful for any to resort unto the public meeting of the Brownists and to communicate with them in the worship of God?

3. Whether such of Brownists as have not renounced their Separation from the Church of England nor yet allow Communion with the public state thereof, may lawfully be received for members of our Church?

6. Whether infants whose parents are not members of the Church may lawfully be baptised according to the manner of these Reformed Churches?

10. Whether it be lawful to receive any as members into the Church, without public examination of them before the whole congregation?

11. Whether a particular congregation hath power to call a minister, without the approbation of the Classis under which it stands?

17. Whether it be lawful for private members of the Church to interpret the Holy Scriptures, at such set days, and places, where sundry members of divers families do ordinarily assemble themselves together?

Several of Hooker's opinions were just as unsatisfactory to the venerable gentlemen of the classis as Paget had predicted. Also, the counter proposals given by the English elders were not very strongly argued; they did what they did because the "congregation was inclined to this person."[55]

The judgment of the classis was predictable. Paget was completely vindicated and thanked for a work of "good conscience" in his actions against Hooker. On Hooker himself, the classis without further examination disqualified him from preaching in Amsterdam; and "the elders shall be warned not to bring him in the future into the pulpit."[56] What a sweet victory for Paget. The English church officials and members were first crestfallen but, on reflection, increasingly outraged. For Paget to be vindicated at their expense was vexing enough, but the anti-Hooker pronouncement (referred to in the English records as the "classis ackt") was absolutely damaging to the Hookerites. The possibility of further negotiation and maneuvering on Hooker's behalf was now almost impossible.

At this point, the Hooker affair merged into a larger question concerning the power and autonomy of local congregations to manage their own affairs. By 1630, only Amsterdam and Utrecht among English churches were joined to their local classes; otherwise the English Reformed

---

[55] Acta Classis, IV, 9; Carter, *English Reformed Church*, pp. 193-200.

[56] Acta Classis, IV, 10. Another copy, with some variations from the classis minutes, is copied into the English register, III, 19.

churches had a more independent status although they were generally dependent upon the municipality for financial sustenance. Throughout the English-Scottish community of churches in the Netherlands, theories of congregational autonomy were rearing themselves. Just so at Amsterdam, where the Dutch Classis obviously assumed authority in English religious matters. The Hookerites were opposed to accepting the classical ruling against Hooker, not only because they were unwilling to be deprived of his ministry but because of the larger issue of a congregation's having some autonomous power.

When the English Consistory next met (October 12), the room was crowded with an angry delegation of members "to the number of 40 or more" demanding redress for Hooker and that they go to the classis, which was scheduled to meet the following day, or to the magistrates. Such agitation and mass pressure was unheard of in the history of the church. The discontented members found the elders in a mood to do business with them, and so a delegation was authorized to go to the next day's classis session. The consistory also drew up a strongly worded protest against the classis and sent it along. The delegation was composed of two elders (William Watson and John Osborn, the latter formerly a Separatist), two deacons (Edward Man and Richard Beauchamp), and two other members (Thomas Farret, reader of the church, and James Crisp).[57] The rejection of Hooker's candidacy had sparked in the church an anti-Paget, pro-Hooker party of large proportions, willing to defy the classis if negotiations failed. To what extent Hooker actively aided the dissidents is uncertain. Although publicly, at least, he avoided the merest hint of agitation, he remained available to the agitators in Amsterdam, and his ideas of congregational independence, as recorded in the twenty questions, were open knowledge. In Paget's eyes, Hooker was unmistakably an encouragement to schism in the church:

> Whiles he maintayned that Churches combined together in the Classis, might choose a Minister, either without or against the consent of the Classis under which they stood. So to practise in these Reformed Churches, is no other than a plain act of Schism, a rending of the Classis, and a breaking off from their communion in the government of the Church.[58]

In presenting the Hookerite case at the classis meeting of October 13, the English delegation declared that the anti-Hooker decision worked as a "muzzle" (*muyl binding*) upon the church and also threw an unfortunate stigma upon *de persoon* (Hooker). The English brusquely demanded that

---

[57] C.R., III, 20; Acta Classis, IV, 11v.
[58] Paget, *Answer*, p. 74.

the entire action of the past meeting "should be annulled." They met with no success. The classis completely reaffirmed its previous decree against Hooker (*de persoon*) and its support for Paget.[59]

After this setback, the English retired; but the next meeting of the eldership raised the fundamental question anew: the Congregational members "demanded howe far theer liberty extended in chusing of a minister?" Four brethren stood, "in the name of the rest," railing bitterly against Paget. They threatened to boycott the Lord's Supper if administered by Paget because of his "cariedg of this busines." The consistory itself was so hostile toward Paget that it would offer no defense of him nor of the classis. The elders instead defended their good names by referring to the "sin" of the classis toward them; "the offence was not geven by us unto others but by others untto us." To the question of congregational liberty in choosing a minister, the elders answered "that the elders weare to goe before in nominating and then the peopell had theer liberty to assent or desent and that nether classes nor consistory could impose any against theer lycking."[60]

At the next week's meeting, the brethren of the Hooker party returned with a defiant scheme; they insisted on scheduling Hooker to preach in the church on communion Sunday, contrary to the classis order. "Seeing wee have protested agaynst the classes ackt, wee should seeme to alowe of it if wee did nott suffer himme to preach." Decision was deferred; but the next night after sermon, "a great number" of members met with the consistory once more to desire that Hooker be allowed to preach for several Wednesdays "as in former tyme hee had done." Faced with this block of resolute Hookerites, the already sympathetic elders and deacons approved the plan, "seeing the evell that might ensue by denieng theer request." One deacon abstained from voting, and Paget unsuccessfully remonstrated against the vote "as beeing as hee sayd a renting from the classes."[61] When Hooker was informed of his preaching assignment, he declined the honor as too explosive.

The painful events of 1631 surrounding Thomas Hooker had until October, 1631, been almost completely omitted from the consistory register, a procedure motivated by the pious hope that the storm would pass. Hereafter, the elders began to record the story in full, as they saw it. By breaking the silence in the official records of the church, the consistory admitted that the Hooker-Paget controversy had gone too far to smooth over. Under the date of November 5, 1631, a full accounting of the events since June occurs, seven closely-written folio pages which praise

---

[59] Acta Classis, IV, 11v; C.R., III, 20-21.
[60] C.R., III, 21.
[61] C.R., III, 22.

Hooker as a good preacher and express open hostility toward Paget. The elders made their case very clear. Another bitter slap at Paget, also dated November 5, was the hasty addition of a new clause, Article 14, to their official "Orders agreed upon by the Eldership":

> 14. That neither anyone of the Eldership or more then one, without the consent of the greater number, shall att any tyme prevent the consistory by propounding ether to the Maiestrate or to classes any minister ether to desyer theer aprobation or reiecktion, but hee or they shall be subieckt to censure as having arogated unto them selues the liberty and power of the whole church.[62]

After a long and rather fruitful ministry, Paget had come to the place where he had little confidence in his people and the people lost confidence in him.

Finally, to make an end to the Hooker business, a classis delegation, after Paget again appealed to the classis, in November 1631 went to the English church, sharply to censure the elders for inviting Hooker to preach "contrary to the classes ackt," and ordering them to cancel Article 14 from the church book, which "they say direcktly contradickts theer resolution." Further, the deputies accused them of unlawful dealing. When called to this account, the consistory justified their contrariness in three points:

> 1. Theer owne disorderly proseeding browght us to frame that acktt. Our congregations urgent desier of restoring Mr. Hooker to his credit & Mr. Pagetts his unkind refusall of our desiers to desist from prosecuting the bisines before the classes weare cause of confirming the same.
> 2. Wee acknolidg that ackt to bee contrary to the resolution of the classis because theer resolution depriveth the church of her dew power.
> 3. We declare that it was resolved on in the full consistory and therefore we desier as yeat the classis resolution & answer upon itt whearby wee suppose the whole matter wilbee ended, for then shalbee seen what power & liberty the church hath.[63]

These declarations summarize the position of the Hookerites at the Amsterdam church: they wanted Hooker and they wanted considerable liberty for congregational decision-making. By this time, however, Hooker had withdrawn from Amsterdam to live in Delft.

Paget was never forgiven by the disappointed Hookerites. In March of 1632 the dissident brethren returned bearing a document "abowght the

---

[62] C.R., III, 337.
[63] C.R., III, 23.

difference betwixt them & Mr. Pagett."[64] Although the elders declined to copy the writing into their book, the gist of it is preserved in the classis minutes after Paget carried his grievances there. The latest outburst from the Hookerites rebuked Paget for his disorderly proceedings and for being "the root of all the troubles in the church." After hearing this, the classis produced another justification of Paget against his detractors.[65] The matter was also dealt with at the Synod of North Holland in 1632 and 1633.[66]

Although forced out at Amsterdam, Hooker found good employment at Delft as assistant to John Forbes in the Merchant Adventurers church. Hooker and Forbes lived together as famously as Basil and Nazianzen, "one soul in two bodies." "And if they had been for any little while asunder, they still met with such friendly and joyful congratulations, as testified a most affectionate satisfaction in each other's company."[67] Hooker had left Amsterdam with his reputation clouded; Forbes determined to clear the situation. Working through Offwood, the chief Amsterdam Hookerite, Forbes requested the English consistory to send him a copy of the classis act against Hooker, because as he explained it, "in regard hee was to receave hime as a fellowe helper in the ministry." Although initially favorable, the elders deferred action and eventually refused in light of their policy of giving out no written copies of the consistory register.[68]

The next month Forbes personally took charge by traveling to Amsterdam, affairs being "at a Dead Lift," and met with the Dutch consistory and the classis on December 15, 1631. At the Dutch consistory, Forbes explained that his church had decided to call Hooker as their preacher; but hearing that Hooker had been declared disqualified for a ministerial call (*onberoepelijk*), he needed to know whether there was any reason for his church to delay.[69] The question was almost superfluous in view of the Delft church's self-supporting existence, but the occasion gave Forbes the opportunity to chide the Amsterdammers for their high-handed treatment of Hooker. The consistory sent Forbes to the classis, where he requested to know precisely why they had rejected Hooker. The classis readily agreed to summarize for him in writing the principal criticisms against Hooker, but Forbes found the reasoning inadequate. Later, after he had received the requested document, he made a further request in

---

[64] C.R., III, 28
[65] Acta Classis, IV, 19.
[66] Acta Synod North Holland, 1632, art. 26; 1633, art. 25; Paget, *Answer*, p. 25.
[67] Mather, *Magnalia*, I, 339.
[68] C.R., III, 24, 29 (Nov. 23, 1631).
[69] Acta Kerkeraad, VI, 304.

late March or early April of 1632 to the classis for an exact copy of the resolution against Hooker, "an Expostulatory letter to the classis which they tooke very unkindly."[70] By now weary of Forbes as much as Hooker, the classis ordered a letter to be drawn up to enumerate to Forbes "his faults, false foundations, and unjust desire," or as Stephen Goffe satirically reported, they thought "that though he [Forbes] complaine against the Bishops of England, yet that himselfe hath more then an Episcopall Spiritt." Forbes was not proud of receiving such a letter and "will not show it."[71]

Still without an associate minister, the elders in 1632 extended a call to Samuel Balmford of The Hague, but he declined, fearing that at his removal the prelatical party would force a conforming Anglican into the Hague church. The Hookerites, moreover, had also organized against Balmford, suspecting that he would be a tool of Paget, and carried door to door a petition against Balmford.[72]

The next candidate most commonly heard of was John Davenport, late of St. Stephen's Church, Coleman Street, London. His support was strongly from the Hookerite party, who still sought a dynamic preacher, "Mr. Hooker under another name." Davenport arrived in the Netherlands by the middle of November 1633, bearded and "in disguised apparell," reported his detractors.[73] According to Paget, he was sent for and "procured" out of England by an anti-Paget group of members of the church, much in the way that Hooker had been solicited two years earlier.[74] Almost immediately, Davenport was invited by the consistory to serve at the church, "a needfull time, when without me they would have been destitute, he [Paget] being unable to preach, or to come to the Church."[75] His name first appeared in the consistory register on January 15, 1634, by which time he had "preached often" and the elders had already extended a call to him. The English elders gained approval for Davenport from the burgomasters (January 31, 1634) and from the classis (February 6, 1634). But like Hooker, Davenport never secured the official post of minister although he did considerable preaching on an interim basis.[76]

---

[70] Acta Classis, IV, 15; B.P., I, 139v.

[71] Acta Classis, IV, 17v; S.P. 16, vol. 237, no. 48.

[72] C.R., III, 35, 41.

[73] Davenport was reported in the Netherlands by Nov. 18/28, 1633 (S.P. 84, vol. 147, fol. 175); he had not yet arrived on Nov. 4/14, 1633 (Dr. Ames "was buried before my arrivall here," B.P., I, 189); S.P. 16, vol. 252, no. 55 (Dec. 16/26, 1633).

[74] Paget, *Answer*, pp. 34-35.

[75] John Davenport, *A Iust Complaint against an Vniust Doer* (Amsterdam, 1634), p. 15; S.P. 84, vol. 148, fol. 1; B.P., I, 169.

[76] On Davenport's career at Amsterdam, see Isabel M. Calder, ed., *Letters of John Davenport Puritan Divine* (New Haven: Yale Univ. Press, 1937), pp. 40-55; W. C. Ford,

Davenport's tenure at Amsterdam (November 1633-October 1634),[77] in fact, carried the inner struggles of the church to a new height and introduced another issue of controversy, the baptism of infants. Davenport accepted the necessity of infant baptism, but he proposed a stricter membership by desiring to baptize only children of members or, at least, of parents who could pass examination for having genuine Christian walk. His convictions on this matter prevented his accepting the call from the elders; and he revealed "his schruple of baptising such infants whose parents were noe members of the congregation not being first examined."[78]

Davenport's vigorous preaching made strong impact, but to secure his permanent ministry, the consistory had to resolve his scruples about membership and baptism. Paget at first treated Davenport quite genially (although Davenport detected hypocritical insincerity); he agreed to an accommodation to Davenport's tender conscience whereby parents of "doubtful" Christian walk would be personally examined by Davenport. "Mr. Paget for his part doth promise to send soo many such persons unto Mr. Damport as shall come unto him."[79] At Davenport's first arrival, Paget tested him out orally by using the Twenty Questions designed in 1631 for Hooker, and Paget passed him as generally orthodox. "He seemed unto me to accord with us, and to dislike the opinions of *Mr. Hooker* generally. The maine or onely difference which he persisted in for a long time, was about the baptisme of infants, whose parents were no members of the Church, nor would submit unto any private examination by him, further then their publick profession of faith before the whole Church." By dredging up the Hooker questions, Paget had set the trap and the "Rock which split Mr. Hooker" now hung over Davenport. Although Paget at first saw baptism as their problem area, eventually the issue of the authority of classes and synods also entered in.[80]

Five Dutch ministers were also called in (January 20, 1634) for consultation and "private judgment;" and although approving Davenport's qualifications and "good zeale and care of having some precedent private examination of the parents," they envisioned the Davenport examinations as voluntary counseling sessions. If immediate baptism was insisted on, the five ministers and Paget assumed that the baptism would be ad-

---

"Davenport-Paget Controversy," *Proceedings* of the Massachusetts Historical Society, 43 (1909), 45-68; Carter, *English Reformed Church*, pp. 81-83.

[77] About April 28, 1634, Davenport referred to having assisted Paget "for allmost 6 Months," *Ivst Complaint*, p. 12.

[78] C.R., III, 46 (Jan. 15, 1634).

[79] C.R., III, 47 (Feb. 11, 1634); Davenport, *Ivst Complaint*, p. 14 (on Paget, "He never did desire it.").

[80] Paget, *Answer*, p. 40; S.P. 84, vol. 148, fol. 2; S.P. 16, vol. 252, no. 55; B.P., I, 181.

ministered and the ignorant parents "be further instructed after the infant be baptized, to wit, because the infants of Christians ought not to bear & suffer the punishment of the ignorance, or yet of such disobedience of their parents or sureties."[81] Paget feared that undue rigidity in baptism would drive the "faulty" parents, being fringe Christians, over to the Brownists for baptism of their babies. Paget asked: "Whether we may suffer their children to dy vnbaptised or to be caryed vnto vnlawfull and false assemblies rather then to baptise them in this case, when the parents refusing other conference do offer them publiquely vnto vs?"[82]

For over a month, January-February 1634, Davenport wavered in his decision over the call and the advice of the five Dutch ministers, and then declined, rather than submitting to Paget's practice, or even to the compromise arrangement for "private examination of parents" worked out by the English elders. "He cannot for the present accept of the call but if the consistory desyred it, he is content to continue in asisting Mr. Paget in that course wherein he now is for a convenyit time, that in the interim, he may accquaint himself with Dutch ministers & the order of the classis and synod and the partickeler state of this congregation."[83] Although disappointed, the English consistory kept him on as assistant to Paget, a "lecturer," with responsibility for preaching the preparation sermon and a weekly sermon on Wednesdays, duties Paget was hardly able to perform because of sickness.[84] Meanwhile, Paget became gravely suspicious of Davenport's real motives, and he decided to lay everything out before the classis and seek their counsel, which turned the Davenport affair (like the Hooker affair of 1631) into a public event.

Because of Davenport's deep support in the English church, the classis urged Davenport to overcome his scruples and accept the call. At least three times they sent deputies to confer with him, but he responded that he needed more time "in order to inform himself through familiar acquaintance and conference with the Dutch ministers." "How much time?" they asked. Davenport asked for "one whole year." The classis granted the time of one month.[85] Davenport had prepared a Latin document for the classis—"which they found very wordy"—summarizing his position: (1) that as for conforming to the orders and customs of the Dutch church, "I doe not yet understand, what those orders and customs

---

[81] C.R., III, 48 (Feb. 15, 1634); Paget gave the date of the five ministers as Jan. 28, 1634 (*Answer*, p. 45), but the writing was already referred to in the C.R. on Jan. 22, 1634. Davenport said the date was Jan. 20, see *Ivst Complaint*, p. 4, and *A Apologeticall Reply* (Rotterdam, 1636), p. 178.

[82] Paget to Hugh Goodyear, May 22, 1634, Goodyear MSS (G. A. Leiden).

[83] C.R., III, 48 (Feb. 15, 1634).

[84] C.R., III, 49 (Feb. 22, 1634); B.P., I, 181.

[85] Acta Classis, IV, 37-38 (Apr. 3, 1634).

are;" and (2) regarding "promiscuous" or "unlimited Baptisinge of all infants, which were presented in the Church," he could not satisfy his conscience "that it is lawfull for him so to doe, yea he greately feareth—least Christ will Iudge him guilty, if he suffer himselfe to be in bondage under such a custom." He could not accept the judgment of the five ministers. He asked for much more time.[86] By May 1, 1634, after another refusal from Davenport, the classis, "having had so much patience, and used so much labour in vayne," closed the book on Davenport's call; "voluntarily refused," they said. The burgomasters also rescinded their approval of Davenport and gave orders to the English to drop his candidacy "ether for pastor or lecturer" and to seek another man but one already in the Netherlands, conformable to the classis, and knowledgeable in the Dutch language "that soe themselves and the classis might receive answere when occasyon required."[87]

The rejection of Davenport, after his strong beginning, was not coincidental. Paget was desperate to stop him, and dealt with a network of "secret friends" (Boswell, who kept Laud informed, the high Anglican Stephen Goffe, professor Gerardus Vossius). Paget promised Goffe as early as December of 1633 that he would minutely examine Davenport in the same manner used so successfully on Hooker, "the same Damport shall undergo." Also around town, Anglican agents spread the story that Davenport was a fugitive from justice, not a religious dissenter, so that he had to "steale out of the land, so many officers (as themselves say) being sent forth to stay him." Although Davenport's friends labeled this as "false information," the damage was done.[88] Boswell and Laud took offense that Davenport was preaching at Amsterdam against kneeling in worship and in favor of the Reformed "gesture of sitting, used in this countrey, in receiving the Sacrament of the Lords Supper."[89] All of these maneuvers of Paget "shuffled the cards" against Davenport, and by the summer of 1634 Boswell could report to England that Davenport was wholly excluded at Amsterdam. Paget, who hated all deviation from Presbyterianism, was willing to go to extreme means. After Paget's meeting with the burgomasters, where Davenport was rejected once and for all, "he came home tould his wife rejoycing, that now the busines is ended."[90]

---

[86] Ibid. (Apr. 3, 1634); Davenport's Latin answer was translated and printed in his *Iust Complaint*.

[87] Acta Classis, IV, 38-39 (May 1, 1634), IV, 41 (July 10, 1634); Paget, *Answer*, p. 57; C.R., III, 54 (July 5, 1634).

[88] S.P. 16, vol. 252, no. 55; vol. 260, no. 13; vol. 308, no. 33; B.P., I, 169.

[89] B.P., I, 189.

[90] Reported in Davenport, *Iust Complaint*, p. 13. S.P. 84, vol. 147, fols. 205-06; vol. 148, fol. 177.

Davenport's dismissal raised much anger among his adherents. The Davenport people rallied on his behalf and once again attacked Paget as being the perpetual roadblock who deprived the church of that "power" which Christ had given unto it. They issued a list of "Grievances and Complaints" (October 18, 1634). "This we prove by his rejecting, and opposing of the most worthy servants of God (who came out of England for the same cause he did) whome the Church with one consent desired, as Mr. Hooker, and Mr. Davenport of later times, and also Mr. Parker, Dr. Ames, Mr. Forbes, Mr. Peters, &c." Further, they said, "he subjecteth this Church under an undue power of the Classis, which he bringeth it under, meerely for his owne ends, as we conceive, without any warrant from the Word of God." So, "we are not to be silent any longer." They testified to the world that Paget "doth not behave himself as becometh a Pastour, neither in government nor doctrine towards us"— moreover his sermons were thin and "sleight." This document of grievances was signed by twenty-one men of the church.[91] Sadly, Paget had never recovered fully his standing in the church after the Hooker actions of 1631, and months thereafter, the Dutch classis and synod were still required to attempt reconciliation among the various parties of the church. The 1634 events brought renewed talk of "division" and schism. Some members refused to take communion if administered by Paget.[92]

The Davenport ringleaders included the core of the former Hookerites, Stephen Offwood, Thomas Farret (reader of the congregation), Thomas Fletcher, Thomas Adams, James Crisp, as well as newer recruits to church agitation, such as William Best, Humphrey Denman, Daniel Burr, and Laurence Coughen (deacon). Davenport's supporters included "the *most* and *cheifest* of the congregation," among them John Webster, the richest English merchant of Amsterdam.[93] Paget tried to dismiss them as malcontents, "divers of them having formerly bene Brownists, and left their separation to come unto us, doe yet shew hereby that they still cleave too much unto some of their opinions."[94]

A delegation of Davenport supporters had a noisy confrontation with Paget in consistory April 12, 1634:

Delegation:	They "required first to know who those degenerate persons were that doo misjudge good acktions of others."
Paget:	"If they would come apart he would answer them but to soe many he would give no answer."

---

[91] Ibid., pp. 17, 19-21.
[92] S.P. 16, vol. 265, no. 35; Davenport, *Ivst Complaint*, p. 16.
[93] B.P., I, 183, 187; Webster paid the highest tax on property of any Englishman in Amsterdam (1631), Fredericks, *Kohier*, p. 67.
[94] Paget, *Answer*, preface.

Delegation:	"When the desiples come to our saviour Christ to be satisfyed in any doubt he refuseth not to answere although there nomber were many more then they are."
Paget:	"The former should be answered to any one of them but not to them all."
Delegation:	"You teach scripture but refuse to follow the example of our saviour Christ."
Thomas Fletcher:	That Paget "allyenated himselfe from being their pastor."[95]

The elders themselves were split, some having "declared, both by word and practise, that they are of *Mr. Davenport* his minde," and Paget found himself much outnumbered, often isolated in consistory affairs, and his opinion was slighted as being "without wayt." "For my part, I abhor this siding," said Paget.[96]

The Davenport people presented their case in a bitter book, *A Just Complaint against an Unjust Doer. Wherein is declared the miserable slaverie & bondage that the English Church of Amsterdam is now in, by reason of the tirannical government and corrupt doctrine of Mr. John Pagett* (1634), printed without Davenport's approval. The publisher was William Best; the printers were Sabine Staresmore and John Canne (two Separatists). The consistory in 1636 proceeded against Best for various offenses, including "schism," but he was very contemptuous of them, "accusinge the consistory of ruyninge the soules and bodyes of those comitted unto them." The entire Davenport candidacy, his people said, could have been handled quietly within the church without going to the classis, had it not been for Paget's "violence."[97] Another tract by John Trasy, although never published, circulated an anti-Paget tirade; "you deprive the church of its free choice of minister which is more than the apostles themselves did dare do." Although the English Reformed Church had begun with free choice of minister and elders, Trasy said, "now you have turned and pretend that when rulers are once chosen, then the whole choyce belongs to them, because they are called governors and because Gods word (say you) hath nothing against it." Trasy, an ex-Brownist, not a member, centered his attack on the two issues of the day: congregational autonomy and unlimited versus limited baptism. "Mr. Paget, how have you stopped the fountains of life? Because the water was clearer then your owne?"[98]

---

[95] C.R., III, 51.
[96] C.R., III, 54; Paget, *Answer*, pp. 98, 104-05; Elder William Whitaker was one of Davenport's strongest supporters.
[97] C.R., III, 66, 67; Paget, *Answer*, p. 64.
[98] Add. MS. 24,666, fol. 1.

Thomas Fletcher, a staunch Hookerite, condemned Paget far and wide; once at Rotterdam, he "over table in the English house vented his rage in so foulmouthed raylinges ... that the abuse was intollerable."[99]

Stung by the widespread hostility, Paget wrote an answer to the critics. At first he expected help from the Dutch classis in preparing an answer to Davenport, and for this purpose a committee was appointed. The English elders, however, strongly advised against printing Paget's book for the sake of "good order" in the church. When the full scope of the division in the English church surfaced, the classis backed away from writing books and also advised against any more polemical tracts.[100] Paget felt an answer was required and published his account, *An Answer to the unjust complaints of William Best, and such other as have Subscribed thereunto. Also an Answer to Mr. John Davenport* (1635). In his book, Paget lauded the wholesome Reformed system of classes and synods, and if Hooker and Davenport or the English church have suffered some inconveniences thereby, "this is not to be imputed unto me, seeing this order was here in these Countries established before my coming unto them: neither is it in my power to alter and change the forme of their government." Paget showed no appreciation for the Hooker-Davenport "new discipline." Nothing but "manifold disorders, confusion and dissipation of Churches."[101] When Davenport perused the *Answer to the unjust complaint*, he found it a tedious book with "some distractions by the vnquiett spirit of the old man."[102] Best issued a counter-response, *The Chvrches Plea for Her Right* (1635) and Davenport printed his story in *Apologeticall Reply* (1636).

With Davenport excluded from the pulpit, his people organized house meetings during the summer and fall of 1634 with Davenport as preacher. These meetings had over 100 attenders. By Paget's own admission, Davenport on Sunday evenings and sometimes on weekdays drew "a great part of the Church with most of the Elders and some of the Deacons." They met at the house of William Whitaker, an elder, and were passed off as merely "Catechysing the family where he lived." Ever concerned about conventicles, the classis sent ministers to warn Davenport and Whitaker against "irregularity and danger"; the meetings ceased in October of 1634.[103] The suppression of the house meetings was the last straw which precipitated the withdrawal from the communion, mentioned above. Davenport left Amsterdam but remained in the Netherlands, at least until 1636, preaching sometimes at The Hague and

---

[99] B.P., I, 230.
[100] Acta Classis, IV, 53, 55-56, 60.
[101] Paget, *Answer*, pp. 18, 72, 126; preface.
[102] Davenport to Lady Mary Vere, July 21, 1635, in Calder, *Letters*, pp. 60-61.
[103] Acta Classis, IV, 46, 47, 51; Paget *Answer*, p. 58; Davenport, *Ivst Complaint*, p. 22.

at Rotterdam. A son was baptized at The Hague April 15, 1635. Davenport returned to England about 1636 and in 1637 sailed to America.[104]

The danger of schism and break-away conventicles did not end with Davenport's departure from the city. In 1635 and 1636, Samuel Eaton, "the *great apostle* for promoting Independency in Yorkshire, Lancashire, and Chester," brother of Nathaniel and Theophilus Eaton, established a small church, perhaps the remnants of the Davenport house church. After being expelled from his church in Cheshire, Eaton came to Amsterdam in 1634 and, according to his *Defence of Sundry Positions* (1645), "joined with others in a Congregational way." The Amsterdam Classis in October of 1635 learned "that some of the English Church were holding particular gatherings in their houses and were censuring sermons." To the Dutch these were "unlawful conventicles." The classis brethren soon identified the unlawful preacher as Mr. Eaton. They admonished him for "holding, without consent of the church, unlawful conventicles," but Eaton revealed an independent spirit by refusing to meet with them "because he himself held their classis to be an unlawful gathering." Such bold talk the classis found astonishing.[105] Eaton's group formally organized; he "erected here a new church, gathered a few members, and enveighed some of ours, that schismed from us," complained Paget; "in summe, as if he would have set up a new forme of government."[106]

At least two pro-Davenport members of the English Reformed Church, Thomas Adams and Henry Poulter, signers of the 1634 "Grievances and Complaints" against Paget, had the bravery to ask for letters of demission "to goe to Mr. Etens." Both requests were denied as ridiculous, and Adams was scolded for going "sometymes to the Brownists and to other unwarantable metings." Poulter was suspended for "havinge unlawfully schismed from the church, and ioyning himself as a member to Mr. Etons company." William Best also may well have been a participant in Eaton's church, being suspended by the consistory about the same time "because of his schisme, in leavinge the church, and joining himselfe as a member to an other companye in disordered

---

[104] E.R.C. The Hague, C.R., I, 12 (P.R.O.); Paget, *Answer*, p. 136. Calder had letters of Davenport from the Netherlands up to Dec. 15/25, 1635, *Letters*, pp. 56-63. There are reports of him in the Netherlands as late as April 27, 1636, B.P., I, 230.

[105] Acta Classis, IV, 61-62, 67, 72-73; Matthews, *Cal. R.*, p. 178; William Urwick, *Historical Sketches of Nonconformity in the County Palatine of Chester* (London, 1864), pp. 76, 342; Morrill, *Cheshire*, pp. 37, 53; R. C. Richardson, *Puritanism in North-West England* (Manchester: Manchester Univ. Press, 1972), p. 40.

[106] Paget to Calderwood, June 16, 1636, Wodrow MS., XLII, 254 (Nat. Library of Scotland).

manner."[107] These disciplines came at the insistence of the Dutch classis.[108] As Amsterdam became too unfriendly, "seeing he saw it was not like to succeed," Samuel Eaton and his family retreated to Rotterdam, where he became a member of the English Reformed Church, Hugh Peter's former church, and sometimes preached.[109] Eaton's church, building upon the ruins of the Hooker-Davenport movement, was the purest non-Brownist Congregational effort at Amsterdam. After Eaton, the conventicle movement ceased.

The aged Paget, "weake, troubled with hoarseness of voyce" was exhausted by the encounters with Hooker, Davenport, and Eaton; nevertheless he outlasted his detractors; and he held the church together. In 1637 he closed his long ministry, thirty years of them at Amsterdam, and received emeritus status with salary. All of his life he had been an unflinching upholder of the "old discipline," as opposed to the Ames-Hooker-Davenport "new discipline." "Though in our particular congregation matters are reasonably well pacifyed," he wrote in 1637, "yett it is a trouble unto me to see so many seekers of reformation, so to oppose the government of the Reformed Churches in Classes and Synods, not onely in opinion but in practick as here at Rotterdam, and as I heare for certaine in new England, yea and in old England also. I feare a great evill to ensue hereupon." His final book, *A Defence of Chvrch-Government, Exercised in Presbyteriall, Classicall, & Synodall Assemblies*, posthumously released by Thomas Paget in 1641, was a last word on behalf of church government. "And for me, I have suffered many things for defence thereof." He died in 1638.[110]

Johannes Rulice (1636-39), Julius Hering (1637-45), and Thomas Paget (1639-46), John Paget's younger brother, carried on the ministerial work. Rulice, a German from Heidelberg who spoke English although not well enough to preach in it at first, was orthodox and no troublemaker.[111] He traveled to England personally in 1637 to recruit an additional minister to replace Paget, "the ablest he can get." He got Julius Hering of Shrewsbury, recently deprived. He had good reason for seeking to leave the country after hearing that Laud said, "I will pickle that Herring of Shrewsbury."[112] Thomas Paget of Blackley, Lancashire,

---

[107] C.R., III, 63, 67, 69.

[108] Acta Classis, IV, 61, 67, 72.

[109] Acta Classis, IV, 75; Wodrow MS., XLII, 254.

[110] Paget to Calderwood, June 16, 1636 and April 23, 1637, Wodrow MS., XLII, 253-54. Carter, *English Reformed Church*, p. 25.

[111] Carter, *English Reformed Church*, pp. 84, 94; Evenhuis, *Amsterdam*, I, 274. In 1639 Rulice transferred to the German Reformed church of the city.

[112] Hering was listed on the register of passengers from Great Yarmouth to Holland, Sept. 15, 1637, Charles B. Jewson, *Transcript of Three Registers of Passengers from Great Yarmouth to Holland and New England, 1637-1639*, Norfolk Record Society, No. 25 (1954), p. 48; Wodrow MS., XLII, 253; *D.N.B.*

intimidated into fleeing the country, described himself as having been "enforced by home-oppressions to seeke for liberty, employment and livelihood" abroad. Like his brother John, he strongly supported Presbyterian government.[113]

The middle years of the seventeenth century, 1640-60, were quieter than the troubled 1630s. The "Congregational" agitation in the church diminished, largely because of Paget's expert strategy in using the Dutch classis as an authoritarian force, also because of the draining away of the most active Congregational ministers over to New England, or, after 1640, back to England. The alienated anti-Paget members were gradually reclaimed. As early as 1636 Daniel Burr was elected deacon and in 1638 Crisp and Denman were elected, Crisp as deacon and Denman as elder—Crisp, however, declining "for causes, knowen unto himself." Crisp and Denman were questioned about what "their judgmente was concerninge the Government of these Churches by Consistoryes, Classis, and Sinods"; and by now, "they answered fully that they agreed wholly with vs."[114] Of the excommunicates, Henry Poulter was restored in 1641, "with many tears, submittinge," and William Best, after professing Arminianism for a time, was readmitted in 1648.[115] Thomas Adams was excommunicated in 1644 for heresy regarding the Sabbath. After several years of agitation about "congregational" reformation (autonomy of the congregation, discriminating membership, congregational decision-making, the covenant) the English church at Amsterdam returned to the middle ground of a conventional Presbyterianism. Thereafter, they talked little about church independence and "due power," and accepted considerable civil and ecclesiastical supervision.

The English Revolution of the 1640s added a new tension to the overseas English community, as some took one side, some the other. Royalist, Anglican refugees came over as well as some Presbyterians out of step with events at home. In a conference with classis deputies, the elders noted the war: "that in these sad divisions of the English nation; wherein the most innocent is traduced by some, if he be not altogether of their mynd, we did easily conceive that many might take occasion to rayse up scandals."[116] In 1645 Julius Hering died. During the interim, John Forbes of Corse, deposed professor of Kings College, Aberdeen, preached several times. For Hering's replacement the call went to Richard Maden, minister of the English church at Utrecht, formerly an

---

[113] "Humble Advertisement" by Thomas Paget, in John Paget, *Defence of Church-Government* (London, 1641); Morrill, *Cheshire*, p. 21; Richardson, *Puritanism*, pp. 67, 137.
[114] C.R., III, 81 (Jan. 21, 28, 1638).
[115] C.R., III, 121, 186.
[116] C.R., III, 204 (May 3, 1651).

Anglican conformist sequestered from St. Mildred Poultry, London. At Utrecht he had adjusted his convictions to pass as a Reformed, but Thomas Paget loudly opposed his coming to Amsterdam. Paget attacked Maden as a prelatical conformist and user of the Prayer Book, not suitable for a presbyterial church. "Seven times he has subscribed to the Prayer Book." To link him with the Reformed church would be "unequall yoking." Among other things, Paget also charged him with Arian heresy and with being a "malignant," whose appointment would be a great offense to the English Parliament and church of God. When the elders refused to harken, Paget carried his case against Maden to the Amsterdam classis, which could be counted on to abhor episcopacy.[117] After long delay, Maden was approved as minister with provision from the classis that "there maye be no innovations brought into our church."[118] Maden served 1647-68 and died at Amsterdam. In the midst of the Maden proceedings, Paget resigned and returned to England in 1646. William Price (1648-59) replaced him. He was a strong Presbyterian member of the Westminster Assembly and opponent of Oliver Cromwell.

Both Maden and Price publicly opposed the English Republic and they were subsequently reported as "violent incendiaryes" by English agents. "I heard Price say, that any man might with a safe conscience kill the protector; and he himself could do it," was one report. Republican members of the church protested against the one-sided Royalist sermons and prayers.[119] In spite of the strong Puritan tradition, the church under Maden and Price remained neutral, if not slightly Royalist, during the revolutionary years.

---

[117] C.R., III, 152-53; Acta Classis, IV, 369; Diary of John Forbes of Corse, in his *Opera Omnia* (Amsterdam, 1703), II, 263-64.

[118] C.R., III, 166.

[119] Thurloe, *S.P.* II, 319, 373-74; C.R., III, 193. On Maden, Matthews, *Cal. R.*, p. 53; on Price, *D.N.B.*

CHAPTER FIVE

CHURCHES AT LEIDEN, THE HAGUE, AND DELFT TO 1660

The first half of the seventeenth century saw English churches established in nearly all the major commercial Dutch cities of Holland. The largest settlements of English and Scots were to be found at Leiden, The Hague, and Rotterdam, with smaller groups at Delft, Dort, and Brielle. Fynes Moryson's *Itinerary* described Holland as the province "first in dignity" and blessed with fine cities: Amsterdam, "famous for trafficke," Rotterdam, where Erasmus was born, Leiden, with its university, and Haarlem, Dort, and Delft, "all very faire Cities." The Hague was "wanting onely wals to make it numbered among the most pleasant Cities, being no doubt a Village yeelding to none for the pleasant seat."[1] Travel from city to city was easily accomplished, and the English commended the Dutch on their unrivaled system of passage boats. "On all sides from City to City, they haue ditches cut, vpon which boates passe almost euery hower to and fro, and giue passage at a low rate."[2] Churches for the English and Scots were planted in the great cities. The city of Amsterdam provided her own stipend for churches, but elsewhere, the provincial States of Holland eventually took over the bill for the foreign churches, sometimes supplemented by municipal stipends and voluntary contributions in the congregations. The cities had responsibility for providing the church buildings and keeping them in repair. The States of Holland book of "Predicanten en kerkelycke saaken" records stipends for English Reformed churches at Dort, Leiden, Delft, The Hague, and Rotterdam, in most cases smaller than for the corresponding Dutch and French churches.[3] Some lists of English churches in Holland report a garrison church under Mr. Day at Gouda, but no records remain of this church.

The English Reformed Church of Leiden

The city of Leiden had two seventeenth-century English churches, one for Separatists and another for the non-Separatist English and Scots. Contrary to Amsterdam, the relations between the two communities

---
[1] Fynes Moryson, *An Itinerary written by Fynes Moryson Gent.* (London, 1617), pt. III, 92.
[2] Ibid., pt. III, 56.
[3] States of Holland, no. 4410 (A.R.A. The Hague).

were quite amiable and produced no polemical books. There are many references to the "Engelse kerk" or "the English church here," meaning in most cases the English Reformed Church, not the later famous church of the Pilgrim Fathers. The early historians of Leiden gave no attention to the Separatists. Van Mieris's *Beschryving der stad Leyden* (1762-84) devoted a few pages to the English Reformed Church but nothing to the Separatists. Not until more recently did Leiden begin to celebrate the Pilgrim Separatists.[4]

Leiden was a prosperous cloth manufacturing city specializing in the "new drapery." The period after 1577 was the time of the "Great Immigration" to Leiden. The first to come were skilled Flemish weavers previously settled in eastern England; and in ensuing years Leiden gained a significant foreign population. Overall, her population grew to about 50,000 in 1640. The studies of N. W. Posthumus show that between 1575 and 1620, 126 persons from England and 18 from Scotland became new citizens of the city, most of them after 1600.[5] This was only a small part of the British population. The same records reveal that the numbers of incoming Germans and Frenchmen were much larger than those of the British. Economically, Leiden was thriving but not exceptional. Where Leiden surpassed all cities was in her university. To the famous University of Leiden came hundreds of England and Scottish students in the seventeenth century (about 950 between 1575-1675).[6] The early seventeenth-century English-Scottish community, composed of both Separatists and non-Separatists, numbered in the hundreds. The English Reformed people claimed 200 families (1609), and the Separatists claimed 100 people in 1609 and by 1620 were a group of 300 or more.

For many years before a formal church was organized, occasional English preaching occurred at Leiden. An English military chaplain served at Leiden in 1587. The real beginning of the church came in 1607 when the growing English-Scottish community petitioned the city government of Leiden for a place of worship. The petition claimed to represent 145 families and a few miscellaneous individuals. The Leiden

---

[4] Frans van Mieris, *Beschryving der stad Leyden* (Leiden, 1762-84), I, 99-101. Leiden now has a special Pilgrim Fathers Museum at the Gemeente Archief.

[5] N. W. Posthumus, *De geschiedenis van de Leidsche lakenindustrie* (The Hague: Martinus Nijhoff, 1908-39), Part II, *De nieuwe tijd*, pp. 40-75; P. J. Blok, *Eene Hollandsche stad onder de republic* (The Hague: Martinus Nijhoff, 1916), pp. 6-7, 60.

[6] Edward Peacock, *Index to English Speaking Students Who Have Graduated at Leyden University*, Index Society Publication, 13 (1883); John W. Stoye, *English Travellers Abroad 1604-1667* (London: Jonathan Cape, 1952), p. 295.

[7] Gerechtsdagboeken van Burgemeesteren, A, fol. 541; F, fols. 160-61; Register van kerkelijke zaken, no. 2148 (Sec. Archief), fols. 39-40, 43-44, 46, 49 (G.A. Leiden).

magistrates seemed favorably impressed and approved the use of the church of St. Catherine Gasthuis although on a shared basis with the Dutch. So far no regular preacher was provided. Sermons were given by local English-speaking preachers (Jonas Volmarius of Oegstgeest, professor Franciscus Gomarus, and Daniel Castellanus of the French Church) and probably by traveling chaplains. Two years later in 1609 the English petitioned again, this time on behalf of 200 families, for financial support for their own preacher; once again the petition was granted, although moderately, with the allocation of two hundred guilders annually for a preacher. In March of 1610 the magistrates approved the calling of Robert Dury (Duraeus, Durie, or to the Dutch often "du Reus"), a Scottish minister of fiery reputation.[7] Although a preacher of some stature, Dury, like John Forbes at Middelburg, was readily available, being at the time in exile and under banishment because of his participation in the prohibited assembly of Aberdeen.

In the first records, the church in St. Catherine Gasthuis was called the English church, or at times the English and Scottish church. The church made two further moves, in 1621 to the Jerusalem church and in 1644 to the Begijnhof church, a site now incorporated into the university library on the Rapenburg.[8] The Begijnhof church after the Reformation had been given over to various university uses, but a part which had been the fencing school was standing vacant and was thus appointed to the English. "The English have part of a church here," wrote a passing traveler in 1695.[9]

In September 1616, Dury died and the church was compelled to search for a successor, someone, they hoped, of great spiritual stature. Then, as on every such occasion, the decisive voice of civil government in church affairs was clear. In the Dutch fashion the church first was required to petition for permission to call a new minister; and after electing the minister, his name required approval by the city magistrates. Aiming for the best, the church first offered the pastorate to the eminent Puritan preacher, Arthur Hildersam (1563-1632), at that very time in hiding from the High Commission for nonconformity. When discovered and visited by John Hartly, an elder of the Leiden church, "making offer to him of the Pastors place, then Vacant," Hildersam voiced interest and might have accepted the assignment "had not his Wives unwillingnesse to go over the Seas, retained him."[10] Disappointed in the first effort, the church proceeded to the election of John Blancquius, an English preacher

---

[8] Van Mieris, *Beschryving*, I, 99-101.
[9] William Mountague, *The Delights of Holland* (London, 1696), p. 100.
[10] Samuel Clarke, *The Lives of Thirty-Two English Divines*, 3rd ed., in *A General Martyrologie* (London, 1677), p. 119.

studying at the university, but this election also miscarried when Blancquius abruptly departed from the city, pleading "indisposition." He also complained about the meager salary offered to him. Discouraging news, but just then another candidate happened on the scene, "the peaceable and pious Mr. Hugh Goodyear."

Goodyear had crossed over to Leiden for study at the university, but the English Church shortly pressed him into service to fill the gap. Approved by the city magistrates on November 16, 1617, at 300 guilders yearly, Goodyear settled in almost permanently as the English Reformed preacher of Leiden until 1661.[11] At the end, Goodyear's cousin, Thomas Goodyear, summarized: "I must not forgett to give God his due praise for my kinsmans long continuance amongst you in those parts which was not much lesse I think then 50 yeares."[12] Not quite that long (forty-four years in fact), but all the same his tenure easily stood in that day as a record among British ministers serving in the Low Countries. After Goodyear, the following were seventeenth-century ministers: Matthew Newcomen (1663-69), Edward Richardson (1670-74), Henry Hickman (1674-92), William Carstares (1688), Robert Fleming Junior (1692-95), and John Milling (1696-1702).

In choosing Goodyear, the church got a staunch Puritan. By birth he came from Lancaster, born in about the year 1590. He had relatives and life-long interests in Manchester, which perhaps was his city. From home he went to Emmanuel College, Cambridge and took the B.A. degree in 1612/13 and the M.A. in 1616. Next he was off to the Continent, traveling with John Bastwick on a pass issued October 26, 1616.[13] By January 14, 1617, they had inscribed themselves in the university album, Goodyear identifying himself as twenty-seven years old, a student of theology, and dwelling at the home of Thomas Brewer. Bastwick and Alexander Leighton lodged at the same house.[14] Brewer, Bastwick, and Leighton were extreme Puritans. Although not as audacious as his friends, young Goodyear in a slightly more quiet way was moving in the same Puritan direction. Before leaving England, he had not yet been ordained minister.

---

[11] Reg. kerk zaken, 2148, fol. 13.

[12] Dec. 6, 1661, Goodyear Papers (Weeskamer Archief 1355), ee (G.A. Leiden).

[13] *Acts of the Privy Council* (Oct. 26, 1616); D. Plooij, *The Pilgrim Fathers from a Dutch Point of View* (New York: New York Univ. Press, 1932), pp. 82-89. Goodyear's family was not prominent, and in 1661 it was reported from England that most of his kindred (and heirs) were "in great want." A reading of his will reveals that his uncle was Roger Goodyear, and Roger's son, Thomas, was a London merchant. Brothers and sisters of Hugh were Isabell (Gilbert), Elizabeth (Radcliffe), Robert, and Elinor (Ketshall). His nephew, William Goodyear, served as a soldier in Holland (see Goodyear Papers).

[14] Plooij, *Pilgrim Fathers*, p. 83.

Rather than returning to England for ordination, Goodyear arranged a quick ordination in Leiden; "he was such a one, who had imposition of hands only by a french minister of this towne, and that by entreaty of his people." Although Huguenot hands were sufficient for Puritan standards, by high Anglican standards Goodyear was never truly consecrated. According to Stephen Goffe, Goodyear was "no minister" because of his lack of authentic Anglican or even classical ordination.[15] Leiden was Goodyear's first and only pastorate. When he arrived in Holland, he was a bachelor, but eventually he married twice, first to Sara van Wassenberch in 1627 and then to Cornelia Schoor in 1648. He had no children. For many years he lived in a house on the Steenschuur and gradually accumulated other property as well.[16] In 1656 it was announced at the South Holland Synod that Goodyear was to be emeritus, but such announcement was premature—perhaps no replacement could be found—and he labored on as minister up to his death in November 1661.[17]

As an officially recognized church, the English Reformed church had its own consistory (*kerkeraad*), distinct from the Dutch *kerkeraad* of the city. All the same, the relationship of the Leiden English Reformed Church vis-a-vis the Dutch Church was cloudy, a problem common to many of the British churches in the Netherlands. What responsibility did the English Church have to the Dutch Reformed Church, its consistories, classes, and synods? What kind of supervision, if any, was the Dutch Church to have over the English? Questions like these were seldom resolved with any precision. In 1641 the Synod of South Holland tried to clarify the situation by asking "whether the English preachers shall be admitted to the classical meetings by form of correspondence with similar rights to all other members?" The answer from the Leiden classis was vague.[18]

The English church under Goodyear's tutelage considered itself a *gereformeerde kerk* like the Dutch Reformed church.[19] However, its reputation grew yearly as a severe, rigid congregation, at least as much as was conceivable in a state-supported Reformed church. Its position in ecclesiastical Leiden was about midway between the exclusive, covenanted Separatists of Robinson on the one side, and the more inclusive Dutch

---

[15] B.P., I, 156 (Dec. 23/13, 1633).
[16] Goodyear Papers.
[17] Knuttel, *Acta Synoden Zuid-Holland*, III (1656). Goodyear was buried Nov. 11, 1661.
[18] Ibid., II, 328, 368-69; Acta Classis Leiden, no. 5, June 24, 1642: "Dat men de selve voor als noch sal laten in statu."
[19] "Stukken betreffende de benoeming van ouderlingen der Engelsche Gemeente," (Weeskamer Archief 4909).

Reformed Church on the other. If Goodyear's church could not compete with the disciplined purity of the Pilgrim Fathers, it nevertheless insisted on very high standards of membership and practice. Goodyear's formal conception of the church was a commonplace of Reformed theology: "A company caled, it may be defined to be the company of the elect that are or that be caled in the gratious acceptable day of the Lord." But in his teachings and practice, Goodyear laid fervent stress on the church as a glorious body (the visible congregation) gathered out from the common company of the world. His lecture on the church put forth the covenant philosophy, the "covenant made before God and the church."[20]

Goodyear was a relentless disciplinarian of the church. The Dutch said he had "a more rigid discipline."[21] Across the years, a succession of incidents dramatized the differing conceptions—or at least differing emphases—of the Dutch Reformed and the Puritan-minded English Reformed Church. Moreover, on at least one occasion, dissension within the English Church on the matter of discipline seriously threatened unity and harmony between minister and his own people.[22] Although so severe, Goodyear's results were short of the mark. In 1633 Goodyear wrote, "The Lord hath placed me over a congregacion wch injoyeth the use of the ordinances, but wanteth that power of godliness wch is in those rare Christians in Manchestre and there about."[23]

So long as the English eventually solved their own problems, no great damage to the peace of Leiden happened. But as some dissatisfied English members sought to escape from their own church and transfer to the Dutch church of Leiden, English problems became community-wide. In 1630 an especially troublesome case arose concerning Richard Parsons, merchant of Leiden and member of Goodyear's church.[24] Because of bitter dissatisfaction with the English Church, he applied to the Dutch to be received as a member; but when asked, he could produce no attestation or demission from his own church. Parsons's primary argument was that part of his family knew little or no English. The Dutch were willing to take him, if he had his document; but without it, they judged themselves unable to overrule a fellow Reformed church constituted under its own consistory. Meanwhile, the English Church refused to issue an attestation of Parsons' good standing. He fell short of their standards, and his publicity of the case was bringing scandal to the

---

[20] Goodyear, "Aantekeningen voor preeken en catechisaties," Lecture for 21st Lord's Day, MSS (G.A. Leiden).
[21] B.P., I, 80.
[22] Acta Kerkeraad Leiden, no. 003, April 16, June 11, July 30, 1632 (G.A. Leiden).
[23] Plooij, *Pilgrim Fathers*, p. 107.
[24] Acta Kerkeraad, No. 003, Mar. 7, 15, Aug. 2, 16, 23, 1630.

church. So an impasse began: The Dutch were willing to receive Parsons, but the English would neither acknowledge Parsons as a good member nor would they dismiss him to the Dutch. For months the agitation jarred relations between the two churches, with the Dutch Church of Leiden almost powerless to act in view of the independent existence of the English Church. "The English church does not stand under us," acknowledged the Dutch.[25] Finally, Parsons tried to settle the case by appealing to the city magistrates, yet nothing moved Goodyear. "The Dutch ministers have commanded him quietnes and constrained him to dismisse some of his flocke, and to send them to the Dutch church."[26]

Similar cases followed in succeeding years. By that time, it was ever more obvious that Goodyear and his elders were of a "more rigid discipline." In 1638 an incident involving Henry Stafford of the English church stirred controversy in the grand style. Stafford was a barber (a surgeon) who because of Sabbath-breaking was suspended from the Lord's Table by Goodyear. The transgression, it turned out, was cutting hair on the Sabbath morning, before the sermon, said Stafford, and for the benefit of the poor. Thoroughly disgruntled, Stafford proceeded to the Dutch consistory and asked to be admitted to their church. The Dutch were willing, but the English once again refused to dismiss him from their discipline. While this case pended, another member of Goodyear's church, Nicolaus Allen (sometimes Oeillaert), was suspended and appealed to the Dutch consistory. According to his story, his transgression was merely that "he had a few times frequented the Dutch preaching and churches." Later, Stafford's daughter also applied for transfer after reporting unendurable harassment. Negotiations between the two churches were far from brotherly, and finally the city officials intervened.[27]

The English church bruskly dismissed the charge that it disciplined members for listening to Dutch sermons. Goodyear's position was that the English dissidents "should be sent to their own consistory and that the Dutch were please not to meddle with his members." The Dutch were "to assume no authority over his church nor take power concerning his members."[28]

In spite of a common Reformed theology, the two churches tried to practice different conceptions of the church. Goodyear insisted on the necessity to discipline relentlessly: never to let the guilty escape to a more permissive brotherhood. He pronounced that his erring members "were

---

[25] Ibid., July 18, 1631; Letters, Portfolio A.
[26] B.P., I, 80.
[27] Acta Kerkeraad, no. 003, July 23, Sept. 17, 1638.
[28] Ibid., Nov. 5, 12, 1638.

scandalous and remained obstinate, and his church judged them worthy of a public censure." The Dutch Church of Leiden had no authority over the English Church; and because the English Church remained aloof from the classis and synod, there was no chance for higher church censure. After hearing the charges against Stafford and Allen, the Dutch consistory concluded "that the reasons are neither sufficient enough to use censure against the persons, nor to prevent them from being received in our Dutch church." Goodyear possessed an abrasive personality, but the base of the trouble was the varying standards of life and church membership between the two churches. In the fall of 1639 the magistrates ordered the transfer of Stafford, Allen, and the daughter to the Dutch church.[29] The consistory records show occasional clashes in later years as well.

For its first forty years, the English Church had no formal ties with larger church organizations. The church was not Separatist, but nevertheless it was isolated from fellowship with English and Dutch churches. After attending the opening meeting of the English Synod in 1622, Goodyear, along with the Amsterdam ministers (John Paget and Thomas Potts), boycotted the synod, a factor significant in bringing on its collapse. Sir Dudley Carleton, English ambassador at the Hague, interpreted the boycott as arising from jealousy, although Goodyear would hardly have agreed.[30] The Amsterdam church was fully incorporated into the Dutch classis and synod; but Leiden, having rejected the English Synod, had nothing to claim except its political tie to the Leiden magistracy. To escape the isolation, Goodyear in 1632 applied for membership in the Classis of Leiden and Neder-Rijnland, but his fellow preachers rejected him. The Parsons case and other controversy in the English Church had prejudiced them against Goodyear as a fit colleague. According to Stephen Goffe, Goodyear "refuseth to be of the English Classis" and in turn "is refused here amongst the Dutch: The reason is, because they conceive him to be of a disagreing disposition in generall; and in particular that he would governe his owne church with a more rigid discipline then is used or thought fitt by the Dutch Classis."[31]

So it went until 1655, when Goodyear applied once again to the classis for membership. This time, although the parties were more amenable than in 1632, Goodyear was admitted only on specific terms which spoke to old, outstanding grievances. His petition, countersigned by his elders, and deacons, read:

---

[29] Ibid., Oct. 25, Aug. 26, 1639.
[30] S.P. 84, vol. 117, fols. 133-34.
[31] B.P., I, 80.

> We, the undersigned elders and deacons of the English church here, acknowledge herewith that our pastor, Hugh Goedyaert, with our permission humbly has requested to become a member of the classis. We promise to make no alterations in our present church practice, nor to do anything in such matters as calling of a preacher and excommunication, without the knowledge and permission of the classis. Also our humble request to the classis is that the above mentioned request may be obtained for God's glory and the edification of our church and in order to prevent all calamity such as schism and like offenses. Acted in Consistory, June 20, 1655.[32]

The marriage of English and Dutch churches proved to be a matter of convenience, not a once-and-for-all event. After Goodyear's death, the English Church lapsed back into its former isolated status, and his successors were seldom if ever members of the classis.[33]

Goodyear avoided the extremes of the Presbyterian-Congregationalist controversies. William Aspinwall of New England wrote to Goodyear once: "I suppose the way of your churches is presbiterian and somewhat differing from our congregationall, but that is not offensive to us, whilst still our common aymes be to be edifyed and built upon the grace of our Lord Jesus."[34] As Congregational ideas made deep inroads at Rotterdam, Amsterdam, and Delft, Goodyear hesitated to take a stand between the old Puritanism of John Paget and the new Puritanism of Hooker and Davenport. During the early 1630s, however, Goodyear, in spite of his traditional Presbyterian stance, showed sympathy for the Hooker-Davenport program. At Amsterdam in 1634 he was reported to be a near-Hookerite. "Mr. Goodyeare, you know," holds "no errors, but such poynts as Mr. Hooker and Mr. Davenport hould."[35] Like them, Goodyear recognized that orthodox words do not necessarily prove faith for membership or baptism. "Every assent is not faith." Although Goodyear and Paget got along tolerably well, Paget still found it advisable to lecture Goodyear on the issues involved in the baptism affair.[36] Goodyear had no deep opposition to classis government and was one of the first English preachers to apply for Dutch classis membership, although unsuccessful in gaining admission.

While not officially in the English Synod group, Goodyear did his part to resist Anglican inroads. The prayer book found no welcome at Leiden. "Some without the licencie of the English Churches here seek to bring us

---

[32] Acta Classis Leiden, no. 5, June 21, 1655. Signatories were Laurens Souter, Henrick Sandby, Allever Knoules, and Jan Houibbot.
[33] Acta Kerkeraad Leiden, no. 006, Feb. 22, May 3, 1675.
[34] (1650) Goodyear Papers, gg.
[35] "Tracts relating to the English Church at Amsterdam," Add. MS. 24,666, fol. 2 (B.M.).
[36] Goodyear Papers, gg.

under the command of the service book in England and I hear that the chiefe in England wil bring it in some congregacion, but cannot so easily bring it in ours."[37] When Egbert Grim propounded theses favorable to Anglican liturgy at the University of Leiden, Goodyear loudly opposed him.[38] On another occasion, Goodyear and John Forbes teamed up to resist the introduction of the prayer book at Utrecht by an interim Dutch preacher, "because they thought it dangerous to let him use our common prayers book."[39] Stephan Goffe, major Laudian agent in the Low Countries, listed Goodyear among the Puritan troublemakers. When asked about his order of service, Goodyear showed Goffe a prayer book of 1586, printed at Middelburg by Richard Schilders. "*Cum privilegio.*" But, asked Goffe, "Who made it?" "What *privilegium?*" Goodyear could not give satisfactory answer except "that it was a book allowed of by all the godly English." Only later did Goffe deduce the horrifying news that the Middelburg book might be the work of Thomas Cartwright.[40]

Late in 1633, Goffe on one of his trips to Leiden applied to Goodyear for permission to take the communion at the English Church. Goodyear refused him. Highly indignant, Goffe demanded explanation. Goodyear in reply talked long about the need to consult the elders, to publish the names of visitors before the congregation and the like, which seemed amazingly weak excuses to Goffe, who pictured himself a martyr for Anglicanism. "It is plain my crime is, that I am of the faith of the church of England." On reflection, Goffe saw that his exclusion was for the best, in light of Goodyear's irregular ordination, "no imposition of hands neither from a Byshop, nor by a Classicall authority." Goodyear was a deficient minister.[41] That was one man's opinion. Six months later Sir William Brereton, traveling through Leiden, stopped off for the Sunday and "heard Mr. Goodier (a worthy, honest man) in the English church, a little (yet neat) place."[42]

Goodyear's old Cambridge connections plus his strategic position at Leiden made him a natural participant in the international Puritan brotherhood of Holland, England, and America. Nearly every English preacher passing through Leiden sought out Hugh Goodyear, perhaps for hospitality as much as for fellowship. In 1627 Goodyear petitioned the magistrates for an increase in salary, the times being so costly, and the burden of entertaining the "foreign preachers and the church members

---

[37] Plooij, *Pilgrim Fathers*, p. 107.
[38] B.P., I, 127-28.
[39] Ibid., I, 86.
[40] Ibid., I, 80.
[41] Ibid., I, 156.
[42] William Brereton, *Travels in Holland the United Provinces England Scotland and Ireland*, ed. Edward Hawkins, The Chetham Society, 1 (1844), 45.

who ordinarily come addressed to him from other kingdoms, provinces, and towns, by virtue of his office." (He got a small raise.)[43] Among the English community in Holland, he had many friends. One was William Ames, professor of theology at the University of Franeker. When the Remonstrants of Leiden attacked Ames's anti-Arminian books, Goodyear jumped to the defense and publicly rebuked Episcopius for disparaging Ames.[44] When Matthias Nethenus was preparing a biography of Ames in 1658, he appealed to Goodyear, for "there is scarcely anybody left who has better knowledge of that man and of his life than you have."[45]

Goodyear had a large, and unusually well-preserved, correspondence with people in England and America. There is one letter from John Cotton (1630), several from Ralph Smith of Plymouth Plantation and William Aspinwall of Boston, and one from Hugh Peter of Salem (1639). Peter wrote to recommend Francis Higginson, the son of the former pastor of Salem, who was coming to Leiden for study. Higginson was the first New Englander to study at Leiden, and the hope was that he would return to Harvard as a teacher. John Cotton and Mrs. John Wilson sent greetings to Goodyear in one of Aspinwall's letters. The correspondence also contains letters with fellow English pastors in Holland, among them Thomas Cawton of Rotterdam, Robert Paget of Dort, and John Paget of Amsterdam.[46] Goodyear published no books or sermons, consequently he made no large scholarly reputation. Nevertheless, he served so long as pastor that he eventually became a pillar of the English preachers abroad. Jacobus Borstius, prominent Dutch Reformed preacher, appreciated Goodyear's friendship and help with the English language. He called Goodyear "his second father."[47]

In relating to John Robinson's Separatist congregation, Goodyear was a moderate. He did not condone their Separatism, but neither did he agitate or publish polemics against them. Separatist and non-Separatist relations were calm at Leiden, in contrast to Amsterdam, and roused few passions. The Pilgrims of New England, after Robinson's death in 1625, asked Goodyear by letters to do some business for them. Letters from abroad sometimes carried greetings for Mrs. Robinson or other Pilgrim friends. Goodyear responded to Ralph Smith in 1633, "as soon as I had received your letter I went unto Mrs. Robinson and acquainted her with

---

[43] Reg. kerk. zaken, 2150, fol. 114v.
[44] Nethenus, "Praefatio introductoria," in Ames, *Opera*, vol. 1 (Amsterdam, 1658).
[45] Plooij, *Pilgrim Fathers*, p. 109.
[46] Goodyear Papers, gg; Goodyear's correspondence with America is analyzed by Plooij, *Pilgrim Fathers*, pp. 82-130.
[47] Jacobus Borstius, *Vyftien predicatien* (Utrecht, 1696), "Kort verhaal van Borstius."

the whole contents of the letter." Goodyear added the note: salute "old master Bruster."[48] Nevertheless, Goodyear was not able to win the Separatist remnant over to his church.

Goodyear's church, unlike Robinson's, lasted for 200 years. Supported by the authority of the state, the English Reformed Church had the resources to go on even during periods when the morale of the congregation dropped low. Goodyear drew his last state stipend in October 1661; he died a month later.[49] Throughout the seventeenth century, the church retained its Puritan character as set by Dury and Goodyear.

The Leiden Separatists

The Separatist church, under the leadership of John Robinson, was not long after the English Reformed Church in establishing itself at Leiden. In 1608 Robinson's church settled in Amsterdam, but they desired to move out on their own. The Scrooby people who had come out of England provided at least a core of the immigrants to Leiden. They petitioned as a group of "100 persons born in England" on February 12, 1609, for admittance to Leiden with provision that they would settle there by May 1 "without being however a burden in the least to any one." They asked for no favors or church subsidies. English ambassador Sir Ralph Winwood protested against their being welcomed in Leiden, but the magistrates replied that they "did not refuse any honest persons free and unrestrained ingress, provided they behaved themselves honestly, and submitted to all the laws and ordinances here."[50] From 1609 to about 1635 the church was established at Leiden; even after the *Mayflower* migration to New England in 1620, a remnant stayed on. They never had a public church building with steeple and bells, but met in Robinson's home. In 1611 Robinson with several friends bought a house and land by the Pieters Kerk, called the Groene Poort (afterwards the Engelse Poort), which they fitted out with several small cottages and a hall for worship. Not all of the congregation could live in this compound; however, it served as their religious and community headquarters.[51] By all reports, they were ordinary people with modest trades (fustian workers, bombazine workers, felt makers, button makers). William Brewster was a printer and also offered lessons in English to university

---

[48] Plooij, *Pilgrim Fathers*, pp. 100, 106-07.
[49] Reg. kerk. zaken, 2155, fol. 107v.
[50] Copies of the original documents of the Pilgrims at Leiden are in D. Plooij and J. Rendel Harris, *Leyden Documents Relating to the Pilgrim Fathers* (Leyden: E.J. Brill, 1920).
[51] Dexter and Dexter, *England and Holland*, pp. 529-32, 541; A. Eekhof, *Three Unknown Documents Concerning the Pilgrim Fathers in Holland* (The Hague: Martinus Nijhoff, 1920), p. 30.

students. "And at length they came to raise a competente and comfortable living, but with hard and continuall labor," wrote their historian, William Bradford.[52] Bradford worked as a fustian weaver.

Their small congregation of 100 grew by 1620 to about 300. Bradford, who estimated the Ancient Church of Amsterdam at 300, said their church at Leiden was "sometimes not much fewer in number; nor at all inferior in able men."[53] Robinson, their only university graduate, was minister and William Brewster, having some university education at Peterhouse, Cambridge, was ruling elder. They also had deacons. Richard Clifton, who had been minister with Robinson at Scrooby, stayed behind in Amsterdam. The Leiden church under Robinson's ministry was a Separatist church in communion with the Ancient Church at Amsterdam. When the Ancient Church split into the two halves in 1610, Johnsonians and Ainsworthians, the Pilgrim church intervened as a sister church (but could not heal the breach). Robinson wrote to Amsterdam in 1624 about the kinship of their church to his church, "which is nearliest united unto you."[54] The doctrinal basis of the church, for Leiden as well as Amsterdam, was the Separatist confession of 1596.[55] Another doctrinal statement, the Seven Articles by Robinson and Brewster (1617), stresses continuity with Reformed theology and acknowledges the 39 Articles, "every Article thereof." Robinson, however, never repudiated the original Separatist confession.[56]

Church life at Leiden, as recorded in all the documents, was harmonious, contrasted to the Separatists at Amsterdam or earlier at Middelburg. No sensational revelations of whorings and fiendish cruelties were shouted about. The Leiden magistrates, in fact, commended the Pilgrims; "these English, said they, have lived amongst us now this 12. years, and yet we never had any sute or accusation came against any of them."[57]

Robinson was the intellectual and spiritual mainspring of the Pilgrim church; and under his leadership Leiden developed into a center of Separatist, and even Puritan, religion hardly inferior to Amsterdam. At Leiden Robinson produced a shelf of theological books which earned him

---

[52] William Bradford, *Bradford's History of Plymouth Plantation, 1606-1646*, ed. William T. Davis (1908; rpt. New York: Barnes & Noble, 1946), p. 39.

[53] William Bradford, "Dialogue or the sume of a Conference," *Publications* of the Colonial Society of Massachusetts, 22 (1920), 139.

[54] Dexter, *Congregationalism*, I, 347; Dexter and Dexter, *England and Holland*, p. 523-24.

[55] B. R. White, *The English Separatist Tradition* (Oxford: Oxford Univ. Press, 1971), p. 157.

[56] Edward Arber, ed., *The Story of the Pilgrim Fathers, 1606-1623 A.D.* (London: Ward and Downey, 1897), pp. 280-81; Walker, *Creeds*, pp. 81-92.

[57] Bradford, *History*, p. 42.

an international Puritan reputation: *A Justification of Separation from the Church of England* (1610); *Of Religious Communion Private & Publique* (1614); *A Manumission to a Manuduction* (1615); *The People's Plea for the Exercise of Prophesie* (1618); *Apologia Justa et Necessaria* (1619); *A Defence of the Doctrine propounded by the Synode at Dort* (1624); *An Appeale on Truths Behalffe* (1624); *Observations Divine and Morall* (1625); *A Treatise of the Lawfulnes of Hearing of the Ministers in the Church of England* (1634, posthumous). A skillful controversialist, he could easily hold his own; his "teeth are like Kniues, and his iawes like swords."[58] Robinson, as an intellectual, entered fully into the academic life of Leiden University, enrolling as a "student in theology" in 1615. He developed contacts with Polyander, Festus Hommius, and Antonius Walaeus.[59] In the scholarly areas, Robinson far outshone Goodyear, whose accomplishments of this kind were modest.

English Separatist religion grew broader and more ecumenical under Robinson's inspiration. In 1609 he came to Leiden as a rigid Separatist, denouncing the Church of England and all her "sour" parish assemblies. In his *Justification of Separation*, although willing to acknowledge that there were some true Christians in the Church of England, he denied any kind of religious fellowship with anyone not of a separated church, no matter how pious. "And it is our great grief, though their own fault, that we cannot have communion with the persons in whom so eminent graces of God are." This bitter spirit carried over to refusing fellowship with non-conforming Puritans, many of them fellow exiles for conscience sake. Robinson's position provoked spirited debate with various visitors, notably with Robert Parker, Henry Jacob, and William Ames, visiting Leiden about 1610-11; and thereafter Robinson began to modify his Separatism to allow fellowship with godly Puritans. William Bradford remembered the days; "wee some of vs knew mr Parker doctor Ames and mr Jacob in holland when they sojourned for a time in Leyden and all three for a time boarded together and had theire victualls dressed by some of our acquaintance and then they liued Comfortable and then they were prouided for as became theire persons." Parker, Jacob, and Ames were a new kind of Puritans (Congregationalists of the non-Separatist kind). In debate with Ames, Robinson wrote his *Of Religious Communion* (1614) and his *Manumission to a Manuduction* (1615) which allowed private fellowship among Christians of all persuasions but refused public fellowship of preaching and worship. However, Robinson's posthumous *Treatise of the Lawfulnes of Hearing of the Ministers in the Church of England*

---

[58] Christopher Lawne, et al., *The Prophane Schisme of the Brownists or Separatists* (n.p., 1612), p. 86.
[59] Plooij, *Pilgrim Fathers*, pp. 52, 93-94.

(1634) gave approval for certain kinds of public fellowship, such as hearing the sermons from godly non-Separatist Puritan preachers.[60]

When the *Mayflower* Pilgrims went out to New England in 1620, Robinson advised "by all meanes, to endeavor to close with the godly party of the Kingdome of *England*." As Governor Winslow put it, "Tis true, I confesse, he was more rigid in his course and way at first, then towards his latter end."[61] To contemporaries Robinson stood out as the most reasonable Separatist. Richard Bernard called him the "one yet nearest the truth unto us, as I heare, and not so Schismaticall as the rest"; others said that "it had been truely a marvel, if such a man had gone on to the end a rigid Separatist." Geoffrey F. Nuttall describes Robinson's mature position as "semiseparatism."[62]

Consistent with Robinson's moderate theology, the Separatist church began to blur the line between Separatist and non-Separatist Puritanism. Instead of insisting on a statement of total rejection of the Church of England for membership, the issue was not much pressed. When new members begin to give their anti-Church of England profession, said Winslow, "I have divers times, both in the one place, and the other, heard either *Mr. Robinson* our Pastor, or *Mr. Brewster* our Elder stop them forthwith, shewing them that wee required no such things at their hands, but only to hold forth faith in Christ Jesus, holiness in the fear of God, and submission to every Ordinance and appointment of God, leaving the Church of *England* themselves, and to the Lord...."[63] John Paget of Amsterdam also heard of these Leiden innovations of receiving "the members of the Church of England into their congregation, and this without any renunciation of the Church of England."[64] When Sabine Staresmore, a member of Henry Jacob's non-Separatist church at London, came to Amsterdam in 1622, he sought admission to the Ancient Church (Ainsworth's) on the ground of transfer from a church for "the most part separated." He was refused. Next, Staresmore went to Leiden and, on the basis of his Jacobite membership, gained admittance to Robinson's church. When he again applied for membership at Amster-

---

[60] John Robinson, *The Works of John Robinson*, ed. Robert Ashton (London: John Snow, 1851), II, 15, 69, III, 377-78; Bradford, "Dialogue," p. 131; Keith L. Sprunger, *The Learned Doctor William Ames* (Urbana: Univ. of Illinois Press, 1972), pp. 37-43; Walter H. Burgess, *John Robinson Pastor of the Pilgrim Fathers* (London: Williams and Norgate, 1920), p. 29.

[61] Edward Winslow, *Hypocrisie Unmasked* (London, 1646), pp. 93, 98.

[62] Robert Baillie, *A Dissvasive from the Errours of the Time* (London, 1645), p. 17; John Cotton, *The Way of Congregational Churches Cleared* (London, 1648), p. 7-8; Geoffrey F. Nuttall, *Visible Saints: The Congregational Way 1640-1660* (Oxford: Blackwell, 1957), p. 10; Burgess, *Robinson*, p. 127.

[63] Winslow, *Hypocrisie Unmasked*, p. 99.

[64] John Paget, *An Arrow against the Separation of the Brownists* (Amsterdam, 1617), p. 127.

dam, on the basis of transfer from Leiden, he was once more "cast out" (by Ecluse, who by then was in charge).[65]

The Leiden Pilgrims built up harmonious relationship with the Dutch Reformed Church of Leiden, quite the reverse of the Amsterdam story. Although Robinson regarded the Reformed churches as falling short of the full mark of the Gospel, he nevertheless acknowledged them as true churches and superior to the Church of England. "Such is our accord in the case of religion, with the Dutch reformed churches, as that we are ready to subscribe to all and every article of faith in the same church," with very few reservations. He professed and held "communion both with the *French* and *Dutch* Churches, yea, tendering it the *Scots* also." Pilgrims were allowed to worship in Dutch Reformed churches when traveling to other cities and Reformed visitors with the Leiden church.[66] When David Calderwood of Scotland came to Leiden in 1619, Robinson invited him to the Lord's Table: "Reverend Sir, You may not only stay to behold us, but partake with us, if you please, for wee acknowledge the Churches of Scotland to be the Churches of Christ." On that occasion, Calderwood declined for fear of giving offense to some of his anti-Brownist brethren.[67] Between Robinson's church and Goodyear's church, however, there seems to have been little movement and fellowship. Nevertheless, the absence of public acrimony is significant.

Robinson's Reformed theology put him on the side of the Contra-Remonstrants against Arminianism. He avidly attended theological lectures on the controverted points of religion, and, according to Bradford's history, entered into public debate against the Arminian professor Simon Episcopius with great success "so it procured him much honour and respecte from those lerned men, and others which loved the trueth." These debates, however, are not recorded in the Dutch church histories. As a Calvinist, Robinson published a book in 1624, *A Defence of the Doctrine propounded by the Synode at Dort*. He was "versed in the Dutch language" and widely known. When Robinson died, Dutch professors and preachers attended his funeral. "Some of the chief of them sadly affirmed, that all the Churches of Christ sustained a losse by the death of

---

[65] Burrage, *E.E.D.*, I, 173-74. A.T., *A Christian Reprofe against Contention* (n.p., 1631), pp. 5-25.

[66] Robinson, *Works*, III, 8; Winslow, *Hypocrisie Unmasked*, pp. 93-96; Alice C. Carter, "John Robinson and the Dutch Reformed Church," *Studies in Church History*, ed. G. J. Cuming, 3 (Leiden: E. J. Brill, 1966), 232-41.

[67] Winslow, *Hypocrisie Unmasked*, pp. 96-97. Winslow did not identify Calderwood by name but as a Scottish divine, author of *Perth Assembly*. John Cotton referred to the same incident but identified the Scot as John Tarbes (i.e. John Forbes); see Cotton, *Way of Congregational Churches Cleared*, p. 8.

[68] Bradford, *History*, p. 43; Winslow, *Hypocrisie Unmasked*, p. 95; Dexter and Dexter, *England and Holland*, p. 584.

that worthy Instrument of the Gospel."[68] Of all the Separatist theologians, Robinson had the most ecumenical outlook. Professor Antonius Walaeus reported that Robinson had confided and "at divers times conversed with me concerning the separation between their congregation and the other English congregations in this country, and that he has at divers times testified that he was disposed to do his utmost to remove this schism; that he was also averse to educating his son for the work of the ministry in such congregations, but much preferred to have him exercise his ministry in the Dutch Churches." Festus Hommius also concurred that Robinson had supported union among the various English churches of the Low Countries. None of Robinson's sons did enter the ministry, either English or Dutch, but after Robinson's death, his "widow, children, and other relatives and friends" joined the Dutch Reformed Church of Leiden.[69]

The flourishing Separatist church at Leiden underwent a major change in 1620 with the immigration of some members to the Plymouth settlement in New England. According to Governor Winslow, the reasons for immigrating were these: "How hard the Country was, where wee lived, how many spent their estate in it, and were forced to return for *England*; how grievous to live from under the protection of the State of *England*; how like wee were to lose our language and our name, of English; how little good wee did, or were like to do to the Dutch in reforming the Sabbath; how unable there to give such education to our children, as wee our selves had received."[70] Only about fifty of the Leiden congregation sailed on the *Mayflower*, the larger part remaining in Holland but with additional people going over yearly. Pastor Robinson stayed at his post in Leiden; elder Brewster went to New England.[71]

The remnant at Leiden grew smaller and smaller. Robinson died in 1625, and the Leiden segment of the church never gained another minister. None of the three main options (disbanding, joining Goodyear's English Reformed Church, or joining the Dutch Reformed Church) occurred as a congregational decision. "What deteyneth the Separatists from ioyning with you, I desire to know at your leasure?" wrote John Cotton to Hugh Goodyear in 1630.[72] Although pastorless, the post-Robinson church had deacons (John Keble and William Jepson).[73]

---

[69] Plooij, *Pilgrim Fathers*, pp. 91, 93-94; Johannis Hoornbeek, *Summa Controversiarum Religionis*, 2nd ed. (Utrecht, 1658), p. 741; Eekhof, *Three Unknown Documents*, pp. 11-17.
[70] Winslow, *Hypocrisie Unmasked*, p. 85.
[71] George F. Willison, *Saints and Strangers* (New York: Reynal and Hitchcock, 1945), pp. 121, 437-53.
[72] April 12, 1630, Goodyear Papers, gg.
[73] Ralph Smith to Goodyear, July 1, 1633: "speake to ye 2 deacons of ye church (yor neighbors)"—Keble and Jepson, Plooij, *Pilgrim Fathers*, p. 100. Plooij interpreted this to

Dissension and splitting occurred in the 1630s over the issue of how far to maintain the Separatist doctrines, following Robinson's approval of the "lawfullness of hearing of the minsters in the Church of England." At the time Robinson's book was printed in 1634, the membership of the church was reduced to a mere one-fifth of former times. Robinson's *Lawfulnes of Hearing* reflected the sentiment of the liberal faction. John Canne of Amsterdam supported the rigid faction. From their standpoint, the church had "declined or apostated."[74] Based on the experience at Amsterdam, where many Separatists were converting to the English Reformed Church, it seemed likely that the shepherdless Separatists of Leiden might also go over to the English Reformed church of Goodyear; however, the remaining records of that church do not reveal former Separatist names. Individual Separatists were reported at Leiden throughout the 1630s (for example Robert Cockyn alias Leonard Verse in 1638).[75] Some circle of pastorless Separatists was still functioning in 1644 (the last known reference) when they took up a collection for the distressed Protestants of Ireland. By this time they were "well-neer vanished."[76]

A few of the Pilgrim Separatists, like Mrs. John Robinson, can be traced into the Dutch Reformed Church. In 1628 Thomas Smith applied for membership, "Englishman, former member of the Brownist church in England but excommunicated from it, because he had listened to a few sermons in the public church of England." He was admitted.[77] In 1639 three Separatist people applied for Dutch membership:

> John Meester and his wife, also Steven Buttersvelt, English, from the congregation of blessed Robbinson, complain that since his death they lack proper exercises so that they are not able to be edified as if they were members of some other church provided with preachers; they seek to become members of our church.[78]

Their request was approved. Meester and Buttersvelt (Masterson and Butterfield) in 1643 were witnesses to the will of Mrs. John Robinson,

---

mean Keble and Jepson were by this time deacons of Goodyear's church, but it is more likely that they were the deacons of the remnant Pilgrim church. Their names do not appear in any of the remaining records of Goodyear's Reformed Church.

[74] Printers to the Christian Reader, in Robinson's *A Treatise of the Lawfulnes of Hearing of the Ministers in the Church of England* (n.p., 1634); A.T., *Christian Reprofe*, pp. 19-20; John Canne, *A Stay against Straying. Or an Answer to a Treatise, intituled: The Lawfulnes of Hearing the Ministers of the Church of England. By John Robinson* (n.p., 1639); Burgess, *Robinson*, pp. 356-59.

[75] S.P. 84, vol. 153, fol. 301. Cockyn was involved in smuggling books into England.
[76] *N.N.B.W.*, V, 605; Baillie, *Dissvasive* (1645), p. 54; Burgess, *Robinson*, p. 359.
[77] Acta Kerkeraad Leiden, no. 003, Sept. 22, 1628.
[78] Ibid., June 17, 1639.

and likely were among that group of Robinson's "widow, children, and other relatives and friends," written about by Johannes Hoornbeek as being "received into the communion of our Church."[79] In 1655 another Separatist, "a certain Englishman of the Brownists," applied for membership. The Dutch ministers raised questions about his views of church order and baptism of children.[80]

Leiden Printers

Leiden, like Amsterdam, served as a Puritan print shop. The "Pilgrim Press" of William Brewster and Thomas Brewer in 1617-1619 became the main purveyor of radical Puritan books in the Netherlands. During these years the press published about twenty books for the Puritan cause.[81] Elder Brewster "also had means to set up printing (by the help of some friends,) and so had imploymente inoughg, and by reason of many books which would not be alowed to be printed in England, they might have had more then they could doe." Two other members of Robinson's congregation, John Reynolds and Edward Winslow, listed their occupations as printer and probably worked with Brewster.[82] Thomas Brewer, so far as is known, was not a member of the Separatist church, and pastor Hugh Goodyear of the English Reformed Church lodged with him in 1617; nevertheless, Brewer was a near-Brownist, having bought a house next door to Robinson, called the *Groenehuis*, and was reported to the English authorities as being a professed Brownist. After returning to England he was called a "patron of the Kentish Brownists." His professed occupation at Leiden was merchant (koopman van de Engelse natie te Leiden) in such products as saltpeter. Brewer was well to do, a "Gentleman of a good house," and he financed the enterprise.[83]

A few of their books were non-controversial devotional and religious tracts and carried the press imprint. A Dutch translation of Dod and Cleaver's book on the Ten Commandments listed Brewster as publisher (voor Guiliaeum Brewster Boeck-drucker, Anno 1617) as did William Ames's *Rescriptio Contracta* (Apud Guiljelmum Brewsterum in Vico Chorali, 1617). More controversial books by Francis Johnson, David

---

[79] Eekhof, *Three Unknown Documents*, p. 35.
[80] Acta Kerkeraad, no. 003, April 23, 1655.
[81] Rendel Harris and Stephen Jones, *The Pilgrim Press: A Bibliographical & Historical Memorial of the Books Printed at Leyden by the Pilgrim Fathers* (Cambridge: W. Heffer and Sons, 1922). During the same period of time, 1617-19, the Amsterdam Separatists put out 8-10 books.
[82] Bradford, *History*, p. 378; Harris and Jones, *Pilgrim Press*, pp. 8-9; Plooij, *Pilgrim Fathers*, pp. 58-60.
[83] Not. Archive 199, fol. 251v, 1617 (G.A. Amsterdam); Arber, *Pilgrim Fathers*, pp. 222, 246.

Calderwood, Thomas Dighton, John Robinson, Robert Harrison, and Thomas Cartwright were published anonymously without any identifying mark, for obvious reasons. Particularly objectionable to king and bishops were two books by David Calderwood, *De Regimine Ecclesiae Scoticanae Brevis Relatio* and *Perth Assembly*, both 1618. Under strict orders to punish the culprit printers, Sir Dudley Carleton played detective and proved their guilt by analysis of printing types used in their anonymous books. After a huge hunt, he broke up the secret press; but Brewster disappeared from the country and Brewer took sanctuary on the university grounds.[84] All of Brewer's type "(which were found in his house, in a garret where he hid them), and his books and papers are all seized and sealed up." After much delay Brewer in December 1619 was transported to England for examination and Sir Dudley assumed the case was closed. Much of the print, however, was spirited away and next turned up as a part of Thorp's Separatist press at Amsterdam. At least, the type used in books after 1623 is a mixture of the two presses, and the clandestine Puritan printing enterprise went on as gloriously as before.[85] During the 1630s Willem Christiaensz, "a master printer," revived the Puritan printing business at Leiden.[86]

Another English printer of a different mind was Thomas Basson (c. 1555-c. 1613), who arrived in Leiden in about 1584. He had a respectable print shop on the Rapenburg, where he translated, printed, and published books in both Dutch and English. During Leicester's short expedition into Holland, Basson was awarded a copyright for certain English documents. Later he became university printer for theses and disputations. Basson was not a Puritan, nor associated with either of the English churches of the city; he was not a promoter of controversial English Puritan literature. In fact, there are hints that he was earlier associated with the Family of Love, and during the Arminian crisis at the university, he printed Arminian books, which set him quite apart from the usual Puritan-minded Englishman of the Netherlands. Basson's son Govert carried on the printing and bookselling business until 1630.[87]

The Hague

English religion had been practiced at The Hague since 1585, when the magistrates provided a place for an English chapel. This chapel,

---

[84] Plooij, *Pilgrim Fathers*, chap. 3.

[85] Ibid., pp. 78-79; Arber, *Pilgrim Fathers*, pp. 195-234; A. F. Johnson, "The Exiled English Church at Amsterdam and its Press," *The Library*, 5th ser., 5 (1951), 230.

[86] S.P. 16, vol. 387, no. 79. See also chapter 11.

[87] J. A. van Dorsten, *Thomas Basson 1555-1613: English Printer at Leiden* (Leiden: Sir Thomas Browne Institute, 1961), pp. 53, 66-68; H. de la Fontaine Verwey, "Thomas Basson en het Huis der Liefde," *Het Boek*, 35 (1961-62), 219-24.

primarily for the edification of Leicester's English soldiers, was in the church of the Sacrament Gasthuis in the Noordeinde.[88] For a long time thereafter the English clergyman at The Hague was officially the chaplain to Sir Horace Vere, governor of the Brill (Brielle) but who resided principally at The Hague. Sir Horace chose a series of Puritan preachers in exile (John Paget, John Burgess, William Ames, and Samuel Balmford) but also some occasional conformists, as John Hassall (1622), forced out of England by debts, and Stephen Goffe (1633-34). In 1610 the States of Holland made a one-time gift of 500 guilders to the English preacher at The Hague "in consideration of his past services, his good reputation and the singular edification of his ministry."[89] The English preacher of 1610 was probably John Burgess. Up to 1627, the Hague congregation was a chapel but not an organized church; however, in 1627 the English congregation, still meeting in the Gasthuis church, became a formal church with its own minister, consistory, and with a provincial stipend of 300 guilders a year for ministerial support. The States raised the stipend to 500 guilders a year in 1628 and to 800 a year in 1661; this however was supplemented by voluntary offerings.[90] The first minister of the church was John Wing, formerly of Flushing, who served 1627-1629. Others were Samuel Balmford (1630-50), George Beaumont (1651-60), John Price (1661-76), Philip Bowie (1676-1715), and David Blair (associate minister 1688-89).

The church in the Noordeinde was an English Reformed church and subsidized by the magistrates as a *gereformeerde gemeente*. According to Thomas Raymond, nephew of Sir William Boswell, the worship "was performed according to the Dutch (not the English manner)."[91] The church was not a part of the Dutch classis or synod. John Wing, the first minister, was inducted by John Forbes of Delft, president of the English Synod, "according to the order of the Dutch and French churches in these lands." At the time of the official foundation in 1627, the church building was "repayred" and outfitted with some new "seates and galleryes."[92] The English building was actually the English-and-German

---

[88] Fred. Oudschans Dentz, *History of the English Church at The Hague, 1586-1929* (Delft: W. D. Meinema, 1929), p. 16; M. G. Wildeman, ed., "Varia Presbyteriaansche Kerk te 's-Gravenhage," (MS, G.A. The Hague).

[89] Dentz, *English Church*, p. 17.

[90] Res. States of Holland, no. 59, Nov. 28, 1626; no. 61, Aug. 17, 1628 (A.R.A. The Hague); Thurloe, *S.P.*, VII, 246. The res. of 1628 refers to *ponden*, that of 1626 to guilders. A *pond Hollands* is equal to one guilder.

[91] Thomas Raymond, *Autobiography*, ed. G. Davies, Camden Society, 3rd ser., 28 (1917), 32.

[92] C.R., no. 67 (1627-76), fol. 2 (P.R.O.). This volume of the register has been published by M. G. Wildeman as *The Eldest Church-book of the English Congregation in the Hague* (The Hague: De Wapenheraut, 1906).

church, because from 1626 onward the German Protestants were given by the magistrates a share in the use of the building, an arrangement that lasted into the eighteenth century.[93] The membership of the congregation had three main factions, the ambassadorial party, the military officers serving with the States, and the usual merchants, craftsmen and servants. The most prominent English members were ambassadors Sir Ralph Winwood (1603-10), Sir Dudley Carleton (1616-28), and Sir William Boswell (1632-50). Another notable member was Elizabeth, Queen of Bohemia, the daughter of James I. Because of the diplomatic corps and royal family, the English church at the Hague had a more than usual aristocratic tone and the consistory register has news of the frequent comings and goings of aristocrats and high military officials. Sir Henry Vane was there in 1630, "Ambassador to the states from the K. of England," and the same year Lord William Craven made a contribution for new communion beakers and silver plate.[94]

In spite of Church of England sympathies among the better sort of members, the church for most of its history followed a Puritan, Reformed course. The first ministers were Puritans and the officers of the church consistory came almost exclusively from the merchant members of the church rather than from the diplomatic or military factions. In worship the congregation prior to 1627 regularly omitted some or most of the prescribed liturgy of the Church of England, sometimes through carelessness but increasingly as a conscious policy. In John Burgess's time (1604?-1610), the practice of kneeling for the communion was dropped and also the cross in baptism and the surplice—the three "nocent" ceremonies despised by Puritans.[95] Ames (1611-19), an extreme nonconformist, made considerable changes in the administering of the sacraments—"some things he left out" and other things he added, but in those days it was allowed to pass. Hassall in his ministry was the exception, for he was a "comfortable man," using the Prayer Book for the most part except that he too "allowed sitting at the communion," this "for feare of giving offense" to the Dutch, who in their canons expressly forbade kneeling.[96] Wing and Balmford carried the congregation, now officially organized, back to the Puritan side and swiftly dropped most of the Prayer Book. Ambassador Sir Dudley Carleton alerted Laud in 1628 to the "novelties" springing up at The Hague under its Puritan leadership—"this place hath servd as a refuge for such ministers of both nations as could not conforme."[97]

---

[93] Dentz, *English Church*, p. 18.
[94] C.R., fols. 4, 8.
[95] William Ames, *A Fresh Svit against Human Ceremonies* (n.p., 1633), pt. 2, pp. 102-03.
[96] B.P., I, 250-51.
[97] S.P. 16, vol. 90, no. 84.

Among the churches of the city, the English church was the least. As he passed through in 1634 Sir William Brereton found two Dutch churches "and one little poor church for the English." In 1695, William Mountague described the English church as "a small one, very plain and ordinary."[98] The English ministers were paid the smallest stipends.[99] The size of the membership can hardly be determined except to note that between 1627-1660 the church recorded 113 baptisms and 16 marriages.[100]

The English Reformed church, moreover, was not the entire story. In 1621, Frederick and Elizabeth, displaced by the Thirty Years War, arrived at The Hague and set up court. Alongside the formal congregation, the king and queen of Bohemia maintained their own chaplain and tiny religious establishment. Here the religion was much more conformable to the Church of England. After Frederick's death in 1632, Elizabeth continued to live at The Hague until 1661 and maintained her chaplains. Her chaplains included Michael Jermyn (1620), John Hassall (1623), Dr. Miles (1632), Griffin Higgs (1627-38), Sampson Johnson (1638-44), William Cooper (1644-48), William Stamp (c. 1650-53), and George Morley (1653-56).[101] She had permission to use the English church building for her separate services, but she participated likewise in some of Balmford's preaching services. Along the north wall of the church was a row of special chairs reserved for notables such as Frederick, Elizabeth, and the English ambassador.[102]

Because of its cosmopolitan character, the English Reformed Church was exceptionally drawn into the Puritan-Anglican struggles of the day. The ambassadorial party, seeking a Laudian style of religion, was on the one side and on the other, the Reformed adherents desiring to maintain the Reformed status quo. For twenty years, 1630-1650, the Reverend Samuel Balmford was the central figure of the church, the one who always stood in the way of Laud's design to reshape the English church. Balmford was a most exasperating fellow. The archbishop called him obstinate and "dyed in grayne."[103] Of his career before coming to The Hague little is known except for his being B.A. and M.A. of Emmanuel

---

[98] Brereton, *Travels*, p. 35; Mountague, *Delights of Holland*, p. 51.

[99] States of Holland, no. 4410, fols. 15-16.

[100] C.R.; a book of baptisms and marriages exists for the period 1677 onward (no. 306, G.A. The Hague).

[101] Mary Anne Everett Green, *Elizabeth Electress Palatine and Queen of Bohemia*, rev. ed. (London, 1909), pp. 255-70. Thomas Raymond mentions Dr. Miles as serving in 1632, *Autobiography*, p. 32. P. S. Morrish, "Dr. Griffin Higgs, 1589-1659," *Oxoniensia*, 31 (1966), 117-38.

[102] Dentz, *English Church*, pp. 105-06.

[103] S.P. 84, vol. 152, fol. 145.

College (1615/16 and 1619) and also for having some exployment with Lady Mary Vere, the great friend of Puritan preachers. By the late 1620s, he had established himself at The Hague with the Veres as household chaplain.[104] When John Wing died in 1629, Balmford succeeded him, chosen "out of Lord Veres family with approbation of the greatest there residing." At least approved by some of the great ones. A few in high places, especially Carleton, were suspicious of Balmford "because of his inconformity" but Sir Horace and Lady Mary Vere interceded and the choice fell on Balmford—Carleton fortuitously then being absent in England and Sir Henry Vane being in charge.[105] In line with the democratic tendency of the church in its early days, Balmford's "election" as minister of the church took place "at a foreappointed generall meeting in the Church," and his installation took place February 24, 1630, with John Forbes in charge.[106]

Once securely established in his ministerial position, Balmford practiced the Puritan style that had become standard at The Hague, but at first circumspectly. His spirit was such that the ambassador could not complain much about him; Balmford "liveth here very orderly, and diligent (without any offence I cann understand of)."[107] Like Ames and Wing before him, Balmford made very sparing use of the English liturgy for baptism, the Lord's Supper, and marriage but did "mangle and pare, and purge it most spittifully."[108] The early 1630s were the most active years for the English Synod, a group of Puritan ministers of Congregationalist sympathies led by John Forbes. Balmford for several years openly identified himself with this dangerous society, which spurned the English Episcopal heritage but at the same time almost equally shunned the Dutch Reformed system of government.

Although Balmford's Congregationalist sympathies can be inferred from his English Synod membership, there are other signs of his inclining that way, a position prevalent among Puritans in Holland prior to 1640. John Davenport claimed Balmford as a fellow believer, holding "the same opinion" on the topic of the church.[109] On the matter of indiscriminate baptizing of infants, Balmford agreed, apparently, to some extent with the Hooker-Davenport position (the strict position) as opposed to John Paget's looser practice. Balmford "expressly denyed you

---

[104] On Balmford see *D.N.B.* and Venn and Venn; John Davenport, *Letters of John Davenport*, ed. Isabel M. Calder (New Haven: Yale Univ. Press, 1937), pp. 29-33.
[105] Add. MS. 17,677, vol. 0, fol. 411v; B.P., I, 250.
[106] C.R., fol. 7v.
[107] B.P., I, 112.
[108] S.P. 16, vol. 310, no. 103.
[109] John Davenport, *A Iust Complaint against an Vniust Doer* (n.p., 1634), p. 15; John Paget, *An Answer to the unjust complaints of William Best* (Amsterdam, 1635), p. 75.

to baptise all."¹¹⁰ Nevertheless, Balmford's position was not extremely outspoken as can be seen in 1632, when he had been proposed as a candidate for the Amsterdam position of co-pastor with John Paget, who examined him and found him somewhat acceptable, at least more so than Hooker, Davenport and Peter, all of whom he vetoed. Paget agreed to offering Balmford the position of co-pastor, but Balmford refused.¹¹¹ After dabbling in "Congregationalist" theology in Holland, Balmford, after returning to England in 1650, functioned in classical presbyterial affairs as a "Presbyterian."¹¹²

For the first few years, Balmford's associations were with the English Synod men and very little with the Dutch Reformed Church of the city. Then, as Laud and Boswell began their campaign to discipline the English ministers of the Netherlands, Balmford saw the situation differently: That the English Synod would be a slender refuge to him in a direct confrontation with the Archbishop but that the Dutch church could be his best hope for safety. As soon as Boswell arrived in 1632, he began to exert pressure on Balmford's church to use the prayer book and ceremonies. Balmford soon decided to apply for membership in the Hague Classis (1634).

Balmford's appeal to the Dutch ministers came in the context of meeting the danger of Episcopal interference at The Hague. Already, some English chaplains in the Netherlands had been dismissed for resisting the introduction of the English liturgy; and such a peril, Balmford insisted, threatened The Hague as well. The good men of the classis shuddered at the prospect and immediately resolved in 1634 that the classis: "take Balmford under her protection and by appeal to the magistrates of these lands and by all possible means to see that Balmford should be kept unmolested in his ministerial service," all of this "to the end that the English church of The Hague be preserved in good rest and unity" and that no strange ceremonies be imported.¹¹³ This show of support was welcome indeed, but what did it mean: "To take Balmford under her protection"?

Throughout the seventeenth century, the relationship between the English Reformed church and the Dutch church remained cloudy. It was a situation where the English minister was never exactly a member of the Hague Classis but "under her protection." Both parties made of it what they wanted, depending on the circumstances. In 1645 the States of

---

¹¹⁰ John Trasy, Add. MS. 24,666, fols. 2, 17-19.
¹¹¹ Alice C. Carter, *The English Reformed Church in Amsterdam in the Seventeenth Century* (Amsterdam: Scheltema & Holkema, 1964), pp. 80-81.
¹¹² Nuttall, *Visible Saints*, p. 9.
¹¹³ Acta Classis The Hague, II, Feb. 6, May 1, 1634 (N.H.A. The Hague).

Holland stated anew that the English church at The Hague "was to be regulated according to the order of the churches of this land."[114] In the second half of the century the issue lay long dormant but occasionally revived. One minister had at least temporary classis membership (Bowie in 1676).

According to the argument of the Hague Classis in 1716 (at that time in a law suit with the English church over the calling of a Mr. Robert Milling as minister), the classis interpreted the resolution of 1645 to mean this: "That the English church is taken under the supervision and government of the Hague classis, but nevertheless, that the English church not be a member of the classis, and also that her minister should take no session in the classis." This "supervision," the classis asserted, had been acknowledged by the English "willingly and unanimously."[115] Not as the English saw it; once the danger of Laud's power had passed, the English church followed a more independent line, having enjoyed the protection during the storm. "Tell them that the English Minister, and Consistory had not any the least dependence upon the Dutch consistory," argued the English on one occasion.[116] Although the legalities were left ambiguous, as the controversy of 1716 revealed, for its time (the 1630s), Balmford's energetic action of associating with the Dutch Classis was a Puritan master stroke that caused much grief to Laud.

In 1632 Balmford was invited to the English Reformed church at Amsterdam as minister, but refused to budge, fearing it was a plot to displace him and install a conformable, pro-Laudian man.[117] Balmford confided to the Amsterdammers about

> the present danger of the church in the Haagh, and the lyke unto other congregations of English in theis contres by the soliciting of sondry ministers at present, which use all means they can to bring into theis churches the booke of Common prayer, and other ceremonies, according as it is used in the church of England, and that their ar som that seeke, if Mr. Balmford should go from the church that then suche a minister should bee put upon that congregation as weare so mynded.

---

[114] Res. States of Holland, no. 78, p. 152; Acta Classis, III, June 3, 1642.

[115] "Stukken betreffende het proces tusschen de Classis van 's-Gravenhage en den Engelschen Kerkeraad aldaar," (1716), no. 83 (N.H.A.); Wildeman, "Bijdrage tot de geschiedenis der Presbyteriaansche Kerk te 's-Gravenhage," *De Navorscher*, 45 (1895), 156-84, 215-57. The issue of church sovereignty "occasioned a tedious lawsuit, wherein the English Consistory got the better," Dentz, *English Church*, p. 28.

[116] C.R., March 30, 1697. Their controversy here, however, was with the Dutch kerkeraad, not the classis.

[117] See above, chapter 4.

Crisis time: "No tyme to speake of his removing in regard of the present Danger."[118]

In 1635 Balmford unwarily made a trip to England to visit his aged mother, over eighty years old; he was recognized, seized and detained by the High Commission at London on orders of the Archbishop of Canterbury. The detention lasted for at least four or five weeks and was a thoroughly harassing experience. After being refused his passport, Balmford appealed to Laud for release: If the fault be nonconformity to the rites of the Church of England, "I humbly desire, it may be considered that I live there [at The Hague] as a minister subiect to the Government of that place, having pay from the States and a linke to the Dutch-classe, who therefore looke I should be regulated by them, not doing ought offensive to the church I liue under."[119] That "protection of the classis," (the "linke") was most valuable to Balmford now.

Dutch ambassador Joachimi looked into the affair: and as he understood it, Balmford was being pressed "that he should bring into his church the rites of the English church, of which he requested to be excused, alleging that he stood under orders of the States General." Joachimi also sent back word that "in the English churches more ceremonies were being brought in than formerly and that the Papists had more freedom than at any time since the death of Queen Mary."[120] After tedious delay, Balmford was released on bond (which he immediately jumped) and hurried back to Holland, a free man, returned "as it were, from prison." He delivered to John Davenport a letter from Lady Mary Vere at Hackney.[121]

Instead of instilling fear, the nerve-racking detention hardened Balmford's resolution to stand firm against Laud. Immediately on his return, Balmford resorted to the classis for counsel: Should he follow the orders from England and begin the English liturgy in his church? Absolutely not, the classis responded, "no such ceremonies to be introduced in the English church."[122] The story was far from over. In 1637 Boswell renewed the campaign to introduce the Prayer Book, hoping that Balmford would be intimidated so that the business could be carried off "without contestacon, or noyse." On His Majesty's command, Boswell again gave order to officiate the church according to the form of the Church of England.[123] Both Boswell and Laud had

---

[118] Amsterdam, C.R., III, 35 (Feb. 1, 1633).
[119] Add MS. 17,677, vol. 0, fol. 411v; also in Liassen Engelandt, no. 5892 (A.R.A.).
[120] Ibid.
[121] S.P. 16, vol. 261, fol. 258v; *Cal. S.P.D.*, June 1637; Davenport, *Letters*, pp. 62-63.
[122] Acta Classis, II, Nov. 26, 1635; B.P., I, 223-24.
[123] S.P. 84, vol. 152, fols. 93-94, 116.

miscalculated on Balmford, whose cooperative spirit had hardly been improved by Laud's High Commission. As soon as he detected Boswell's direction, Balmford raised the alarm among his Dutch friends. The chance for a quiet *coup* at the English church was lost.

The Hague Classis, as always in those years, backed Balmford against Laud and Boswell. The classis produced a resolution and buttressed its position by appealing to the States General Resolution of 1633 (the "No Novelties" resolution). So exasperated was Boswell that he viciously scolded the classis for such meddling in English affairs: "I layed open at full," on the classis "that they had put an indignity upon my self, the English frequentants of this church, and the Church of England." After such sharp reproof, Boswell predicted a quick accommodation from the Dutch "in some quiet, and handsome maner."[124] Soon the Prayer Book.

But once again, Balmford proclaimed his link to the Dutch church. At its next meeting, instead of retreating from Boswell, the classis stood firm. As a classis, they had no authority to allow Anglican changes in the English Reformed church, "nor to allow the least innovation or alteration in ceremonies, order, or liturgy."[125] Next, they threw Boswell's complaints and petition upstairs to the Synod of South Holland, where they were soon lost in the machinery. "Delay and Temporize" was the synodial response to the classis, and nothing ever came of Boswell's petition to eliminate Dutch supervision of the English church.[126]

Blocked again by Puritan tactics, Boswell's anger boiled over at Balmford: "He had done very ill to flye unto the Dutch Classis." And when Balmford was called upon to explain his obstinacy to English authority, he gave no satisfaction at all, being full of talk about responsibility to the Reformed status quo. "For which reason he said, he could not change his course."[127] By establishing his own noncomfornist ways as the traditional mode of the English church at The Hague, and thus in the spirit of the Reformed order, he tagged Boswell and Laud as the innovators and troublemakers.

Having made little headway against Balmford by using threats, the Anglicans hatched the plan to get rid of him by manufacturing a call for him in 1636 and again in 1637 to the Amsterdam English Reformed church. This would then open the way for importing a conformable preacher to The Hague. Although they dangled the temptation of a better position before him, either in Amsterdam or even in England (a good place of perhaps £140 a year), Balmford always refused the

---

[124] Ibid., fols. 112-14.
[125] Acta Classis, III, May 4, 1637.
[126] Knuttel, *Acta Synoden Zuid-Holland*, II, 141-42 (1637, art. 43).
[127] S.P. 84, vol. 152, fols. 116-17.

blandishments, considering "his service in keeping out comon prayers ... more considerable then the increase of his meanes."[128]

While Balmford controlled the church, the other English preacher at The Hague, the chaplain of Elizabeth of Bohemia, proved much more friendly to Laud. When Sampson Johnson replaced Griffin Higgs as Chaplain in 1638, the Church of England gained a strong champion. Johnson was Laud's man and chosen by him for the position in consultation with Elizabeth. Step by step, Johnson instigated Anglican worship as an alternative to Balmford's Puritanism; for example, in 1639, while performing a baptism in the English church building, Johnson suddenly used the sign of the cross, of course, over the protests of Balmford.[129] This was duly reported to the classis. Johnson further tried to ingratiate himself with Laud by advertising to the Dutch the merits of the Church of England, thus to create a better image. "I think I have performed that office to sett them right, and have desired them not to believe the partiall reports of ignorant and malicious vagabonds." Also, Johnson detected real progress in undercutting Balmford, for now Johnson's own sermons made great impact and the people go "very unwillingly to heare their own shepheard." By 1640 Johnson reported to Laud, "our church here begins to wish much for common prayers.[130]

In spite of such reports, Johnson's threat as a rival to Balmford did not last long. He was not nearly so persuasive as he imagined himself, and was naive besides when it came to Dutch politics. Johnson made a nearly ruinous blunder in 1639 by commenting favorably on the doctrines of Socinianism, this on top of using the sign of the cross and other ceremonies. Although Johnson always claimed to be misquoted, the report went far and wide—being "in the mouths of most all the preachers"—of his commending the Socinian writers "for their Rationall and cleere expression of themselves" and even that their doctrines were *"vera et solida theologia."*[131] On learning about Johnson's use of the cross, the classis felt obliged to send investigators to the English church; and in the local Dutch consistory, the topic of Johnson's alleged Socinianism caused distress. Observers were set on Johnson to uncover the extent of his heresy by listening to his sermons, "especially the brethren who understand the English language."[132]

During the heresy scandal, Johnson's employer, the queen of Bohemia, also suffered by association. While investigating Johnson, the

---

[128] B.P., I, 238, 315; S.P. 84, vol. 155, fol. 254.
[129] Acta Classis, III, Feb. 2, 1639.
[130] S.P. 16, vol. 441, no. 47.
[131] S.P. 16, vol. 417, no. 96; vol. 418, no. 49.
[132] Acta Classis, III, Feb. 2, 1639; Acta Kerkeraad, no. 102, Mar. 28, 1639 (N.H.A.).

Dutch added various complaints against her as well, most notably her attendance at stage plays and her occasional indecent dress. The consistory preachers urged Johnson "to preach against bare necks, by reason her majesty uses to go so," but he declined such sermons.[133] Although Balmford's role in discrediting Johnson is not clear, it is certain that he made complaints to his Dutch Reformed friends and thus set the classis and consistory machinery in motion. The charge of Socinian heresy resulted from Johnson's own indiscretion, but one can well imagine Balmford fanning the flames since it served so well the purpose of eliminating Johnson as a serious rival. With such discredited agents as Johnson, Laud could expect to make little progress at The Hague. Laud grimly rebuked Johnson for his blundering: "You did extremely ill."[134]

Taken as a whole, Laud's designs at The Hague produced very little, being frustrated by Balmford and the Puritan-minded Dutch churchmen. Among the military chaplaincies and at the Merchant Adventurers at Delft, Laud's program basically succeeded. The different outcome at The Hague grew from the masterful way in which Balmford used "political" techniques by fortifying himself with the Dutch governmental and ecclesiastical authorities. Instead of a two-way combat between the archbishop and the English preacher, Balmford turned it into a three-sided affair with the Dutch churchmen and magistrates aiding him against Laud. "Treacheries or Conspiracies," lamented Boswell to Laud, "Evil contrivances ... to make your Grace and the Episcopacy odious." "They esteem our clergy little better than Papists."[135] Working behind the scenes, Balmford had done a superb job of ecclesiastical and political manipulation.

Balmford and the Hague Classis proved to be the main roadblocks to the archbishop. When the Hague Classis refused to abandon Balmford at its May meeting of 1638, Laud labelled the event a "May-Game in May." And, said Boswell, "if Balmford had not been peevish it might haue been as easily compassed heer in the Haghe, as in the Regiments." How true, Laud agreed; Balmford was peevish, and his "Peeuishnes hath done a greate deale of Harme there and Crossed or Delayed at least the Progresse of that, which could not but haue done a greate deale of Honor to the English Church."[136] The English Revolution put an end to Laud's meddling.

---

[133] Green, *Elizabeth*, p. 355.

[134] S.P. 84, vol. 155, fol. 79v; S.P. 16, vol. 417, no. 96.

[135] Richard Parr, *The Life of James Usher, with a Collection of Three Hundred Letters* (London, 1686), pt. 2, pp. 27-28.

[136] B.P., I, 291; S.P. 84, vol. 154, fols. 17-19.

The 1640s, however, proved no time of comfortable ease for the church, even though Laud was behind bars. Boswell remained at The Hague as a Royalist agent until his death in 1650, and as increasing numbers of Royalist emigrés came over, the Puritan-versus-Anglican turmoil became worse instead of better, especially when Balmford attempted to introduce new Puritan practices commended by the Westminster Assembly. To this time, Balmford had retained a few passages of the English liturgy in the Lord's supper ("We have in use our English Liturgy in administering the Sacraments," he had told Laud in 1635), but now Balmford proceeded to drop every trace of them. So intense became the inner struggles in the church that Balmford in despair suspended the Lord's Supper in 1645 and appealed once more to the Hague Classis. Its counsel was that Balmford act peaceably and in all things follow the order of the Dutch Reformed Church *quod substantiam et materiam*, "hoping that therein everybody shall take good contentment."[137] Boswell, in fact, presented memorials to the States General and the States of Holland in 1645, protesting against the "innovations" proposed in the church; and to buttress his argument, he appealed to the States General resolution of 1633 (the "No Novelties" resolution) to head off any further Puritan inroads in the church. The 1633 resolution had always before been the refuge of Puritans like Balmford; but now Boswell turned the tables. Both the States General and States of Holland, nevertheless, found Boswell's logic unconvincing and affirmed the English church as being "regulated according to the order of the churches of these lands."[138]

In 1650 Balmford closed his ministry at The Hague and returned to London, where he found a pastorate at St. Albans, Wood Street, and also a wife. Initially, in April of 1650, Balmford asked permission of the classis to be absent from The Hague for two or three months and in the meanwhile gave to the classis the "supervision over his church." He left, and four months later the report traveled back to The Hague of Balmford's betrothal and acceptance of another call at London. His intention not to return to Holland was confirmed in November, when he requested from the classis his testimony of "life and walk among us."[139] The English church was rather provoked at being dropped so lightly, but nothing could be done.

---

[137] Acta Classis, III, June 26, 1645; B.P., I, 371, 373; Liassen Engelandt, no. 5892, fol. 198.

[138] Res. States General, no. 3204, fols. 408, 409v, 410; Liassen Engelandt, no. 5897, fol. 160; Res. States of Holland, no. 287, fols. 141, 152.

[139] Acta Classis, III, April 25, Aug. 25, Nov. 7, 1650. This was his second marriage; he had married Dorothy Bennet in 1630, C.R., fol. 8.

Balmford left behind him an unsettled church split between the Royalist emigrés and the old Reformed core of the congregation entrenched in the consistory. The situation "had fallen into great unrest," noted the classis.[140] As Balmford's replacement, the church secured George Beaumont (1651-60), formerly chaplain to the Merchant Adventurers and most recently minister of the English church at Huesden and chaplain to Colonel John Cromwell. As Forbes's successor at Delft in 1634, Beaumont had been regarded as an agent of Laud and so came with an Anglican taint. The Hague Classis had a large part in supervising the church during the interim period and took the occasion to fasten some authority over the English church. The congregation and classis made agreement that Beaumont was to officiate according to the:

> confession and order of the Churches in this Countrey under the inspection of the Classes of the Hage, bringing in no novelties without the consent of the Classes: and in matter of difference hearkning to their advice unto which we all desire to submit our selves, haveing liberty to apeale from them to the Synod of South Holland. And seeing there are at this present som Ministers that do not conforme to the doctrine and orders of the Churches of this Countrey, we especially desire him not to admit any such to preach in this Congregation without consent of the Elders and Deacons.[141]

The classis claimed that all the interim events were "under the supervision of this classis."[142] The influx of Royalist emigrés made the church more Anglican in membership than previously.

The Royalists found great rapport in religion with the chaplains of the Queen of Bohemia and Mary, Princess of Orange. Elizabeth of Bohemia, who had been receiving a pension from the royal family for years, during the revolution had her funds cut off so long as she kept chaplains like Sampson Johnson. Parliament insisted on dismissing Johnson and installing some "godly, learned, conscionable divine" of their own choosing. Elizabeth yielded and took William Cooper, a Puritan approved by the English Parliament. Accepting Cooper was the price of her pension. After the execution of King Charles, Elizabeth's brother, "she temporized no more." She proclaimed herself openly Royalist, and after the departure of Cooper back to England, she sought out Anglican chaplains, first William Stamp and then George Morely. On May 8, 1649, Parliament cut off her pension and she launched a private war with Walter Strickland and Oliver St. John, the "so-called English Ambassadors." She warned that anyone associating with the

---

[140] Acta Classis Hague, III, Dec. 1, 1651.
[141] C.R., fol. 22.
[142] Acta Classis, III, Jan. 2, 1651.

Republicans would be flung down the stairs and kicked out of her door.[143] William Stamp (1650-53), a former chaplain to Charles as Prince of Wales, preached Royalist sermons and published them in a book, *A Treatise of Spiritual Infatuation*, "being the present visible disease of the English Nation." His main text was, "Rebellion is as the sinne of witchcraft." (I Sam. 15:23) Stamp also preached once each Sunday at the English church.[144] After Stamp's death in 1653, Elizabeth called George Morley, deprived canon of Christ Church, Oxford, who had come into exile with Prince Charles. After the Restoration he became Bishop of Winchester. He was one of the chief upholders of Anglicanism-in-exile during the Republic. The queen's finances had sunk so low, however, that although promised £50 a year, he never in his two and one half years service received anything above board for himself and his servant. Morley always gloried in the fact that while abroad he had lived solely by the liturgy of the Church of England—"did not submit my self to the Classis or comply with any of their novel Usages and Practises." When he left the Queen in 1656, he turned the chaplaincy over to George Beaumont, minister of the church, who promised to read the Prayer Book to her.[145]

All Anglican liturgical innovations alarmed the Dutch churchmen. The ministers had particular suspicion about Thomas Browne, chaplain to Mary, Princess of Orange, the eldest daughter of Charles I. Browne, chaplain 1651-59, was a Royalist refugee and former chaplain to Archbishop Laud. Earlier chaplains had also fallen under suspicion (John Dury, Malachi Harris, and Robert Sheringham). The Dutch consistory in 1649 raised much alarm about "English ceremonies" and sent deputies to the Prince of Orange for his assistance.[146] In 1651-52 the Hague Classis singled out Thomas Browne, *Hoff-Predikant* to the Princess of Orange, and sought to force his subscription to the Dutch Reformed confession. The classis urged that subscription would show his unity with the Reformed church, but Browne said he had already subscribed as an English minister to the 39 Articles and that was sufficient. The classis quizzed him about two rumors: (1) That he preached "in a manner deviating from the truth," and (2) that he dishonored the Dutch Reformed Church as schismatic. Browne completely denied the allegations but did grant that he sometimes used controversial quotations from the

---

[143] Green, *Elizabeth*, pp. 359-70.
[144] William Stampe, *A Treatise of Spiritual Infatuation* (The Hague, 1650), title page; C.R., fol. 38.
[145] "Unpublished Letters from the Queen of Bohemia," *Archaelogia*, 37 (1857), 242; George Morley, *Several Treatises* (London, 1683), p. viii.
[146] Acta Kerkeraad, no. 102, fols. 185, 188-90.

Church Fathers, which may have been misunderstood. The classis advised against bringing obscurity and deviation into the pulpit. Although not fully satisfied, the classis brethren let the matter drop except for keeping a watch on him.[147] In 1658 the classis received reports of Browne's further mischief in preaching "very harmful, even blasphemous theology, smacking of pure Socinianism." Deputies were again dispatched to remonstrate with him. Browne refused to respond except to send back a signed copy of the 39 Articles—he said, "he never taught any thing other."[148]

In 1658 George Downing, who had come over as English ambassador, visited the English Reformed Church; he discovered that Beaumont was using old-fashioned prayers that prayed for Charles the king (Charles II). When Downing complained, Beaumont responded that "he could not leave off the doing thereof without command, (being bound, at his entrance into that place, to make no innovation or change)." Downing thereupon caused an order to be drawn up by the Dutch Council of State "that the English ministers here doe pray no more for Charles Stuart," and Beaumont ceased. Rather a trimmer, Beaumont did not jump so far as to offer prayers for Oliver Cromwell but he did "insinuate" that England was most prosperous under Cromwell. Downing took Ambassador Boswell's old chair. Beaumont's assistant, however, a Scotsman, "so much a cavallier," resigned his place. Elizabeth of Bohemia also angrily withdrew—"she having taken away her hanging and cushions"—and only reluctantly returned. To repair the finances lost by Royalist withdrawals from the church, Downing secured a subsidy from the English Republic which, of course, ended in 1660. Downing, who found himself much in the role of Boswell in the 1630s, complained about the church as a "nursery of cavallierisme"; "the vilest of our nation flocked hither, pleasing themselves with the notion of praying for their king, as they call him, and having the church at their command."[149] Beaumont in 1660 removed to a church in Ireland to "the remotest citadell in his majesties Kingdom of Ireland among a congregation of Scottish men" but later advanced to prebend of Westminster and Dean of Derry. On leaving The Hague, he gloomily warned that the Dutch churchmen might try to take over the English church by installing a Dutchman as minister. However, this proved to be an unfounded rumor.[150]

---

[147] Acta Classis, III, Aug. 14, 1651; April 29, July 1, 1652.
[148] Ibid., Nov. 4, 1658, July 23, 1659.
[149] Thurloe, *S.P.*, VII, 246, 257-58; Dentz, *English Church*, pp. 21-22.
[150] Add. MS. 18,744, fols. 39, 41.

Delft

The picturesque city of Delft, situated between Rotterdam and The Hague, impressed English visitors as a "fair and well built" place. Fynes Moryson commended Delft for its beer, "called Delphs-English," which he judged almost, but not quite, as good as English beer.[151] The Merchant Adventurers made Delft their Dutch staple port from 1621 to 1635; and throughout the seventeenth century, after the Adventurers left, an English community remained. A monument to the wife of Sir Charles Morgan (Elizabeth, daughter of Philip Marnix) was in the Old Church, and there was an "English House," which Samuel Pepys found in 1660 and stopped "to drink in."[152] The church of the Merchant Adventurers under the ministry of John Forbes was one of the most pro-Puritan churches, but with the removal of the Merchant Adventurers to Rotterdam in 1635, the church transferred away from Delft. Their church building in the Prinsenhof was taken over by the French church. The remnant of the English community petitioned in 1636 to have a regular English Reformed church established in the city.

The English petitioners of 1636 claimed to speak for "over 70 families," and they promised the magistrates that if a church were allowed, "they would procure a preacher, and diverse famillies Tradsmen, to come out of England to dwell in their towne." On March 6, 1636, the burgomasters approved an English church and secured a provincial stipend of 500 guilders for a preacher.[153] The congregation met in the Gasthuis Church and continued as an organized English Reformed congregation until 1724.[154] The promised growth did not occur; instead the congregation diminished considerably, to only 27 in 1645 and 34 members in 1668. The consistory register shows 41 baptisms 1645-60 (a total of 103 to 1724) and 9 marriages 1645-60 (a total of 28 to 1724).[155]

John Forbes's Puritan spirit carried over into the newly-organized church. In early 1636 Patrick Forbes, John's son, became interim preacher. However, he did not last long. He preached a "rayling sermon" which was reported to Sir William Boswell for being a "Publick Scandall" against the Church of England. Using a text from Isaiah,

---

[151] John Ray, *Travels through the Low-Countries, Germany, Italy and France*, 2nd ed. (London, 1738), I, 22; Moryson, *Itinerary*, pt. I, 47.

[152] Steven, pp. 372-73; Samuel Pepys, *Diary*, ed. John Warrington (London: Dent, 1906), I, 58.

[153] Memoriaalboek van de Burgemeesteren, III, 334v, 335 (G.A. Delft); B.P., I, 212-13. On the English church see Dinant P. Oosterbaan, *Het oude en nieuwe Gasthuis te Delft* (Delft, 1954), pp. 261-68.

[154] *Beschryving der Stadt Delft* (Delft: Reinier Boitet, 1729), p. 327.

[155] C.R., nos. 101, 102, also called doopboek and trouwboek (G.A. Delft).

Forbes proved that the defenders of the Prayer Book "were traytours to the King of Heaven." Boswell, together with Captain Henry Hexham and some of the Dutch preachers, raised such a stir that Forbes found it prudent to slip out of town.[156] In the 1630s Delft was a center of Puritan book printing and exporting. James Moxon was printer.[157] The first established minister of the new church was Robert Park (1636-41), an Emmanuel College graduate, former vicar of Bolton, Lancashire. He received his first pay in September of 1636 but little more of him or the church is heard until 1640, when he became involved in controversy with the Dutch consistory of Delft. It is unclear whether he remained at Delft throughout this period. About 1640 Park reorganized the church and gave it renewed activity.[158] Succeeding minsters of the church were: Patrick Forbes (1641-42), Edward Richardson (1643-45), Alexander Petrie Junior (1645-83), Alexander Hodge (1668-69), John Sinclair (1684-87), Thomas Hoog (1689-94), and Wilhelm van Schie (1694-1724).

The Dutch Reformed Church of Delft claimed a supervisory responsibility over the little English church, referring to them "as the members of our church, being of the English Nation."[159] Behind the scenes, Captain Henry Hexman, a grammarian and longtime military officer with English forces in the Netherlands, a moderate Anglican in religion, and Dionysius Spranckhuysen (his cousin, Delft minister), composed a little core working against the Puritan influence at the church. After the Patrick Forbes incident, Spranckhuysen led the Dutch consistory to demand that English ministers of the church "should be conformable to the customary church order of the land," or, as Spranckhuysen confided to Hexham, even conformable to the Church of England. According to Hexham, "For, the English Lithurgie he hath a reverend opinion of it, hath read the book of Common prayer," and if at Austin Friars in London, "if the King, or the Arch Bishop of Canterbury, should enioyne him to read it: he would make noe scruple to doe it." When asked whether their church would conform to the Church of England or the Netherlands church, the English replied, "That they had rather conforme themselves to the order of the Netherlandish Church."[160] The

---

[156] B.P., I, 212-13, 217, 219-20, 229.

[157] S.P. 16, vol. 387, no. 79; see below chapter 11.

[158] Memoriaalboek van Burg., III, 334-35, 385-86; [Alexander Forbes], *The Anatomy of Independency* (London, 1644), p. 20.

[159] Acta Kerkeraad Delft, V, 225; VI, 15 (Old Church, Delft).

[160] Acta Kerkeraad, V, 176v; B.P., I, 212-13, 217. On Hexham, see G. Scheurweghs, "English Grammars in Dutch and Dutch Grammars in English in the Netherlands before 1800," *English Studies*, 41 (June 1960), 133-34; on Spranckhuysen, see *N.N.B.W.*, V, 789-90.

English church, however, maintained a considerable independent line without acknowledging much Dutch supervision.

During 1640-41 Park became embroiled with the Dutch consistory, the Classis of Delft en Delfland, and the Synod of South Holland regarding his calling to the church and the general nature of ecclesiastical government. "He does not wish to submit to the order of the Dutch church."[161] The Park controversy may well appear to be merely theological hair splitting until it is noted that Park was one of the new Congregational Puritans in league with Burroughes, Ward, and Bridge of Rotterdam. He transferred in 1641 to succeed them as minister of the Rotterdam church; the Delft experience had been a trial run of his emerging Congregational ideas. The Dutch Reformed churchmen did not find Park's ideas worthwhile nor did they acknowledge Park's English church, lacking an established consistory, as being a genuine Reformed church. The extent of Park's innovations within the church are unknown; however, it is clear that he was influenced by the Rotterdam theology and perhaps he attempted a covenant. He argued for the independence of the church to choose its own minister without classical supervision. The consistory register does not exist before 1645, Alexander Petrie's ministry. Within the church several members opposed Park and petitioned to the Dutch consistory that their church be brought into line with Dutch Reformed practice. They asked that their minister be required to join the classis. Captain Hexham and two associates, George Tuevelt and John Tomason, headed up the anti-Park faction and solicited support among the Dutch, but Park counter-attacked by smearing them as "slanderers, calumniators, false witnesses, liars, haters of peace and salvation." He brought absentee members and ex-members from Rotterdam and The Hague to assist him.[162]

The Dutch clergy made the largest complaint about Park's refusal to submit to Dutch Reformed authority, as if he were an independent person. The Dutch consistory insisted that Park must "conform in doctrine and order with the churches of this land," and although he subscribed to several articles, his exceptions were so large as to make his confession "absolutely not satisfactory."[163] In 1641 the consistory drew up four conditions for satisfaction: (1) That the consistory must examine the instrument of Park's induction as minister; (2) that he must be called and confirmed in his office like other preachers of the consistory, since

---

[161] Acta Classis Delft, no. 138, fol. 321 (N.H.A.); Oosterbaan, *Gasthuis*, p. 265.

[162] "Memorie van aen de kerkeraad tegen Ds. Park," no. 61, "Stukken van de Engelse predikanten te Delft," no. 60 (Archive of the Kerkeraad of Delft); Forbes, *Anatomy*, pp. 20-21, 23-24.

[163] Acta Kerkeraad, V, 213v.

there is here no established (*gereformeerde*) English church; (3) that Park must conform in everything of doctrine and in church order; (4) that Park, since he does not have an established church, shall stand under this consistory, but after he shall have established a consistory, he shall stand under the classis and synod.[164] The Delft consistory was one of the most diligent in attempting to impose control over the English church.

When Park refused to submit, the much exasperated consistory complained to the magistrates and then to the classis and synod.[165] Park in turn solicited theological judgment from the universities of Leiden and Utrecht, but only Voetius gave him any support. The South Holland Synod found Park obstinate to work with, and in spite of repeated conferences, "he seeks only a *judicium dogmaticum* and will not submit himself to the judgment of the Synod, but says he stands alone under the magistrates of Delft."[166] By September 23, 1641, Park was reported as having gone to Rotterdam without any demission or testimonials. The consistory alerted the magistrates to search "for a capable English preacher who might be called and inducted according to the order of the Dutch Reformed Church."[167]

For a short time Patrick Forbes was recalled for minister, 1641-42; but so many questions were raised about him that he was put on a provisional status.[168] Edward Richardson, B.A. from Emmanuel, 1640, became the next minister, 1643-45; and although the Dutch church by now assumed a supervisory watch over the English church, the English still acted rather independently. In fact, the Dutch consistory was chagrined to learn that after Forbes's departure, the English brought in trial preachers without consultation and then called and installed Richardson as preacher "without the knowledge of this consistory." Whereupon they sent deputies to instruct Richardson on the "justness of the order of the Dutch Reformed churches" and as best they could to regularize *ex post facto* his calling and establishment.[169] In approving Richardson's call, the magistrates, at the urging of consistory, laid down conditions intended to regularize the system of calling English ministers. In future any English minister must be approved by both the magistrates and classis, and then he was to be enrolled as a member of the Classis of Delft en Delfland.[170]

---

[164] Ibid., V, 214-15.

[165] Ibid., V, 213v, 216; Knuttel, *Acta Synoden Zuid-Holland*, II, 326-28.

[166] Knuttel, II, 327. Papers on Park are in the Archive of the Synod of South Holland, III, 35, iii, 29, fols. 201-07. J. A. Cramer, *De theologische faculteit te Utrecht ten tijde van Voetius* (Utrecht: Kemink en Zoon, 1932), pp. 51-52, 229-36.

[167] Acta Kerkeraad, V, 218v.

[168] Memoriaalboek van Burg., III, 385-86; Acta Kerkeraad, V, 220.

[169] Acta Kerkeraad, V, 225, 232v, 233. Richardson's letter of calling (July 18, 1643) is found in "Stukken," no. 60.

[170] Memoriaalboek van Burg., III, 393v-394; Acta Kerkeraad, V, 235-36.

Richardson subscribed to the Dutch Reformed confession October 10, 1643, but he never became a member of the classis. In 1645 Richardson resigned his position to return to England as minister at Deighton, Yorkshire. The records show that he also became minister at Ripon.[171]

Richardson's replacement was Alexander Petrie Junior, a thorough Presbyterian, son of the Scottish preacher at Rotterdam. Educated at St. Andrews and for a short time minister at Brielle, he had good Reformed credentials. He had undergone Dutch Reformed examination and exhibited all proper testimonials of doctrine and life "in conformity with the order of our church."[172] Nevertheless, the English church continued to harbor some Congregationalists and to practice a few of Park's Congregational doctrines, perhaps inadvertently. Until Petrie came in 1645, the church "had no established consistory." Petrie moved quickly to organize elders and deacons (one was Captain Hexham, first a deacon, later an elder), but the tiny membership made it more practical to function in many cases on a congregation-wide basis. Elections, when held, were "by the joint voyces of all."[173]

Although Petrie apologized for resorting to congregational meetings, church business sometimes had to go forward on the basis of congregational decision-making. "The Minister declares that hee calles all the members together not that hee thinkes the power of governing belonges to all the members and not to the Elders onlie but in regard of the small number wee have necessitie forceth us to it, having so few that Elders and Deacons cannot be elected out of them."[174] Petrie sometimes preached "against Independents, Brownists and sectaries," and this caused some of his members to absent themselves, in particular one of the deacons, Robert Amersone. Petrie's position was "that hee wold never forbeare speaking against errors, and on further dispute hee descovered his dislike of paedo-baptisme."[175] Except for a short break in 1668-69, Petrie continued as minister until his death in 1683. He worked harmoniously with the Dutch church, and under his ministry the anti-classis, anti-synod talk at the English church ceased. Although some later English ministers of Delft did apply for membership in the classis, they were not automatically received as members.

---

[171] Acta Kerkeraad, VI, 3; Matthews, *Cal. R.*, p. 410.
[172] *F.E.S.*, VII, 545; Acta Kerkeraad, VI, 15-16, 25.
[173] Acta Kerkeraad, VI, 13; C.R., no. 102, fol. 38.
[174] C.R., no. 102, fol. 40 (Jan. 22, 1651).
[175] Ibid., Jan. 15, 1651.

CHAPTER SIX

CHURCHES AT ROTTERDAM, BRIELLE, AND DORT TO 1660

Rotterdam was the second greatest city of the Netherlands, and after Amsterdam, "the second great Emporium of this Trading People."[1] In numbers of English and Scottish residents, Rotterdam for a large part of the seventeenth century exceeded all other Dutch cities. According to ambassador Sir Dudley Carleton in 1619, Rotterdam had "many families" of English and Scots; they supported "two considerable Churches," and for a time even a third, as well as a Scottish school and the English School.[2] When Thomas Bowrey visited Rotterdam in 1698, he discovered that the north-west sector of town was the Scottish quarter "and is Inhabited mostly by Scotch."[3] The English Reformed Church was founded in 1619, the Scottish Church in 1643, and the chapel for the English Merchant Adventurers was established at Rotterdam 1635-1655. There was also occasional mention of a Rotterdam Brownist church, but no records survive.[4] Because of Rotterdam's reputation for shipping and trade, the English-Scottish settlers were almost exclusively commercial people, merchants, "skippers-underlings and tappers of beere and makers of Tobacco-pipes." The English community lived in the vacinity of the Nieuwehaven and Haringvliet.[5]

The English Church of Rotterdam

In 1611 the English settlers in the city petitioned for an English Reformed church, but they merely received permission to hold occasional meetings "in such places as they find suitable" and without any financial support. The official foundation of the English church dates from 1619, when the English received approval for a church and preacher, and the provincial States of Holland, at the urging of Sir Dudley Carleton, voted a subsidy of 400 guilders a year.[6] The Rotterdam Dutch preachers

---

[1] John Northleigh, *Topographical Descriptions* (London, 1702), p. 7.

[2] Ibid., p. 11; Carleton, *Letters*, p. 378.

[3] Thomas Bowrey, *The Papers of Thomas Bowrey*, Hakluyt Society, 2nd ser., 58 (1925), 29-30.

[4] William Brereton, *Travels in Holland the United Provinces England Scotland and Ireland*, ed. Edward Hawkins, The Chetham Society, 1 (1844), 7-8.

[5] S.P. 84, vol. 90, fol. 111. See also "Engelsche tabakspijpmakers in oud-Rotterdam," *Rotterdam Jaarboek* (1916), p. 44, and *Jaarboek* (1922), pp. 19-20.

[6] Res. van Vroedschap Rotterdam, no. 18, fol. 94 (Aug. 1, 1611); Res. States of Holland, no. 52, fol. 240 (Oct. 16, 1619). On the English church, see *Rotterdam in den loop der eeuwen* (Rotterdam: W. Nevens, 1906-09).

reported to the Classis of Schieland (Rotterdam's classis) in April 1620 that the English church "had grown much and increased daily" and was about to call a regular minister.[7] The first two ministerial candidates refused the position. John Douglas, Scottish military chaplain, declined in favor of a pastorate at Utrecht; his reason was that the Rotterdam people were so ordinary socially "with whom I know not how to converse." John Hassall after some trial preaching also refused the new church on grounds that the 400 guilders would be too thin for him and the English burgers too poor—Hassall, it seems, was financially pinched, having fled England because of debts[8]

Finally, during 1620, the English congregation secured Thomas Barkely, formerly of Heusden, and he served until 1628 or 1629. The Classis of Schieland resolved "goede correspondentie te houden" and specified that the English minister should become a member of their classis.[9] However, for various reasons, the English church remained independent of classis membership until 1816. The first orders and constitution of the consistory are dated 1622.[10] After Barkely the following seventeenth-century ministers served the church: Hugh Peter (1629-35), William Ames (1633), John Davenport (1636-37?), William Bridge (1636-1641 or 1642), John Ward (1636-41), Jeremiah Burroughes (1639-41), Sydrach Simpson (1639-41), Joseph Symonds (1641-47), Robert Park (1641-49), Thomas Cawton (1651-59), Richard Maden (1660-80), Nathaniel Mather (1663-71), Joseph Hill (1678-1705), John Spademan (1681-98), and Joseph Hill Junior (1699-1717). The position of co-pastor was established from 1633 to 1647 and again after 1680.

Their first church building, apparently, was the St. Peter's Church. It was known already during the 1620s as the Engelse Kerk. In 1632 the city magistrates assigned the English a wooden building on the Glashaven, known as the "Academie" or the "Rederijkers Schouwburg," a theater used by a "company of pretended rhetoricians." In spite of a tainted history, the English cleansed the hall, burned the old theatrical properties, and "converted to a better use to a church." In 1651 the congregation moved to another building on the Haringvliet (rebuilt in 1715), which served until the church closed in 1876.[11]

---

[7] Acta Classis Schieland, IV, April 5, 1620 (G.A. Rotterdam).
[8] S.P. 84, vol. 89, fol. 47, vol. 90, fol. 111, vol. 92, fol. 99a; B.P., I, 251.
[9] Acta Classis, IV, April 5, 11, 1620; Res. Vroedschap, no. 19, fol. 225. By Jan. 24, 1629, Barkely had been replaced by Hugh Peter.
[10] Copied into the English C.R., no. 342 (1668-1761).
[11] Steven, pp. 325, 333; Brereton, *Travels*, p. 6; Charles B. Jewson, "The English Church at Rotterdam and its Norfolk Connections," *Norfolk Archaeology*, 30 (1952), 329. J.

The Rotterdam English Church was an ordinary English Reformed Church during the Barkely years, "sub ordine presbyteriali, cum nostra Belgica."[12] Hugh Peter, who came in 1629, one of the new Congregational-minded Puritans, thoroughly shook up the church and led it into a period of exceptional activity, transforming the presbyterial church of the 1620s into a model Congregational church of the 1630s. Peter remodeled the church on the basis of a "new" covenant. In a memorable congregational meeting of 1633, John Forbes, president of the English Synod, and Peter presented the covenant, "a precise thing," to the inner core of the congregation, thus constituting the church on a new basis. "Peter wanted not to be caled by the vulgar English of Rotterdam but by the Godly;" and the newly covenanted congregation, voting by hand, extended a new call to Peter, who thereupon asked for a new ordination by Forbes to his charge. Such doings were unheard of in the Reformed churches of the Netherlands—men and women alike clamoring and voting. "I see the men choose him, but what do the women do?" asked Forbes. "Hereupon the women lift up their hands too."[13] Those who did not sign the covenant Peter immediately dropped from the church; and, as one of the excommunicated members complained, "so that it seemes to me our Church formerly was noe Church: but what authorite he hath to doe those thinges: I knowe not."[14]

The Rotterdam 1633 covenant had fifteen articles:

1. To be contented with meet triall for our fitnes to be members.
2. To cleave in hart to the truth and pure worship of God and to oppose all wayes of innovation and corruption.
3. To suffer the Word to be the guider of all controversies.
4. To labor for growth of knowledge and to that end to confer, pray, hear, and meditate.
5. To submite to brotherly admonition and censure with out envie or anger.
6. To be throughly reconciled one to another even in judgment before we begin this work.
7. To walk in all kind of exactnes both in regard of our selves and others.

P. van der Weele, "De Schouwburg der Rederijkers in 1631," *Rotterdam Jaarboek* (1940), 66, 75. A map of 1626 by Balthasar Floris van Berckenrode shows the St. Peter's church with the name *Engelsche Kerk*. (G.A. Rotterdam).

[12] Johannis Hoornbeek, *Summa Controversiarum Religionis*, 2nd ed. (Utrecht, 1658), p. 777.

[13] Reports of Peter's covenant and ordination are found in the following: S.P. 16, vol. 286, no. 94 (April 26, 1633); B.P., I, 139-40 (Nov. 1633); B.P., I, 146 (Nov. 1, 1633); S.P. 84, vol. 147, fol. 174v (Nov. 18/28, 1633).

[14] B.P., I, 146.

8. To forbear clogging ourselves and harts with earthly cares, which is the bayn of religion.
9. To labor to gett a great measuer of humilitie and meekness and to banish pride and highnes of spirit.
10. To meditate the furthering of the Gospell at home and abroad as well in our persons as with our purses.
11. To take nearly to heart our Bretherens condition and to conform ourselves to these troublesome tymes both in our diet and apparell that they be without excesse in necessitie.
12. To deale with all kynde of wisdom and gentlenes towards those that are without.
13. To study Amitie and brotherly love.
14. To put one another in mynd of this *Covenant*, and as occasion is offered to take an accounte of what is done in the premises.
15. And for the furthering of the Kingdome of Christ: diligently to instruct children and servants, yea, and to look to our wayes and accountes dayly.[15]

According to Hoornbeek and Hornius, Peter's Congregational reforms were inspired by letters of instruction from John Cotton from New England; however, the chronology hardly allows for this.[16] Moreover, covenant-making was already established in the Netherlands before New England covenant-making was very far along, as evidenced in the covenants at Middelburg (1623) and Amsterdam (about 1631) and in the theology of Dr. William Ames, professor at the University of Franeker, whose *Medulla Theologiae* (1627) and *De Conscientia* (1630) extolled the church covenant doctrine.[17] Hugh Peter's Congregational church at Rotterdam owed more to Ames's theology than to any "letters" from New England. Peter himself referred to his work at Rotterdam as "Independency." To further the work, in 1633 he succeeded in bringing Doctor Ames himself to Rotterdam to serve as co-pastor, "who left his professorship in *Friezland* to live with me because of my Churches Independency at *Rotterdam*, and charged me often, even to his death, so to look to it, and if there were a way of publik worship in the world, that God would owne it was that."[18] Ames died a few months after taking up his post at Rotterdam.

---

[15] Ibid., I, 154.
[16] Hoornbeek, *Summa Controversiarum*, p. 777; George Hornius, *Historia Ecclesiastica et Politica* (Leiden, 1665), pp. 253, 267.
[17] William Ames, *Medulla Theologiae* (Amsterdam, 1627), I, 32, 14-15; Keith L. Sprunger, *The Learned Doctor William Ames* (Urbana: Univ. of Illinois Press, 1972), p. 227.
[18] Hugh Peter, *Mr. Peters Last Report of the English Wars* (London, 1646), p. 14; Sprunger, *Ames*, p. 242.

With the church fully-established on the covenant, Peter used vigilant discipline to protect the purity of the fellowship. "This saith Mr. Paget was a kind of Excommunicacion to above two parts of the congregation in former times and hath caused the difficulty of administering the sacrament because he will give it to none but them whose names are at his New Covenant." The vulgar non-subscribers were excluded, even gentlemen "of very good worth." The non-subscribers complained "of the difficulty of the way to Heaven here more then in England or the Gospell."[19] The church register records 99 baptisms from 1621 to 1634 and 216 marriages to 1634, at which point there is a break in the register until 1653. Thomas Cawton, who became minister of the church in 1653 began once again to record baptisms and marriages in the book with this sarcastic note: "In the year 1635 to about 1650 were Mr. Hugh Peters, Mr. William Bridges, Mr. Jeremiah Burroughs, Mr. Sydrac Simpson, ministers of the Church. Who being Independents did baptize none but such as were children of the members of their church, which were but few I suppose. And therefore it seems they thought not good to Register them in this church book. However, if they did it in any of their owne, they took the same away with them."[20] In fact, the church did grow considerably during the 1630s, up to a membership of 1000 or more.[21]

Neither the Classis of Schieland nor the Rotterdam magistrates interfered much with the English Church in its Puritanical innovations, so that Rotterdam in the 1630s was without rival as the radical Puritan center of the Netherlands. Thomas Hooker, John Davenport, and William Ames all were at Rotterdam with Hugh Peter; thus the Puritan plans multiplied. Peter masterminded a scheme of erecting a Puritan school for the refugee English young people to function along side the church. The magistrates were persuaded to extend Dr. Ames a joint call as both pastor and teacher for the school for 1000 guilders a year.[22] Peter felt great satisfaction in receiving official subsidy to undergird this cluster of Puritan institutions-in-exile. Ames's sudden death in Novermber of 1633 dealt an incalculable blow. "Now the pillars," lamented Peter, "were fallen and the great good intended to be done in his Colledge at Rotterdam all disapoynted."[23] Although Hooker spent some time at Rotterdam with Hugh Peter before leaving the country in 1633 (about

---

[19] B.P., I, 139, 172.
[20] Baptism and Marriage Register, no. 356 (The archive of the English church is in the possession of the Scots Church of Rotterdam).
[21] Acta Kerkeraad Rotterdam, I, Dec. 4, 1641 (G.A. Rotterdam).
[22] Res. Vroedschap, no. 20, fols. 453, 463, 464. Ames was approved April 9, 1632, but did not take up his duties till Aug. or Sept. of 1633, Sprunger, *Ames*, pp. 92-93.
[23] S.P. 16, vol. 250, no. 28.

March), he never was an officially-inducted minister.[24] John Davenport, after his rejection at Amsterdam, assisted Peter but also without magisterial appointment. In 1635, however, the church was known as "Mr. Peters and Damports English church." In 1636, after Peter left, Davenport agreed "to be their Doctor but another must be pastor." This was not a long arrangement.[25] Another innovating minister, Samuel Eaton, came to Rotterdam in 1636, after unsuccessfully attempting to organize a Congregational church at Amsterdam. He sometimes preached at the Rotterdam church.[26]

In 1635 the Merchant Adventurers moved to Rotterdam. According to Article 7 of the contract between the city and the Adventurers, they were to have use of St. Peter's Church, "where they may exercise the Christian Reformed religion according to the discipline and order of the Church of England." The magistrates also promised "not to tolerate or allow any other public English church in our city except the church of the aforenamed Society of Merchant Adventurers," nor to tolerate anyone preaching against the teaching or discipline of the Church of England.[27] The contract was a great victory for Laud, at least in words. They were empty words, however, because the magistrates put no restrictions and did not cut off funds for the Hugh Peter church. Far from it; in fact, the Merchant Adventurers were soon complaining of taking a back place behind the Puritan English Reformed Church. When the States in 1635 issued a call for public prayers in the churches on behalf of a campaign of the Prince of Orange, they summoned Peter's church "as the English church, and the Companies church neglected: As if theirs were the only church allowed by authority, and ours an obscure or schismaticall church." Calvinist prayers, it was believed, were superior to the read prayers of the Church of England. To clear up the situation, the English Reformed consistory requested assurances from the burgomasters, who promised "that the church shall be maintained in the free exercise of its religion as at present."[28]

In the late 1630s the English Reformed Church came under new leadership. Hugh Peter departed in 1635 for America; John Davenport and Samuel Eaton in 1636 or 1637 also sailed for America. In March of 1636 the church received permission to elect a new minister. Rotterdam's hospitality to the Puritans and the open Independency of the English

---

[24] Keith L. Sprunger, "The Dutch Career of Thomas Hooker," *The New England Quarterly*, 46 (Mar. 1973), 42-44.
[25] S.P. 16, vol. 291, no. 71; B.P., I, 230 (April 27, 30, 1636).
[26] Acta Classis Amsterdam, IV, 75 (June 2, 1636).
[27] C. te Lintum, *De Merchant Adventurers in de Nederlanden* (The Hague: Nijhoff, 1905), p. 241.
[28] Res. Vroedschap, no. 21, fol. 83 (Mar. 19, 1636); S.P. 16, vol. 291, no. 71.

church attracted a new wave of English immigrants, both ministers and lay people, escaping from the severe policies of Archbishop Laud and Bishop Wren of Norwich.[29] Eight Puritan ministers were deprived in Norwich in 1636 and others from the surrounding areas. On May 13, 1636, Bishop Wren received a report that "Warde of S. Michels and Bridges and Allen as we heare are all three at Rotterdam or some other Place in the Low Countries." Within the next two or three years, John Ward, William Bridge, Jeremiah Burroughes, and Edward Wale, deprived by Wren of Norwich; and Sydrach Simpson and Joseph Symonds, deprived at London, were all at Rotterdam and active in the church. Paul Amyraut, another minister deprived by Wren, settled at Utrecht. Thomas Allen and William Greenhill, also deprived by Wren, returned to England in 1637 after short visits to Holland.[30]

The Puritan exodus included a goodly company of "wealthy Citizens and Clothiers," and the congregation grew. The church books of the Congregational churches at Norwich and Yarmouth give this account: "The urging of Popish ceremonies, and divers innovated injunctions in the worship and service of God by Bishop Wren and his instruments; the suspending and silencing of divers godly ministers; and the persecuting of godly men and women, caused divers of the godly in Norwich, Yarmouth, and other places to remove, and to pass over into Holland, to enjoy the liberty of their conscience in God's worship, and to free themselves from human inventions. After they came into Holland, divers joined themselves to the church in Rotterdam, and abode members of that church five or six years."[31] The Rotterdam church included in its membership three of the Five Dissenting Brethren (Bridge, Burroughes, Simpson). The English church at Arnhem was established as a result of the same immigration of the 1630s.

Bridge and Ward joined the Rotterdam church as "private men." "They conformed themselves to the Discipline which Master *Peters* had planted; they renounced their English Ordination and Ministeriall Office." Then, the congregation being bereft of ministers, "did choose and ordain both them to be their Ministers."[32] This took place in 1636.

---

[29] B.P., I, 225-26; R. W. Ketton-Cremer, *Norfolk in the Civil War* (London: Faber and Faber, 1969), pp. 76-79; Kenneth W. Shipps, "Lay Patronage of East Anglican Puritan Clerics in Pre-Revolutionary England," Diss. Yale 1971, pp. 289-99.

[30] Tanner MS. 68, fols. 3v, 7, 10, 115, 207v (Bod., Oxford); Ketton-Cremer, *Norfolk*, p. 80.

[31] Thomas Edwards, *Antapologia* (London, 1644), p. 35; the quotation from the church books is quoted in Browne, *Congregationalism*, pp. 208-09.

[32] Robert Baillie, *The Dissvasive from the Errours of the Time* (London, 1645), p. 75. On the Five Dissenting Brethren, see Berndt Gustafsson, *The Five Dissenting Brethren: A Study of the Dutch Background of Their Independentism*, Lunds Univ. Arsskrift, 51 (1955).

By October 1636, Stephen Goffe reported about a "fresh" minister having come over from Norwich "to be Peters successor."[33] Sydrach Simpson came over in 1638, and he also renounced his ordination and joined as a private member.[34] Bridge was sometimes called "teacher" rather than minister, but the Dutch records refer to both Ward and Bridge as "ordinary ministers." The English church practiced a democratic church life with most decisions being made in the congregational meetings. The magistrates allowed stipends for two ministers.[35]

Although enjoying financial favor and patronage from the magistrates, the officials exercised little supervision over the church. Unlike Amsterdam where Paget kept the situation stirred up, the Rotterdam classis kept a distance; and in fact relationships between Dutch and English churches were slight. This free, unsupervised situation generated divisive tendencies and splitting into factions. Trouble began in the congregation over the issue of prophesying ("that the people on the Lords dayes should have liberty after the Sermons ended, to put doubts and questions to the Ministers"). Simpson, a private member of the congregation, supported it and Bridge opposed it, except possibly on a weekday. Ward was caught in the middle, and the congregation cleared the situation by deposing Ward (January 1639) for his siding against Bridge on prophesying and also on grounds that he was preaching old sermons previously used at Norwich. To replace Ward, the church in January 1639 chose Jeremiah Burroughes, who had come over in 1638, deprived at Tivetshall, Norfolk. Thereafter the church was known as the Burroughes-Bridge church.[36] Simpson withdrew to establish a second English Reformed Church, assisted by Joseph Symonds. The Simpson-Symonds church, "a Church against a Church," advertised itself as "for a purer Church and for more ordinances." It was a completely voluntary church without government sponsorship or subsidy.[37]

The splitting of the church and deposing Ward was the occasion for the assembly of churches referred to in the *Apologeticall Narration*. The church at Arnhem, pastored by Thomas Goodwin, Philip Nye, and John Archer intervened after judging the deposing as "too sudden" and "too severe." A conference of the two Independent congregations was called, a "solemne assembly," and Ward's troubles were patched up. "That Church, which had offended, did as publiquely acknowledge their sinfull

---

[33] B.P., I, 240.
[34] Baillie, *Dissvasive*, p. 75; Paul S. Seaver, *The Puritan Lectureships: The Politics of Religious Dissent 1560-1662* (Stanford: Stanford Univ. Press, 1970), pp. 257-58.
[35] Res. Vroedschap, no. 21, fol. 140 (Feb. 16, 1637); [Alexander Forbes], *Anatomy of Independency* (London, 1644), p. 23.
[36] Edwards, *Antapologia*, pp. 142-43; Res. Vroedschap, no. 21, fol. 274 (Jan. 10, 1639).
[37] Edwards, *Antapologia*, p. 143; Acta Kerkeraad, I, Dec. 4, 1641.

aberration in it, restored their *Minister* to his place again, and ordered a solemn day of fasting to humble themselves afore God and men, for their sinfull carriage in it; and the party also which had been deposed did acknowledge to that Church wherein he had likewise sinned."[38] Ward's restoration apparently did not occur until the summer of 1641. The Ward affair went down in early Congregational history as a sample of how Congregational brethren used synods for advice, counsel, and removing offenses. Presbyterian scoffers laughed at the pretentious claims of the little conference of two churches—"the Synod of Rotterdam." Grandiose language covered manifold disorder. "In a word," said the ever caustic Thomas Edwards, "all things are loose in independent Government."[39]

The schisms and other signs of loose practice (no consistory, absent ministers) alerted the Dutch Reformed Church to possible trouble. The Dutch Reformed Consistory of Rotterdam, at the urging of the synod, in 1641 investigated the English religious situation with particular attention to how the English preachers came to Rotterdam, why they were leaving, and what procedures were being followed for admission and demission.[40] The report, dated November 26, 1641, made these points:

1. Rotterdam has three English reformed churches. The first one is the English Court (Merchant Adventurers) Church, which has no connections with the other two churches. The second church is a public church receiving a proper subsidy from the province and city for the maintenance of two ministers. The third church separated from the second church about two years ago because of certain misunderstandings over prophesying and now supports its own two ministers. This happened without the knowledge of magistrates, classis, or consistory.
2. Ministers for the Merchant Adventurers church are sent out of England and are chosen by the Archbishop of Canterbury.
3. The calling of ministers in the other two churches was done by vote of all the male members of the respective churches. The ministers came into exile because of the governance of the bishops; this is their reason for having no certificate of demission or other documents of their life and doctrine.
4. The admission of ministers was done without letter of calling and without any communication with classis, consistory of the Dutch Reformed Church, or magistrates.

---

[38] *Apologeticall Narration, Hvmbly Svbmitted to the Honourable House of Parliament* (London, 1643), pp. 16, 20, 21.
[39] Edwards, *Antapologia*, pp. 178-79; Baillie, *Dissvasive*, p. 76.
[40] Acta Kerkeraad, I, Aug. 30, 1641.

5. The second church for two or three years deposed Waert (John Ward) its ordinary established preacher, and this past summer they again received him as minister, all of this without knowledge of classis, consistory, or magistrates.
6. Borris (Jeremiah Burroughes), ordinary preacher of the second church and Bridge (William Bridge) last winter travelled to England for a certain time. Bridge returned but Borris remained in England and resigned his position by letter, although not having any particular call in England. The church is displeased with Borris and has expostulated with him.
7. For the last two or three months, Bridge and Waert, ordinary preachers, and Wael (Edward Wale), established elder and sometimes preacher with support from the congregation, went to England with intention to stay over the winter. They have no particular ministerial call in England but wish to advance the good cause of the churches of England. Some fear they will not return. This leaves the church, consisting of 1000 persons, without any ordinary and established minister or elder.
8. The church has no board of elders as in the Dutch Reformed and French churches. All discipline, calling of ministers, and ongoing governance is done by the whole congregations, *praeentibus pastoribus*, whenever pastors are present.
9. Meanwhile, while the regular ministers are in England, the church, so they need not be without ministry, has called Perck (Robert Park) by provisie and only for preaching for six months. He was formerly at Delft. This was done without knowledge of magistrates, consistory, or classis.
10. During this six months, the church has no sacraments, being without any established minister. Their children hence were baptized in the Dutch church.
11. In the third church, Simpson had returned to England, like the ministers of the second church, leaving Simons his colleague to serve the church. He also, however, is considering leaving. In this case, some of the congregation and many in the city hope that perhaps this third church will be re-united with the second church.

Appendix: The second church stands by itself, having over it no ecclesiastical assemblies or judgments, so that when great discontent arose over the deposing of the minister, the discontented persons withdrew into their church apart. The church also has no means of appeal for those under censure or otherwise troubled.[41]

---

[41] The report is in the Archive of the Synod of South Holland (III, 35, iii, 29), "Engelsche predikanten: 1641," fols. 209-13 (N.H.A.); also entered in Acta Kerkeraad Rotterdam, I, Dec. 4, 1641.

This document gives the clearest picture available of the status and organization of the three English churches of Rotterdam. Particular attention was drawn to the democratic life of the churches, their being left without regular ministry in 1641, and that the churches proceeded without consultation with the magistrates or Dutch Reformed church. By 1641, the anti-Laudian immigration was slowing down and beginning to reverse to England. Ministers and members were returning home. By November 1641 all the original ministers had returned to England (Bridge, Ward, Burroughes, Simpson, Wale), however, Bridge, Ward, and Wale were expected back and may have served a short while in 1642.

The history of the Rotterdam English churches has close connection with Norfolk. Charles B. Jewson called the Rotterdam church "the mother church of Congregational Dissent in Norfolk."[42] People and letters moved easily back and forth. No sooner was Bridge at Rotterdam than he began writing "fierce Letters to some of his old friends in *Norwich* to come from the Church of England." In Congregational enthusiasm he told them "not to be content with the ordinance of hearing, but to looke out after the plat-forme of Government, left by Christ and his Apostles."[43] When the way cleared in England, the Rotterdam congregation, well experienced in Congregationalism as a way of church life, sent some of its members back to Norfolk to become core people in establishing Congregational churches at Norwich and Yarmouth. They took with them lawful demission from the Rotterdam church "to join together into a body in church-fellowship."[44] The Rotterdam church provided much leadership for Congregationalism in England and America: John Ward, William Bridge, Sydrach Simpson, Edward Wale, Jeremiah Burroughes, and Robert Park, ministers of the church, returned to England to serve Congregational churches. John Davenport, Hugh Peter, and Thomas Hooker became Congregational ministers in New England. Samuel Eaton served both in England and America. Several Rotterdam lay people went on into the ministry, namely James Gedney, a weaver, Stephen Gooch, and William Ames Junior, serving Congregational churches in Norfolk and Suffolk. Francis Hillen, a limner, sometimes "a public preacher," opened a school at Rotterdam and also edited a grammar, *The English and Low Dutch Instructor* (1664).[45]

---

[42] Jewson, "English Church at Rotterdam," p. 324.

[43] Edwards, *Antapologia*, p. 18.

[44] Browne, *Congregationalism*, p. 209. Jewson has identified 57 persons who transferred membership from Rotterdam to the Yarmouth and Norwich churches, 1642-55 (p. 334).

[45] On Gedney, Gooch, and Ames, see Charles B. Jewson, "Return of Conventicles in Norwich Diocese 1669," *Norfolk Archaeology*, 33 (1962), 425-28. On Hillen see G. Scheurweghs, "English Grammars in Dutch and Dutch Grammars in English in the Netherlands before 1800," *English Studies*, 41 (June 1960), p. 135, which concludes that

The Rotterdam churches were reunited in 1643 under Robert Park and Joseph Symonds at the strong insistence of the magistrates, who resented that so much had been done without their consent. George Beaumont, ejected chaplain of the Merchants Adventurers, reported in 1643 "that our magistrates of Rotterdam will no longer suffer the other congregation folk to have their repetetious meetings."[46] The union was very fragile, however, and the old Simpson-Symonds people were not much at ease. They were allowed prophesying only in a private home on a week day.[47] The Congregational foundations laid by Hugh Peter held strong throughout the ministries of Park and Symonds, with Peter's great approval; "I thanke the Lord such a Church it continues to this day," he wrote in 1646 after a visit to Rotterdam as Parliamentary agent.[48]

The English Reformed Church at Rotterdam was the most theologically innovative of the English churches, except perhaps for the Arnhem church. It was famous for its Independency, covenants, democratic decision-making without even an eldership (which the synod investigators had noted with astonishment), and women's participation. Women had voted at the adoption of the covenant, although not in congregational meetings thereafter; women for several years met for their own weekly communion, prayer, and fasting meeting.[49] John Bachelor visited Rotterdam in 1641 and praised the church as "the beautifull face of holinesse, the lively representations of Jesus Christ in his ordinances, the sweet and blessed communion of the Saints in all love and dearenesse." He proclaimed his full conversion to Congregationalism: "mine heart is convinced."[50] After elder Edward Wale left in 1641, the consistory of elders was not reconstituted. Neither branch of the church, Bridge's or Simpson's, had an eldership. "For many yeers they have had none," and so "have governed all their affaires by the voices of the people," wrote Robert Baillie (1645). Whether the omission of elders, which lasted over ten years, was an ideological policy or related to lack of suitable candidates, is uncertain. Nevertheless, it was one of the most distinctive features of the church and most surprising to outsiders. Congregational decision-making took time, and the poorer members complained they could not afford to take time from their jobs. On at least one occasion, the Rotterdam-Arnhem assembly, the richer members

---

the schoolmaster Francois Hillenius is the same as the Congregationalist Francis Hillen, member of the Rotterdam church.

[46] Acta Kerkeraad, I, Aug. 28, 1641; B.P., I, 343 (Sept. 21, 1643).
[47] Baillie, *Dissvasive*, p. 77.
[48] Peter, *Last Report*, p. 14; Hugh Peter had visited Rotterdam in 1643.
[49] Forbes, *Anatomy*, p. 29; Baillie, *Dissvasive*, p. 111.
[50] Edwards, *Antapologia*, p. 185.
[51] Forbes, *Anatomy*, p. 34.

reimbursed the poorer members for wages lost while attending meetings.[51]

The church was open to many opinions from the leftward wing of Puritanism (Brownist and Anabaptist), giving rise to charges of "undeniable" pro-Brownism. When in Amsterdam, the Dissenting Brethren "have gone to Mr. *Canne's* (the Separatist) and to his Church." Symonds seems particularly to have verged on Separatism, urging his friends back in England to "a totall Secession from the Church of England because of its corruptions." Symonds complained of an invasion of Anabaptist pests in his congregation. More orthodox Puritans regarded him as also deviant, "turning aside to ways of separation."[52] Both Park and Symonds, however, retained their state-supported positions in the English Reformed Church and claimed no total secessions from anyone.

After Park and Symonds returned to England, Symonds in 1647 as rector of St. Mary Abchurch, London and Park in 1649 as Congregational lecturer at Bolten, Lancashire, the church once again began a ministerial search.[53] The Congregational refugee ministers had nearly all returned to England or gone on to America, but men of other persuasion, currently out of favor in England, were to be had. Two Presbyterians, Thomas Cawton and James Nalton, implicated in Love's Plot against Cromwell, came to Leiden in 1651, "intending to sit down a while there, till the storm in *England* was blown over." They became the next ministers of the church. The Rotterdammers sent a Macedonian call, "Come and help us," and they came. Cawton and Nalton found their main support in Mr. Harris and Mr. Shepheard, whose membership went back to the old days before Hugh Peter's Independency. Working with the Presbyterian remnant, Cawton and Nalton dispersed the Independent adherents, and according to Cawton's story, "being vanquished they vanished and never appeared after to molest them or the English Church, which before was Independent, but now was brought off, and remains so to this day."[54]

After six months, Nalton returned to England, but Cawton was admitted as regular Reformed minister in June of 1652 and remained minister

---

[52] Edwards, *Antapologia*, p. 56; John Quick, "Icones Sacrae Anglicanae," I, i, 491 (D.W.L.); Brook, *Puritans*, III, 39; Geoffrey F. Nuttall, "Some Bibliographical Notes and Identifications," *T.C.H.S.*, 16 (1950), 157.

[53] Res. Vroedschap, no. 22, fol. 168 (June 3, 1647), fol. 285 (Nov. 19, 1649). Joseph Hunter reports that Richard Heywood in 1644 went to Rotterdam and persuaded Park (Pike) to return to Bolton (1644); see *The Rise of the Old Dissent Exemplified in the Life of Oliver Heywood* (London: Longman, Brown, Green, & Longmans, 1842), p. 37. If so, Park's return was short since Dutch records place Park at Rotterdam in 1647 and 1649.

[54] Thomas Cawton, Junior, *The Life and Death of That Holy and Reverend Man of God Mr. Thomas Cawton* (London, 1662), pp. 51-52.

till August 1659, when he died. Having "brought off" the church into Presbyterianism, Cawton restored traditional practices, including records in the old marriage and baptism registers and establishing a consistory of elders. Cawton confirmed to the Dutch consistory that the church had no elders except for Mr. Harris, who had served under the old presbyterial government two decades before. The classis sent deputies to help re-establish the consistory.[55] Cawton was a diligent pastor, preaching two sermons every Sunday, "not assisted by any but Gods alsufficient assistance." Although growing weaker, he never ceased his preaching, though towards the end, at every trip into the pulpit, "every one thought he would either faint or die before he came down." Once he did faint in the pulpit, but as he swooned his only thought was, "The pulpit is a good place to die in." He died August 7, 1659—not preaching at the moment—and was buried at Rotterdam.[56] Cawton's Presbyterian ministrations, however, did not totally banish the old Independent ghosts. Although called Presbyterian thereafter, the church long retained a reputation for Independent tendencies.[57]

The Scots Church of Rotterdam

The Scots of Rotterdam did not gather into a separate Scots church, a third British congregation, until 1642-43. Prior to that they were amalgamated into the English Reformed Church, which the earliest documents sometimes refer to as "the English and Scottish church," or with the Dutch Reformed church.[58] The impetus for a distinct Scottish church in the 1640s arose from the heightened national consciousness of the Scottish Revolution and perhaps from the controversies in the English church about militant Independency, so abhorrent to Scottish Presbyterians. The Scots petitioned for an officially-sponsored church for the Scottish nation, co-equal with the churches of the English and French nations. The campaign began with petitions to the burgomasters of Rotterdam (July 14, 1642) and the consistory of the Dutch Reformed Church (October 1, 1642); the petitions were on behalf of "the Scottish nation, also at the request of the Scottish skippers, craving permission for the founding on their behalf of a Scottish Congregation." The Scots were said to be 300 to 400 strong.[59] The Rotterdam magistrates forwarded the

---
[55] Acta Kerkeraad, IV, May 29, June 5, 1652; Cawton, *Life*, p. 53.
[56] Cawton, *Life*, pp. 53-54, 67.
[57] Steven, p. 333.
[58] Res. Vroedschap, no. 18, fol. 490; Scots C.R., I, 1 (The archive of the church is in the Scots Church building).
[59] Res. Vroedschap, no. 21, fol. 458; Acta Kerkeraad, I, Oct. 1, 1642; Acta Classis Schieland, V, Oct. 14, 1642. A collection of early documents about the church, 1642-50, has been printed by the church, "Copie van de officieele documenten betreffende de oprichting van de 'Schotsche Kerk' te Rotterdam, in 1643" (n.p., n.d.).

petition to the States of Holland, who on July 19, 1642, approved the establishment of a Scots church and voted an annual stipend of 550 guilders for ministerial salary. The Rotterdam burgomasters provided the church building and a supplementary stipend of 380 guilders, making a total of 930 guilders, in order to bring the Scottish minister equal to the English minister.[60] The financial and legal foundations had been laid by October of 1642, but the new congregation still lacked a preacher. The Scots with the help of the Dutch Reformed consistory appealed to the Presbytery of Edinburgh to send over a preacher. In July of 1643 Alexander Petrie, former minister of Rhynd came, "commissioned from Scotland to be minister for the Scottish congregation here."[61]

Petrie appeared before the Dutch Reformed consistory July 31, 1643, presenting his credentials from Edinburgh; he preached his first sermon to the church August 2; he was inducted into his office by William Spang of Veere on August 30.[62] The election of a Scottish consistory took place on September 13, 1643, "under the supervision of the Deputies of the Dutch consistory." William Muire and Mathew Patoun were elected elders, Andrew Delap and Robert Burt deacons. The new officers were all transfers from the Dutch Reformed church of Rotterdam. With the installation of preachers and consistory, the Scottish church was considered established. Dominee Berckel on behalf of the Dutch classis and consistory gave the church his blessing: "That now this Scotish kirk is established, and these elders and deacones being received, this is a free congregation in itself as any other, and the Consistorie therof is absolute as the consistorie of the dutche kirke is."[63] The Scots themselves interpreted their commissioning as a church as authorization to become a branch of the Church of Scotland, comparable to the Scots Church of Veere. They made a careful study of the resolutions of the general assembly of the Church of Scotland and entered into the consistory register: "This kirk is granted to be erected according to the discipline of the kirkes of Scotland."[64]

The first Scots church building was in a remodeled warehouse, "the warehouse of Ambrosius situated in the Wynstreet, and viewing on the Wynhaven." The congregation met here from 1643 to 1658. From 1658 to 1697 they met in St. Sebastian's chapel in Lombard Street; but because it was small and remote from the Scottish quarter of town, the

---

[60] Res. States of Holland, no. 286, p. 173; Steven, p. 2; Res. Vroedschap, no. 21, fols. 474, 524; no. 22, fol. 168. The Rotterdam contribution was raised to 700 guilders in 1649 (no. 22, fol. 258).

[61] Acta Kerkeraad, I, Oct. 23, 1642, Feb. 25, July 31, 1643.

[62] Ibid., I, July 31, 1643; C.R., I, 1.

[63] C.R., I, 1; Acta Kerkeraad, I, Aug. 13, 1643.

[64] C.R., I, 1.

Scots persuaded the burgomasters to build a more commodious church, completed in 1697, on the Vasteland next to the Schiedam Dike, or called "vulgarily from the many Scots Inhabitants there, the Scots-Dijck."[65] The seventeenth-century Scottish population of Rotterdam was considerable, and the membership grew rapidly. The first year (August-December) they had 24 baptisms, and in 1644 there were 83 baptisms. The church gathered in the scattered Scots among the Dutch Reformed churches of the area and also some English people, especially those not of Congregational persuasion.[66] Each of the British churches had its own flavor. The English Reformed Church had a strong Congregationalist tradition; the Merchant Adventurer Church used the Prayer Book; the Scots Church was Presbyterian. The ministers of the church were exclusively Scottish Presbyterians: Alexander Petrie (1643-62), John Hoog (1662-89), Robert MacWard (1676-77), Robert Fleming (1677-94), James Brown (1691-1713), Robert Fleming Junior (1695-98), and Thomas Hoog (1699-1723).

Petrie, who served the church single-handedly for nineteen years, was a dedicated Covenanter and Scottish nationalist. He kept the church attuned to Scottish politics and religion. He was the author of two books, *Chiliasto-mastix* (Rotterdam, 1644), an anti-millennial treatise, and a church history, *A Compendious History of the Catholick Church, from the year 600 until the year 1600* (The Hague, 1662). The hasty appearance of *Chiliasto-mastix*, within the first year of his coming to Rotterdam, reveals the urgency Petrie felt in combatting millenarianism in his flock: "For you have heard this errour preached in stead of the doctrine of Christ ... by some of the Authoures of the Apologeticall narration for Independencie."[67] One of Petrie's sons, Alexander Petrie Junior, was reader at the church for a short time in 1644-45 and then became minister of the English church at Delft; a daughter married Andrew Snype, minister of Veere.[68]

As a national church in a foreign land, the Scots church had the double mission of relating to the new country of the immigrant while at the same time maintaining the Scottish identity. The church had close connections with the Dutch city and provincial officials and the national Dutch Reformed church. The political government paid the bills and gave magisterial supervision; the Dutch Reformed church gave ecclesiastical

---

[65] Steven, pp. 5, 17, 125-26; C.R., III, 3.
[66] C.R., I, 1; Baptism, marriage, membership register, no. 47. Alexander Petrie, *Chiliasto-mastix* (Rotterdam, 1644), dedicated his book to "the Scotes and Englishes of the Scots Congregation of Rotterdam."
[67] *Chiliasto-mastix*, dedication.
[68] *F.E.S.*, VII, 541, 550.

supervision. The entire work of establishing the church was done under the watchful eyes of burgomasters, kerkeraad, and classis. The Rotterdam consistory in 1642 sought advice from Amsterdam about the functioning of their English Reformed church, since the Amsterdam church was considered the best regulated of the Netherlands British churches. The intention was to follow the same policies at Rotterdam, not to repeat the mistakes made with the already-existent Rotterdam English church.[69] The burgomasters had decreed during the establishing of the church that "the Scottish Nation shall not proceed to calling a minister until they shall have established good order in everything, which is to be arranged by the Dutch consistory together with the classis subject to approval by the magistrates."[70] Installation of ministers, election of elders and deacons, and all other important steps in founding the congregation occurred "under supervision." The close link between church and city was manifested in the communion silver, the wine being served in four silver cups embellished with the arms of the city of Rotterdam issued by the burgomasters in 1644.[71]

The church at some point united with the Dutch Reformed Classis of Schieland. The Reformed officials, following the Amsterdam example, had resolved that the Scots church be attached to the classis, but early attempts to enroll the church were postponed by the Dutch churchmen (1642, 1643, 1644). In June 1644, nearly a year after Petrie's entrance at Rotterdam, he was still postponed from membership "for various weighty reasons."[72] There is no clear record of Scottish membership in the Classis of Schieland at any time in the seventeenth century. In 1816 the Scots were formally enrolled in the Classis of Rotterdam, and they may have had membership somewhat earlier. William Steven in 1833 lauded the Scottish connection to the classis as being "singularly beneficial to the congregation." Financial and political backing provided long-term stability:

> Whatever immunities the Dutch clergy have enjoyed from the State or the city, the Scots ministers have always had their full share. And during the troubles by which the continent of Europe was agitated, more especially when Holland was under French domination, the circumstance of the Scottish church forming part of the Dutch ecclesiastical establishment, was, as will afterwards be seen, of immense avail; and, under a gracious Providence, has mainly contributed to its existence to the present time.[73]

---

[69] Acta Kerkeraad, I, Oct. 5, 1642; Res. Vroedschap, no. 21, fol. 474.
[70] Acta Kerkeraad, I, Oct. 13, 1642; Res. Vroedschap, no. 21, fol. 474.
[71] O.A.R., no. 2744 (G.A. Rotterdam); Steven, p. 6.
[72] Acta Kerkeraad, I, Oct. 13, 1642; Acta Classis, V, Oct. 14, 1642, Nov. 23, 1643, June 20, 1644.
[73] Steven, p. 7. Steven assumed a membership in the classis as early as 1643, but his source does not bear this out.

The church assumed it had a special responsibility for overseeing the Scottish community religiously, educationally, and even materially. Religiously the Scots were nourished with Presbyterian doctrine; but this was not enough. The church also provided poor relief for the indigent of the Scottish nation, gave education to the Scottish youth, and took at least a partial responsibility for the well-being and good behavior of the entire Scottish community. The concurrence of church and politics was close. Robert Baillie and George Gillespie, who visited Rotterdam in 1645, being "drivien hither by storme" while traveling to London, urged Lord Forbes, Conservator of Scottish privileges in the Netherlands, to uphold the minister and elders in the work of discipline, "seeing ther be so many inordinate and stubborne persones of our nation in this towne."[74] Petrie spent long hours gathering into the church the Scots of the vicinity and subjecting them to Scottish Presbyterian discipline. Some of the Scot residents of Rotterdam falsely claimed Dutch Reformed membership in order to evade Petrie's ministrations; or if legitimate Dutch Reformed members, some refused to transfer. To avoid such cases, Petrie asked to have all Scots transferred to the Scots church. Also Petrie and the elders sought to have all proclamations and marriages of Scots done only in the Scots church, likewise all Scottish baptisms and communion. In particular, Petrie complained about backsliding Scots under church discipline, who resorted to the Dutch Reformed Church for baptism of their children.[75] The church was large; between 1643 and 1660 there were 734 baptisms and over 1100 members were added (Amsterdam, the other large church, had 493 baptisms for the same period).[76]

Events in Scotland were of vital concern to the Rotterdam Scots. Through the church, Scots were kept involved in the Covenant movement. As nearly the first action at the church, Petrie in October 1643 introduced the Scottish Covenant as a requisite for membership: "Agreed that the covenant or Confession of the kirk of Scotland shalbe read from the pulpite on Sunday, to the end, that all may know it, and after consideration thereof all the members of this congregation who ar receved or ar to be receved heerafter at any time shall subscrive it." On January 6, 1644, the Covenant was publicly subscribed by the church; "many hundreds swear unto it by solemne lifting up of their handes and by subscriving it."[77] The church kept fast days in the 1640s for the suc-

---

[74] C.R., I, 20.
[75] Acta Kerkeraad, I, Aug. 26, Sept. 2, Sept. 9, 1643, Jan. 6, 1644, Jan. 25, 1645.
[76] A. L. Schenk, "The Golden Book of the Scots Church," MS. 1011 (Scots Church); Baptism Register, no. 47. Cf. Amsterdam register, no. 82.
[77] C.R., I, 2, 4. Baptism register, no. 47, fol. 81; the confession of 1580 and 1638 must be subscribed "by all the members of the Scottish kirk at Rotterdam ere they receive the communione."

cess of Scotland. Moreover, many individual Scots of Rotterdam went much further and provided financial and military supplies for the armies.[78]

The inner life of the church during Petrie's ministry was unsettled. Many controversies occurred. Some were between the Scottish majority and the English minority (1645). Another great debate stirred the church about whether the reader should be allowed to make a few expository comments or was merely to read clearly without comments. Some suspected that expository commentary "bordered on Brownism or Papistry." In 1645 Robert Baillie and George Gillespie on their visit were called upon to promote a reconciliation in the church; in 1650 Petrie was forced to appeal to the Dutch Reformed consistory for help in restoring peace.[79] Petrie, a man "of a hasty and warm temperament," ran into many obstacles in keeping a firm Scottish Presbyterian regime. William Steven, a nineteenth-century successor of Petrie, evaluated Petrie; "at times, he seemed to forget that he was in a foreign country, and that it is next to impossible for a clergyman so situated, to put in force that salutary discipline, which, judiciously directed, is productive of the happiest results."[80]

Brielle

The English garrison church in St. Jacob's Church, dating from 1585, disbanded soon after 1616 when Brielle ceased to be an English cautionary town and the troops were removed. The long-time English minister, Michael Seroyen, died soon after 1616 and was not replaced.[81] The English families who continued to live at Brielle, a city important for English trade and travel, made repeated efforts to re-establish worship in their church building (the Engelse Kerk). In 1622 some of the "English congregation" requested the appointment of Nicholas Rushe of Ouddorp as English preacher, but the Brielle consistory refused to support him on grounds that an English preacher for Brielle was no great necessity and because of his bad reputation in the Classis of Brielle.[82] Nicholas Rushe, apparently, was the Christ's College fellow expelled from Cambridge in

---

[78] David Stevenson, *The Scottish Revolution 1637-1644* (Newton Abbot: David & Charles, 1973), pp. 128, 189.
[79] C.R., I, 20; Acta Kerkeraad, IV, Aug. 5, 1650; Steven, pp. 7-11.
[80] Steven, p. 22.
[81] By 1620 Mrs. Seroyen was "widow Seroyen," H. de Jager, *De Brielsche Vroedschap in de jaren 1618-1794* (Rijswick, 1904), p. 222. For the earlier history of Brielle, see above chapter 2.
[82] H. de Jager, "Engelsche predikanten te Brielle," *De Navorscher*, 43 (1893), 598-99. Also on the church at Brielle see Cornelis Veltenaar, *Het kerkelijk leven der gereformeerden in den Briel tot 1816* (Amsterdam: A. H. Kruyt, 1915), pp. 98-106.

1610 for preaching at St. Mary's about "gorbellyed clergye" and "develish parasytes." Rushe, "having left his service in England, came to Holland," and was admitted to the Dutch clergy in spite of his incompetence in Dutch; but as pastor at Ouddort he offended with his strange manner of preaching and praying. After he was refused at Brielle, Rushe served at St. Anthonypolder 1623-27.[83] Without a shepherd, the congregation dwindled.

In the 1640s several attempts were made to revive the church. In 1644 an English delegation petitioned to secure a minister for the increasing English-Scottish community, and the magistrates of Brielle agreed to sponsor the church. The magistrates took note of "the aforesaid inhabitants, together with all the passengers and travelers, who came and wait for a favorable wind, and all the others arriving daily because of the trouble in England." The magistrates promised a subsidy of 300 guilders and summoned assistance from the Dutch Reformed ministers of the city in finding a minister candidate.[84] After looking around, by August they found young Alexander Petrie, son of the Scottish minister of Rotterdam, highly recommended for "learning, life, and disposition." The magistrates hired Petrie and promised him maintenance for several months at the least.[85] The Brielle congregation contained "a number of respectable Scotch families," who were no doubt well pleased with the Scottish tongue of Petrie, M.A. of St. Andrews.[86] The English half of the congregation, however, was not satisfied with Petrie. In exasperation, the magistrates cancelled the church, which had barely begun to revive and dismissed Petrie because of "disagreements arisen between those of the English and Scottish nations of this city, being such that the establishment of a preacher to serve these nations can bring forth no fruit." Petrie's entire service at Brielle lasted only from August 20 to September 11, 1644.[87]

In 1647 the English tried again, led by "some English ship masters and merchants;" and although a certain preacher was brought in temporarily, the English church was not officially re-established. In 1649, Robert Prickett, an English Royalist, on recommendation of the Prince of Orange sought the position of English minister, but the magistrates refused him when they discovered that the English and Scots of Brielle would

---

[83] Acta Classis Brielle, E3a, April 26, 1622 (N.H.A.); Charles H. Cooper, *Annals of Cambridge* (Cambridge: Warwick, 1842-52), III, 31-33; Knuttel, *Acta Synoden Zuid-Holland*, I, 63, 233.

[84] Jager, "Engelsche predikanten," pp. 599-600.

[85] Ibid., pp. 600-01.

[86] Steven, p. 8.

[87] Res. Vroedschap, no. 9, fols. 53v-54v (G.A. Brielle); Veltenaar, *Kerkelijk leven*, pp. 104-05.

not support him.[88] The English and Scottish congregation, or what was left of it, received another setback when the magistrates in 1653 assigned the English Church building to the French congregation, after which the Engelse Kerk became known as the Fransche Kerk. Only scattered reports of English or Scottish religion at Brielle are found thereafter. In 1697 arrangements were made for Scottish preaching in the French Church for the benefit of some Scottish travelers and sailors laying over because of the wind. Again in 1713, the English families of Brielle petitioned for a church, but their request for a provincial stipend, although supported "in the most earnest manner" by the British churches of Rotterdam, was not approved.[89] In spite of the continued existence of a British community at Brielle throughout the seventeenth century, the church was not established on a regular basis after 1616.

Dort

Dort (Dordrecht) was another of the prosperous south Holland trading cities. John Ray in 1663 described it as "a large city, very rich and populous, well built with tall houses of brick, not inferior to those of *Antwerp*."[90] English and Scots were attracted for trade (the Merchant Adventurers in 1655) and military service. A company or two of English or Scottish soldiers were often garrisoned at Dort.[91] One part of the town where the English settlers lived and had their business was known as the English Quay. The Scottish merchants also designated Dort as a staple port in 1668, but without much effect; "as the measure was far from popular, comparatively few merchants repaired to this place." The famous Synod of Dort of 1618-19 attracted English and Scottish delegates, who carried on English worship for a few months. A settled English Reformed Church was first established in 1623.[92] From 1655 to 1700 the Merchant Adventurers had their own church, which made the second English church. When Sir William Brereton visited in 1634, he thought he detected a few Brownists lurking about.[93]

The English and Scots of Dort in 1623 obtained a church building and subsidy for minister. The first minister was John Oswald (1623-25). The church seal of 1771 refers to the church as the *Ecclesia Britanica*. The

---

[88] Res. Vroedschap, no. 10, fol. 183v. On Prickett see *D.N.B.*; Jager, "Engelsche predikanten," p. 602; *Notes and Queries*, 3rd ser., 2, p. 469.
[89] Jager, "Engelsche predikanten," p. 603; Steven, p. 286.
[90] John Ray, *Travels through the Low-Countries, Germany, Italy and France*, 2nd ed. (London, 1738), I, 20.
[91] Brereton, *Travels*, pp. 12-13.
[92] Steven, pp. 297-98.
[93] Brereton, *Travels*, pp. 7-8.

church was sometimes known in early documents as the Church of "the English and Scottish nation"; however, more frequently it was simply "the English Church,"[94] The English established a consistory, composed in 1623 of Henry Lodge and Vincent Johnson, elders, and Giles Langley and George Waters, deacons. Waters was well known as a printer of Puritan books. The English Reformed Church in the 1620s used the Gasthuis Church, later the Augustijn Church (forenoons) and the New Church (afternoons); and in 1635 the magistrates assigned them to an old warehouse in the Orphan Hospital, the former Molkenhuis or dairy house of the Mariënborn Klooster. The Merchant Adventurers met in the old Wine Street guild chapel (the Wijnkoopers Kapel). The orphanage chapel served the congregation until 1700, when the English Reformed Church and the Merchant Adventurers combined and used the Wine Street church building.[95]

The English Reformed congregation was small with 86 members in 1643, a high of 120 in the 1650s, and 78 in 1664. The church books record 75 baptisms 1629-60 (a total of 82 to 1700) and over one hundred marriages 1625-60 (a total of 120 to 1700).[96] These numbers were greatly swelled by military people who came to the Dort minister for marrying and baptizing without being part of the settled congregation. In 1642 the church could not supply a proper candidate for elder and asked for a man from the Dutch church as elder, "onley in the way of lending, untill the foresayd church be provided with fitt men of their owne nation."[97]

John Oswald, the first minister, a Scot, "did not perform well." He was inducted into his office by John Forbes, his father-in-law; and although he held the office of minister for two years, he was mostly absent in Scotland, leaving the congregation "as sheep without a shepheard." The outraged congregation made complaints to the English ambassador, the States of Holland, the city magistrates, and finally appealed to the English Synod for redress, but nothing came of it. In fact, the Synod even issued Oswald "a honorable testimoniall or Attestation." Meanwhile the church made do with various visiting preachers (Mr. Rush, Mr. Roystone, Mr. Palmer, Mr. Bachelor). Some of the chief members in

---

[94] J. L. van Dalen, *Geschiedenis van Dordrecht* (Dort: C. Morks, 1931-33), II, 799-801; Matthys Balen, *Beschryvinge der stad Dordrecht* (Dort, 1677), pp. 173-74; C.R., no. 5, fols. 1, 5, 8 (G.A. Dort).

[95] Van Dalen, *Dordrecht*, II, 799-800; C. J. P. Lips, *Wandelingen door Oud-Dordrecht* (Zaltbommel: Europese Bibliotheek, 1974), I, 51-52, 251-52.

[96] Membership book, no. 38, and baptism and marriage register, no. 42 (G.A. Dort); see also C.J. Wasch, "Het doopboek der Engelsche gemeente te Dordrecht van 1629-1811," *De Nederlandsche Leeuw*, 5 (1887), 104-06.

[97] C.R., no. 5, fol. 28; Acta Kerkeraad Dordrecht, no. 13, Oct. 23, 1642 (G.A. Dort).

exasperation transferred to the Dutch Reformed Church.[98] Succeeding ministers were: John Vincent (1625-35), Francis Dibbet (1635-37), Robert Paget (1638-83), and Samuel Megapolensis (1685-1700).

After they were finally rid of Oswald, who swindled some extra pay while leaving, they turned to John Vincent, an army chaplain and, according to Sir William Brereton, "a man of mean parts."[99] Vincent, usher of the Latin School as well as preacher, died in 1635. Next the church called Francis Dibbet (Dibbetius) from St. Anthonypolder, "a Dutchman which speaks English"; his assignment included a Dutch sermon on Sunday afternoon at the New Church. In 1637 Dibbet accepted a call to the Dutch church of Arnhem.[100] The most notable of the Dort ministers proved to be Robert Paget, who carried on a ministry of 45 years, 1638-83. Paget was a nephew of John Paget of Amsterdam; he was born in Leicestershire, educated at the University of Leiden, and thoroughly integrated into Dutch society, having friendly contact with important people, like Jacobus Borstius, the Dort preacher, and the de Witt family. He wrote Latin poetry and gained reputation as a good poet.[101]

Paget's roots were very deep in Dort, and although receiving calls to other churches, he would not move. The English church at Utrecht called him as minister in 1655, claiming the challenge of a large congregation and many young scholars from the university, but the magistrates refused to release him from Dort. "He cannot yet assure us of another Minister," they said. Members of the congregation pleaded against his leaving because of "the doubtfull and dangerous condition our Church which in case he did leave it might come to be broken or scattered."[102] In 1668 the English Church at Amsterdam urged him to come as their minister, but again he refused, citing his great satisfaction at Dort, "such tranquillity and contentment in the issue, that he was thereupon resolved for the future never to listen to any motions for a remoovall."[103] With his long tenure and reputation Paget became one of the patriarchs of English religion in the Netherlands.

The English church followed the general policies of the Dutch Reformed Church, so that Dort was free of the ecclesiastical controversies that disturbed English-Dutch church relations at Rotterdam, Amsterdam,

---

[98] C.R., no. 5, fols. 3, 5-7; on Oswald, see *F.E.S.*, VII, 543.
[99] Brereton, *Travels*, p. 13.
[100] C.R., no. 5, fol. 10; Acta Classis Dordrecht, VII, 104 (N.H.A.).
[101] *N.N.B.W.*, V, 419-20; Alice C. Carter, *The English Reformed Church in Amsterdam in the Seventeenth Century* (Amsterdam: Scheltema & Holkema, 1964), p. 25; Van Dalen, *Dordrecht*, II, 800. Several of Paget's letters are in the Goodyear Papers at Leiden.
[102] C.R., no. 5, fols. 92-97.
[103] Ibid., fol. 123.

and Delft. The pages of the consistory register record the customary Reformed British attention to discipline. Cases of slanders, witchcraft, drunkenness, wife beating, marital unfaithfulness, and non-attendance at church were some of the besetting sins of the congregation. As primarily a church of merchants and craftsmen, there was much concern for business ethics. Non-payment of lawful debts was punished by suspension from the communion table.[104] The elders approached their disciplinary work seriously and legalistically; they required fair rules of evidence and sufficient witnesses before punishment. While waiting for the discipline to take a moral effect, the offenders were suspended from the Lord's Table. For this reason the elders were thoroughly annoyed when a suspended offender was given church fellowship elsewhere, as in 1645 when suspended member Peter Clayton went over to Heusden's English church and received communion several times. The elders complained that Heusden encouraged his "offensive courses, to the prejudice of good order and Ecclesiasticall Discipline." Of the 120 names on the membership lists of 1643-56, 10 persons were suspended at one time or another for disciplinary reasons.[105]

The English ministers, especially Paget, accepted the Presbyterian system enthusiastically and administered the church with discipline and order. Paget was one of the editors of his uncle John Paget's Presbyterian treatise, *A Defence of Chvrch-Government* (1641). Independency, Robert said, was a great error, a pleading "for a meere Democracy." He believed Presbyterianism to be "the Church-government allowed by the word of God."[106] Nevertheless, the English church slid back and forth between being integrated into the Dutch Reformed system and having an independent existence. In 1633 the English applied to the Classis of Dort for membership, so that "in all incidents and difficulties they might address the classis." The classis replied by inviting the English minister to attend classis meetings "with an advisory voice and not more."[107] When Dibbet became minister in 1635, the classis closed the door and announced that the "English church shall no longer be a member of the meeting."[108] In 1641 the Synod of South Holland offered to assume a supervisory responsibility over the church, but the English declined, "that we should not yeeld that our Church should accept of such unequall motions." The English instead offered to join the classis on "equall termes." The English renewed their proposal for membership in

---

[104] Ibid., fols. 15-18, 67.
[105] Ibid., fols. 53, 62, 64-65; membership book, no. 38, fol. 48.
[106] Robert Paget, "The Publisher to the Christian Reader," in John Paget, *Defence of Chvrch-Governement, Exercised in Presbyteriall, Classicall, & Synodall Assemblies* (London, 1641).
[107] Acta Classis Dortrecht, VII, 85v.
[108] Ibid., fol. 104.

the Classis of Dort in 1645, hoping thereby to strengthen their system of discipline. The consistory attempted to keep the congregation in good discipline, but frequently their members slighted their authority or complained of ill treatment. With the entire Dutch church to back them up, "all occasion of such complaint should ere long be taken away." As Paget and the elders reasoned it, having classis membership "we might have a readier and surer way for the ending of all differences and judging of such causes as cannot so easily or conveniently be judged by ourselves." Disciplined members would be awed and "we may the better stop their mouthes." "If need be," the elders thought, they could "proceed the more resolutely unto heavier censures against offendours."[109]

Paget with his Dutch education and experience in Dutch Reformed religion was very willing to have membership in the classis. The English and Dutch churches in 1645 finally negotiated an agreement of nine articles which set forth the conditions of English membership: (1) That the English church submit to the order of the Synod of South Holland; (2) that they regulate themselves according to the laws of the Classis of Dort; (3) that the English preacher pay widow money and all other classis expenses; (4) that the English church should be visited by the regular classis visitors; (5) that no elders of the English church would attend classis meetings; (6) that the calling and examination of English ministers be done with the approval of the classis; (7) that the English enjoy all privileges of classis membership including vote, classical committees, and widow's money; (8) that this membership be approved by the magistrates; (9) that the classis should have liberty to remove the English church without giving reasons. The English consistory, concerned that they join on an equal basis with other churches, added two clauses of their own to the contract: That the English church retain the liberty to withdraw when "they see fit cause, without being accountable to the Classis," and that they never be dismissed from the classis without permission of the magistrates. After negotiations, Paget in April 1646 took session with the classis.[110] This set the pattern for the next fifty years, one of the most genial arrangements enjoyed by any of the English churches. Even then the English felt slighted in some classis activities. In 1703, the English reversed themselves and voted "to separate our selves" because their minister was not allowed a decisive vote and other prerogatives of membership "which our minister had often desired."[111] In 1816, at the general reorganization of the churches, the English church was once again put into the classis.

---

[109] C.R., no. 5, fols. 23-24, 39, 46-47.
[110] Ibid., fols. 50-52; Acta Classis Dordrecht, VIII, 57, 64-65.
[111] Ibid., fol. 199.

CHAPTER SEVEN

THE CHURCHES IN ZEELAND: MIDDELBURG, FLUSHING, AND VEERE TO 1660

English and Scottish settlements in Zeeland had deep roots. The Brownist and Merchant Adventurer churches in Middelburg, going back to 1581-82, and the Flushing garrison church of 1586 were the oldest English churches established in the United Provinces. The Zeeland cities carried on a vigorous trade with England and Scotland, and British passengers in many cases made Flushing and Middelburg, hardly more than a mile or two apart, their first stops in the Low Countries. From there, the extremely sharp-eyed Fynes Moryson claimed, "you could see ... in a cleere day, the Downes of Kent in England." He labelled Middelburg "the chiefe place of trafficke in *Zealand*, as *Amsterdam* in *Holland.*"[1] A thriving seventeenth century city, Middelburg impressed visitors as "large, well built, having spacious streets, populous, full of wealthy merchants, and well fortified." Foreign merchants congregated in Middelburg because of its superb commercial situation; the Hanse merchants and the English Merchant Adventurers came, while the Scottish merchants settled nearby at Veere.[2] The Merchant Adventurers were at Middelburg 1582-1621. During this time they had their chapel in the Gasthuis Church. The Brownist church faded away in the middle 1580s.

The English House on Lange Delft, headquarters of the Adventurers, was the center of English activity, not only of the members but also of visiting "English Gentlemen both to lodge & eat there."[3] During the seventeenth century, as Amsterdam and Rotterdam flourished, Middelburg declined relatively in its standing among commercial cities. This decline prompted the Merchant Adventurers to pull out and go to Delft. The merchants made four arguments for removing from Middelburg: (1) Middelburg was on the uttermost part of the United Provinces, away from other places of trade; (2) the competition of the interlopers in Holland; (3) the lack of commodities for return traffic for otherwise empty ships; and (4) Middelburg was a "verie unhealthfull place, which is

---

[1] Fynes Moryson, *An Itinerary written by Fynes Moryson Gent.* (London, 1617), pt. I, 50.
[2] John Ray, *Travels through the Low-Countries, Germany, Italy and France*, 2nd ed. (London, 1738), I, 19; W. S. Unger, *Geschiedenis van Middelburg im omtrek*, 2nd ed. (Middelburg: Zeeuwsch Genootschap der Wetenschappen, 1966), pp. 42-43.
[3] Moryson, *Itinerary*, pt. I, 50.

the cause that wee can by no meanes get men of age and quallitie to furnish the goverment of our Company," leaving too many young and disorderly men to carry on company business.⁴ The removal of the Merchant Adventurers diminished the trade of the city, certainly regarding England, and James Howell found the city "much crest-falen since the Staple of *English* cloth was removed hence." With the English Adventurers gone, the magistrates turned the Gasthuis Church over to the use of the Dutch Reformed Church.⁵

Not long after the Merchant Adventurers had moved out, an English Church was re-established in 1623 for the benefit of the continuing English-Scottish population. After receiving petitions, the magistrates voted to sponsor an official English Reformed Church, which would meet in a part of the old English House, being used in 1623 as a sugar refinery. In 1629 the magistrates transferred the English to the church building of the Cellite or Alexian Brothers (de Kappel van het Cellebroeders Klooster), thereafter known as the Engelse Kerk.⁶ The English and Scots were not a large group, only about "threescore," and the magistrates gave them no money subsidy at first beyond the use of the building.⁷ The founding members issued a call to minister Samuel Bachelor of Heusden, but he refused. Their second choice was John Drake, who was recommended to them by Dr. William Ames of Franeker University. Drake was inducted as minister September 3, 1623, simultaneously with the election of elders and deacons and adoption of a covenant; thus they "did imbody themselves into a Christian Society." The church counted its "direct beginning" from September 3, 1623, when they established their minister and subscribed to the covenant.⁸ After Drake, who served 1623-42, the following seventeenth-century ministers pastored the church: Petrus Gribius (1642-52) and while he was absent, Johannes Teellinck (1646-47) and John Skase (1648); William Spang (1652-64); David Anderson (1664-66); Joseph Hill (1667-73); Nicolas Shepheard

---

⁴ S.P. 84, vol. 83, fols. 31-32 (document of 1618).

⁵ James Howell, *Epistolae Ho-Elianae. Familiar Letters Domestic and Forren*, 2nd ed. (London, 1650), II, 17; *Naamlyst der predikanten, ouderlingen en diakenen* (Middelburg, 1770), p. 3, no. 32, archive of Middelburg E.R.C. (R.A. Zeeland). Howell's letter was dated 1619; however his dates are untrustworthy and the condition he describes was post-1621. Moreover, the Middelburg Adventurers had been in crisis since the Cockayne Project of 1614.

⁶ *Naamlyst*, p. 4. On the Middelburg church, W. S. Unger, "De voormalige Engelsche kerk te Middelburg," *Buiten*, 17 (May 5, 1923), 213-14.

⁷ John Quick, "Icones Sacrae Anglicanae," (MS, D.W.L.), I, i, 253-54; *Naamlyst*, p. 5.

⁸ C.R., I, 1 and 21; Quick, "Icones," I, i, 253-54; *Naamlyst*, p. 5. Drake may have been one of Ames's students at Franeker. His background is obscure, being reported variously as a native of Buckinghamshire and Devonshire; see Quick's life of Drake in "Icones," I, i, 249-77.

(1674-79); John Quick (1680-81); William Spang Junior (1682-83); Robert Tory (1683-91); John Leask (1692-97); and Cornelius Coorne (1698-1724).

For the first eight years, the English congregation raised all of its own funds, apart from having the building provided, from voluntary collections. They paid 300 guilders ministerial salary, although sometimes it was "extremely delayed." In 1631, "as the church fell behind because of the dying and leaving of many members," the Middelburg magistrates began making yearly cash contributions for support "by reason our congregation demyneshith and that people ar nott so well able to pay as formerly." This brought the jointly supported salary to 600 guilders.[9] In 1641 the English Church appealed to the States of Zeeland for additional support, which was granted, bringing the combined stipend up to 1000 guilders. Gradually the States increased their support until in 1659 the English churches at Middelburg and Flushing received "regular and ordinary salary" as enjoyed by the Dutch ministers.[10] As the city and province took over the financial burden of the church, the English elders decided in 1644 to buy a house in the Lange Geere as a parsonage, and which they sold again in 1667 over the great objections of minister Joseph Hill—"sacrilegious alienation," he complained.[11]

Although one of the longest-lived British churches in the Low Countries (to 1921), the Middelburg church was never a large church. In the 1630s the church complained of financial weakness because of members leaving and dying, and the remainder "having poor trades, such that they can bring nothing or very little to the maintenance of a minister."[12] In 1642 the church had 47 members and then grew in 1652 to 84 members and to 105 members in 1664 (the high point of membership). In 1692, at John Leask's coming, the church had dropped back to 41 members. The church had 185 baptisms 1624-1660 (a total of 258 to 1700) and 147 marriages 1624-1660.[13]

The church, although known as the English Church, always had a mixture of English and Scots. William Spang, the first Scottish minister of the church, 1652-64, began calling it a "British Church" and even the "Scottish Church" because, he explained, the church "is equally con-

---

[9] Deacons' Account Book, no. 41, Jan.-Feb. 1632; *Naamlyst*, pp. 5-6; C.R., I, 58.

[10] *Naamlyst*, p. 6; C.R., I, 99; II, 202; *Notulen van Staten van Zeeland* (1641), p. 403; (1659), p. 123 (printed annual volumes, R.A. Zeeland).

[11] *Naamlyst*, p. 6; Quick, "Icones," I, i, 268.

[12] Petition to Magistrates of Middelburg (1635), in C.R., I, 71.

[13] Marriage, baptism, and membership register, no. 27; C.R., I, end of book. The number of marriages 1661-1700 was very high (252), far beyond usual for this size congregation; 196 of these came during the 1690s.

sisting of English and Scots."[14] This Scottish aggressiveness brought out some ill will from the English side of the congregation who detected favoritism towards Scots and prejudice against the English tradition of the church. They said, it is "a most uncontestable Truth, that the church originally was purely English."[15]

A distinctive feature of the English church was its foundation on the basis of a written covenant. John Drake, under the influence of William Ames, was a covenant enthusiast, and his ordination on September 3, 1623, was combined with adoption of the covenant. The covenant reads as follows:

> We and everyone of us, doe, in the sighte of God, and before all men, from the very heart and conscience testifye and professe that, in the sense of our most wofull case in our selves both by the very guiltinesse of our first parents sin lying on us, and by reason thereuppon of our owne corrupt nature fear our birth and our sinfull lives ever since, we are wholly to seek for salvation unto the Lorde Jesus Christe and through him alone, by fayth in him according to the Scriptures, (there being no help for us ever to be saved els without the truthe of this faith) and so to give up our selves in our hearts and lives for ever to be his, to have them ruled and working onely accordding to his will reveiled in the scriptures. Therefore doe we here binde our selves to all these premises and what ever of rights belongeth thereto; and doe accordingly professe eache of us personally, as for the aforsayd, so farther thus: I do in my heart and conscience receive the whole divinely inspired scripture of the Olde and New Testament to be guided in all things fully thereby, and to yeald willingly unto any truthe shall be soundly shewed me foorth of the same by any whomsoever. Unto which end, for my full help in learning the sayd word of God and framing my whole life thereafter, I joyne now a member to the bodie of this churche and submit my self, according to the scripture and any sound reason to be shewed me from the same, unto all the communion, oversight and government of this sayd churche in admonitions, censures, and whatsoever doth by the same rule belong to the good order of a churche.[16]

This is the oldest non-Separatist English covenant in the Netherlands, except for the rejected Francis Johnson covenant of 1591 at the Merchant Adventurer's Church in this same city of Middelburg.[17] The English

---

[14] C.R., I, 91, 197.
[15] Quick, "Icones," I, i, 271.
[16] C.R., I, 1r and v.
[17] See above, chapter 2.

Reformed congregation in its early years gave high esteem to the covenant as the basic foundation "in setting a righte beginning, to give patterne ... and a help for best building up of the church." They instituted the covenant at "the gathering" of the church "and were accordingly willing to professe the same at any good occasion."[18] In 1624 at the first anniversary of the ordination and covenant, they celebrated "a yeare beeing now past since our churches first settled beginning." The year 1623 "allso was especially the first open and evident making a covenant with the Lorde by our church: such covenant still beeing the chief ground thereoff."[19] According to John Quick's researches, "it was by the advice of our famous *Dr. Ames* that this church founded itself upon this particular covenant."[20]

Among the controverted points of theology in the English churches of the Low Countries (membership, baptism, and congregational decision-making) the Middelburg church inclined toward the Ames-Hooker-Davenport side. Drake as minister was "by joynt suffrages elect" and elections for elders and deacons were decided by male members in congregational meetings by "billes of choyse" or "plurality of voyces."[21] Drake, a Puritan, was also scrupulous to baptise only infants of members of the congregation, or at least one parent being a member; and very few exceptions were made. In 1634 three children of non-members were baptized by only after careful examination, "uppon very earnest motions, and promise of great care in using the churche."[22] Drake was a member of the English Synod.

The Middelburg church was a strong example of the Puritan, Reformed worship and church life practiced among the British churches in the Netherlands. Drake was known as a diligent preacher and disciplinarian, "very taking and edifying," and was commended by one of his successors, Joseph Hill, as "a very Reverend and worthy Person, and a mute pattern to be followed by all his successors."[23] At first, Drake spent many hours "through all the towne" rounding up the scattered English residents of Middelburg, "there being divers of them came not so muche as to churche." Drake exhorted them "of their dutye."[24] Drake and the succeeding ministers carefully guarded admission to the Lord's Table. Before the communion, held every eight weeks, minister and elders

---

[18] C.R., I, 1r and v.
[19] C.R., I, 21.
[20] Quick, "Icones," I, i, 258.
[21] Ibid., p. 254; C.R., I, 29 (1626), I, 75 (1637).
[22] C.R., I, 69.
[23] Quick, "Icones," I, i, 261-62.
[24] C.R., I, 22-23.

followed the Dutch examples of a house to house visitation of members to examine and exhort. John Quick found the visitation duties taxing almost beyond his strength. "This work would take me up full three days from Morning to Evening: So that when I have returned to my Lodgings, I have not been able, as we say, to move a foot, being quite spent and tyred with the fatique of my walks and visits." Before communion, the church issued tokens to members in good standing which served for admission. Without a token, no one was admitted.[25]

In discipline the English church held to high standards, more severe than the Middelburg Dutch church. The English church required public confessions from sinners. In one case, a fornicator, who brought scandal "to the shame, as it must needs be, of us all," was required to make a public congregational confession in spite of pleas that in discipline the English demanded more than the Dutch church. The offender thought the Dutch practice of private confession before the eldership much preferable, but the English elders insisted on stricter standards of public confession. "Answer was made, that though the Dutch Churche of this city might have good reesen for such their lesse publique course..., Why then doe we not rather follow the generall example of all reformed Churches in all Countries.... Why not of the English churches comonly throughout all these dominions here?" All the English churches here—including the Flushing church and the Merchant Adventurers when at Middelburg—"all which generally, I say every where doe (as they ought) require this publique presence of the offendour." As one concession, however, the elders ordinarily did not record in the register the name of the offender being dealt with, for "we finde no need to sett downe his name in writing here."[26]

As the only English institution in Middelburg, the church took responsibility for upholding the reputation of the English community, both morally and economically. The sin of one might be regarded as the sin of all, "much spoken of to the reproche of our churche," perhaps even, "a special judgment of God upon this church." Debtors and bankrupts, considered as blights upon the honesty of the church, were counselled spiritually and on financial management, then dropped from the Lord's Table until they had settled their affairs.[27] The consistory also kept a little store of money for poor relief gathered by collections and doled this out to

---

[25] Quick, I, ii, 787; C.R., I, 52. "Avondmaalloodjes bij de Engelsche gemeente te Middelburg," *Jaarboek Muntk.* 13 (1925), 103-04.

[26] C.R., I, 34-36 (June 13, 1626); his confession, as given to the congregation, is recorded on fols. 39-40. Later, the elders relented in some cases and allowed a private confession in the consistory, thus acting "in mildnesse unto adification & not unto destruction" (C.R., I, 111, Dec. 23, 1643).

[27] C.R., I, 50 (1629); I, 62 (1632); I, 111 (1643).

needy members, and sometimes to indigent travelers. When poor funds ran short (minister's and reader's stipends were in hard times drawn out from the fund), strangers were excluded and sent to the Dutch for relief. By the consistory rules of 1643, "noe pensioner shall be taken on but those that are members of the church, neither without advice of the church councle duely assembled." The elders, with business-like efficiency, in 1658 refused membership to a begger woman on suspicion that "the chef end of her desyr to be admitted, was thereby to get the church engadged to a weekly contribution." They offered passage back to England to get her out of the way and admonition "to leave of that shameful course of making a trade of begging from door to door." After being refused, she carried on "so passionatly and undiscretly," thought the elders, "that she deserved reproof."[28]

When Drake died in 1642, he was succeeded by Petrus Gribius (1642-52), *gente Germanus*, who transferred from the Dutch church at Oost Duiveland. Gribius was married to a daughter of Willem Teellinck, which gave him good credentials with Puritans. He had studied in England, where he met John Cotton, and earlier with William Ames at Franeker. Cotton referred to him as "a German who lived some time here with us" in England. Gribius in 1645 translated the Dutch liturgy into English "such English as it is," but the Middelburg people did not appreciate his worship liturgies, "nor indeed at that time could they endure the usage of them." From 1646 to 1648, Gribius was on leave to the West India Company in Brazil; and during his absence two young ministers served, Johannes Teellinck, his brother-in-law, one-time minister of the Dutch church at Maidstone, and John Skase, a ministerial proponent recently examined by the Classis of Walcheren. After Brazil, Gribius returned to the church until 1652, when he was called to the German church at Amsterdam.[29] William Spang, minister 1652-1664, formerly of Veere, was the first Scottish minister and "a most zealous champion of Presbytery."[30]

Middelburg's English church followed an independent, self-governing course for the first twenty years of its existence, being "itself independent from the Dutch classis of Walcheren," with little supervision attempted by magistrates or Dutch Reformed Church.[31] Although a member of the English Synod, Drake had congenial relations with the Dutch Reformed

---

[28] C.R., I, 113 (1644); I, 105; I, 201 (1658).
[29] *Naamlyst*, pp. 6-8; Quick, "Icones," I, i, 270; B.P., I, 168; D. Plooij, *The Pilgrim Fathers from a Dutch Point of View* (New York: New York Univ. Press, 1932), p. 86; Franeker Univ. *Album*, p. 74.
[30] *Naamlyst*, p. 8; Quick, "Icones," I, i, 271; F.E.S., VII, 547-48.
[31] Quick, "Icones," I, i, 268.

ministers of Middelburg. Moreover, the Zeeland churches had a long tradition of contacts with the Puritan movement in England. Of the Dutch Middelburg and Flushing ministers, Willem Teellinck, married to an English woman, and his sons Maximiliaan and Johannes Teellinck, and later Johannes Thilenus, all had long associations with England. As Middelburg minister, Willem Teellinck generously supported the establishment of the English church, "whereof he was a chief procurer at the first." His sons, Johannes and Maximiliaan, and his son-in-law Gribius were all at some time ministers of English churches in the Netherlands.[32] Puritans often looked to the Zeelanders as the most fervent people of Dutch religion—almost the Dutch equivalent of the Puritans—for which reason William Ames dedicated his *Cases of Conscience* to the States of Zeeland: "It is reported over all places neere hand, that the Doctrine according to Godlinesse, is both more Practically Preached by the Pastors, and more put in practise by the Hearers in your Churches, then yet hath been marked in many others, though they hold the same Doctrine. That worthy Servant of the Lord, Master William Teeling, who was by this meanes in great admiration, and famous throughout all the Low-Countrey Churches ... tooke such painfull paines this way, both publikely and privately, by word and writing, that it may be truely said, The zeale of Gods house hath eaten him up."[33]

At the time of John Quick's pastorate in 1680-81, he found sweet spiritual communion with six of the stricter Middelburg ministers (six out of twelve), "who were strict Puritans, and my particular friends, who loved me as if I had been their naturall Brother." His most intimate confidant was minister Johannes Thilenus, a loving and generous spirit, far different from "that of the generallity of the Nether dutch Ministers, who were of a more narrow and meaner spirit, more closed and reserved in conservation." How could this be, Quick would ask, and Thilenus would always reply: "My deare *Brother*, I am no Dutchman, I am an Englishman borne." Since Thilenus had, in fact, been born in London when his father was minister at the Austin Friars church, Quick adopted him as an English brother and included him in his "Icones Sacrae Anglicanae," the only foreigner so honored.[34] In theological doctrines, the Zeeland and English ministers were agreed. The greatest friction between the two churches came when the English, lacking suitable candidates for elders, would sometimes elect Dutch members, without prior

---

[32] C.R., I, 47; on Willem, Johannes, and Maximiliaan Teellinck, see *N.N.B.W.* and Willem J. M. Engelberts, *Willem Teellinck* (Amsterdam: Scheffer, 1898).

[33] William Ames, *Conscience with the Power and Cases Thereof* (n.p., 1639), Dedication "To the Illustrious and Mightie Lords, the States of Zeland."

[34] Quick, "Icones," I, ii, 775-80.

arrangements, to serve in their eldership (1625, 1627, 1631, 1644). The English referred to this as election "by way of borrowing;" the Dutch, if not consulted beforehand, felt slighted and complained "not very kindely, nor in the friendeliest manner."[35]

As the city and provincial magistrates began providing subsidy to the English church in the 1630s and 1640s, the cords of governmental control were fastened on. When Gribius was elected minister in 1642 (80% of his salary being provided by city and province), the church followed the usual Zeeland procedure of calling in the magistrates to form a *Collegium Qualificatum*, a distinctive Zeeland committee composed of magistrates and church officials which acted on ministerial elections. The magistrates promised the English they would continuee the stipend "providing they receyve content in the person who should be called."[36] After receiving repeated English petitions for subsidy, the States in 1645 approved a new subsidy but on condition that the English churches of Middelburg and Flushing "being of no ecclesiastical conference, should be brought under the Classis of Walcheren," in conformity with the practice of English churches in Holland and to prevent all disorder and confusion.[37] This was a condition for receiving 400 guilders a year, and the English elders quickly perceived the proposed order to be "according to Gods ordinance, and without doubt would prove manie wayes beneficiall and comfortable." They made immediate application for classis membership. Gribius and John Roe of Flushing attented the next classis meeting and appealed for English membership, citing the "great difficulties and calamities which they sometimes were aware of because they were independent and under no classis and synod." Both churches in September, 1645 were admitted as members.[38] The Scottish church at Veere joined the Classis of Walcheren in 1669; its conditions for admittance were that the church never acknowledge the English bishops or the episcopalian government.[39]

Classis membership brought the English churches of Zeeland greater ecclesiastical respectability and gave them access to financial support. As members of the classis, the Middelburg and Flushing churches applied to the States for support "like the Dutch, since they were now members of the classis," and by 1659 they were brought up to the ordinary ministerial stipend allotted in Zeeland.[40] Gribius and his immediate suc-

---

[35] C.R., I, 42; I, 114.
[36] C.R., I, 92.
[37] *Notulen* van Staten van Zeeland (1645), pp. 280, 328-29.
[38] C.R., I, 127 (Aug. 8, 1645); Acta Classis Walcheren, III, 95-96.
[39] Acta Classis Walcheren, V, 142.
[40] *Notulen* van Staten van Zeeland (1649), p. 184; (1659), p. 123; Flushing C.R., no. 4469, June 28, 1651 (G.A. Flushing).

cessor, Spang, a Scottish Presbyterian, had no hesitations in accepting the overlordship of magistrates and classis. They were grateful for the greater stability achieved.[41] One of the later ministers, however, John Quick greatly lamented the 1645 decision to join the classis as being "many ways prejudiciall to the succeeding Pastors." "Besides it hath given the Classis a Negative upon the very Acts of the English Consistory in their Election of a Pastor." Although Presbyterianism was one issue at stake, Quick thought the more serious issue to be the church-state matter. "Erastianism was the trump card at Middelburg, the Lords haveing ingrossed all Church-power into their own hands." Quick was reputed to be a Presbyterian in England, but in Middelburg he acted like a Congregationalist.[42]

In 1655 Middelburg and Flushing received a visitation of Quaker missionaries from England. John Stubbs and William Caton "went a shoare in the name & power of the Lord" and immediately "sounded the word of the Lord vp one street, & downe another." Van Laren at Flushing pleaded with them to stay away from the English church, but they could not be silent. At the church, according to Stubbs, they stood forth as "signes and wonders." Then "after all was ended the one of vs begun to speake, but the priest said Sirrah you should haue put of your hatt, and came running hastily downe without his hatt or gloues to preuent vs. Soe his example to the people did the more stirr them vp in soe much that they did violently fall vpon vs after the same manner that hath been often practized in England. The first that had hand of vs was a man of Douer in England, for he knew vs, & said he had enough of vs, and he with some others (but especially the Scotts) did offer much abuse to vs by haylinge of vs: but the Lord stirred vp some to restrayne the ruder sort, whose intent was exceeding bloody towards vs...." At Middelburg, having been forewarned, Spang preached against them and declared "that it was in the magistrates power to apprehend vs, and not only soe, but also to put vs to death, and brought seuerall scriptures to proue it, as Nebucadnezers example." In spite of such omens the two prophets attended the services at Middelburg and "the one of vs stood vp to speake the word of the Lord which is contrary to the will of man." Their boldness caused Spang and others to be "so much the more against us, and some especially were very violent against us, and did beat me much." After a few days of witnessing, "we left them in great heat and rage, and that night took Shipping for the City called Rotterdam."[43]

---

[41] Quick, "Icones," I, i, 271.

[42] Ibid., pp. 270-71; C. G. Bolam, et al., *The English Presbyterians: From Elizabethan Puritanism to Modern Unitarianism* (London: George Allen & Unwin, 1968), p. 85.

[43] William I. Hull, *The Rise of Quakerism in Amsterdam 1655-1665* (Swarthmore: Swarth-

Shaken at the Quaker commotion, the English eldership of Middelburg resolved to censure a few members who had given audience to the "two disturbers" and they voted thanks to the minister and elder Dickenson "for their care in hindering thes two quakers from trubling the congregation upon sunday." The elders further asked help of the magistrates, who agreed "that we wold not only hinder such inordinat intruders but also acquaint the magistrates with it."[44] In 1657 Christopher Birkhead, another Quaker, received heavy sentence for interrupting Spang in the midst of his sermon. The magistrates punished him with two years of hard labor in the *rasphuis*.[45]

Flushing

Flushing was a major port, like Rotterdam and Brielle, for English travelers entering into the Netherlands. The cross-channel trip to Flushing was the shortest across. Trade and military location made the city "very considerable for its strength and riches" although less impressive than Middelburg, the capital city of the province.[46] Flushing depended on the sea for livelihood; navigation and trade, as well as less honorable callings, were the lifeblood of the city. William Steven of Rotterdam in his day reputed it as a place "notorious for the smuggling propensities of some of its inhabitants."[47] Flushing in 1572 had been one of the first Dutch cities to rise in revolt against Spain, a historical mark which the city treasured. Thereafter at Flushing they commemorated their "delivery from Spanish tyranny, which was stopped here on the 6th of April, 1572, when the citizens unassisted and unsupported by any foreign power, drove out the Walloons, opened their gates, and laid the corner stone of that singular and always remarkable revolution, which placed seven small provinces in a state of independency."[48]

When England entered the war on the side of the Dutch, Flushing in 1585 was handed over to the English as a cautionary town, garrisoned by English soldiers, and supported by Dutch funds. As the victory was won, the Zeelanders came to resent this foreign overlordship, so that Sir John Throckmorton, lieutenant-governor of Flushing, in 1616 complained that "these people of Zealand openly grumble and grudge us the money

---

more College Monographs on Quaker History, no. 2, 1938), pp. 103-08. Stubbs and Caton in their journals did not mention the ministers by name; they may be inferred by the dates.

[44] C.R., I, 183-84 (Sept. 22, 29, 1655); I, 184-85 (Oct. 10, 1655).
[45] Hull, *Rise of Quakerism*, p. 178.
[46] Moryson, *Itinerary*, I, 50; Ray, *Travels*, I, 19.
[47] Steven, p. 302.
[48] Bicentennial service by Justus Tjeenk, minister of the English church, April 5, 1772, quoted by Steven, p. 304.

that they provide for our maintenance."[49] The English garrisoning of Flushing ended in 1616 with the return of all the cautionary towns to the Dutch.

As long as the English soldiers held the town, 1585-1616, they maintained an active garrison church in their own building, the Engelsche Kerk. The longest-established minister was Thomas Potts (chaplain 1605-16), entertained with a stipend of £120 a year.[50] Potts was a "vehement" Puritan with a dynamic preaching style popular with the soldiers. He often took the side of the common soldiers in disputes with the officers, who came to resent his interference as a "factious partisan."[51] In 1614 Potts interceded for the sergeant major, who was under discipline for brawling. "The Sunday after this disorder was committed, the Sergeant Major sent for Mr. Pott our minister and told him that only the grace of God had withheld him from murdering three men." Said Potts, "Why then you weare drunk." "Noe," answered the soldier, "I was not, but I think I was mad." The commanding officer warned against interfering, "that herein I oppose myself to him and to the whole garrison."[52]

Potts also had a long-standing debate with the governor and officers about the "soldier's oath," by which recruits were entered on the muster roll week by week for extra watching and warding, service not performed, and for which the captains collected pay for the bogus names.[53] Lieutenant-governor Throckmorton reported to Lord L'Isle that Potts was continually preaching to the men about the oath and dishonest payrolls: "He presseth all men, that take that oath, with perjury who do not receive their full pay and perform their actual duties in watching and warding accordingly. His bitterness is extreme in this point, yea in the pulpit itself." Potts preached that these practices were mortal sins and a great cheating of the common soldier. "Whether it be not a wrong to a poor soldier, who hath charge of wife and children, to deny him liberty to help himself by working on his free days?" he asked. Potts reported a death room scene, where "I could lately give a souldier of the garrison no comfort in this case on his death bed, but upon his faith and repentance,

---

[49] H.M.C., *De L'Isle and Dudley MSS.*, V, 385.

[50] Ibid., V, 339. Potts's background before Flushing is obscure. Quick referred to Thomas and his brother Lawrence, one-time minister to the Merchant Adventurers at Middelburg, as exiled ministers from the diocese of Norwich, younger brothers from a "gentle" family of Norfolk, "Icones," I, i, 251-53. Other reports make them natives of Cheshire; see also Venn and Venn, III, 384, 386. Thomas Potts was betrothed at Flushing in 1610, Steven, p. 301.

[51] *De L'Isle and Dudley MSS.*, III, 173, 442; V, 202.

[52] Ibid., V, 194, 190.

[53] Ibid., IV, 312-14.

he promiseing to leave off this bad practice if he might live, but he dyed."⁵⁴

When preaching failed, Potts threatened to debar offenders from the Lord's Table. A new suit of clothes given by the captains of the garrison "to gratify him with" did not sweeten the situation. "I protest, my lord, I knowe not what to saye unto him," wrote Throckmorton, and he longed for some quiet complacent chaplain, "wourthey precheres that observed the government, and weare not inquisidours after bussines that did not conserne thire vocacion." Under such preaching as Potts gave them, the captains claimed they were "not edified by him," and for a time in 1616 they actually withdrew from the communion table.⁵⁵ All the same, Potts's preaching hit its mark and Throckmorton proposed some revision in the garrison rules, "For, in trewthe, it is to hevie a burthen for me to beare to heare the preacher perpeteually to rake them upp and to laye the suffering of these abuses upon my concyence, the which how trewe or howe untrewe soever, yet the common man and the strainger whoe maye heare it dothe beleave it to be soe because the preacher speaketh it and preacheth against it."⁵⁶

In the garrison church, the less sharp the preaching, the better. The best chaplain, according to the officers, was a bland, non-political fellow who did not excite the troops. By this standard, Potts was overly powerful and painful, "too collorick and fierye to be a preacher, especyalle to men of armes, yeet trewly sumtimes he will speake well, and perhaps he willbe a fytter man for some other auditorye then is ours."⁵⁷ In 1608, in Potts's absence, the Flushing people recruited the occasional services of two Scottish ministers, John Forbes and Robert Dury. They also preached at the Merchant Adventurer church at Middelburg. Respectable English and Scottish ministers were scarce in the Low Countries, and these able ministers were a godsend, much superior to the usual ministerial failures drifting about overseas. Although the garrison officers claimed ignorance "that they were banished by our King's command out of Scotland," Forbes and Dury, in fact, were exiles under sentence of perpetual banishment for associating with the forbidden Assembly of Aberdeen in 1605. When news of their being at the garrison reached England, swift was the explosion. The king sent thundering orders that Forbes and Dury "be some unruly Scottish ministers who were banished" and that His Majesty was "unwilling that any of his good subjects should be instructed with their poisoned doctrine," least of all the soldiers. The unhappy

---

⁵⁴ Ibid., IV, 312-13; V, 361.
⁵⁵ Ibid., IV, 288, 316; V, 323, 338, 381-85.
⁵⁶ Ibid., V, 382 (Jan. 1616).
⁵⁷ Ibid., V, 340.

lieutenant-governor, Sir William Browne, had great embarrassment in explaining how such traitors could have been received, even though, it was said, they had preached only about four sermons and very uncontroversial ones. "Neither never did I ever hear a man [Dury] with more zeal so particularly pray for his Majesty, the Queen, the Prince and all the royal issue." Browne also admitted that he had requested Dury "for this one time" to baptize his baby boy, even knowing Dury to be a convicted traitor, rather than having "hazarded him to be kept unchristened"—it was either Dury or no one at all.[58]

With the departure of the garrison in 1616 the English church ceased as an officially recognized church with paid minister and building. Potts petitioned the States of Zeeland to continue as English minister at Flushing, but the request was denied. The States, however, did vote him a one-time grant of 500 guilders "for his good service." The Dutch church took the occasion to annex the "Engelsche Kerk" building totally to its own use.[59] For a space of four years, 1616 to 1620, the church was allowed to lapse although some preaching continued. Potts in 1617 accepted a call to Amsterdam as assistant to John Paget. Ludovicus de Dieu, one of the Dutch ministers of Flushing, occasionally preached to the remaining English settlers.[60] The English government in its negotiations with the Dutch government had specified that at Flushing and Brielle "many of his Majesty's subjectes have long lived in these townes, and there have planted themselves and their familyes," some to remain. Between 1598 and 1625 at least ten English and Scots became citizens (poorter) of Flushing.[61]

The English-Scottish remainder hoped to see a church re-established. In 1619 they petitioned for a church, claiming "in number above 112 housholderes." Altogether 126 householders supported the petition. Such a church would be beneficial to inhabitants and "also to many passengers lying often a long time wind-bound in that towne." The petitions and letters spoke of a church "for the good of that poore people at Vlushing, who be destitute of the foode of their soules." Briefly one impediment raised itself, "the old emulation between Middleborrow and Vlushing," but without waiting for provincial stipend the Flushing magistrates gave approval for the church.[62] The city of Flushing provided the church building, but at the first, as at Middelburg, the congregation

---

[58] Ibid., IV, 23-25 (June 2, 1608); H.M.C., *Salisbury MSS.*, XX, 184.

[59] *Notulen van Staten van Zeeland* (1616), p. 208; H. G. van Grol, "Iets van de oudste geschiedenis der Engelsche Kerk te Vlissingen," Bijlage, *Jaarverslagen betreffende het archiefwezen en de oudheidkundige verzameling der Gemeente Vlissingen* (1913), pp. 10-11.

[60] *B.W.P.G.N.*, II, 496.

[61] P.C. *Acts* (1515-16), pp. 541-42; poorter list, no. 5010 (G.A. Flushing).

[62] S.P. 84, vol. 88, fols. 225-26; vol. 89, fol. 172; vol. 90, fol. 81.

raised the remainder of its own support. On June 19, 1620, John Wing was ordained as minister of "this renewed English Church" with assistance from John Paget of Amsterdam, Willem Teellinck of Middelburg, who preached the ordination sermon, and other Dutch ministers and magistrates. A consistory was established with George Browne and Henry Corker, elders, and Philip Baker and John Basset, deacons.[63]

Although the Engelsche Kerk building had been assigned to the Dutch church, the magistrates gave the new English congregation some shared use of the building, and about 1637 the congregation moved into a chapel of the Groote Kerk (St. Jacob's Church). The English church continued in the same place until 1911, when a ruinous fire destroyed the building, and entirely ceased in 1921.[64] For a time, the English church also maintained a school for their children.[65] The church received some occasional subsidies from the Flushing magistrates and in the 1640s began receiving funds from the States of Zeeland. In 1651 Reverend Van Laren got the Flushing ministerial "full stipend" and in 1659 the States took over and "al was brought upon the land."[66] Following John Wing (1620-27), other seventeenth-century ministers were: Maximiliaan Teellinck (1627-28); John Roe (1628-45); Thomas Potts Junior (1645-51); Arnold van Laren (1651-76); Samuel Megapolensis (1677-85); Hugo Fitts (1689-1700).

The first minister, John Wing, was formerly chaplain to the Merchant Adventurers at Hamburg, and one time a minister at Sandwich. He considered himself a scholar and while at Flushing published five books of sermons, *The Crowne Conjugall* (1620), *Jacobs Staffe* (1621), *Abels Offering* (1621), *The Best Merchandise* (1622), *The Saints Advantage* (1623). Another edifying project was his translation and printing of the Dutch catechism into English for use of the children of the church.[67] He made an unhappy try at political writing in 1624 in support of the Dutch position after the Amboyna massacre. For some unknown reason, he anonymously translated into English a Dutch pamphlet justifying the massacre, thus associating himself with an action highly displeasing to the English government. Ambassador Sir Dudley Carleton, without realizing Wing's involvement, asked him to trace down the culprit author who put such trash into English. Wing was very embarrassed to reveal himself as the translator—"ignorance, and simplicity, are my only errors," he

---

[63] C.R., no. 4469, fol. 3 (G.A. Flushing).
[64] C.R., Jan. 22, 1628; Van Grol, "Engelsche Kerk te Vlissingen," pp. 13-14.
[65] C.R., Dec. 11, 1627.
[66] C.R., June 28, 1651; *Notulen* van Staten van Zeeland (1659), p. 123.
[67] C.R., Apr. 16, 1630. Burrage surmised that Wing may have been an ex-Jacobite; *E.E.D.*, II, 293-95.

pleaded.⁶⁸ Wing transferred to The Hague in 1627 as first minister of that English church.

Maximiliaan Teellinck, son of the famous Willem Teellinck, served for a short period in 1627-28 before moving on to the Dutch church at Zierikzee. John Roe, preacher of the garrison church at Zwolle, came in 1628. Teellinck and Roe had both received education at the University of Franeker, "bred up for some years time under our most R. Dr Ames." Roe, probably of Suffolk, had enrolled at Franeker in 1622, at the same time as Robert Snelling.⁶⁹ He was a Puritan, a member of the English Synod, and in the Davenport-Paget controversy over membership and baptism, he sided with Davenport. According to Davenport, Roe "in answer to a letter which Mr. Paget sent to him concerning this matter professed himselfe to be of my judgment."⁷⁰ In 1645, Roe received an urgent call to a church in England (the various letters came from Frostenden, South Cove, and Wrentham Suffolk); and although the Flushing elders at first refused to give him leave since "themselves to have more right in him, as being theirs by calling, though born in England," at last they reluctantly released him as having a "calling from God" (August 28, 1645).⁷¹

As successor to Roe, the Flushing congregation thought of young Thomas Potts Junior, son of the former garrison chaplain, living at Amsterdam as student of divinity (Leiden University), "of very good hope and well liked of for his preaching." When he received a call form Flushing, he refused on grounds of his young years, his weakness in the English language, the desire to live in England for a year or two, also "the churches lack of meanes and not combining with other churches."⁷² At this response, the church enlisted the city magistrates; and they sent a formal letter (April 4, 1645) strongly supporting the call and soon after that a promise of 716 guilders a year.⁷³ Potts's presbyterial reluctance about the church's "not combining with other churches" was soon resolved, because the English church joined the Classis of Walcheren in September, 1645 at the same time as the Middelburg church. Potts reconsidered and accepted the pastorate. He moved to Flushing in

---

⁶⁸ S.P. 84, vol. 120, fols. 99, 138.

⁶⁹ Quick, "Icones," I, i, 269. See Franeker Univ. *Album*, pp. 69, 75; as a disputant under Ames in 1623 (*Medulla*), Roe dedicated his piece to William Ames, Christopher Young, and John Phillips of Wrentham, Suffolk, Ames's brother in law. Ames's mother was a Snelling of Ipswich.

⁷⁰ *Letters of John Davenport*, ed. Isabel M. Calder (New Haven: Yale Univ. Press, 1937), p. 55; Ad. MS. 24,666, fol. 2 (B.M.).

⁷¹ C.R., Jan. 3, 15, Aug. 28, 1645.

⁷² C.R., 1645.

⁷³ No. 750 (G.A. Flushing); C.R., April 2, 1645.

November of 1645 and was ordained to the church on January 19, 1646, by Maximiliaan Teellinck. In his opening sermon he preached about how "God did bring about great matters by weake and unlikely meanes, and so desiring the people that none might stumble or despise him for his youth." He was twenty-five years old.[74]

Potts was minister during a difficult time for the English churches, many congregations being disrupted by the Revolution in England. In 1651 the elders "tooke into consideration some passages which had happened in our church, tending to a breach amongst us, in regard of inter medling of the affaires of England and Scotland." They decided that "the minister shal study the peace of the church, and that strangers if they preach amongst us, shal have the liberty to pray or not to pray for the King as their conscience shal lead them unto."[75] The ministry of Potts was only for five years. In 1651 he received a call from the English church of Utrecht, which "could no otherwise be considered of him but divine." He proposed to accept the call as God's will unless it turned out that the Utrecht church was smaller than the Flushing church. The Utrecht English church at that time had about 145 members. When challenged that way, the Flushing elders released Potts and began looking for another minister.[76] In his later career Potts, after Utrecht, returned to Flushing as Dutch minister; John Quick who met Potts in 1680 commended him as "a strict disciplinarian, and a severe enemy to all debauches, and to the noveltys."[77] Securing competent English or Scottish ministers for the Zeeland churches became ever more difficult, in fact nearly impossible, as the eldership had feared in 1645 in releasing Roe, "that in regard of these parts, in which an English minister, especially such an one as they esteemed him for can hardly be found."[78]

As outside financial support from city and province increased, the church was required to defer in church matters to the burgomasters who paid the bills. For election of minister, at least two magistrates from Flushing would join the consistory, constituting a *Collegium Qualificatum* ("the qualifyed colledge ... to wit the church council accompanied with the Burgemaister Lampsen, and the Lord quirijn Willemse Schepen"). Next they secured approval from the Classis of Walcheren.[79] To replace Potts they found Arnold van Laren, Dutch minister at Veghel; he had

---

[74] C.R., Dec. 28, 1645; Jan. 19, 1646; Leiden Univ. *Album*, cols. 305, 347.

[75] C.R., Apr. 4, 1651.

[76] C.R., 1651; on the size of the Utrecht church, "Memoriaal van visitaties der kerken," no. 7, pt. 1, archive of Classis of Utrecht (R.A. Utrecht).

[77] Quick, "Icones," I, i, 252.

[78] C.R., Jan. 15, 1645.

[79] C.R., Apr. 4-May 5, 1651.

[80] C.R., June 28, 1651; E.R.C. Amsterdam, C.R., III, 218.

once lived in England and learned to preach in English.[80] The Flushing church had even less success than Middelburg in attracting native English or Scottish preachers. Except for Wing and Roe (1620-27 and 1628-45) the church was served exclusively by English-speaking Dutchmen: Teellinck, Potts (of English family but born and educated in the Netherlands, having "lack of utterance in English"), Van Laren, Megapolensis, Fitts, and in 1700 Van der Pyl.

The Flushing church upheld discipline. "The anxiety and active vigilance of the kirk-session to discountenance, in our countrymen, every impropriety in speech and behaviour especially merits commendatory notice."[81] Cases of drunkenness, violence, fornication, ribaldry, and "cholerik humor" were repressed in the highways and byways. In 1633 the consistory took action: "Determined that an elder and deacon shal on the Lords dayes in the beginning of the foore noons sermon go and visit the tap houses of English, that so there may be order taken by the church and civil magistrate to reforme them of such disorders and profanenesse as is wont at such times to be in them."[82] Like the Middelburg English church, the Flushing church practiced open confession before the congregation. A back-slidden elder, after falling out with another member of the church in a public place, made this public confession:

> Beloved brethren it is not unknown unto you that about a yeare ago it pleased God to suffer me to give a great offence, not onely to himselfe, but also to many of the congregation, for the which I have bene grieved even to my very soule, especially when I consider whereunto God and your selves have called me. But when I consider how it pleased God many times to let his nearest and dearest children to fall into heavy and grievous sinnes, that thereby he may let man see what he is when God pleaseth to restraine his spirit in us for a time: I then comforted my selfe with Paul (Rom. 7:18-19) when he saith, I know that in me dwelleth no good, etc. If the dearest children of God have so often fallen, what am I then O Lord that am so inferiour to the rest of them. Wherefore I beseech you in the name of God that you wil be pleased to passe by this my offence as if it had never bene committed, that so I may not be a patron unto others hereafter to imitate mee in evil, but rather to follow those which walke before you in the wayes of God. ... This is al which I would impart, the rather because the sacrament draws neare, whereunto I am desirous to come, and that with comfort: which God grant us al.[83]

During the pastorates of Wing, Teellinck, and Roe (to 1645), the church was independent of supervision from Dutch Reformed

---
[81] Steven, p. 302.
[82] C.R., Aug. 18, 1627, Apr. 23, 1633.
[83] C.R., Aug. 18, 1627.

assemblies, and the church was associated with the English Synod. Wing, Teellinck, and Roe were all members of the Synod. John Forbes and Jeremiah Elborough, as officials of the English Synod, examined Teellinck in 1627, gave their "approbation," and had charge of the ordination.[84] In searching for a successor for Teellinck in 1628, the church relied on the English Synod once again for help in choosing a minister. As a first step the church sent a letter to the synod president, and the Flushing church received answer desiring them "to take notice of Mr John Roo." After Roe had accepted the call to Flushing, the church requested the synod to send representatives for Roe's ordination; but because of delays and poor communication with Forbes, synod president, the church finally had to proceed to the ordination without the English Synod. They called in neighboring Dutch and English churchmen—not intending "any prejudice to the Synod."[85] Flushing's negotiations with the English Synod in 1627 and 1628 are the clearest picture available of the workings of the synod at the local level. The difficulties and delays of the English Synod's dealings with Flushing indicate the problems of a scattered synod attempting to supervise affairs at such a distance. Moreover, the synod functioned very loosely and seldom met, and by 1633 it had become completely defunct. By 1630 both Roe and Drake of Middelburg had largely ceased to participate;[86] and by their continued independence from the Classis of Walcheren, they were all the more isolated from wider religious fellowship.

When the States of Zeeland in the resolution of July 22, 1645, decreed that the Flushing and Middelburg churches should join the Classis of Walcheren in exchange for financial support, Flushing made no more delays. The elders in making their application judged it "expedient for the better strenthning of our church and ordering of all things in it ... that entrance into brotherly fellowship in councel meetings of Eldership be sought."[87] After classis membership, the Flushing ministers received better stipends and the church could count on financial security. In 1661 the town magistrates repaired the consistory chamber with new windows and a little chimney; they also "had given us a new church-porch, and new windows, which heretofore had oft in vain bene desired."[88]

Although fully incorporated into the Dutch church system, the English churches of Zeeland imagined themselves still as second class churches. Van Laren and Sprang felt slighted in classis business, even though taken

---
[84] C.R., June 10, 1627; Middelburg C.R., I, 41.
[85] C.R., (1628).
[86] B.P., I, 168.
[87] C.R., Aug. 9, 1645.
[88] C.R., Feb. 22, 1661.

on as "ordinary members of this Classis, and have the same entertainment and stipend with the rest of the Dutch brethren;" they felt passed over for special assignment and had no turn as "deputies *ad res Indiae Orientalis.*" The Dutch ministers "did studio passe us by," and "would never accept of us." Finally Spang of Middelburg became classis scribe (1657) and pushed for his turn as deputy *ad res Indiae Orientalis.* Because of resistance from the Middelburg ministers, he "desired of the Classis that we might have our turn among the brethren of the Durp ministers (van het platte lant) which accordingly was granted by the Classis, and so he had his first turn there; but having supplied that place but a very short time, dyed, and so I [Van Laren] succeded this day in his place"—in the consistory register "this is written down here for posterity."[89] A few of the Dutch ceremonies the English church omitted. Thomas Potts in 1647 requested to omit preaching on the after-Christmas feast days as it was the Dutch "custome to preach on these dayes (according to the articles agreed on in the Synod at Dort)." The classis left this matter to the English conscience to decide.[90]

Veere

About four miles north of Middelburg is Veere (also known in former times as Campvere and Tervere). As the long time Scottish staple port, Veere was the center of Scottish settlement in Zeeland, and at times of the entire Netherlands. In 1444 Wolfert van Borselen, lord of Veere, married Mary Stuart, daughter of James I of Scotland, bringing the two places into close political and economic association. Veere became the exclusive staple port for Scottish trade with the Netherlands. The Scottish factory at Veere was composed of merchant factors presided over by a lord conservator appointed by the king of Scotland. The Scottish company with its carefully prescribed privileges continued at Veere with only temporary interruption from 1541 to 1799, when the Dutch at last declared the staple contract void. Veere contained a cluster of Scottish economic and religious institutions: company, court, church, warehouses, and houses.[91] The company headquarters were in the Scottish conciergerie on Wijngaard Straat, "a very roomy building with large rooms, apartments, attics, basements, and other places for the use and convenience of all the Scottish merchants." On the quay were the two impressive sixteenth-century "Schotse Huizen" (*Het Lammeken* and *De*

---

[89] C.R., Sept. 4, 1664.

[90] C.R., Jan. 13, 1647; G. D. J. Schotel, *De openbare eeredienst der Nederl. Hervormde Kerk in de zestiende, zeventiende en achttiende eeuw* (Haarlem: A. C. Kruseman, 1870), pp. 238-40.

[91] On the Scottish staple, see John Davidson and Alexander Gray, *The Scottish Staple at Veere* (London: Longmans, Green, & Co., 1909); and Steven, pp. 288-94.

Struys) owned by wealthy merchant families.[92] The Van Borselens called their mansion Lauderdale House in honor of their Scottish connections.[93] To serve the spiritual needs of the Scottish merchants, the staple contract allowed for the maintaining of a Scottish church at Veere. Erecting a church among foreign settlers faithful to the worship of the old country "satisfies at once the instinct of religion and the instinct of nationality."[94]

The staple contract of 1541 called for "the choice and option of a suitable place in the collegiate church of our town of Campvere, with a chaplain so as it shall please the said nation." The contract of 1578 also specified a Scottish staple church; "the said Magistrate grants unto them the quire of the great kirk, and their ministers to have off the town their dwelling house, with free exercise of beer and wine of his household and family."[95] The contract of 1612 made promise of a separate building for the Scots church, rather than a piece of the great church, also a church yard and a parsonage; however the city of Veere never carried through on these provisions.[96] In spite of provisions for a church in the staple contracts, the Scottish merchants did not succeed in establishing a permanent church until the seventeenth century, whereas English Merchant Adventurers at Antwerp and Middelburg had been far quicker in this matter. The name of at least one sixteenth-century staple minister is known (John Dawson in 1552), but otherwise until the seventeenth century, the office of minister was often unfilled. The Convention of Royal Burghs in 1586 regretfully noted the omission of a church at Veere as contributing to "thair uncumlie behaviour in thair civill lyfe and outwarth manner is contrair the lawis of God and civill polecie."[97]

Until a permanent appointment of minister, Veere relied on traveling and short-term ministers for occasional religious services. In one case, John Forbes and Robert Dury, banished ministers, lived briefly at Veere in 1608 until driven forth by order of King James; "they, having been supplied amongst the Scottish merchants in the town of Campheire where they have their staple, upon direction sent to the Conservator of the privileges of our nation, were put forth of that town."[98] Finally in 1614, the Convention of Burghs arranged for the establishing of an

---

[92] P. H. Damsté, *Veere: Vier eeuwen markiezaat* (De Bilt: J. W. H. Patist, 1966), pp. 42-47.

[93] Steven, p. 289.

[94] Davidson and Gray, p. 270. The consistory register of Veere was destroyed by fire in 1940. Thus, I rely most on Davidson and Gray, who made extensive use of the register for their book. They are, however, rather hostile to the religion of the seventeenth-century Scottish church (inquisitorial methods" and the "tyranny of the Kirk Session").

[95] Ibid., pp. 270-71.

[96] Damsté, *Veere*, p. 35.

[97] Davidson and Gray, p. 271.

[98] H.M.C., *Salisbury MSS.*, XX, 184; Davidson and Gray, p. 273.

organized church and named as first resident minister Alexander MacDuff and as reader Thomas Ewing. A kirk session of deacons and elders was elected.[99]

Although the town provided the place of worship in a chapel in the Grote Kerk, the merchants and the Convention of Burghs were responsible for other financial support, principally the minister's salary (1600 guilders by 1652).[100] During the French invasion of the 1790s, the Scottish chapel, no longer used because of the closing of the staple, was desecrated and "entirely stripped of its internal furnishings and sacrilegiously conveyed by the French into a house of correction."[101] The list of seventeenth-century ministers includes the following: Alexander MacDuff (1613-25); George Sydserff (1625-27); John Forrett (1628-29); William Spang (1630-53); Robert Browne (1653-54); George Robertson (1657-60); Thomas Mowbray (1660-64); Andrew Snype (1664-86); Charles Gordon (1686-91); Thomas Hoog (1694-98); John Chalmer (1699-1729).[102]

Throughout its history, the Scottish church at Veere was an extension of the staple company and dependent on it. The chief company official, the lord conservator, was also the leading member of the church and was given the position of ruling elder. Both minister and reader were required to carry out assignments given them by the king as well as the government of the company. To prevent unwanted rebels from using Veere as a center for agitation, the Privy Council in 1614 gave orders that the minister was responsible to issue certificates for passengers. No ship was to take on passengers at Veere without testimony from the minister "bearing that the persone or personis who desyris to be transportit into this kingdome doeth hant the Scottis kirk at Campweere and are knowne to be professouris of the trew religion presentlie profest and be law establissit within this kingdome."[103] This system of certificates, however, was not much enforced. Because the company saw the church as useful, "care was taken to strengthen the hands and add to the comfort of the officiating minister." All merchants of the company were required to attend services under a penalty of paying thirty stivers for each absence.[104] The various lord conservators, depending on their theologies, had opportunity to push the church in one direction or another. Sir Patrick Drum-

---

[99] Davidson and Gray, p. 274.
[100] Quick, "Icones," I, i, 270; about £133 in 1621; 1,200 guilders in 1643, Davidson and Gray, pp. 276, 281.
[101] Steven, p. 293.
[102] *F.E.S.*, VII, 541-42.
[103] Davidson and Gray, p. 275.
[104] Steven, pp. 290-91; James Yair, *An Account of the Scotch Trade in the Netherlands and of the Staple Port of Campvere* (London, 1776), p. 217.

mond (conservator 1625-40), a faithful royal servant and promoter of prelacy, tried to impose his Episcopal theology on the church. Minister John Forrett complained in 1628-29 that Drummond "did encrotche" upon the church.[105] After Drummond's removal, his successor was Thomas Cuningham (conservator 1644-60); Cuningham was a Presbyterian and guided the church into adopting the Solemn League and Covenant.[106]

The church at Veere held to the tenets of Scottish religion and made every effort to be the faithful Scottish Presbyterian church overseas. Preaching, sacraments, and discipline all had high priority. At the kirk session "at each meeting 'search for scandal' was made, seeking out and laying bare in the face of the congregation every detail of unfortunate lives."[107] By bringing over ministers from Scotland, the church kept in communication with the larger Church of Scotland. The early ministers, however, did not leave much of a mark on the church. MacDuff died in 1625. George Sydserff, his successor, served till 1627, but he returned to Scotland claiming ill health. "The aire of that cuntrey does not agrie with his complexioun."[108] The strongest minister was William Spang (1630-53), 23 years old, M.A. from the University of Glasgow, and for several years teacher in the High School of Edinburgh. Spang was a cousin of Robert Baillie and was one of the correspondents in the Baillie letters. In 1652 Spang transferred to the English Church at Middelburg, which Spang insisted on calling the "British Church" of Middelburg.[109] Spang's resignation left a ministerial gap at Veere which was very inadequately filled by temporary clergymen until 1660.

With the rise of the Covenanters in Scotland, Veere was drawn into national Scottish affairs. In 1639 Thomas Cuningham and fellow merchants, early supporters of the Covenant, began shipping over to Scotland "great quantity of armes, ammunition, cannon and other warre-like necessaries."[110] Drummond as lord conservator stood in the way of pro-Covenant activity, so Cuningham challenged his authority and succeeded in deposing Drummond. Cuningham took over as lord conservator in 1644. On May 29, 1644, the Solemn League and Cove-

---

[105] Thomas Cuningham, *The Journal of Thomas Cuningham of Campvere 1640-1654*, ed. E. J. Courthope, *Publications* of the Scottish History Society, 3rd ser., 11 (1928), preface, pp. ix-xvi.

[106] Andrew L. Drummond, *The Kirk and the Continent* (Edinburgh: St. Andrew Press, 1956), p. 81.

[107] Davidson and Gray, p. 284.

[108] Ibid., p. 277.

[109] *F.E.S.*, VII, 547-48; Quick, I, i, 271. After transfer to Middelburg, he continued to serve Veere until 1653.

[110] Cuningham, *Journal*, p. ix.

nant was adopted in the church.¹¹¹ Veere followed the lead of the Church of Scotland on most political issues and called appropriate fasts and thanksgivings as the wars progressed. In 1644 Veere set aside a day for "solemn thanksgiving to the Lord for his mercifull gratious assistance given to the armies of our land ingadgit in the cause of relligioune and liberty." On September 2, 1651, the church held a day of prayer for blessing upon the king and the Scottish army; but the next day at the battle of Worcester, Cromwell prevailed.¹¹² Spang as minister kept close to events in Scotland through his correspondence with Baillie and his occasional trips to Edinburgh. Baillie much commended Spang for condemning Laud's prayer book (1639), for refusing fellowship with John Forbes of Corse (1644), and for propaganda work among the Zeeland church on behalf of Scotland (1644).¹¹³ Spang was the author of several books on the times, *Brevis et Fidelis Narratio* (1640), *Historia Rerum Nuper in Regno Scotiae Gestarum* (1641), and *Motuum Britannicorum Verax Cushi* (1647).

Covenanters and Royalists came into conflict in 1643 at the church when the Porterfields and Drummonds (Royalists) erected a coat of arms and memorial stone in the church in commemoration of Elizabeth Cant, widow of John Porterfield and mother-in-law of Sir Patrick Drummond. The kirk session, led by Spang and Cuningham, opposed the memorial as an innovation smacking of scandal, pride, and idolatry. Such ostentatious memorials in a Scottish church, said the kirk session, were appropriate only for great persons or other rare members who had greatly benefitted the church—not applicable to Elizabeth Cant. The Porterfields made "bloody threatenings" against anyone who would lay a finger on the memorial, but Spang and Cuningham got the upper hand by appealing to the General Assembly of the Church of Scotland and gaining its support for removing the memorials. Soon after, in 1644, Cuningham received official appointment from Scotland as lord conservator; Drummond, however, had been removed from authority in 1640 and had therefore long lost his place as elder of the church.¹¹⁴

Up to 1641, the Scottish church had no formal ties with any classis or synod in Scotland or the Netherlands. Like the English churches of Flushing and Middelburg it was independent. Alexander MacDuff made a small exception in 1622 and 1623 by attending the English Synod, but

---

[111] Ibid., p. xv; Davidson and Gray, p. 291.
[112] Davidson and Gray, pp. 292-93.
[113] Robert Baillie, *The Letters and Journals*, ed. David Laing (Edinburgh, 1841-42), I, 113; II, 166, 169. On Spang and Baillie, see chapter 13.
[114] Davidson and Gray, pp. 295-99; Cuningham, *Journal*, pp. xix-xx.

thereafter he was not active in the synod.[115] The 1641 General Assembly of the Church of Scotland meeting at Edinburgh voted to take in Veere as a member; and Spang and an elder of Veere were invited to come to the 1642 Assembly "at which time they should be inrolled in the books of the Generall Assembly."[116] Spang alone from his church attended the Assembly of 1642, no elder being available to make the trip with him, at which time the Veere church became an official member of the Church of Scotland. The Assembly admonished Veere as a full member of the church to observe all things Scottish in worship and discipline and to attend Assembly meetings at least once in three years. For "counsel and advice" in matter of discipline the church was placed under the Presbytery of Edinburgh; however, the General Assembly was to act "as their immediate superior judicatory."[117] From their overseas location the church at Veere found it difficult to participate in presbytery and assembly affairs; and minister and elders seldom attended the General Assembly meetings. From 1668 to 1675 the staple was moved briefly to Dort, which left the church, remaining in Veere, on an uncertain foundation. In 1669, the Veere church joined the Classis of Walcheren, without, however, renouncing its Church of Scotland membership. The Dutch classis took the church in under conditions "that the Scottish church not stand under the jurisdiction of the bishops or that Reverend Snype never go over to the episcopal government, also that he conform in everything concerning the formula of unity."[118] The Walcheren ministers were ever suspicious of Episcopalian religion. In 1693, Veere ceased to participate in the Dutch classis and claimed independence from the Dutch Reformed Church.[119]

---

[115] Minutes of the English Synod, 1622 and 1623, S.P. 84, vol. 106, fol. 84; S.P. 84, vol. 110, fol. 3.

[116] *Acts of the General Assembly of the Church of Scotland 1638-1842* (Edinburgh, 1843), p. 52; Davidson and Gray, p. 279.

[117] *Acts of the General Assembly*, p. 335 (under 1704, which referred back to acts of 1642).

[118] Acta Classis Walcheren, V, 142.

[119] Acta Classis, VIII, 336, 358; William Mair, *A Digest of Laws and Decisions Ecclesiastical and Civil*, 4th ed. (Edinburgh: William Blackwood, 1923), pp. 371-72.

CHAPTER EIGHT

THE UTRECHT AND ARNHEM CHURCHES TO 1660

Unlike the military-dominated garrison churches of Gelderland, Overijssel, and Utrecht provinces, the city churches of Utrecht (Utrecht province) and Arnhem (Gelderland province) developed into established congregations with a settled, civilian membership. Holland and Zeeland had the largest network of well-established city churches, but among inland cities Utrecht drew the largest British settlement, composed of merchants, soldiers, and after 1636, students attending the University of Utrecht. The Arnhem church was short-lived, but during its brief existence it played a powerful role among Netherlands English churches. Utrecht had an old English community; and the fifteenth-century Merchant Adventurers sometimes held a cloth fair there.[1] During the wars with Spain, Utrecht was the headquarters for English regiments in the province, which much swelled the British population.

The students also came, because next to Leiden, Utrecht University was the favorite place of study. The university album contains 203 English and Scottish names for the period 1640-99; and although a significant number, it is far from the actual number of British students coming into the city. A majority of students, those not necessarily intending to take a degree, never bothered to register. At one point in 1693, when Utrecht had seventy to eighty English and Scottish students in town, only seventeen British had officially enrolled themselves in the entire past five years. The venerable *Zwolse Bijbel*, which was kept in the English church after 1656 and used by visiting British students as a visitor's book, contains the signatures of about 500 names, most from the period 1680-1720.[2] When the English-Scottish civilian inhabitants petitioned in 1622 for the establishment of a church, they had already reached the number of 120 families. The province of Utrecht had only one other English church, a garrison church at Amersfoort.[3]

---

[1] C. H. D. Grimes, *The Early Story of the English Church at Utrecht* (Chambéry: Imprimeries Réunies, 1930), pp. 5-6.

[2] A. Hulshoff, "Britsche en Amerikaansche studenten op bezoek of voor studie te Utrecht," *Historia*, 12 (Oct. 1947), 230-31; "Schotten en Britten te Utrecht," *Maandblad van "Oud-Utrecht,"* 27 (Jan. 1954), 124; G. W. Kernkamp, *De Utrechtsche Academie 1636-1815*, vol. 1 of *De Utrechtsche Universiteit* (Utrecht: Oosthoek's, 1936), p. 180. If the university album and the Zwolse Bible are collated, they contain about 500 different English and Scottish names from the seventeenth and early eighteenth centuries.

[3] B.P., I, 234. The history of the Amersfoort church is given in chapter 10 on garrison churches.

An English military chapel existed at Utrecht at various times prior to 1622, the time of the formal establishment of the English Reformed Church. Following the Earl of Leicester's visit in 1586-87, the English were given use of the Maria Kerk, and thereafter as troops were stationed at Utrecht, the chaplains continued to hold English worship services in St. Mary's, St. Peter's church (1610), or St. Catherine's church (1621).[4] John Douglas, chaplain to Colonel John Ogle and Colonel Edward Cecil (1617, 1619), and George Clark (1619-22), both Scots, put the chapel on a more organized basis. Douglas received "a little small gratuity" from each company, "cheefly to make the more intire and mutuall obligation between the officers and the preacher," and he further received a provincial subsidy of 400 guilders a year, which was afterwards continued for Clark.[5] A consistory of three elders, all military officers, was chosen. Douglas described the task of church building: To merge the officers of five regiments plus the horse troops into one congregation, "to make up more formally one Body without schisme." The military officers had also paid a small gratuity from each company for use of hiring a reader, coster, carpenter, and making up a purse of charity funds for Douglas's "disposeing for our countrymen."[6] Douglas applied for and was accepted as a member of the Classis of Utrecht after subscribing to the Dutch Reformed confession.[7] He had been rumored by some to be a secret Arminian, but this was never proved. The biggest obstacle encountered by Douglas was the hostility of Cecil, his former regimental commander. Cecil opposed his being continued as Utrecht preacher and labelled Douglas as treacherous and "unfitt."[8]

Although preaching and worship were provided by Douglas and Clark for the benefit of all English-Scottish civilian and military people of the city, the Utrecht English citizens were far from satisfied with the garrison-dominated church. During the winter season it went well enough, but when the troops went into the field, they took their chaplain with them, leaving the resident congregation "utterly unprovided both of Church and preacher."[9] Tensions between English and Scots troubled the waters. Consequently, in 1622 the town residents, "finding their own strength, if their scattered numbers were once collected into one body ... made a full muster of their numbers" (120 families) and applied to the

---

[4] Grimes, *Utrecht*, pp. 7-9; Hulshoff, "Studenten te Utrecht," p. 188; Kernkamp, *Acta et decreta senatus ... de Utrechtsche Academie* (Utrecht: Kemink, 1938-40), II, 7, 11-13.

[5] S.P. 84, vol. 90, fol. 107; Res. Staten van Utrecht, no. 231, Aug. 28, 1618 (R.A. Utrecht).

[6] S.P. 84, vol. 92, fol. 5.

[7] Acta Synod Utrecht, Reitsma and Van Veen, VI, 425.

[8] S.P. 84, vol. 80, fol. 154, vol. 90, fol. 170.

[9] Utrecht C.R., 1657-1757, no. 848, pt. 1, fol. 288 (G.A. Utrecht).

States of Utrecht and to the city magistrates for establishing a civilian English Reformed Church under official sponsorship. Ambassador Sir Dudley Carleton of The Hague supported the campaign for a church.[10] The city magistrates provided a church building and the provincial and city governments jointly gave stipends, 150 guilders each for a total of 300 guilders a year; Thomas Scott of Gorinchem was called as minister. Thereafter, the congregation dated its foundation from 1622, not from the prior garrison church. "What happened before the year 1622 we have already observed has no connection with us, or our Church," asserted an eighteenth-century minister of the church. "We have shown that our Church was first erected in the year 1622, that it is a Burger Church."[11]

The English Reformed church of Utrecht, which existed 1622-1841, was served by the following seventeenth-century ministers: Thomas Scott (1622-26), Jeremiah Elborough (1626-29), Alexander Leighton (1629), Ralph Clayton (1629-30), Isaac Fortry (1630-37), Paul Amyraut (1637-38), John Hering (1639-42), Malachi Harris (1643-44), Richard Maden (1644-46), Walter Bowie (1647-50), Thomas Potts (1651-55), John Best (1655-96), James de la Faye (1696-1748). John Douglas and George Clark served the garrison church 1617-22. In 1621 the English moved from St. Peter's to St. Catherine's church, and in 1625 they returned to St. Peter's.

In 1656 the burgomasters transferred the English congregation to St. Mary's church, which remained the *Engelse Kerk* until the congregation's demise.[12] At St. Mary's (the Maria Kerk) the English met in a partitioned-off place within the nave with use of the south chapel as a consistory chamber.[13] Although a well-built, commodious place of worship, St. Mary's was also used for secular business purposes, much to the dismay of the English, for selling books and prints at the time of the annual Utrecht market, even as a lumber shop in the old choir.[14] The English protested indignantly—and in vain—"that on the very walls is this in Latin, to let them know such sacred places are not to be prophan-

---

[10] Ibid., fol. 288; Carleton's letter to the States of Utrecht is in the archives of the States, "Brieven," no. 289 (R.A. Utrecht).

[11] C.R., I, 295, 297; "Aanteekeningen uit de resolutiën der Staten van Utrecht omtrent de geschiedenis der Engelsche gemeente te Utrecht over 1618-1753," no. 6192, pt. 2712 (G.A. Utrecht).

[12] G. G. Calkoen, "Beschrijving der St. Pieterskerk te Utrecht," MS, fols. 84-85; Calkoen, "De kapittelkerk van St. Marie," MS, fol. 57 (G.A. Utrecht); Kernkamp, *Acta et decreta*, II, 7, 11-13.

[13] Calkoen, "St. Marie," fols. 6, 56-57.

[14] C.R., II, 9 (July 20, 1757); Acta Kerkeraad Utrecht, H, July 1, 1661 (G.A. Utrecht); Calkoen, "St. Marie," fol. 57. John Northleigh, *Topographical Descriptions: with Historico-Political, and Medico-Physical Observations* (London, 1702), p. 81.

ed: Flecte Genu, domus haec venerabilis, hospite Christo."[15] Among the famous distinctions of St. Mary's church was its ancient foundation pillar laid upon a bull hide, "like the sole of a shooe" and decorated with a carved ox in the animal's honor. Preserved in the old library was a collection of world curiosities—some old Bibles, an elephant's tooth, some heathen idols, and five unicorn horns.[16]

At the establishment of the congregation in 1622, the financial support for the minister came half from the city and province (300 guilders) and another 300 guilders from the congregation itself, making a total of 600 guilders.[17] As a part of the congregation's share, the soldiers provided "2 guilders by the short month of each single company, and rateably of the rest." The burden of raising 300 guilders per year by subscription proved heavy, and within the year the congregation petitioned the city and the province for greater subsidy and received several increases (a subsidy of 500 guilders in 1623; 850 in 1641; 1000 in 1650).[18] The church prided itself on being an officially sponsored English Reformed Church with close and genial connections to the magistracy. "The magistrates of this city have always acted the part of its Christian governors."[19] The church added a combined reader-ziekentrooster (provincial subsidy of 72 guilders in 1637), a school and schoolmaster (1630 to about 1656), and kept a poor relief fund, "being we have a relation to such of the English nation, who being in distresse resort to us."[20] Among the English churches of the Netherlands, Utrecht ranked as a good-sized church. Membership was 145 persons in 1652, 180 in 1658 and 1665 (the highest membership recorded), 113 in 1670, 50 in 1690, 40 in 1700.[21]

The Utrecht church had a marked Puritan flavor, and the preachers, almost without exception, were Puritans. Thomas Scott, former chaplain of King James I and rector of St. Saviour's, Norwich, was in exile because of writing an anti-Spanish, anti-Catholic book, *Vox Populi* (1620), in which he had attacked "Spanish pretences" in general and Gondomar in particular. While in exile in Gorinchem and Utrecht, Scott continued to produce at a great rate Puritan books dealing with high

---

[15] Northleigh, *Top. Descriptions*, p. 81.

[16] Ibid., pp. 77, 81; Edward Brown, *A Brief Account of some Travels*, 2nd ed. (London, 1685), p. 101; William Mountague, *The Delights of Holland* (London, 1696), p. 197.

[17] C.R., I, 288-289; B.P., I, 263.

[18] B.P., I, 264; for a summary of financial arrangements, see "Over een geschil tusschen den kerkeraad der Engelsche gemeente en de classis van Utrecht," no. 364, pt. 231 (R.A. Utrecht).

[19] C.R., I, 293.

[20] "Eng. gemeente en de classis," fol. 10 (also Res. Staten van Utrecht, Sept. 21, 1637); Calkoen, "Pieterskerk," fol. 85; C.R., June 7, 1658.

[21] Memoriaal van classis visitaties, Archive of Classis of Utrecht, no. 7, pt. 1 (R.A. Utrecht).

politics.²² Scott's ministry came to a tragic end of June 18, 1626, when he was murdered on the open street by John Lambert, a soldier of Lord Wimbleton's company. Although a Catholic conspiracy was suspected, no motivation for the murder was ever proved in spite of racks, whips, and tortures laid on Lambert; to the very time of his execution he maintained "he was never hired or induced, by the perswasions of any Priest, Iesuit, or other person." The sensational event inspired a book, *A Briefe and Trve Relation of the Mvrther of Mr. Thomas Scott* (London, 1628).²³ His successor, Jeremiah Elborough, formerly a regimental chaplain to Colonel Levistone at Montfoort, arrived in time to witness Lambert's torture and execution. Both Scott and Elborough were active in the English Synod. After Utrecht, Elborough transferred to Hamburg as minister to the Merchant Adventurers.²⁴

Dr. Alexander Leighton (March-May, 1629) was the most vehement Puritan thus far at Utrecht. A medical doctor educated at the University of Leiden but more interested in politics and theology, he was the writer of several unlicensed Puritan books. He came to Utrecht just after printing his most recent blast, *An Appeal to the Parliament; or Sions Plea against the Prelacie* (Amsterdam, 1628). With such a record of anti-prelacy, he could hardly return to England in safety, and the vacancy at Utrecht seemed to him a God-given call, "which was so freely and forciblie put upon me that I could not avoyd it." The strong-minded Leighton, however, lasted only about three months at Utrecht and was then forced out for refusing to conform with the Classis of Utrecht on the practice of feast days. Returning to London in the summer of 1629, Leighton fell straightway into the hands of the High Commission, where he suffered vicious punishments.²⁵ A call to another renowned Puritan, Samuel Ward, lecturer at Ipswich, was extended in 1637 but refused.²⁶

Another of the Utrecht Puritan preachers was Paul Amyraut (November, 1637-August, 1638). He was a Palatinate German, rector of Wolterton, Norfolk, who had been driven out by Bishop Wren in 1636 *ob eius manifestam contumaciam* and for not bowing at the name of Jesus.²⁷

---

²² *Aphorismes of State* (Utrecht, 1624); *The Belgick-Souldier* (Dort, 1624); *Votivae Angliae* (Utrecht, 1624); *Workes* (Utrecht, 1624). A Dutch translation of *Vox Populi* (Utrecht, 1625) was done by Jacobus Hughes of Hagestein in 1625; he also did translations of *Vox Dei* and *Vox Regis* (Utrecht, 1624-25).

²³ *D.N.B.*; *Briefe and Trve Relation*, pp. 1-3, 10.

²⁴ B.P., I, 264-65.

²⁵ D. Butler, *The Life and Letters of Robert Leighton* (London: Hodder and Stoughton, 1903), pp. 31-33; *D.N.B.*; S.P. 16, vol. 138, no. 23. His successor Clayton was chosen by Sept. 22, 1629 (Acta Classis Utrecht, I, May 19-20, 1629).

²⁶ B.P., I, 266.

²⁷ B.P., I, 266-67, 236; *D.N.B.*; Matthews, *Cal. R.*, p. 10; R. W. Ketton-Cremer, *Norfolk in the Civil War* (London: Faber, 1969), p. 72.

Amyraut escaped over to the Low Countries by a ship from Great Yarmouth, masquerading as an ordinary traveler. After a short time as chaplain at Breda, he was called to Utrecht. Ambassador Boswell considered Amyraut "a most unfit Minister," the more so after reports poured in that he "demeaned himself very irreverently towards our Church, in publique." Amyraut's Puritan ministry, supported by the civilian core of the congregation and by Professor Voetius of the university, offended some of the gentlemen and higher officers of the regiment, "who haue obstejned from the congregacon since his comming in."[28] Amyraut belonged to the bitter Puritans who fled the land after 1636, and his strident anger marked a new level of the Puritan struggle. In spite of the shelter from the prelates provided at Utrecht, Amyraut did not long survive there because of unresolvable disputes with the classis. Having refused conformity at home, he also refused Dutch Reformed conformity in the Netherlands and resigned. His conscience, he said, would not permit him to become subject to their church.[29] The church revealed its theological soul by its repeated choosing of Puritan ministers.

The ministers of the 1640s were a more mixed group, generally reflecting a difficult time of ministerial recruitment because of the return home of the Puritans. John Hering (1639-42) came from a Puritan family, being the son of Julius Hering of Shrewsbury. Julius and John, a young men of twenty-three years, came over in 1637, a few months after Amyraut, well disguising their Puritan identity. They traveled as gentleman and son on educational business, "to passe into Holland, to place his Said Sonne and to Retorne in 2 months."[30] In fact, Julius was going over to assume the pastorate of the Amsterdam Reformed church, and John, who indeed may have taken some education, fell into Amyraut's vacant position at Utrecht after first assisting on an interim basis. Young Hering's name was presented to the States of Utrecht as an unordained proponent not bound by any episcopal ordination in England. Hering had the strong support of the English contingent of the congregation, especially the English garrison officers, who insisted upon upholding the "honor of the English nation."[31] In spite of hopeful beginnings, Hering did not strengthen or unify the congregation, and in 1642 the English consistory began action to remove him for non-performance of duties, being absent without leave, and, even worse, that "he was

---

[28] S.P. 84, vol. 153, fols. 300-01; Charles B. Jewson, *Transcript of Three Registers of Passengers from Great Yarmouth to Holland and New England 1637-1639*, Norfolk Record Society, 25 (1954), 25; *N.A.K.*, 4 (1893), 282-87.
[29] Acta Classis Utrecht, II, Aug. 14-15, 1638 (R.A. Utrecht).
[30] Jewson, *Transcript*, p. 48.
[31] C.R., I, 290; "Eng. gemeente en de classis," fol. 11r & v.

most guilty of scandalous and unproper life" in connection with "a certain widow Bagger." Shortly after these allegations, Hering found it expedient to resign.[32] Malachi Harris (1643-44), who came recommended by Sir William Boswell, harbored high Anglican loyalties and so gained "very good" acceptance among some of the military officers and gentlemen but ill will from the Calvinistic core of the congregation, headed by Mr. Bor, former elder, who wanted to oust him and bring in from England a son of lecturer Samuel Ward of Ipswich. "Such unworthy dealing doe somewhat trouble," complained Harris.[33] Bor's faction accused Harris of preaching Popery and opposing Scripture-reading; and to document their accusations they made notes from his sermons and submitted them to the classis. Harris faced accusations of Popery, Arminianism, ceremonies, and of preaching "that none could be fitt to expound Scripture without these 3 languages, the Hebrew, the Greeke and the Logick-tongue."[34]

The Anglican-Puritan controversy, sparked by Harris, carried over to the Utrecht Classis, where Harris was called to answer the charges: (1) Arminianism—Harris said he was opposed, but the classis was suspicious, noting that he was A.B., M.A., and B.D. from Emmanuel, Cambridge, and Cambridge was reputed to be "over-runne with Arminianisme." (2) Church government by elders—Harris dissembled and evaded a direct answer whether lay elders were *jure divino* but promised to observe all practices required of him. (3) "Popish" Anglican ceremonies—Harris reiterated his loyalty to the Church of England and its ceremonies, "nor doe I thinke them to be Popish." He promised, nevertheless, to conform faithfully to the Dutch Reformed church while at Utrecht and was eventually admitted as a member of the classis, all the while defending the Anglican church from aspersions of Papism. After the ordeal, Harris gloated at how he had poured back coals of fire on his Dutch Reformed accusers; they complained of Popish tendencies in England while at the same time Popish priests were allowed to function in their own province. Harris had leaped at them: "I never heard of any such matters in England. Some of the Professors held downe their heads."[35] After spending eighteen dismal months "cloistered" at Utrecht, Harris was reprieved in 1644 by a call from Prince Frederik

---

[32] Acta Classis Utrecht, II, May 1-2, 1642, sess. 1 & 2, June 9-10, 1642; Acta Kerkeraad Utrecht, D, June 13, 17, 20, 1642.

[33] B.P., I, 322, 326; he arrived in Utrecht in late 1642 but was not invested until 1643.

[34] B.P., I, 327, 331.

[35] Ibid., I, 333-35. On June 6/16, 1643, Harris wrote, "yesterday I took my session in the classis."

Hendrik to be chaplain to his daughter-in-law Mary, Princess of Orange at The Hague.[36]

Richard Maden (1644-46), a displaced Anglican sequestered from St. Mildred Poultry, London, was willing to subscribe to the Dutch Reformed confession. Although he served without incident, he was nevertheless suspected by some Puritans of being a secret Anglican prelaticist.[37] He resigned to accept the pastorate of the Amsterdam English Reformed Church. The next years were a time of bitter divisiveness in the congregation, reflecting schism between garrison and civilians and between English and Scots. The garrison officers strongly supported Robert Remington (1647) "with intention to force him upon the Consistory," but he was refused after the consistory wrote to the Westminster Assembly and got "no favorable account of him."[38]

The English consistory, which at this period tended to be more partial to the Scots than to the English, instead gave a call to Walter Bowye, a Scottish preacher. Although the consistory prevailed in installing Bowye as minister (1647-50), the resulting acrimony was the most serious experienced in the history of the church. Unheeding the opposition within the congregation, the consistory proceeded with Bowye's call and gathered the required support from magistrates and classis, thereby achieving a *fait accompli*.[39] The anti-Bowye faction refused to accept him and began a furious counter-campaign to prevent his officially assuming the office. Speaking on behalf of "officers, gentry, and others," they petitioned the English consistory against Bowye and made four complaints: (1) That Bowye prayed "that god would breake the kings hart and to convert the Queene that she doe noe more mischiefe"; (2) That he preached dangerous, subversive doctrines "contrary to the duty of a subject," saying, for example, "the king and Independents were likely to bring in Popery, and through toleration of Religion Atheisme"; (3) That in the communion he used neither the Dutch nor the English forms; (4) That he was a Scotsman and "doth not speake perfect English." When the English consistory still refused to back down, the military petitioners, 102 persons strong, carried their cause to the States of Utrecht, the city magistrates, the Dutch consistory, and the classis, always complaining

---

[36] "Eng. gemeente en de classis," fol. 12v; B.P., I, 337.

[37] Alice C. Carter, *The English Reformed Church in Amsterdam in the Seventeenth Century* (Amsterdam: Scheltema & Holkema, 1964), pp. 95-96; Matthews, *W.R.*, p. 53.

[38] C.R., I, 291; Res. Staten van Utrecht, Aug. 26, 1647, Sept. 3, 1647.

[39] Whether the consistory of elders and deacons was becoming predominantly Scottish in nationality by the 1640s is not known. The consistory register and record of elections before 1647 is mostly lost. Some of those serving in the late 1630s and 1640s were: John Bor and Thomas Skynner (1637); Oliver Moore, John Ree, elders 1647, and Tob van Hobooken, Rogar Botham, Caleb Gooding, deacons, 1647.

that Bowye demeaned the English king and queen "by various scandalous words" and that the English members "could not well understand him." They demanded a new election "of a good English Minister." Sir William Boswell, still functioning in the Netherlands as Charles I's agent, worked with the dissident English officers.[40] At the height of the controversy in 1647-48, some of the English military people withdrew from the main congregation and established their own church served by English chaplains of the area. Bowye's short and troubled ministry ended with his sudden death in 1650.[41]

The 1650s, served by Thomas Potts (1651-55) and John Best (1655-96), were a more settled time for the church. Potts, who transferred from the Flushing English Reformed Church, the son of the former Flushing and Amsterdam minister of the same name, provided a unifying influence on the Utrecht church—"the church is now at rest"—and also enjoyed good rapport with the surrounding Dutch churches. In 1654, in fact, the Dutch church of Utrecht tried to induce Potts to come over to their church as minister, but he declined their offer. However, in 1655 he took a call to return to Flushing as minister of the Dutch church.[42] His successor, John Best, a Dutchman formerly minister at Schermer, served for over forty years. He too received an invitation from the Utrecht Dutch Reformed church, having made a good impression with his "gifts," but decided against deserting the English church. One factor in Best's decision was fear of displeasing the city magistrates, who did not approve the transfer, and the suspicion in the English church that no replacement minister would be appointed very quickly.[43] During the revolutionary period, 1640-60, numerous Royalist English and Scottish preachers, out of favor in Britain, took refuge in Utrecht (Michael Honywood, Robert Creighton, Edward Martin, William Sancroft, Herbert Thorndike, and others).[44] William Colvill, a Scottish minister suspended by General Assembly in 1648 for supporting Hamilton's expedition, lived at Utrecht in 1651-52. Tradition refers to him as a minister of the English church and it is well possible that he did some

---

[40] B.P., I, 384-98; Res. Vroedschap, Aug. 27, 1647 (G.A. Utrecht). Boswell's letter is in "Brieven" (R.A. no. 289).

[41] B.P., I, 398; Acta Kerkeraad Utrecht, E, Jan. 10, 1648, fol. 47v.

[42] Acta Kerkeraad Utrecht, F, Aug. 23, 1653, Nov. 14, 1654; Steven, pp. 301-02n.

[43] C.R., I, 294; Acta Kerkeraad Utrecht, F, Aug. 11, 18, 22 and Sept. 4, 6, 1656. Edmund Calamy refers to Best as a Dutchman, *An Historical Account of My Own Life*, 2nd ed. (London, 1830), I, 144. Alice Carter, *English Reformed Church*, p. 107, believes him to be the son of an Englishman, William Best of Amsterdam. See baptism register, Amsterdam E.R.C., no. 82, 1619 and 1621. John Best was enrolled at Leiden Univ. in 1637 (*Album*, col. 285) and at Franeker Univ. in 1643 (*Album*, p. 128).

[44] Paul H. Hardacre, *The Royalists during the Puritan Revolution* (The Hague: Nijhoff, 1956), pp. 284-94.

preaching following Bowye's death; however, there is no record of his having been elected an official minister. He returned to Scotland in 1652, after being elected principal of Edinburgh University, but Cromwell prevented his assuming office.[45]

The consistory register, which commences with 1657, reflects a church life by that time of a routine kind. Preaching, the sacraments, and discipline followed the usual Reformed pattern. The consistory, after weathering the strife of the 1630s and 1640s, concerned itself primarily with routine discipline matters: Sabbath breaking, swearing, drunkenness, and such "course of life," also with a businesslike administration of the finances and poor relief of the congregation. Chrysie Farmer in 1658 had to be reproved for her "begging at the doores ... which being not to be borne in a member of the church, as being offensive to good Christians."[46] In the quarterly pre-communion visitation, the minister and officers made regular surveys of the congregation and seldom found anything remarkable: "found things indifferently well" (1657); "things were all indifferently well" (1658); "reasonable good estate, but that some few did give offense by their sinnes" (1659).[47]

Finding a workable relationship with the Dutch church and state was a long and uneven story for the English church of Utrecht. Because of receiving official financial subsidy from the magistrates, the church found itself bound by state policies relating to established Reformed churches; the church was obliged to turn to the magistrates on matters of meeting place, salary, furniture and benches, and, above all, for approval for calling of ministers. Except for taking notice of some controversies with unseemly publicity, the city magistrates did not concern themselves with the day-to-day affairs of the congregation, provided the overall prescribed policies were followed, for example, "that they (to witt, the congregation) shall not goe to thee Calling of a minister then with dew Correspondence, and examination of the Minister."[48]

The Dutch Reformed Church (the Dutch consistory, the Classis of Utrecht, and the Synod of Utrecht) gave much attention to insure English conformity with Reformed theology and practice. John Douglas in 1619 joined the classis and subscribed to the confession, with the slight reservation that "he excepted against that Article of Faith which speaks of the equality of ministers."[49] Thereafter, the Dutch Reformed church-

---

[45] *F.E.S.*, I, 134. Covill was nominated as minister at Flushing in 1651 (C.R., June 28, 1651) and at Middelburg in 1652, when he was said to be "residing at Utrecht" (Middelburg C.R., I, 169).
[46] C.R., I, Dec. 5, 1659.
[47] C.R., I, Dec. 30, 1657; Oct. 1658; Sept. 22, 1658.
[48] B.P., I, 263v.
[49] Acta Synod Utrecht, 1619, Reitsma and Van Veen, VI, 425; C.R., I, 297.

men harked back to Douglas's conformity as an excellent precedent.[50] After Douglas's pastorate, however, the link was broken and the next two ministers (Scott, Elborough) belonged to the English Synod rather than to the Dutch, leaving the English church nearly independent. Scott was inducted into ministerial office in 1622 by John Forbes of the English Synod, as was Elborough in 1626. Fortry in 1630 was inducted by Hugh Goodyear, the English minister of Leiden, not a member of any classis or synod.[51]

The aloofness of the English ministers of the 1620s troubled the Utrecht consistory and classis, and moreover, rumors were flying across the Low Countries about a general condition of disorderliness among English preachers. Utrecht Synod in 1625 resolved that English preachers should "stand under the supervision and censure of the Dutch consistory of the place where they were established and reside," further that the magistrates be persuaded to insure that no English churches would be permitted to function until their ministers exhibited to the local classis proper *testimonia vitae et doctrinae* and conform to all classical laws. The Synod renewed this resolution in 1626 and 1627.[52] Inasmuch as the Utrecht English church was the only English church in the entire province, except for some garrison preaching at Amersfoort, the intent of the synodical resolution was clear.

The major English policy instituted by the Dutch church in the 1620s was to impose conformity on the English church and bring their preachers into the Utrecht Classis—"a condition not wholly to the liking of some of the English preachers," admitted the classis.[53] Elborough, the English preacher most affected by the synodical resolutions, refused to cooperate with the Dutch "because he was not yet minded to join himself to the Classis of Utrecht." Since Elborough was already functioning in office, the synod agreed to let the matter rest for a time, but by "repeated remonstrances to the magistrates" they determined to arrange affairs that no further English ministers be admitted without conforming.[54]

After Elborough's tenure, which ended in 1629, the English church was put under much tighter supervision, and their ministers were compelled to conform by taking classis membership. The Utrecht Synod received wide approval from other provinces for their firm stand, but for the incoming English and Scottish ministers, enforced conformity was in-

---

[50] Acta Synod Utrecht, I, 1627, sess. 4, art. 3. The acta of the synod after 1620 are not printed and are found in R.A. Utrecht.

[51] B.P., I, 264-66.

[52] Acta Synod Utrecht, I, 1625, sess. 4, art. 4; 1626, sess. 2, art. 9; 1627, sess. 2, art. 9, sess. 4, art. 3.

[53] C.R., I, 273.

[54] Acta Synod Utrecht, 1627, sess. 4, art. 3; 1628, sess. 3, art. 5; C.R., I, 296.

convenient indeed, certainly *niet geheel na den smaak*.[55] The church asked: "But will the Gecommitteerden [the Classis officers] show but one example that the church erected in 1622 was under the Classis before the year 1629; or that then they came underst upon their Request?"[56] When Leighton came in 1629, he fell under the full provisions of the synodical and civil regulations, and he was soon forced out for refusing to fully conform in observance of feast days. Although a part of the congregation supported Leighton, the English elders accepted the inevitability of full conformity, if their subsidy of 500 guilders a year were to continue, and pushed Leighton to submit without "disorder." Faced with the ultimatum of "no innovation nor dispensation," which his conscience would not permit, Leighton resigned.[57]

Ralph Clayton, the next preacher, was put to a similar test; and although his conscience, "without the least difficulty," permitted taking classis membership, he remained at Utrecht only about seven months.[58] Isaac Fortry was approved by the classis in 1630 but only after giving assurances that "he would engadge to preach the feast texts," which had been Leighton's stumbling block.[59] Paul Amyraut (1637-38), who immigrated from Norfolk in the same wave as some of the Independents, refused to take session in the classis. The nature of his scruples is not recorded, whether he shared the "independent" scruples of the Dissenting Brethren or was perhaps straining at some particular gnat (e.g. feast days) in the Dutch Reformed church order.[60] Taken as a whole, the English church and its preachers yielded to the Dutch church with a minimum of enthusiasm, thus, said the English preacher of a later day, "to prevent its being thought, that we greatly at a loss how to dispose ourselves, had fled to the very reverend Classis with tears in our Eyes beseeching their protection."[61] In relations between the English and Dutch churches at Utrecht, the most influential go-between was Professor Gisbertus Voetius. His great standing in both churches made him a spokesman to be heeded. One English visitor, Edward Brown in 1668 included him among the sights of Utrecht. Voetius, "often frequenting the English Church," befriended many an English and Scot of the Puritan side and gave full support to the Puritan wing of the Utrecht con-

---

[55] Acta Synod Gelderland, 1626, art. 32 (R.A. Gelderland); C.R., I, 273.
[56] C.R., I, 295.
[57] Acta Classis Utrecht, May 19-20, 1629; Acta Kerkeraad Utrecht, D, fol. 9v.
[58] Acta Synod Utrecht, 1629, sess. 4, art. 4; Acta Classis Utrecht, Sept. 22, 1629, Feb. 16-17, 1630, May 11-12, 1630.
[59] C.R., I, 297; Acta Classis, Nov. 2-3, 1630. Fortry is listed in the Leiden Univ. *Album* (Isaacus Forterius Londonensis 22 A 1627), col. 202.
[60] Acta Classis Utrecht, pt. 2, Aug. 14-15, 1638; B.P., I, 267-68.
[61] C.R., I, 296.

gregation. "I profess to be almost a member of this church," Voetius declared.[62]

During the 1640s and onward, after Amyraut's unsuccessful campaign to be independent, the English church fell into an uncomplaining role as a Reformed congregation within the general framework of the Dutch Reformed church. The English church viewed itself as one of the Utrecht town churches, albeit the smallest, on equal level with the Dutch church of the city. In the classis the English minister spoke in his turn, "the last of the Citty divines and before the rurall;" and if he were a recently arrived minister, "not understanding their dutch," he would use Latin.[63] The consistory register contains a definition of the church:

> A particular congregation, or certain number of Christians of the reformed Religion, Burgers and Inhabitants of the City of Utrecht, lieveing under the ministry of one or more clergymen lawfully called and admitted unto their office; and under the governance of their own consistory, as their most immediate ecclesiasticale superiors; and under the civil government of the magistrates as their lawfull governors and Christian superiors.[64]

So the matter stood until the eighteenth century, during the ministry of William Brown (1748-57), when the issue of the status of the English church was raised anew, this time by the Dutch classis, which proposed to demote the English church from a town church of the first *locaat* to some lesser rank among the village churches. Brown was even assigned to a lower place at the dining table, "in itself a great trifle," Brown granted, "yet it ceised to be so, as soon as it was Considered as an expression of esteem or disregard which any man or Society of men are entitled to; and in this case could be considered as a trifle by none, but Such as have lost all sense of honor, all regard to the opinion of mankind, and their influence among them."[65] In contrast to the reluctant seventeenth-century ministers, Brown carried on a great effort to prove that the English church belonged in the first rank of the classis churches, not to be demeaned as some relic of the old English garrison chaplaincy. Brown's position was finally upheld by the States of Utrecht.[66]

The church was composed of four main components: English and Scots, soldiers and civilians. The relationship of the English garrison to the settled English-Scottish civilians was a long unsettled matter, as was

---

[62] Brown, *Travels*, p. 102; B.P., I, 394, 267v; Duker, *Voetius*, III, 133, 145.
[63] B.P., I, 339-40 (the experience of Malachi Harris).
[64] C.R., I, 287.
[65] C.R., I, 268-69.
[66] The English side of the story is given in extended version in C.R., I, 268-300; Steven, pp. 341-42; Grimes, *Utrecht*, p. 19.

the national division between English and Scots. The church before 1622, the garrison church, was served by a military chaplain and organized with a consistory of military officers, but after the formal establishing of 1622, the civilian part of the congregation took charge and made it into a "Burger Church." The regiments, admittedly, provided a part of the financial support (two guilders per month per company), but otherwise the soldiers were not admitted to places of power. "Shew us one example that since that time either any officer or soldier was elder or deacon of our church."[67] The burger core of the congregation was mercantile and had a strong Scottish contingent—"men of mean fortunes and merits" said the officers—whereas the garrison faction was more strongly English and through their main spokesmen, the high officers, more aristocratic and conformable to Church of England religion. Their petitions came in the name of "the officers and gentry" of the church.[68]

Many of the inner controversies of the church involved a split between the civilian and military components of the church. In 1637, when the strict Puritan Amyraut was given a call by the congregation, it was over the strong protests of the officers, both English and Scots, who complained bitterly that the elders had "fownd means to exclude the commander and officers from any part in the election of the minister." The elders, however, had the support of Professor Voetius, who supported the election of Amyraut. The officers caused a short secession as some "abstejned" from the congregation.[69] In 1639 the officers insisted on the election of John Hering, in which the elders concurred but soon regretted as an unhappy choice. At the time of Hering's election, the consistory laid down a policy of accepting no further financial support from the company payrolls and instructed Hering that "he must not receive any means (as formerlie hath been used by Mr. Fortree and others) from the English and Scottish Companies here garrisoned."[70] The civilian-military rivalry was a painful fact throughout the 1640s: The military officers supported Malachi Harris whereas the elders worked to undermine him; the officers supported the candidacy of Robert Remington (rejected in 1647), the elders opposed him; the elders pushed through the election of Bowye in 1647 and the officers opposed him, even seceding temporarily from church.[71] Among Netherlands British churches, Utrecht had the most equal balance between military and civilian members, producing years of bickering, and also a near balance between English and Scots. As the

---

[67] C.R., I, 297.
[68] S.P. 84, vol. 153, fol. 300; B.P., I, 384, 385.
[69] S.P. 84, vol. 153, fols. 300r & v.
[70] C.R., I, 290.
[71] B.P., I, 322-31, 384-98; C.R., I, 289-91.

elders saw it, "frequent disputes indeed happened between the garrisone and consistory, the first endeavoring to encroach upon the rights of the latter, and of the burgers they represented."[72] As late as 1650, the preacher of the church needed to refer to himself as "preacher of the English and Scottish nation and of the English and Scottish garrison."[73]

Arnhem

Arnhem, the capital city of Gelderland, was the site of a small but vigorous seventeenth-century English church (1638 to about 1645 or 1650). Unlike the other Gelderland churches at Nijmegen, Zutphen, Doesburg, and Tiel, which were garrison churches serving military people, the Arnhem church was established by substantial English civilian immigrants fleeing from the Laudian religion of the 1630s. The roster of Arnhem settlers composed the most prestigious colony-in-exile to be found in the Netherlands, men of the stature of Sir William Constable, Sir Matthew Boynton, Sir Richard Saltonstall, Yorkshire gentry; Henry Lawrence of St. Ives, Huntingdonshire; and Edward Ask, town recorder of Colchester—"worthy gentlemen."[74] Others of lesser quality were: Anna Crosbe, widow of William Crosbe, who was admitted to the tailors guild and to town citizenship in 1638; Mathias Forrester or Faster, tailor, admitted as citizen in 1640; and John Vright, tailor, admitted 1640. Forrester was in the service of Boynton.[75] The core of this Arnhem congregation had come over from England in 1637 and temporarily resided at "Viana" and Utrecht.[76]

The Viana and Utrecht people, or some of them, pushed on to Arnhem in 1638. On September 20, 1638, application was made to the city magistrates on behalf of some "Englishmen of quality and mark" (10-12 families, more than 100 persons), who had left England because of conscientious objection to the ceremonies of the Church of England. They proposed to settle at Arnhem, if suitable housing could be found and if

---

[72] C.R., I, 298.

[73] Petition to the States of Utrecht by Walter Bowye, "Eng. gemeente en de classis," fol. 15.

[74] Tanner MS. 65, fol. 24 (Bod.); J. T. Cliffe, *The Yorkshire Gentry from the Reformation to the Civil War* (London: Athlone Press, 1969), pp. 17, 307-09; Kenneth Shipps, "Lay Patronage of East Anglican Puritan Clerics in Pre-Revolutionary England," Diss. Yale 1971, p. 323; Daniel Neal, *The History of the Puritans* (Rpt. Westmead, Farnborough, Hants: Gregg International Publishers, 1970), II, 288-89.

[75] Burgerboek, O.A.A., no. 1223, fols. 71, 74, 75; Res. de Magistraat Arnhem, O.A.A., no. 16, fols. 140, 235, 236 (G.A. Arnhem).

[76] Thomas Edwards, *Antapologia* (London, 1644), pp. 22-23, 35, 187. Constable came over April 7/17, 1637, Archer July 27, 1637. "Viana" is not a current spelling; it could be Viane in Duiveland or more likely Vianem in Utrecht province since Archer refers to the city and university of Utrecht in his letters.

they could be provided with a building for the public exercise of the Reformed religion in the English language. They brought with them their own minister in the person of John Archer, who had already been ministering among them in Viana in 1637. The Arnhem burgomasters, pleased at the arrival of people of such quality, gave hearty welcome and assigned them a meeting place in the choir of the Broeren Kerk, a part of the old Franciscan cloisters, which they were to share with the French garrison church. As the cold winter weather came on, the English made further request in December for a pulpit and for hangings for the wall "because of the cold."[77] Although provided with meeting place, like other Reformed churches, the English church did not ask for the usual subsidy for minister's salary. The well-to-do congregation met expenses by its own offerings. After sermon and prayer, "the greatest companie present theire offeringes, which amounte to aboute two or 3 hundred pounds a year Sterlinge. The Ministers content themselfs with a hundred pounds a man per annum the Remainder is reserued for pious vses."[78] Francis Dibbet, former minister of the English church at Dort, 1635-37, came to Arnhem as Dutch Reformed minister in 1637; he may have been of assistance to the new English church.

Three ministers served the church in overlapping pastorates: John Archer (beginning at Viana in 1637 until his death about 1642); Thomas Goodwin (1639-41); and Philip Nye (1639-40 or '41). Thomas Edwards called Archer "pastour" and Goodwin and Nye "teachers." The church had for several years two, even three ministers, preaching "by turns."[79] All three were nonconformist Puritans in exile and outspoken advocates of the new Congregationalist theology; Goodwin and Nye became members of the famous Five Dissenting Brethren. Henry Lawrence was elder of the church and did some preaching. What drew this particular group of people to Arnhem is unclear, especially in view of the much more centrally-located English colonies in Rotterdam and Utrecht. Under Archer, Goodwin, and Nye, the Arnhem church became fully Congregational, with a zeal matched only, if at all, by the Rotterdam church, pastored since 1629 by Hugh Peter, William Ames, William Bridge, Jeremiah Burroughes, and Sydrach Simpson. If Archer, their "precious" colleague had not died early, he would certainly have joined the other Dissenting Brethren in their Congregational apologia. The

---

[77] Res. de Magistraat Arnhem, O.A.A., no. 16, fols. 134-36, 143v. See Van Hasselt, *Kronijk van Arnhem* (Arnhem, 1790), pp. 279-80.

[78] Tanner MS. 65, fol. 24.

[79] Edwards, *Antapologia*, pp. 22-23, 35; Edwards, *Gangraena* (London, 1646), pt. 3, p. 100. The exact dates when Goodwin, Nye, and Archer were at Arnhem are not completely certain. Nye and Goodwin both signed a letter of 1639 from Arnhem (Calamy, *N.M.*, II, 423); apparently both returned to England by 1641 (*D.N.B.* and Calamy).

Arnhem church, although claiming adherence to the tenets of Reformed religion, had very little intercourse with surrounding Dutch Reformed or even English Reformed churches, except for Rotterdam. Because the congregation was financially self-supporting, it was freed from the usual supervision of magistrates and classis, and theologically the church believed in being "Independent." At the time of John Ward's deposition at Rotterdam in 1639, the Arnhem church intervened by sending Goodwin, Nye, Henry Lawrence, and one other elder to conciliate. This consultation of sister churches the *Apologeticall Narration* grandly referred to as "that solemne assembly."[80]

While awaiting some change in the religious situation in England, which would permit a return home, the Arnhem people seemed to live a comfortable life. "Your frinds, Mr Laurence and his wife," came one report, "are in good health att Arnheim, the ayer of which place is uery agreeable vnto them, as to the rest of the good sosietye that liue there."[81] John Archer proclaimed life in the Netherlands to be better than ever: "For Holland, it is much better then I expected, for pleasantnesse, health, plenty of flesh and foule: we alter not our English diet in any thing." From Utrecht, before moving to Arnhem, he wrote, "a man may live as pleasantly there as at Hartford." Others commended the country as "so healthfull and pleasant as to resemble them to Bury in Suffolke."[82] Critics of the Arnhem and Rotterdam Independents accused them of resting abroad in a high and easy life, with "wives, children, estate, suitable friends, good houses, full fare." Thomas Edwards sneered at "poor" Archer, silenced and deprived at home, reportedly in failing health, yet on coming over to Arnhem had a regular ministry with good income and even the "strength to beget a sonne," whereas in England he was married many years and never had any child.[83] The miracle was temporary, however, and by 1642 Archer had relapsed and died.

The Arnhem church in its short life was innovative and experimental among the Netherlands English churches. "An humour of innovating at least, if not a spirit of errour, did much predominate among them," charged the Presbyterians onlookers.[84] The Independent-spirited Arnhem church was one of the two model churches of the Dissenting Brethren. From the beginning, the church was organized on the basis of a

---

[80] *An Apologeticall Narration* (London, 1644), p. 20; Robert Baillie, *Dissvasive from the Errours of the Time* (London, 1645), p. 76.

[81] Thomas Meauty (May 6, 1639) in Jane Lady Cornwallis, *Private Correspondence of Jane Lady Cornwallis* (London: n.p., 1842), pp. 289-90.

[82] Edwards, *Antapologia*, pp. 187-88.

[83] Ibid., pp. 25-26, 187-88; Baillie, *Dissvasive*, p. 79.

[84] Baillie, *Dissvasive*, p. 79.

church covenant, which Thomas Goodwin defined, as "an assent and resolution professed (by them to be admitted by us) with promise to walk in all those ways pertaining to this fellowship, so far as they shall be revealed to them in the gospel."[85] Edwards mocked them as a church of "pick't Christians." No one was admitted unless "truly godly." Newcomers were thoroughly scrutinized. A respectable visiting British minister, asking to be admitted to the communion, was barely received by them, and then only on condition of defending his church as a true church.[86] John Forbes of Corse lived at Arnhem for several months in 1645, but made no mention of fellowship or even of visiting the English church, whereas at all other cities he was a habitual sermon goer and guest preacher at the British churches.[87] Decisions and discipline were done in the congregation. As refugees of conscience, the Arnhem people took their worship very seriously. Their service of worship took this form: "They haue two Preachers, and this the discipline of theire Church; Vpon euery Sonday a Communion, a prayer before sermon and after, the like in the afternoone. The Communion Table stands in the lower end of the Church (which hath no Chancell) altar-wise, where the Chiefest sit and take notes, not a gentlewoman that thinkes her hand to faire to vse her pen and inke." The offering followed.[88]

Independency, however, was only the first step. Much new light was breaking forth at Arnhem. The innovations put in action, or at least debated, included anointing the sick with oil, laying on hands on the sick for healing, solo singing ("one man alone to sing in the midst of the silent Congregation"), prophesying, and the holy kiss. Archer was said to be preaching fantastic doctrines about the state of the soul after death and of imagining God to be the author of sin, for which his book, *Comfort for Beleevers* (1645) was condemned by the Westminster Assembly and Parliament and burned by the common hangman. "With such fine new speculations do the Independent Pastors feed their Flocks."[89] Millenarianism, another theological speculation, also took root at Arnhem in the teachings of Goodwin and Archer. "They run themselves over head and ears in the deepest gulph of that old Heresie." They "set

---

[85] Thomas Goodwin to John Goodwin, in response to a letter received by Thomas Goodwin, Nov. 20, 1639, Thomas Goodwin, *Works* (Edinburgh: James Nichol, 1861-66), XI, 536.
[86] Edwards, *Antapologia*, p. 37; [Alexander Forbes], *Anatomy of Independency* (London, 1644), p. 21.
[87] "J. Forbesii vita interior" (diary), in John Forbes, *Opera Omnia (Amsterdam, 1703)*, II, 264-65.
[88] Tanner MS. 65, fol. 24; Baillie, *Dissvasive*, p. 123.
[89] Edwards, *Antapologia*, pp. 35-37, 60; Baillie, *Dissvasive*, pp. 80-82, 87-88.

up the whole Fabricke of *Chiliasme.*"[90] Goodwin's fast sermon, *A Glimpse of Sions Glory*, preached at Arnhem or one of the other Netherlands churches in 1641, was filled with as much Millenarianism as Independency. Goodwin outraged orthodox Presbyterian Puritans by his assertion that Independency is the first step of Christ's coming kingdom. "Independency of Congregations *God* will honour," said Goodwin.[91] Archer's preaching and his book, *The Personall Reign of Jesus Christ upon Earth* (1642), were enthusiastically Millenarian.[92] Such teachings dismayed orthodox Dutch and British Calvinist theologians. Georgius Hornius, Leiden professor, denounced the Arnhem Independents of Archer's time as *crassi Chiliastae.*[93]

The Arnhem church was a church-in-exile, waiting for the doors to reopen to England. Beginning in 1640, "when the coasts were cleered," ministers and congregation began traveling home, and "were entertain'd and receiv'd with all respects and applause."[94] Nye returned to England in 1640-41 and became minister at Hull and Kimbolton, Huntingdon; Goodwin with some of the flock returned in 1641 and established an Independent church at London.[95] Nearly all the prominent members of the church, with the exception of Henry Lawrence, hurried home to work for the Parliamentary cause. After Archer's death, about 1642, the church was left without ordained ministers. Thereafter the church made do with lay preaching, "gentlemen preaching ordinarily in the absence of their Ministers." Elder Lawrence "a Gentleman and no Preacher, yet he preached all this while at Arnhem, while his brethren were in

---

[90] Baillie, *Dissvasive*, pp. 79-80, 244; Peter Toon, ed., *Puritans, the Millennium and the Future of Israel: Puritan Eschatology 1600 to 1660* (Cambridge: James Clark, 1970), pp. 62-68.

[91] *A Glimpse of Sions Glory: or the Churches Beautie Specified* (London, 1641), p. 33. This sermon was published in two printings, one with anonymous title page. Consequently, its authorship has been debated, but Goodwin is the most likely author. There is a variant edition, the Emmanuel College copy, which has a title page with the words: "Briefly layd open in a Sermon, at a generall Fast day in Holland. By T. G."; see John F. Wilson, "A Glimpse of Syons Glory," *Church History*, 31 (Mar. 1962), 66-73, and Toon, *Puritan Eschatology*, pp. 131-36. Recently Paul Christianson, *Reformers and Babylon* (Toronto: Univ. of Toronto Press, 1978), pp. 213-19, 251-52, has argued for Burroughes' authorship.

[92] John Archer, *The Personall Reign of Christ vpon Earth* (London, 1642), p. 3; Baillie, *Dissvasive*, p. 80.

[93] Georgius Hornius, *Historia Ecclesiastica et Politica* (Leiden, 1665), pp. 268, 331; Geoffrey F. Nuttall, *Visible Saints* (Oxford: Blackwell, 1957), p. 148.

[94] Edwards, *Antapologia*, p. 2.

[95] There is evidence that Goodwin, as the author of *A Glimpse of Sions Glory*, was still in the Netherlands in 1641, based upon interval evidence in *A Glimpse* (pp. 32-33). See also Murray Tolmie, *The Triumph of the Saints* (Cambridge: Cambridge Univ. Press, 1977), p. 122. According to the *D.N.B.*, Nye traveled to England on the same boat with John Canne in 1640 (other sources indicate, however, that Canne was in Amsterdam throughout 1640). Calamy says Goodwin and Nye returned at the beginning of the Long Parliament.

England."[96] At one point (1639) the church had solicited Edward Reyner of Lincoln to come over as an additional preacher, "but hoping that better times were approaching in England, he sent them a denial."[97]

The steady emigration and death of ministers and congregation left the church of the late 1640s in a low position. "The Arnhem people lived for many years without a pastor."[98] The church had never had a mercantile or military population as a core group; consequently, when the civil wars overturned the Laudian regime, the one firm factor motivating the chuch, its reason of being, disappeared. How long the church actually continued to exist after Archer's death is unknown. There is mention of Arnhem as a live church in *Anatomy of Independency* (1644), in Robert Baillie's *Dissvasive* (1645), and perhaps in Thomas Edwards's *Gangraena* (1646). Baillie, however, implied that the church had ceased active preaching services; lay preaching, he said, "these of *Arnhem* did to the last day of their churches standing maintain it." Edwards reported that the Arnhem sectaries were returning to England in 1645 or 1646 ("the Spring last").[99]

In the mid 1640s, the Arnhem church, already notorious for its Independency and Chiliasm, developed Anabaptist tendencies. "They all generally and their families were Anabaptist," came reports.[100] The remnant, bereft of ordained ministers, refused to fraternize with more conventional English Reformed churches of the provinces; when orthodox Puritan preachers were available, they "staid at home, and would not heare the English Reformed ministers." Some of the Arnhem people said, "If those Ministers would promise never to preach for Baptisme of children, nor against their way, they would hear them." When Archer's book *Comfort for Beleevers* was condemned by Parliament, the Arnhem remnant, now called "sectaries" by more respectable Puritans, defended Archer's memory and "justified all in that book." They spoke much against the Westminster Assembly, the covenant, and the Parliament.[101] Although many of the stories about Anabaptism come from hostile witnesses, they are confirmed, in part, by two writings of elder Henry Lawrence, *Of Our Communion and Warre with Angels* (Amsterdam, 1646) and *Of Baptisme* (Rotterdam, 1646). The latter book is an argument for adult believer's baptism and against infant baptism.[102]

[96] [Alexander Forbes], *Anatomy of Independency*, p. 25; Baillie, *Dissvasive*, p. 174.
[97] Calamy, *N.M.*, II, 423.
[98] Hornius, *Historia Eccl.*, p. 274.
[99] Baillie, *Dissvasive*, p. 174; Edwards, *Gangraena*, pt. 3, pp. 99-100.
[100] Edwards, *Gangraena*, pt. 3, pp. 99-100.
[101] Ibid.
[102] The two books were published anonymously but are attributed to Henry Lawrence (B.M.). *Of Our Communion* is dedicated to Lady Lawrence, mother of the author.

Whether the church functioned at all after 1650, or even 1645 is doubtful, at least with regular worship services. However, there may have been a slight revival or resurrection after 1660, after the Restoration when some Republican exiles took refuge at Arnhem.[103] The English church of Arnhem left few traces in the histories of Arnhem and still less in the records of the Dutch consistory and classis. There is a vague reference to an English church at Arnhem in the Dutch consistory register of 1667. At that time the Dutch laid down the policy that attestations would be required for members to transfer from the English or French churches to the Dutch, or back again.[104] William Steven's conclusion on the church was "that the members of this church who remained in Holland, gradually becoming acquainted with the Dutch language, attended the native clergy," thus accounting for names such as Beverly, Brown, and Hereford in the Dutch Reformed church.[105] In spite of a very short existence, the Arnhem church left a mark in the history of Puritanism.

---

[103] S.P. 29, vol. 90, no. 1.

[104] Acta Kerkeraad Arnhem, no. 2, fol. 97, Oct. 13, 1667. The reference is, however, inconclusive since it may refer to a general Gelderland policy for English churches, not specifically to an existing Arnhem church. See also Van Hasselt, *Kronijk*, pp. 279-80; and *Arnhem: zeven eeuwen stad* (Arnhem: Arnhem Genootschap van Oudheidkunde, 1933), pp. 175-76.

[105] Steven, p. 284.

CHAPTER NINE

THE MERCHANT ADVENTURERS

The chief seventeenth-century English trading company was the Merchant Adventurers. This mighty cloth exporting company was sufficiently powerful to control nearly half of the exports of London, and even in spite of reverses during the course of the century, the Adventurers overall maintained a position of prestige and wealth.[1] The Merchant Adventurers had the monopoly for shipping unfinished white cloth into designated staple ports in Germany and the Low Countries. Their seventeenth-century German staple port was Hamburg, and in the Low Countries they used Middelburg (1582-1621), Delft (1621-35), Rotterdam (1635-55), and Dort (1655-68). In 1668 the Adventurers lost their monopoly in the Netherlands; however, the company continued to operate under competitive conditions until the end of the century and maintained a church at Dort until 1700.

Wherever established overseas, the Merchant Adventurers had a preacher and church as a part of the company community. The company churches, far removed from Church of England supervision, fell into a Reformed-Presbyterian pattern and were almost invariably served by nonconformist Puritan preachers. "I fynde the Disciplyne therof presbyterian, and that the Company fell into this Fashion at the first graunt of Free Exercise of Religion vnto them, and hath soe continued from tyme to tyme, and from place to place of theyr Residence,'' reported Ambassador Sir William Boswell in 1633.[2] The early chaplains in the Low Countries were an illustrious roster of Puritans: Walter Travers, Thomas Cartwright, Dudley Fenner, Francis Johnson, Matthew Holmes, Henry Jacob, Hugh Broughton, Lawrence Potts, and John Forbes.[3]

The sixteenth-century Merchant Adventurers church, when at Antwerp and Middelburg, established many Reformed precedents. The church was governed by elders and deacons chosen from the greatest

---

[1] Astrid Friis, *Alderman Cockayne's Project and the Cloth Trade* (Copenhagen: Levin and Munksgaard, 1927), p. 70; Charles Wilson, *England's Apprenticeship, 1603-1763* (New York: St. Martin's Press, 1966), pp. 69-70. On the Merchant Adventurers in the Netherlands see C. te Lintum, *De Merchant Adventurers in de Nederlanden* (The Hague: Nijhoff, 1905) and Jürgen Wiegandt, *Die Merchants Adventurers' Company auf dem Kontinent zur Zeit der Tudors und Stuarts* (Kiel: Kommissionsverlag Walter G. Mühlau, 1972).

[2] S.P. 16, vol. 234, no. 8.

[3] On the early history of the Merchant Adventurers, see chapter 2.

merchants and politicians of the place. The preachers put the priority on preaching the word and showed no enthusiasm for the official Prayer Book, which was used minimally by Travers and Cartwright and thereafter dropped altogether. The *Book of the Forme of Common Prayer*, the Puritan worship book printed by Schilders of Middelburg (1586, 1587, 1602), was substituted in place of the Anglican prayer book in the late sixteenth-century period. By the 1630s, all worship books had been eliminated and the situation had gone so far that the company preachers "will observe no formes of prayer, nor admit of any Liturgy or divine service ... nor will they administer the Sacraments in any forme, but their owne."[4]

As warrant for these Puritan deviations from the Anglican norm, the company stood upon two historical precedents: (1) the grant of religious liberty to the company at Antwerp by Archduke Matthias in 1579, and (2) the sixteenth-century policies established by ambassadors Davison and Gilpin and the Earl of Leicester.

> In the yeer 1579 at the request of the Queens majesty by her Ambassador (Davison) was graunted by (Mathias) then governor in these countryes, free liberty of a church and government for all the english marchants and there her Majestys subjects then living at Antwerpe, on the back syde of the same act, is the same approved by the magistrates of Antwerpe with this provise that wee conforme ourselves both in doctrine and discipline with these churches of the reformed religion, which the English did. And Mr Davison was chosed the first elder of the church. ... In the yeere 87 [1586?] when Leycester was heer governor, there was a generall sinode whereine the discipline of the church was sett down in a forme and articles to be practized in her Majestys name, and by Mr Gilpin her Majestyes agent. A copy werof was sent unto our church then resident at Middelburg, which forme of government wee have always since observed and still observe.[5]

Said the company, "Wee haue conformed our selues to the Government established in the Churches of the United Provinces, by the joint authority of our State, as well as of this State under which wee live, as our predecessors haue done." Any alteration from Reformed religion toward Anglicanism, the Adventurers feared, "without sufficyent authority had been a great disobedyence to his Majesty and a dangerous aberracion from the Accord between his Majesty and these States."[6]

---

[4] S.P. 16, vol. 224, no. 57; Horton Davies, *The Worship of the English Puritans* (Westminster: Dacre Press, 1948), pp. 124-25.

[5] B.P., I, 104; S.P. 84, vol. 144, fols. 139v-140r. The national synod referred to was the Hague Synod of 1586; no general synod was held in 1587; F. L. Rutgers, *Acta van de Nederlandsche synoden der zestiende eeuw* (The Hague: Nijhoff, 1899), pp. 622-43.

[6] S.P. 84, vol. 145, fol. 151; S.P. 16, vol. 234, no. 8.

After the foundations laid by Travers and Cartwright, the preacher most influential in shaping the church was John Forbes (1610-34). A Scot, formerly minister of Alford in Aberdeenshire, Forbes was one of the six preachers forced into exile in 1606 after participating in the unlawful Assembly of Aberdeen (1605). Taking refuge in the Netherlands, Forbes began preaching on an interim basis for the merchants at Middelburg in 1610 and in about 1612 became official minister, displacing Lawrence Potts. In exile Forbes was an active organizer of nonconformist Puritan activity, both English and Scottish, and was a chief promoter of the English Synod. He had a skilled political hand and succeeded outstandingly in manipulating affairs to the Puritan advantage at the States General. By his powerful preaching and leadership he achieved a great reputation in the congregation, which honored him by putting several of his sermons into print. In theological matters Forbes advanced far beyond his Scottish Presbyterian upbringing and often innovated in worship. His Anglican detractors labelled him "chief of these Refractory ministers," and the "oracle of all the rest." Another enemy (albeit a demon-possessed lunatic) accused him of being a "blockhead."[7]

The ability of Forbes to survive as Merchant Adventurer preacher for twenty-four years, in the face of official London displeasure, proves the substantial independence of the Merchant Adventurers in religious affairs; his survival also proves his own agile political skills. Both James I and Charles I were once or twice resolved to remove him; and although he was summoned back to London several times for reprimand and dismissal, Forbes charmed his way through each situation until 1634 when Laud put an absolute end to his ministry. When Forbes was admitted at Middelburg, King James "in great displeasure rebuked the company for entertaining such a one," but Forbes was saved by Scottish connections at court.[8] Forbes lived such a prosperous life at Middelburg and Delft that other exiled Scots almost believed him to be some secret agent of the Crown. "We feare that Mr John Forbese bee the king's agent and intelligencer," suspected David Calderwood in 1618.[9] There is, however, no evidence of his being a secret turncoat, in spite of having occasional communications with King James and Dudley Carleton.[10]

Forbes's success in the presence of majesty depended on his adroit mixture of prophetic preaching—the man of God—and doses of flattery.

---

[7] S.P. 84, vol. 146, fols. 73-74; S.P. 16, vol. 250, no. 28; William Brereton, *Travels in Holland the United Provinces England Scotland and Ireland*, ed. Edward Hawkins, Chetham Society, 1 (1844), 26; *F.E.S.*, VII, 542-43.
[8] S.P. 84, vol. 146, fol. 40v.
[9] S.P. 14, vol. 104, no. 26.
[10] Carleton, *Letters*, p. 506; S.P. 84, vol. 98, fols. 77, 86.

In one interview with King James, near the end of the reign, the king (by Forbes's own account) gravely asked Forbes for counsel: "He disired him to give him a Reason, why it came to pass that he had found the Scotish church good and left it bad, and that he found the English Church bad, and should leave it far worse." Forbes's answer: "It proceeded from the Bishops whose government was antiChristian." Forbes also advised the king that remedy was still possible, especially so in Scotland "where that Government was not yet so strongly settled, and in England also it might be done, so it were wisely managed."[11] Forbes returned safely to his charge at Delft after that encounter.

When summoned before Charles in 1633, Forbes again spoke bluntly but also winsomely enough that the king hinted at a bishopric in exchange for conformity. Even though Forbes "flatly refused" to conform, he did it so well that the king sent him back to his church for one last chance.[12] Laud, however, thought otherwise, especially after Forbes had imprudently expounded to Laud "such things as I thought did most concern your graces good both here and hereafter." Laud immediately caused his dismissal as Merchant Adventurer preacher (1634).[13] Forbes, who refused all blandishment for official preferment lived hazardously, never knowing when the next purge would come; he managed very well to have held his position for twenty-four years. He once wrote to his cousin Andrew Melville, "I am not moved by the foolish judgement of vain courtiers, nor by the empty triumphs of the bishops: such winds cannot shake the foundation on which we rest."[14]

The Merchant Adventurer preachers were supported financially by the company, not by Dutch stipends. The host city, however, provided the church building. Forbes at Delft received 260 pounds annually guaranteed plus some voluntary gifts from the congregation. Of this sum sixty pounds was for a curate, "or in their reformed language an Assistant."[15] When the company moved to Delft in 1621, they had the use of the Prinsenhof church.[16] The company headquarters, known as the English House, were also in the Prinsenhof, an honorable location where William of Orange had once lived. "The company of English cloth merchants live here bravely, accommodated with all necessaries, and invested many privileges; their house rent free, victuals excise free; a stately room to dine in; a dainty bowling-alley within the court; a pair of

---

[11] Eg. MS. 784, fol. 193 (B.M.).
[12] Ibid.; S.P. 84, vol. 147, fols. 155-56.
[13] S.P. 16, vol. 260, no. 5.
[14] Thomas M'Crie, *The Life of Andrew Melville* (Edinburgh, 1819), II, 434-36.
[15] S.P. 16, vol. 260, no. 13.
[16] Dinant P. Oosterbaan, *Zeven eeuwen. Geschiedenis van het oude en nieuwe gasthuis te Delft* (Delft, 1954), p. 261.

butts; accommodated with fair, convenient lodgings."[17] Financial independence meant ecclesiastical freedom from Dutch authority but not from the English government, which frequently attempted to control the Adventurer's church.

Forbes at Delft kept us the Antwerp-Middelburg tradition of drawing elders and deacons from the important members of the company, except for excluding the deputy, Edward Misselden (1623-33), a supporter of Anglican religion and known agent of Laud. The slighted deputy became Forbes's most bitter enemy. Forbes and his elders (Samuel Avery, Timothy Williams, and Andrew Kenrick)[18] governed the church according to Presbyterian standards, at least until the 1630s, when Forbes began to innovate and move the church into freer, more Congregational directions. Forbes was assisted in his church innovations by Thomas Hooker, his assistant 1631-33, and by Hugh Peter and Samuel Bachelor, neighboring ministers who preached occasionally in the church. Cotton Mather records that Hooker's first sermon at Delft was from Philippians 1:29, "To you it is given not only to believe, but also to suffer." Mather further records that Forbes and Hooker worked together so closely that they were like Basil and Nazianzen, "one soul in two bodies." They made an invincible Puritan team.[19]

Before Forbes's pastorate, the church followed the Travers-Cartwright precedents but had no set consistorial rules or church constitution. The consistory register, by reports of 1633, recorded "certain ecclesiasticall censures used by the church against consenage, swearing, drunkennes, raylings, fornications, etc, wherin our predecessors haue been more exact and diligent then the present times. ..."[20] The original consistory register from Antwerp went with the segment of the merchants settling at Middelburg and Delft, rather than to the Hamburg court. The register, however, and all other papers of the church disappeared at some time after 1633, except for copies of a few pages collected by Boswell in that year as a part of his investigations into Puritan activities at Delft.[21] Forbes proclaimed enthusiasm for Dutch Reformed religion, and he had excellent rapport with the Dutch ministers; nevertheless, his ministry was taking an independent direction. He "doth neither conforme to the church of England, nor to the churches of the States, nor to the government of the Company," the anti-Puritans charged.[22] He never used the Prayer Book, and although he made some use of Dutch worship forms, as

---

[17] Brereton, *Travels*, p. 19.
[18] P.C. Acts, no. 43, fol. 185 (P.R.O.); S.P. 84, vol. 145, fol. 151.
[19] B.P., I, 114-16; Mather, *Magnalia*, I, 339.
[20] B.P., I, 96.
[21] Ibid., I, 101-07.
[22] S.P. 84, vol. 146, fol. 73v.

reading chapters and singing psalms before sermons, even these forms he revised, not using "the very same words verbatim."[23] Earlier he used the Lord's Prayer, but this he too dropped.[24] Like other English and Scottish preachers in the Netherlands, he served the communion to the congregation seated.

Forbes so detested the words of the English liturgy, and eventually all liturgies, that he refused all set forms of any kind, "no not in Baptising, nor in the celebration of the Lords Supper, nor in Marriage, but every time speake as the Spirit enableth them, of this sort Mr Forbes is most eminent, and therefore is sent for, farre and neare to Baptise Children after the New way."[25] The Spirit-filled Forbes gradually eliminated all prayers for the king as "supreme governor" of the church, observance of the holy days of Christ's birth and death, and the Lord's Prayer, "but doth all things according to his owne judgment and minde, both in doctrine and administration, and the discipline of the church."[26] The ritual of the Lord's Supper, and all rituals, were not central to worship in the Merchant Adventurer church; during Forbes's controversies with deputy Edward Misselden, 1631-1633, Forbes omitted serving the Lord's Supper for eighteen months rather than having Misselden participate. Preaching was primary. The church scheduled at least three sermons each week.[27]

Forbes's associations with Thomas Hooker, Hugh Peter, and William Ames, of the newly-emerging Congregationalist party, carried Forbes far to the radical side. As these Puritans talked of selective membership and church covenants, Forbes was drawn into some of their doctrines. While Hooker was his assistant, 1631-33, the church began a more spiritual policy of baptizing, with Hooker refusing to baptize some babies "because he knew not the faith of their parents."[28] To bring greater spiritual improvement, Forbes and his elders carried through a strict reorganization of the church in 1633, based on Four Propositions, only a few weeks after Hugh Peter had completed the famous church covenanting at Rotterdam. In a somewhat similar step, the Merchant Adventurer church adopted Four Propositions or articles:

1. That they acknowledge that Gods word is trulie preached and the Sacraments rightlie administered in the church of Delfe according to the work of God.

---

[23] B.P., I, 96v.
[24] S.P. 84, vol. 146, fols. 202-03.
[25] S.P. 16, vol. 310, no. 103.
[26] S.P. 84, vol. 146, fol. 73v.
[27] S.P. 16, vol. 260, no. 13.
[28] S.P. 16, vol. 310, no. 103.

2. That the discipline there used in the church, is also according to the word of God.
3. That they submitt to be ruled by their Pastor and Elders according to the word of God.
4. That whosoever will not submit to the said discipline and censure of the said Pastor and Elders shall bee held as an heathen and publican.[29]

With the entire congregation assembled, men, women, and children, Forbes "read to them his presbyterian and consistoriall canons and constitution and caused them to submit themselves therewith, and to be governed therby and by no other authority; and thereupon hath administred to them the communion which he forbare before, 16 or 18 monthes."[30] The church reorganization took place about May of 1633, some forty years after Francis Johnson had first attempted unsuccessfully to introduce a written covenant into their church, then residing at Middelburg.[31]

The Four Propositions are harsh and rigid, intended to produce a disciplined congregation. Misselden, moreover, interpreted them as punitive, anti-episcopal maneuvers designed to exclude him and other Anglicans from power. Taken within the context of the popularity of covenant-making in the Netherlands English churches of the 1630s, however, the propositions suggest a theological preference for a more Congregational conception of the church. Forbes was not ignorant of the significance of adopting "propositions" or covenants, having recently presided at the congregational meeting at Hugh Peter's church in Rotterdam, April 1633, when Peter's covenant was consecrated. Ambassador Boswell included Forbes's Four Propositions in his collection of suspect covenant documents forwarded to Laud. The other covenants were John White's Dorchester covenant and Hugh Peter's Rotterdam covenant.[32] However, in spite of attraction to some of the Hugh Peter-William Ames Congregational doctrines, Forbes did not become a full-fledged Congregationalist; and in 1634, having moved with his family to Rotterdam, he was considered out-of-step by the Rotterdam Congregationalists.[33]

---

[29] S.P. 16, vol. 252, no. 29; S.P. 84, vol. 147, fol. 45.
[30] S.P. 84, vol. 147, fol. 45 (Misselden's report of July 16, 1633). R. P. Stearns in his *Congregationalism in the Dutch Netherlands* (Chicago: The American Society of Church History, 1940), p. 37, mistakenly presents the Four Propositions as imposed from London as an anti-Forbes program.
[31] On Francis Johnson in 1591, see chapter 2.
[32] B.P., I, 152-54; S.P. 16, vol. 252, nos. 29, 32.
[33] [Alexander Forbes], *The Anatomy of Independency* (London, 1644), p. 23.

As perennial president of the English Synod and minister of a prominent church, Forbes was looked upon in the Netherlands as the most responsible spokesman of British religion. Boswell, on the contrary, deeply distrusted Forbes as a Puritan ringleader, and during a conference with the Dutch Council of State, attempted to expose Forbes's religious singularities, hoping to undermine his prestige.

> Said one of the Dutch politicians: Forbes "obserues our formes and constitucions."
>
> Boswell responded: "I held yt neither impertinent, nor iniuriouse to tell them, that upon enquiry I believed their lordships would finde, He neuer vsed any Cathechisme in his church, without which a Church could not subsist; He neuer vsed any set forme for mariage, baptisme, or communion, expresse termes for the same being inioyned in our and their churches: That he was wont rarely to vse, and of late hath vtterly forborne the Lords prayer: He kept no anniuersary solemnisation of our Sauiours birth or passion: neither kept orderly correspondence and vnity with any part of their churches."[34]

The Dutch councillors were surprised at such news.

Forbes, although enjoying strong support among the merchant congregation, could never win over Misselden, the deputy, who denounced him as a very poor pastor. Misselden resented Forbes's great standing in the company, which overshadowed his own position; and beginning in 1631, they came into open conflict. As a writer of books, one on *Free Trade* and another on *The Circle of Commerce*, a man experienced in business and politics, Misselden expected to be treated respectfully. Honor was due to the deputy of the Merchant Adventurers. How exasperating to be slighted by Forbes and the inner Puritan core of elders. Misselden could only surmise that Forbes was a cunning schemer reaching far above his proper station, a sly Scot, who "wound himself unto familiarity with yong men of our Company beyond the seas, and so got himself to be entertained for their preacher; whereby he hath corrupted them exceedingly with his presbyterian doctrine and discipline. ... This man is of an imperious spirit, and full of singularities."[35] What Misselden most resented was never being elected a church elder, as the old precedent for the deputy was. Forbes and the elders "never advised with him in anything concerning the church." In 1631 Forbes overstepped his authority by admitting into the congregation as voting members non-company Englishmen of Delft, who attended services. These were mere "handicrafts men, and others unfree of this fellowship." When

---

[34] S.P. 84, vol. 146, fols. 202-03.
[35] S.P. 84, vol. 147, fol. 45.

Misselden confronted Forbes about this, Forbes backed down, but bad will prevailed. The elders saw Misselden as an enemy agent, "as if he went about to alter the course, they now are in, and to have the church governed by the Governor or his Deputy and Assistants."[36] In a short while, Misselden found himself ostracized by the merchants of Delft, who solidly supported "honest Mr. Forbes."[37]

The beleaguered Misselden began a furious campaign (1632-33) to discredit Forbes and force his removal, thus to restore his own authority. Misselden's strategy was a combination of appeals to the company officers of London plus anti-Forbes conspiracies with ambassador Sir William Boswell and Archbishop Laud. Boswell and Laud were already active in broader schemes to repress all Puritanism in the Netherlands. Consequently, Misselden's personal grievances at Delft made him a ready agent of the high officials and one of their most useful informants. For the next several years, Misselden prepared a barrage of memoranda justifying his own affairs and condemning Forbes and, in time, the entire company of merchants at Delft—"in truth there are none fit."[38]

Misselden was an astute observer of Dutch-English affairs; and in spite of obvious prejudices, he was an informative witness. His correspondence covered a host of Merchant Adventurer matters, religious and economic. In a memo of 1633 entitled "The Constitucion or Government of the United Provinces: with a brief observacion of some essentiall matters of state relative to the king and kingdome of England," Misselden surveyed the Dutch situation. "For as these countries are well styled the schole of warre; so are they become the Councel of State, and place of Agitation, of all the great actions of the Christian world." Concerning the people as a whole, "The people of these parts, are naturally subtile: and the government is managed by as many learned and able men, as are any where in the world." He lifted out three great issues of state policy, religion, war, and trade, and proposed a remedy for each problem. First, in religion, the Dutch, although Reformed in faith, extended toleration "by way of connivence, of all other corrupt Religions," and according to Misselden this was done merely for cunning reasons of state "to draw people and trade to their Countries." Dutch toleration affected England by way of giving refuge to British religious refractories, Forbes included among them. The remedy was to close the door to the

---

[36] B.P., I, 48-49.
[37] S.P. 84, vol. 144, fol. 240; on the controversy at Delft, see Stearns, *Congregationalism*, chapter 3, "Trouble at Delft," and Robert P. Brenner, "Commercial Change and Political Conflict: The Merchant Community in Civil War London," Diss. Princeton 1970, chapter 8, "The Merchant Adventurers."
[38] S.P. 16, vol. 257, no. 12.

religious deviants by forcing the Dutch government to refuse admittance or employment to any nonconformist Puritan preachers. If this policy would be enforced, predicted Misselden, the Delft church would be brought to swift conformity.

The second issue was national power and war, in which the Dutch, although a small handful of people, were able to wage war and prevail against Spain, and throughout to finance their way by taxes and borrowing. If the Dutch States were to prevail in all seventeen provinces, they might become intolerably powerful. He recommended as remedy that King Charles intervene as *Rex Pacificus* to arrange an immediate peace, short of full Dutch victory, between Spain and the United Provinces, perhaps thereby happily gaining for England some territory in Brabant and Flanders. The third issue was trade. "They have nothing of their owne and yet they abound in trade, raising trade out of forreine trade, brought home unto them," to the detriment of England. The Dutch were the greatest threat to the English fishing and cloth trade, the former being already almost stolen away and the latter under severe pressure. The Dutch imported Irish and English wools and fullers earth, as well as Spanish wools, and were so efficient in their draperies manufacturing that they produced good quality drapery at cut prices. Misselden's remedy was absolutely to cut off trade of English wools and fullers earth into the Netherlands, enforcing the ban by making such trade a felony. Or better still, said Misselden, let the English occupy Flanders and Brabant and re-establish the Merchant Adventurers at Antwerp.[39]

The most urgent letters from Misselden warned of the troubles in the church of Delft. Only if he were retained as deputy of Delft with full authority could the situation be set right. He portrayed himself as a martyr persecuted by the merchants "because I have shewed my selfe in my place, to stand for his Majesty's government, and the Church of England"—he had no other faults.[40] Everyone at Delft abused him, and none were to be trusted. "One part of them is lay elders: another part is such as are married to strangers; and the rest are apprentices and young men."[41] However, the deepest blame for the controversy he laid squarely on John Forbes, and no improvement was possible until a conformable minister would be sent to replace him, and also an Anglican Prayer Book, to be "immediately sent over to Delff, and read in the church, ... and to receive the Communion kneeling." As the long term solution, Misselden urged that the government of the company be revoked to London, "under His Majesty's eye," away from the young men who

---

[39] S.P. 84, vol. 146, fols. 73-74 (1633).
[40] S.P. 84, vol. 146, fol. 71.
[41] S.P. 16, vol. 257, no. 12.

lived abroad. Puritanism could never have infiltrated so deeply into the Merchant Adventurers, Misselden judged, except for the immature youthfulness of the Delft and Hamburg merchants. Left to themselves, the young men fell in with Forbes, assisted him in his radical innovation of the church, and next "our yong men returne home, worse then they came, and so become ill members to our Mother Church, and Country."[42]

Religious immaturity among the merchants was only part of Misselden's problem. During the first half of the seventeenth century, the Merchant Adventurers dropped into a permanent economic decline, which recent historians label as "prolonged crisis" or "long-term depression." Misselden attributed this depression to the youthful inexperience of the merchants.[43] Although he granted that the Dutch gave clever competition, Misselden laid almost sole blame on the incompetence of the young Forbites of Delft and Hamburg. The Adventurers, "by their intrusting of their chief government to yong men, in forreigne parts, they have almost lost the trade of cloth, and brought 80 thousand clothes a yeare, which not long since were exported out of this kingdome to their places of residence, to 40 thousand."[44]

What began as a misunderstanding between Misselden and Forbes in 1631 turned by 1632 into an all-out war between Misselden versus the entire Delft Merchant Adventurer company. Most of the Hamburg merchants, at least the chief officers, were also hostile to Misselden. When his slanders against the Delft people became known, his position among them was completely undermined. No one trusted him. Samuel Avery was the chief spokesman of the merchant factors at Delft (elder of the church, also son-in-law of Edward Bennet, the deputy governor at Hamburg, and brother of the Hamberg secretary); he efficiently rallied opinion for having Misselden removed. "We have no reason to ... suffer such a man to be our deputy."[45] After Misselden's letters to London had accused the Delft Adventurers of being schismatics and refractories, seventeen of them prepared a petition to Sir William Boswell, November 27, 1632, asserting their total loyalty to king and church—it was just that while living abroad they felt obliged to conform to Dutch Reformed prac-

---

[42] S.P. 84, vol. 147, fol. 45v, vol. 146, fol. 71.

[43] Wilson, *England's Apprenticeship*, p. 53; B. E. Supple, *Commercial Crisis and Change in England 1600-1642* (Cambridge: Cambridge University Press, 1959), pp. 136-37; Wiegandt, *Merchants Adventurers' Company*, pp. 102-05.

[44] S.P. 84, vol. 147, fol. 46. On the role of young merchants abroad, see Friis, *Cockayne's Project*, pp. 81-82.

[45] S.P. 84, vol. 144, fol. 240. On Bennet, see Heinrich Hitzigrath, *Die Kompagnie der Merchants Adventurers und die engelsche Kirchengemeinde in Hamburg 1611-1835* (Hamburg: Johannes Kriebel, 1904), p. 95.

tice "as our predecessors have done."[46] The merchants were convinced that Misselden was irrationally bent on vicious revenge, "being resolved to spend the last peny in his purse, and the last blood in his body to be revenged of us."[47]

In July of 1633 Misselden was voted out as deputy by action of the head Merchant Adventurer court at Hamburg, but this only drove him on to still more desperate schemes of revenge, more penny and blood. Because the Merchant Adventurer's charter was vulnerable to governmental manipulation, Misselden bitterly urged that the Adventurers be summoned into Star Chamber for minute examination of their charter; "and if these grounds will beare a bill in the starre chamber, I suppose, it will bring ten thousand pounds to the king, and besides a perfect reformacion of all these evills." Then, *ex malis moribus, bona nascunter leges*. Although the prolonged commotion about the Merchant Adventurers had no success in regaining Misselden his lost position, one result was a thorough review of the organization in the Privy Council and a redrawing of the charter in 1634. However, any attempted alterations in the government of the company in the 1630s proved to be temporary. The General Court and the holding of elections remained overseas at Hamburg.[48]

Misselden's anti-Forbes agitation served Ambassador Boswell very well, because Delft was already one of the main targets of his campaign to destroy Dutch nonconformity. The suggestion of revoking the company's charter impressed Boswell as sound advice; and any scheme for the removal of Forbes had Boswell's vehement support. The king was also urging such action. Secretary John Coke dispatched instructions to Boswell, February 15, 1633, to give "diligent inspection" to the Merchant Adventurer's church; thereupon Boswell went to Forbes: "I now playnely tould him, that his Majestie had taken a resolucion (as he had reason) in his owne Peculiars, to exempt Societies of his Subjects so imediately depending uppon him, to have Divine Service performed according to the Lawes of his owne Church, and Kingdome."[49] Further, Archbishop Laud in March of 1633 presented to the Privy Council a tenstep program for bringing conformity to English religion in the

---

[46] S.P. 84, vol. 145, fol. 151. The names were: Will. Cockeroft, Fr. Tichburne, Ric. Gaye, Ric. Archer, Christoph. Tomlinson, John Quarles, Ed. Morgan, Laur. Goff, Andrew Kenrick, Tim. Williams, Sam. Avery, Will. Fox, Barny Reymes, Ed. Bolle, John Ainsworth, Th. Clotterbook, Will. Colmer.

[47] S.P. 84, vol. 144, fol. 240.

[48] S.P. 84, vol. 147, fol. 46; Te Lintum, *Merchant Adventurers*, pp. 99-100.

[49] B.P., I, 109; S.P. 84, vol. 146, fols. 65-67. Already when sent over in 1632, Boswell had instructions to supervise the church of the Merchant Adventurers, S.P. 84, vol. 144, fol. 167v.

Netherlands, including special regulations for the Merchant Adventurers:

> That the Company of Merchants there residing, or in any other parts, shall admit no Minister as Preacher to them but such as are so qualified, and so commended as aforesaid (i.e. "such as should conform in all things to the Church of *England*, to be commended to them by their Lordships, the Advice of the Archbishop of *Canterbury* and *York* being taken in it.")
>
> That every Minister or Chaplain in any Factory, or Regiment, whether of *English* or *Scots*, shall read the Common Prayers, Administer the Sacraments, Catechise the Children, and perform all other publick Ministerial duties, according to the Rules or *Rubricks* of the *English* Liturgie, and not otherwise.[50]

Laud intended to close all the doors to Puritans. The ten-step program was found good and was formalized as an Order in Council in October of 1633. Under the new regulations the Merchant Adventurers were to transfer their government back to London, submit to the liturgy and discipline of the church of England, and in religion to be under the Bishop of London as diocesan.[51] The Privy Council also attempted to frighten the Delft Puritans into quick submission by ordering home for discipline Forbes, Avery, and seven others, being the "chief actors" of the "Presbyterie."[52]

Meanwhile, Boswell at The Hague was expounding the necessity of the anti-Puritan policies to the Dutch Council of State. "For as the Company was a Corporation immediately depending upon his Majesty like a little Republique among them, but not of them; so was the church in that Republique. A peculiar of his Majesties, which he would cause to be visited and ordered in his owne good tyme."[53] Forbes refused to bend, stiffened by the backing of Avery and other Delft merchants, everything having "been done by consent of all the Company here," not by any particular ones.[54] After Forbes had been called before Boswell for discipline and twice ordered over to England, without backing down, Boswell concluded that he "for certaine will not read the prayers." Before the face of

---

[50] Peter Heylyn, *Cyprianus Anglicus* (London, 1668), pp. 232-33. These were articles 2 and 4 of Laud's program.

[51] S.P. 16, vol. 247, no. 2; Privy Council Acts, no. 43, fols. 185, 261.

[52] P.C. Acts, no. 43, fol. 185 (Oct. 31, 1633).

[53] S.P. 84, vol. 146, fol. 202.

[54] S.P. 84, vol. 144, fol. 240. At least one of the merchants, John Quarles, who publicly supported Forbes and Avery was aiding Boswell by surreptitious letters, B.P., I, 94, 96; see also R. Bijlsma, "Rotterdams handelsverkeer met Engeland tijdens het verblijf der Merchants Adventurers (1635-1652)," *Bijdragen voor vaderlandsche geschiedenis en oudheidkunde*, 5th ser., pt. 4 (1917), 104.

the king, Forbes not only refused personally to use the Prayer Book but "said he would hinder it to his power." King Charles in October of 1633 gave him one more chance to conform at Delft, and when that failed to happen, Forbes was dismissed after twenty-four years of service.[55] In one of his last sermons at Delft, he preached from I Timothy 6:15 on the Christian's duty to God and to kings. "We must not obey the king against that king that made him a king."[56]

After returning from his interrogation before the king in October 1633, Forbes had only a few weeks to put his affairs in order. The elders sought frantically for some subterfuge which might save their preacher and their Reformed worship. One clever plan, based upon the old lecturer system from England, proposed bringing in to assist Forbes a second minister who would do the official duties requiring the Anglican service book—"the prayer businesses"—and freeing Forbes as "lecturer" to preach. Henry Sibbald of Nijmegen or Mr. Oldsworth of England were rumored as Forbes's new assistants. "Dr Sibbald they say ... is to be but as it were the curate, and that Mr Forbes shall stilbe entertained as the preacher, which (I use the words of one of the marchants) is the choice worke, for as for those litle things to baptize children and administer the sacrament the Apostles were not wont to do them. And thus Mr Forbes will find as good entertainement as before. ..."[57] So they hoped. Boswell, however, exasperated at the sly maneuvers of the Delft Puritans, put an end to Forbes's lectureship scheme by demanding full conformity or immediate dismissal. Boswell wrote: "He is in to returne unto his charge in Delft, if he will conforme himself and his congregacion to the ordres of our Church. ... I dare confidently averre, that His Majesty will skarce recouer in thrice seuen yeares, as at present, so handsome a concurrence, and advantage of bringing our Liturgie, and Church Discipline into that Company."[58] In February of 1634, Forbes gave up the struggle and in a letter to Laud submitted to being removed without further resistance. Hugh Peter, a part time preacher in the church, had shortly before, October 1633, also closed his service at Delft.[59]

Forbes moved himself and his family from Delft and sought employment at Rotterdam but nothing permanent could be arranged. He died at Veere in August 1634, "being taken there with a fit of the stone, which caused a burning fever."[60] To the Puritan zealots of the Netherlands the

---

[55] S.P. 84, vol. 146, fol. 182v; S.P. 84, vol. 147, fols. 155-56; Eg. MS. 784, fol. 193.
[56] John Forbes, *Fovr Sermons* (n.p., "Published by S.O.," 1635), p. 57.
[57] S.P. 16, vol. 250, no. 28; S.P. 16, vol. 252, no. 55.
[58] S.P. 84, vol. 147, fol. 174.
[59] S.P. 16, vol. 260, no. 5; S.P. 84, vol. 148, fol. 1; B.P., I, 146.
[60] He was buried "Saturday last," i.e. August 9/19 (report of August 14/24, 1634), S.P. 84, vol. 148, fol. 177.

twice-deprived Forbes ranked among the great heroes of the faith; "this truth of God he witnessed more then 30. yeares, not onely unto the losse of his living, and unto bonds; but also unto banishment, for defending that it is not lawfull for any Prince or Potentate to commend anie human devises, for to compell them to be used in the worship of God, and for mainteyning this endured these great tryalls."[61] He had survived at Delft longer than his arch-enemy Misselden, but only by about six months.

In trying to save his own job, Misselden had made himself odious to the majority of Merchant Adventurers. The court at Hamburg, which had jurisdiction over the company at Delft, voted to remove him in July 1633. In his place they elected Robert Edwards. Misselden's removal, however, offended the Privy Council, who were grateful for Misselden's intelligence of the last years, and they declared the election null and void.[62] At the October meeting of the Hamburg court, Edwards was removed, as ordered, but instead of reinstating Misselden they elected Samuel Avery, the chief Forbite (also the son-in-law of the Hamburg governor), as deputy.[63] The Adventurers were absolutely insistent that they could never endure Misselden, "that they will use him with such respect, as belongs to a bankrupt or insolvent"—the ultimate insult among merchants.[64] Provocative action, perhaps, but by October of 1633 the Adventurers judged that it was safe to bypass Misselden, who had made such a tedious nuisance of himself that Boswell and even the king were tired of him.[65] In spite of repeated petitions, Misselden never recovered his prestigious position.

With Forbes out of the picture, the Delft church entered a new period of its history. "Nowe in steed of preacheinge wee should have a littell seruice starvice read," predicted the Anglicans.[66] Under close scrutiny from London, the church was to be remodeled theologically, and Archbishop Laud took personal charge of installing a conformable minister to succeed Forbes. His first choice was Stephen Goffe, Lord Vere's zealous Anglican chaplain, one of the few Netherlands chaplains showing enthusiasm for the Prayer Book. His religion was nearly opposite to Forbes and the merchants despised him. Although Goffe was willing to venture much on behalf of Anglican religion, he found excuses to refuse the assignment at Delft. "There I shalbe penned up in one narrow corner among men that hate me," he complained. "They have beene used to

---

[61] "To the Reader" by S. O. (Stephen Offwood), in Forbes, *Fovr Sermons*.
[62] P.C. Acts, no. 43, fol. 185.
[63] S.P. 16, vol. 257, no. 12; Stearns, *Congregationalism*, p. 46.
[64] S.P. 16, vol. 257, no. 12.
[65] S.P. 84, vol. 147, fols. 86-87 (Sept. 15/5, 1633) and fols. 155-56 (Oct. 26, 1633); P.C. Acts, no. 43, fols. 280-81 (Oct. 23, 1633).
[66] B.P., I, 146.

heare three extemporary sweating sermons every weeke, and ergo unless I bring them at least two sermons I shall never be reckened a preacher amongst them."[67]

Next, Laud put forward George Beaumont, also a conformist, and arranged for his election as company preacher. Beaumont, who served the Adventurers 1634-43 (and later had churches at Heusden and The Hague), was commended by Laud as "learned, sober, and conformable to the doctrine and discipline established in the Church of England." Laud gave orders to the merchants: "You are to receive him with all decent and courteous usage," and further, "it is his Majesty's express command, that both you, the Deputy, and all and every other merchant, that is or shall be residing in those parts beyond the seas, do conform themselves to the doctrine and discipline settled in the Church of England; and that they frequent the Common Prayers with all religious duty, and reverence." They were to name churchwardens and sidesmen. Any refractory merchants were to be reported to the Bishop of London for punishment.[68] So began the new order at Delft.

In 1635 the Merchant Adventurers moved to Rotterdam, which remained the Dutch staple port until 1655. The Adventurers had not pros-pered at Delft; and although their decline was far more deep-seated than the shortcomings of any one port, the Adventurers laid the blame on Delft. Delft was miserable, they said, "the worst of a sea towne in all Holland, a town that neither had trade to sea nor shipps, nor marchants, that trade by sea, neither indeed was the towne capable of trade." Misselden judged Delft an "vnfit place of Residence."[69] Because Delft offered insufficient trade for their goods, the English merchants were using the city primarily as a "warehouse" for trade with more bustling surrounding cities. From their depots at Delft, they reshipped their woolen cloths to other cities; and for goods for the return trip, they had to send to Amsterdam and Rotterdam.

For several years, the Merchant Adventurers searched for a suitable city to transfer their residence. In a memorandum of 1629-30, "Whether the Province of Zealand or the Province of Holland were most comodious for the residence of the Merchant Adventurers," the merchants studied the alternatives. Zeeland, where their previous Middelburg residence had been located, was judged to have a fine location but serious inconveniences such as lack of fresh water and too much competition from the interlopers operating in Holland. Holland, which had prosperous trade,

---

[67] S.P. 16, vol. 260, no. 13.
[68] S.P. 16, vol. 270, no. 3; also in Laud, *Works*, VI, 380-81.
[69] S.P. 84, vol. 144, fols. 146-47; Edward Misselden, *Free Trade. Or the Meanes to Make Trade Flourish* (London, 1622), p. 50.

also had drawbacks, mainly the hazards of bringing ships into Amsterdam by Texel and the matter of the tare. Nevertheless, the merchants found the weight of the arguments strongly on the side of Holland, Delft, of course, excluded. Amsterdam, Rotterdam, and Dort were attractive. "Itt cannot be gainsaid but that Holland, for the trade of the Company of Merchant Adventurers is more comodious then Zealand." Deputy Misselden, before his removal, favored Amsterdam, "the principal Emporium of this part of the world: and that's in one word the best residence, where there is most trade;" Rotterdam he downgraded as second-rate, "it being the nursery of the Arminians, and a much rougher people then those of Delft, though but Hollanders at the best." The king, however, vetoed Amsterdam "for manie respects."[70] By 1635 negotiations were completed for the Adventurers to move to Rotterdam. Boswell advised that the religious issue be thoroughly studied, and that as a part of any contract, the company church be specified as Church of England in practice and that any existing English churches at Rotterdam be closed down.[71]

Minister Beaumont and his Prayer Book transferred along with the Merchant Adventurers to Rotterdam. Boswell, on behalf of Laud, succeeded in inserting a restrictive clause on religion, article 7, into the contract with the city:

> We (the magistrates of Rotterdam) have granted the Merchant Adventurer Society a suitable and well-located church, St. Peter's Church, where they may exercise the Christian Reformed religion according to the discipline and order of the Church of England as presently used in their church at Delft. Their church is to be kept in proper repair without cost and to the satisfaction of the aforenamed Society; and they are granted complete freedom of sepulchre and Christian burial for their dead within the church. We promise not to tolerate or allow any other public English church in our city except the church of the aforenamed Society. We shall take steps to prevent any preaching by anyone in their congregation which might be against the doctrines or discipline of the Church of England.[72]

While at Rotterdam, the Merchant Adventurer church was established in the recently remodeled St. Peter's church, already known locally as the "Engelsche Kerk" because of its previous use by the English Reformed Church.[73] Preachers of the church were George Beaumont (to 1643),

---

[70] S.P. 84, vol. 144, fols. 146-47, 107-08, 167v. The undated memorandum (fols. 146-47) refers to the Merchant Adventurers as being 8 years at Delft, i.e. 1629-30.

[71] S.P. 84, vol. 148, fol. 186.

[72] Te Lintum, *Merchant Adventurers*, p. 241.

[73] J. H. W. Unger and W. Bezemer, eds., *Bronnen voor de geschiedenis van Rotterdam* (Rotterdam, 1892-1907), II, 363, 466; St. Peter's church, or the Boshuys church, was already referred to as "the Engelsche Kerk" in the map of Balthasar Floris van Berckenrode, 1626 (G.A. Rotterdam).

John Dury (1644-45), Henry Tozer (1648-50), Thomas Marshall (1650-72), and others.

So long as Beaumont ministered, the church was regulated according to Laudian religion, and in accordance with instructions from Laud. Beaumont eliminated obvious Reformed practices, and he gave the church an Anglican appearance by installing railing about the communion table and making the altar a little sanctuary—"clergy inside, the people outside."[74] Beaumont's church had little contact with Dutch Reformed preachers or with the Puritans. In a report of 1641 prepared by the Dutch consistory of Rotterdam, the Merchant Adventurer church was said to have no connections with the English Reformed churches of the city, and "ministers for the Merchant Adventurer church are sent out of England and are chosen by the Archbishop of Canterbury."[75] The drastic swing of the church from the Puritan side to the extreme Anglican side was hardly to the liking of the merchants, certainly not to Deputy Samuel Avery, who had long upheld the ministry of Forbes. However, rather than provoking a confrontation with Laud, Avery and the remainder of the congregation, of which only a small minority appreciated Beaumont, followed a course of unenthusiastic, minimal conformity. Beaumont's reading of the Prayer Book fell on a lethargic congregation. Because Rotterdam had another English church, the English Reformed Church ("Peters and Damports English church"), there was an alternative worship available to merchants dissatisfied with their own church. Some of the merchants did move to the other church, "who out of conscience had renounced the Merchants Church, when Master *Beaumont* became Pastor to it."[76]

Article 7, which promised the Merchant Adventurers the exclusive monopoly of English religion in Rotterdam, was a great victory for Laud. However, much to Anglican grief, the article was unenforceable. Instead of disbanding the older Puritan "Peters and Damports English church," the magistrates allowed it to exist and even continued to provide regular funds for it. Fresh ministers were approved as replacements for Peter and Davenport, when they emigrated. Throughout his years at Rotterdam, Peter had assiduously cultivated friendship with the burgomasters. He lavishly dedicated to the "Amplissimus, Prudentissimus, Consultissimus" lords and Senate of Rotterdam his edition of William Ames's *Lectiones in CL. Psalmos* (1635); and in all consequent affairs the

---

[74] Unger and Bezemer, *Bronnen*, II, 466. The *Cal. S.P.D.*, 1639-40, p. 213, reports a case of nonconformity in the Merchant Adventurer church in 1639. The document is misdated, and should be dated 1633.

[75] Acta Kerkeraad Rotterdam, no. 1, Dec. 4, 1641 (G.A. Rotterdam).

[76] Forbes, *Anatomy*, p. 23.

"most excellent, most prudent, most learned" magistrates never deserted the church.[77] Edward Misselden, hoping for reinstatement as deputy, in 1635 tried to discredit Avery for being lukewarm in defense of Anglican religion. Soon after the Adventurers moved to Rotterdam, the ink barely dry on article 7, their church and minister were neglected in the planning for an official day of prayer. The states turned for prayers to the Peter-Davenport church, "as the English church, and the Companies church neglected." Deputy Avery, whose duty it was to uphold the church's honor, had allowed the insult to pass without protest. Misselden took this as one more evidence that the Merchant Adventurers had turned into a "violent faction of malicious men ... their malice, or rather madnes." Avery, who had been publicly linked with Forbes for many years, was removed as deputy in late 1635 by pressure from London.[78]

Beaumont had many discouragements in his ministry. He was angered because article 7 was not enforced by law, and his great goal was "the vindication of our 7th Article against concurrence of English Churches."[79] The other English church, however, refused to disband and survived at Rotterdam until 1876. Beaumont also complained of the inconvenient Dutch practice of burying some of their dead in St. Peter's, even during divine service on some holy days. On the positive side, he reported the abolishing of the Presbyterian eldership and its replacement with a vestry with himself having the final vote over all business. Thereafter, church affairs were much more manageable. Abolishing the eldership was in line with Laud's instructions that the church name churchwardens and sidesmen as prescribed by canon.[80] Beaumont himself considered his major achievements at Rotterdam as the pacifying and unifying of the congregation. "When other English congregations here have bin at dissention, you had (and ever may you have) peace."[81] Beaumont's Anglicanism did not endear him to the congregation, and the company paid him much less than they had formerly paid Forbes.[82] The Beaumont ministry (1634-43), by fastening Laudianism upon the church, caused a sharp break in the fifty-year Puritan Reformed tradition of the church.

In 1642, with Laud brought down in England, Beaumont found himself under severe threat of dismissal. An order of dismissal from London, signed by company official Robert Edwards, came November 18,

---

[77] Raymond P. Stearns, *The Strenuous Puritan: Hugh Peter, 1598-1660* (Urbana: University of Illinois Press, 1954), p. 86.
[78] S.P. 16, vol. 291, no. 71.
[79] B.P., I, 277.
[80] S.P. 16, vol. 316, no. 14; S.P. 16, vol. 270, no. 3.
[81] B.P., I, 320.
[82] S.P. 16, vol. 316, no. 14.

1642; but Beaumont fought back and held office until late 1643. Sir William Boswell, the king's agent, supported Beaumont against his detractors by praising his great diligence, "having preached twise every Sunday since he was there Chaplen, some times 6 sermons in 8 daies. Against whose life, and conuersation no man can make exception."[83]

During the English Revolution, although the pressures from king and archbishop were removed, the Adventurers instead found themselves under orders from Parliament to take a stand on the Parliamentary side. Beaumont's continued presence in the church gave suspicion of pro-Laudianism, and the Adventurers were advised by Parliamentary friends to remove their preacher. Hugh Peter visited Rotterdam in 1643 and thereafter reported that their preacher "preaches against the proceedings of the Parliament." "Truly," answered Beaumont, "tis more than I know of."[84]

When the Adventurers, under Parliamentary supervision, dismissed Beaumont in 1643, they also swept out his altar and railings.[85] His successor was John Dury (1644-45), the son of Robert Dury, former Scottish minister of Leiden. John Dury was a long-time worker on behalf of ecumenical unity between Lutherans and Reformed—considered eccentric on that account—and, although from a zealous nonconformist family, in politics he was more Royalist than Parliamentarian. As a young minister he had briefly served the Merchant Adventurers at Elbing, West Prussia (1628), but after that he became "a traveller in the work of peace among the churches." During 1642-44, he had been living nearby at The Hague as chaplain to Mary, Princess of Orange.[86] Although ordained in the Reformed church of the Netherlands, he had adopted many tenets of Anglican religion during the Laudian regime, even to the point of undergoing an Episcopal re-ordination at the hands of Bishop Joseph Hall—so "to be sure, that he entereth in by the door into the Sheepfold, least if he enter in another way, he be counted a thief and a robber." William Prynne later attacked him over his re-ordination as the "time-serving Proteus;" the hope of "Archbishops preferments made Mr. Dury an Episcopall Proselite, and marr'd his Presbyterianship."[87]

---

[83] B.P., I, 319, 324, 347, 353. Beaumont was still at Rotterdam Oct. 24/Nov. 4, 1643, but by Feb. 20, 1644, he was at Paris.

[84] B.P., I, 319, 347, 353, 363.

[85] Bijlsma, "Rotterdams handelsverkeer," pp. 95-96; Unger and Bezemer, *Bronnen*, II, 466.

[86] John Dury, *A Summarie Account of Mr Iohn Dury's Former and Latter Negotiation* (London, 1657), pp. 1, 23-24; *D.N.B.*; B.P., I, 359, 367.

[87] J. Minton Batten, *John Dury: Advocate of Christian Reunion* (Chicago: Univ. of Chicago Press, 1944), pp. 16, 47-48; William Prynne, *The Time-serving Proteus, and Ambidexter Divine, Uncased to the World* (n.p., 1650), pp. 1-2.

The irenic Dury, whose grand ecumenical vision encompassed Christian fellowship among Calvinists and Lutherans, Anglicans and Puritans, English and Scots, Presbyterians and Independents, attempted a middle road at the Rotterdam church, hoping to bridge the dissensions. He adopted a service of worship that incorporated unobtrusive pieces of the traditional Prayer Book liturgy into the Reformed framework, so that it was "neither strictly formal, nor altogether informall." He called it a "middle way." "And by this rule I made use of the Leiturgie at Rotterdam, neither laying it wholly aside in respect of the substance of prayers; nor bending myself to the whole formality of it." In August of 1645 Dury resigned at Rotterdam and returned to London, having been elected to the Westminster Assembly, "where in the service of the Churches, for the composure of Domestick differences, he imploied himself between all emergent parties."[88]

The Merchant Adventurers have reputation for consistently supporting the Parliamentary side,[89] but taken as a whole, their Rotterdam preachers of the 1640s and 1650s leaned toward the Royalist side. Although the Royalist persuasion of the preachers may have resulted from the easy availability of such preachers during the Revolutionary period, that hardly is an adequate explanation since several of the deputy governors leaned in the same direction. Henry Tozer (1648-50) was a "puritan royalist" who had refused to participate in the Westminster Assembly. Because of his Royalism he was deprived from his fellowship at Exeter College, Oxford. He was author of an oft-printed devotional book, *Directions for a Godly Life*.[90] Thomas Marshall (1650-72) was also a Royalist during the revolution and "borne arms therein for his majesty." He was a notable scholar, B.D. of Oxford, "distinguished by his uncommon acquaintance with the Septentrional and Oriental languages," but upon word of the approaching Parliamentary visitation to Oxford, "went beyond the seas," eventually to Rotterdam.[91] Deputy William Cranmer in 1645 and deputy Jones in 1649 were reported to be anti-Parliamentarian and dangerous. Walter Strickland, agent of Parliament, sent back several unflattering dispatches in 1649 about the Adventurers. He complained of Jones as "a weake man" and the secretary as a "knave." Strickland warned, "you know not the hurt that company

---

[88] Dury, *A Declaration of John Dury* (1660), quoted by Batten, *Dury*, pp. 97-99; Dury, *Summarie Account*, p. 24.

[89] See William E. Lingelbach, *The Merchant Adventurers of England*, in *Translations and Reprints from Original Sources*, 2nd ser., vol. 2 (1902), pp. xxi-xxiii; Bijlsma, "Rotterdams handelsverkeer," p. 96; Te Lintum, *Merchant Adventurers*, pp. 172-74.

[90] *D.N.B.*; Wood, *Ath. Oxon.*, III, 273; IV, 171. He died at Rotterdam Sept. 11, 1650.

[91] Wood, *Ath. Oxon.*, IV, 171; *D.N.B.*; Steven, p. 326.

doth."[92] The Adventurers offended Republican sentiment by inviting as guest preacher William Price of Amsterdam, not just once but several times. Price was an outspoken critic of Cromwell. "The last Lord's day, Price of Amsterdam, the fowlest-mouthed priest in the world, preached before the company of English marchants at Rotterdam, a fellow who makes not onely pulpits, but all places weary of his invectives against the state of England, and the counsell of state."[93] During the 1650s, the Merchant Adventurers jumped on the Republican band wagon and put the company in better official favor.

The company of merchants moved to Dort in 1655. By this time they were a rapidly declining fellowship compared to their splendid history. The contract with the city of Dort specified in article 7 that the city would provide a suitable church building for a Merchant Adventurer church:

> We (the magistrates of Dort) have granted the aforenamed Society a suitable and well-located church, where they may exercise the Christian reformed religion. Their church is to be kept in proper repair without cost and to the satisfaction of the Society; and they are granted complete freedom of sepulchre and Christian burial for their dead within the church. The aforenamed church and churchyard are not to be used for the burial of any others without the prior consent of the Society.[94]

Much of the language of the contract is taken over verbatim from the previous contract of Rotterdam with several important exceptions. The Dort contract dropped the Anglican phraseology of the Laudian period, inserted at Rotterdam at Laud's and Boswell's insistence; also because of unhappy controversies with the Dutch at Rotterdam over burials, the Adventurers demanded exclusive burial rights in their new church. However, no attempt was made to write into the contract a monopoly of English religion at Dort, or to disturb the already existent English Reformed Church pastored by Robert Paget.

Thomas Marshall transferred with the company from Rotterdam to Dort and served another sixteen years until 1672. The "English Court Church" (also referred to by Dort historians as the English Episcopalian church) was given possession of the old Iron Weigh House on Wine Street (the Wijnkoopers Kapel). In addition to the church building, the city magistrates paid rent for houses for the preacher and reader.[95]

---

[92] Thurloe, *S.P.*, I, 118-19; *Cal. S.P.D.*, 1644-45, p. 603; *Cal. S.P.D.*, 1649-50, p. 258.
[93] Thurloe, *S.P.*, I, 118.
[94] Pieter Hendrik van de Wall, *Handvesten, privilegien, vrijheden, voorregten, octrooijen en costumen ... der stad Dordrecht*, vol. 3, pt. 8 (Dort: Pieter van Braam, 1770-90), pp. 1746-47; Lingelbach, *Merchant Adventurers*, p. 241; J. L. van Dalen, *Geschiedenis van Dordrecht* (Dort: C. Morks Czn., 1931-33), II, 801. The contract was signed Nov. 29, 1655.
[95] Van Dalen, *Dordrecht*, II, 801; Matthys Balen, *Beschryvinge der stad Dordrecht* (Dort, 1667), pp. 194-95.

In Matthys Balen's *Beschryvinge der stad Dordrecht* (1667), the merchant church was described: "There are no elders in this church," only deacons for poor relief. "Service is generally performed there every Sunday morning and afternoon. Before the singing, the minister reads (*in inferiori cathedra*) a psalm and two chapters from the Bible. A sermon also is always preached in the said Court Church upon the 25th of May, that being the day for solemnizing the anniversary of the king's birth. The deacons at present are Mr. Samuel Bubwith and Mr. Robert Hartley."[96] After Marshall's return to England in about 1672, he became rector of Lincoln College, Oxford and royal chaplain; eventually he was dean of Gloucester. Other Merchant Adventurer preachers known to have served at Dort were Philip Bowie (1672-76), later minister at The Hague, Augustine Freezer (1685), and Mr. Whittel (1688). Following the Restoration the Merchant Adventurers showed much enthusiasm for the king and Church of England, duly celebrating coronation days and royal birthdays with wine and fireworks and mourning royal deaths. Freezer in 1685 preached a sermon in the church on the death of Charles II, *The Divine Original and the Supreme Dignity of Kings, no Defensive against Death*. He lauded princes and "the divine authority of Kings."[97]

While residing at Dort, the company reached the end of its history as a privileged company in the Netherlands. In 1668, with the English and Dutch at war, the States General revoked the privileges of the Merchant Adventurers. Thereafter the England merchants who remained at Dort became ordinary, individual merchants without the privileges of a monopoly company, trading like English merchants in other Dutch cities. In 1688, the Merchant Adventure monopoly was abolished in England itself.[98] Their one privilege retained at Dort was the exemption from the beer and wine excise tax. The Merchant Adventurer church, however, was continued by the merchant community, although ever shrinking, until about 1700, when it merged with the English Reformed congregation. The combined congregations took over the merchant's Wine Street building and in 1700 called Samuel Masson as their joint minister. The merged congregation existed until 1839 and was in all essentials the old Dort English Reformed Church; it "all along retained its Presbyterian aspect."[99] Nevertheless, the Adventurer's component of

---

[96] Balen, *Beschryvinge*, pp. 194-95.

[97] Freezer's sermon was printed at Rotterdam in 1685 (see the dedication to the Merchant Adventurers and the foreword to Mary, Princess of Orange); C. J. P. Lips, *Wandelingen door Oud-Dordrecht* (Zaltbommel: Europese Bibliotheek, 1974), I, 302-03.

[98] Wiegandt, *Merchants Adventurers' Company*, pp. 108-09; Te Lintum, *Merchant Adventurers*, pp. 216-17.

[99] Van de Wall, *Dordrecht*, vol. 3, pt. 8, p. 1747, writes, "The exact time when this happened cannot be specified" but at least by the time of the calling of Samuel Masson, 1700; Steven, 299.

the church retained a small identity, at least until the mid eighteenth century. As late as 1751, Samuel Jay, the minister, together with the sexton and bell ringer, petitioned for the old Adventurer's exemption from the beer and wine excise, and they were upheld by the States General, "in consideration that all the persons just named are survivors (leftovers) of the English Court by whom they were chosen and appointed, should have and enjoy freedom of the country's imposts."[100]

Hamburg

Although Hamburg is geographically outside the Netherlands, the Merchant Adventurer church at Hamburg deserves mention because of its many connections with the Netherlands English churches. Ministers and members moved freely back and forth between the two areas. After the Merchant Adventurers were compelled by war circumstances to leave Antwerp in 1582, their headquarters (governor and general court) were moved to Emden, then to Stade, and finally in 1611 to Hamburg, which remained the chief Adventurer port until the final demise of the company in the early nineteenth century. At Hamburg the Merchant Adventurers achieved a great heighth of prosperity and then gradually ran downhill to a final decay. Hamburg and the Dutch staple city were the two centers of Merchant Adventurer religion.[101]

The Hamburg church was in the English House, the company headquarters building. The Lutheran magistrates of Hamburg at first granted liberty of English worship rather reluctantly for fear of promoting Reformed theology. The 1567 charter, during an early residence of the Adventurers at Hamburg, forbade the public dissemination of Zwinglianism, but in later contracts the restrictions disappeared.[102] The Merchant Adventurers at Hamburg, like their brethren in the Netherlands, carried on the Puritan tradition of Cartwright and Travers. Their early seventeenth-century preachers were Richard Sedgwick (c. 1601-15), at Stade and Hamburg; John Wing (c. 1615-19); William Loe (1619-20); Thomas Young (1620-27); and Jeremiah Elborough (1629-65). All but Doctor Loe were Puritans.

Sedgwick sought service abroad, like many of the merchant chaplains, after trouble in England arising from nonconformity. According to

---

[100] Lingelbach, *Merchant Adventurers*, p. 253.

[101] On the Merchant Adventurer church at Hamburg, see William E. Lingelbach, "The Merchant Adventurers at Hamburg," *A.H.R.*, 9 (1904), 275-76; J. M. Lappenberg, "Die Capellane der englishchen Court," *Zeitschrift des Vereines für hamburgische Geschichte*, 2 (1847), 649-51; the baptism, marriage, and communicants register is in the Hamburg Staatsarchiv, "Eng. Kirchenbuch, 1617-1738"; Hitzigrath, *Engelsche Kirchengemeinde in Hamburg*.

[102] Lingelbach, "Hamburg," 275-76.

Brook, "he happily introduced a purer church discipline, and the Lord abundantly blessed his labours."[103] John Wing, who moved to Flushing as English preacher in 1620, was an active worker in the Puritan movement of the Netherlands. Two of his books, *Jacobs Staffe* (1621) and *Abels Offering* (1621), are sermons preached at Hamburg. His service among them, he said, was "like a *litle heaven* to me;" however, he also sadly referred to "foule and vnworthy imputations" against him.[104] Young is primarily known as having been John Milton's tutor, before coming over to Hamburg. Milton wrote a Latin elegy for Young in 1627 ("Dearer he to me than thou, most learned of the Greeks").[105] Between 1627 and 1629, there is a gap in the Hamburg church book. Elborough, who came in 1629, was former minister of the English church of Utrecht and an officer of the Puritan English Synod of the Netherlands. Doctor William Loe (1619-20), on the contrary, was no friend of Puritans. He had been royal chaplain and prebend of Gloucester cathedral. He crossed over to Hamburg because of personal disagreements with Laud, his dean at Gloucester. When Loe came, Archbishop Abbot "commanded the use of the book of Common prayer, and kneeling at the Communion." One of the Puritan merchants, John Fenwick of Newcastle, later complained that Loe had caused injustices against him, at orders from the king and Abbot, being "driven from my employments and means of preferments there." While at Hamburg, Loe wrote a book of hymns, *Songs of Sion* (1620), for the Adventurer's church.[106]

In spite of Doctor Loe's Anglican innovations, the church remained at core Presbyterian in worship and discipline. The church was organized on the basis of three canons or "questions to be demaunded by the pastor and answered affirmatively before him and elders by every one that is to be admitted a member of the church":

1. First whether you doe constantly believe the Scriptures conteyned in the old and newe testaments only to be an absolut rule of all

---

[103] Brook, *Puritans*, II, 488; Paul S. Seaver, *The Puritan Lectureships* (Stanford: Stanford Univ. Press, 1970), pp. 185-86.

[104] John Wing, *Jacobs Staffe* (Flushing, 1621), Dedication, and pp. 204-05. Wing began as assistant minister (i.e. weekly lecturer) and moved to a full time position. His exact tenure is not known. *Abels's offering* was preached at Hamburg in 1617; he was admitted at Flushing June 19, 1620. He also served at Sandwich but whether before or after Hamburg is not known.

[105] David Masson, *The Life of John Milton* (1881, rpt. New York: Peter Smith, 1946), I, 72. The last mention of Young in the Hamburg church register is November 1627.

[106] S.P. 16, vol. 257, no. 12; *D.N.B.*, s.v. "Loe"; on Elborough see B.P., I, 263-68; John Fenwick, *Christ Ruling in the Midst of his Enemies* (1643), in *Reprints of Rare Tracts & Imprints of Ancient Manuscripts* (Newcastle, n.d.), I, 30. Loe's *Songs* was dedicated to eleven English merchants of Hamburg. Another book of sermons by Loe, *The Merchant Reall*, was printed at Hamburg in 1620. Loe was appointed minister in 1618 but did not take up his duties until 1619; Hitzigrath, *Engelsche Kirchengemeinde*, pp. 7-8.

righteousnes, and sufficient to teach all Christians whatsoever is necessary for salvation.
2. Secondly whether you believe yourselfe to stand bound to frame the course of your life according to the rules of the sayd scriptures framing the whole course of your life, sutably to the sacred doctrine conteyned in them so farre as by gods favor and your own best endeavor you shalbe enabled.
3. Thirdly whether you will submitt yourselfe to the government and discipline of Christ established in this congregation, and be ordered by the same in case of your offense or miscariage.[107]

These three canons, which tightened up standards of membership, dated from about the time of Richard Sedgwick's reforms of "a purer church discipline." They stand at the beginning of the Hamburg "English Churchbook" (1617-1738). Although the circumstances of their adoption are unknown, they bear much resemblance to John Forbes's four canons at Delft in 1633 but come much earlier. In discipline the church governed in a presbyterial manner by lay elders. According to Edward Misselden of Delft, the Hamburg church, except for a meager use of the Prayer Book, "fashion themselves in other things after their owne garbe."[108] Although the Hamburg church, under Puritan preaching, put on Puritan "garbe," the Hamburg merchants were not attracted to extreme Congregationalist theology like some of the Delft merchants.

During the 1630s the Hamburg church, like Delft, laid aside the Prayer Book. The two Merchant Adventurer churches had manifold opportunities for conference and communication. Forbes of Delft and Elborough were old colleagues from the English Synod; and moreover, Forbes had presided at Elborough's installation at Utrecht.[109] The Avery family was another connection between the two churches. Samuel Avery of Delft, elder of Forbes's church, and Joseph Avery of Hamburg, company secretary, were brothers and the deputy governor at Hamburg was Samuel Avery's father-in-law, Edward Bennet. Bennet was an ex-Brownist, "at first brought in by Mr. Forbes, and taken out of the Brownists church at Amsterdam; whereof he was a principall member, untill he came to be Deputy of our Company."[110] Samuel Avery mobiliz-

---

[107] Hamburg church register, fol. A (Hamburg Staatsarchiv).
[108] S.P. 16, vol. 257, no. 12.
[109] B.P., I, 265.
[110] S.P. 84, vol. 147, fol. 45; S.P. 16, vol. 257, no. 12 (1633). Bennet was "courtmaster" of the company 1630-38 (Hitzigrath, p. 95). "Edward Benet" and a Benet family were members of Francis Johnson's church at Amsterdam. See J. Soutendam, "De Engelsche Court of Lakenstapel te Delft, 1621-1635," *Bijdragen voor vaderlandsche geschiedenis en oudheidkunde*, N.R., vol. 6 (1870), 22; also Christopher Lawne, *The Prophane Schisme of the Brownists* (n.p., 1612), pp. 4, 11, 12.

ed the Merchant Adventurers of both places against deputy Misselden of Delft. "He hath gone up to Hamburghe himself in person, to draw them there to his faction," complained Misselden; "he hath got me out of my place, and a man after his owne mind, to be put in my rome." For a short while, Avery succeeded in installing himself in Misselden's place.[111]

Laud's campaign against Puritanism in the Merchant Adventurers, backed up by the Order in Council of October 1633, applied to Hamburg as much as Delft. Although Elborough behaved himself less belligerently than Forbes, Laud did not trust him or any of the church. Laud put them down as a gang unfaithful to the mother church; "they retained nothing of a Church of *England*, governing themselves wholly by *Calvin's* Platform." Their worship was psalms and sermon "according to the *Genevian* fashion."[112] On one occasion in 1632, when English dignitaries were visiting Hamburg (two ambassadors and an admiral), the lack of the Prayer Book raised a commotion. Dr. Ambrose, visiting Church of England preacher, was asked "to exercise" in the congregation. As the service began with singing of psalms, Dr. Ambrose asked for the use of the church's Bible and Prayer Book.

> Deacon: "They had no such thing as a *Common-Prayer* Book, and that the Common Prayers were not used amongst them."
> Ambrose: "Why then ... the best is, that I have one of my own;" (which being presently taken out of his pocket, he began with the Sentences, and invitation, and was scarce entred into the Confession, when all the Church was in an uproar).

The elders sent the deacon back a second and even a third time to Ambrose, admonishing him to get on with the sermon and cease the liturgy, but he replied "that if they would have no Prayers they should have no Sermon." When the elders and deacon cut him short again, "on the receiving of which Message he puts the book into his pocket, and goes out of the Church, the two Embassadours following him, and the Admiral them."[113]

John Dury in 1635 and again in 1640, being unemployed, solicited Laud and the company governor to be appointed as Hamburg minister. He had heard rumors that Elborough was leaving; and when these proved false, he pleaded to be appointed even as "curate." If appointed,

---

[111] S.P. 84, vol. 147, fol. 45.
[112] S.P. 16, vol. 257, no. 12; Heylyn, *Cyprianus Anglicus*, p. 231.
[113] Heylyn, *Cyprianus Anglicus*, pp. 231-32. Dr. Ambrose was perhaps John Ambrose, a naval chaplain, Venn and Venn, I, 26. James Howell, *Epistolae Ho-Elianae*, ed. Joseph Jacobs (London: David Nutt, 1892), reports on the trip to Hamburg but does not mention the church service (I, 292-300).

Dury promised to introduce the Prayer Book and "take occasion to speake of it to others to gain their affections toward it." At the time of these petitions, Elborough was being assisted by Mr. Warren, whom Dury hoped to displace.[114] Although nothing came of his petitions at Hamburg, Dury in 1644-45 did become Merchant Adventurer preacher at Rotterdam.

During the Republican period of the 1650s, the Cromwell party considered the Hamburg Adventurers too lukewarm in politics and religion. Elborough's old-fashioned nonconformity lacked Republican fervor. When Richard Bradshaw, Oliver Cromwell's son-in-law, became English agent at Hamburg, he demanded higher standards. "Our Church government goes on in the Presbyterian form, by Elders and a Consistory solemnly supported; here be some could wish these formalities were laid aside, and the power of godliness more pressed."[115] Bradshaw's "power of godliness" people rallied to John Gunter, assistant preacher and chaplain of Bradshaw (1655-56), for spiritual ministry. Bradshaw, in fact, favored removing Elborough for being a hindrance to Gunter's "honest partie." Gunter was appointed at Hamburg on the recommendation of Thomas Goodwin, "but not having his health, he staid only two years." He was re-established in England in 1658.[116] Elborough continued to serve past the Restoration.

The Adventurers after the Restoration received strict orders from London to worship according to the Prayer Book. Elborough went through the motions, but only with "cold and careless cariage in what he does read." The Congregationalist faction meanwhile withdrew into their own house church at the home of Samuel Richardson for fervent preaching and prayers. The Richardson congregation was suppressed by the company deputy in 1663. Elborough's neglect of the Anglican liturgy caused his dismissal in 1665 for "nonconformity." His seventeenth-century successors were: Thomas Griffin (1665-82), George Walls (1682-89), and Lionel Gatford (1690-1702), all conformists. The Hamburg church closed in 1806.[117]

Although the Merchant Adventurers showed a strong commitment to Puritan religion, the merchants, except for the brief period in the 1630s when Forbes and Avery were in charge at Delft, avoided the most extreme positions. As the "little republic" under his majesty, the Adventurers depended for their prosperity on governmental charters and

---

[114] H.M.C., *10th report*, VI, 133; S.P. 16, vol. 457, no. 66.

[115] H.M.C., *6th report*, appendix, 433 (Oct. 29, 1650).

[116] Calamy, *N.M.*, III, 460; Thurloe, *S.P.*, III, 345, IV, 322; Joseph Foster, *Alumni Oxoniensis* (Oxford: Parker, 1891-92), II, 620.

[117] Hitzigrath, *Engelsche Kirchengemeinde*, pp. 18-22, 94.

privileges, and they found it prudent to avoid sectarianism and religious controversy. When they could have their choice, they took a non-liturgical, Puritan style of worship and discipline, but in periods requiring Anglican conformity, they gave a nominal conformity. Unlike the zealous ideologues on either extreme, the Merchant Adventurers did not feel called to sacrifice everything on the altar of religion, being "more for a trade than a crowne or a church."[118]

---

[118] Peter Mews in *The Nicholas Papers*, ed. George F. Warner, Camden Society, N.S., 50 (1892), II, 267.

CHAPTER TEN

CHURCHES ON THE MILITARY FRONTIER IN BRABANT, GELDERLAND, AND OVERIJSSEL

Many of the two-dozen English and Scottish churches were military chapels in Brabant, Gelderland, and Overijssel, short-lived and not thoroughly established, as opposed to the settled town churches. Each of the four English regiments and two or three Scottish regiments had its own chaplain. In 1632 when Sir William Boswell made a survey of English religion, the chaplains were Stephen Goffe for Lord Horace Vere, Samuel Bachelor for Colonel Charles Morgan, Gamaliel Day for Colonel Philip Paginham, and Mr. Sclaer for Colonel Herbert. Andrew Hunter was the longtime "preacher to the Scots Regiments" (1598-c. 1630); and he was succeeded in the 1630s by Henry Sibbald, George Clark, Patrick Forbes, and others.[1] The chaplains in addition to serving in the field were also, when in residence, ministers to the congregations in the garrison towns, ministering to the whole English-Scottish military and civilian population.

During the seventeenth century, garrison churches existed at Gorinchem, Gouda, Geertruidenberg, 's-Hertogenbosch, Heusden, Bergen-op-Zoom, Nijmegen, Wesel, Tiel, Doesberg, Zutphen, Grave, Amersfoort, Zwolle, and Maastricht. At first, these churches did not have regular provincial or municipal stipends, and except for a few exceptions they were not organized with consistories and constitutions. Their expenses were met by pay from the regimental officers and by occasional payments from the local Dutch officials or the provincial states assemblies. "Of the Garrisons none have any Meanes from the States but only Utrecht. 500 g. per ann. and Bergen 200 g. per ann.; the rest are payed by the Captaines, which is about 2 gulders a weeke, as long as they bee in the Garrisons."[2] Eventually, most of the garrison chaplains had a small allowance of about 200 guilders plus ministerial housing allowance from the States General.[3] The cities supplied buildings for their use.

---

[1] B.P., I, 168; Ferguson, *Scots Brigade*, I, 57, 245, 294, 438; S.P. 84, vol. 106, fol. 84. Vere's regiment went to Col. George Goring in 1633; Morgan's regiment had formerly been under Col. John Ogle; Paginham's regiment was formerly under Col. Edward Cecil (Viscount Wimbledon); Herbert's regiment had been under Edward Harwood. Among the early chaplains serving Vere were Mr. Vincent, Mr. Norringham, John Paget, John Burgess, William Ames, John Hassall, and Obadiah Sedgewick.

[2] B.P., I, 168 (1632). For lists of seventeenth-century English and Scottish churches, see S.P. 16, vol. 170, no. 8 and B.P., I, 160 and 168.

[3] B.P., I, 303.

Most of these churches existed only for a few months or years, depending on the movement of troops; the longest surviving were Breda, Bergen-op-Zoom, and 's-Hertogenbosch, which existed until the 1670s. The garrison churches were centers for preaching, marrying, and administering the sacraments to a mobile military population. The military preachers served a necessary role because of the thousands of English and Scottish troops continually serving in the Netherlands. The Scottish regiments, who stayed longest, served in the Netherlands until 1782.

The military camps were hardly pious places. The chaplain's work was uphill effort, if taken seriously, and he was constantly thwarted by wickedness and indifference. Many of the chaplains in the field, it must be said, were a dreary lot, uninvigorating and barely competent. Dutch churchmen complained much about the low quality of English chaplains, being reputed for disorderly preachers without good testimony or proper attestation of their calling.[4] Sir John Fortescue has described the routineness of the chaplain's life: "Before each relief marched off for the night to the trenches it drew off in parado to the quarters of the colonel in command, heard prayers, sang a psalm and so went to its work; but though there was a sermon in the colonel's tent, there was no compulsion to attend, and there were few listeners except a handful of well-disposed persons."[5] During times of mortal battle, interest in religion notably revived. Chaplain Stephen Goffe in 1633 found his work quite leisurely, and except for the pay, better than a regular ministry; "in my present place I find the liberty of 9 months at least in the yeare to make use of the university and such learning as may be found here. And as for the affaires of the church I can fixe my selfe sometimes in one town, and sometimes in another, where I can learne, and see, and prevent and do what is my duty to do."[6]

Charles Cruickshank's history of the Elizabethan army gives low ratings to the army chaplains; using the example of Ireland in 1600, fourteen preachers had been appointed but of them three were absent "and the rest were said to be useless."[7] In spite of some unworthy chaplains, the religious situation in the seventeenth-century Netherlands army was better because of the well-motivated refugee Puritans available for service, some of considerable theological eminence (William Ames, Robert Parker, John Burgess, John Paget, Thomas Scott). The Puritan noncon-

---

[4] Knuttel, *Acta Synoden Zuid-Holland* (1625, 1626, 1627).

[5] *A History of the British Army*, Part One, *To the Close of the Seven Years' War* (London: Macmillan, 1899), I, 170. For a contemporary description of the chaplain, see Thomas Raymond, *Autobiography*, ed. G. Davies, Camden Society, 3rd series, 28 (1917), 37-38.

[6] S.P. 16, vol. 260, no. 13.

[7] Charles G. Cruickshank, *Elizabeth's Army* (Oxford: Oxford Univ. Press, 1946), p. 44.

formists found regular employment in the regiments, and as ambassador Sir Dudley Carleton explained it, "This place hath servd as a refuge for such ministers of both nacions as could not conforme (and without such these churches by reason of theyr short maintenance can not be supplied)."[8] Until Laud launched a campaign, the chaplains were almost unanimously Puritans, who had abandoned their Prayer Books.

In spite of indifferent success in the camps, many of the Puritan chaplains were energetic and hopeful of spiritual reformation. Samuel Bachelor, Colonel Morgan's chaplain, wrote a book on religion in the camps, *Miles Christianvs, or the Campe Royal* (1625), which likened the war against Spain to ancient Israel against the heathen, "they, the defense and propagation of Religion in spite of the Canaanites: we, the *mysticall warre* of these *Provinces* for the same ends, against the *Papacie*." The military life was fraught with much wickedness, violence, adultery, fornication, drunkenness, murmuring, and mutiny. "Manie come sober and civill," lamented Bachelor, "yet, when they betake themselues to the warres, loose all civilitie and frugalitie."[9] The English mercenaries in Holland had reputation for loose living, as one traveler discovered when recognized as an Englishman; he was barely able to get overnight lodging in Leiden, having been refused at six inns and barely admitted at the seventh, "which made me gather that they do not willingly entertaine Englishmen" due to the "licentiousnesse of our Souldiers."[10] Bachelor urged three steps of spiritual uplift in the camps: (1) Let every man begin to reform himself, especially the officers, for "if the fountaine be bitter, the streames can be no better"; (2) The churchly ordinances of suspension from the Lord's Table and military discipline must be used to punish open sins, "els your preachers may teach holynes, till their braines fall out at their browes, and to none end"; (3) The army must recruit better men, not "the skumme of men, fitter to fill *prisons* and *Iayles*, then places of better note."[11] John Hales of The Hague preached against duelling as the besetting military sin, "men of hot and fiery disposition, mutually provoking and disgracing each other."[12]

Puritanism rooted itself deeply in the army among chaplains and troops, proving, said the Puritan preachers, "that Piety can enter into Tents, and follow after camps, and that God had his *Iosua's* and his *Cor-*

---

[8] S.P. 16, vol. 90, no. 84.

[9] Samuel Bachelor (or Bachiler), *Miles Christianvs, or the Campe Royal* (Amsterdam, 1625), Preface, and p. 15. Another edition was printed at London in 1629; a Dutch edition at Gorinchem in 1628.

[10] Fynes Moryson, *An Itinerary written by Fynes Moryson Gent.* (London, 1617), pt. III, p. 98.

[11] Bachelor, *Miles Christianvs*, pp. 43-47.

[12] John Hales, *Golden Remains*, 2nd impression (London, 1673), pp. 68-89.

nelius'es in all ages."[13] Many of the officers made special efforts to employ Puritan chaplains and could be counted on to support nonconformist causes. A good part of Cromwell's officers of the 1640s were veterans of Dutch service, having experienced the Puritan religion of the Netherlands. Thomas Scott, exiled Puritan from Norwich serving at Gorinchem and Utrecht, praised "the glorious splendor of the Christian Campe, which should resemble heaven, where Michael fought with the old Dragon."[14] When Archbishop Laud in 1633 began his campaign against Puritanism in the Netherlands, he could find scarcely a single conformable chaplain, except for Stephen Goffe, who volunteered his services as an Anglican agent.

Bergen-op-Zoom

Bergen-op-Zoom, which withstood a furious Spanish seige in 1622, was a strategically located garrison town of Brabant. From the time of Leicester's command, English and Scottish soldiers were on permanent duty. Traveler John Ray as late as 1663 found two English companies at Bergen-op-Zoom.[15] Long before the Spanish wars, which brought in the English army, English traders had established themselves and gave some English flavor to the town: the Engelse Kaai, the Engelsestraat, and Londonstraat. Sir Charles Morgan is buried in the Grote Kerk, his wife, however, at Delft.[16] A chapel for the English troops, in charge of chaplain Richard Hyts, was founded in 1592 on the efforts of Leicester, but thereafter there is a break in the records until 1614.[17] In that year the Bergen-op-Zoom Dutch consistory noted that a new English preacher was coming, and they resolved to summon him into their meeting for the purpose of examining his credentials.[18]

The Bergen-op-Zoom English church met in St. Margaret's Cloister. During times of high military action, the city bustled with English and Scottish people, and the church would prosper accordingly. In 1623, following the great seige, the church had over 120 members plus other ordinary attenders.[19] Then again, when the army went into the field, the

---

[13] Richard Sibbes, *The Bruised Reede, and Smoaking Flax* (London, 1630), "Epistle Dedicatorie."

[14] Scott's poem, "The Campe's a Schole," in Bachelor, *Miles Christianus*.

[15] John Ray, *Travels through the Low-Countries, Germany, Italy*, 2nd ed. (London, 1738), I, 20.

[16] Paul C. Bloys van Treslong Prins, *Genealogische en heraldische gedenkwaardigheden in en uit de kerken der provincie Noord-Brabant* (Utrecht: A. Oosthoek, 1924), I, 38; Steven, p. 372.

[17] J. van der Baan, "Engelsche gemeente te Bergen-op-Zoom," *De Navorscher*, 32 (1882), 77. For the earlier history of the Bergen-op-Zoom church, see chap. 2.

[18] Acta Kerkeraad Bergen-op-Zoom, I, 12 (G.A. Bergen-op-Zoom).

[19] Ibid., fol. 18; S.P. 84, vol. 117, fol. 113.

church would nearly disappear. In 1629 the Bergen minister was guest pastor at Middelburg, "his owne charge beeing even wholly absent at the seige of Bosch."[20] One of the earliest chaplains was Thomas Morton (1617-21), a Scot, formerly of Zutphen, who exhibited credentials of lawful calling to the Dutch consistory and was approved by *provisie* for service without power to administer the sacraments.[21] Peter Rogers (1619), an English preacher, served briefly, but the Dutch refused him permission to minister there because of irregularities in his credentials. He had no passport, no testimonials from his previous church, no plausible reason for having left England, and he seemed incompetent. After Bergen-op-Zoom he found a position at Nijmegen.[22] Two Scots, George Clark and Alexander Clark, served off and on during the seige years and immediately after (1622-27), but Alexander, who sought to have a permanent position at Bergen, was declared unworthy by the English Synod and "by their Authority they had deprived one Mr. Clarke the Scotch regiment Preacher to the Earle of Bucklough."[23] The next minister was Steven Paine (1627-62), and the final minister was Petrus Domcelius (Domsel) who served 1662-77.

The church had a building provided by the town and received a small subsidy of 200 guilders from the States General. Nevertheless, the church was never put on an officially established basis like the English Reformed Churches at the surrounding cities of Middelburg, Flushing, and Dort. Alexander Clark in 1623, when the garrison was reduced after the lifting of the seige, petitioned the magistrates and the Dutch Reformed Church to receive an official appointment, but the request was not approved. The magistrates thought it best that the church remain under the *Krijgsraad* (war council) and receive military stipend.[24] Consequently, the ministers were closely dependent upon pleasing the captains, who paid much of the bill. George Clark in 1626-27 was boycotted by some of the English captains who refused to pay, saying they had not been "rightly served by him," and Steven Paine in 1648 complained that his officers, because of reduced forces, "no longer would or could pay his ordinary weekly payment."[25] Apart from having no adequate financial subsidy, the con-

---

[20] Middelburg C.R., I, 48 (R.A. Middelburg).
[21] Acta Kerkeraad, I, 14; Res. States General, no. 3180, fol. 483r.
[22] Acta Kerkeraad, I, 16.
[23] B.P., I, 168; Alexander Clarke is referred to in Acta Kerkeraad (1623) and in S.P. 84, vol. 117, fol. 113 (1624); George Clarke is listed at Bergen-op-Zoom in Ferguson, *Scottish Brigade*, I, 350-52 (1626-27). The Acta Kerkeraad of 1626 refers merely to Du Clerus and Clerc. The Clarks had long careers as Scottish chaplains. The Franeker Univ. *Album* has Georgius Clerck (1642), a chaplain "who had served Scottish troops in our camps for 14 years," p. 124.
[24] B.P., I, 168; Acta Kerkeraad, I, 18; S.P. 84, vol. 117, fol. 113.
[25] Ferguson, *Scottish Brigade*, I, 351-52; Baan, "Eng. gemeente," p. 77.

gregation functioned as an English Reformed Church with close association with the Dutch Reformed Church. The congregation was organized with elders and deacons, and in 1644 Paine applied for membership in the Classis of Tholen en Bergen-op-Zoom and was admitted. Paine's career in the classis, however, proved to be more a courtesy granted to him than an official standing. The classis in 1649 decided to exclude the English elders and declared that Paine was merely to participate in general discussion and to have no regular vote. He continued to attend and sometimes vote; he even served occasionally as chairman of the session. Through the years, the mains issues between the English and Dutch churches related to whether the English minister could perform marriages for Dutch members or even for mixed marriages of English and Dutch. The Dutch Reformed ministers considered such action a "matter of confusion."[26]

Steven Paine, the long-time minister, was a thorough Puritan. Previous to serving at Bergen, he had been a common soldier, "being no minister" ("a Silly common Soldier"), in Sir Horace Vere's regiment; but having a religious bent, he had risen to reader and then to minister. He was ordained at Utrecht in 1626 by John Forbes of the English Synod. The Synod in 1627 arranged for his transfer from Schoonhoven to Bergen-op-Zoom, where he ministered until 1662.[27] Paine collaborated closely with the radical Synod Puritans and kept the church pointed in a Puritan direction. Rather than use the Prayer Book, he used the Dutch forms, much altered, as they had been translated by Captain Henry Hexham and written into the leaves of his Bible.[28] When some of the officers in outlying camps around Bergen began using the Prayer Book for religious exercises, Paine joined with Dutch ministers of the town "in admonishing of the Captain, and forbidding the thing to be done againe."[29] After the demise of the English Synod, Paine moved closer to the Dutch Reformed Church and worked with the ministers of the town. He married twice, in 1630 and again in 1655, and had at least five or six children. One of his sons, John, he commended for advancement to the "Lord off Seulekom" in 1642.[30]

Paine died in 1662, still at his pulpit, and according to reports, leaving the church "in a prosperous condition."[31] The elders of the English church sought help from the Classis of Tholen en Bergen-op-Zoom to get

---

[26] Acta Classis Tholen en Bergen-op-Zoom, 1638-58, fol. 71r & v, 107v (N.H.A.); Acta Kerkeraad, I, 18-19, 20, 45, 50 (1626, 1629, 1670, 1674).
[27] B.P., I, 78, 161; S.P. 16, vol. 310, no. 103.
[28] S.P. 16, vol. 310, no. 103; B.P., I, 377-78, 161.
[29] S.P. 84, vol. 147, fols. 104 and 174v.
[30] H.M.C., *Lang MSS*, I, 211; Baan, "Eng. gemeente," pp. 77, 311.
[31] Acta Classis Tholen, 1659-75, fol. 95 (April 10, 1662).

another minister; and in a few weeks the church secured Petrus Domcelius, a Dutchman who had formerly served the Dutch congregation at Sandwich, England. Domcelius was a questionable choice. At Sandwich he had not been a successful minister, having been removed from his place at the request of members of his church. He had originally gone to England, it seems, primarily to learn the English language; and after being deposed, preached "in broken English" in various conventicles.[32] At Bergen he took classis membership, like Paine, but he soon came into controversy for suspicion of heresy after preaching a sermon on I John 2;21.[33] Although cleared of this charge, other complaints followed from his church, especially about non-residence. From July 1676 to April 1677, when he left the English church altogether, he jointly served the Dutch church at Rucphen and the English church.[34] After Domcelius, no replacement was appointed and the church ceased. In 1685 St. Margaret's Church was turned over to the French congregation.

Breda

Another of the great fortified cities of Brabant was Breda, a much desired prize in the battles of the Eighty Years War. Huge walls gave a military atmosphere to the fortress city. Entering the city, reported an English traveler, required passing through two gates and over five draw bridges.[35] The Spanish seized Breda in 1625, an event memorialized by Velázquez's *The Surrender of Breda*, but a turn in the war brought Breda back to the United Provinces in 1637. After the recovery of Breda, the area once again swarmed with British troops, producing almost overnight a large English-Scottish population, as had been the case before the Spanish victory. In 1638 six English and five Scottish companies were stationed at Breda, and when John Ray visited in 1663, he still found two English companies, the same as at Bergen-op-Zoom.[36] English and Scottish chaplains followed the troops to Breda, and churches were begun, supported by the military payroll. The first English chaplain was reported at Breda in 1614.[37] Prior to the Spanish occupation of 1625, the following chaplains served at Breda: Walter Whetstone (1618-19), Andrew Hughes (Hewes), preacher to Edward Cecil's regiment (1619),

---

[32] Ibid., fol. 98v; Hessels, *E.L.B.A.*, III, 2356, 2383. Domcelius recorded himself in 1662 as formerly of St. Margritt, England.

[33] Acta Classis Tholen, 1659-75, fol. 101 (May 30, 1662) and fols. 162v, 163 (July 1, 1664).

[34] Baan, "Eng. gemeente," pp. 78-79.

[35] Ray, *Travels*, I, 20.

[36] S.P. 84, vol. 153, fol. 302; Ray, *Travels*, I, 20.

[37] A. Hallema, "De Engels-Hervormde gemeente te Breda gedurende de 17de eeuw," *De Oranjeboom*, 1 (Jaarboek, 1948), 73.

Alexander Clark, a Scottish proponent (1621), and Daniel Widdows (1624).[38] The English troops hired an English chaplain, the Scots chose a Scottish chaplain; but they used the same church building. During the Spanish occupation the British church disappeared.

Following the recovery of Breda in 1637, the English church was reinstituted, for all practical purposes an arm of the military establishment. The congregation met in the Wendelinus Kapel, which was shared with the French church.[39] By the 1640s the English had moved to the Gasthuis Kerk in Bosch Straat.[40] Like Bergen-op-Zoom and other garrison towns, the Breda church received a modest stipend for minister, 240 guilders from the States General and from the Breda burgomasters 40 to 50 guilders more. Daniel Widdows in 1624 was receiving 40 guilders for house rent from the burgomasters, and this practice of 40 or 50 guilders per year continued throughout the life of the church.[41] The Breda church, because of Breda's location in a barony responsible to the Prince of Orange, had considerable dealings with the stadholders of the House of Nassau, to whom petitions for financial assistance were directed. In addition to the Dutch stipends, the preachers also received support from the military officers in the usual regimental fashion.[42] Ministers who served the Breda garrison church after 1637 were: Paul Amyraut (1637), Richard Dell (1637-46), Sampson Johnson (1646-53), Andrew Kier (1655-56), David Michael (1656-60), Zacharias Denman (1661-70), and John Butler (unofficially as supply pastor 1664-66 and officially 1670-72). Patrick Forbes served the Scots at Breda in 1637-38.

The British garrison church was immediately caught in two furious controversies, an English-Scottish split and an Anglican-Puritan controversy. The English captains brought in Anglican Richard Dell in 1637, former preacher at Geertruidenberg "a discreet, studyng, man, and fully obedient to the Laws of the Church of England."[43] The Scottish officers, however, refused to accept Dell and appointed their own minister, Patrick Forbes, "sonne of old Forbes." As the son of John Forbes of Delft, Patrick came from strong nonconformist stock, upholding the Scottish Covenanter tradition as well as the Puritan. He had just come from Delft, where his "rayling" anti-Anglican sermons had made him notorious. In 1638 he signed the National Covenant on a

---

[38] For Whitestone, S.P. 84, vol. 92, fol. 210; for Hewes, S.P. 84, vol. 93, fol. 159a; for Clark, Hallema, "Breda," p. 99; for Widdows, Stadsrekening, 9 (1624), after fol. 42 (G.A. Breda).
[39] S.P. 84, vol. 153, fol. 302v; Hallema, "Breda," 78.
[40] Hallema, "Breda," p. 72.
[41] Ibid., 79, 87; Stadsrek., 9, fol. 42f.
[42] Archief van Nassause Domeinen, no. 1086, fol. 566 (A.R.A.).
[43] B.P., I, 257.

visit to Glascow.⁴⁴ Neither nation nor preacher would yield to the other, and as a result, for over a year the British community split into rival English and Scottish churches, each with its own minister. Sir William Boswell and Archbishop Laud pushed Dell to institute the worship of the Prayer Book, while Forbes preached mightily against the Book and agitated against Dell for being one of the "formalists, tyme servers and viperlike." Forbes further stirred up his Scottish congregation by praying "that it would please god to put into the kings hart, to remove and purge out all abominasens and evills out of his Sanctuarys and that god would strengthen the harts of those of Scotland to stand out and never yield unto them." With such preaching and praying the Scots were well edified and "do peremptorily say they will have Mr. Forbes to be their Preacher, and will give nothing to any other minister that shalbe chosen whosoever." They would not listen to the Prayer Book.⁴⁵

The Scottish anti-episcopal faction headed by Forbes drew support from some of the Puritanically-inclined English people of Breda, but Boswell ordered Forbes to admit no English to his services. Dell charged Forbes with being "the vanest young man in these netherlandes ... and so he hath made a rent betweene the Scots and English; which (for ought I can learne) hath never beene in any Garrison in these landes."⁴⁶ Wild, bitter talk arose from the Breda Puritans: The Church of England is a whore, the bishops are evil men. One of Forbes's deacons, John Foot, was heard to say: "Take the Archbishop and Bishops and put them all into a sacke; He that comes out first is a knave, and so he that comes out last is a knave." Another time Foot called the Prayer Book "a teacher of lys." What proof did he have? Foot recited a syllogism:

> That which maintaines and upholds lys is a teacher of lys.
> But our comon prayer booke maintaines and upholds lyes.
> Ergo it is a teacher of lyes.

Irrefutable Puritan logic. Under the influence of the Congregationalists of Rotterdam (Bridge, Ward, Burroughes) Foot derided Dell for being a Prayer Book minister with Episcopal ordination, and accused him of being no true minister, as Dell reported, "unless I had a new ordination as the ministers at Rotterdam have done."⁴⁷

Dell was showered with abuse as Forbes adeptly rallied the Dutch and French ministers of Breda against Anglican innovations, as if Dell and

---

⁴⁴ B.P., I, 213, 217, 219, 229; *D.N.B.*, s.v. Patrick Forbes. On Forbes at Delft, see chapter 5.
⁴⁵ B.P., I, 272, 293, 257.
⁴⁶ Ibid., 272.
⁴⁷ Ibid., 293.

his Prayer Book were some disturber of the peace. The French minister demanded of Dell: "Who sent and called you heere?" When Dell referred to his calling from the English captains, the French minister sneered: "Oh, the English Captaines: What, are they not Christienes?" Dell sustained courage by writing letters to Boswell and by imagining himself a genuine martyr for the Church of England, not willing for gain to stoop, like Forbes, to preaching about the church as a "whore"—"(as some heere) are not ashamed to publish it to there hearers."[48] Among the persecutions suffered, Dell's congregation had great difficulty in securing seats and benches for their meetings, and Dell himself for a long time was hindered in receiving the customary chaplain's subsidy from the States General. Dell, however, did outlast Forbes, who dropped out of the Breda scene in 1638; his next Netherlands pastorate was at Delft in 1641. Ambassador Boswell gave Dell every support in introducing Anglican ceremonies into Breda and sharply rebuked Forbes for standing in the way: "What way of division and trouble you runne, which (lett me tell you plainly:) will lead you into a Wildernesse before you be aware, and so leave you at a losse, during your whole life." Boswell warned, "I told him also I would keep an eye upon him."[49] As a whole, Dell's ministry at Breda, which lasted until his death in 1646, was not very happy. "We dwell in a remote place and among a people of strange Humours," he complained.[50]

After riding out the storm stirred up by Forbes, Dell and Boswell took satisfaction in making the Prayer Book a regular part of English worship at Breda, the first "Publique Exercise of our Common Prayers in that Towne, where for ought I can learne, they have never been used before."[51] The English church, nevertheless, was financially maintained by the Dutch as an English Reformed Church; and in spite of much grumbling, the English were tied into the system of Dutch Reformed classes and synods. Although the church functioned until 1672, its dependence on the military population made it a rather fragile congregation without the stabilizing core of long-term settled members. A consistory was not established until 1648 and qualified candidates were few, "the scarcity of material for such offices and the refusing of some to serve."[52] The captains, who would have been desirable elders because of their prestige, were reluctant to serve "because they had no certain and

---

[48] Ibid., 290, 293.
[49] S.P. 84, vol. 153, fols. 138, 303; B.P., I, 293, 301.
[50] B.P., I, 351.
[51] S.P. 84, vol. 153, fol. 303.
[52] Acta Classis Breda, II, 97r & v (N.H.A.).

secure residence at Breda;" whereupon the classis urged the church to organize on the basis of the chief non-military citizens of the church.[53] The first consistory (1648) included Captain Courtney, Valentine Buck, Simon Kerke (elders), and Edward Clark, Tobias Reedeclyff, and Robert Cooper (deacons). A petition of 1655 listed 26 members of the church;[54] as troops were transferred, the British population shrank to a small colony.

The English Reformed Church of Breda, after Forbes's departure, developed into the most Royalist and Anglican church in the Netherlands. This arose from the association of Breda with important persons from the Stuart and Orange families. Mary, Princess of Orange (1631-60), daughter of Charles I, had a residence at Breda and promoted Anglican ceremonies and Episcopal religion. Her brother Charles II, while in exile up to 1660, also occasionally resided at Breda, which further made Breda a center of Royalism and Anglicanism in exile. Although the Dutch Calvinists of Breda did their best to keep the church on a Reformed course, the congregation and its powerful patrons brought in ministers who were militant Church of England exiles. Both the Dutch consistory and the classis made it a policy to examine the orthodoxy of the English ministers, and the Breda classis, after some hesitation in 1639, insisted on enrolling them as members of the classis and requiring subscription to the Dutch creeds and canons. The main go-between of the two churches was Dominee Hanckius, who knew the English language.[55]

Initially, during the Forbes-Dell schism, the Reformed churchmen had been cool toward Dell, suspicious that he threatened to subvert Reformed religion.[56] By 1643, however, the classis had taken Dell under wing and promised to support his request for a subsidy from the States General under condition that he take classis membership and "stand in life and doctrine under the jurisdiction of this classis."[57] He subscribed and got the subsidy. After that, the classis insisted on similar membership from all succeeding ministers, not so much for ministerial fellowship as for insuring Dutch Reformed conformity. Dell's successor, Sampson Johnson (1646-53), was the former pro-Laudian chaplain to Elizabeth of Bohemia, dismissed in 1644 at the insistence of Parliament. At the Hague he had been reputed a Socinian; and back in England, where he held the livings at Fobbing and Stebbing, Essex, he had been sequestered in 1645,

---

[53] Ibid., II, 127v; Hallema, "Breda," pp. 80-84.
[54] Ibid., II, 129-30 (art. 30); Arch. Nass. Domeinen, no. 1086, fols. 544, 550.
[55] Hallema, "Breda," p. 81.
[56] Acta Kerkeraad Breda, I, 37 (G.A. Breda).
[57] Acta Classis Breda, II, 81v; Hallema, "Breda," p. 79.

after returning to the Netherlands as a Royalist agent, for "malignancy against the Parliament." "Dr. Johnson ... is gone beyond sea, where he employeth himself against the Parliament."[58]

With such a record, few of the Netherlands English churches would have chosen Johnson; but Breda in 1646, with the encouragement of the Prince and Princess of Orange, welcomed him. The Classis of Breda approved his election, with the proviso that he give the usual Reformed subscription, and they stressed again the need to establish an English consistory in order to put the church on a sounder Reformed basis. The classis register book (1625-58) includes signatures of ministers subscribing to the Reformed confession and canons, and among them Johnson's name is boldly inscribed as chaplain extraordinary to Queen Elizabeth and pastor of the English Church of Breda. Several times the classis returned to the topic of Johnson's ministry in the church, and the requirement that he adhere to the "order and forms of these Dutch churches." The classis in 1649 exacted a promise from him that he would preach the prescribed sermons of Reformed catechetical instruction. In most things Johnson gave satisfaction; and when he desired to return to England in 1653, the classis issued him a testimony of his good service.[59]

The church went two years without finding a regular minister and then secured Andrew Kier (1655-56), a Scot who followed the precedent of joining the classis. He died in 1656.[60] The church next brought in David Michael, or Mitchell (1656-60), another Scot, former rector of St. Giles, Edinburgh, who had been deprived by the Covenanters. The classis insisted on the customary subscription from Michael, but he dallied so long that after three years had passed, he was still not inscribed in the classis book. Michael admitted having a few scruples about the Dutch confession, but in 1659 the classis warned him that his time for studying the issues had expired and that he must subscribe and join. He reluctantly conformed in January of 1659, inscribing himself, being a Scot, as *pastor ecclesiae Britanniae* and noting some qualifications. At the Restoration of 1660 he resigned to return to a benefice in England "by his majesty's special favor." His reward was to be named Prebendary of Westminster and shortly thereafter bishop of Aberdeen, 1662-63.[61] The successor, Zacharias Denman (1661-70), although ordained in England,

---

[58] Matthews, *W.R.*, p. 156; Davids, *Annals*, pp. 230, 475; for Johnson's career at The Hague, see chapter 5.

[59] Acta Classis Breda, II, 129-30, 156; Hallema, "Breda," pp. 82-85.

[60] Arch. Nass. Domeinen, no. 1086, fols. 548, 550, 572; Hallema, "Breda," pp. 89-91.

[61] Arch. Nass. Domeinen, no. 1086, fols. 580-87; Acta Classis Breda, III, 2-3, 24, 69; Hallema, "Breda," pp. 91-92; Robert S. Bosher, *The Making of the Restoration Settlement: The Influence of the Laudians, 1649-1662* (London: Dacre, 1951), p. 291; *F.E.S.*, I, 70.

came to Breda from Loppersum in Groningen. He was sick much of the time and barely able to carry on his duties.[62]

The last minister of the church was John Butler, fellow of Magdalen College, Oxford, a staunch Anglican. For two years, 1664-66, during Denman's tenure, Butler functioned temporarily as Breda minister without official appointment; he then returned as official minister in 1670-72. Butler was proud of his record during his first ministry of never subscribing to the Dutch Reformed religion; "there behaved himself as became a true Son of the Church of England in refusing to Subscribe the Articles of the Synod." During the second Anglo-Dutch war of 1665-67, he showed a touch of bravado by "continuing his prayers in publick for your Majestie after the Rupture with the States."[63] In his second ministry, 1670-72, he found no way of avoiding attendance at the classis; but he did not sign the book. Butler carried credentials signed by two bishops, attesting to his license as *Diaconatus et Presbyteratus*. The classis brethren, slightly suspicious of such credentials, examined him carefully and found him orthodox enough in doctrine.[64] The lingering anti-Episcopal prejudices of the Breda churchmen led to a debate, after Butler passed examination, about other Anglican preachers: "What was to be done with some English preachers who had received the laying on of hands from English bishops and then being called to pastorates in the Netherlands have been found during examination to be very bad ministers?" The worthy brethren of the classis thought best to submit this concern as a particular gravamen at the next synod.[65]

Butler found plausible excuses to postpone signing the book for many months; and when, in June of 1672, the classis checked further into him, it was discovered that he had departed for England. "Nothing further can be done," decided the classis.[66] With the renewal of war between England and the Netherlands, the English mercenary troops in service of the states were withdrawn, and Breda, like some other garrison towns, disbanded its England church. On August 5, 1672, the remaining elders and deacons of the English Reformed Church (Horst, Byemortel, Brucker, Zweebruggen, and Philips) turned over to the keeper of the stadhuis the valuable items of the church, being one large Bible, one sermon book, two silver cups, one damask table cloth, one pewter dish, one writing book, and one copper poor box containing 59 guilders.[67]

---

[62] Hellema, "Breda," p. 93; Acta Classis Breda, III, 186.
[63] S.P. 29, vol. 157, nos. 64, 65.
[64] Arch. Nass. Domeinen, no. 1086, fol. 598; Hallema, "Breda," pp. 94-96.
[65] Acta Classis Breda, III, 586-87.
[66] Hallema, "Breda," p. 96.
[67] Ibid., p. 98.

Gorinchem, Heusden, 's-Hertogenbosch, Geertruidenberg

Across the provinces of Brabant and Holland was a line of fortresses where English-Scottish churches were established in the first half of the seventeenth century. Gorinchem, across the Waal River on the border of Holland, with huge earthen walls was "a Town well seated."[68] The English had a church in the chapel of the old St. Agnieten Klooster. Thomas Scott was minister in 1622, and following him, Samuel Bachelor served at Gorinchem during the 1620s and 1630s; he was also chaplain to Colonel Morgan's regiment. Bachelor had transferred in 1622 from Heusden, and soon after arriving, refused a call to Middelburg.[69] Other regimental preachers who gave some service at Gorinchem were Daniel Widdows, who in a petition of 1634 referred to his previous service at Zutphen, Heusden, and Gorinchem, and Walter Bowye, who in 1647 was at Gorinchem "attached to the Scottish regiment." The Gorinchem church was almost exclusively a military chapel, ministering to "the honourable officers, and all honest Souldiers of the English Nation."[70]

Samuel Bachelor, the long-term Gorinchem minister, was a fervent Puritan and close collaborator of John Forbes and Hugh Peter. He belonged to the English Synod and held the office of scribe. Bachelor was a great enemy of Anglican ceremonies and refused the Prayer Book except for a few excerpts in baptism, the Lord's Supper and marriage, but "purged" of impurities; he "thinkes he shall suffer gloriously in refusing to use the same booke in the beginning of divine service."[71] Boswell labelled him a preacher "mean in abilities of learning, and discretion, or powre to doe harme, as he is in fortunes."[72] At Gorinchem he wrote his book on the chaplain's calling, *Miles Christianvs, or the Campe Royal* (printed by Richard Platter at Amsterdam, 1625; in Dutch, as *Koninglijk Veldleger*, Gorinchem, 1628). In 1633 through pressure from England, he was dismissed by Colonel Morgan and ordered back to England for discipline, but Bachelor refused to go. The king was furious at Bachelor, and to escape the royal wrath, Bachelor signed up to go to Pernambuco with the West Indies Company although it is uncertain that he actually emigrated.[73] His name is found in Gorinchem records until 1647. He was always on the edge of poverty, "endebted, and desperately

---

[68] Edward Brown, *A Brief Account of some Travels in divers Parts of Europe*, 2nd ed. (London, 1685), p. 103.
[69] W. F. Emck, *Kroniek van Gorinchem* (Gorinchem: Noorduyn, 1929), p. 75; S.P. 16, vol. 310, no. 103; S.P. 84, vol. 106, fol. 84; Middelburg C.R., I, 1v.
[70] B.P., I, 177; Steven, p. 341; Bachelor, *Miles Christianvs*, "Preface."
[71] S.P. 16, vol. 310, no. 103.
[72] S.P. 84, vol. 146, fol. 196v.
[73] B.P., I, 191.

poore, having at present a wife in childbed and eight little ones" (1633).[74] The Gorinchem Classis in 1647 referred to him as a "former English minister," burdened with six or seven children, weak of judgment and understand-ing, and seeking subsidy from the States General or States of Holland. In 1650 he returned to England; and by this time the church had ceased, because in 1650 the city of Gorinchem sold the former Engelsche Kerk building for private use.[75] In the nineteenth century William Steven discovered the old cloister building, "converted into a private residence, and now occupied by the chief magistrate." Within was a "large apartment, which tradition points out as the place where the British met for divine service."[76]

Heusden, another of the fortress cities, established an English church which met in the Vrouwen Klooster on a shared basis with the French church.[77] The following ministers are known to have served: Thomas Barkely (1619); Samuel Bachelor (1620-22); Daniel Widdows (1630-40); John Stone (1642-49); and George Beaumont (1651). Financially, the church was supported by the army payroll and occasional modest stipends from the Heusden magistrates. Very likely, the chaplain also received the ordinary chaplain's subsidy from the States General. In 1621 the English officers supported Bachelor's petition for a small subsidy to get him through the winter; the Heusden burgomasters granted him twelve guilders.[78]

Barkely, Bachelor, and Widdows were all Puritans who belonged to the English Synod. However, when Widdows was caught in the Laudian campaign for Anglican conformity in the garrisons, he gradually bent with the times. Stephen Goffe, Laud's chief agent among the English preachers, reported in 1633 that Widdows was beginning to read the service from the Prayer Book. Widdows, quite intimidated, pleaded with Goffe: If he "would do him no good to do him no harme."[79] Widdows was necessitated to petition the States General for an extra allowance in 1634 on grounds of being "a poore man, that lived long in the land, and now by reason of his age and his wifes blindnes stood in need of helpe

---

[74] S.P. 84, vol. 146, fol. 196v.

[75] Acta Classis Gorinchem, IV, Oct. 12, 1648 (N.H.K. Heusden); Knuttel, *Acta Synoden Zuid-Holland*, III, 53, 98, 158, 219; Emck, *Kroniek*, pp. 75, 546. Bachelor did not get the special subsidy. Possibly he did serve at Pernambuco, as suggested in 1633, since the synod noted (1648) that once "he had gone into another service and there became impotent."

[76] Steven, pp. 306-07 (1833).

[77] Jacobus van Oudenhoven, *Beschryvinge der stadt Heusden* (Amsterdam, 1743), p. 217.

[78] On Barkely and Bachelor at Heusden, A. C. Duker, *Gisbertus Voetius* (Leiden: Brill, 1897), I, 374 and bijlage 136; S.P. 84, vol. 106, fol. 84.

[79] S.P. 16, vol. 250, no. 28; B.P., I, 172.

being in a garrison where he had but three captaines." Widdows imagined himself a "poore pilgrim who complaines not only of persecution but Martyrdome."[80] His name appears occasionally in the Dutch records of Heusden as *pastoris Anglicani* between 1630 and 1640.

John Stone (1642-49) and George Beaumont (1651), the last two ministers of the church were Prayer Book Anglicans. Because of his Anglican doctrines, Stone had great difficulties with local Dutch Reformed ministers. The Dutch Classis of Gorinchem, having jurisdiction at Heusden, approved Stone only on condition that "he conform in learning and liturgy with the churches of these lands," but Stone offended by brazenly practicing Anglican ceremonies.[81] In 1648 he baptized an English baby by using "English episcopal ceremonies." "A great disorder," said the Dutch ministers of the town. They complained that he openly practiced some forbidden Anglican ceremonies; consequently the classis ordered him to desist.[82] Beaumont, his successor, who served as Colonel Cromwell's regimental chaplain as well as Heusden minister, was well known as a former follower of Laud. He had supplanted John Forbes as Merchant Adventurers preacher and was the first to introduce Anglican ceremonies into their church, for which Boswell commended him as a "most approved good preacher."[83] When Beaumont removed to The Hague in 1651, the place at Heusden apparently was left unfilled. Nothing further is heard of the Heusden English church. In 1656 twelve English officers with their wives were admitted with attestation as members of the Dutch Reformed Church of Heusden; if the English church had still survived, they would have been referred there.[84]

An English church was established in 1630 at 's-Hertogenbosch ("the *Bosch, Hertogenbosch* the *Dutch* call it, the *French Bois le duc*, i.e. *Sylva Ducis*"). The fortress city had fallen to the Dutch army in 1629. The city was reputed to be "one of the greatest cities in *Brabant* ... a very good Frontier against all Enemies on this side." The Spanish had considered it nearly impregnable to attack, "yet hath it been taken in the late wars."[85] As soon as the Protestants took charge of the city, Reformed churches were speedily opened, including churches for the French, German, and English Protestants. The first reference in the Dutch consistory records pertaining to the English church is an entry of July 17, 1630, where the Dutch ministers appealed to the English, German, and French ministers

---

[80] B.P., I, 177, 193.
[81] Acta Classis Gorinchem, IV, Oct. 13, 1642.
[82] Ibid., Oct. 12, Nov. 24, 1648, April 12-13, 1649.
[83] B.P., I, 324; Steven, p. 311.
[84] Membership register, no. 18, Feb. 5 and June 4, 1656 (N.H.K. Heusden).
[85] Brown, *Travels*, p. 103; Ray, *Travels*, I, 41-42.

for help in curbing the homicides terrorizing the city.[86] The English church continued until 1670. They met, at least in later years, in the Beguinage church (Begijnen Kerk).[87]

The 's-Hertogenbosch English ministers included these men: Petrus Gribius (1632-33); Thomas Dennis (1639); Elie Delme (1641-42); and Alexander Wedderburn (1644-70). Another minister, William Cooper of Nijmegen, was appointed as minister in 1640 but apparently declined the position.[88] Gribius, an English-speaking German with many Puritan connections, tried to put the congregation on an organized basis by seeking fellowship with the Dutch ministers in the consistory and classis and by attempting to form an English consistory of his own. The Dutch obliged by dispatching Dominee Udemans to install Gribius in his ministerial charge, and admitted him to the classis, but Gribius's further plan to have elders and deacons did not materialize. He "would erect a presbytery among the Capteines who will not learne that new hard lesson." Gribius proved his Reformed loyalty by submitting his credential for examination and promising to subscribe to all the confession of the Synod of Dort.[89] Gribius had a short pastorate. He seriously weighed but declined in 1633 a call to the Dutch church at Helmond, but in the same year he accepted a call to the Dutch church at Oost-Duiveland.[90] He later served the English church of Middelburg, 1642-52.

In 1639 Thomas Dennis was serving the church. There were complaints that he was not conformable to the Dutch Reformed confession.[91] In 1641-42, Elie Delme, who could preach in both English and French, filled the pulpit.[92] In 1644 Alexander Wedderburn began a long pastorate that lasted until 1670; his widow in 1671 received a widow's gift from the city magistrates. His son John became a prominent physician of Middelburg.[93] The English church barely survived the demise of minister

---

[86] Wigger Meindersma, *De Gereformeerde gemeente te 's Hertogenbosch 1629-1635* (Zalt-Bommel: H. J. van de Garde, 1909), p. 217.

[87] A. F. O. van Sasse van Ysselt, *De voorname huizen en gebouwen van 's-Hertogenbosch* ('s-Hertogenbosch, 1911-14), II, 394. Until 1653, however, this was a Roman Catholic church.

[88] Resolutiën van Stadsregering, no. A 39, fol. 76 (G.A. 's-Hertogenbosch).

[89] B.P., I, 141, 168; Meindersma, *Hertogenbosch*, p. 218; D. Plooij, *The Pilgrim Fathers from a Dutch Point of View* (New York: New York Univ. Press, 1932), pp. 86-87. For Gribius's later career at Middelburg, see chapter 7.

[90] Meindersma, *Hertogenbosch*, pp. 218-20.

[91] D. Nauta, *Samuel Maresius* (Amsterdam: H. J. Paris, 1935), p. 152. Thomas Dennis, M.A. Exeter, Oxford, received Privy Council passes in 1634 and 1637-38 to go over as preacher to Morgan's regiment; Leiden Univ. *Album*, col. 267.

[92] Nauta, *Maresius*, p. 489. Maresius called him "noster Dalmaeus." In 1642 he was suggested as a candidate for the English church of Middelburg. Leiden Univ. *Album*, col. 291, refers to him as "Anglo-Britannus."

[93] Resolutiën van Stadsregering, B 150, fol. 69v; no. A 69, fol. 178v; Steven, p. 284.

Wedderburn (1670), terminating about the same time. By 1672 the English church building had been for some time abandoned by the English and was handed over for use as a school.[94]

Geertruidenberg, "no great town, but well fortified and intrench'd," had English troops and a short-lived church.[95] Some of its ministers were Alexander Clark (1622), Mr. Firsby (1632-33), Richard Dell (mid 1630s), and Francis Harris (1637). Firsby during the Laudian campaign became conformable, and earned Stephen Goffe's approval as a "good honest man."[96] The church was almost totally dependent upon the stationing nearby of one or more of the English companies. Like the other Brabant garrison churches, it dissolved with the transfer of the soldiers.

Nijmegen, Zutphen, Doesburg, Zwolle, Amersfoort

The English churches of Gelderland and Overijssel were small and temporary, much dependent on the vicissitudes of the military campaigns. The Dutch classes of the area (Nijmegen, Zutphen, Zwolle, and Amersfoort) as well as the Synod of Gelderland showed constant concern that these small English congregations be decent and orderly; consequently most references in Dutch classis and synod records relate to matters of credentials for ministers and supervision of the tiny churches.

Nijmegen sponsored an English church which functioned from about 1621 to 1664 or perhaps a little longer. The Nijmegen consistory resolved in 1621 concerning an English preacher who was shortly expected to arrive, that good order be maintained in his ministry.[97] The Nijmegen ministers were: Peter Rogers (1622), James Forme (1623-24), William Howell (1626), Henry Sibbald (1633), Timothy Batt (1639), William Cooper (1640), Thomas Butler (1641; 1644), Louis Morgan (1644-59), Gamaliel Day (1662-64). The Nijmegen consistory in 1641 referred to two English ministers thereabouts, "both the English preachers to serve in the English church this winter."[98] The English-Scottish congregation met in St. John's chapel (the "sale van S. Johans huijs"). In 1633 the city magistrates paid a carpenter three guilders and fifteen stuivers for making new benches for the church,[99] and in 1649, after the English had

---

[94] Sasse van Ysselt, *De voorname huizen*, II, 394. A John Mackinzie, Scottish chaplain, was living at 's-Hertogenbosch around 1680, but he had no appointment as town minister (Steven, p. 284). The Gemeente Archief has a register book of English marriages, 1668-70 (no. 213). Only four marriages are recorded; the entries are in Dutch.

[95] Ray, *Travels*, I, 20. Ray (1663) reported one company of English foot there.

[96] For Alexander Clark, S.P. 84, vol. 106, fol. 84; for Firsby, S.P. 16, vol. 310, no. 103, B.P., I, 133, 141-42; for Harris, B.P., I, 259; for Dell, B.P., I, 257.

[97] Acta Kerkeraad Nijmegen, I, May 6, 1621 (N.H.K. Nijmegen).

[98] Ibid., Dec. 19, 1641.

[99] Raadsignaat, no. 95, Feb. 27, 1633; Stadsrekening, Mar. 13, 1633, no. 847, fol. 7410 (O.A.N., G.A. Nijmegen).

protested, the burgomasters transferred some guilds who had shared the building to another place.[100] Although a garrison church, they organized sufficiently to have elders and deacons. The church received a modest subsidy from the city, which drew upon the endowment of the St. John's House, a Roman Catholic hospital secularized in 1638, for the use of schools and churches. This endowment (the St. Jansgoederen) gave some support for lodging of the English and French ministers of Nijmegen, who lived in the St. John's ordenshuis (1638) and also from 1638 on, 100 guilders a year, eventually 150 guilders, for the salary of the English minister.[101]

A garrison church like Nijmegen did not ordinarily attract a high quality of ministers; the more able went to the settled churches of Holland and Zeeland. Peter Rogers, for example, before coming to Nijmegen had been rejected as unqualified at Bergen-op-Zoom.[102] James Forme had "many and divers debts."[103] William Howell was judged unqualified by the Dutch preachers, who labeled him "a certain pretended English preacher."[104] Timothy Batt disgraced himself by espousing Anabaptism, although his deviance was not discovered until after he had left Nijmegen. Although the Dutch consistory became perturbed at Batt's Anabaptism, the one consolation was that the news of his Anabaptism superseded another rumor, now proved false, that he had converted to Papism.[105] The most renown of the Nijmegen ministers was William Cooper, former Puritan vicar of Ringmer, Sussex and chaplain at The Hague to Elizabeth of Bohemia, 1644-48. He later held various ecclesiastical appointments under Cromwell.[106]

The Nijmegen Dutch Reformed churchmen distrusted most of the frequently changing English and Scottish chaplains; they doubted they were really legitimate preachers of the Word. The Synod of Gelderland resolved in 1626 and 1627 that for the prevention of disorders, no foreign English or French ministers were to be allowed without submitting attestations of their calling, doctrine, and life.[107] William Howell in 1626

---

[100] Raadsignaat, Apr. 18, 1649.

[101] Johannes Smetius, *Chronijk van de stad der Batavieren, waar in nevens de beschrijving van Nijmegen* (Nijmegen, 1784), p. 184; Raadsignaat, May 23, 1638; Rekening St. Jansgoederen, 1648 (fol. 89), 1649 (fol. 93), 1650 (fol. 91), etc. Payments to English ministers Louis Morgan to 1659 and Gamaliel Day, 1662-1664, are recorded in the municipal records of Nijmegen.

[102] Acta Kerkeraad Bergen-op-Zoom (1619), I, 16.

[103] Ferguson, *Scots Brigade*, I, 343-44.

[104] Acta Kerkeraad Nijmegen, I, April 2, 1626.

[105] Ibid., II, May 19, 1639; Mar. 21 and April 18, 1641.

[106] Ibid., II, Mar. 8, 1640; Matthews, *Cal. R.*, pp. 134-35. Cooper had a call to Bosch in 1640, but there is no indication of his having accepted it.

[107] Acta Synod Gelderland, I, 1626, art. 32; 1627, art. 21 (R.A. Gelderland).

was delinquent in handing in his credentials and also careless in performing his duties. The Dutch consistory admonished Howell, the "pretendeerde predicant," to cease all ecclesiastical ministry until he produced his lawful attestation; and from time to time the preachers sent further messages about the necessity of "good church order" to the English officers in charge.[108] Several of the English ministers cooperated voluntarily with the Dutch ministers (e.g. William Cooper in 1640 and Thomas Butler in 1641).[109] The Dutch church assumed they had a supervisory responsibility over the foreign English church. They determined to hold "goede ende billicke correspondentie" between the two churches; the Dutch requested that the English marriage banns be read in both churches and that the marriages be recorded in the Dutch consistory register.[110] When a controversy arose in the English church in 1657 between minister and members, the Dutch churchmen felt a responsibility to bring about reconciliation. Several of the English members had asked for transfer to the Dutch Reformed church.[111] The English ministers did not become members of the Nijmegen Classes; some, however, were members of the English Synod (Rogers, Sibbald).

During the height of war activity, Nijmegen had a large English and Scottish population. Following the campaign of 1629, Smetius's *Chronijk* reports that the town was overflowing with 500 or 600 sick and wounded, "bloody and wounded, the majority Scots." In 1633 Nijmegen was the headquarters of seventeen foreign regiments, English, Scottish, and German.[112] The city also accumulated a small civilian British population. Between 1592 and 1651 twenty-five English and Scots took citizenship at Nijmegen, the majority before 1640.[113]

The records of the Classis of Zutphen mention two English-Scottish garrison churches, one at Zutphen and the other at Doesburg. The church at Zutphen met in the former Dominican Broederen Kerk, beginning on November 14, 1611: "On this day the English began their first preaching service." Again in 1623 the English officers of the garrison asked permission anew for English services.[114] Among the Zutphen ministers were Thomas Morgan (1611), a Scot, former preacher at

---

[108] Acta Kerkeraad Nijmegen, I, Apr. 2 and 8, 1626; Sept. 14, 1628; Nov. 13, 1631. Howell performed marriages without banns.

[109] Ibid., II, Mar. 8, 1640; Dec. 5, 1641; May 19, 1644. Butler came from Bridewell, London.

[110] Ibid., I, Aug. 17, 1623.

[111] Ibid., III, Dec. 23, 1657; Jan. 16, 1658.

[112] Smetius, *Chronijk*, pp. 172-73, 176.

[113] J. A. Schimmel, *Burgerrecht te Nijmegen, 1592-1810* (Tilburg, 1966).

[114] Acta Kerkeraad Zutphen, I, Nov. 24, 1611; July 13, 1623 (G.A. Zutphen).

Dublin, Ireland; Miles Maling (1622), and Daniel Widdows (before 1632). The church continued to function well beyond this time but the ministers are not known. The Classis of Zutphen in 1649 brought an item to the synod about the English minister of Zutphen.[115]

The town of Doesburg to the south, also under the jurisdiction of the Classis of Zutphen, had English worship services for several years, at least during the period 1613-33. Ministers were Robert Parker (1613-14), the Puritan exile author of *Scholasticall Discourse against Symbolizing with Antichrist in Ceremonies, Especially in the Signe of the Crosse* (1607); followed by William Howell (1621-22); and Thomas Parsons (1630-33). Because of Parker's notable Puritan reputation, he proved too controversial for more choice positions at Amsterdam and was reduced to taking the out-of-the-way post at Doesburg.[116]

The Zutphen Classis took on itself the responsibility of close supervising of the foreign preachers. Howell, who had an ill reputation wherever he served, proved to be a suspiciously slippery character; in spite of all requirements laid down by the Zutphen Classis he refused to produce his ministerial credentials. In June of 1621 the classis issued the ultimatum that he must produce his credentials from England within six to eight weeks (the end of July); but even by August 29, still no attestation—"expected any day," he kept saying. The exasperated classis finally offered him 40 guilders to make a trip to England to fetch his papers, but nothing came of it, and in 1622 the Zutphen ministers turned the matter over to the new English Synod.[117] After transferring to Nijmegen, Howell had similar problems in proving his genuineness of ministry. Parsons, Howell's successor, belonged to the English Synod and had no problems with the Dutch Classis. In 1630 Parsons (Peirsonus), "English preacher in some garrisons around here," asked approval from the Synod of Gelderland for authority to perform marriages and the communion in the English congregation (*Engelsche vergaederinge*). The Synod, however, declined to give a definitive answer because of the broadness of the issues; "the matter concerns not only us but the other synods as well."[118] The fact that the Dutch churches did not judge some of the Gelderland garrison churches to be worthy of performing marriages and the sacraments reveals, perhaps, some Dutch prejudice but mainly indicates the lax

---

[115] On Thomas Morton, Acta Kerkeraad Zutphen, I, Oct. 13, 1611; on Miles Maling, Acta Classis Zutphen, I, 162; on Daniel Widdows, B.P., I, 177; Acta Synod Gelderland, I (1649, gravamina).

[116] On Parker, see Acta Classis Zutphen, I, 92v, Sept. 21, 1613 (G.A. Zutphen); for Parker at Amsterdam, see chapter 4.

[117] Acta Classis Zutphen, I, 152, 158, 161v, 162, 173 (1621-22).

[118] Acta Synod Gelderland, I, 1630, art. 10.

religious organization and practice prevalent among the British on the military frontier.

Zwolle in Overijssel had an English church during the 1620s and up to about 1633, but no records remain except for the names of three ministers: John Palmer (during the 1620s); John Roe (1628), "preacher of the garrison laying at Swoll"; and John Black.[119] Roe, later of Flushing, belonged to both the Classis of Zwolle and the English Synod.[120]

Brief references to other garrison churches appear here and there: Amersfoort (Petrus Gribius, preacher), Gouda (Gamaliel Day, preacher), Tiel (Mr. Sclaer, preacher), Grave (served by a Scottish regiment preacher), and Wesel, Germany (with "a Dutchman which speakes English"), all in the period 1630-33.[121] Maastricht in 1663 had an English preaching place, which the French and English used alternatively.[122] All of these were cities "where publike Churches are allowed unto his Majestyes subjects."[123]

The Amersfoort church, in Utrecht province, lasted 1630-33 and perhaps longer.[124] Petrus Gribius began his ministerial career as a proponent at Amersfoort in 1630. Although he "gave good content" when examined theologically by the Classis of Amersfoort, neither the classis nor the Dutch consistory of Amersfoort admitted Gribius as a member as he requested. The Earl of Oxford (Robert de Vere), the regimental commander, created a crisis at Amersfoort by ordering Gribius to use the Prayer Book and the prescribed Anglican ceremonies; but Gribius made long excuses and gained support for his stand from the Classis of Amersfoort and the Synod of Utrecht. The Synod instructed Gribius not to bring in any ceremonies of kneeling and the like and to pattern himself after the prevailing order of the Reformed churches of the province. After Gribius transferred to 's-Hertogenbosch in 1632, the English officers announced they were seeking a reader or preacher who would use edifying books, not a militant firebrand, lest the congregation would split over

---

[119] Steven, p. 344; Flushing C.R., no. 4469 (1628). John Palmer of Zwolle is probably the same man as Mr. Palmer of Dort (1624-25).

[120] C.R., Flushing E.R.C., fol. 9; Acta Synod Overijssel, 1628, art. 62, gravamina from Classis of Zwolla; B.P., I, 160.

[121] B.P., I, 160, 168; S.P. 16, vol. 170, no. 8. Gouda is mentioned, as Tergoo, only in B.P., I, 168. Other garrison churches having brief mention are Camphere (Kampen?) and Tervere (Veere).

[122] Ray, *Travels*, I, 43.

[123] S.P. 16, vol. 170, no. 8.

[124] Acta Classis Amersfoort, I, Aug. 31, 1630; Mar. 12-13, 1633 (in Archive of Classis of Utrecht, no. 23).

the issue of ceremonies.[125] No ordained replacement for Gribius was found. The Earl of Oxford thereupon designated a common soldier to read service from the Prayer Book. The practice became common in camps administered by Anglican officers, in the absence of a regular preacher, to have prayers read.[126]

---

[125] Acta Classis Amersfoort, Aug. 31, Nov. 9-10, 1630; Mar. 12-13, 1633; Knuttel, *Acta Synoden Zuid-Holland*, 1631, I, 379; Acta Synod Utrecht, I, 1630, sess. 7, art. 8, sess. 8, art. 1 (G.A. Utrecht).

[126] B.P., I, 161.

CHAPTER ELEVEN

THE ENGLISH SYNOD, PRINTING, AND OTHER PURITAN ENTERPRISES

The Netherlands was the Puritan refuge. "The old Puritan Ministers, who could not of conscience conforme ... did shelter themselves from the storms of Episcopall persecution, and from the tyranny of the High Commission Court, in the English Army, and English churches of the Netherlands, as in a Sacred Sanctuary, and a most safe hideing place, which the Lord in his good providence prepared for them."[1] Without employment in the Netherlands, many nonconforming Puritan ministers would have been impoverished and, as the bishops grimly hoped, forced back into conformity. Ambassador Sir Dudley Carleton acknowledged the incongruity of allowing Puritan zealots silenced at home to minister to the British merchants and soldiers abroad. But who else was willing to serve such out of the way places? "Inconformable men were there used ... being at hand and ready to be had." The choices were "to be either quite destitute, or else to entertaine ministers conformable to the articles and canons of our Church indeede but such otherwise as were of debauched life, and for their unworthinesse left unprovided for at home and consequently forced to seek their fortune abroad."[2] The Dutch Raad van State in 1633 specifically querried Ambassador Sir William Boswell, "If the English Ministres in these parts were chased out of their contrey?" Boswell replied, with some exaggeration, that of the English Synod preachers "not above one or two ... durst live at home in England: their disobedience to the lawes therof was such."[3]

Several hundred English and Scottish ministers served in the seventeenth-century Netherlands. Many of these were nonconformists silenced in England, or barely a step or two away from deprivation. Before the Puritan Revolution the nonconformist immigration came primarily from three dioceses, London, Norwich, and Chester.[4] The

---

[1] John Quick, "Icones Sacrae Anglicanae," I, i, 11 (MS, D.W.L.).
[2] B.P., I, 250-51; S.P. 16, vol. 90, no. 84.
[3] S.P. 84, vol. 146, fol. 202.
[4] From London diocese: Hugh Peter, John Davenport, Thomas Hooker, Alexander Leighton, Sydrach Simpson, Joseph Symonds, John Archer, Philip Nye, Thomas Weld, and William Ames. From Norwich diocese: Thomas Scott, Thomas Allen, William Bridge, Jeremiah Burroughes, William Greenhill, Edward Wale, John Ward, and Paul Amyraut. From Chester: John Paget, Thomas Paget, Samuel Eaton, Julius Hering, and Robert Park. This does not mention the Separatists, an additional large group.

Puritan build-up in the Netherlands was swelled in the 1630s by lay immigrants from Yorkshire, East Anglia, and other places. The East Anglians had "better opportunity of sudden and easy slipping over."[5] Puritans bitterly laid the blame for forced immigration on archbishops Laud and Neile and underlings like Bishop Wren of Norwich. The prelates and their accusers all acknowledged the fact of a large Netherlands immigration but disputed the motives for it. The Puritans claimed to have been harried out; the prelates argued that immigration proceeded from many motives.

The 1641 articles of impeachment against Wren charged him (as bishop at Norwich 1635-38) with driving forth from his diocese fifty godly ministers in a mere twenty-eight months of his oppressive episcopacy, "whereby some of them were forced to go beyond Sea," further he "caused 3000 of the King's Subjects (many of whom using Trades employ'd 100 poor People each) to go into *Holland* and other Places beyond Sea. ..."[6] An anti-Wren petition from Norwich gave specifics of over fifty families (500 persons) chased out by Wren, having "villifyed their persons and burdened their consciences that he forced them to fly the land." Diverse Norwich ministers ("their consciences not permitting obedience) were for their safegard of conscience forced to fly the land as Mr Bridge Mr Ward and Mr Wales and Mr Allen."[7] Wren's defense, quite correctly, stressed that economic motivations moved many of the thousands going abroad and that the emigration had begun before his being bishop of Norwich and continued well after his leaving. Nevertheless, he granted that some were, no doubt, motivated by "the utter Dislike of all Church Government, and of the Doctrine and Discipline, by Law here establish'd."[8]

The deprived ministers carried some of their pious followers with them to the Netherlands and established new churches, as at Arnhem, or enlarged existing churches, as at Rotterdam, which grew to over 1000

---

[5] Christopher Wren, *Parentalia* (London, 1750), p. 102; Carl Bridenbaugh, *Vexed and Troubled Englishmen, 1590-1642* (New York: Oxford Univ. Press, 1968), pp. 395, 466. On the Yorkshire immigration see J. T. Cliffe, *The Yorkshire Gentry from the Reformation to the Civil War* (London: The Athlone Press, 1969), pp. 307-08; on East Anglia, see R. W. Ketton-Cremer, *Norfolk in the Civil War* (Hamden, Conn.: Archon Books, 1970), pp. 62-85, and Kenneth W. Shipps, "Lay Patronage of East Anglican Puritan Clerics in Pre-Revolutionary England," Diss. Yale 1971. On the Chester immigration, primarily clerics rather than lay people, see J. S. Morrill, *Cheshire 1630-1660* (London: Oxford Univ. Press, 1974), p. 191; William Urwick, *Historical Sketches of Nonconformity in the County Palatine of Chester* (London, 1864), pp. 76-77, 138-39, 473.

[6] Wren, *Parentalia*, pp. 14, 100; John H. Horton, "Two Bishops and the Holy Brood: A Fresh Look at a Familiar Fact," *New England Quarterly*, 40 (Sept. 1967), 357-63.

[7] Tanner MS. 220, fols. 124-25 (Bod., Oxford).

[8] Wren, *Parentalia*, p. 102; Ketton-Cremer, *Norfolk*, pp. 76-79.

members by 1640. "It was no hard matter ... to perswade them to remove their dwellings, and transport their Trades." The militant preachers urged: "The Sun of Heaven, say they, doth shine as comfortably in other places, the Son of Righteousness much brighter: Better to go and dwell in *Goshen*, find it where we can, than tarry in the midst of such an *Egyptian* darkness as was then falling on this Land." In Holland "they filled up their Congregations to so great a number."[9]

Puritans in the Netherlands, whether ministers or congregation, did not fade out of English-Scottish affairs. "Such of us of the English nation, who have been enforced by home-oppressions to seeke for liberty, imployment and livelihood," they said, "not daring through forgetfulnes to let goe out of minde our most endeared native countrey."[10] A Puritan network, in league with the movement in Britain, functioned throughout the Netherlands. The main elements of the Puritan enterprise were: (1) the various British churches, which gave employment to the refugee ministers, (2) the English Synod (also known as the English Classis), and (3) the Puritan printing shops. Other schemes flourished. Some of the exiles used the Dutch universities for refuge; moreover, Hugh Peter and William Ames laid plans for a Puritan college at Rotterdam (a Puritan Douai). Ames was to be professor for the "educating and fitting of some studious youths, that should be sent him out of England, for the holy ministry, and so keep up the Orthodox Truths, and power of Godlyness, which were in a very declineing condition in his native country." This particular project failed with Ames's death in 1633.[11] When Sir William Boswell came to The Hague in 1632 he discerned the spider-like strands of a Puritan conspiracy. "At my first entry and view I spied to be a spider of divers thrids, uneven, very much entangled."[12] The "network" was an informal conglomerate of Puritan activities which gave employment and marshalled the resources of the angry exiles.

The numerous British town churches were uniformly Puritan-minded and anti-Episcopal. They wanted preachers of Puritan sermons. The Merchant Adventurers and many of the military officers also employed zealous Puritans. Sir Horace and Lady Mary Vere almost singlehandedly sustained a large troop of pious preachers unemployable back in England. In Holland Lady Mary could do even more good than at home, Puritan associates told her, "in respect of the helpe and encouragment the ministry and course of Religion in the Hague may have by your

---

[9] Peter Heylyn, *Cyprianus Anglicus* (London, 1668), p. 367.
[10] Thomas Paget, "Humble Advertisement," in John Paget, *A Defence of Chvrch-Government* (London, 1641).
[11] Quick, "Icones," I, i, 44.
[12] B.P., I, 109.

countenance and example."[13] Without such opportunities in churches and chaplaincies, many of the exiles would have been ruined by poverty, few of them, because of language difficulties, being capable of ministering in Dutch churches. One typical exile, Nicholas Rushe, applying for a Dutch position at Arkel, was refused because the congregation "could not well understand his language."[14] Without positions and sanctuary in the Netherlands, they could not have maintained their ceaseless Puritan activities abroad and at home.

Before Laud's elevation to archbishop in 1633, the English government had no systematic plan of combating Puritanism in the Netherlands. It was a matter "never urged nor pressed; but the governors of the Church of England connived at it; for ought I know," reported ambassador Carleton.[15] Laud for the first time conceived a comprehensive "design" to reverse the situation, the effort in the Netherlands being merely part of the larger design to impose conformity and discipline on Anglican religion world wide, England, Scotland, Ireland, America, the Netherlands, embassies "in all Courts of Christendom," ships at sea. In March 1633 he presented to the Privy Council a program of ten steps for bringing conformity to English religion overseas. He outlined these policies: (1) That no chaplains be admitted to the English regiments unless conformable, (2) That the Merchant Adventurers admit no ministers unless conformable, (3) That unconformable ministers already employed be dismissed, (4) That every minister, whether English or Scottish, serving merchants or the regiments be required to use the Prayer Book and liturgy, (5) That all ministers abroad be prevented, through the foreign state, from disseminating any bitter words or writings against the English church or state, (6) That no temporary ministers be admitted to preach unless conformable, (7) That no deputy governor be sent to Delft or other Merchant Adventurer factory unless conformable in religion and approved by the Privy Council, (8) That a clause concerning the above regulation be inserted in the Adventurer's charter, (9) That all royal agents in the Low Countries be instructed on these policies and be required to give an annual report "of the Progress of the business," (10) That the English Classis or Synod of

---

[13] Add. MS. 4275, fol. 160. On the Veres, see Clement R. Markham, *The Fighting Veres* (Boston: Houghton Mifflin, 1888); Samuel Clarke, *The Lives of Sundry Eminent Persons in This Later Age* (London, 1683), pt. II, pp. 145-51 (Life of Lady Mary Vere). Chaplains to the Veres, household and military, included John Paget, John Burgess, William Ames, Obadiah Sedgewick, Samuel Balmford, John Hassall, Stephen Goffe, all except the latter two Puritans. For a sample of Lady Mary's correspondence with Puritan divines, see *Letters of John Davenport*, ed. Isabel M. Calder (New Haven: Yale Univ. Press, 1937).
[14] Acta Classis Gorinchem, III, Sept. 7-8, 1620 (N.H.K. Heusden).
[15] B.P., I, 250.

Holland be prevented from functioning. An order in council of October 1, 1633, instituted the policies regarding the Merchant Adventurers, and thereafter Laud's program went at full speed.[16] Just as zealously, the Netherlands Puritans resisted, "resolved still to maintain the cause," stubbornly confident that the Laudian Babylon would not prevail.[17]

The English Synod

The desire for an ecclesiastical organization of the English and Scottish churches of the Netherlands was often expressed. John Paget of Amsterdam with the help of Ambassador Sir Ralph Winwood had proposed an English classis in 1608 and again in 1611 and 1612, but without result.[18] At that point only Amsterdam and Leiden had established English churches, and Flushing and Brielle had military chapels. By 1621, when the movement came to fruition, the need was greater, new English churches having been formed at Rotterdam, Flushing, Veere, Heusden, Utrecht, and Gorinchem; and the number of chaplains had similarly increased. Most of these, except for Paget and Potts of Amsterdam who belonged to the Dutch classis, had no Dutch or English ecclesiastical supervision. Various chaplains disgraced their calling, "some with their rashness, drunkenness, and strange opinions, causing great offense." Itinerant ministers practiced their ministry, "preaching and serving the sacrament," without undergoing any examination of doctrine or life.[19] A new plan for an English Synod in 1621 gathered support from many reputable British preachers in the Netherlands and had strong backing from the Dutch Synod of South Holland.

Arguments in favor of the synod were pious and persuasive. According to the advocates of a synod, a synodical organization would bring orderliness to British religion by "reformation of such disordres and confusions as menn did too well and openly perceave in dyvers of the English and Skotch ministers as they sayde or pretended to be." Thus, "the stragling and infamous ministers of England cominge hither, may bee hindred from preaching." Another reason for a synod was the example of the French churches of the land who had their own synod, the Walloon Synod. It was logical that "the States should doe our Nation the like

---

[16] Heylyn, *Cyprianus Anglicus*, pp. 231-33; S.P. 16, vol. 247, no. 2; H. R. Trevor Roper, *Archbishop Laud 1573-1645*, 2nd ed. (London: Macmillan, 1963), chapter 7.

[17] William Ames, quoted in Advertysement of *Fresh Suit against Human Ceremonies* (n.p., 1633).

[18] Amsterdam C.R., I, 36; S.P. 84, vol. 117, fol. 132v; see above chapter 4.

[19] Documents on the English Synod, 1621-22, Synod of North Holland, no. 388 (archive of Classis of Amsterdam, G.A. Amsterdam).

honor."[20] John Forbes, John Wing, Thomas Scott, Thomas Barkely, Samuel Bachelor, and several chaplains, eleven in all, took the lead in establishing the synod.[21] The Synod of South Holland in 1621 supported them by sending a petition to the States General on behalf of an English synod.[22] Meanwhile, Sir Dudley Carleton, ambassador at The Hague, "procuring and assisting in the passing of that Commission," had the difficult task of persuading King James I to acquiesce in an English Synod. The king was instinctively opposed because it would be independent of the Church of England. When finally won over, James approved an organization with very limited powers: "To suppress those who tooke upon them the function of preachers without lawfull vocation or Admission to the Ministery, And 21y, to examine, restraine, and punish the ill manners of such as give scandall by their vitious lives." Nothing more. Carleton informed the synod organizers "they must hold themselves to the first intention of the grant of theyr meetings, which was not to establish any thing new."[23]

The States General, having received recommendations from the Council of State (Raad van State) and Carleton, formally commissioned a synod for the English and Scots on October 20, 1621. The *Hoogmogende Heren* were persuaded of the necessity of acting by reports about "the scandalous and inordinate doings among the English and Scottish preachers in the garrisons." The English Synod was to be modeled after the example of the Walloon Synod. The Council of State, which handled many details of government, gave special direction that the new synod examine the lives, doctrines, fitness, opinions, qualifications, and condition of such as are entertained to the ministry.[24] The 1621 States General resolution put the English Synod upon a legal basis and also for the first time gave a specific legal foundation to all British churches in the Netherlands: That they be conformable to the pattern of the Walloon Reformed churches and, by obvious implication, conformable to the Dutch Reformed churches.[25] The synod was called by the Dutch the *Engelse Synod.* Among the English it was known both as "English Classis" and "English Synod."

---

[20] S.P. 16, vol. 310, no. 103; B.P., I, 16-17. For a history of the English Classis/Synod, see Raymond P. Stearns, *Congregationalism in the Dutch Netherlands* (Chicago: American Society of Church History, 1940).

[21] B.P., I, 11.

[22] A copy of the petition, July 13, 1621, is in Documents on the English Synod, no. 388; Knuttel, *Acta Synoden Zuid-Holland*, I, 48.

[23] S.P. 16, vol. 90, no. 84; B.P., I, 35-38; Stearns, *Congregationalism*, pp. 96, 135.

[24] Res. States General, no. 3180, fol. 437v, 503v; S.P. 84, vol. 104, fols. 96-98; Documents on English Synod, no. 388.

[25] S.P. 84, vol. 120, fol. 237.

Sir Dudley Carleton summarized the early history of the synod in a dispatch of 1624 to the king:

> The number of your Majesties subiects, both English and Scottish as well soldiers as inhabitants, being great in these provinces, who have divers churches and preachers of both nations, all, two onely excepted, allowed and stipendiated by the States, the inconveniences for want of government amongst the said preachers which ... moved my predecessor Sir Ralphe Winwood, to be a suiter to the States in their behalfe, that they might have their clasicall meetings after the same manner as the Wallon and French churches have: which was then crossed by the Arminian faction as contrary to their ends. Soone after the Nationall Synode at Dort, these of South Holland holding a provincionall synode, amonst other cautions for preventing new disorders in the churches of these provinces, revived this motion of classical meetings ... which being made knowne unto me by some of the chiefe English and Scottish preachers, and my assistance desired, by example, of my predecessor, to procure them of the States the like libertye as the Wallons have, I excused my self untill I might know therin your Majesties pleasure: which being signified unto me the 11th of August in answare of my dispatch of the 19th of July 1621 in conformity to what was desired, I layd hold of the opportunity of the motion of this Synode of South Holland and by that meanes brought that to effect which otherwise I could not promise myself to have obtayned: and accordingly an act was graunted for the classicall assemblyes of your Majesties subiects. ..."[26]

The synod preachers consequently claimed three basic foundations for the synod: the 1621 resolution of the Synod of South Holland, the 1621 resolution of the States General, and the approbation of King James "as wee understood by his Majestys Ambassador."[27]

Although come to life, the English Synod was faced with two immediate hazards. The first came from King James's lingering suspicions that the synod, headed by his old adversary John Forbes, was too Puritan. For several months in 1621, before finally giving support to the action of the States General, James insisted on naming a "moderator" to superintend the synod.[28] The synod preachers, however, absolutely resisted any moderatorship, seeing it as a wedge for imposing Anglican religion upon them. When Alexander MacDuff of Veere sought advice about the synod by writing home to the Archbishop of St. Andrews, he received answer strongly urging a synod moderator, a *moderatorem perpetuum*, "that is, in effect, a superintendent, and in order to avoid controversy, that the king nominate the moderator."[29] The mention of a

---

[26] S.P. 84, vol. 117, fols. 132-33.
[27] B.P., I, 16.
[28] B.P., I, 12-15; S.P. 84, vol. 116, fol. 78.
[29] Documents on English Synod, no. 388 (Reasons of the English Preachers of Amsterdam, no. 2).

perpetual moderator raised sinister fears, but the Puritans fended off the odious proposal by arguing that the Dutch Reformed church and the States General would never admit of any such outside official. Because all but one or two British churches received financial support from the Dutch magistrates, the synod preachers pleaded that they were absolutely forbidden by law to deviate from Reformed practice or accept any foreign governor. Although desirous of being obedient subjects of His Majesty, the preachers made the point that Dutch law strictly prevented the practice of Anglicanism (for which they were secretly grateful). In the meantime, they promised to privately esteem the Church of England—"and our continuall prayers."[30] Although the king finally relented from imposing the moderator, he renewed the demand in 1622 and nearly every year thereafter. In 1624, James sparked a crisis in the synod by decreeing that a moderator must immediately be appointed. The annual meeting was already assembled, under the presidency of Thomas Barkely; but when pressed by Carleton to accede to a kingly-appointed moderator, the synod dissolved their meeting rather than comply.[31]

The other hazard to the success of the synod was the refusal of several English ministers to cooperate (John Paget and Thomas Potts of Amsterdam and Hugh Goodyear of Leiden). The Amsterdam English Reformed church was the largest and most important British church in the entire country; its failure to join was an embarrassing setback. Although Paget himself had in 1611-12 been the promoter for a similar English Synod, he would have nothing to do with the new body organized by John Forbes. Paget and Potts, both members of the Amsterdam Classis, received invitations to the first English synodical meeting held at Delft in 1622; but instead of joining the new group or extending a hand of fellowship, they opposed it. Paget and Potts hurried to the Dutch classis and complained about "the pretended English synod." They stirred up agitation in the classis, in the Synod of North Holland, and among the Amsterdam magistrates. The two English preachers proclaimed that their membership in the Dutch classis suited them very well and that they had no reason to make a change to a new synod. When Forbes came to Paget to recruit him to the new enterprise, Paget said bluntly, "that as we had no will, so we had no power to withdraw or disjoyne ourselves from the Classis."[32]

---

[30] B.P., I, 12-15.

[31] S.P. 84, vol. 121, fols. 237-39; vol. 116, fol. 78; vol. 117, fol. 132.

[32] Acta Classis Amsterdam, III, 30-33 (May 2 and July 4, 1622); B.P., I, 139; John Paget, *An Answer to the unjust complaints of William Best* (Amsterdam, 1635), p. 87; Alice C. Carter, *The English Reformed Church in Amsterdam in the Seventeenth Century* (Amsterdam: Scheltema & Holkema, 1964), pp. 71-73.

The sum of Paget's anti-synod arguments are contained in a list of seven questions forwarded to the Synod of South Holland, "Objections of the English ministers of Amsterdam against the classical meetings of the English." He charged that:

1. The English Classis had been instituted without the suffrage and even knowledge of the ministers of the English church of Amsterdam.
2. It consisted of only seven or eight ministers who have an actual ministry.
3. The classis raised fears of confusion in ecclesiastical order and government because the King of Great Britain sought to bring in a Perpetual Moderator.
4. The classis contained some members affected with Brownism, some of dissolute life, and some addicted to the Episcopal order.
5. The first meeting of the classis had confusions and dissensions.
6. There was reason to fear that, if this English classis did conform to the order of the Belgic churches, then the Belgic churches in England might be compelled to conform themselves to the Church of England.
7. There were some in this classis which held the opinion "that our Lord Jesus Christe hath committed the power of ecclesiasticall discipline to everie particular Church; and for that reason the disposing and supervising or overseeing therof belonges not to anie Classical or Synodall Assemblie."[33]

In spite of obstacles from Amsterdam, the English Synod was launched. Nevertheless, the refusal of the Amsterdam ministers to join the synod was a sharp rebuff, being "some bleamish upon their meeting it self, and reproch upon the persons that assembled therein."[34]

What motivated Paget to react so bitterly to Forbes's synod? The motives for establishing the synod seemed good. Sir Dudley Carleton (1624) attributed the hostility of Paget, Potts, and Goodyear to personal grievances at not having the top places; "and the English Ministers of Amsterdam and Leyden upon causeles jealousyes not onely refused to appear at their assemblyes, but indeavored to interrupt them by poisoning the waters even at the fountayne."[35] Potts and Goodyear did attend the organizational meeting of 1622 but not thereafter. Paget never attended. Paget had old animosities toward Forbes, going back at least to

---

[33] S.P. 84, vol. 106, fol. 141. Other versions are in Acta Classis Amsterdam, III, 32-33 and Documents on the English Synod, no. 388.
[34] Amsterdam C.R., II, May 10, 1623.
[35] S.P. 84, vol. 117, fol. 132v.

1610, when the Scot had been nominated, over Paget's objections, by some of the congregation as co-pastor. Paget had vetoed him. Carleton's analysis, although accurate as far as it went, skipped over an important theological aspect of Paget's criticism of the synod, which Sir Dudley himself had not yet perceived. The stated purpose of the synod was pastoral and organizational (ending confusion and bringing orderliness to the ministerial calling); all of this could have been secured by having the English ministers affiliate with a Dutch Reformed classis in the region where they served. Because of his knowledge of the organizers of the synod, Paget surmised that the real intent was to use the synod as a headquarters for militant Puritanism in the Netherlands. He further feared that the synod would be dominated by radicals committed to Henry Jacob's doctrines of church government. Paget had a great fear of "Jacobites."[36] Although cloaking itself under the garb of orthodox Reformed churchmanship, Paget predicted that the synod would soon become a tool of unorthodox Jacobites and near-Brownists (points 4 and 7 of his Seven Questions). He warned his Dutch friends that some of the synod preachers denied the authority of classes and synods except for advice and counsel, "saying that each particular church itself had received the power to practice discipline immediately from Christ, which they would not grant to any synod." What kind of a "synod" would this new English Synod without synodical authority be? Paget did not mention by name which of the synod preachers he considered to be Jacobite or Brownistically-inclined. Perhaps he referred to John Wing.[37]

The newly-chartered synod held its first organizational meeting at Delft in April of 1622. The following ministers attended: Andrew Hunter (Scottish chaplain), John Forbes (Delft), John Hassall (chaplain to Sir Horace Vere), Thomas Potts (Amsterdam), Thomas Barkely (Rotterdam), John Wing (Flushing), Peter Rogers (Nijmegen), William Howell (Doesburg), Barnaby [Walter] Whetstone (chaplain to Lord Lisle), Andrew Hughes (chaplain to Sir Edward Cecil), Thomas Scott (Gorinchem), Alexander MacDuff (Veere), Hugh Goodyear (Leiden), Samuel Bachelor (Heusden), George Clark (Utrecht), Alexander Clark (Geertruidenberg), Miles Maling (Zutphen). Forbes was elected synod president. The outlines of a synodical organization were established and twice-yearly meetings were prescribed (changed to an annual meeting in 1623). Each settled town congregation was invited to send an elder to synod meetings. In general form, the English Synod was "to be the same with the dutch and french churches," as stated in the commission from

---

[36] Paget, *Answer*, p. 28 and preface; B.P., I, 139.

[37] Documents on the English Synod, no. 388. Burrage, *E.E.D.*, II, 293, surmises that John Wing may have been an associate of Jacob at London.

the States General. They made a start at cleaning up ministerial scandals by calling for a full examination of all English and Scottish ministers in Dutch service. Each member was to bring to the next meeting "a Testimonie of his warrantable calling to the ministerie, and cariage therein to be considered and censured by the Synod."[38]

The second meeting took place one year later, April 12, 1623, also at Delft. Forbes continued as president and John Wing was named scribe. At this meeting the membership of the synod was formalized, after examining all the ministerial credentials, "proof of their calling to the Ministery and carriage." Fourteen were enrolled as members: John Forbes, Andrew Hunter, John Hassall, Thomas Scott, Thomas Barkely, Walter Whetstone, Andrew Hughes, John Wing, Alexander MacDuff, James Fayem (Forme), John Oswald, Samuel Bachelor, George Clark, Alexander Clark. All but two, Fayem of Nijmegen and Oswald of Dort, had been attenders at the 1622 meeting; five of the 1622 attenders were not enrolled (Potts and Goodyear, who were now opposing the synod, and three chaplains, Howell, Maling, and Rogers). Some who applied, probably the three chaplains, were turned down for having insufficient credentials or for not bothering to attend, knowing they could not qualify. Ministers who did not appear for examination, or who were refused, were therewith declared to be suspended from all ministerial functions.[39] Such pronouncements had little or no effect on Paget, Potts, and Goodyear, who were well entrenched in their positions at Amsterdam and Leiden; for chaplains like Howell (Howle), Rogers, and Maling, who were already among the weakest preachers around, the synod's blacklisting virtually eliminated them from practicing in the Netherlands.[40] Carleton commended the synod's vigilance; "some unlearned and scandalous persons, who tooke upon them the function of preachers without vocation or admission to the Ministerye, not daring to appeare, and abyde the tryall, were deposed, some unfitt men presenting themselves not admitted, and others of better lyfe and doctrine receaved in their places."[41]

In another action, the synod in 1623 passed a resolution declaring uniformity with Reformed doctrine and practice:

---

[38] Minutes of the 1622 meeting, S.P. 84, vol. 106, fols. 84-85.

[39] Minutes of the 1623 meeting, S.P. 84, vol. 112, fols. 3-4.

[40] Rogers had earlier been removed as minister at Bergen-op-Zoom in 1619 because of inadequate credentials; nothing more is heard of him after 1622. Howell never could produce ministerial credentials to the satisfaction of any English or Dutch church officials, being known around Zutphen as a "pretendeerde predikant." No reference to Maling is found after 1622.

[41] S.P. 84, vol. 117, fol. 132v.

> For ordering and ruling all matters of our ministeriall function in administration or discipline, it is concluded that all the members of this synod shall subscribe the last Nationall Synod holden at Dort 1618, together with the ordinances of all preceding synods in force to the same effect, and that no liturgy be used in any church amongst us, but that which is in use in the churches of these United Provinces; by reading onely of a chapter or two, and the ten Commandements out of the Bible, and singing of a Psalm before the sermon: and that in administration of the sacraments, the onely order there specified, bee practised both in delivering, and receiving; and that every pastor endeavour to perswade his people thereunto, so farr as may bee without schisme and in case of not prevailing to acquaint the Synod with their successe.[42]

No Prayer Book was to be allowed. By their interpretation of the law (the States General resolution of 1621) the Reformed-Puritan religion was made obligatory and the Anglican liturgy virtually illegal.

The synod's energetic action in silencing notorious preachers enhanced its reputation among Dutch churchmen. Even the Synod of North Holland, previously unfriendly because of Paget's agitation, took a more cordial view in 1623. The North Holland Synod joined the South Holland Synod in agreeing to further the success of the English Synod.[43] Sir Dudley Carleton was favorable to their work and reported their activities to London in the most positive light. Among the bishops, George Carleton of Chichester was supportive, having heard of the "fruit" of the synod.[44] The English Synod continued to meet almost yearly: at Rotterdam in 1624 (Barkely president, Scott scribe), Utrecht in 1626, The Hague in 1627 (Wing president), Rotterdam in 1628, and Dort in 1631 (Forbes president, Bachelor scribe). The meeting of 1624 was adjourned early and no meeting apparently was held in 1625 due to conflicts with King James. "The devill is busy by all means to hinder good workes," they said.[45] The 1629 meeting was definitely cancelled, and whether the synod met in 1630 is unknown. The last official meeting was in 1631. Forbes of Delft served as president several times, so that the synod, the "Delph Classis," became strongly associated with him—"that is indeed nothing else but Mr. Forbes his Superintendency," mocked Stephen Goffe.[46] In addition to the original fourteen members of 1623, other newcomers joined from year to year (Hugh Peter, Samuel Balmford, Steven Paine, Daniel Widdows, Henry Sibbald, Gamaliel Day, Thomas

---

[42] S.P. 84, vol. 112, fol. 4.
[43] Acta Synod North Holland, 1623, art. 8; however, by 1626 the synod had again turned against the English Synod.
[44] S.P. 14, vol. 164, no. 11.
[45] S.P. 84, vol. 131, fol. 220.
[46] B.P., I, 100; S.P. 16, vol. 237, no. 48.

Hooker, Jeremiah Elborough, Thomas Parsons, John Roe, John Drake, Maximilliaan Teellinck). Most were English ministers, but several Scots were active as well. Mr. Sclaer and Egbert Grim, English-speaking Germans serving in the regiments in the 1630s, were fringe members of the synod; they could gain employment and stipends from the States only with attestation from the English Synod. Sclaer, who had lived in England and was licensed by the Bishop of Bristol, depended on synod recommendations for his job. He told Goffe, "he was so much engaged to the Delph Classis ... that he could not well tell how to come off."[47] In the 1630s, as Laud applied heavy pressure to destroy the synod, participation dropped to about one-third of the active British preachers (eight or ten out of thirty).[48]

The most visible activities of the synod in its first half-dozen years, 1621 to 1627, were in fulfilling the original 1621 mandate of the States General. They licensed and examined ministers and weeded out the worst of them, and in other ways provided encouragement to the scattered British preachers. When asked what the synod did at its meetings, Steven Paine "sayd sometymes reformed vices, as if ther were that lived in fornication, or committed adalteri; they did use to summon them and examined the matter."[49] "Blessed effects were soone discerned in the removing and silencing of many unworthy and offensive persons who eyther intruded themselves into the ministerie without lawfull calling or entring regularly had abused that holy profession."[50] The results of reforming the ministerial corps, however, were not all that could be desired, as new scandals regularly appeared. The Synod of South Holland made fresh complaints in 1625, 1626, and 1627 about disorder in the English garrisons; "various vagabonds, being of scandalous life, have forced their way in."[51] Thus chided, the synod in 1626 sent new letters to the British officers asking that great care be taken in choosing chaplains. The synod also urged that all chaplains be required by their officers to join the English Synod. Of the four English colonels, only Sir Horace Vere and Sir Edward Harwood completely cooperated with the synod.[52]

Some of the synod's work was with the local congregations. The synod officers could be useful to the congregations seeking new ministers, as in

---

[47] S.P. 16, vol. 232, no. 23; B.P., I, 100.

[48] The active members of the 1630s were: Forbes, Peter, Balmford, Bachelor, Paine, Widdows, Sibbald, Hooker, Ames, and possibly Parsons; B.P., I, 168; S.P. 16, vol. 310, no. 103.

[49] B.P., I, 78.

[50] Sir Dudley Carleton (1626), S.P. 84, vol. 131, fol. 220.

[51] Knuttel, *Acta Synoden Zuid-Holland*, I, 137, 171-72, 207.

[52] S.P. 84, vol. 131, fol. 220.

1628 when the synod helped to bring John Roe from Zwolle to Flushing. The Flushing church in 1623 had developed a document, the Flushing "Protestation," affirming the relation of congregation and classis.[53] In other cases, the local churches called upon the synod for arbitration between minister and congregation. In 1625 the church at Dort appealed to the synod for "redress" because of the inadequacy of their minister, John Oswald. Forbes went to Dort but no discipline was applied to Oswald (who was Forbes's son-in-law).[54] Ministers transferring from one church to another were ordinarily ordained into their new charge by officers of the synod; and more controversially, in a few cases the synod ordained new people into the ministry. This was strictly beyond the limits of their original authorization from King James; and the English prelates were alarmed at the prospect of never-ending Puritan ordinations being produced abroad. One of the newly-created ministers was Steven Paine, a common soldier in Sir Horace Vere's company, who was ordained by John Forbes in 1626.[55] When Hugh Peter reorganized the Rotterdam church in 1633, adopting a written covenant and having himself ordained anew, he asked John Forbes, synod president, to be in charge.[56]

In spite of considerable activity, the synod faced serious organizational and practical problems in becoming an efficient, functioning synod for the British churches. The churches and preachers were so scattered among the cities that regular consultation was impossible. One meeting per year was the best that could be arranged, and even this had to be omitted several years. Travel by synod officers to the local congregations was irregular, so that the churches were required to proceed alone in many occasions. Modeled after the Walloon Synod, the English Synod suffered similar problems and worse: only annual meetings "and that then there is such trouble in their gathering together, some dwelling in one province and some in another, at such great distance that they never all meet and by reason of their few meetings there grow up many enormities in particular congregations unpunished."[57]

The pastoral function was nearly overshadowed in the later history of the English Synod. The synod was an organization of zealous Puritans, many of them exiles of conscience, and as such it upheld a vision of aggressive Puritan mission. The synod tried to control its membership by requiring subscription to the Reformed religion "in use in the churches

---

[53] Minutes of 1623, S.P. 84, vol. 112, fol. 4v; for further details of the relationship of the synod to a local congregation (Flushing), see Flushing C.R., no. 4469, for 1627-28.
[54] Dort C.R., no. 5, fol. 7; Add. MS. 17,677, vol. N, fol. 318.
[55] B.P., I, 161; S.P. 16, vol. 90, no. 84.
[56] S.P. 16, vol. 286, no. 94.
[57] B.P., I, 139.

of these United Provinces," which corresponded very well with their deeply-held Puritan theology. Some of the rank-in-file members were nondescript men of no public views; however, the leadership was a core of ideologically dedicated men committed to the international Puritan movement of England and America. The articulate members were Presbyterians or, eventually, Jacobites (soon to be known as Independents or Congregationalists). One of the early members, John Hassall, was an Anglican conformist, a *non residens* having left his charge in England because of debts. The synod gave him a special dispensation for membership. While in Holland, he adapted himself to the Reformed system, using only a few parts of the Anglican liturgy for the sacraments but allowing sitting at the communion. After he returned to England about 1625, having put his financial affairs in order, he resumed his Anglican priesthood and eventually became Dean of Norwich. Back in England he revealed himself as a great enemy of the Puritans.[58] Other than Hassall the members were all professed Puritans. Gamaliel Day, who came over in 1627, aspired to use some parts of the Prayer Book in his services. The synod at its 1623 meeting had gone on record as requiring the Dort confession and the Dutch Reformed style of worship; however, Day understood John Wing, synod president, to say "that their Classis should no way hinder him from using the orders and prayers of the church of England." Later, John Forbes at another synod meeting "admonished by way of advice but not authority not to read them any more."[59]

In the last years of the synod's existence, about 1628-1633, the Puritan program became more militant. The synod Puritans skillfully extracted precedents from the Treaty of Nonsuch (1585), Leicester's governorship, and the States General resolution of 1621 to buttress their Puritan, antiprelatical campaign. They claimed: "Her Majestie Queene Elizabeth, by an Act under her hand and seale yeilded to the States, that her owne subiects in this land should not use the formes and discipline of their owne church, but wholy conforme themselves unto the Dutch Church. Now that noe man may diminish this priviledge of the States graunted by the Queene, they pretend that an English Classis is necessary. ... And this act of the Queene, they prove was graunted when Flushing and Brill were putt into her hands."[60] Sir Dudley Carleton marked the synod's turning point toward radicalism as 1628. Carleton particularly objected

---

[58] Acta Classis Amsterdam, III, 31; B.P., I, 251; S.P. 84, vol. 112, fol. 3.
[59] B.P., I, 165.
[60] S.P. 16, vol. 310, no. 103. The Treaty of Nonsuch, in fact, did not specify that the English should follow Reformed worship. Leicester's decisions as governor, however, did approve such policies; see above, chapter 2.

to theological novelties, and he named innovations of liturgy, some designing their own pattern of worship "after thyr owne fancyes betwixt the English and the Dutch," and the synod's ordaining of ministers in the Netherlands. According to Carleton, "heertofore it hath bin left at liberty to such as would use eyther the English or the Dutch liturgy in any place;" but the synod had henceforth turned to a direction "prejudiciall to our English church government." Carleton, who had earlier been a strong supporter of the synod, ordered the synod to cease all meetings. He dispatched a letter to William Laud, at that time Bishop of Bath and Wells, warning of the situation.[61]

When the synod attempted to hold its annual meeting in June of 1628, Carleton delivered to the assembled preachers six "Articles" from King Charles, which in substance ordered them to allow no innovations or meddling in liturgy, ordination, ceremonies, doctrines, and printing. The harassed ministers concocted a long answer, claiming to have been misunderstood and disclaiming novelties. However, they defended their right to perform ordinations.[62] Both Carleton and the English Synod appealed to the States General for clarification, Carleton to restrict its activities, the synod for confirmation of its privileges. The synod got the better of it. The States General in a new resolution of 1628 confirmed and strengthened the resolution of 1621 and resolved "that the English Synod shall regulate itself according to the order of the land," that is, according to Dutch Reformed practice.[63] The Puritans were jubilant at the renewed support but thought it prudent to omit the meeting in 1629. After John Forbes drew up a petition pleading that the synod was "more moderate and temperate," King Charles gave them leave to resume meetings.[64] The synod met again in 1631.

The political and propaganda activities of the English Synod came to the fore in the 1630s in response to Laud's "design" in the Netherlands. Laud in 1633 urged the Privy Council to abolish the synod:

> That the *English* Ministers in *Holland*, being his Majesties born Subjects, be not suffered to hold any *Classical* meetings, but howsoever not to assume the power of *Ordination*; from which if they should not be restrained, there would be a perpetual Seminary for building up men in Schisme and Faction, to the disturbance of this Kingdom.[65]

---

[61] S.P. 16, vol. 90, no. 84 (Jan. 14, 1628); see William Laud, *Works* (Oxford, 1847-60), VII, 12-14.
[62] B.P., I, 35-38; Stearns, *Congregationalism*, pp. 23-26.
[63] Res. States General, no. 3187, fol. 360v.
[64] S.P. 16, vol. 152, no. 74.
[65] Heylyn, *Cyprianus Anglicus*, p. 233; Trevor-Roper, *Laud*, pp. 248-49.

While directing affairs from England, Laud gave the day-to-day operations into the hands of Ambassador Sir William Boswell, who had assumed the office in 1632. In face of such thunderings, the synod preachers became bolder in their anti-Anglican resistance, which seemed to them a life and death struggle. "This now dying classis will at this time use all their force," warned Goffe.[66] Forbes, having resumed the office of president, and Bachelor, scribe, spearheaded the synod program, but they were well reinforced by some new anti-Laudian preachers recently come over, Hugh Peter, Samuel Balmford, Thomas Hooker, and John Davenport. Intimidation from the English government at the same time frightened away some of the faint-hearted members. Dr. William Ames, professor of theology at Franeker University, although not an official synod member, functioned as chief Puritan intellectual in the Netherlands. He collaborated with the synod Puritans, and briefly, after moving to his Rotterdam pastorate in 1633, became more active. Boswell contemptuously labelled the synod members (the "Classisarians") as mischievous troublemakers illegally absent from England, "all of them Exiled and some of them highly criminous persons, and bitterly disaffected against our state and church." Could anything be more ludicrous than to give a synod of such men the supervision of religion? "As if in England wee should erect a Colledge of Canters to prevent Rogues."[67]

Forbes, Peter, and Bachelor proved to be clever politicians and masters of agitation and propaganda. The legal status of the English Synod was seemingly secure because of the States General resolutions of 1621 and 1628, but the Puritans took nothing for granted in the political realm. Forbes, a frequent visitor in the political halls of The Hague, kept friendly links with key politicians of the Council of State and States General. The resolution of 1628 was a great triumph for the synod, which had lobbied heavily for it, by requiring the English to use Reformed practice and not permitting the Anglican. When Boswell ordered chaplains Bachelor and Sclaer back to England for discipline, Forbes interposed the authority of the States General to shield the chaplains from the English government. Because the chaplains received a Dutch subsidy, Bachelor waved aside the king's commandment by saying, "If the States will commaund him to go, he will obaie them."[68]

The Council of State took up the case of Sclaer and Bachelor and posed the issues: (1) "Whether it were fitting to suffer the ministres and preachers, who were stipendiated by the States, and so in their service to depend upon a forein powre? (2) Whether it were fitting to leave the Cor-

---

[66] B.P., I, 100.
[67] S.P. 16, vol. 310, no. 103.
[68] S.P. 84, vol. 146, fol. 144.

onells powre to send the Ministres of their Regiments out of the States dominions, in case of delinquency and offence?" The Council thought it not wise to allow such things.[69] Samuel Balmford similarly shook off Laud's orders for conformity because of being "subiect to the Government of that place, having pay from the States."[70] Boswell could never deliver Bachelor and Sclaer across to London, thanks to the synod's connections with the politicians, much frustrating the ambassador. "And most likely in the end they will wholly decline the delivery of his person: because they hold that a prejudice to their independence, and (as I understand, have heertofore refused the French King upon the like point.)"[71] Forbes, Bachelor, and Peter, the most active synodians, seldom rested in their political endeavors—now at The Hague, now at Amsterdam, now at Leiden University. It was such that whenever they appeared in town, Boswell braced himself for "some crosse caper."[72]

Most Dutch churchmen and politicians had a deep-seated aversion to English Episcopal religion. "Our ceremenies which are to be brought in here are counted by the Majistracts and people nothinge but popery."[73] The synod Puritans skillfully played on these prejudices to reinforce their own position. They filled the air with rumors about the ill intentions of the Church of England, guaranteed to keep the States General aroused. Puritans made great impact with reports that Anglican religion was Papism in disguise and that Laud conspired to obtrude the Prayer Book on the Netherlands, not only upon the hapless English preachers, but upon the entire Dutch church. Laud, the story ran, schemed to "contrive an Episcopall jurisdiction, not only over the English, but also over the Reformed Belgic churches themselves in these parts." Who was responsible for these scare stories? "For which," complained Boswell, "wee may thank our English Refractories."[74] At Amsterdam, the Puritans "bester themselves ... to belye our Bishops whom they make to project aery bishopriks in these lands, and some intended power over the Dutch themselves."[75] Sinister stories about Prayer Books and lordly prelates were always effective in exciting the Dutch. "Mr. Peter he playes mightely upon the Latine service that would be brought in, and warnes men to tak heed on't, and of those high priests that trewly will keep men in ignorance."[76]

---

[69] S.P. 84, vol. 146, fol. 200.
[70] Liassen Engelandt, no. 5892, fol. 198 (A.R.A.).
[71] S.P. 84, vol. 146, fol. 196.
[72] B.P., I, 111v.
[73] S.P. 16, vol. 258, no. 62.
[74] S.P. 84, vol. 146, fol. 204; vol. 148, fol. 2.
[75] B.P., I, 169.
[76] B.P., I, 116.

Laud persisted in his anti-Puritan campaign whereas previous archbishops had eventually allowed the Dutch Puritans to go their own way. Consequently, the synod leaders in 1633 petitioned the States General for additional protection. The atmosphere had been well prepared by horror stories about Laudian innovations. In April of 1633, with Forbes at The Hague urging "the busines," the States General obliged with a strong resolution forbidding any innovation or Prayer Books in English religion: "The situation of the English and Scottish preachers ministering in the cities of these provinces in any churches shall by provision be left in the same state as at present without permitting any novelties or unaccustomed things."[77] Outmaneuvered again, Boswell complained to the Council of State for siding with the synod preachers, "and into whose hands by their Act for a Classis, they had committed the custodie of our English Ministers." Further, demanded Boswell: Who will watch these so-called custodians, *Nam quis demum custodiet ipsos custodes*? The Councillors of State in some surprise retorted by asking Boswell "whether I would have no course held for government of them" if not a synod? Boswell's answer: "I presumed they would leave them to his Majesties owne wisdom, and piety."[78]

In combatting the synod Puritans, Boswell built up a tiny corps of agents who, for one reason or another, were willing to serve Laudian religion. Boswell's most zealous agent was Stephen Goffe (B.A. Merton College, M.A. St. Albans Hall, Oxford), chaplain to Sir Horace Vere, 1632-34. He volunteered to introduce the Prayer Book into his regiment and began reading in the summer of 1632; gradually he inserted the ceremonies, with the exception of omitting the prayers for the king "because I durst not read them," being "very offensive to some."[79] Goffe was the first English preacher to openly defy the synod by proclaiming sympathy for Laudianism. Others in Boswell's service were Edward Misselden, the Merchant Adventurers' deputy at Delft, also a few of the newer preachers, including George Beaumont, who succeeded Forbes at Delft, and various of the chaplains of the Queen of Bohemia (Griffin Higgs, Sampson Johnson). Even venerable John Paget, Puritan exile of 1604, because of his hatred of Forbes and the synod gave Boswell good help.[80] Boswell also put pressure on the English officers to dismiss all nonconforming chaplains, in line with Laud's Privy Council order of 1633. Boswell hoped to undermine the synod by causing unemployment among the synod preachers. The States General resolutions of 1621,

---

[77] Res. States General, no. 3192, fol. 365v; B.P., I, 123.
[78] S.P. 84, vol. 146, fol. 203.
[79] B.P., I, 80, 157-59; S.P. 16, vol. 232, no. 23, vol. 236, no. 30.
[80] S.P. 16, vol. 286, no. 94.

1628, and 1633 gave protection to the established town churches, but the military chaplaincies and the Merchant Adventurers church were vulnerable. Laud and Boswell arranged to have several new men more to their liking (in the style of Goffe) come into the chaplaincies. Each of the colonels received express orders from the king to take action "in pressing at their chaplains to like conformitie."[81]

The last great work of the synod was a campaign to withstand the attempted incursions of the Prayer Book. Whenever a preacher went over to the Laudian side, he could count on bombardment from all around. Goffe found it no easy matter to speak up for the Church of England in Holland. Some of the soldiers refused to attend; Colonel Hollis "forsooke the church," and Colonel Morgan conspicuously remained absent until after the prayers were done. Samuel Bachelor, synod scribe, rebuked Goffe in name of the English Synod and ordered him to desist; when this failed, he and Sclaer instigated the States General to send investigatory agents, "as if some new and superstitious thing had been introduced." The synod Puritans so strenuously condemned Goffe as "an Innovator and dangerous troubler of the church" that the States in 1633 cut off his stipend.[82] After hearing about Goffe, the president of the Council of State (Francois van Aerssen) declared that he "ought to be looked unto," being "desirous to bring in those things which might trouble their church."[83] At Leiden Hugh Goodyear refused to admit the odious Mr. Goffe to the Lord's Table. It was all very embarrassing, "the Dutch ministers and schollars I light in company with when they heare my name they startle at me." Sir Horace finally secured a resumption of Goffe's stipend but only on promise of future conformity to the Dutch Reformed Church. Goffe paraded himself as a martyr for the Anglican faith.[84]

Others who followed Goffe's Anglican practices received a similar harsh treatment from the synod. Sclaer and Grim, the Germans, got letters and scolding for attempting a few readings from the Prayer Book. When Captain Clerk from Bergen-op-Zoom arranged to have one of his soldiers read prayers from the Prayer Book, Stephen Paine, preacher of the place, incited the Dutch Reformed preachers to put a stop to it.[85] Deputy Edward Misselden of Delft tried to uphold Anglican religion against the wishes of John Forbes, preacher of the church; in the ensuing uproar Misselden was dismissed by the Merchant Adventurers for

---

[81] S.P. 16, vol. 233, no. 4.
[82] B.P., I, 133; S.P. 16, vol. 232, no. 23.
[83] B.P., I, 100.
[84] B.P., I, 156; S.P. 16, vol. 286, no. 94; vol. 232, no. 23.
[85] S.P. 84, vol. 147, fol. 104; B.P., I, 141-42.

meddling. The merchants sided with Forbes, who denounced Misselden as "an Enemy to God and man."[86] It was a terrible thing for a preacher to be caught between the two sides.

Increasingly in the 1630s, the synod became a close fellowship of men of like theological mind, more than a formal ecclesiastical organization. The theological development of the synod membership was away from the old Presbyterian-style Puritanism toward a more radical, free style. The core synod members (Forbes, Bachelor, Peter, Hooker, Davenport, and their close friend Ames of Franeker) all were distinguished by a Congregationalist style of Puritanism. Their Reformed religion, in deviating from the Church of England, did not conform to Dutch Reformed practice on several points. They rarely in worship used the Dutch liturgy, even in English translation which was available to them, but instead experimented with their own simple worship. Some used no set forms at all (Forbes and Hooker), or else on their own initiative chose a mixture of agreeable parts from the English liturgy, the 1586 Middelburg worship book, and their own words (Bachelor, Balmford, Peter), all "wilbe absolute in their own parishes," administering the sacrament, baptism, and marriage, not according to the forme of both churches, but "as the speritt moves them."[87]

The attitude toward the authority of synods was the most revealing clue of the transformation of the synod into a headquarters of early Congregationalist religion. Although united by a loose synod organization, the synod functioned more as an offensive weapon against the bishops than as any authoritative organization over preachers and congregations. The synod never met often, only once in every year or two. Under these circumstances, the amount of business that could be transacted was slight, but in time this defect turned itself into a positive ideological good. A weak synod reinforced the theories of congregational autonomy being elaborated by Ames, Peter, Hooker, and Davenport. Paget had warned at the foundation of the synod of a "Brownistic" and Jacobite faction; and his early shrewd observation was well born out in the 1630s.[88] After the unhappy experience of seeing Davenport and Hooker vetoed by the Amsterdam classis the synod Puritans had practical reasons for questioning the Dutch Presbyterian system as much as the Episcopal one back home. After such examples, said Paget, "the forbesian and preciser puritans abhor" Presbyterianism as much as Episcopal religion.[89]

---

[86] B.P., I, 68; see chapter 9.
[87] S.P. 84, vol. 146, fol. 144; S.P. 16, vol. 310, no. 103.
[88] S.P. 16, vol. 286, no. 94.
[89] S.P. 16, vol. 252, no. 55.

The English Synod for more than a decade had been remarkably successful in maintaining itself in the face of persistent English opposition. In the military chaplaincies and the Merchant Adventurers, Boswell and Laud made headway by causing the dismissal of the most recalcitrant Puritans. Forbes was removed as Merchant Adventurer minister in early 1634 and Bachelor, although spared the ordeal of going before the High Commision, was dismissed by Sir Charles Morgan as regimental chaplain. All the English colonels received direct orders from King Charles to have conformable chaplains.[90] These were partial victories for Laud's design.

Several leading members of the Puritan network were lost to the synod in 1633-35 through death or emigration. Peter, Hooker, Davenport went for America. Forbes and Ames died. Bachelor applied to go to South America with the West India Company. Boswell gloated: "I perceive Mr. Forbes his removall and Doctor Ames his death hath much dismayed that party, being wont to magnifie the wisdom, and gravity of the one, and learning and industry of the other, Qualities very rarely to be found among our Classarians, and their Brethren who servive here."[91] The English Synod faded away by the end of 1633 or early 1634. It never met after 1631; and although the core membership continued to function as a Puritan brotherhood, the loss of many key members over the course of a few years meant the end of a specific organization labelled as the English Synod or Classis. Forbes, the last president, died in 1634 and was not replaced.

Omitting meetings after 1631 was a conscious policy by the synod leadership to concentrate on legal and propaganda activities rather than risk the infiltration or take over of the synod by Laud's agents in a formal meeting. King Charles was demanding "that he might have a commissioner of his own to Represent himself in those Synods." Consequently, the English preachers "did of their own accord drop these synodicall meetings and refused all of them to attend upon them."[92] Laud took great delight in his success over the synod. However, the Puritan network had other resources. After the death of the synod, Puritans were still entrenched in many pulpits in the towns and the printing shops were busy.

Puritan Printing Enterprises

Puritan writers put vast confidence in the power of the printed word. They saw the potential for influencing literate public opinion through a

---

[90] S.P. 84, vol. 146, fol. 100.
[91] S.P. 84, vol. 147, fol. 174v.
[92] Voetius reported this to John Quick, "Icones," I, i, 269.

wide dissemination of books, which, like Puritan preaching, relied on a popular style geared to the widest possible audience. Francis Johnson proclaimed the Puritan commitment to book evangelism: "I have published (gentle Reader) for thy good, and for the truthes sake which we witnes to the world."[93] The Amsterdam Separatists were the early masters of propagandistic journalism—homely illustrations, interesting, even titilating anecdotes—but Puritan preachers of all varieties took to the printing press with desperate enthusiasm. In England printing was under control of government censorship. With the bishops in control of the presses, the extreme Puritans were at a great disadvantage in the battle of ideas. To the Netherlands they went. Many Puritan writers would have been absolutely silenced except for recourse to the foreign printers. "If there be but a Printing-house in any of the Cities in the Provinces of Holland, I will cause this letter to be printed," proclaimed John Lilburne. The Separatist theologians (Francis Johnson, Henry Ainsworth, John Smyth, Robert Browne, John Robinson, John Canne) were totally dependent on overseas printers; and numerous controversial non-Separatist Puritans, of the stature of Thomas Cartwright, Walter Travers, Dudley Fenner, Henry Jacob, William Ames, Robert Parker, and William Bradshaw were nearly as dependent on Dutch and other foreign printers.[94] Without the overseas print shops, some of the most creative voices of English religion would have been stifled.

Dutch printers, highly skilled in their craft, welcomed the printing trade of all Europe. Whatever could not be printed elsewhere was sent to the Dutch. Although the Netherlands printing shops are significant for the topic of Puritanism, other groups, such as Roman Catholics, French Jansenists, Jews, and Polish Socinians, relied equally on the Dutch "Citty of Refuge." It has been calculated that more books were printed in the seventeenth-century Netherlands than all other countries combined.[95] Thousands of copies of Puritan books were printed in the Netherlands, either at established Dutch printers or in special Puritan shops, and then smuggled back to England. The Dutch and Puritan printers also did a

---

[93] Francis Johnson, *Certayne Reasons and Arguments* (n.p., 1608), To the Reader.

[94] Lilburne, *A Coppy of a Letter* (n.p., 1640), pp. 7-8. For a beginning to the topic of 16th-17th-century British books printed abroad, see C. E. Sayle, *Early English Printed Books in the University Library Cambridge* (Cambridge: Cambridge Univ. Press, 1900-07); Pollard and Redgrave, *Short-Title Catalogue*, under individual authors and index of printers; Leona Rostenberg, *The Minority Press & the English Crown* (Nieuwkoop: B. de Graaf, 1971), chapter 15, "A Liberty of Printing"; Stephen Foster, *Notes from the Caroline Underground* (Hamden: Archon Books, 1978).

[95] Wytze Hellinga, *Copy and Print in the Netherlands* (Amsterdam: North Holland Publishing Company, 1962), introduction by H. de la Fontaine Verwey, p. 29; Quick, "Icones," I, i, 13-14, 84-86.

thriving business in pirated editions of the English Bible, which they printed excellently and cheaply for import into England. The one sort of printing threatened the well-being of the English church-state establishment; the other sort underminded the prosperity of the English printing monopoly. Archbishop Laud was outraged at the Bible traffic, first because many of the Bibles were Genevan editions, "the worst, and many of the notes very partial, untrue, seditious, and savouring too much of dangerous and traitorous conceits," second, on pragmatic grounds. Regardless of which edition, the smuggled Dutch Bibles were so good, they threatened to undercut the entire monopolistic English Bible trade. "For the books which came thence, were better print, better bound, better paper, and for all the charge of bringing sold better cheap. And would any man buy a worse Bible dearer, that might have a better more cheap?" In Laud's overall anti-Puritan design, destroying the Netherlands trade in Bibles and nonconformist books was high priority. So, said Laud, "to preserve printing here at home, as well as the notes, was the cause of stricter looking to those Bibles."[96]

Through the years, many printers served the Puritan cause. The first Dutch printer of Puritan books was Richard Schilders of Middelburg (active 1579-1634). At Dort the Separatists published several volumes by "one Hanse" (identified likely as Hans Stell); some English books were also printed by Isaac Canin and George Waters (Joris Watersz), an Englishman, deacon of the English Reformed Church of Dort. Waters printed several important Puritan treatises, including William Bradshaw, *The Unreasonablenesse of the Separation* (1614) and William Ames, *Manuduction for Mr. Robinson* (1614). Thomas Scott, the exile from Norwich, author of *Vox Populi* (1620) printed several books at Gorinchem and Utrecht.[97] At Leiden and Amsterdam, the Separatists set up presses as a close adjunct of the churches. The Brewster-Brewer press of Leiden (the Pilgrim Press) for two years produced much reading matter for the Puritan cause until Ambassador Carleton closed it down in 1619. Nevertheless, much of the Leiden type and supplies were transported to Amsterdam to the Separatist's press, and Harris and Jones have surmised that the press itself may have been carried to Plymouth plantation with

---

[96] Laud, *Works*, IV, 262-63, 349-50; Harry Carter, "Archbishop Laud and Scandalous Books from Holland," *Studia Bibliographica in Honorem Herman de la Fontaine Verwey*, ed. S. van der Woude (Amsterdam: Hertzberger, 1967), p. 46.

[97] J. G. C. A. Briels, *Zuidnederlandse boekdrukkers en boekverkopers in de Republiek der Verenigde Nederlanden omstreeks 1570-1630* (Nieuwkoop: B. de Graaf, 1974), pp. 212-19, 543-44; *The Writings of Henry Barrow, 1590-1591*, ed. Leland H. Carlson (London: George Allen and Unwin, 1966), p. 75; Sayle, *Early English Printed Books*, III, s.v. Utrecht and Gorinchem. See above, chapter 2 for Schilders and Hanse.

Brewster (the "great iron screw").[98] Temporarily, Leiden lacked a Puritan printer.

During the 1630s the Puritan writers kept the printing presses swiftly moving. Amsterdam was the chief center for Dutch printing and likewise the most active place of Puritan printing. There "were ever some pestilent rayling bookes printed and writed against the Church of England and the Bishops."[99] The Separatists for many years had kept a printing concern managed by printer Giles Thorp (1604 to 1622). Thorp was an officer of the Ancient Church. In 1619 Matthew Slade told Sir Dudley Carleton, who was in pursuit of William Brewster of Leiden, that there was little likelihood of a new English printer settling at Amsterdam, "there being another English printer named William Thorp, also a Brownist setled here." Richard Plater succeeded Thorp as manager of the press. Sabine Staresmore, although not a full time printer, was also active in the Separatist printing shop in the 1620s-1630s. "He was an English Printer." Francis Hill, another printer, worked in Amsterdam, perhaps at the Thorp-Plater press or elsewhere in the city. In 1624 Hill acted as a paid undercover agent for Carleton about events in the Amsterdam-Leiden printing underworld. He was able to pass on bits of information about the publishing plans of Alexander Leighton, David Calderwood, and William Ames.[100] John Canne, preacher of the Ancient Church from 1630 onward, turned printer after coming to Amsterdam. He kept the press in his house. Several of his books of the late 1630s carried the motto "Richt-Right" or "Right-Right"; thus his press has been nicknamed the "Richt-Right Press."[101]

Many English authors, in need of a printer but eschewing close dealings with the Separatists, dealt with Dutch printers for pay. Jan Fredericksz Stam and Johannes Jansson had reputations for collaborating with Puritan writers. Stam in the 1630s, in addition to printing thousands of English Bibles, in quarto, folio, and duodecimo, turned

---

[98] A. F. Johnson, "The Exiled English Church at Amsterdam and its Press," *The Library*, 5th ser., 5 (1951), p. 230; Rendel Harris and Stephen K. Jones, *The Pilgrim Press* (Cambridge: W. Heffer and Sons), p. 4; see above, chapter 5.

[99] Thomas Raymond, *Autobiography*, ed. G. Davies, Camden Society, 3rd ser., no. 28 (1917), 32-33.

[100] S.P. 84, vol. 92, fol. 41; vol. 117, fol. 157; vol. 118, fols. 24, 70; B.P., I, 139; Johnson, "Exiled English Church," pp. 220, 230-31. R. B. McKerrow, *A Dictionary of Printers and Booksellers in England, Scotland and Ireland 1557-1640* (London, 1910), p. 137. On Staresmore, see William Best, *The Chvrches Plea* (Amsterdam, 1635), p. 1 and Paget, *An Answer*, preface; Foster, *Notes from the Caroline Underground*, pp. 21-23. See also chapter 3 on the Separatist printers of Amsterdam.

[101] S.P. 84, vol. 154, fol. 151; vol. 153, fol. 293; Sayle, *Early English Printed Books*, III, s.v. Amsterdam; John F. Wilson, "Another Look at John Canne," *Church History*, 33 (Mar. 1964), 40-42.

out books for John Paget, Alexander Leighton, Henry Burton, William Prynne, and John Bastwick. Jansson was printing Bayly's *Practise of Piety* "by tenn thousand at time."[102] Many of the Amsterdam printers and booksellers were in the big business of English Bibles. Joseph Athias boasted of himself having printed more than a million, enough for every plow boy and servant girl; Jan Jacobsz Schepper, Steven Swart, Joost Broerss, Joacham Nosche.[103]

The Puritan printing enterprise included more than merely a printer with a printing press. The second essential was the financial patron who paid the cost of the particular book in press or, better still, provided long-term backing. Thomas Brewer at Leiden took this responsibility for the Pilgrim Press; and although the Amsterdam press did not have so devoted a wealthy financial backer, the Ancient Church membership and a host of individual merchants in England or the Low Countries kept the work moving.[104] If no support could be found, the author himself paid at a "painfull" cost.[105] The third essential of Puritan printing was transporting the books into England and Scotland, where they would do the most good. Hugh Peter in 1633 reported from Holland about the printing of Ames's *Fresh Suit*, "but how the bookes will come into mens hands is a question."[106] The transportation in Puritan books involved a great part of the merchants and ship captains who went back and forth between Britain and the Netherlands. It was common practice to tuck a few forbidden books or pirated Bibles into the ship cargo and smuggle them across. Some merchants shipped books by the thousands. Matthew Symmons, a printer at Leiden, told the police that merchants of all persuasions were involved in the book traffic, Separatists and also orthodox pillars of the community. They financed, printed, transported, and peddled Bibles and books. "Manie merchantes bye great quantities of them there and packe them up in towe and other goodes and so bring them over." Of the

---

[102] S.P. 16, vol. 387, no. 79; A. F. Johnson, "J. F. Stam, Amsterdam, and English Bibles," *The Library*, 5th ser., 9 (1954), 185-86.

[103] T. H. Darlow and H. F. Moule, eds., *Historical Catalogue of the Printed Editions of Holy Scripture in the Library of the British and Foreign Bible Society* (London: The Bible House, 1903-11); I. H. van Eeghen, *De Amsterdamse boekhandel 1680-1725* (Amsterdam, 1960-67), IV, 101-02, 135-38; I. H. van Eeghen, "De befaamde drukkerij op de Herengracht over Plantage (1685-1755)," *Amstelodamum* Jaarboek, 58 (1966), 83.

[104] For a list of merchants involved in book printing, 1637-38, see S.P. 16, vol. 387, no. 79.

[105] Alexander Leighton received only £50 help from friends for his *Appeal to the Parliament* (1629), printed by both the Thorp-Plater and the Stam printeries, which was but a "poore-pittance of that which it cost me"; Leighton, *An Epitome or Briefe Discoverie* (London, 1646), p. 2. John Davenport had his *Apologeticall Reply* (1636) printed by Isaac van Waesberge of Rotterdam and paid "the whole charge of all himself," which came to 450 guilders, half the yearly salary of an English minister of Rotterdam; B.P., I, 230.

[106] S.P. 16, vol. 241, no. 52.

ship masters, said Symmons, "they are all together that I know not who to name ... there is not one that I know but bring over anie prohibbeted goodes."[107]

Many strategems were invented to smuggle the books into England. Single copies were peddled in the Dutch ports to individual travelers bound for England. Some lots of books came with false title pages to ease their way past careless customs agents. Other shipments slipped over disguised as "white paper" for the stationer "and so never looked into, or lett passe by negligence, or falshood of the searchers." Even the zealous Anglican Edward Misselden of Delft found himself an unwitting tool of the Puritan smugglers, who secreted a supply of the latest "blew book" in a cloth ship bound for England among Misselden's goods, but without his or the master's knowledge. The captains with books to bring in bragged of having strategies sufficient "to cozen the devell."[108]

The motivation of the merchants for investing and smuggling books was more than monetary gain. Some profits, no doubt, were made in book trading, especially in the Bibles, but such was not the mainspring of the action. For the printers in exile, the authors, and many of the financial supporters, the motivation was high religion. As Harris and Jones write in their history of the Pilgrim Press, "the establishment of the Leyden Printing-house was of the nature of a new religion; at all events it was a religious act at the centre of a new religion." Even the financial capitalist "must be or become something of a believer."[109]

The network of printers of the 1630s extended into many cities outside of Amsterdam. At Leiden Willem Christiaensz van der Boxe, a Dutch printer, was busy with nonconformist books. Somewhere, Christiaensz had become ideologically committed to the cause of Puritan printing, so much so that some books by William Prynne he himself initiated and financed. During 1637 and 1638 he printed Prynne's *Newes from Ipswich*, in both English and Dutch (*Hier, Wat nieuws uyt Ipswich in Enghelandt*), another edition of *An Abridgement* of 1605 by the Lincoln ministers, John Bastwick's *Answer to Sir John Banks*, a part of George Gillespie's *A Dispute against the English-Popish Ceremonies Obtruded upon the Church of Scotland* (the latter printed jointly with Canne of Amsterdam), and Thomas Hooker's *The Souls Preparation for Christ*. Hooker's book, according to the title page, was "printed for the use and benefit of the English Churches in the Netherlands" (1638). "The saide William printeth much english."[110]

---

[107] S.P. 16, vol. 246, no. 56; vol. 387, no. 79.

[108] B.P., I, 135; S.P. 16, vol. 246, no. 56; vol. 387, no. 79; S.P. 84, vol. 148, fols. 43-44.

[109] Harris and Jones, *Pilgrim Press*, p. 5.

[110] S.P. 84, vol. 153, fol. 271; S.P. 16, vol. 387, no. 79; Briels, *Boekdrukkers*, pp. 184-85; Carter, "Laud," p. 48; A. F. Johnson, "Willem Christiaans, Leyden, and His English Books," *The Library*, 5th ser., 10 (1955), 121-23.

The translating and printing of Prynne's *Nieuws uyt Ipswich* was Christiaensz's own project, with notes out "of his owne head." This was an ideological labor, and he promised to also put the book into French. Asked "the reason why," Christiaensz exclaimed, "He would make the Bishops crueltie knowne to all nationes."[111] In 1639 Christiaensz printed a Dutch translation and abridgment of Prynne's *Histrio-Mastix* (translated by I. H.) with a new preface telling of the latest prelatical cruelties against Prynne. Boswell thought Christiaensz "a mean fellow."[112]

Where had Christiaensz imbibed the Puritan zeal? He is not known to have been a member of either Robinson's or Hugh Goodyear's church. However, he had earlier lived at Middelburg, and his first wife was English, Anna Perkins.[113] Both at Middelburg and Leiden he had ample opportunities to fraternize with Puritan exiles. Several refugee English printers assisted Christiaensz, including Benjamin Allen, "lately fled from England and lodging at Christian's house," another person called "Wheelers," and Matthew Symmons, "lately come out of England" (November of 1637). A forced interrogation of Symmons by the Leiden magistrates, at Boswell's insistence, produced much of the information known about the workings of the Puritan printers in 1637-38.[114]

Leiden also had means for transporting books into England. One of the book smugglers was Robert Cockyn, alias Leonard Verse, "a Brownist inhabitant of Leyden, and frequenting England under pretence of a privat foot-post ... employed for conveighance of letters, and pamphlets." He knew all the ports and craftily "takes his passage at the port where he thinks to find least security for his person and papers he carieth."[115] Leiden attracted many authors in the 1630s desperate to find a printer. One of them, using the pseudonym of Mr. Daniel, went about town violently threatening the assassination of Laud and Wren; saying

---

[111] S.P. 16, vol. 387, no. 79; Ethyn W. Kirby, *William Prynne* (New York: Russell & Russell, 1972), pp. 35-36. The printed copy does not have Christiaensz's name: *Hier, wat nieuws, In het Nederduytsch overgheset, uyt den vrienden druck van het Engelsche exemplaer, dat ghenaemt wordt, Nieuws van Ipswich, In Engelandt.* Ghedruckt in't jaer 1637.

[112] S.P. 84, vol. 154, fol. 113; *Histrio-Mastix ofte schouw-spels treur-spel, dienende tot een klaer bewijs van de onwetlijckheden der hedendaechsche comedien* (Leiden: Ghedruckt bij Willem Christiaens, wonende op't Rapenburgh bij de Toelen-Brugghe, 1639), voor-reden by I. H.

[113] Briels, *Boekdrukkers*, p. 184.

[114] S.P. 84, vol. 153, fols. 183-90. Symmons statement, "The Informacion of M.S.," is in S.P. 16, vol. 387, no. 79. On Allen, see Henry R. Plomer, *A Dictionary of the Booksellers and Printers Who Were at Work in England, Scotland, and Ireland from 1641 to 1667* (London, 1907), pp. 1-2; on Simmons, Plomer, p. 164.

[115] S.P. 84, vol. 153, fol. 301.

"that he should doe God good service that should rid the world of them."[116]

Delft had an English printer of Puritan books in James Moxon. He printed Henry Hexham's *True and Brief Relation of the Famous Seige of Breda* (1637), an uncontroversial book, and also some of "Dr. Bastwicke thinges" (the four parts of his *Leteny* of 1637). Delft, whose English church was under the fiery preaching of Patrick Forbes, functioned in 1637 as a headquarters for large-scale printing and transporting of Puritan books. A "Mr. John" (perhaps John Foot), merchant, "hath a pasel of boockes of several sortes lying in Delfe which are of all sorts of those which are against the preletes—the like can scarce be seene together." Mr. John paid for Moxon's printing of the *Leteny* and shipped 1000 copies, plus many other forbidden books, to England through a ship to Newcastle.[117] John Lilburne, an apprentice in Holland, began his Puritan career by having books printed at Delft in 1637, for which he paid a savage price at the hands of the Star Chamber. Having returned to England, he was arrested on charges of masterminding the libelous traffic in Bastwick's *Leteny*. In 1637 the Star Chamber punished Bastwick, Burton and Prynne by chopping off their ears for authoring objectional books, including the *Leteny*, which Lilburne was now accused of transporting. Lilburne and John Wharton, it was charged, had caused ten to twelve thousand books to be printed at Rotterdam and other places and then stored them in a chamber at the house of John Foot of Delft. All of this Lilburne denied, but nevertheless the Star Chamber in April 1638 found him guilty and had him whipped at cart's end and set in the pillory.[118] Another sign of Moxon's printing was a shipment of books from Delft containing Bastwick's *Leteny* intercepted at Yarmouth in November 1637. Also on board the ship were the fugitive ministers Jeremiah Burroughes and William Greenhill, slipping back into the country, "factors for venting such stuff."[119]

---

[116] S.P. 84, vol. 152, fols. 219, 228. Daniel, reported at Leiden in 1637, "had made a book, which he saith, would make his Lordship and others scratche their heads (these were his words) where it did not itche." He was a preacher or lecturer from Norwich diocese and thought to be associated with the publishing of *News from Ipswich*.

[117] S.P. 16, vol. 387, no. 79; Joseph Moxon, *Mechanick Exercises on the Whole Art of Printing 1683-4*, ed. Herbert Davis and Harry Carter, 2nd ed. (London: Oxford Univ. Press, 1962), p. xix.

[118] John Lilburne, *A Worke of the Beast* (Richt Right, 1638), pp. 10-11; Lilburne, *The Christian Mans Triall*, 2nd ed. (London, 1641), p. 2; M. A. Gibb, *John Lilburne, The Leveller* (London: Lindsay Drummond, 1947), pp. 38-49. Wendy Oxford, *Vincit qui patitur* (n.p., 1653), p. 2, says he had the same printer of Delft as Lilburne in the 1630s. On Puritan book printing, Lilburne in particular, see William Haller, *The Rise of Puritanism* (New York, Columbia Univ. Press, 1938), chapter 7, and pp. 432-40; Foster, *Notes from the Caroline Underground*, chapter 5.

[119] Tanner MS. 68, fols. 9v, 10.

In late 1637 or early 1638, Moxon moved his print shop to Rotterdam. The relationship between church and printer was as close as at Amsterdam. Moxon was permitted to set up his printing press in the church building, the Academie, used by the English Reformed Church. The church at that time was under the ministry of John Ward and William Bridge. Soon after arriving at Rotterdam, Moxon undertook to print 4000 Bibles and 2000 Psalms for Edmund White, Christoffel Huling, and Catarijn Dorrel, who in effect became his patrons and partners. "These men pay every Saterday night ... and thus marchantes are turned printers." Presumably, the three were members of the church. In 1643 Moxon returned to London.[120] Another Rotterdam printer and bookseller was Henry Tuthill. He did a printing of the *Book of Psalms in English Meter* in 1638.[121]

The heavy punishment of authors before the Star Chamber in 1637-38 corresponded with Laud's systematic anti-printing campaign in the Netherlands. The English government was determined to uncover the Puritan book conspiracy: "Who Printed all these Bookes?" "Who was at the charges of Printing of them?" "Who transported them?"[122] When Sir William Boswell came as ambassador in 1632, he had orders to move equally severely against the printers and the English Synod. His official instructions told him, "specially not to suffer our sectarie fugitives to plant themselves ther: and by scandalous pamphlets sent from thence to defame our church government."[123] Boswell ran to and fro in search of the latest "blew coat" such as Ames's *Fresh Suit* of 1633 and the anonymous *Crown of a Christian Martyr* of 1634. In 1637 Laud determined that stiffer policies must be administered, and so began new press decrees in the Star Chamber and fresh orders to Boswell. The ambassador in 1637 warned of a troublesome upsurge of Dutch radicalism, "flyes in swarmes out of England with clamours about our church affairs." Laud agreed: "Swarmes of Waspes (for Bees they are not) are flowne over to those parts."[124]

Boswell mapped out a strategy aimed at silencing Christiaensz of Leiden and Canne of Amsterdam. The Netherlands had press control laws on the books (the States General *plakkaten* of July 7, 1615 and January 16, 1621), but, as Boswell well knew, the laws were seldom en-

---

[120] E. Wiersum, "Te pand gegeven drukkersgerief," *Tijdschrift voor Boek- en Bibliotheekwezen*, 8 (1910), 266-68; S.P. 16, vol. 387, no. 79; Moxon, *Mechanick Exercises*, pp. xx-xxi.
[121] S.P. 16, vol. 387, no. 79.
[122] The first two were questions demanded of John Lilburne; *Christian Mans Triall*, p. 2.
[123] S.P. 84, vol. 144, fol. 164v.
[124] B.P., I, 291; S.P. 84, vol. 154, fols. 17-19.

forced because they depended on local officials and "considering the fashion of locall officers heer to oppose or elude the command and directions of General States in like cases." The *Plakkaat* of 1621, to which Boswell appealed for enforcement, prohibited the printing, giving forth, selling, scattering, or carrying about of any scandalous and seditious books, libels, rhymes or the like, "especially concerning foreign kings and ecclesiastical governments," on pain of 300 guilders fine and worse punishments for a second offense.[125] By expert diplomacy and ceaseless pressure, Boswell pushed the magistrates of Leiden to apply the punishments against Christiaensz, a 300 guilders fine on April 13, 1638, for printing Prynne's *Nieuws uyt Ipswich*, part of Gillespie's *Dispute*, and Bastwick's *Answer to S:. John Banks* (a part of the *Leteny*). During this action, Matthew Symmons, one of Christiaensz's printers, was examined and required to give information.[126] Next to Canne of Amsterdam.

Boswell lectured the Amsterdam magistrates about Canne's evil activities, how "it was against the rules of humanity and good neighborhood to suffer such viperouse beasts to nestle themselves in their towne where they meant to spitt their venome against their Soveraigne and native country."[127] Canne was brought to court July 3, 1638, and, like Christiaensz, given a fine of 300 guilders for causing others to print his *Necessitie of Separation* (1634) and for himself printing the *Brief Relation* of Bastwick, Burton, and Prynne (1637), a news sheet called *Newes from Scotland*, and a part of Gillespie's *Dispute*. The burgomasters were urged by Boswell "to be very vigilant and severe for preventing the like in wayes hereafter." At these little triumphs, Boswell took great delight. "It is more then I can learne hath ever ben before, much more then any man thought I could have gotten done at all. For it is the first tyme that the Placcarts have been executed."[128]

As it turned out, the 300 guilder fine did not long silence the presses of Christiaensz or Canne. Christiaensz in 1639 published *Histrio-Mastix* and Canne actually increased his output (over fifteen books 1638-40). From Canne came forth such fiery blasts as *The Beast is Wounded* (1638, identified by Le Maire as authored by Canne himself); Canne's *The Stay against Straying* (1639); three books by Lilburne, *The Work of the Beast* (1638), *Come out of Her My People* (1639), *The Poore Mans Cry* (1639); and

---

[125] Res. States General, no. 3180, fol. 17; S.P. 84, vol. 154, fols. 113, 148-49.

[126] S.P. 84, vol. 153, fols. 183-90, 271; vol. 154, fols. 150-53; "The Informacion of M. S.," S.P. 16, vol. 387, no. 79.

[127] S.P. 84, vol. 154, fol. 113v.

[128] S.P. 84, vol. 153, fols. 188, 271, 293-96; vol. 154, fols. 114, 151-53. A copy of the "Right-Right" *Brief Relation* (1638) is bound with the B.M. copy of Laud, *Divine and Politicke Observations* (Right-Right, 1638).

many others.[129] Johannes Le Maire, the old Dutch preacher of Amsterdam, aided Laud and Boswell by keeping a close surveillance on Canne to prevent more of his printing. Whenever Le Maire caught scent of a new English or Scottish libel, he dispatched the praeter and demanded the full rigor of the press laws. This "hindered in the very birth" the coming forth of books and caused Canne to be dragged into court again in January 1639. Le Maire assured Laud of his resolution "to hinder these evil-doers in all places."[130] Through joint efforts from Le Maire and Boswell, some new proclamations were issued, a municipal one against libelous printing at Amsterdam April 16, 1639, and a resolution on libels by the States of Holland, May 19, 1639: "Resolved that every city in its own jurisdiction should take care to hinder and suppress books touching on English-Scottish matters."[131]

Never before had the English government had a collaborator like Le Maire of Amsterdam, so willing to be the watchdog over Puritan printing. Consequently, for a few years the Puritan printing enterprise was driven deeper underground. Some booksellers were frightened off from handling the Puritan wares and occasional authors had trouble finding printers. "None dares to medle with any seditious kinde of libels more," boasted Le Maire. Andrew Melville in 1639 had a Latin book for printing, commentaries on Ephesians with pungent remarks on the duties of subjects and obedience to king, but could find no printer.[132] However, in retrospect, it can be seen that the output of Puritan books at Amsterdam, although less visible, increased 1638-40. Some of the selling of books shifted to Rotterdam. There *The Beast is Wounded* and Bastwick's *Leteny* were openly hawked, such libels "they dare, I say, hang before their dores."[133] Boswell thought much could be accomplished by cutting off the financial backing of the printers. He tried to ruin Thomas Crafford, one of Canne's financial patrons. By various strategems, he forced Crafford out of the city in 1639; and when he next turned up in Rotterdam, Boswell followed hot after him with threatenings to the Rotterdam magistrates (de famosis libellis suppresses, Thomas Craffordo capiendo). Promised Boswell, "I have now allmost this moneth together, been in chase of this vermyn (Craffort) from place to place; with a Resolution never to give him over." Crafford was hardly given more than a bad

---

[129] S.P. 84, vol. 138, fol. 44; vol. 154, fol. 256; vol. 155, fol. 32; Wilson, "Canne," pp. 40-41.

[130] S.P. 84, vol. 154, fol. 256; vol. 155, fol. 93.

[131] S.P. 84, vol. 155, fols. 93, 102, 136; Willekeuren der stadt Amsterdam, L, fol. 82v. On book censorship in Holland, J. Diederich, A. C. J. de Vrankrijker, et al., *Vijf eeuwen boek in Nederland* (Haarlem: De Librije, 1940), pp. 70-71.

[132] S.P. 84, vol. 155, fols. 93, 260; Carter, "Laud," p. 51n.

[133] S.P. 84, vol. 155, fol. 93.

scare, it seems, and he continued at Amsterdam throughout the 1640s in the book business and other affairs.[134]

Puritan authors condemned Laud's campaign against printing in the Netherlands as one of his most hateful policies. During the revolution, when Laud came to trial, one of the charges against him was that he had suppressed book printing in Holland, the evidence being his correspondence with Le Maire. Laud had no trouble answering this accusation to his own satisfaction. As an unswerving upholder of the royal-hierarchical establishment, Laud could imagine no other prudent course than total press control encompassing Great Britain and the Low Countries. "Till this was done, every discontented spirit could print what he pleased at Amsterdam. ..." As for his own actions, "where's the Fault?" "I neither am nor can be sorry for it."[135]

The books of the 1630s printed in Holland (by Prynne, Burton, Bastwick, Lilburne, Leighton, Ames, Hooker, Forbes, and Canne) carried Puritan militancy to new extremes. The authors, hardened by savage experiences with the Star Chamber or High Commission, used their books to evoke nightmarish visions of blood, gore, and prelatical bestiality. Books "written in a desperate way to throw all loose," said Laud.[136] The master stroke of the Puritan journalists was their propaganda skill with cruelty and atrocity stories (making "the Bishops cruelties knowne to all nations"). Spine tingling stories: "the slitting of Bastwickes and Burtowns nose, the burning of Prinnes cheeke, the cutting of Lightouns eares, the scourging of Lilburne through the cittie, the close keeping of Lincolne, the murthering of others by famine, cold, vermine, stinke, and other miseries in the caves and vaults of the Bishops houses of inquisition."[137] Monstrously bestriding the world, the prelates knew only cruelty and unquestioning obedience. "All the Arguments that I see to this day," cried Leighton, "were *Prison, Fire, Brands, Knife* and *Whip*, which as all know are unanswerable *Arguments*." How long "the bloody prelates?" How long "their barbarous crueltie?" "How long, Lord?"[138]

The "beastly" imagery—"the Beast is wounded," the "worke of the Beast"—served the double propaganda purpose of dehumanizing the bishops and at the same time evoking the powerfull apocalyptic horrors of Revelation 13. Within a few pages in *The Beast is Wounded*, the bishops

---

[134] S.P. 84, vol. 155, fols. 137, 145; Van Eeghen, *Amsterdamse boekhandel*, IV, 101.
[135] Laud, *Works*, IV, 262-64.
[136] Ibid., VII, 544.
[137] Robert Baillie, *Ladensium* (n.p., 1640), preface.
[138] Leighton, *Epitome*, p. 69; Lilburne, *Worke of the Beast*, Publisher to the Reader; Samuel R. Gardiner, *History of England 1603-1642* (New York: AMS Press, 1965), VIII, 228.

are dragged forth as thieves and murderers, vermin, great foxes, spiritual wolves, prelatical dogs, crocodiles, asses, dunghill worms, locusts, venomous snakes, and Amalekites to be put to the sword. Bishop Wren was "the Norredge Beast" and the Archbishop "little great Laud" and "butcher Laud." Le Maire said, "I was mightly astonished to see the extreme bitterness, which they are full of."[139]

Dutch book printing was an essential arm of the English-Dutch Puritan movement, closely related to the work of the local churches, the exiles, and the English Synod. So close was the connection that the printing press was in the church building at Rotterdam and in the pastor's house at Amsterdam. "But what can a poore pilgrim, a banished man doe?" John Davenport once asked.[140] The ceaseless work of the Dutch Puritans demonstrated that pilgrims-in-exile, with careful support and organization, could be fully involved in the Puritan brotherhood. They awaited a not-too-distant victory. William Ames, the learned doctor of the Synod Puritans, in 1633, "less than a month before he departed this world," said: "The age comming may see these superstitious ceremonies upholden in our Land, have been witnessed to be unlawfull, and by this it shall appear we haue not betrayed the cause of Christ but witnessed this trueth against his adversaryes."[141]

---

[139] *The Beast is Wounded* (Richt Richt, 1638), pp. 3-20; S.P. 84, vol. 155, fol. 93.
[140] Davenport to Lady Mary Vere, Dec. 15/25, 1635, *Letters*, p. 63.
[141] Ames, *Fresh Suit*, "Published by S. O."

CHAPTER TWELVE

DEVELOPMENTS IN THEOLOGY AND CHURCH GOVERNMENT

The Netherlands was a sixteenth- and seventeenth-century school and seminary of British religion. The Netherlands gave opportunity to refugee nonconformists for unlimited theological speculation and experimentation in churchmanship. "Seminaries of disorderly preachers," complained the bishops. The basic pattern of British religion practiced in the Netherlands was Puritan and Reformed. By the 1630s, there were at least twenty-five churches, plenty of preachers, and several thousand English and Scottish population.[1] All of the established city churches and most of the garrison churches, because of their official Dutch subsidies, were considered to be *gereformeerde gemeenten*, Reformed churches, English-language equivalents of the Dutch Reformed churches. The conditions imposed on them by their financial subsidies necessitated a Reformed stance, and from every indication this was the desire of the preachers and congregations themselves. The first of these Reformed English churches was the Merchant Adventurers church of Antwerp and Middelburg; next came the garrison churches at Flushing and Brielle in the 1580s; and in the early seventeenth century came the officially-sponsored English churches at Amsterdam (1607), Leiden (1607), Rotterdam (1619), Flushing (1620), Utrecht (1622), Middelburg (1623), and elsewhere. The Separatist churches of Amsterdam (1596) and Leiden (1609) provided an alternative church model in several aspects but also drew heavily upon the Reformed tradition.

English theologians in the Netherlands, freed from the restraints at home, made notable contributions to Puritan theology. Although often busied with controversial polemics, the theologians addressed many concerns of systematic and practical theology. The early Merchant Adventurer preachers, Walter Travers, Thomas Cartwright, and Dudley Fenner, by their writings intellectually developed the theology and ecclesiology of English Puritanism. Schilders of Middelburg printed Travers's *Defence of Ecclesiastical Discipline* (1588) and at least eight of Fenner's books.[2] In the seventeenth century, the most eminent of the theologians-in-exile was Doctor William Ames, professor of theology at

---

[1] B.P., I, 132.
[2] J. Dover Wilson, "Richard Schilders and the English Puritans," *Transactions* of the Bibliographical Society, 9 (1909-11), 65-134.

Franeker University. His *Medulla Theologiae* (1627, in English, *The Marrow of Sacred Divinity*) and *De Conscientia* (1630, in English, *Conscience with the Power and Cases Thereof*), resulting from his professorial career, were major textbooks of the Puritan brotherhood of England and America. The other half of Ames's energies were poured into Puritan polemics (two *Replies* to Doctor Morton, the *Fresh Suit*, all published in Amsterdam).[3] Other major Puritan theologians writing and publishing in Dutch exile were Hugh Broughton, Henry Jacob, and Robert Parker.[4] In addition, nearly the entire output of serious Separatist theology, after the migration of 1593, came from Amsterdam and Leiden.

The Puritan, Reformed theology produced in the Low Countries drew upon the body of Calvinist doctrines and liberally added doses of English practical piety. Another ingredient commonly found in the Puritan books was the philosophy of Peter Ramus. Ramism provided a methodical framework for organizing religious doctrine: precise definitions, dichotomies, outline charts, and a conspicuous emphasis upon "use." In the late sixteenth century Dudley Fenner produced at Middelburg a Ramist manual in English, *The Artes of Logike and Rethorike* (1584). Cartwright and Travers were Ramists. Henry Jacob used Ramist dichotomies in his *Reasons Taken ovt of Gods Word* (Middelburg, 1604). The chief of the Puritan Ramists in exile was William Ames. His *Medulla* and *De Conscientia* are organized by Ramist method, and in his *Philosophemata* (Leiden, 1643) he laid out the full theory of theological Ramism. Ames's friends Hugh Peter and Thomas Hooker practiced Ramism, and Hugh Goodyear was a collector of Ramist books.[5] However, Ramus was not the exclusive property of Puritans. One of the most zealous Netherlands Ramists was Edward Misselden, the Merchant Adventurers' anti-Puritan deputy of Delft. He brought Ramism to the

---

[3] Keith L. Sprunger, *The Learned Doctor William Ames* (Urbana: Univ. of Illinois Press, 1972), pp. 127-52. John D. Eusdon has edited a modern version of the *Marrow* (Boston: Pilgrim Press, 1968).

[4] For Broughton, see *D.N.B.*, also his *Works* (London, 1662) for his career back and forth between England and the Low Countries (about 1589-1611); for Jacob, see Robert S. Paul, "Henry Jacob and Seventeenth-Century Puritanism," *The Hartford Quarterly*, 7 (Spring 1967), 93-96, and Stephen Brachlow, "Puritan Theology and Radical Churchmen in Pre-Revolutionary England: with Special Reference to Henry Jacob and John Robinson," Diss. Oxford 1979. Jacob's career in the Netherlands is vague. Tradition places him at Middelburg in 1599; however he was in England 1603-05 and in Holland about 1610-16. At least ten of Jacob's books were printed by Dutch printers. For Parker, see Frank B. Carr, "The Thought of Robert Parker (1564?-1614?) and his Influence on Puritanism before 1650," Diss. Univ. of London 1965.

[5] Sprunger, *Ames*, pp. 105-42; Sprunger, "John Yates of Norfolk: The Radical Puritan Preacher as Ramist Philosopher, *Journal of the History of Ideas*, 37 (Oct.-Dec. 1976), 697-700; Lee W. Gibbs, ed., *William Ames Technometry* (Univ. of Pennsylvania Press, 1979).

service of economics by inserting dichotomies and Ramist definitions into his treatises on commerce. Ramus is "so admirable in all the *Arts*," said Misselden, "and aboue all the rest, in this Logicall skill of Dichotomizing."[6] Puritanism owed much to the flow of books and the example of the churches from the Netherlands.

The Theology and Practice of English Reformed Religion in Exile

The Dutch-based English-language churches of the first generation (1575 to about 1630) and the Puritan preacher-theologians followed the main outlines of international Calvinism.[7] The models were the churches of Geneva, France, Holland, and Scotland. The early Merchant Adventurer preachers in their books proved the godliness of the Reformed pattern of worship and governance. Fenner in *A Defence of the Godlie Ministers* (1587) asserted that churches organized by pastors, doctors, elders, deacons, and synods were "prescribed by Christ" and moreover were "ordinarie, perpetuall, and the best." Even his pious songbook, *Song of Songs* (1587), dedicated to the worthy company of Merchant Adventurers for their mealtime devotions, slipped in the exhortation that Christ's "church" (Song of Solomon, chapter 6) means a church organized with "Teachers, Pastors, Elders, Deacons, Church seruantes." His main complaint with the Church of England was "onely in some weightie and necessarie partes of Church-gouernement."[8] The sixteenth-century precedents of the presbyterian-ordered *Engelse Kerken* (Antwerp, Middelburg) buttressed by the writings of the sixteenth-century theologians, set the main direction for the seventeenth-century development of English Reformed churches in the Netherlands.

The seventeenth-century churches aimed for a simplified worship with emphasis on preaching and sacraments. A few of the sermons preached in Holland survive in printed or manuscript form.[9] There was at first some minimal use of the Prayer Book in a few town churches, as at The Hague and Utrecht, but it swiftly disappeared from the regular worship service. Although the Anglican Prayer Book was rejected by the chur-

---

[6] Edward Misselden, *The Circle of Commerce* (London, 1623), p. 73.

[7] The description of church practices will be drawn from the records of the British churches at Amsterdam, Leiden, Utrecht, Rotterdam, Delft, Dort, Flushing, Middelburg, and Arnhem, which are the churches with the fullest records.

[8] Dudley Fenner, *A Defence of the Godlie Ministers, against the Slaunders of D. Bridge* (n.p., 1587), pp. 132-33; Fenner, *The Song of Songs* (Middelburg, 1587), chapter 6.

[9] John Forbes, John Wing, William Ames, John Hales, Samuel Bachelor, Thomas Goodwin, and William Bridge have printed sermons preached in Holland. Some manuscript sermons also survive, by Hugh Goodyear (G.A. Leiden, no. 66751), by Robert Fleming, Jr. (Bod., Rawl. MS. E, 44-48); by Joseph Hill, Henry Hickman, and Matthew Newcomen (B.M., Sloane MS. 608).

ches, the worship had structure and the preacher frequently used a printed service book. The godly example was Calvin's *La Forme des Prières* and Knox's *Forme of Prayers and Ministration of the Sacraments*. These Genevan service books inspired an almost identical English Puritan version, *A Booke of the Forme of Common Prayers, Administration of the Sacraments, &c. Agreable to Gods Worde, and the Use of the Reformed Churches*, published by Waldegrave of Edinburgh in 1584 and in further printings by Schilders of Middelburg in 1586, 1587, and 1602. The Waldegrave and Middelburg service books, concluded Horton Davies, were probably the work of Cartwright or Travers and Fenner.[10] Contemporaries believed them to be the product of Cartwright.[11] The book laid down directions for orderly worship: confession of sins, Psalms, prayers, Scripture reading, sermon, Apostles' Creed, blessing. The point, it seems, was not to be against all "prayers in a forme, but against the contagion and perill of our booke" (the official Prayer Book). Laudian Anglicans resented the Middelburg book because of its Reformed order of teachers, prophesying, and elders, making "every thing to be Christs owne order, and necessary to be done."[12]

The Middelburg book served as a Reformed alternative to the bishop's Prayer Book in several English churches. Said Hugh Goodyear of Leiden, "It was a book allowed of by all the godly English." John Paget had a copy which he lent to Boswell in 1636, his only copy, "neither know where they are to be got." Paget thought the book largely modeled on the Dutch forms.[13] Other liturgies were available. The Dutch liturgy in translation was endorsed by the English Synod in 1623. The Synod resolved: "That no liturgy be used in any church amongst us, but that which is in use in the churches of these United Provinces," meaning that the churches could read a chapter to two, say the Ten Commandments, and sing a Psalm before sermon.[14] Forbes of Delft adapted the Dutch format to his usage, "only reading chapters, singing psalmes before sermon." For the sacrament he drew on the Dutch model, yet "doth not say the very same words verbatim."[15] Petrus Gribius of Middelburg in 1645 translated the Dutch liturgy into English and had it printed at London, but according to reports, the Middelburg church did not take to his

---

[10] Horton Davies, *The Worship of the English Puritans* (Westminster: Dacre Press, 1948), p. 116-27; Davies, *Worship and Theology in England: From Andrewes to Baxter and Fox, 1603-1690* (Princeton: Princeton Univ. Press, 1975), pp. 405-06.
[11] B.P., I, 86.
[12] Ibid.
[13] Ibid., I, 80, 221.
[14] S.P. 84, vol. 112, fol. 4.
[15] B.P., I, 96.

translated liturgies.[16] Steven Paine of Bergen-op-Zoom used the Dutch liturgy as translated personally for him by Henry Hexham. Some preachers attempted to frame their own hybrid service forms, "after theyr owne fances betwixt the English and the Dutch."[17] In every case, the emphasis was on Reformed simplicity and orderliness of worship.

The sacraments of communion and baptism were administered according to Reformed practice. Nevertheless, several of the English preachers who rejected the Prayer Book for regular worship made some paraphrases or used sentences from the book for baptism and communion. Sir William Brereton gave a visitor's report about the communion at the Amsterdam English Reformed church in 1634. The bread and wine were taken sitting at tables. "All receivers coming up and sitting at a long table whilst they received; all the men first successively, and then the women, and when they have received, return to their places." The Separatists, however, had communion sitting in the benches, being served by the deacons.[18] The usual English communion, administered quarterly or bi-monthly, was preceded by a house to house visitation, at which time spiritual health was evaluated and communion tokens were issued. The tokens were tickets of admission to the Lord's Table. Following the service, a check was made of the tokens which were identifiable by name for taking of attendance.[19] Strict congregations, like Rotterdam and Arnhem, at the time of the Dissenting Brethren, had weekly communion.[20] Some late seventeenth-century "Sacramental Discourses" by Robert Fleming Junior, minister at Leiden and the Rotterdam Scots Church, set forth the practice of the 1690s. Fleming used a pattern of a Wednesday or Thursday fast, where tokens were given out, a Saturday preparation sermon, and the Sunday morning communion. He administered the elements to members seated at tables.[21] John Quick of Middelburg (1680-81) described the pre-communion visitation as extremely arduous, so fatiguing that by nightfall "I have not been able, as we say, to move a foot."[22] So long as the regular home visitation prevailed (the later seventeenth century in most churches), the church officers

---

[16] John Quick, "Icones Sacrae Anglicanae," I, i, 270. It was printed by Field for Ralph Smith, London, 1645.

[17] S.P. 16, vol. 310, no. 103; S.P. 16, vol. 90, no. 84; B.P., I, 377-78.

[18] William Brereton, *Travels in Holland the United Provinces England Scotland and Ireland*, ed. Edward Hawkins, the Chetham Society, 1 (1844), 63; Robert Baillie, *A Dissuasive from the Errours of the Time* (London, 1645), p. 121.

[19] Amsterdam C.R., II, 28; Middelburg C.R., I, 52. "Avondmaalloodjes bij de Engelsche gemeente te Middelburg," *Jaarboek Muntk.*, 13 (1925), 103-04.

[20] Thomas Goodwin, et al., *An Apologeticall Narration* (London, 1644), p. 8.

[21] Rawl. MS. E, 47 (Bod.).

[22] Quick, "Icones," I, ii, 787.

kept an accurate up-to-date surveillance of the spiritual condition of the congregation, whether "indifferently well," or "reasonable good estate."[23]

The inner organization of the churches was government by pastor, elders, and deacons. Numerous garrison churches, lacking a permanent membership, omitted elders and deacons because of lack of suitable candidates; even so, the omission was considered harmful. Churchly perfection could only be achieved by establishment of a consistory.[24] Officers were chosen by election ("by the most voyces of the whole congregation," Amsterdam, 1607, or "by all our members," Middelburg, 1626), indicating a large degree of congregational participation.[25] The elected elders and deacons were from the prominent families of the congregation, often the most successful merchants. However, the democratic element in decision-making deteriorated in many churches across the century. At Amsterdam in the 1630s, congregational participation gave way to a more powerful eldership, which chose its own membership and announced decisions to the congregation as facts accomplished. The congregation was asked to pray for the decision-making elders and to ratify formally the decision already made. Some early ministers were chosen by congregational elections (John Drake at Middelburg in 1623 "by joynt suffrages elect"), but the more usual pattern was election in the consistory with announcement to the congregation and inviting comments previous to installation.[26]

The office holders and electorate were the male members of the church. None of the churches allowed women to participate in preaching or elections. The preachers condemned the notion as outlandish and unscriptural. Ainsworth, Johnson, and Robinson, the great Separatist spokesmen, all wrote against female church leadership or voting. "Absolutely unlawfull," said Ainsworth; "it was never our judgment or practice, that in Elections women or children should *give their voices*." Non-Separatist John Paget was adamant against women in church affairs, "as if they had had power to give voyces in the election of Ministers."[27] Only John Smyth, the Anabaptist, allowed a place for women in congrega-

---

[23] Utrecht C.R., I, Mar. 8, 1658; Sept. 22, 1659.
[24] B.P., I, 141.
[25] Middelburg C.R., I, 29; Amsterdam C.R., I, 6.
[26] Quick, "Icones," I, i, 254; Alice C. Carter, *The English Reformed Church in Amsterdam in the Seventeenth Century* (Amsterdam: Scheltema & Holkema, 1964), p. 29.
[27] Henry Ainsworth, *An Animadversion to Mr. Richard Clyftons Advertisement* (Amsterdam, 1613), pp. 33-34; Ainsworth, *Covnterpoyson* (n.p., 1608), p. 176; John Paget, *An Answer to the unjust complaints of William Best* (Amsterdam, 1635), p. 92.

tional discipline and censures.[28] During the 1630s, however, the issue was raised anew and became a point of controversy in some churches.

In regard to membership in classes and synods, the English or British churches did not follow the Reformed practice. Except for the English Reformed Church of Amsterdam, which always had membership in the Classis of Amsterdam, the English-Scottish churches had minimal ties to the presbyterial organization of the Dutch Reformed church until rather late. Utrecht did not join the classis until 1629, Middelburg and Flushing in 1645, Dort in 1646, and Leiden in 1655. Even then, the tie was loose. The English Synod of 1621-33 was an effort to remedy the lack of inter-church structure. The Scots church of Veere in 1642, seeking larger church relations, became a constituent member of the Church of Scotland, eligible to attend general assembly; but because of distance and local circumstances this membership proved more honorific than practical.[29] The Merchant Adventurers church, the mother church of English Reformed congregations in the Low Countries, although famous for its presbyterianism, was no member of any synod, "never classically subordinat unto them for appeales or otherwise."[30] The avoidance of full participation in Dutch Reformed synods during the 1620s-1630s had an ideological "Congregationalist" dimension, but the longer-term explanation for the independent course was the isolation of the scattered British congregations, who felt distant from the neighboring Dutch Reformed churches in language and culture. Rather than be dependent on foreign governance, the British consistories preferred to be independent. Relationships with the hierarchy of the Church of England were few—the fewer the better—and in the Netherlands the Puritan preachers made it clear that because of Dutch law they could not recognize the jurisdiction of the prelate nor use the English liturgy. Most of the preachers in the English churches were expatriates from England, having come over with episcopal ordination. Only a rare few felt compelled to renounce their English ordination in favor of a new Reformed ordination. The English Synod ordained two or three persons into the ministry. Hugh Peter at Rotterdam was ordained anew into his charge, without specifically repudiating his old ordination; his successors William Bridge, John Ward, and Sydrach Simpson, went further and renounced their prelatical ordination and received a fresh Puritan ordination.[31]

---

[28] John Smyth, *Paralleles, Censvres, Observations* (n.p., 1609), p. 63; Walter Burgess, *John Robinson* (London: Williams and Norgate, 1920), p. 292; Johannes Bakker, *John Smyth* (Wageningen: H. Veenman & Zonen, 1964), p. 125.

[29] John Davidson and Alexander Gray, *The Scottish Staple at Veere* (London: Longmans, Green, 1909), p. 279.

[30] S.P. 16, vol. 234, no. 8.

[31] B.P., I, 139; Baillie, *Dissvasive* (1645), pp. 75, 82.

The Puritan abhorrence of lax discipline in the Church of England prompted an especially scrupulous discipline in the Puritan Reformed churches. These English churches were renown throughout the Netherlands for stern discipline (a "rigider discipline") and this provoked unending controversies with the more tolerant Dutch Reformed churches.[32] The English churches leaned toward the scrupulous side in membership matters. At first baptism presented no problems. Babies were baptized when presented to the church by English-Scottish families in line with current Dutch Reformed practice. Ideally, one or both parents should be members of the church and known to the pastor, but in actual fact, every infant brought in was baptized, with very few exceptions recorded in any church. However, the issue of baptism emerged as a matter of contention in the 1630s.[33] The English consistories kept a sharp eye over their membership, and against every wickedness punishment was swift, whether by admonition, suspension from the Lord's Table, or final excommunication. Non-attendance and moral turpitude (Sabbath breaking, whoring, drunkenness, fighting, and the like) were common sins. Unlike the parish churches at home, the Netherlands English churches aimed at confronting and finally excluding all open sinners.

As the leading, and usually the only, English or Scottish institution in a Dutch city, the church felt obliged to serve as a moral, social and even economic governor for the British community. A scandal by one person reflected on the entire community, and consequently the consistories of the churches took responsibility to maintain respectable economic and social standards. In a commercial society like the Netherlands, the sanctity of contract and debt payment was counted a religious duty as much as an economic duty. The English followed the example of the Dutch Reformed Church in enforcing economic discipline and debt repayment. The church accepted that the ultimate business sins were bankruptcy and defrauding of creditors; the Synod of North Holland in 1618 laid down policies for dealing with bankruptcy, in which a bankrupt was to be excluded from the Lord's Table until he made restitution or satisfactory arrangements with the creditors.[34] At Middelburg, a debtor in 1632 was "advised" to abstain from the communion, meanwhile the elders took responsibility to help him make peace with his creditors; in 1651 the wife of a bankrupt, guilty of "scandalous breaking," was refused a positive attestation; Elnathan Negus, a deacon, went bankrupt in 1660 and was

---

[32] B.P., I, 168.
[33] Carter, *English Reformed Church*, p. 82.
[34] Reitsma and Van Veen, II, 23-24 (articles 11, 12); these articles were copied into the Amsterdam C.R., I, 112.

swiftly suspended from his office as well as from the communion.[35] At the Dort church, a fallen member in 1639 was declared unfit for the Lord's Table because of the double sins of lying and not paying debts; in 1645 Edward Tyre was refused attestation for transfer because he departed the city with unpaid debts.[36] The disciplinary arm could be long. Kracht Kenderman in 1641, newly come over from London to The Hague, was summoned before the English consistory of The Hague and questioned sharply about things left amiss in London. The elders had two letters, "one from my landlord in London, demanding his rent, the other from my wife ... that I left her in poor circumstances."[37] English theology in Holland absorbed many of the economic values of the surrounding Dutch society. After several years' residence in the Netherlands, William Ames began to condone usury as somewhat consistent with clear reason and Scripture, which brought rebuke to him from Nathaniel Holmes: "We must remember how this learned Doctor lived where the people are intolerable vsurers."[38]

On Sabbath observance, a social concern dear to the Puritan conscience, the English-Scottish churches fell out of step with majority Dutch practice. English travelers and settlers to the Netherlands, whether Puritan or not, were offended at the Dutch use of the Sabbath. Ambassador Sir Dudley Carleton reported that Sunday seemed a mere day of labor, "for they never knew yet how to observe the Sabbath." Sir William Brereton, Puritan gentleman, made a similar judgment; "here is little respect had to sanctify the sabbath." Edmund Calamy (1671-1732) found the situation absolutely hazardous to spiritual health. While a student at the University at Utrecht in 1688-91, he never once partook of the Lord's Table and his observance of the Sabbath slipped badly. "I was too apt to be influenced by common examples, as to my conduct on the Lord's day."[39] By English and Scottish standards, the Sunday was altogether too much used for labor, dancing, beer and brandywine parties, markets, baking and brewing. No "Scottish Sabbath" here.[40]

In face of such lax Sabbath standards, the English and Scottish churches gave high priority to enforcing Sabbath observance in their own congregations. The English church at Leiden in 1638 suspended the barber

---

[35] Middelburg C.R., I, 62, 161, 208.
[36] Dort C.R., no. 5, fols. 15-18, 67.
[37] Hessels, *E.L.B.A.*, III, 1856 (no. 2613).
[38] Nathaniel Holmes, *Usury Is Injury* (London, 1640), p. 5.
[39] Carleton, *Letters*, p. 380; Brereton, *Travels*, p. 6; Edmund Calamy, *An Historical Account of My Own Life*, 2nd ed. (London, 1830), I, 146-47, 187.
[40] L. Knappert, *Geschiedenis der Nederlandsche Hervormde Kerk gedurende de 16ᵉ en 17ᵉ eeuw* (Amsterdam: Meulenhoff & Co., 1911), pp. 187-88.

Henry Stafford for cutting hair on Sunday mornings. The Flushing church sent the elders and deacons forth into the English taverns on Sunday forenoons during the sermon to search for English Sabbath backsliders. John Paget at Amsterdam was an unswerving disciplinarian of the Sabbath. Paget dealt with one Richard Tomlins, after noting him drunk at the Sunday communion table and then asleep during the sermon.[41] That was the heart of the matter—double and triple sins—one sin attracted others. Almost invariably, the Sabbath breaker was also a drinker, a party-goer, a truant from church services, "forsaking the publique assemblies ... profaning the Sabbath, despising admonition."[42]

The campaign to clean up the Sabbath encountered many obstacles. English-Scottish Sabbath values were not accepted by Dutch society as a whole. The churches were a flickering light upon a hill. The more the churches played lords of the Dutch Sabbath, the more likely were troublesome incidents with neighboring Dutch Reformed churches. Paget ran into controversy when he publicly rebuked William Best for Sabbath breaking and permitting his wife, a member of the Dutch church, to maintain a shop where she sold fruit on Sundays—"evill-example a stumbling block to many." Best, twice a deacon at the English church, refused the admonition and argued that Sunday selling was necessary for the benefit of the sick and for merchandising perishable goods. "There are many scoores, constantly breakers of this day," why pick on him? Best reminded Paget that the Dutch preachers had never forbidden his wife's trade. Paget's discipline was frustrated.[43] At Leiden, where Stafford had been suspended for Sunday barbering, the Dutch church agreed to accept him and his family into membership, the trivial offense of barbering being "not sufficient enough to hinder their being received in our Dutch church." This clash of standards caused such hard feelings between the English and Dutch churches that the burgomasters finally intervened and ordered Stafford to be transferred to the Dutch church.[44] The Puritan position on the Sabbath did not prevail in the Netherlands. Instead, the English and Scots gradually accommodated themselves to the prevailing values. Alice C. Carter observes that "this was a matter in which alien migrants could hardly afford, in spite of their pastor's views, not to follow the custom of the country of their

---

[41] Acta Kerkeraad Leiden, no. 003, July 23, 1638; Amsterdam C.R., III, 74-75, Sept. 16, 30, 1637; Flushing C.R., no. 4469, April 23, 1633; Carter, *English Reformed Church*, p. 30.

[42] Amsterdam C.R., II, 43; Utrecht C.R., I, Mar. 8, 1658.

[43] Paget, *Answer*, pp. 92-94; William Best, *The Chvrches Plea for Her Right* (Amsterdam, 1635), pp. 5-8.

[44] Acta Kerkeraad Leiden, no. 003, July 23, Aug. 6, Nov. 11, 1638; Aug. 26, Sept. 2, Oct. 28, 1639.

adoption."⁴⁵ For the British churches to insist on severe Sabbath observance, in spite of the dominant Dutch practice, was a losing battle; and, the Sunday profaners insisted, it was also bad business. Mrs. Best kept her shop open at Amsterdam, and at Utrecht, John Longworthy pleaded "necessity" for Sabbath work. "Otherwise he cannot maintaine his family."⁴⁶

Although the Reformed pattern was the norm, during the "second generation" of the churches (1630-60) theological and ecclesiological innovations became the rule. The innovations were associated with the English Synod movement (Ames, Peter, Forbes) and later with the new immigrants of the 1630s, many of them outspoken preachers of the Jacobite or Congregational way (Hooker, Davenport, Goodwin, Nye, Burroughes, Simpson, and Bridge). The English Reformed churches of the Low Countries had reputation in Puritan eyes as superior to the average Anglican parish church, but were the churches as good as they should be? Their formalism and routine, some feared, detracted from a true experience of warm religion. During the 1630s, a renewing spirit of change swept the churches, especially at Rotterdam, Arnhem, and Delft, and wrought reforms of freer, more Spirit-filled worship, greater democratic participation (both men and women), and stricter standards of baptism and membership. Puritan reformists aimed toward "the doctrine of godliness," which they judged to be sadly lacking in conventional English and Dutch churches.⁴⁷ "They would constitute a number of new Practises as Prophecying which they have done tymes, and a New Liturgy ... and they would condemn all manner of Holy dayes, not allowe so much as Christmas, nor Good Friday, nor Easter, nor Whitsontide."⁴⁸

Liturgy and worship practices went in many novel directions. In 1633, in a report to ambassador Boswell, the churches were categorized into four ways of worship:

1. Some use no set forme at all no not in Baptising, nor in the celebration of the Lords Supper, nor in Mariage, but every time speake as the Spirit enableth them. Of this sort Mr. Forbes is most eminent, and therefore is sent for, farre and neare to Baptise children after the New Way, and Mr. Hooker by his discourses is reckoned of this

---

⁴⁵ Carter, *English Reformed Church*, p. 122.
⁴⁶ Utrecht C.R., I, June 30, 1665.
⁴⁷ The "Doctrine of Godliness" or "power of godliness" is discussed by William Ames, *Conscience with the Power and Cases Thereof* (n.p., 1639), dedication; by Thomas Hooker in a letter from Rotterdam, Mather, *Magnalia*, I, 340; by the Dissenting Brethren, *Apologeticall Narration*, p. 4.
⁴⁸ S.P. 16, vol. 310, no. 103.

order. ... And for children hee is sayd to refuse to baptise them, because hee know not the faith of their parents. [John Forbes in the 1630s began to omit the Lord's Prayer. He and Thomas Hooker were of the Merchant Adventurer church at Delft.]

2. Some use the Dutch formes translated into English, as those doe who are mingled in the Dutch Classis, and Mr. Paine doth at Bergen ... yet the Dutch formes are much altered according to the iudgement of the English Classis.
3. Some use an English Liturgy put out by Cartwright (as it is conceived) which was printed at Middleborough 1586. cum privilegio. ... This Mr. Goodyer [Leiden] useth and Mr. Peters [Rotterdam] saith it hath been always used, hee found it in his Consistory. Whether hee use or noe I cannot tell. I believe hee runnes the Forbesian way.
4. Some use our English Liturgy in baptisme, and the Lords Supper and Mariage, but mangle, and pare, and purge it most pittifully ... of this sort are Mr. Balmford [The Hague] and Mr. Batchelour himselfe [Gorinchem], who yet thinkes hee shall suffer gloriously in refusing to use the same booke in the beginning of divine service.[49]

Orthodox Anglicans accurately discerned that the innovations in Puritan religion were a hybrid, as much at variance with the Dutch Reformed system as the Church of England. "They are as opposite to the Dutch Church as unto ours." "These churches of our English yett not Anabaptists neither conforme to the Liturgy of the Church of Englande: Nor to that of the Netherlands, nor of any other Church in the worlde."[50]

The English Reformed Church of Rotterdam, presbyterial until the coming of Hugh Peter in 1629, underwent a transformation, Forbesian and Jacobite. In 1633 Peter reconstituted the church on the basis of a written covenant, revised the membership rolls to include only those giving personal adherence to the covenant, and received fresh ordination to the newly-organized church. The deadwood and merely routine members were swept out to produce a purified church—"more then in England or the Gospell," exclaimed the omitted members.[51] Rotterdam and its sister church at Arnhem would admit only the "truly godly." Woe to the person who came without good credentials or from a church of only average spirituality. The Congregationalist church model received a good testing in the Netherlands: they "require every Church member to be a Saint, really regenerate and justified who at their admis-

---

[49] Ibid.; the notes about Forbes are from B.P., I, 114.
[50] S.P. 16, vol. 170, no. 8; S.P. 16, vol. 310; no. 103.
[51] B.P., I, 139-40, 172.

sion have publikely satisfied the whole Congregation of convincing signes of their true holiness."[52]

At Peter's reordination and covenanting, women were called on to vote; however, Rotterdam did not retain the female vote thereafter, nor did any of the Netherlands congregations allow "any women any publike Ecclesiastick power." Women, however, did have a special role in the Rotterdam church through their own weekday prayer, praise, and communion service.[53] In the next step of Rotterdam church reformation, the board of elders was eliminated, so that in the late 1630s all discipline, calling of ministers, and governance was done "by the whole congregation" (the male members).[54] Peter was assisted by William Ames and John Davenport; and after 1636 the church was pastored in turns by John Ward, William Bridge, Jeremiah Burroughes, Sydrach Simpson, Joseph Symonds, and Robert Park. The Rotterdam church, disillusioned with the practice of Dutch Reformed religion, avoided all ecclesiastical connection with the classis and synod. Said Hugh Peter to Davenport, "Take heed Mr. D. what you do, for you were as good yeald to the English Bishops as to the Dutch classis."[55] William Ames, who accepted a call as co-pastor in 1633, praised the Rotterdam "Independency" as God's "way of publik worship."[56]

The Arnhem church, under the ministry of Thomas Goodwin, Philip Nye, and John Archer, was an associate church of Rotterdam. Arnhem carried through a large program of church innovations, not only the covenant and other Congregational practices adopted at Rotterdam, but charismatic, spirit-filled actions. Arnhem practiced anointing the sick with oil, laying hands on the sick for healing, and the holy kiss. Archer and Goodwin preached a vivid millenarianism.[57]

The doctrine of the millennium had many advocates among the Netherlands Independents. A generation before, Hugh Broughton of Middelburg began the apocalyptic teaching among the Dutch Puritans, but it remained a controversial point. Doctor Ames of Franeker, in correspondence with Joseph Mead, a millenarian Puritan, showed skepticism about any literal reign of Christ upon earth. "Yet methinks that Millenary state spoken of may well be understood of the Church raised from a dead condition, and so continued for that space." Ames "could

---

[52] [Alexander Forbes], *The Anatomy of Independency* (London, 1644), pp. 21-23; Baillie, *Disvassive* (1645), pp. 105-06. Baillie paid the Congregationalists an unintended compliment on the purity of their lives ("truly godly").

[53] Forbes, *Anatomy*, p. 29; Baillie, *Disvassive*, p. 111.

[54] Acta Kerkeraad Rotterdam, I, Dec. 4, 1641; Baillie, *Disvassive*, pp. 45, 109.

[55] B.P., I, 191.

[56] Hugh Peter, *Mr. Peters Last Report of the English Wars* (London, 1646), p. 14.

[57] For details on the Arnhem church, see above, chapter 8.

not approve of any of the Millenary tenets."[58] Goodwin's *Glimpse of Sions Glory* (1641) neatly tied together Independency and the thousand-year reign of Christ, the one leading to the other. Christ shall reign personally. "But when shall these things be?" Goodwin, following Thomas Brightman's calculations, predicted the Lord's return as early as 1650 or possibly in 1695. The work of Independency in 1641 (gathering an Independent church), was preparatory to the coming of the kingdom in 1650. "And this worke is a Foundation of abundance of glory that *God* shall have, and will continue till the comming of *Christ.*"[59] Goodwin referred to his congregation as "gathering a church together," an ambiguous phrase. If the sermon was preached at Arnhem—and the notation simply says "Briefly layd open in a Sermon, at a general Fastday in Holland"—was he referring to the upbuilding and improving of the Arnhem church? The Arnhem church had been functioning with a covenant since 1638-39. Goodwin may have referred to a fresh covenanting of a core of members preparing to return as a church to England.[60] Possibly the sermon was preached at another of the Netherlands English churches. The church at Delft was being renewed by Robert Park in 1640-41.

Archer, Goodwin's colleague, in *The Personall Reign of Jesus Christ upon Earth* (1642) sketched in many details about the Millennium. "Hee will governe as earthly Monarches have done, that is universally over the world." Archer calculated that the Millennium would most likely begin in 1661.[61] Although not a Fifth Monarchist, Archer was respected and quoted by them during the English Revolution.[62] The Rotterdam Independents also dreamed millenarian visions. Burroughes in *Moses his Choice* (1641) and Bridge in *Babylons Downfall* (1641) predicted the ruin of Babylon and the swift coming of Zion. John Canne of Amsterdam in 1640 was talking the language of "Kingdome" and "Sion"; upon his return to England he became a Fifth Monarchist.[63] Alexander Petrie,

---

[58] Ames to Mead, May 27, 1630, *The Works of the Pious and Profoundly-Learned Joseph Mede, B.D.*, 4th ed. (London, 1677), pp. 782-83; John Worthington, *The Diary and Correspondence of Dr. John Worthington*, ed. James Crossley, Chetham Society, 13 (1847), I, 250.

[59] [Thomas Goodwin], *A Glimpse of Sions Glory: or the Churches Beautie Specified* (London, 1641), pp. 13, 31, 33; Peter Toon, ed., *Puritans, the Millennium and the Future of Israel: Puritan Eschatology 1600 to 1660* (Cambridge: James Clark, 1970), p. 64. Goodwin's *Exposition upon the Revelation* (1639) also comes from the Arnhem period; Bryan C. Ball, *A Great Expectation* (Leiden: E. J. Brill, 1975), p. 87.

[60] Murray Tolmie, *The Triumph of the Saints: The Separate Churches of London 1616-1649* (Cambridge: Cambridge Univ. Press, 1977), pp. 91-92.

[61] John Archer, *The Personall Reign of Christ upon Earth* (London, 1642), pp. 3, 52-53.

[62] B. S. Capp, *The Fifth Monarchy Men: A Study in Seventeenth-century Millenarianism* (Totowa, N.J.: Rowman and Littlefield, 1972), pp. 45-46.

[63] Ibid., pp. 30-31; see letters of John Canne (1640) in Add. MS. 4275, fols. 143-45.

Scottish Presbyterian of Rotterdam, tried to refute the swiftly moving millenarian tide with *Chiliasto-mastix* (1644). He feared the joint forces of Independency and millenarianism in the Netherlands.[64]

At least two other Dutch churches carried through sufficient reforms to qualify as Independent, the English Reformed Church of Delft (a not fully-successful church reorganization under Robert Pack in 1640-41) and Samuel Eaton's "Congregational" church at Amsterdam in 1635-36.[65] Other churches, although not as publicized as there four, experienced some of the new life. Written covenants appeared in at least three other churches (Middelburg, 1623, Amsterdam, 1630-31, and the Merchant Adventurers of Delft, 1633). John Quick, in fact, believed that all the English churches of the Netherlands at some time adopted a covenant, "a written Federall Transaction betwixt them and God." If so, only the covenants of Middelburg, Amsterdam, Delft, Rotterdam, and Arnhem survive.[66] The concern for stricter membership, inspired by the campaigns of Hooker and Davenport, prompted many of the preachers—who hesitated to go the whole way like Peter—to institute scrupulous policies for baptism and transfer. Balmford of The Hague, Goodyear of Leiden, and Roe of Flushing took steps against indiscriminate baptizing in their churches.[67]

The Amsterdam English Reformed Church in the 1630s was deeply affected by the Hooker-Davenport doctrines. A majority faction of the congregation, many of them ex-Brownists, favored the Hooker-Davenport Congregational innovations, but they were thwarted by John Paget, the old, conservative Presbyterian pastor. The issues in contention boiled down to two: (1) "promiscuous baptism"—baptism to be only of parents of the visible church, (2) "due power of the church," ("every particular Congregation, is independent, and may, yea ought to practise Ecclesiasticall Government").[68] Both of these reforms had been achieved at Rotterdam, but after long turmoil they were defeated at Amsterdam. Like the innovating party at Rotterdam, the Hooker-Davenport people at Amsterdam sought to mobilize the entire congregation. In a canvassing of the members, women as well as men signed petitions ("women and maydes"), which Paget denounced as completely scandalous. In consistory, Paget cross-examined the petition leaders (all men) about the women's role in election of ministers: Some did not allow women to have

---

[64] Alexander Petrie, *Chiliasto-mastix* (Rotterdam, 1644), p. 3.

[65] On Eaton's church, see chapter 4; for Delft, see chapter 5.

[66] Quick, "Icones," I, i, 46. For copies of the covenants, see chapters 4 (Amsterdam), 5 (Rotterdam), 7 (Middelburg), 8 (Arnhem), 9 (Merchant Adventurers).

[67] Paget, *Answer*, pp. 75-78; for Balmford and Roe, Add. MS. 24,666, fol. 2; for Goodyear, see Paget letter, Goodyear Papers gg.

[68] Best, *Chvrches Plea*, preface.

a voice in ministerial elections, some did not know; some defended it on the basis of "the judgement of certain Ministers."[69]

In *The Apologeticall Narration* of 1644, the Congregationalist Brethren praised their Dutch experience as a fruitful period of spiritual growth. Congregationalism in Holland steered a "middle way" between Brownism and the over-authoritarianism of Presbyterianism.[70] Although powerful examples, these experimentations in the "second generation" churches did not permanently transform the British churches of the Low Countries. In the 1640s Congregationalism moved back to England. During the remainder of the seventeenth-century, the churches reverted to a more conventional Reformed church mode. The Arnhem church closed down and even the Rotterdam church was "brought off" by Thomas Cawton in the 1650s and became "Presbyterian" once again.[71] Occasional incidents flared up in the late seventeenth century over pastors or churches not happy with Dutch Reformed policies or practice, but not on the scale of the tumultuous days of earlier century. John Quick resigned at Middelburg in 1681 because of disagreements over the liturgy and governance practiced in Zeeland. Several Scots, after calls to British churches, were unable to observe the prescribed Dutch liturgy and feast days.[72]

The discussion thus far has been strictly on developments in British Calvinism. In spite of the strong Arminian movement in the Netherlands, the overseas English and Scots were little affected by it. The preachers, and the congregations so far as they publicly expressed themselves, were almost unanimously supporters of strict Calvinism and the Synod of Dort. Several of the exiled preachers disputed and wrote on behalf of the Calvinist side. William Ames in the Netherlands wrote four books against the Arminians and attended the Synod of Dort as an advisor to president Johannes Bogerman.[73] John Forbes (Forbesius Scotus) disputed with Simon Episcopius at Leiden and published anti-Arminian sermons. In a sermon at Delft, Forbes wove together a Calvinist interpretation of the words, "Who will have all men to be saved" (I Tim. 2:4). Another vigorous Contra-Remonstrant was Matthew Slade, rector of the Amsterdam Latin school and author of a sharp book against Vorstius, *Cum Conrado Vorstio* (1612).[74] Among the Separatists, Francis

---

[69] Paget, *Answer*, p. 21; Amsterdam C.R., III, 44.

[70] *Apologeticall Narration*, p. 24.

[71] Steven, p. 333.

[72] David Blair at The Hague, Steven, pp. 308-09, 320; Robert MacWard at Utrecht, Steven, pp. 30-32; Thomas Potts at Flushing, C.R., Jan. 13, 1647.

[73] Sprunger, *Ames*, pp. 45-51.

[74] Ibid., p. 47; John Forbes, *A Sermon Discvrsing the true Meaning of these Words*, I Tim. 2:4 (Delft, 1632), p. 39. On Slade's Contra-Remonstrantism, C. Van der Woude, *Sibrandus Lubbertus* (Kampen: J. H. Kok, 1963), which details his correspondence with Lubbertus.

Johnson wrote substantially against the Remonstrants in *Christian Plea* (1618), because they "derogate from Gods glorie, and advance fraile man." John Robinson publicly disputed with Episcopius at Leiden and published *A Defence of the Doctrine propounded by the Synode at Dort* (1624).[75] Defections to the Arminian side were extremely rare, except for John Smyth and Thomas Helwys, the Anabaptists, who adopted the Anabaptist position of free will. John Douglas, chaplain at Utrecht, ambitious for preferment in England, was reputed to be an occasional Arminian but denied it. Sampson Johnson, chaplain to Elizabeth at The Hague, spoke a little on behalf of both Arminianism and Socinianism. Thomas Dennis, minister at 's-Hertogenbosch, could not in conscience acknowledge the resolutions of the Synod of Dort. Thomas Basson, English printer of Leiden, printed Arminian books. William Best, Paget's arch rival at Amsterdam, after being suspended from the church for schism, joined the Arminians and temporarily adopted their views of predestination.[76] Except for extremely scattered exceptions like these, the English-Scottish churches were solidly in the Calvinist camp.

Separatist Contributions

The adoption of covenants and other strict practices in the non-Separatist churches suggest a Separatist influence. Most of the new Congregational reforms had been long practiced in the Dutch Separatist churches. Although no respectable non-Separatist Puritan would dare admit inspiration from the Brownists, the constant example and competition of the Separatists undoubtedly made an impact. When Ames, Jacob, and Parker were with Robinson at Leiden in 1610, the conversation went both ways. The non-Separatists did "freely communicate light to him, and received also some things from him," said John Cotton.[77] Separatist churches carried to the extreme certain Puritan-Reformed values of the movement as a whole: godliness, purity, discipline, the Holy Spirit. They de-emphasized other Puritan values, orderliness, form, and the brotherhood of international Calvinism. The goals of worship and governance, which more cautious Puritans talked and yearned for, the Separatists claimed to be practicing in full. "Wee (through Gods great

---

[75] Francis Johnson, *A Christian Plea Conteyning Three Treatises* (n.p., 1617), p. 243; William Bradford, *Bradford's History of Plymouth Plantation, 1606-1646*, ed. William T. Davis (1908; rpt. New York: Barnes & Noble, 1946), pp. 42-43.

[76] S.P. 84, vol. 80, fol. 154; vol. 81, fol. 76; vol. 89, fol. 47; S.P. 16, vol. 417, no. 78; D. Nauta, *Samuel Maresius* (Amsterdam: H. J. Paris, 1935), p. 152; J. A. van Dorsten, *Thomas Basson* (Leiden: Sir Thomas Browne Institute, 1961), p. 53; Best, *Chvrches Plea*, p. 7.

[77] John Cotton, *The Way of Congregational Churches Cleared: In Two Treatises* (London, 1648), p. 8.

mercy) obteyned them before their faces." What more could the nonseparatist Puritans desire? The Separatists demanded: "For what is it they [Separatists] practise you professe not and teach others both to pray for and practise?" Robinson sincerely believed and "would often say" that their severest Puritan critics "if they were in a place wher they might have libertie and live comfortably, they would practise as they did."[78]

The Separatists had their largest churches in the Netherlands, three to four hundred members at the Ancient Church of Amsterdam and three hundred or more members at Leiden, and as leaders they had the most talented Separatist intellectuals of the early seventeenth century. Matthew Slade, elder of the church, became one of Amsterdam's leading scholars, a "walking library" and rector of the Latin School. Henry Ainsworth, although not a university graduate, by enormous effort mastered the Hebrew language and was among the keenest Hebraists of the day. The egoistic Hugh Broughton challenged Ainsworth's standing in Hebrew, smearing him as an "unspeakeable" ignoramus, but he could not undermine his reputation.[79] Johnson, Robinson, Smyth, and Canne were thought-provoking, creative theologians, capable of making a good showing in theological debate.

The Separatists made notable contributions by their example of the separated church in English history and their commitment to simplified, spiritual worship.[80] Their reforms occurred independent of the state. Separation of church and state was no intrinsic Separatist value but only the practical outworking of their policies in England and the Netherlands. "Reformation without tarying for anie" so antagonized state authorities that the Separatists were cut off from all official favor. Their separation, they were convinced, was a necessary secession from evil. The Church of England was irreparably evil, and the Separatist Confession of 1596 denounced it as "false and counterfeit, deceyving hir children with vaine titles of the word, Sacraments, Ministerie, &c. having indeed none of these in the ordinance and powre of Christ emongst them."[81] These were no small blemishes. Johnson in his debate with Henry Jacob listed 96 Antichristian abominations still retained in the English church, such dread corruptions as "confusion" ("of maner of people though never so wicked and prophane"), her "false doctrines," her "fundamental errors," also such flaws as idol-temples, persecutions,

---

[78] Confession of 1596, Walker, *Creeds*, p. 56; Sabine Staresmore, *The Vnlawfvlnes of Reading in Prayer* (n.p., 1619), p. 44; Bradford, *History*, p. 45.

[79] C. P. Burger, Jr., "Een Metselaar-Latinist," *Het Boek*, 20 (1931), 305-10; *D.N.B.*, s.v. Ainsworth, Slade; Broughton's canards are in Broughton, *Certayne Questions* (n.p., 1605), pp. 4, 25, and in *Works*, "An Admonition to Mr. Francis Blackwell."

[80] Davies, *Worship of the English Puritans*, p. 97.

[81] Walker, *Creeds*, p. 51.

speaking lies in hypocrisy, will-worship, and superstitions.[82] Separation was supported powerfully by Scriptures from Genesis to Revelation: Genesis 6:2, "Then the sonnes of God saw the daughters of men"; Isaiah 52:11, "Departe ye, departe ye"; Jeremiah 50:8, "Fly from the middest of Babylon"; Hosea 4:15, "Come not yee to Gilgall"; Acts 2:40, "Save yourselves"; Revelation 18:4, "And I heard another voice from heaven, saying, Come out of her, my people." Who, being tender of conscience, could do less than separate? "That separation which is onely from syn, and communion therewith, is of God, & is al good mens dutie."[83]

"But you excommunicate in effect all Churches," rebuked the anti-Separatists.[84] Not entirely so. The Separatist relationship to the foreign Reformed churches was not absolute renunciation. Separatists considered themselves to be Reformed churches, standing with "all faythfull people at this day in Germanie, France, Scotland, the Low-Contries, Bohemia, and other Christian Churches rownd about vs."[85] No established Reformed church welcomed fraternal ties with the Separatists because of their notorious reputation; moreover, the Separatists made themselves further obnoxious by being habitually critical of the practices of the Dutch Reformed Church. The position of the English Separatists to the Reformed Churches was comparable to the position taken by the non-Separatist Puritans to the Church of England: although a true church, it was defective. Separatist members of Amsterdam were disciplined for attending the Dutch church, and Ainsworth and Johnson scolded much about deficiencies of the Reformed. Deep hostility had been generated between the two churches by the rigid Separatist discipline, nor was it forgotten that Jean de l'Ecluse had withdrawn from the French church because of alleged sins in their public worship. Neither side trusted the other. The accusations went back and forth—"If you esteem us as no church, we certainly esteem you as no church."[86]

Throughout the debates, however, the Separatist theologians were careful to avoid any unconditional renunciation of the Dutch Reformed Church. Theologically they accepted the predestinarian tenets of Calvinism; and when not embroiled in some public dispute, they were willing to give a good word for the Reformed churches, including the

---

[82] Quoted in Henry Jacob, *A Defence of the Chvrches and Ministry of Englande* (Middelburg, 1599), pp. 26-28; also Francis Johnson, *An Answer to Maister H. Jacob* (n.p., 1600), pp. 63-66 and index.

[83] Jacob, *Defence*, p. 5; Johnson, *Answer to Jacob*, preface; Ainsworth, quoted by Paget, *Arrow*, p. A3v.

[84] Broughton, *Works*, p. 722.

[85] Confession of 1596, Walker, *Creeds*, p. 55.

[86] Paget, *Arrow*, p. 46; R. B. Evenhuis, *Ook dat was Amsterdam* (Amsterdam: W. Ten Have, 1965-74), II, 227.

Dutch, which "may for the faith of Christ which they professe, wel be estemed."[87] Robinson of Leiden had a positive relationship with the Dutch Reformed church and readily acknowledged communion with them "in the substance of things." Ainsworth and Canne were the most scrupulous Separatists but even they found some hope for Reformed churches. The Reformed churches exceeded the Church of England in all respects, said Canne, "for in theire constitution, ministry, worship, and government they are as opposite as light and darknesse one to another."[88]

Having renounced evil and lukewarm Christianity, the Separatists gathered the saints into congregations. They expected to be but a handfull, because the gathered church "when it is at the greatest, is but a little flock and smal remnant."[89] The Separatist doctrine of the gathered church began with Robert Browne, the first Separatist theologian; "the Church planted or gathered, is a companie or number of Christians or beleeuers, which by a willing couenant made with their God, are vnder the gouernment of god and Christ, and kepe his lawes in one holie communion." The Confession of 1596 (printed at Amsterdam) called for joining "together in Christian communion and orderly couenant."[90] The instrument of gathering was a double covenant, first the promise to keep the faith in God by Christ, and second, to observe God's laws in love and to walk in God's ways. The positive aspect was to profess faith, the negative was to renounce evil and separate. "Unto this ar all that make profession of faith and obedience, to be admitted, without respect of persons."[91]

The covenants of the Ancient Church and Robinson's church at Leiden were more spiritual than legal written documents. Written legalistic covenants survive from some of the stricter non-Separatist English Reformed Churches (Rotterdam, Amsterdam, Middelburg, the Merchants Adventurers, Arnhem) but not from the Separatists. John Quick, who resided in the Netherlands 1680-81, made a search for written covenants in the Netherlands churches and found a few but none at

---

[87] Johnson, *Christian Plea*, "To the Reader," and p. 245.

[88] Ainsworth, *Covnterpoyson*, p. 16; John Canne, *A Necessitie of Separation* (n.p., 1634), p. 188; John Robinson, *Works*, III, 48; Alice C. Carter, "John Robinson and the Dutch Reformed Church," *Studies in Church History*, ed. G. J. Cuming, vol. 3 (Leiden: E. J. Brill, 1966), 232-41.

[89] Henry Ainsworth, *The Commvnion of Saincts* (n.p., 1615), p. 340.

[90] Browne, *Book which sheweth*, in *The Writings of Robert Harrison and Robert Browne*, ed. Albert Peel and Leland H. Carlson (London: George Allen and Unwin, 1953), p. 253; Champlin Burrage, *The Church Covenant Idea: Its Origin and Development* (Philadelphia: American Baptist Publication Society, 1904), pp. 36-39, 58-59; Walker, *Creeds*, p. 69 (art. 33).

[91] Ainsworth, *Commvnion of Saincts*, pp. 340-44; Johnson, *Answer to Jacob*, p. 196.

Leiden or Amsterdam for the Separatists, "all of them having been lost by the negligence of church officers."[92] The actual procedure for admission to the church was described by John Canne as a three-step process: (1) to go for examination and instruction before the elders who would propound the name to the congregation; (2) to go before the public assembly of the congregation and "there he is to make a profession of Faith, and to be asked sundrie needfull questions"; (3) "being found worthie," by the consent of the whole church, he is joyfully to be taken into their communion.[93]

Separatist worship differed from ordinary Reformed worship by its greater simplicity and spontaneity. Along with throwing out the official Prayer Book, Separatists went a step further and eliminated all written service books and formal prayers, even the Lord's Prayer. Forms and ritual, they warned, were merely "stinted" and "imposed"—"a read and dead service" instead of spiritual worship. Prayer and worship could not be forced into old forms. "Prayer is a powring out of the hart before God, by making requests or giving of thanks according to present need ... through the help & working of the Holy ghost. ... We find that al the holy men of God vsed thus to pray in the spirit, without reading or saying by rote any number of words."[94] At best this free style fostered warmth and participation, at worst it degenerated into noisy pandemonium ("another Westminster Hall").[95] A child, infidel, or idiot can read prayers and service from a book, but a free worshipping congregation of saints opens the door to "the spirits motion in us."[96] John Smyth and Thomas Helwys exceeded everyone else in sweeping out stinted worship by refusing all songbooks and even written Bible translations. Smyth would have had preachers translating by voice from Hebrew and Greek originals, since New Testament worship was spiritual and proceeds from the heart, not books. The Johnson-Ainsworth Separatists thought this an extreme position.[97]

Separatist theology taught that all the saints, male at least, had gifts for prophesying in the congregation and helping in its governance. However, rumors of a Separatist "democracy" were much exaggerated.

---

[92] Quick, "Icones," I, i, 258.

[93] Canne, *Necessitie of Separation*, chapter 4. The identical process, nearly word for word is found in the anonymous *A Guide unto Sion or Certain Positions* (n.p., 1638), p. 30.

[94] Ainsworth, quoted by Paget, *Arrow*, p. A3v; Ainsworth, in *Certayne Questions*, pp. 11-12; Staresmore, *Vnlawfvlnes of Reading in Prayer*, p. 1; Johnson, *Christian Plea*, pp. 245-49.

[95] Add. MS. 29,492, fol. 11.

[96] Staresmore, *Vnlawfvlnes of Reading in Prayer*, pp. 22, 26.

[97] Henry Ainsworth, *A Defence of the Holy Scriptures, Worship, and Ministerie* (Amsterdam, 1609), pp. 1-4; Walter Burgess, *John Smith the Se-Baptist, Thomas Helwys and the First Baptist Church in England* (London: James Clark, 1911), pp. 122-33.

Random members did not preach, administer the sacraments, and handle the discipline; "we deny it," Ainsworth said.[98] Nevertheless, the Separatist congregations pioneered in wide congregational participation. Officers were elected "by the free choyse of the congregation wherein they are to administer." Discipline was handed out in the congregation. Congregational business meetings and even services of worship were open to the gifts of the ordinary lay members. Johnson upheld lay participation in the "exercise of prophecy" including interpretation of Scripture, disputing points of religion, answering of question, "els the diversities of gifts in men, are not knowen, nor used, as they might be." Ainsworth, although decrying "popular government" one moment, the next was urging strong lay participation. Ordinary members were not to be forbidden all speaking and expounding in public nor excluded from congregation decision-making. Excommunication, said Ainsworth, belongs not to bishops with Latin writ nor to aristocratic elderships. Thus "our difference also and dislike of the Presbyteries practice where people are excluded, and deprived of a great part of their Christian liberty and benefit therby."[99] The degree of congregational participation actually to be practiced was a determining factor in the Johnson-Ainsworth split of 1610. Johnson took the more authoritarian position, "advancing the Elders, disgracing the people"; Ainsworth took the more democratic position of shared responsibility between elders and congregation.[100]

The most disturbing Separatist issue, the relationship to outside churches, went to the heart of Separatism's reason for being. Ainsworth and Canne took the position of rigid separation of all religious interaction with the Church of England, and Johnson and Robinson also began at this point. Late in his career, Johnson in *Christian Plea* (1618) moved to a more liberal position of acknowledging the lawfulness of the Church of England, and even the Roman Catholic church in some respects, but, because of their great corruptions, refusing communion with them. Baptism of the Roman Catholics must be regarded as an ordinance of God, not to be despised in an Anabaptistical manner; and at this late date, Johnson also discovered that the Church of England had possession of the covenant and baptism of the Lord and many "precious doctrines."[101] Although still Separatist in all practical respects, Johnson's position

---

[98] Ainsworth, *Covnterpoyson*, pp. 174-77.
[99] Canne, *Necessitie of Separation*, p. 7; Johnson, *Christian Plea*, p. 281; Ainsworth, *Covnterpoyson*, p. 178.
[100] Francis Johnson, *A Short Treatise Concerning the Exposition of These Words of Christ, Tell the Church* (n.p., 1611); Ainsworth, *Animadversion*, preface; Ainsworth, *A Reply to a Pretended Christian Plea* (n.p., 1620), preface.
[101] Johnson, *Christian Plea*, pp. 215-16.

rocked the Separatist boat, and Ainsworth felt obliged to answer in a *Reply to a Pretended Christian Plea* (1620).

As theology began to diverge, so did practice. Robinson's church at Leiden moved to a generous membership policy which admitted some Christians, not previously Separatist church members, without requiring a full Separatist declaration; but the Ancient Church held to the traditional strict position. Sabine Staresmore tried to transfer into Amsterdam from Henry Jacob's Independent church at London, a church not absolutely Separatist, being composed of people who "never intended separation from the Church of England." He was turned down at Amsterdam; he then traveled to Leiden and applied for membership there, which was given.[102] Returning to Amsterdam, Staresmore was briefly admitted and then excommunicated. His previous church membership was judged to be not separated and thus unlawful. Jacob, they said, had a Samaritan church with a "Samaritanesh covenant," meaning a church with a confused or mixed religion. The Leiden church, without fanfare or public declaration, quietly began a de facto communion with some churches outside the Separatist fold. Thereafter, the strict Amsterdam Separatists regarded the Leiden church as having "declined or apostated," and the posthumous publication of Robinson's *Lawfulnes of Hearing of the Ministers in the Church of England* (1634) was a further embarrassment to the Separatist brotherhood. Canne was inspired to write a rebuttal, *A Stay against Straying* (1639).[103]

Robinson's broadening views, although never absolutely renouncing his past Separatism, brought him to a semi-Separatist position little different in its functioning from the non-Separatist Congregationalism of Jacob, Ames, and Parker. Robinson's late writings are a bridge across the Puritan factions and his church was a "bridge" of practical churchmanship. Robinson "opened so many pathe wayes."[104]

Church Groups: Presbyterians, Congregationalists, Anabaptists, Quakers, and Anglicans

In the free environment of the Netherlands, the Puritan movement split into many factions. Presbyterianism, Congregationalism (Separatist and non-Separatist), Anabaptism, and Quakerism all had adherents.

---

[102] A. T., *A Christian Reprofe against Contention* (n.p., 1631), pp. 5-19, 33-34; Tolmie, *The Triumph of the Saints*, pp. 12-19; Burgess, *John Robinson*, pp. 291-97.

[103] A. T., *Christian Reprofe*, pp. 19-20.

[104] Ibid., pp. 19-20. On Robinson's relationship to Separatism, see B. R. White, *The English Separatist Tradition* (Oxford: Oxford Univ. Press, 1971), pp. 158-59, and Stephen Brachlow "More Light on John Robinson and the Separatist Tradition," *Fides et Historia*, 13 (Fall 1980), 6-22.

Some English people retained loyalty to Church of England Episcopalianism. The theologians and practicing congregations of the Netherlands helped to develop the doctrines of the various groups; they also argued polemically among themselves. Puritans started with the Bible. William Bradshaw's much-valued treatise, *English Puritanisme* (1605) began with the right Puritan note: "The word of God contained in the writings of the Prophets and Apostles, is of absolute perfection, giuen by Christ the head of the Churche, to bee vnto the same, the sole Canon and rule of all matters of Religion, and the worship and seruice of God whatsoeuer."[105] Then he proceeded to draw strictly Congregationalist conclusions. Presbyterians, also starting with the Bible, assumed the Word led invariably to Presbyterianism. John Smyth thought the rule of Scripture led to Anabaptism. No matter how much dedicated to the Word of God, free Biblical speculation led not to one but to many conclusions. New situations, not detailed in the Bible, called for fresh interpretations. Even so thorough a Biblicist as Henry Ainsworth admitted as much in his book of Psalms for singing, "Englished both in Prose and Meeter" in which he had to resort to human tunes for the music, having found no tunes dictated personally by God.[106] Francis Johnson found himself in the ironical position of accusing the Papists and the Anabaptists of being too Biblical, the Papists for rigidity on "This is my body," the Anabaptists for pressing literally "Teach all nations and baptise them."[107] Puritan theologians, who accused the Anglican prelates of being loose in Biblical interpretation, themselves sometimes found it necessary to go beyond the very words of the Bible and deduce obvious grounds or some "pregnant consequence" of the Bible.[108] Thus the factions.

The most long-standing theological position of the Netherlands Puritans was Reformed or Presbyterian. Beginning with the Merchant Adventurers church of Cartwright, Travers, and Fenner, the church practiced Reformed worship and church government. During the seventeenth century, the chief Dutch Presbyterian defenders were the Pagets (John, Thomas, and Robert) and some of the Scottish preachers. In fact, Michael Watts credits the Dutch Presbyterians with the most consistent Presbyterian stand of their day. "For the first forty years of the seventeenth century English Presbyterianism survived only among the congregations of English Puritans in the Netherlands, and in particular in the Amsterdam church of which John Paget was pastor." John Paget

---

[105] William Bradshaw, *English Pvritanisme* (n.p., 1605), p. 1.
[106] Staresmore, *Vnlawfvlnes of Reading in Prayer*, p. 3.
[107] Johnson, *Short Treatise*, To the Reader.
[108] Mr. Hy (William Hinde of Banbury), quoted by Thomas Morton, in *A Defence of the Innocencie of the Three Ceremonies of the Chvrch of England* (London, 1618), p. 2.

defended Reformed religion against the Separatists in his *Arrow against the Separation* (1618) and thereafter in his later books, *An Answer to the unjust complaints of William Best* (1635) and *A Defence of Chvrch-Government, Exercised in Presbyteriall, Classicall, & Synodall Assemblies* (1641), against the Independents. John with his brother Thomas Paget (Amsterdam preacher 1639-46) and his nephew Robert Paget (Dort preacher 1638-83) made a formidable phalanx of Presbyterians. Their analysis of recent events was that Protestantism was beset by two extreme evils, on the one side tyrannical bishops and pope, on the other side the Brownists and their allies the Independents. The latter (the Jacobites) they traced to Henry Jacob, "when Orthodox men began first to be stained with it."[109] Presbyterianism, said John Paget, is "appointed by God."[110]

The two doctrines most necessary for Paget to defend were the power of the eldership and the presbyterial power of classes and synods. Paget was pathetically saddened to see his Presbyterian life work of nearly forty years undermined by the Jacobite-Amesian Puritans. He wrote to David Calderwood in 1637, "it is a trouble unto me to see so many seekers of reformation, so to oppose the government of the Reformed Churches in Classes and Synods," especially at Rotterdam. "I feare a great evill to ensue hereupon."[111] Paget's last years were painfully troubled by a Congregationalist faction in his church, headed by Hooker and Davenport, but he outlasted all of his enemies. Throughout its history, the Amsterdam church belonged to the Amsterdam Classis and the Synod of North Holland.

William Spang of Veere and Middelburg, a cousin of Robert Baillie, was a proponent of Scottish Presbyterianism. Through Baillie he became a Presbyterian agent for rallying Dutch Reformed opinion against English Independency. His books, *Brevis et Fidelis Narratio Motuum in Regno & Ecclesia Scotica* (1640) and *Historia Rerum Nuper in Regno Scotiae Gestarum* (1641) gave a glorious history of the Church of Scotland and reveal him to be "a most zealous champion of Presbytery."[112] Alexander Forbes (or Patrick Forbes) wrote *The Anatomy of Independency* (1644), a sharp answer to the *Apologeticall Narration*. Forbes, apparently from the family of John Forbes of Delft, had lived in Holland and had first hand information about Dutch church affairs. He slanted his material in favor

---

[109] Robert Paget, "The Publisher to the Christian Reader," Thomas Paget, "Humble Advertisement to Parliament," in John Paget, *Defence of Chvrch-Government* (London, 1641). Michael R. Watts, *The Dissenters* (Oxford: Clarendon Press, 1978), I, 60. For the use of the term "Jacobite," see B.P., I, 139 (1633); S.P. 16, vol. 286, no. 94 (1633).

[110] Paget, *Defence*, p. 29.

[111] Wodrow MSS, Folio XLII, fol. 253 (Nat. Library of Scotland).

[112] Quick, "Icones," I, i, 271. For Baillie's negotiations with Spang, see Baillie's *Letters and Journals*.

of the Presbyterians and against the Independents.[113] Another of the Dutch Presbyterian group was Thomas Edwards (of *Gangraena* fame). He came to Amsterdam as a lay person in 1647, still at work on "some treatises," and died there in 1648.[114] A problematic book is Robert Parker's posthumous, *De Politeia Ecclesiastica Christi* (1616). Both Presbyterians and Congregationalists claimed the book as supporting their side. Parker was an old friend of Ames, Jacob, and Robinson; however, when he moved to Amsterdam, Paget boasted of converting Parker back to Presbyterianism. "After much conference with him he plainly changed his opinion."[115] Although somewhat ambiguous, the book has served the Congregationalists much better than the Presbyterians, and it is more accurate to treat Parker with the discussion of the early Congregationalists.

The second major grouping was the Separatist Congregationalists. The Separatist colonies in the Netherlands, whose main immigration was prior to 1610, kept the Separatist faith alive and propagated to the world. In its strictest form, however, Separatism failed to grow much beyond its original families of 1610, and in fact began to decline and fragment. Members were lost to other Puritan factions. Paget had considerable success in winning them back to the English Reformed Church of Amsterdam. Congregationalism or Independency became a major religious movement in England and the Netherlands, not through Separatism, but through the non-Separatist Congregationalists.

This phase of the Congregationalist movement was headed by Henry Jacob, William Bradshaw, William Ames, and Robert Parker.[116] They claimed not to be Separatists from the Church of England, thus hoping to escape the odium of Brownism; nevertheless they were committed to the Congregationalist goals of covenants, gathered churches, independent church government, and Spirit-filled worship. As Separatist goals they

---

[113] The identity of the author of *Anatomy of Independency*, said to be Alexander Forbes, is questionable to me. Alexander Forbes's name is written into the B.M. title page, which is otherwise anonymous. Patrick Forbes might be a more likely author; see Baillie, *Letters and Journals*, II, 181, where he refers to Mr. Forbes of Delft (presumably Patrick Forbes or even James Forbes, sons of John), having sent over "a very prettie piece against the Apologetick. I like it very well, I wish it were in print." (1644) An Alexander Forbes was a medical student at Franeker in 1623 (*Album*, p. 71) and the same or another of the same name was at Leiden in 1624 (*Album*, col. 175).

[114] Edwards's confession of Dec. 17/27, 1647 and his will of Feb. 3, 1648 are in the archives of the Amsterdam E.R.C., Carter, *English Reformed Church*, pp. 201-03.

[115] Paget, *Defence*, pp. 90, 105.

[116] For a discussion of Non-Separatist Congregationalism, see Perry Miller, *Orthodoxy in Massachusetts 1630-1650* (1933, rpt. Boston: Beacon Press, 1959), chapter 4. For a critique of the concept of Non-Separatist Congregationalism, see Geoffrey Nuttall, *Visible Saints* (Oxford, Basil Blackwell, 1957), pp. 9-10.

had been unattainable except in a few scattered conventicles. The goal of the non-Separatist Congregationalists (known in Holland often as "Jacobites" and in England as Independents) was to establish a midway position between Presbyterianism and Separatism, something never before achieved. "Learn a mean betwixt All and Nothing," said William Ames. Goodwin, Nye, Simpson, Burroughes, and Bridge called it "a middle way."[117]

The development of non-Separating Congregationalism is, like Separatism, closely connected with the Netherlands. Its other early center, also overseas, was New England. The leading theologians of the movement did much of their work in Dutch exile, and most of its early books were printed in the Netherlands. One of the earliest manifestoes of Congregationalism was Bradshaw's *English Puritanisme* (1605). It contained "the maine opinions of the rigidest sort of those who are called Puritanes in the Realme of England." By "rigidest sort" was understood "the forward professours which stand out against the Ceremonies," just short of Separatism.[118] Bradshaw's books was taken up by William Ames, who translated it into Latin as *Puritanismus Anglicanus* (Frankfurt, 1610). According to the Bradshaw-Ames approach, rigid Puritanism was Biblically pure and Congregationalist in polity. "They hould and maintaine that euery Companie, Congregation or Assemblie of men, ordinarilie ioyneing together in the true worship of God, is a true visible church of Christ." Increase Mather, speaking for the New England churches, called the book "perfect Congregationalism."[119]

Jacob, Ames, and Parker used the Netherlands for their place of work and refuge. The chief of these non-Separatist theologians was Jacob (Merchant Adventurer preacher about 1599, back in England 1603-05, again in Holland about 1610). Some of his writings and nearly all of his printing was done in the Netherlands. His book presented the case for non-Separatist independent, covenanted churches. "Only a Particular ordinary constant Congregation of Christians in Christes Testament is appointed and reckoned to be a visible Church." In at least one of his writings he spoke of "covenanting" (1605). Jacob returned home and

---

[117] Ames, "To the Reader," in Bradshaw, *The Vnreasonablenesse of the Separation* (Dort, 1614); *Apologeticall Narration*, p. 24. The term "Jacobite" was used in the 1630s (see above, no. 109); Congregationalism and Independency were terms used in the 1640s; Watts, *Dissenters*, I, 94-98.

[118] *Syons Prerogatyve Royal* (Amsterdam, 1641), pp. 36-37. According to Robert Paget, the author of *Syons Prerogatyve* was John Canne; *Defence*, "The Publisher to the Christian Reader."

[119] Bradshaw, *English Puritanisme*, p. 5; Increase Mather, *A Disquisition Concerning Ecclesiastical Councils* (Boston, 1716), pp. v-vi.

established a church of his kind at Southwark in 1616.[120] The church began with a covenant, but unlike the Separatist covenantings, "none of them were separated" from the Church of England.[121] Jacob's theology threw aside all the layers of classical-synodical apparatus and left the independent congregation in charge of its own affairs. Paget interpreted Jacob as creating a new discipline with only one layer of authority, "an independent, single uncompounded policie." "The old discipline of french, Scottish, belgique churches is rejected. And for me," Paget lamented, "I have suffered many things for defence thereof."[122]

Parker's book, *De Politeia Ecclesiastica Christi*, whether or not misunderstood, as Paget claimed, advanced the cause of Jacobite Congregationalism. The publishing of it was in the hands of Congregationalists.[123] Parker laid great stress on the primacy of the local congregation. It "speaks down-right in this thing," claimed John Canne, who enjoyed the book.[124] Congregationalists were fond of quoting the passage, "all ecclesiastical power is always in the whole congregation"; and although such teachings do not absolutely exclude all functions of synods, they suited Congregationalists much better than Presbyterians.[125] Ames's edition of *Puritanismus Anglicanus* was taken as "a peremptory restraint of all Ecclesiasticall authority unto particular Congregations." His two most powerful books, *Medulla Theologiae* and *De Conscientia* interpreted Scripture in favor of independent congregations; "such a congregation or particular Church is a society of believeres joyned together by a special bond among themselves, for the constant exercises of the communion of Saints among themselves." "This bond is a

---

[120] Henry Jacob, *Reasons Taken ovt of Gods Word and the Best Hvmane Testimonies Proving a Necessitie of Reforming Ovr Chvrches in England* (n.p., 1604), p. 5; Tolmie, *Triumph of the Saints*, chapter 1. Jacob's *Divine Beginning* has a preface signed Leiden, 1610; his *Declaration and Plainer Opening* was signed at Middelburg, 1611. On Jacob's career in Holland, see above chapter 2, note 55.

[121] A. T., *Christian Reprofe*, p. 6; Stephen Offwood, *An Advertisement to Ihon Delecluse, and Henry May the Elder*, pt. 2, "Heady and Rash Censures" [Amsterdam, 1632], p. 1.

[122] Paget, *Defence*, p. 30; Jacob, *The Divine Beginning and Institution of Chrtsts Church* (1610), preface; Paget to Calderwood, June 16, 1636, Wodrow MSS, Folio XLII, fol. 254.

[123] The preface was most likely by John Robinson or William Ames, see Frank B. Carr, "The Thought of Robert Parker," pp. 124-25; Marius Bouwman, *Voetius over het gezag der synoden* (Amsterdam: Bakker, 1937), pp. 50-53.

[124] *Syons Prerogatyve Royal*, p. 36.

[125] *De Politeia Ecclesiastica Christi* (Frankfurt, 1616), Lib. III, pp. 24, 28, "Quasi tota authoritatis Ecclesiastica ab ea fluat tanquam a fonte & ad eandem refluat tamquam ad mare," (p. 28) and "Ab initio certe sic fuit, ecclesiae quaeque totae ecclesiasticam potestatem & jurisdictionem exercuerunt semper" (p. 24). Canne in *Syons Prerogatyve Royal*, p. 36 and Best, *Chvrches Plea*, p. 86 quoted this. Paget, *Defence*, p. 106, and Forbes, *Anatomy*, p. 35 claimed Parker for the Presbyterians.

covenant."[126] Ames helped to publish abroad several books of friends of similar opinion. Paul Baynes's *Diocesans Tryall* (Amsterdam, 1621) and William Bradshaw's *Vnreasonablenesse of the Separation* (Dort, 1614) advanced the "new discipline."[127] The New England Congregationalists claimed much inspiration from this Dutch-English circle. The doctrines of the church, John Cotton asserted, "we received by the light of the Word from Mr. *Parker*, Mr. *Baynes*, and Dr. *Ames*."[128]

Congregationalism further advanced intellectually and in practice in the Netherlands during the 1630s. The English Synod had a strong Congregationalist cast. The exiles Peter, Ames, Hooker, and Davenport were active in the cause of writing books and building churches based on the New Puritanism. Peter, Hooker, and Davenport went on to further the movement in England and America. Several of the early figures of Congregationalism in England took refuge in Holland in the late 1630s. The Five Dissenting Brethren (Goodwin, Nye, Simpson, Bridge, and Burroughes) were ministers at Rotterdam and Arnhem, the center of a vigorous Independency-in-exile. The five also spoke of "precious" friends and companions with them, who died in exile (John Archer and Mr. Harris, probably George Harris, reported as having died abroad in 1638).[129] Others of their persuasion were Samuel Bachelor; John Bachelor, who praised Rotterdam Independency in 1641 as "the beautifull face of holinesse"; Samuel Eaton, founder of a Congregational church at Amsterdam; Joseph Symonds and John Ward of Rotterdam; Robert Park of Delft.[130] In the churches at Rotterdam and Arnhem, Eaton's church at Amsterdam, and to some extent at Park's church at Delft, the Congregationalists put their heavenly theories into action, contemporaneous to the development of Congregational churches in New England. When the Netherlands Independents swarmed back to England in 1640 and after, they became the founders of Independent churches in East Anglia, London, and Hull.[131] "All the English ministers of Holland, who are for New England way, are now here," said Robert Baillie (London, March 15, 1641).[132] The Five Brethren on the basis of their experiences at Rotterdam and Arnhem produced *The Apologeticall*

---

[126] Ames, *Marrow*, I, 32, 6 and 15; Paget, *Defence*, p. 106.
[127] Both had prefaces by Ames.
[128] Cotton, *Way of Congregational Churches*, p. 13.
[129] *Apologeticall Narration*, p. 12. Edwards, *Antapologia*, p. 187, identified the friends who died in the Netherlands as Archer and Harris. On Harris, see Venn and Venn, II, 311. For the Dissenting Brethren in the Netherlands, see above chapters 6 on Rotterdam and 8 on Arnhem, and Berndt Gustafsson, *The Five Dissenting Brethren: A Study of the Dutch Background of Their Independentism*, Lunds Univ. Årsskrift, 51 (1955).
[130] For Bachelor's confession of Independency, see Edwards, *Antapologia*, p. 185.
[131] Tolmie, *Triumph of the Saints*, pp. 95, 104-07.
[132] Baillie, *Letters and Journals*, I, 311.

Narration, a milestone document of Congregationalism, and expounded their position in the Westminster Assembly.

The vigor of the Dutch Congregationalists provoked many controversies with old, entrenched Presbyterian Puritans. Forbes in his pro-Presbyterian *Anatomy of Independency* identified the dividing issue as the nature of the church, whether gathered or parishional; Forbes would confine congregations within the bounds of a distinct parish whereas the Congregationalists would gather their churches without any such confinement.[133] In the face of habitual controversy, Separatists and non-Separatists ("Congregationalists" or "Independents") gradually converged in the Netherlands, America, and England. Robinson urged the immigrants to Plymouth to "endeavour to close with the godly party of the Kingdom of England: and rather to study union than division."[134] After the Restoration of 1660, in Amsterdam the venerable Ancient Church, nearly the mother church of Separatism, became known simply as the Independent Church.

Divisions between Congregationalists and Presbyterians in Holland were quarrels within the Reformed bailiwick. The emergence of English Anabaptist and Quaker groups pulled English dissent much farther afield. English Anabaptism had a long history in the Netherlands, at first as an offshoot of Brownism. The first true English Anabaptist congregations were established at Amsterdam by Smith and Helwys. Smyth's church became Anabaptist in 1608, and Helwys's was founded in 1610. Neither church remained long as a distinct congregation in Amsterdam, Smyth's merging with the Dutch Mennonites and Helwys's immigrating back to England in 1612. Thereafter English Anabaptists at Amsterdam joined the Dutch Mennonites. Smyth and Helwys were the chief theologians of early English Anabaptism, especially of the General Baptist wing. The distinctive theological tenets of Smyth were believer's baptism, free will, pacifism, and the general atonement.[135] Smyth's deviations aroused great hostility among Calvinistic Puritans, who attacked him as an unclean pariah stricken with "blindnes."[136] Nicholas Rushe, a non-Separatist, violently attacked all Mennonites and threatened them with "gallows and halter."[137]

---

[133] Forbes, *Anatomy*, p. 21; C. G. Bolam, et al., *The English Presbyterians* (London: George Allen & Unwin, 1968), pp. 93-94.

[134] Edward Winslow, in Edward Arber, *The Story of the Pilgrim Fathers, 1606-1623* (London: Ward and Downey, 1897), p. 183. On definitions and relationships among Separatists, Congregationalists, and Independents, see Watts, *Dissenters*, pp. 94-98, where he refers to all three as "branches of the larger tree of Independency."

[135] For Anabaptism in Amsterdam, see above, chapter 3.

[136] Ainsworth, *Defence of Holy Scripture*, p. 3.

[137] Acta Classis Brielle, vol. E3a, April 26, 1622 (N.H.A.).

After the early seventeenth century, the Smyth-Helwys period, no additional Anabaptist congregations were formed in the Netherlands, and only one preacher, Timothy Batt, converted to Anabaptism. Batt, who was a chaplain serving with English troops at Nijmegen in 1639, became a "wederdooper" (Anabaptist) after leaving his charge. He wrote a letter in 1641 to the Nijmegen Dutch consistory "in which he showed the reasons, by means of a booke he sent along, for his having become an Anabaptist." Whether the Anabaptist book was his own writing or from another author is not stated.[138] Batt became active as a Baptist in England in the 1640s.[139]

During the 1640s and 1650s Anabaptist ideas gained ground among some members of the experimental English congregations at Arnhem and Rotterdam, being accounted "a very tolerable errour," but no large groups were won over. Symonds of Rotterdam complained of being "pestered" with Anabaptists in his church—"grosse Anabaptists."[140] A faction at Arnhem, after Archer's death, was "generally" Anabaptist and would listen to no preaching in favor of baptism of children. One of their lay preachers, Henry Lawrence, preached Anabaptist sermons.[141] At Delft a Robert Amersone shocked the church by announcing for Anabaptism and separatism in 1651. His reason was that he doubted the Reformed practice of "baptisme, separatione, and publike worship." He expressed an "opinione of the inutilitie of infant baptisme, he said. Yea, and after long reasoning said, he knew no benefite of his own baptisme, and that it made no distinction twixt us and others, and that wee in baptizing did not according to the word." The remainder of the consistory felt obliged to suspend him from office and vote excommunication.[142] Anabaptism, although the smallest of the English theological groups in the Netherlands, made a distinct contribution to English religion. Apart from its distinctive denominational message, Smyth and his circle were the earliest English Puritans to stand for absolute democracy in the congregation and religious freedom for all Christians.[143]

Quakers began appearing in the Netherlands in 1655. William Caton and John Stubbs started the work with a missionary journey in 1655 to

---

[138] Acta Kerkeraad Nijmegen, II, Mar. 21, 1641 (N.H.K. Nijmegen).

[139] Batt of Nijmegen is probably the Timotheus Batt of John Stalham and Timotheus Batt, *The Summe of a Conference at Terling in Essex, Januarie 11, 1643* (London, 1644). Batt is mentioned in *Transactions* of the Baptist Historical Society, 3, p. 122, and vol. 6, p. 222. Thomas Edwards, *Gangraena* (London, 1646), pt. I, 35, 93, also mentions a person of this name.

[140] Forbes, *Anatomy*, pp. 6-7; Petrie, *Chiliasto-mastix*, p. 3; Baillie, *Disvassive* (1645), p. 119; Brook, *Puritans*, III, 39.

[141] Edwards, *Gangraena*, pt. III, 99-100. See Lawrence's, *Of Baptisme* (1646).

[142] Delft C.R., no. 102, fols. 2-3 (Jan. 15, 22, Feb. 5, May 7, 19, 1651).

[143] Watts, *Dissenters*, I, 44-48.

Flushing, Middelburg, and Rotterdam. William Ames (the Quaker, not the Franeker professor of the same name) began missionary journeys in 1656. At Amsterdam "seuerall receiued my testimony." Ames, the chief apostle of Quakerism to Holland, was an ex-Baptist preacher; he died at Amsterdam in 1662. The Quaker missionaries came back every year and built up permanent Quaker meetings at Amsterdam, Rotterdam, Leiden, Haarlem, and other towns.[144] Unlike the Presbyterians, Congregationalists, and Anabaptists, who functioned among expatriate English and Scots, the Quakers were a missionary fellowship converting English, Dutch, and all creatures. Because of preaching success among the Dutch, Holland Quakerism became culturally Dutch and functioned in the Dutch language, nevertheless with many contacts with English Quakerism. When William Penn visited the Rotterdam meeting in 1686, he preached "a good Ingenious English Sermon, to his Dutch Congregation"; fortunately he had a good translator.[145] The Quaker message was for extreme simplicity of life and worship (rejection of tithes and outward sacraments, no distinction between clergy and laity, also refusal to remove hats and observe other social niceties). Ames's sermons laid great stress upon the Inner Light.[146]

Quaker missionaries went first to the British churches but made little headway among the English-Scottish settlers. The Quakers were not welcome in any of the English churches, because when they attended, they tried to take over the service and proselytize. Caton and Stubbs in 1655 received hard treatment from the Flushing and Middelburg English churches ("great Indignation, and some Violence," but not imprisonment). Christopher Birkhead visited Middelburg in 1657 but fared worse, receiving a workhouse sentence of two years at hard labor for interrupting the worship at the English church.[147] When William Ames first came to Amsterdam in 1656, he took his message to the English churches, both English Reformed and Brownist, but the word fell on stony hearts. The Brownist preacher, being interrupted in the service, "thrust me out & shutt ye door to keep me out" (1656). The indomitable Quakers raised specters of social disorder and chaos: visions of new Münsterites. They refused to take off hats before magistrates. They

---

[144] William I. Hull, *The Rise of Quakerism in Amsterdam 1655-1665* (Swarthmore: Swarthmore College Monographs on Quaker History, no. 4, 1938), pp. 17-28, 102-110; William C. Braithwaite, *The Beginnings of Quakerism*, 2nd ed. (Cambridge: Cambridge Univ. Press, 1955), p. 412. See also J. Z. Kannegieter, *Geschiedenis van de vroegere Quakergemeenschap te Amsterdam, 1656 tot begin negentiende eeuw* (Amsterdam: Scheltema & Holkema, 1971).

[145] William I. Hull, *William Penn and the Dutch Quaker Migration to Pennsylvania* (Swarthmore: Swarthmore College Monographs on Quaker History, no. 2, 1935), p. 117.

[146] Hull, *Rise of Quakerism*, pp. 25, 230-31, 306.

[147] Middelburg C.R., I, 183-85; Hull, *Rise of Quakerism*, pp. 105, 178.

disturbed Reformed worship services. Ames and a co-worker, Humble Thatcher, were arrested in 1657 and banished from Amsterdam for disturbing the peace—but they soon returned.[148]

Robert Mercer, the English Reformed minister, preached anti-Quaker sermons and stirred up the magistrates against Ames. After Ames refused to retreat, and even continued to witness during Mercer's sermons, he was on Christmas day "dragged out, unanswered, by violent hands, severely beaten, kicked by their feet and shamefully mishandled" (1658). This was the second time, Ames complained, that he had been dragged out of the congregation, so he wrote a rebuke against "priest Mercer," *The Protection of the Harmless* (1659).[149] Another missionary, John Higgins, came over to witness to the British, but had equally barren results. At Amsterdam Higgins, like Ames, "was haled out of their Assembly here, by some of the ruder sort."[150] The Middelburg consistory records have entries about the Quaker intruders, but the Amsterdam records omit mentioning them. Having won few adherents among the British, the Quakers turned to preaching among the Dutch. Most of their converts came from the Dutch, the Mennonites and Collegiants being a richly fertile field—"white unto harvest," said Ames. Among the earliest Mennonite converts were Jakob Willemszoon Sewel and Judith Zinspenning of Amsterdam, the parents of historian William Sewel.[151]

Because their message was strange, the early Quakers faced surprisingly vicious opposition from Dutch magistrates and churchmen. The Dutch had learned to tolerate Brownists, Anabaptists, Independents, Jews, and Socinians, but it took a long time to love the Quakers. In the first few years Quakers received penalties of fines, banishment, or imprisonment at Amsterdam, Gouda, Leiden, Haarlem, Middelburg, Flushing, Utrecht, Zutphen, Rotterdam, and Schiedam. Mobs frequently attacked Quakers.[152] William Ames was seized by Dutch officers at Moordrecht and thrown into the dolhuis (madhouse) for several weeks; but he turned the persecution into a triumph. Ames considered it worthy of a book, *An Account of the persecution and imprisonment of William Ames and Maerten Maertensz, servants of Jesus Christ, and imprisoned for his name's sake in*

---

[148] Hull, *Rise of Quakerism*, p. 24; Kannegieter, *Quakergemeenschap*, pp. 14-15; William Sewel, *The History of the Rise, Increase, and Progress of the Christian People Called Quakers* (Philadelphia: Friends' Book Store, 1856), I, 220.

[149] Hull, *Rise of Quakerism*, pp. 60-62; Ames's book was in Dutch, *De Bescherminge der onnoosele tegens ... Priester Mercer*. Robert Mercer was assistant minister at the English 1656-59.

[150] Ibid., p. 189.

[151] Braithwaite, *Beginnings*, p. 409; Hull, *Rise of Quakerism*, p. 267.

[152] Hull, *Rise of Quakerism*, pp. 231-32; H. A. Enno van Gelder, *Getempeerde vrijheid* (Groningen: Wolters-Noordhoff, 1972), pp. 72-74.

the mad-house at Rotterdam (1659).[153] In spite of early persecutions, the Netherlands was a busy place of Quaker preaching and printing. They were not a large group but they were persistent. "Quakers they are not without, no more then we," wrote an English traveler.[154]

The Anglicans, the conformable Church of England ministers, compose the final theological group. Prior to the English Revolution they were few, but having steady support from Laud and ambassador Boswell, the loyal Anglicans were able to preserve a minimal presence of the Prayer Book. The English town churches were *gereformeerde gemeenten*; and because of their close ties with the Dutch Reformed Church and the Dutch government, Episcopal Anglican influences were small among them. The military chaplains serving under English officers were more suspectible to Laudian pressure. The sixteenth- and early seventeenth-century chaplains possessed Prayer Books and frequently read some parts of the service, although omitting ceremonies of kneeling and adoration. Sir William Boswell obtained information that the Prayer Book had been somewhat used in the regiment of Sir Horace Vere until about 1620, one captain recalling the use of the book at the seige of Ostend (1601-04). Thomas Scott had a Prayer Book at Utrecht, but Elborough, who came in 1626, ceased reading it. Although the book may have been brought to service, the Puritan chaplain made grudging use of it, "some things he left out," or substituted "words of his owne."[155]

During the reign of the English Synod, the Prayer Book and Anglican liturgy, whatever little remained of them, were virtually eliminated from the Netherlands. In the 1630s Laud and Boswell began the rebuilding of a conformist Anglican party. This was accomplished by bringing over from England trustworthy conformists and appointing them into places controllable by Laud, such as the military chaplaincies and the Merchant Adventurers church. From this time forward, a core of Anglican conformists, ideologically believing in Episcopal religion, was re-established in the Netherlands. The most zealous of them was Stephen Goffe, Vere's chaplain. Other conformists were Richard Dell of Breda, Malachi Harris of Utrecht, and George Beaumont of the Merchant Adventurers. Elizabeth of Bohemia at The Hague employed several conformable chaplains (Griffin Higgs, Sampson Johnson, William Stamp, and

---

[153] William I. Hull, *Benjamin Furly and Quakerism in Rotterdam* (Swarthmore: Swarthmore College Monographs on Quaker History, no. 5, 1941), p. 207; Hull gives the title in English translation; it was written in Dutch, *Een beschrijvinge van de vervolginge ende het vangen van William Ames ende Maerten Maertensz., dienst-kneghten Jesu Christi, ende gevangene om sijn getuigenis wille in het dollhuis tot Rotterdam.*

[154] John Northleigh, *Topographical Descriptions* (London, 1702), p. 11. Northleigh's trip to the Netherlands was about 1700.

[155] B.P., I, 161, 250.

George Morley), and Mary, Princess of Orange, preferred similar chaplains (Malachi Harris, Thomas Browne, Robert Sheringham). The marriage contract between Mary and William II guaranteed her right to exercise religion according to the Church of England.

The Anglican chaplains before 1640 were sustained from above by the English church-state apparatus. They had little grass roots support from the English settlers themselves, who preferred the Puritan religion. The authority of high military officers and the Privy Council kept preachers like Goffe and Beaumont in their pulpits. The Laud-Boswell party admitted as much in a petition of 1635: The Anglican church order has "as yet no other ... bottome, but the Colonels power." It was feared that if the power of the colonels over their chaplains were diminished or the captains and lower officers given a voice in choosing them, the conformable chaplains "will find either small or no entertainment if they conforme unto our church, some of the captaines through an indifferency and coldnes, fearing to displease, others through opposition, desiring to please the Dutch upon whom they hope."[156] To be an Anglican conformist during the 1630s, surrounded by Synod Puritans, required daring and a sense of mission. "The honor of our English Church," said Griffin Higgs, "doth stand, or fall in the judgment of men in these parts, by the preaching of us Conforming ministers."[157]

Boswell thought much good could be achieved by building up a positive image of the Church of England among the Dutch. He distributed books by Laud as propaganda pieces, so that "any upright judge may discerne that we are not so black as the malice of men doth paint us." He gave out samples of the Anglican Prayer Book. As a counter measure, Puritans printed and scattered about their own versions of Laud's speeches. Canne of Amsterdam printed Laud's Star Chamber speech against Prynne, Burton, and Bastwick (June 14, 1637), *Divine and Politike Observations* (Right-Right, 1638). This was a butchered version calculated to reveal Laud's ugliness.[158] The Prayer Book was translated into Dutch as a project of Elizabeth of Bohemia and printed at Rotterdam in 1645 and again at Amsterdam in 1711.[159] The establishment of Church of England congregations did not occur until the end of the seventeenth century, Amsterdam in 1698, Rotterdam in 1700.

---

[156] S.P. 84, vol. 149, fol. 37v.
[157] B.P., I, 210.
[158] S.P. 84, vol. 155, fols. 143-44; B.P., II, 34.
[159] Steven, p. 264; Fred. Oudschans Dentz, *History of the English Church at The Hague* (Delft: W. D. Meinema, 1929), pp. 29-30.

CHAPTER THIRTEEN

RELATIONS BETWEEN THE DUTCH AND BRITISH CHURCHES

The English and Scottish churches of the Netherlands, because of their scattered locations, had infrequent contact with one another. They maintained some ties with the churches of their mother countries; other links connected them to the churches of their adopted country. As outposts of English and Scottish religion, the Netherlands British churches were small links in the network of Protestant relationships among England, Scotland, and the United Provinces. The churches of all three nations had a common Reformation heritage; the presbyterial churches of Scotland and the Netherlands had the closest kinship but not excluding the Episcopal Church of England. The clergy of the Dutch Reformed Church accepted the Church of England as orthodox in doctrine albeit somewhat less "reformed" in matters of ceremony and liturgy. The English clergy from their side also expressed reservations about the Dutch church because of some things not to their liking. Puritans praised Dutch religion for its theological excellence but regretted the lack of practical piety. Episcopal Anglicans regarded the Dutch church as unduly tolerant of sects and discerned a deficiency in organization. Bishop George Carleton lectured the Synod of Dort that much of the Arminian disorder would have been remedied by having bishops over the Netherlands church.[1] Sir Clement Edmonds, in the Netherlands on a diplomatic mission in 1615, analyzed the Dutch Reformed Church as having "the shew of a reformed church and their publique exercises make a good face and presence of a Christian Congregacion." Nevertheless, he was offended at the proliferation of Jews and sects. A man might live there all his life and be of no congregation. "Not many eclesiasticall orders nor much ceremony in their service," was another complaint from Anglicans. King Charles I rather sneered at Reformed liturgy as mere "naked and indigested formes."[2]

---

[1] Matthias Graf, *Beyträge zur Kenntniss der Geschichte der Synode von Dordrecht* (Basel, 1825), p. 93.
[2] Tanner MS. 216, fol. 6v; Peter Mundy, *The Travels of Peter Mundy*, Hakluyt Society, 2nd ser., 55 (1924), 68; S.P. 16, vol. 233, no. 4; Norman Sykes, *The Church of England & Non-Episcopal Churches in the Sixteenth & Seventeenth Centuries* (London: S.P.C.K., 1948), pp. 14-23.

Religious ties between Britain and the Netherlands

Two events of the early seventeenth century brought England and Scotland deeply into Dutch church affairs. The first was the Vorstius affair of 1611-12. King James I (James VI of Scotland) cherished exalted visions of himself as the theological governor of Reformed Europe, including some religious superintendency over the Netherlands. When Konrad von der Vorst was named to succeed Arminius as professor of theology at Leiden in 1611, James warned of Socinian dangers. He gave no peace until Vorstius, "this blastphemous monster," had been banished from the university.[3] Ever the master theologian, James instructed ambassador Sir Dudley Carleton (at The Hague 1616-28) never to forget "that you are the minister of that master, whom God hath made the sole protector of his religion."[4]

The other prime event of seventeenth-century British-Dutch church history was the Synod of Dort (1618-19). Because of his early Calvinist upbringing, James took the orthodox side against Arminianism. The early seventeenth century saw furious controversy in the Netherlands between the followers of Arminius (the Remonstrants) and the strict Calvinists (the Contra-Remonstrants). The religious issues became mixed with politics, and finally to settle the free will-predestinarian dispute once and for all, the States General issued a call for a great international Reformed assembly to meet at Dort in 1618. In sending delegates, King James appointed sound, orthodox divines: George Carleton, the bishop of Llandaff; Joseph Hall, the dean at Worcester; John Davenant, master of Queens' College, Cambridge; Samuel Ward, master of Sidney Sussex, Cambridge; Walter Balcanqual, of Scotland; and Thomas Goad, chaplain to Archbishop Abbot, not one of the original five delegates but sent over to replace Hall partway through the synod. The Arminians lost on every controverted point, and the outcome of the synod was the promulgating of a thoroughly Calvinist set of canons. The Canons of Dort affirmed predestination, the limited atonement, the irresistability of grace, and the perseverance of the saints.[5] The Arminians were routed—for the moment.

---

[3] Winwood, *Memorials*, I, 295; Jan den Tex, *Oldenbarnevelt* (Cambridge: Cambridge Univ. Press, 1973), II, 522-37; Frederick Shriver, "Orthodoxy and Diplomacy: James I and the Vorstius Affair," *E.H.R.*, 85 (July 1970), 449-74; W. Nijenhuis, "Saravia en het optreden van Jacobus I tegen de benoeming van Vorstius te Leiden," *N.A.K.*, N.S. 55 (1975), 171-91.

[4] Carleton, *Letters*, p. 6.

[5] A. W. Harrison, *The Beginnings of Arminianism to the Synod of Dort* (London: Univ. of London Press, 1926), chapters 9-10; G. P. van Itterzon, "Engelse belangstelling voor de Canones van Dordrecht," *N.A.K.*, N.S. 48 (1968), 267-80.

The Synod of Dort was a milestone alike of Calvinist and Arminian theology. Even the Arminians in their defeat had gained publicity for their cause. The English excursion into Dutch theology had a double effect, first of advertising official commitment to Calvinism, but second, unintentionally, of scattering new seeds of Arminian free will into British theology. Arminian free will had taken root in a few English hearts prior to the Synod of Dort, but its rapid growth came after 1619. At the Synod the British delegates maintained a Calvinist solidarity except for a slight wavering on article two, the extent of the atonement. Carleton, Goad, and Balcanqual held to the strict interpretation whereas Ward and Davenant learned toward universal atonement. Ward recalled how "some of us were held by some half Remonstrants, for extending the Oblation made to the Father, to all."[6] The delegates returned as heroes of Calvinism, and the king praised their Calvinist contribution to the Synod. He denounced the Remonstrants as "intolerable," and Archbishop Abbot declared them "pertinacious."[7]

The Synod of Dort touched many corners of British theology. In addition to the official six delegates, several more English and Scots attended the conference (among them William Ames, as an advisor to the synod president; John Brinsley, Hall's nephew and secretary; and the ever-memorable John Hales, chaplain to Sir Dudley Carleton).[8] Hales at Dort saw too much of Calvinist rigidity, and there and then bade John Calvin "good-night."[9] Within a few years Arminianism began to infect a good part of the non-Puritan Church of England. Hardly had Joseph Hall returned from the Synod when he saw signs of his "own church begin to sicken of the same disease, which we had endeavored to cure in our neighbours." After Laud succeeded Abbot as archbishop, the theological balance shifted sharply against Calvinism in favor of Arminianism. The Laudians disdained the heavy and inelegant decrees of Dort, nor would they be indebted to some Dutch "village" for their theology.[10] Arminianism played the opposite role in England than in the Netherlands, in the latter associating with the liberal tolerant party, in England with the authoritarian state-church establishment.

---

[6] Richard Parr, *The Life of the Most Reverend Father in God, James Usher* (London, 1686), p. 68.

[7] *Cal. S.P.D.*, 1619-23, pp. 64, 67.

[8] Keith L. Sprunger, *The Learned Doctor William Ames* (Urbana: Univ. of Illinois Press, 1972), pp. 54-57; Matthews, *Cal. R.*, p. 75; John Hales, *Golden Remains* (London, 1673), which contains his reports from Dort.

[9] Hales, *Golden Remains*, "Mr. Fairndon's Letter."

[10] Joseph Hall, *Works* (Oxford, 1837-39), I, xxxii; H. Hensley Henson, *Studies in English Religion in the Seventeenth Century* (London: John Murray, 1903), pp. 29-30; Irvonwy Morgan, *Prince Charles's Puritan Chaplain* (London: George Allen & Unwin, 1957), p. 162; William Laud, *Works* (Oxford, 1847-60), VI, 246.

In Scotland the Canons of Dort gained a wide acceptance. Although the Scots had been given slight representation at the synod, only Balcanqual, the strongly Calvinist decisions of Dort coincided so congenially with Knoxian theology that they immediately were received as statements of excellent religion. Scotland considered the Canons of Dort to be thoroughly agreeable with Scripture, right reason, and the Scottish temperament.[11] Theological connections between Scotland and the Netherlands held firm throughout the seventeenth century. Both churches were avowedly Calvinist and Presbyterian, allowing many occasions for fellowship. Scotland as the poorer area looked to the Netherlands as a strong leader in international Reformed religion. Scots read Dutch theology (favorites were the Canons of Dort, Burgersdijk's logic, and the *De Veritate Religionis Christianae* by Grotius), studied at Dutch universities, served in the Dutch army, and cultivated friendships with Dutch scholars. Many of the students at Leiden University in 1700 were Scots. "Scotland was very much indebted to Dutch theology in the seventeenth century and this influence remained strong until the nineteenth."[12]

The pronouncements of the Synod of Dort helped to set the direction for the Netherlands British churches. English and Scottish preachers, as servants of the Dutch state, were required to adhere to the Canons of Dort. Consequently, Arminianism made almost no headway among preachers or congregations. None of the British preachers deserted the Calvinist cause except for the Anabaptists John Smyth and Thomas Helwys, who adopted the free will and universal atonement tenets of Dutch Mennonitism. William Ames, John Forbes, John Robinson, and Francis Johnson wrote books, or substantial chapters, in defense of the Synod of Dort. If preachers had Arminian doubts, they did their best to restrain them.[13]

Religious intercourse between England and the Netherlands, although not so vigorous as Dutch-Scottish relations, proceeded by many channels, but most strongly via the Puritan wing of the church. English Calvinists cultivated fellowship with orthodox Dutch Calvinists; many ties were built between Puritan pietists and Dutch precisionists. Puritans appreciated Dutch skills in systematic theology. They commended the Dutch for stripping away so thoroughly "the *drosse* of that *overlaying,* &

---

[11] G. D. Henderson, *Religious Life in Seventeenth-Century Scotland* (Cambridge: Cambridge Univ. Press, 1937), pp. 84-86.

[12] Ibid., pp. 72, 78; Andrew Drummond, *The Kirk and the Continent* (Edinburgh: St. Andrew Press, 1956), p. 137.

13 The Scot John Douglas was suspected of Arminianism but cleared himself, Hales, *Golden Remains*, p. 145. Thomas Dennis of 's-Hertogenbosch was suspected of Arminianism, D. Nauta, *Samuel Maresius* (Amsterdam: H. J. Paris, 1935), p. 152.

tyrannizing Prelace. ... They cashiered the Bishops."[14] In spite of Dutch Reformed doctrinal excellence, its daily practice did not measure up to Puritan standards. Puritans looked in vain for visible signs of the "Doctrine of Godliness." William Ames, Thomas Hooker, and the Dissenting Brethren (Goodwin, Nye, Burroughes, Simpson, and Bridge) all repeated the lament, after living in the Netherlands, that "heart religion" was hardly to be found. "The power of godliness, for ought I can see or hear, they know not," wrote Hooker.[15] "The Practicall part, *the power of godlinesse* and the profession thereof, with difference from carnall and formall Christians, had not been advanced and held forth among them, as in this our owne Island," wrote the five brethren.[16] William Ames was warned by Paul Baynes at his immigration to Holland to beware of a "strong head and a cold heart."[17] Nearly every English Puritan preacher to the Netherlands became a missionary of English practical divinity.

Historians of pietism trace a distinct link between English Puritanism and seventeenth-century Dutch pietism.[18] Puritanism with its emphasis upon personal conversion, devotional piety, and strict morality was one of the factors inspiring a reformist, precisionist faction in the Dutch church. The early forerunners of the movement were Jean de Taffin (1529-1602), Godefridus Cornelisz Udemans (1580-1649), and especially Willem Teellinck (1579-1629).[19] In the later seventeenth century Dutch Reformed pietism centered around Gisbertus Voetius, Matthias Nethenus, Jodocus van Lodenstein, Theodorus a Brakel, Jacobus Koelman, Petrus van Mastricht, and the pious woman, Anna Maria van Schurman.[20] The connections between the precise factions in each nation

---

[14] Alexander Leighton, *An Appeal to the Parliament* (n.p., 1629), p. 222; Samuel Balmford, *Habakkuks Prayer Applyed to the Churches Present Occasions* (London, 1659), p. 108; Marvin A. Breslow, *A Mirror of England: English Puritan Views of Foreign Nations, 1618-1640* (Cambridge: Harvard Univ. Press, 1970), chapter 4.

[15] Mather, *Magnalia*, I, 340.

[16] Thomas Goodwin, et al., *The Apologeticall Narration* (London, 1644), p. 4.

[17] Mather, *Magnalia*, I, 245. For Ames's view of the doctrine of godliness see his *Conscience with the Power and Cases thereof* (n.p., 1639), "To the Reader."

[18] Wilhelm Goeters, *Die Vorbereitung des Pietismus in der reformierten Kirche der Niederlande bis zur labadistischen Krisis 1670* (Leipzig: J. C. Hinrichs'sche Buchhandlung, 1911), pp. 21-27; Heinrich Heppe, *Geschichte des Pietismus und der Mystik in der reformirten Kirche, namentlich der Niederlande* (Leiden: E. J. Brill, 1879), pp. 140-43; F. Ernest Stoeffler, *The Rise of Evangelical Pietism* (Leiden: E. J. Brill, 1965), p. 117; Wilhelm Broes, *De Engelsche Hervormde Kerk, benevens haren invloed op onze Nederlandsche, van den tijd der Hervorming* (Delft: De Wed. J. Allart, 1825), II, 163-66.

[19] Stoeffler, *Evangelical Pietism*, pp. 121-33.

[20] Ibid., pp. 148-62; Heppe, *Pietismus*, pp. 144-204; Martin H. Prozesky, "The Emergence of Dutch Pietism," *Journal of Ecclesiastical History*, 28 (Jan. 1977), 29-37; James Tanis, "Reformed Pietism and Protestant Missions," *Harvard Theological Review*, 67 (1974), 65-73.

were maintained by way of books sent back and forth, letters, and by personal visits.

Among the English Puritans in the Netherlands, none was more effective than William Ames in stirring up zeal for practical divinity. From his professor's chair at Franeker University, 1622-33, Ames preached a theology that put dogmatics and practice on an equal footing. "Theology is the doctrine of living to God" (*theologia est doctrina Deo vivendi*).[21] As a teacher of theological students Ames counteracted barren intellectualism by stressing conversion and simplified biblical divinity. In an "Exhortation to the Students of Theology" (1623), Ames made a plea for heart religion, "because I saw that something necessary was lacking." His goal was less controversy and more piety. Having himself been converted by the preaching of William Perkins, Ames exhorted that to be merely *bonus ethicus* ("a well cariaged man outwardly") was not enough; a converted Christian must be *bonus theologus* ("a sincere hearted Christian").[22] At the university Ames gained a kind of notoriety for extreme moral preciseness in matters of drink, piety, hard study, and Sabbath observance. His students were "astonished and stunned."[23] Some received the word gladly, and through missionaries like Ames, the Dutch precisionist movement was fed with choice Puritan doctrines. From the English sprang forth practical divinity "as from a perennial spring," praised Voetius. According to Nethenus, Voetius's colleague at the University of Utrecht, "in England ... the study of practical theology has flourished marvelously; and in the Dutch churches and schools, from the time of Willem Teellinck and Ames it has ever more widely spread, even though all do not take to it with equal interest."[24]

The translation into Dutch and printing of Puritan books in Holland was an enterprise for spreading the Puritan doctrines of Godliness among the Dutch. Writings of William Perkins, William Ames, William Whately, Lewis Bayly, William Whitaker, Thomas Hooker, Richard Sibbes, Paul Baynes, Robert Bolton, Richard Baxter, Daniel Dyke, Thomas Adams, William Prynne, Thomas Cartwright, Henry Ainsworth, and Thomas Goodwin are a few of the Puritan books put into Dutch. The

---

[21] William Ames, *Medulla Theologiae* (Amsterdam, 1627), p. 1.

[22] "Paraenesis ad studiosos theologiae," trans. Douglas Horton, "An Exhortation to the Students of Theology" (1958); Ames, *A Fresh Svit against Human Ceremonies in Gods Worship* (n.p., 1633), pt. I, p. 131.

[23] Sixtinus Amama, "De barbarie oratio," *Anti-Barbarus Biblicus* (Franeker, 1656); Sprunger, *Ames*, pp. 71-95.

[24] Gisbertus Voetius, *Selectae Disputationes Theologicae*, in *Reformed Dogmatics*, ed. John W. Beardslee (New York: Oxford Univ. Press, 1965), p. 269; Matthias Nethenus, introduction to Ames, *Omnia Opera*, trans. Douglas Horton, *William Ames* (Harvard: Harvard Divinity School Library, 1965), p. 15.

traffic in books also went the other way, worthy Dutch books being put into English. Several of Willem Teellinck's books were translated into English.[25]

Among Dutch printers, Willem Christiaensz van der Boxe was the most zealous to bring the Puritan moralistic writings into Dutch. He printed in 1633 *Den witten duyvel*, a translation of Thomas Adam's *The White Devil or the Hypocrite Vncased* (1613), a treatise against the vices of the flesh—immoderate diet, vainglorious building, thieving, and unconcern for the poor. In 1637 he printed Prynne's *News from Ipswich* (in Dutch, *Hier, wat nieuws uyt Ipswich*) and in 1639 Prynne's anti-theater polemic, *Histrio-Mastix (in Dutch, Histrio-Mastix ofte schouw-spels treur-spel*, translated by I. H.). The Christiaensz edition boiled the over 1000 pages of the original text into 136 pages. Why translate Prynne into Dutch? According to I. H.'s preface, "it is necessary to speak out against the theater." Until then, only one small book existed in Dutch on the evil of the theater, written by Georgius Nolthenius and printed at Kampen in 1600. In the precisionist spirit of Prynne and Teellinck, Christiaensz's version speaks out against the Dutch sins of the day: licentious holidays, plays, cursing, and Sabbath breaking.[26]

Two Dutch men stand out as strong confederates of the Puritans, Teellinck and Voetius. Willem Teellinck was their firmest ally of the early seventeenth century, being well acquainted through travel with England and Scotland. As a young man he studied at St. Andrews in Scotland and later made several visits to England, where he entered into the Puritan fellowship of John Dod and Arthur Hildersam. In England in 1604, he lived for eight months at Banbury in the home of a very spiritual Puritan citizen. He married an English wife, Martha Grijns (Greenston) of Derby. In his *Huys-boeck* (1618) he testified to the fruits of the religion he had experienced in England: Daily devotions, faithful attendance at sermons, a loving home life. "The fruits which this religion brought forth were ... faith working powerfully through love ... a simple performance of one's daily calling, charity for the poor, visiting the sick, comforting the sorrowing." After theological education at Leiden, he became

---

[25] Stoeffler, *Evangelical Pietism*, pp. 117-18; see also Matthias A. Shaaber, *Check-list of Works of British Authors Printed Abroad, in Languages Other Than English, to 1641* (New York: The Bibliographical Society of America, 1975); Broes, *Eng. Herv. Kerk*, II, 66.

[26] "Voor-reden" by I. H. and "Den Drucker tot den Leser" by Christiaensz, in Prynne, *Histrio-Mastix ofte schouw-spels treur-spel, dienende tot een klaer bewijs van de onwetlijckheden der hedendaechsche comedien* (Leiden: Ghedruckt by Willem Christiaens, wonende op't Rapenburgh by de Toelen-Brugghe, 1639); Harry Carter, "Archbishop Laud and Scandalous Books from Holland," *Studia Bibliographica in Honorem Herman de la Fontaine Verwey*, ed. S. van der Woude (Amsterdam: Hertzberger, 1967), p. 48. I have not been able to identify the book by Nolthenius; he was a preacher of Kampen.

preacher at Middelburg and propagator of practical divinity through preaching and many writings. He authored sixty books, many with a strong devotional tone, among them translations of William Perkins and William Whately. He was a strong advocate of Sabbath observance.[27] Teellinck had great credit among Englishmen for devoutness far beyond the ordinary. In the doctrine of Godliness he "tooke such painfull paines this way, both publikely and privately, by word and writing, that it may be truely said, the zeale of Gods house hath eaten him up." At Flushing and Middelburg he worked closely with the English churches. Two of his sons served as preachers of Netherlands English churches, and one of his daughters married Petrus Gribius, another preacher at an English church.[28] Several of his books were published in England by Thomas Gataker.

Gisbertus Voetius, professor of theology at Utrecht University 1634-76, was the mightiest Dutch Puritan of all. He gave leadership to the later seventeenth century precisionists (with him were Anna Maria van Schurman, Jodocus van Lodenstein and others). Voetius often used the word "preciseness" (*precijsheyt*), which he defined as "the exact or perfect human action conforming to the law of God as taught by God, and genuinely accepted, intended, and desired by believers." Voetius's "Puriteinsche precijsheyt" owed a great debt to English practical divinity; and he deferred to the English, who "labored more than any other Reformed people in this branch of theology." Ames and others had done well but "Perkins, the Homer of practical Englishmen to this day, stands above all."[29] The strict English and Scots looked to Voetius as the champion of orthodox Reformed religion, the Dutch theologian closest to the spirit of Puritan heart religion. He and the ministers trained by him "were men of our old English Puritan stamp, burning and shineing Stars both for light and life, for learning and holyness, painfull practicall Preachers ... vigorous opposers of all antiscripturall Noveltys and Innovations in Doctrine."[30] During the tenure of Voetius, Utrecht University attracted many Presbyterian Scots and nonconformist English students. Thomas Cawton, preacher of Rotterdam, was one of many fathers who sent their sons to study at Utrecht precisely because of the orthodox presence of Voetius.[31] From his powerful position at the universi-

---

[27] Willem J. M. Engelberts, *Willem Teellinck* (Amsterdam: Scheffer, 1898), pp. 1-25, 115-32; Heppe, *Pietismus*, pp. 106-40; *N.N.B.W.*, V, 890; *B.L.*, 373-75.

[28] Ames, *Conscience*, dedication; on the Teellincks' pastorates, see above, chapter 7.

[29] A. C. Duker, *Gisbertus Voetius* (Leiden: E. J. Brill, 1897), I, 352-53; II, 203-70; Voetius, *Reformed Dogmatics*, pp. 274, 317.

[30] John Quick, "Icones Sacrae Anglicanae," I, ii, 775.

[31] Thomas Cawton, *The Life and Death of That Holy and Reverend Man of God Mr. Thomas Cawton* (London, 1662), pp. 68, 73.

ty, Voetius could be of especial service to English and Scottish friends. He was a steady upholder of the English Reformed Church at Utrecht, "often frequenting the English Church," and aiding the strict Calvinist faction of the church, reputed to be "a faction depending on Doctor Voutious."[32]

At the level of the local congregation, relationships between the British and the Dutch Reformed churches were generally good. In Zeeland, where Teellinck's influence was strong, the British churches of Flushing, Middelburg, and Veere had sweet fellowship with the Dutch church. The Dutch Zeeland churches, moreover, were especially admired in Puritan eyes, the "doctrine according to godliness" being "both more Practically Preached by the Pastors, and more put in practise by the Hearers in your Churches, then yet hath been marked in many others."[33] When John Quick became English minister at Middelburg in 1680, the legacy of Teellinck was still strong. "The ministry of the Word was exceeding Successfull, many Hearers would weep at Sermons ... multitudes were converted." Quick had precious communion with Johannes Thilenus, Dutch preacher, and indeed with six of the twelve preachers, "who were strict Puritans, and my particular friends." Quick and his strict friends were bitterly opposed to the influence of Johannes Cocceius, "a dark Eclipse upon true Piety."[34] Zeeland had the earliest Dutch churches to speak out in favor of the Puritan, Parliamentary side during the English Revolution.

In Leiden, a university town, Hugh Goodyear and the English church found many persons interested in England and the English language. Professor Gomarus (François Gomaer), former student at Oxford and Cambridge, knew the English language and sometimes preached to the English congregation.[35] Professor Andreas Rivetus visited England several times and learned to know many officials of the Church of England through which he became increasingly tolerant toward Anglicanism.[36] The Leiden theological faculty several times was called upon for some judgment about the English churches. Their advice was moderate and not inflamatory to either Puritans or Anglicans. In 1633 Polyander, Walaeus, and Thysius gave advice to the Council of State about the suspected introduction of Anglican ceremonies into the Netherlands British churches; in even-handed fashion they refused to

---

[32] B.P., I, 268, 394.
[33] Ames, *Conscience*, dedication.
[34] Quick, "Icones," I, ii, 781-82, 791, 799.
[35] G. P. van Itterzon, *Franciscus Gomarus* (The Hague: Martinus Nijhoff, 1929), pp. 27-30.
[36] H. J. Honders, *Andreas Rivetus als invloedrijk gereformeerd theoloog in Holland's bloeitijd* (The Hague: Martinus Nijhoff, 1930), pp. 24, 29.

condemn or censure the Anglican liturgy but raised question about the means used by the English Episcopalians, "without the authorization of the States General or the Dutch Reformed synods." In 1634 they examined Ames's *De Conscientia* and advised that its anti-Anglicanism be toned down. Little wonder that the high Anglican Stephen Goffe regarded the Leiden professors as nearly his best Dutch friends.[37] Jacobus Borstius, student at Leiden University in the 1630s, later preacher at Dort and Rotterdam, learned the English language from Goodyear, his "second father." At Dort he was a friend of the English preachers Robert Paget and Thomas Marshall and at Rotterdam of Thomas Cawton and Alexander Petrie. He befriended various distressed Scottish exiles.[38]

At the top levels of the Church of England, the bishops maintained their own contacts with the Dutch church, Arminians as well as Calvinists, quite different from the Puritan channels of communication. Anglican links most frequently were to the liberal Dutch intellectuals. Archbishop Laud and such prelates were not trusted by the rank-and-file Calvinist Dutch preacher, but among more sophisticated and wider-traveled scholars, the Church of England had better reputation.[39] Foreign scholars enjoyed traveling to England; and, if the proper impression was made, they might develop prestigious friendships, even subsidies or offices. Several prominent Reformed churchmen with high church predilections took positions in the Church of England, among them Hadrian Saravia, Isaac Casaubon, Gerardus Joannes Vossius (a non-resident canon of Canterbury), and later in the century his son Isaac Vossius. Ambassadors Carleton and Boswell worked behind the scenes to counteract the Puritan influence in the Low Countries, hoping to produce a positive Anglican image. Boswell counted on Hugo Grotius, Gerardus Vossius, and Johannes de Laet as being very well-affected to the Church of England (when help was needed in some anti-Puritan business); and Johannes Le Maire of Amsterdam, a correspondent of Laud, was several times useful in snuffing out Puritan printing.[40]

---

[37] For various pronouncements of the Leiden theology professors see A. Eekhof, *De theologische faculteit te Leiden in de 17de eeuw* (Utrecht, 1921), pp. 139-43, 160-62; J. A. Cramer, *De theologische faculteit te Utrecht ten tijde van Voetius* (Utrecht: Kemink en Zoon, 1932), pp. 299-300; B.P., I, 80, 86, 100.

[38] Jacobus Borstius, *Vyftien predicatien* (Utrecht: Thomas Appels, 1696), "Kort verhaal van het leven."

[39] Rosalie L. Colie, *Light and Enlightenment: A Study of the Cambridge Platonists and Dutch Arminians* (Cambridge: Cambridge Univ. Press, 1957), pp. 1-21; C. W. Roldanus, "Nederlandsche-Engelsche betrekkingen op den boden van 'Arminianisme'," *Tijdschrift voor Geschiedenis*, 58 (1943), 6-21; C. R. Dodwell, ed. *The English Church and the Continent* (London: Faith Press, 1959), pp. 77-78.

[40] Thomas Raymond, *Autobiography*, ed. G. Davies, Camden Society, 3rd ser., 28 (1917), 36; C. S. M. Rademaker, *Gerardus Joannes Vossius* (Zwolle: W. E. J. Tjeenk Willink, 1967), pp. 141-44, 238-39.

Stephen Goffe considered Vossius "a zealous excellent instrument for our church." To a Saravia, Grotius, or Vossius, the Laudian Church of England commended itself for its roots in the Church Fathers, its beauty, its uniting of piety and learning: "a true *via media*, characterized by comprehensiveness and a 'virtuous mediocrity.'" Vossius assured Laud that "nothing was so highly precious to him as to be able to please the high princes of the English church."[41]

The liberal intellectuals, when they could, watered down the anti-Anglican utterances of the Dutch preachers. Overall, however, the huge majority of Dutch preachers clung to their negative image of Laudian religion, so well stirred up by the Puritan agitators. Boswell complained many times of the all too effective Puritan propaganda "to make your Grace and the Episcopacy odious." Among the Calvinists, "the main things that they hit in our teeth are, our Bishops to be called Lords; the Service of the Church; the Cross in Baptism; Confirmation; Bowing at the name of Jesus; the Communion Table placed altar-wayes. ..." "They esteem our Clergy little better than Papists."[42]

With the onset of the English Revolution in the 1640s, the Dutch church stepped into further involvement in English-Scottish affairs. The Dutch synods, responding to reports of needy Protestants in Ireland, launched a drive to collect relief funds. The overthrow of the bishops and the sweeping reform of English religion gained swift support from the Dutch preachers; however the churches thought it best to aid the church reformation in England "by churchly means," avoiding a show of politics. The Synods of North Holland, South Holland, and Zeeland in 1643, 1644, and 1645 voted days of prayer, relief collections, letters to England and Scotland, and petitions to the States General in support of the British reform.[43] They gave special thanks to God for the removal of bishops from the Church of England and the presbyterial work of the Westminster Assembly.[44]

Some of the Dutch churchmen quickly became embroiled in the Presbyterian-Congregationalist controversies in the Westminster Assembly. Both parties appealed to the Dutch Reformed Church for sup-

---

[41] Roldanus, "Nederlandsche-Engelsche betrekkingen," pp. 8-10; Dodwell, *English Church and Continent*, p. 78; S.P. 16, vol. 252, no. 55; vol. 260, no. 13.

[42] Boswell to Laud, June 12, 1640, Parr, *Usher*, pp. 27-28.

[43] Knuttel, *Acta Synoden Zuid-Holland*, II, 424-25 (1643), 466 (1644), 504-05 (1645); Acta Synod Zeeland, as reported in Knuttel, I, 399-402 (1643); Acta Synod North Holland, no. 101, 1643, art. 54 (G.A. Amsterdam). Many of the Classes also took collections and sent statements of support to the Westminster Assembly (Amsterdam, 1643, 1644; Brielle, 1644; Haarlem, 1644; Walcheren, 1643, 1644).

[44] Knuttel, *Acta Synoden Zuid-Holland*, II, 504-05 (1645); Acta Synod North Holland, no. 101, 1645, art. 52.

port of their positions, the Presbyterians to the formal presbyterial confession and organization of the church, the Congregationalists to their experience in the Netherlands wherein "the magistrates paid the salary" and otherwise left them to their own activities. Even the bishops appealed to their Dutch friends for some good word on behalf of Episcopacy.[45] Robert Baillie, working through his cousin William Spang of Veere, masterminded a grand anti-Independent strategy encompassing the three nations: "Forbes is on the presse. Hold Apollonius on. ... Edwards's piece we expect the next week at furthest. Strange! that your divines of Holland will learn nothing from England. Doe they sitt still while we are a-dying!" The books he referred to were Alexander Forbes (or Patrick Forbes), *Anatomy of Independency* (1644), written in the Netherlands, Thomas Edwards, *Antapologia* (1644), and a book in process by Willem Apollonius on behalf of the Classis of Walcheren.[46]

The Dutch Reformed clergy gave thanks for the swing toward Presbyterianism in England, but they feared the Congregationalism of the *Apologeticall Narration*, like the Brownism of an earlier period.[47] After hearing news reports from the Westminster Assembly, and urged along by Baillie and Spang, the Classis of Walcheren sent official letters to the Assembly (1644) and commissioned Willem Apollonius to write a book in aid of Presbyterianism. This culminated in *Consideratio quarundam controversiarum, ad regimen ecclesiae spectantium quae in Angliae regno hodie agitantur; ex mandato et jussu Classis Walachrianae conscripta* (London, 1644). It soon appeared in English translation, *A Consideration of Certaine Controversies at this time agitated in the Kingdome of England, Concerning the Government of the Church of God* (London, 1645). John Norton of Ipswich in New England wrote a rejoinder, *Responsio ad totam quaestionum* (London, 1648). Appolonius dealt with seven questions at stake in the Presbyterian-Congregationalist dispute: qualifications for church membership, church covenants, the nature of the visible church, the exercise of church government (whether by the congregation as a whole or by the consistory), the power of the minister, the power of classes and synods, and set prayers. In his presbyterial rebuttal to Congregationalism, Apollonius reflected the consensus of the Dutch Reformed church.[48] A copy was given to

---

[45] Cramer, *Theologische faculteit te Utrecht*, p. 299.

[46] Robert Baillie, *The Letters and Journals of Robert Baillie*, ed. David Laing (Edinburgh, 1841-42), II, 193. For the problem of authorship on the *Anatomy of Independency*, see chap. 12, note 113.

[47] D. Nauta, *De Nederlandsche Gereformeerden en het Independentisme in de zeventiende eeuw* (Amsterdam: H. J. Paris, 1936), pp. 9-18.

[48] Ibid., pp. 19-27; John Norton, *The Answer to the Whole Set of Questions of the Celebrated Mr. William Apollonius*, trans. Douglas Horton (Cambridge: Harvard Univ. Press, 1958), introduction.

every member of the Assembly, and Baillie was well pleased with Apollonius. "Surely he hes done a piece of good service to God and his churches here."⁴⁹ Baillie, like many Dutch Reformed churchmen, equated Presbyterianism and Godliness.

More help for Presbyterianism came from the Netherlands in years to come. The Synods of North Holland and South Holland in 1645 in a well coordinated campaign passed resolutions in favor of the Presbyterian policies of the Westminster Assemblies. In almost identically worded resolutions, the synods sent their approval for the Presbyterian reforms to the Parliament of England, being informed that the religious reforms in England would make "the English and Dutch churches united in the matter of doctrine, also in the matter of church government, through God's grace."⁵⁰

Meanwhile, the Assembly had sent over to Holland for more information to be used against the Congregationalists. This was in the form of four questions to be submitted to the theological faculties of Leiden and Utrecht, copies also being sent to five of the British ministers in the Netherlands (John Dury, Alexander Petrie, William Cooper, William Spang, and Samuel Balmford, apparently considered to be safe Presbyterians). The first of the questions from London asked for evidence about the Reformed system of governance by pastors, elders, deacons, and teachers and the power of classes and synods—how can such be proved to be of divine institution out of the Word of God? The remaining questions concerned the power of the congregation, the authority of elders and deacons, and the lawfulness of human institutions in the church (referring to the episcopal system). The faculties of Leiden and Utrecht each received copies, and moreover John Dury, a self-appointed spokesman of reconciliation among churches, sent a personal letter with another copy of the questions to Voetius. Nothing much to the advantage of either side came of the questions. Leiden brushed the queries off as being purely church questions, not proper for the university to meddle in, and apparently Utrecht declined any answer whatsoever.⁵¹ In addition to Apollonius, several further anti-Independent books emanated from the Netherlands. From the British churches came John Paget, *A Defence of Chvrch-Government* (1641, published posthumously for him by Thomas

---

⁴⁹ Baillie, *Letters*, II, 246. In addition to Baillie's account, John Lightfoot also tells about the anti-Independent dealings of the Assembly and the Dutch church; Lightfoot, *The Whole Works*, ed. John R. Pitman (London: J. F. Dove, 1822-25), vol. 13.

⁵⁰ Knuttel, *Acta Synoden Zuid-Holland*, II, 505 (art. 39); Acta Synod North Holland, 1645 (art. 52). The planning on behalf of English Presbyterianism among the synods is revealed in a letter of S. Cabeljou to Voetius in Cramer, *Theologische faculteit te Utrecht*, pp. 295-99.

⁵¹ Cramer, *Theologische faculteit te Utrecht*, pp. 52-53, 294-300.

and Robert Paget); Samuel Maresius, *Decisio academia* (1648), which proved that Presbyterianism is *jus divinum*; and two books by Johannes Hoornbeek, the *Summa controversiarum religionis* (1653) and *Epistolae ad Johannem Duraeum de Indepentissmo* (1660).[52]

The most interesting writer contributing to the debate was Voetius. He had many English friends in both the Presbyterian and Congregationalist camps; moreover, his analysis was subtle, not so unswervingly hostile as the ordinary Dutch Reformed writer on Independency. His doctrine of church polity was Reformed, and he spared no words in criticizing certain aspects of Congregationalism. Nevertheless, he laid such importance on the "particular church" and church covenants that he gave considerable comfort to Congregationalists and some despair to the Presbyterians.[53] He taught that ecclesiastical power was in the whole church, local as well as synodical.

Two times Voetius spoke out on matters related to the English Presbyterian-Congregationalist controversy. First in 1641, he gave judgment on the dispute in the English church of Delft, which pastor Robert Park was reorganizing on Independent lines, claiming the authority of particular congregations to elect and induct a minister without supervision from the neighboring Reformed churches. Park appealed to the theological faculties of Leiden and Utrecht for judgment, in which case Voetius gave partial support to the Delft Congregationalists on grounds that a "combination of the faithful bound together in a corpus was in essence the church of Christ, with power to elect their minister."[54] The question of a congregation's authority to elect and ordain ministers was repeatedly dealt with in Apollonius and the other Dutch writings on Congregationalism. Secondly, in response to frequent urgings, Voetius presented his overall position on church government. His position was set forth in his theses "De potestate et politia ecclesiarum" (1644) and fully in *Politica Ecclesiastica* (1663).

However, in these writings, much awaited by all parties, he left his position so divided as to be of little help to the Presbyterians. They were "verie evill satisfied with Voetius's Theses." Better that "he had written nothing in this purpose." Voetius stressed the *ecclesia prima* (congregation), in the style of Robert Parker, and put the origin of the particular congregation in a covenant. Baillie, who had helped to speed the publica-

---

[52] Marius Bouwman, *Voetius over het gezag der synoden* (Amsterdam: S. J. P. Bakker, 1937), pp. 44-49.

[53] Ibid., pp. 56-62; Douglas Nobbs, *Theocracy and Toleration: A Study of the Disputes in Dutch Calvinism from 1600 to 1650* (Cambridge: Cambridge Univ. Press, 1938), pp. 153-54.

[54] Nobbs, *Theocracy*, p. 156; Cramer, *Theologische faculteit te Utrecht*, pp. 51-52, 229-36. See chapter 5 for the Delft church.

tion of the chief anti-Independent books of the day, Forbes's *Anatomy of Independency*, Apollonius's *Consideratio*, and Edwards's *Antapologia*, was bitterly distressed that Voetius could not be recruited to write a similar book. Voetius, with many friends of the Congregationalist persuasion, was the Dutch Reformed theologian most favorable to their position. He believed both in synodical authority and the independence of the congregation; the business of condemning the Congregationalists he left to others.[55]

The Church-State Connection: The Legal Status of the English and Scottish Churches

The material prosperity of the English and Scottish churches depended to a large extent on the goodwill of the local and provincial Dutch governments. Like the Dutch Reformed churches, the English-Scottish Reformed city churches were established with sponsorship and financial support from the city magistrates and in most cases from the provincial states. Buildings and ministerial salary were provided. The garrison churches with chaplains as preachers were in a separate category, being provided with church buildings by the local government and some small stipend from the States General. The Separatists received no buildings or subsidies of any kind. Government sponsorship meant government control. Magistrates assumed that paying the bills gave them possession: "their" church, "their" preachers. The Reformed churches were expected to uphold the state, according to Romans 13, and collaborate in the work of the general welfare. At Amsterdam, says Brugmans, the churches were bound to the city "with silver chains," but chains nevertheless, and such was the case in every Dutch city and province.[56] The state gave financial and political support (the substance of the "silver chains"), and the churches in return rendered unto Caesar what they were asked to do. Ministers of the state as well as ministers of God, as John Northleigh put it, "and as a man may modestly say, seem to be bound to serve both God and Mammon, for they have neither Church Land nor Tythes, nor any Contributions but what their Masters pay them."[57] The English language churches fell under the same rules as the Dutch.

Foreign congregations had a complex situation. A large majority of the membership of the English and Scottish churches expected to return

---

[55] Baillie, *Letters*, II, 65, 205, 240, 246; Nobbs, *Theocracy*, pp. 172-77, 271-73; Bouwman, *Voetius over synoden*, pp. 55-56.

[56] H. A. Enno van Gelder, *Getempeerde vrijheid* (Groningen: Wolters-Noordhoff, 1972), pp. 35, 60-61; Alice C. Carter, *The English Reformed Church in Amsterdam in the Seventeenth Century* (Amsterdam: Scheltema & Holkema, 1964), p. 41; H. Brugmans, *Geschiedenis van Amsterdam* (Amsterdam, 1930-33).

[57] John Northleigh, *Topographical Descriptions* (London, 1702), p. 109.

home someday. The King of England and the bishops of the Church of England held to the position that British subjects abroad should retain loyalty to their native religion. The long range design of Laud was to bring all overseas British churches into line with Anglican practice. Legally, however, the British churches of the Netherlands were bound by Dutch law. Caught between two possibly contradictory allegiances, the British churches learned to work within the situation and at times to put it to good advantage. In the 1620s-1630s, at the time of the English Synod, some of the churches developed a theology of congregational autonomy; but when the pressure of Laudianism pressed upon them, the churches threw aside their autonomous theories and drew close to the Dutch Reformed Church, using it as a counterweight to the English governmental interference. When the dangers had passed, the churches lessened the ties and moved back to a middle position.

Two sets of treaties and laws provided the legal foundation of the churches. The first was the English-Dutch treaty of August 10, 1585, the Treaty of Nonsuch, in which Elizabeth committed large-scale English troops to the Netherlands and in return received command over the towns of Flushing and Brielle. Article 11 set forth that in the cautionary towns the governors were to preserve "the true religion as it is presently exercised in England and in the United Provinces." Article 14 read: "The governor and garrison are permitted the free exercise of religion as in England, and for this purpose will be provided with a church in each city."[58] In 1616 the towns were returned to Dutch authority, and the treaty clauses were no longer operative. Nevertheless, the 1585 treaty had functioned for over thirty years and set important precedents. Although the treaty seemingly allowed the exercise of Anglican worship with Prayer Book and liturgy, almost the reverse happened. Under the administration of the Earl of Leicester, general of the English forces, and the various governors of the cautionary towns, the practice of religion was allowed to be Reformed and Puritan. Leicester and his Puritan chaplains, in spite of the words of the treaty, established Puritan churches at Flushing and Brielle.

Leicester's policies proved more potent than the articles of the treaty themselves. The sixteenth-century precedents were very long-lasting, and Puritans thereafter harked back to the treaty, at least as administered by Leicester, as the legal basis for requiring Reformed English churches in the Netherlands:

> Because her majestie Queen Elizabeth, by an Act under her hand and seale yielded to the States, that her owne Subiects in the land should not use the

---

[58] Jean DuMont, *Corps universel diplomatique der droit des gens* (Amsterdam, 1728), vol. 5, pt. 1, 454-55.

formes and Discipline of their owne church, but wholy conforme themselves unto the Dutch Church. ... And this Act of the Queene, they prove was graunted when Flushing and Brill were putt into her hands. And this is very true that such a Graunt was made, and is now to bee seene.[59]

Such was the common view among Puritans. Sir Dudley Carleton tried to argue the opposite, that in the treaty the clear meaning was "expressely capitulating the use of the established publick forme of Gods service in the Church of England."[60] Interpretation differed on whether to stress the formal words of the treaty or the historical functioning of the treaty. Although some regiments in the field, contrasted to the established city churches, used the Prayer Book, the prevalent practice was Puritan.[61] The treaty of 1585, as administered by Leicester, gave a quasi-legal status to Puritan practice in the Netherlands. The Merchant Adventurers also relied on precedent to perpetuate their Presbyterian form of worship and governance: We practice what "hath bene ever practiced, since it was first established at Antwerp" by authority of the Ambassador of Queen Elizabeth.[62]

The second legal foundation for the British churches was the body of legislation passed by the States General in 1621, 1628, and 1633. Before that time, there had been no overall policy in writing for the British churches apart from the precedents established in the sixteenth century. The impetus for Dutch legislation arose from the forming of the English Synod in 1621 and the aggressive policies of Laud in the 1630s. Dutch Reformed churchmen regarded the Laudian form of the Church of England as little better than "popery." Consequently, churchmen and magistrates threw up legal roadblocks to thwart any possible Anglican designs in the Netherlands. The English-Scottish churches were intended to be *gereformeerd*, not creatures of the bishops.

The States General resolution of October 20, 1621 established the English Synod (1621-33). By chartering a synod, the Dutch desired to bring some orderliness to the disorganized troop of British chaplains and preachers. The resolution specified that the synod be organized "according to the pattern of the Walloon churches in these lands."[63] The Walloon churches were Reformed in doctrine and practice; consequently the law of 1621 applied the same standard to the British churches. By a second resolution, July 12, 1628, the States General specifically required that the English and Scottish preachers must observe the ecclesiastical

---

[59] S.P. 16, vol. 310, no. 103 (1633).
[60] B.P., I, 250v.
[61] B.P., I, 161.
[62] S.P. 84, vol. 144, fol. 240.
[63] Res. States General, no. 3180, fol. 503v (A.R.A.).

order of the land as practiced by Dutch preachers. This was intended as a defense against Anglican agents coming into the Netherlands.[64] By a third resolution, April 22, 1633, the States General, having information about Anglican liturgy in use among some chaplains, decreed "that the situation of the English and Scottish preachers ministering in the cities of these provinces shall by provision be left in the same state as at present without permitting any novelties or unaccustomed things."[65] This third resolution (the "No Novelties" law) proved to be extremely useful to Puritans warding off pressure from Laud or Boswell. All three of the laws had come about through Puritan campaigning among friendly clergy and politicians.

A fourth law, passed by the States of Holland July 14, 1645, was also applicable on a more limited scale. Because of some Anglican-Puritan controversies at The Hague, the provincial States resolved that the English Church of The Hague "in the celebration of the Holy Communion and other ecclesiastical affairs shall be regulated according to the order of the Reformed churches of these lands."[66] This was regarded as being a logical extension of the laws of 1621, 1628, and 1633 and although specifically designed for The Hague had a general application to the churches of the province of Holland (Amsterdam, Leiden, The Hague, Delft, Rotterdam, Gorinchem, Heusden, Dort). Taken as a whole, the four resolutions provided a political-ecclesiastical framework for British religion in the Netherlands. The English-Scottish churches were required to be Reformed churches.

As a part of the religious establishment, the English-Scottish churches had to bring the magistrates into many of their decisions. The choosing of ministers, the amount of ministerial salary, and the handling of controversies became matters for the magistrate along with the congregation. Elders of the British churches were regularly deputed to go to the magistrates of their city for permission to proceed with this or that action. In some cities, burgomasters attended consistory meetings when ministerial elections were being held; they were prominently in attendance at the installation of new preachers. In Zeeland the system of joint collaboration was institutionalized into a body known as the *Collegium Qualificatum*, a committee of burgomasters and church officials formed ad hoc for the election of ministers in each church. This was the practice at the English churches of Middelburg and Flushing.[67] The system of col-

---

[64] Res. States General, no. 3187, fol. 360v.
[65] Res. States General, no. 3192, fol. 365v.
[66] Res. States of Holland, no. 78, pp. 141, 152; Res. States General, no. 3204, fols. 408-10.
[67] Flushing C.R., no. 4469 (1651, 1676); Middelburg C.R., I, 96; G. D. J. Schotel, *De openbare eeredienst der Nederl. Hervormde Kerk in de zestiende, zeventiende en achttiende eeuw* (Haarlem: A. C. Kruseman, 1870), p. 325.

laboration and joint consultation easily turned into official dictation. In Amsterdam in the late seventeenth century, the burgomasters virtually dictated English ministerial elections.[68]

Links with the Dutch Classes and Synods

The Dutch Reformed Church had two primary concerns about the British churches of the Netherlands, first to prevent the practice of Anglican ceremonies, second to have a supervisory authority over the British churches. Without some English or Dutch classical organization, the Dutch clergy feared that English-Scottish religion would be in perpetual disorder. The ordinary Dutch Calvinist preacher had deep hostility toward the ceremonies. In every city where Laudian innovations were attempted, the local Dutch preachers raised an alarm: Amersfoort in 1630, Bergen-op-Zoom in 1633, 's-Hertogenbosch in 1633, The Hague in 1635-37, Breda in 1638, Heusden in 1648.[69] The Classis of Utrecht in 1643 examined Malachi Harris, minister of the English church, about his stand on the "popish" ceremonies of the Church of England. In spite of his stout defense, nothing could convince the Utrecht clergy of the lawfulness of Anglican ceremonies, "since many of them savour so much of Popery."[70]

The churches of South Holland helped to promote the English Synod in 1621, but when King James talked of appointing a superintendent of his own choice—which the Puritan clergy suspected would become a quasi-bishop—the Dutch clergy threatened to dissolve the synod rather than see an Anglican agent at its head.[71] During Anglican-Puritan controversies in 1632, the States of Holland, instead of allowing Anglicanism to slip in amongst the English, debated "that ere long they might par adventure have never an English preacher in the land."[72] Nearly every Dutch synod with British churches within its jurisdiction went on record as opposed to Laud's Anglican ceremonies, either in response to a particular incident in the local British churches or simply on general principle. The Synod of Utrecht in 1630 acted on a complaint from Petrus Gribius, chaplain to the English at Amersfoort. His chief officer, Robert de Vere, the Earl of Oxford, had ordered him to use the Prayer Book and kneeling at the communion. The synod urged Gribius to hold to Dutch practice and refuse the ceremonies.[73]

---

[68] Carter, *English Reformed Church*, pp. 100-05.
[69] See chapters dealing with these churches.
[70] B.P., I, 333-34.
[71] S.P. 84, vol. 121, fol. 237v.
[72] Add. MS. 17,677, vol. N, fol. 317.
[73] Acta Synod Utrecht, I, 1630, sess. 7, art. 8 (no. 18, Classis of Utrecht).

The Synod of South Holland spoke out several times against English ceremonies: in 1631 in support of Gribius in the Amersfoort affair; in 1637 in support of Samuel Balmford at The Hague; in 1651 against ceremonies being used in the chapel of Mary, Princess of Orange.[74] The Synod of North Holland, having only Amsterdam of the British churches, had no reports of ceremonies in its area; nevertheless, the synod thought it wise to go on record against the ceremonies being pressed at The Hague and at any other place in the land.[75] The Synod of Overijssel resolved in 1638 that the ceremonies should be hindered by all means.[76] Ambassador Sir William Boswell tried to persuade the Dutch Calvinists that the Church of England was agreeable with them "in substance of true Religion, and only different in ordre or maner." However not many were convinced.[77]

The English church of Amsterdam was the first of the British churches to have membership in a Dutch classis. Its membership began at the foundation of the church in 1607 and continues up to the present. No further British churches took membership in a Dutch classis until the Utrecht English church was united with the Utrecht Classis in 1629. In the interim, the British churches had organized their own English Synod. Except for Amsterdam and Leiden, the preachers of all the churches joined the English Synod, at least for a time. The Synod of South Holland was the firmest supporter of the separate English Synod, believing that such a synod would be able to regulate the disorderliness among the military chaplains. The Synod of South Holland had resolutions year after year about "the coming in of English ministers with unlawful calling or, having taken up service in the garrison, who administer improperly" (1622, 1623, 1625, 1626, 1627, 1641, 1642, 1643).[78] The Synod of North Holland and the Classis of Amsterdam, incited by John Paget, were almost consistently unfriendly toward any separate synod for the English. Paget charged that the English Synod was in the hands of schismatics and pro-Brownists.[79] The Synod of Utrecht, which at first had allowed the Utrecht English Church to join the English Synod, followed the lead of Amsterdam and withdrew its support in 1625. Rather than allowing the English to regulate themselves, the Utrecht Synod resolved that supervision of English preachers in Utrecht province

---

[74] Knuttel, *Acta Synoden Zuid-Holland*, I, 379, II, 141-42, III, 278.
[75] Acta Synod North Holland, no. 101, 1637, art. 34; 1638, art. 21.
[76] Acta Synod Overijssel, 1638, sess. 4, art. 47 (Zwolle Classis archive, N.H.A.).
[77] S.P. 84, vol. 146, fol. 201v.
[78] Knuttel, *Acta Synoden Zuid-Holland*, I, 48, 84, 137, 171-72, 207; II, 312, 313, 326-28, 368, 416.
[79] Acta Synod North Holland, no. 99, 1622, art. 28; 1623, art. 20; 1624, art. 18; no. 100, 1625, art. 45; 1627, art. 34; 1628, art. 20; 1629, art. 17; 1630, art. 11, etc.

should be by local consistories and classes. However, the incumbent Utrecht minister Jeremiah Elborough, who was active in the English Synod, declined to join the Dutch. After his departure in 1629, the Dutch clergy saw to it that subsequent English preachers would be required to take session in the Utrecht Classis as a condition of their employment.[80]

On the military frontiers of Gelderland, Brabant, and Overijssel, the British churches were small and weak. The Dutch Reformed policy in these areas was to give supervision without extending membership in classes. The Synod of Gelderland (with jurisdiction over Nijmegen, Arnhem, Zutphen, Doesburg, and Grave) thought supervision over the British chaplains to be urgently necessary. The Dutch regarded the British chaplains on the whole as spiritually low quality and the congregations to be little more than informal preaching places. The various classes of Gelderland did not admit the preachers of such ephemeral churches to membership. They supervised the coming and going of the chaplains and examined credentials of doctrine and calling; otherwise there was little fellowship. The consistories of Nijmegen and Zutphen and the Synod of Gelderland in 1626 and 1627 adopted a policy similar to the Utrecht policy: No English chaplain to be admitted "without knowledge of the magistrates of the respective cities and without presenting to the respective Dutch consistories proper attestation of mission and calling, also his doctrine and good conduct."[81] In Overijssel, the English preacher at Zwolle, John Roe, enjoyed double membership, having session at the same time in the English Synod and the Classis of Zwolle.[82] The States General resolved in 1660 that in the "Bailiwick of 's-Hertogenbosch and in other Quarters of like nature, belonging under the Generality" the preachers of the English churches or the English and Scottish regiments "must subscribe to the order of the classes under which they have been called or admitted."[83]

After the English Synod went defunct in 1633, there was no substitute organization of English-Scottish churches except for some supervision given by the Dutch classes. Many churches were completely isolated. In 1641 the Synod of South Holland, which encompassed an area of many churches, drew up a new policy for the British churches. This was set forth as a proposal, "Project of Regulation for the English Preachers in

---

[80] Acta Synod Utrecht, I, 1625 (sess. 4, art. 4), 1626 (sess. 2, art. 9), 1627 (sess. 4, art. 3), 1628 (sess. 3, art. 5), 1629 (sess. 4, art. 4).

[81] Acta Synod Gelderland, I, 1626, art. 32; 1627, art. 21 (R.A. Gelderland); Acta Kerkeraad Nijmegen, I, April 8, 1626 (N.H.K. Nijmegen).

[82] Acta Synod Overijssel, 1626, art. 62. For Roe's connection with the Zwolle classis at the time of his calling to Flushing in 1628, see Flushing C.R. (1628).

[83] Nikolaas Wiltens, *Kerkelyk plakaatboek* (The Hague, 1772), p. 20.

the Cities under the Synod of South Holland, Who Serve in Public Churches and Enjoy Public Financial Support." The proposal had seven steps: (1) No English preacher to be admitted to the ministry without showing an attestation or testimonial of life and doctrine and evidence of calling to the holy ministry to the classis where the church is located; (2) If called to an established Reformed church with its own consistory, the preacher should present his credentials to the classis; if coming to an unorganized congregation without consistory, he must have authorization from the classis before beginning services; (3) The English preacher must subscribe to the formularies of the Synod of Dort and thus demonstrate his conformity with the teachings of the Dutch Reformed Church; (4) The English preacher must use only the established church order and liturgy of the Netherlands; (5) English churches are to be governed by their own minister and consistory, but in cases of unresolvable controversies, they may appeal to the Dutch consistories, classes, and synod of South Holland for arbitration; (6) The Synod deputies will consult with the States of Holland and some qualified English preachers about instituting these policies; (7) The Synod shall present these articles to the English churches with friendly inducements and, so far as is feasible, shall seek to make them attractive (*smakelick te maken*).[84] This comprehensive proposal was never enacted into law. When the proposal for English classis membership was sent out to the various classes for study, their replies were not conclusively in favor of the change.[85] Also, consultation with leading English preachers revealed opposition to so sweeping a regulation. The preachers declared the proposal *niet smakelick was*. The Synod of South Holland, nevertheless, expressed the hope that the scattered, independent English preachers would of their own choice seek membership in the Dutch classes.[86]

A long-range policy of inducements and pressure from the magistrates and clergy eventually brought many of the British churches, like Amsterdam and Utrecht, under the local Dutch classes. The English church at The Hague joined in 1634 (a "link," not full membership), Breda in 1643, Bergen-op-Zoom in 1644, Middelburg in 1645, Flushing in 1645, Dort in 1646, Leiden in 1655, and Veere in 1669. The motivations varied. The minister of The Hague sought classis membership because of Laudian intimidation. The Flushing and Middelburg churches joined because of an edict from the States of Zeeland, who voted to give financial subsidy only on condition of membership in the Classis of

---

[84] Knuttel, *Acta Synoden Zuid-Holland*, II, 326-28 (1641, art. 60).
[85] Acta Classis Leiden, no. 5, June 24, 1642; Acta Classis Delft, no. 138, June 12, 1642; Acta Classis Schieland, V, June 23, 1642; Acta Classis Hague, III, June 30, 1642.
[86] Knuttel, *Acta Synoden Zuid-Holland*, II, 368-69, 416.

Walcheren. At Utrecht and Breda there was strong pressure from the Dutch Reformed Church to exclude from employment British preachers who refused to take membership in the classis. The English Reformed Church at Rotterdam had the clearest position as an independent congregation, from Hugh Peter's time onward. In spite of some later contacts between preacher and classis, no official tie was developed. Richard Maden, minister 1660-80, had his theological examination from the Classis of Schieland, but in 1662 when Maden formally requested membership, the classis put him off.[87] According to Steven, the Rotterdam English church "was the only one which might be said not to be united to the Classis."[88]

Once "the ministers of our churches became members of the Classis, the Dutch clergy seldom interfered in their settlements."[89] Going under the classis proved for many British ministers not a very fruitful experience. After being pressed to join, they found themselves not taken seriously and sometimes demoted to low membership status. Amsterdam, the original classis church, had no such problems, but elsewhere the relationship, supposedly finalized by classis membership, remained cloudy. At The Hague the successors of Balmford were seldom active in the classis, and the classis interpreted their relationship to mean "that the English church is taken under the supervision and government of the Hague Classis, but nevertheless, that the English church not be a member of the Classis."[90] The successors of Goodyear at Leiden were seldom members in the classis. At Bergen-op-Zoom the English preacher was admitted as a member in 1644, but five years later the classis reinterpreted his membership and allowed him merely a discussion role in sessions and no vote.[91] The church at Dort withdrew from classis membership in 1703.[92] The Utrecht church because of its small size was relegated to a status below all other Utrecht churches. The English minister in 1753 unloosed a tremendous campaign to have the church restored to full classis status.[93] The reorganization of the Dutch churches in 1816 finally settled the question of the relationship of the English and Dutch Reformed churches by incorporating all English and Scottish

---

[87] Acta Classis Schieland, VI, June 19, Sept. 4, Oct. 2, 1662; Knuttel, *Acta Synoden Zuid-Holland*, IV, 214.

[88] Steven, p. 399. In spite of Steven's statement, I also find no evidence of the Rotterdam Scots church having joined the classis in the 17th century.

[89] Steven, p. 400.

[90] "Stukken betreffende het proces tusschen de classis van 's Gravenhage en den Engelschen Kerkeraad aldaar" (1716), no. 83, Hague Classis (N.H.A.).

[91] Acta Classis Tholen en Bergen op Zoom, III, 107v (April 21, 1649).

[92] Dort C.R., no. 5, fol. 199.

[93] Utrecht C.R., I, 269-98 (1753).

churches into the Dutch. Article one reads: "The Dutch Reformed Church consists of all Reformed congregations in the Kingdom of the Netherlands, Walloon, English and Scottish Presbyterian, as well as Dutch."[94]

---

[94] "Algemeen regelement voor het bestuur de Hervormde Kerk in het Koningrijk der Nederlanden" (1816).

CHAPTER FOURTEEN

TIMES OF WAR AND REVOLUTION
1640-1670

The middle part of the century with its revolutions and wars was a profoundly troubled period for the overseas English and Scottish churches. Whether they wanted to or not, the churches were dragged into the upheavals, first the English and Scottish Revolutions, then the Anglo-Dutch wars of 1652-54, 1665-67, and 1672-74. The revolutionary events of England and Scotland overturned the Royalist-Episcopalian regime and prepared the way for the return home of the exiled Puritans. Always the refuge, the Netherlands during the 1640s-1650s turned into the "citty of refuge" of exiled Royalists.

In 1640-41 the English refugees began moving back to England. "It pleased God to bring us his poor *Exiles* back again in these revolutions of the times," said the *Apologeticall Narration*.[1] Goodwin, Burroughes, Nye, Bridge, and Simpson, the five brethren, were among the first to go back, also John Ward, Edward Wale, and Paul Amyraut. They returned in glory, and found their old persecutors thrown down. Laud and Wren were in the Tower. Several of the returning Puritans were called to preach before Parliament. In one of the Parliamentary sermons, Burroughes preached a joyful note: "Now we are come and finde peace and mercy here, the voice of joy and gladnesse. ... We scarce thought we should ever have seene our Countrey, but behold we are with our Honorable Senators and Worthyes of our Land ... oh! who is like unto thee, O Lord."[2] Goodwin and Simpson organized churches in London. The cities of Rotterdam and Arnhem lost large parts of their English populations in the great return. "Hoping that if episcopy were abolish'd they might peacably live at home and enjoy their consciences," they said.[3] The Covenanters of Scotland and both sides in England recruited men and supplies in the Netherlands, "a nursery of good and useful men."[4]

---

[1] Thomas Goodwin, et al., *An Apologeticall Narration* (London, 1644), p. 22.

[2] Jeremiah Burroughes, *Sions Joy* (London, 1641), p. 41. Other Dutch exiles who preached to Parliament were Nye, Bridge, Goodwin, Simpson, Symonds, Dury, and perhaps John Ward; John F. Wilson, *Pulpit in Parliament* (Princeton: Princeton Univ. Press, 1969).

[3] J. T. Cliffe, *The Yorkshire Gentry from the Reformation to the Civil War* (Hamden: Archon Books, 1970), p. 258.

[4] Clements R. Markham, *The Fighting Veres* (Boston: Houghton, Mifflin, and Co., 1888), pp. 450-57; C. H. Firth, *Cromwell's Army*, 3rd ed. (London: Methuen, 1921), p. 15.

Royalists and Anglicans in Exile

As the Puritans returned westward to England, an immigration to the Continent of Royalists and Anglicans began. The emigrés of the English Revolution scattered to many countries, but a good share of them to the Netherlands. Sir John Denham wrote: "At Paris, At Rome, At the Hague they are at home; the good fellow is nowhere a stranger."[5] Those who had been on top just months before were now ruined. The world had turned upside down. Sir John Reresby, traveler and chronicler, turned into a bitter immigrant: "I left England in that unhappy time when honesty was reputed a crime, religion superstition, loyalty treason; when subjects were governors, servants masters, and no gentleman assured of any thing he possessed." Abroad he fled; England was intolerable, "to live there appeared worse than banishment."[6]

While the war between king and Parliament continued, the Royalists came over to raise funds, buy arms, and hire soldiers. Queen Henrietta Maria made a Dutch trip in 1642, ostensibly to deliver Princess Mary to her husband in Holland, but in fact, to raise money and supplies. As the cause became more desperate the queen had to sell or pawn her jewels, and the king his paintings and other valuables, to keep the army going.[7] Royalist agents criss-crossed the provinces in search of aid, among them Stephen Goffe and Sampson Johnson, former preachers in Holland.[8] Several wealthy English merchants remained loyal to the crown and kept the money and supplies flowing. The most faithful of these was John Webster, one of the biggest merchants of Amsterdam. He handled many affairs for the king and queen. In 1642 he sent over to King Charles 300 carbines, 300 pairs of pistols and holsters, 300 saddles; in 1644 he shipped an order of 500 muskets and 200 picks, which however were intercepted by a parliamentary ship.[9] Parliament in 1644 put him on a list of Amsterdam and Rotterdam "incendiaries and enemies to the Parliament," the others being Theophilus Baynham, Edward Manning

---

[5] P. H. Hardacre, "The Royalists in Exile during the Puritan Revolution, 1642-1660," *Huntington Library Quarterly*, 16 (Aug. 1953), 356.

[6] John Reresby, *The Memoirs and Travels of Sir John Reresby, Bart.* (London, 1813), p. 1. He went abroad in 1656.

[7] John W. Stoye, *English Travellers Abroad 1604-1667* (London: Jonathan Cape, 1952), pp. 306-09; Quentin Bone, *Henrietta Maria: Queen of the Cavaliers* (Urbana: Univ. of Illinois Press, 1972), pp. 142-50; R. Bijlsma, "Rotterdams handelsverkeer met Engeland tijdens het verblijf der Merchants Adventurers (1635-1652)," *Bijdragen voor Vaderlandsche Geschiedenis en Oudheidkunde*, ser. 5, pt. 4 (1917), 95-96.

[8] Stoye, *English Travellers*, pp. 308-09, 319-20; Matthews, *W.R.*, pp. 156, 356; H.M.C., *Pepys MSS*, pp. 215-16.

[9] S.P. 84, vol. 158, fols. 9-10, 16; Not. Archive 701, fol. 551; 1480, fol. 85v (G.A. Amsterdam).

(Man?), Richard Ford, and James Yard. They were declared outlaws for aiding the Royalists; consequently it was necessary for Webster to remain in Amsterdam, where he had purchased citizenship.[10] Webster later claimed to have expended £20,000 on behalf of the king, most not repaid. Among his papers he kept as a souvenir a note for 2000 guilders signed by Charles R, April 1649, and a letter of commendation from Charles as Prince of Wales for his "great zeale for his Majesties service upon all occasions" (1648).[11]

When the king was overthrown and the revolution seemingly decided, the Royalists streamed over by the hundreds. Charles, Prince of Wales, and the remainder of the royal family withdrew to the Continent to establish the court in exile; some of the exiles found refuge with him. The households of Elizabeth, Queen of Bohemia, sister of Charles I, living at the Hague, and the court of Mary, Princess of Orange, daughter of Charles I, became havens for emigré Royalists. Amsterdam, Rotterdam, The Hague, Breda and Utrecht were temporary centers of Royalism.[12] The Royalist network in exile, like the Puritan exiles of the previous generation, were a danger, or at least a nuisance, to the English Republic. Sir William Boswell, a skilled diplomat, kept at his place as agent for the Stuarts until his death in 1650; thereafter affairs were handled by William MacDowell.[13] The Royalists in exile printed books, plotted, cursed their ill situation, and kept alive the faith of the Church of England. As the revolution changed directions in England, new exiles kept slipping over (anti-Cromwell Presbyterians like Thomas Edwards, William Price, James Stephenson, Thomas Cawton, and James Nalton; the radical Leveller John Lilburne). As in times past, the English government protested against seditious rebels in the Netherlands. This time it was the turn of Republican ambassadors (Walter Strickland and George Downing) to fulminate against "rebels and declared enemies of the Republic."[14] Many complaints were delivered to the Dutch about pro-Royalist "scandalous books" being shipped over from the Netherlands.[15]

When "Laud fell," said Peter Heylyn, "the Church fell with him."[16] During the English Revolution the active center of Anglican religion was

---

[10] *Cal. S.P.D.*, 1644, pp. 312, 320; Res. States General, no. 3203, fols. 456v-458.

[11] S.P. 29, vol. 225, no. 6, 6i; vol. 229, no. 190; *Pepys MSS*, pp. 204, 218.

[12] Thurloe, *S.P.*, II, 373-74.

[13] *D.N.B.*, s.v. MacDowell; Samuel R. Gardiner, ed., *Letters and Papers Illustrating the Relations betwixt Charles the Second and Scotland in 1650*, in *Publications* of the Scottish History Society, 17 (1894), pp. 82, 123.

[14] Downing's letter of Sept. 10, 1658, Liassen Engelandt, no. 5901 (A.R.A.).

[15] *Cal. S.P.D.*, 1649-50, p. 411.

[16] Robert S. Bosher, *The Making of the Restoration Settlement: The Influence of the Laudians 1649-1662* (London: Dacre Press, 1951), p. 1.

in exile on the Continent. Bosher has collected a list of 149 Anglican clergy in exile 1645-60, of which about 50 had all or part of their exile in the Dutch Netherlands, "rendered notorious at home by their Laudian views and Royalist activity."[17] It was a despairing time for the fallen Church of England—what was the future of the Episcopal church? There were many temptations to cross over to the Church of Rome or for the sake of advancement to accommodate to the Presbyterianism of the Reformed churches; nevertheless, most of the emigré Anglicans kept faithful to the orthodox *Ecclesia Anglicana*, often under extreme hardship. The tiny chapels of the Stuarts or other great Royalist emigrés preserved the remnant of Anglican worship in exile, at Paris, Brussels, Antwerp, Breda, The Hague.[18]

The emigré community clung to the Prayer Book and liturgy as precious beyond price. Dean Richard Steward preached: "I must hence hold it a duty I owe to that venerable Church that baptized us all, though our now afflicted Mother, to keep the fruit of her own womb from thus trampling on her, to keep them, as much as in me lies, from being gulled and cheated from her unity, and withal from communicating too deeply in sin with those who have now cast her on the ground."[19] George Morley administered the Anglican service in chapels at Paris, Caen, Antwerp, The Hague, and at Charles's peripatetic court, "according to the Liturgy of the Church of England without any subordination to the Classis ... because I think I am obliged to live and dye (if I can) in the publick exercise of mine owne profession."[20] The emigré spirit is well preserved in a book of sermons, *A Treatise of Spiritual Infatuation*, preached at The Hague in 1650 by William Stamp, "the imprisoned, plundered, exilde Minister of Gods word." He gave a lamentable but persevering sermon on "spiritual infatuation," being a presumptuous disease destroying the church and government of England. "*Desolation, & Devastation* at *home*: *Banishment*, and I feare, too generall a Desertion of us, that are *abroad*."[21]

---

[17] Ibid., pp. 49, 284-94; see also Matthews, *W.R.* Other than those mentioned in the text, the exiles included: James Aitken, John Arnway, William Brough, Daniel Bullen, Thomas Cade, Guy Carleton, Francis Corker, Robert Creighton, George Davenport, John Forbes, Michael Honywood, George Jay, William Johnson, Thomas Jones, Paul Knell, Henry Leslie, John Lowen, John Maplet, Edward Martin, Peter Mewes, John Michaelson, Degory Polwheel, John Rowland, William Sancroft, James Stephenson, Herbert Thorndike, George Wishart.

[18] C. R. Dodwell, ed., *The English Church and the Continent* (London: Faith Press, 1959), pp. 78-79.

[19] Bosher, *Restoration Settlement*, p. 51.

[20] Harley MS. 6942, fol. 149 (letter of July 12, 1653); George Morley, *Several Treatises* (London, 1683), preface.

[21] William Stamp, *A Treatise of Spiritual Infatuation Being the Present Visible Disease of the English Nation* (The Hague, 1650), pp. 25-26.

Some of the refugee Anglican ministers found place as chaplains at the court of Charles (in 1649 Richard Steward, Andrew Clare, and John Earle, later William Stamp, John Lloyd, and George Morley).[22] Princess Mary of Orange, residing at The Hague and sometimes at Breda, employed first John Dury, ecumenical churchman, then several Anglican chaplains: Malachi Harris, Thomas Browne, and Robert Sheringham. Elizabeth of Bohemia, living at The Hague, had Sampson Johnson, William Stamp, George Morley, and George Beaumont. Under financial pressure from Parliament, who threatened to cut off her pension, Elizabeth dismissed Johnson in 1644 and took on a Puritan chaplain, William Cooper (1644-48). After her brother's execution in 1649, she threw out the Puritans and sought the most Royalist chaplains to be found.[23] A few of the Anglicans found places as preachers in the established English Reformed churches, Richard Maden at Utrecht and Amsterdam, Malachi Harris at Utrecht, Sampson Johnson and David Michael at Breda, John Stone as military chaplain at Heusden, John Dibdale as chaplain at Sluis. Richard Chalfont, Henry Tozer, and Thomas Marshall found employment with the Merchant Adventurers of Rotterdam. Some set their sights too high and found nothing. Archibald Hamilton, Bishop of Cashel, sought to become a professor at Leiden University but was passed over.[24] Although the chaplains serving in private chapels had a free hand in worship, as dictated by their patrons, those who took pastorates in the public English Reformed churches were limited by law (the Resolutions of 1621, 1628, 1633, and 1645) from practicing a genuine Anglicanism. They were further limited by the watchfulness of the Dutch Reformed clergy. The most that the Anglican-minded preachers might do was to slip in some parts of the liturgy at the communion or an occasional sign of the cross at a baptism.

The Dutch consistories and classes kept a close eye on the new Anglican refugee preachers. The Princess Mary's chaplains were reputed to be extreme ceremonialists. Chaplain Malachi Harris in 1645 complained about vicious rumors at Breda; "our Princesse was reputed here for a Papist, on all hands, and my officiating in the presence must be saying of masse, as my cassock makes me a Jesuit."[25] Mary's next chaplain, Thomas Browne, was hounded by the Hague preachers to desist from Anglican ceremonies, but he shook them off with a Laudian superiority.

---

[22] *Pepys MSS*, pp. 255-56.
[23] Mary Anne Everett Green, *Elizabeth Electress Palatine and Queen of Bohemia*, rev. ed. (London, 1909), pp. 359-64, 369-70.
[24] J. van Beek, "Archibald Hamilton, een gevluchte Anglicaansche aartsbisshop in Nederland," *N.A.K.*, 4 (1907), 148-80.
[25] B.P., I, 376.

Although the Dutch preachers urged that he should demonstrate solidarity with the Dutch Reformed Church, Browne refused to identify with them by subscribing to the required Dutch confession. The Dutch took offense at reports that Browne preached disparagingly about the Reformed Church and called it "schismatic." Browne tried to mend the damage by declaring that he really believed that "these churches were true churches and the preachers lawfull preachers"; however he would not make a formal submission to the Canons of Dort.[26] Other Anglicans had similar harassing experiences. Richard Maden was admitted at the English Reformed Church of Amsterdam in 1647 only on the explicit condition that he subscribe and practice conformity to Dutch Reformed religion—no Anglicans wanted.[27]

At Breda the classis kept a minute supervision over the ministers of the English church, which was full of Royalists. Charles sometimes kept court at Breda and Princess Mary and Queen Elizabeth lived part time there. Of all the established English churches, Breda was the most influenced by Anglicanism. During Laud's campaign to place Anglicans in Netherlands churches, Richard Dell in 1637 came to Breda; gradually he inserted bits and pieces of the Anglican liturgy. By 1645 he had advanced to the point where he used the liturgy exactly as printed and the people received the communion kneeling, "nor hath he received any the least check from the Classis for so doing."[28] His successors in the Breda pastorate, Sampson Johnson, Andrew Kier, and David Michael were required to subscribe to the Dutch Reformed confession and go under the classis. Michael's subscription, however, was given only with qualifications.[29] John Stone of Heusden used "English episcopal ceremonies" for baptisms; thereupon the classis summoned him in and admonished him for acting against lawful regulations.[30] John Dibdall of Sluis, another of the exiles of "shipwracked fortune," had a long controversy with the Classis of Walcheren. He refused to acknowledge their authority; "they have pressd hard upon me, to submitt onder their jurisdiction but I have refused."[31]

For the Anglican preachers, the farther away from the Dutch classis, the better. Reformed worship to them seemed pale and uninspiring, the preachers meddlesome. George Morley, with over three years service in the Netherlands, boasted that he "never had anything to do with the

---

[26] Acta Classis Hague, III, April 29, July 1, 1652.
[27] Amsterdam C.R., III, 152-53, 166; Acta Classis Amsterdam, IV, 369.
[28] B.P., I, 377-78.
[29] Acta Classis Breda, II, 111-12, 300, 321v.
[30] Acta Classis Gorinchem, IV, Nov. 24, 1648, April 12-13, 1649.
[31] B.P., I, 380.

Classis, nor they with me."[32] However, while chaplain to Elizabeth at The Hague he occasionally preached in the English Reformed Church —near apostatizing to high Anglicans—"for which his Lordship suffered much in his reputation."[33] Chaplain Thomas Browne would never allow the Princess of Orange to mingle with the English Reformed congregation at The Hague, when she lived there, "though in the worst of times, when there was hardly any face of a church of England."[34]

Anglicans did not have the Dutch field to themselves. Puritans also organized in the Netherlands on behalf of the revolution. The Parliamentary agents (among them George Strickland, Samuel Glover, and Isaac Dorislaus) campaigned among the politicians, and meanwhile the preachers worked in the churches. Hugh Peter, long-experienced in the Netherlands, returned in September 1643 as Parliamentary agent. His commission "combined the objects of a financial representative, propaganda agent, and counterspy."[35] He visited the Amsterdam English Reformed Church, "having biene sent into these United Netherlands by a Committee of the Parliament in England, with commission to try if he could borrow some money for the Parliaments use." Although the elders would not open the pulpit to him, he met with private groups of English people and preached political sermons, "rebellious matters of dangerous effect" tending to "continuation of the war in England." Sir William Boswell complained to the States General about him.[36] Peter visited many of the other English churches and some Dutch churches: he was at Amsterdam in November 1643 and January 1644, and from November to January he visited Rotterdam, Bergen-op-Zoom, Goes, Flushing, and Middelburg. While at Rotterdam he stirred up trouble for George Beaumont of the Merchant Adventurers church, a Laudian conformist, who was consequently dismissed by the London Court of the Adventurers.[37] Peter explained his mission to the Dutch Reformed Church of Bergen-op-Zoom as "to thank the churches of Zeeland for their affection to the churches of England," also to explain the war, "that Parliament sought nothing other than to maintain her privileges and to reform the discipline of the churches." He urged the Dutch churches to continue their good affection to the English church.[38] Parliament also arranged to send over

---

[32] Morley, *Seven Treatises*, preface.
[33] Edward Lake, *Diary*, ed. G. P. Elliott, *Camden Miscellany*, 1 (1847), 26.
[34] Ibid.
[35] Raymond P. Stearns, *The Strenuous Puritan: Hugh Peter, 1598-1660* (Urbana: Univ. of Illinois Press, 1954), pp. 218-20.
[36] Amsterdam C.R., III, 137; Res. States General, no. 3202, fol. 601.
[37] B.P., I, 347; Flushing C.R., no. 4469, Jan. 1, 1644; Acta Classis Walcheren, III, 66.
[38] Acta Kerkeraad Bergen-op-Zoom, I, 29 (Jan. 6, 1644).

representatives from the Dutch church at London to itinerate among the Dutch churches to raise funds.[39] Robert Baillie by letter and William Spang of Veere through personal contacts were also urging the Dutch church to get involved in the affairs in England and Scotland.[40]

The Dutch churches, acting through their classes and synods, spoke out enthusiastically in favor of the Puritan, Parliamentary reforms. They accepted the English Revolution as an uprising of fellow Christians for the sake of the Reformed religion. In a letter to the Church of Scotland, July 18, 1643, the Synod of Zeeland commended their new found freedom and warned them never again to be seduced by Episcopal ceremonies. "Freed from the yoke of the bishops and cleansed from Anti-Christian ceremonies and filth, the Scots should beware not to fall again into the same slavery."[41] Dutch Reformed prayers went up in support of Covenanters and Puritans against the bishops. Throughout all the synods, the clergy organized fast and prayer days, sent petitions to the politicians of the States General, and gathered collections for the relief of Irish Protestants. The money collections for Ireland were channeled through London, causing Boswell to object that the relief funds were being misused and instead were going to Scotland for military purposes.[42] The States General and the provincial states were not happy to see the *Predikanten* initiating policies towards England and Scotland. In 1649, when the preachers of The Hague sent condolences to Prince Charles for the execution of his father, the States of Holland rebuked their meddling and gave them strict orders against any communications with foreign princes or mention of politics in sermons and prayers. Decreed the States: The task of Dutch preachers is not politics; their task is "to hold fast to their profession of proclaiming the word of God edifyingly and purely to the church."[43]

The overseas English and Scottish churches felt many reverberations of the revolution within their congregations. The Merchant Adventurers, being dependent on a royal charter, were quickly affected. Although they had tilted toward the Royalist side early in the war, they shifted the other

---

[39] Dirke Hoste and Maurits Stampsis were in Zeeland in 1643; D. Nauta, *De Nederlandsche Gereformeerden en het Independentisme in de zeventiende eeuw* (Amsterdam: H. J. Paris, 1936), p. 44.

[40] Robert Baillie, *The Letters and Journals of Robert Baillie*, ed. David Laing (Edinburgh, 1841-42), II, 169, 181, 193.

[41] Quoted in the records of the Synod of South Holland, Knuttel, *Acta Synoden Zuid-Holland*, II, 399-402; [Pieter Le Clercq], *Het leven van Willem den II* (The Hague, 1738), pp. 100-09.

[42] Res. States of Holland, no. 77, pp. 169-70.

[43] Res. States of Holland, no. 82, p. 32; Edward Hyde, *Clarendon: Selections from the History of the Rebellion and Civil Wars and The Life by Himself*, ed. G. Huehns (London: Oxford Univ. Press, 1956), p. 322 (Chapter 49).

way when the Parliament gained the ascendancy. The merchant church at Rotterdam made suitable adjustments in 1643, first by dismissing pastor George Beaumont, the conformist forced on them when Forbes resigned, and then by cleansing the liturgical furnishings (altar and railings) which Beaumont had installed.[44] Several of the Merchant Adventurers, who had given money and supplies to the king, were outlawed by Parliament in 1644 after Hugh Peter's visit to Rotterdam. One of them, Theophilus Baynham stubbornly refused to recognize the supremacy of Parliament. In 1645 the officers at London ordered that the Solemn League and Covenant be administered at Hamburg and Rotterdam; all the Rotterdam merchants subscribed except for Baynham. A few months later Baynham fell into a canal and drowned—reportedly drunk from toasting the king. Puritans declared that Baynham had been punished by the "remarkable hand of God."[45]

At the Middelburg church, composed mainly of merchants, the dilemma of whether to deal in war goods with the king or Parliament was a keen question. One merchant had been reported to England for having "fraughted a ship with ammunition for the King," and his ship was seized by a Parliamentary vessel. When he got back to Middelburg, he brought charges in the eldership that fellow church members had reported him and "had a great hand" in his humiliation. Another of the merchants, who had apparently reported him, declared, "He had done no more than his duty, having taken the nationall covenant of England."[46] The English church at The Hague, having many of the new Royalist emigrés, was deeply split about the revolution. Samuel Balmford, a staunch Puritan, found the character of his congregation substantially changed. When he attempted in 1645 to introduce into the church the new Westminster *Directory*, the Royalists made such an outcry that the communion had to be postponed. Boswell, still working hard for the king, led the attack on the *Directory*, "for by submitting thereto I had de facto acknowledged a Powre above my Soveraigne." Cleverly, Boswell turned the old tables on Balmford by appealing to the "No Novelties" Resolutions of 1633, which had originally been created to forestall Laudian innovations. This time Boswell hoped to prevent Presbyterian innovations.[47] Balmford resigned to return to London in 1650, and his place was taken by George Beaumont. For the next seven

---

[44] J. H. W. Unger and W. Bezemer, eds., *Bronnen voor de geschiedenis van Rotterdam* (Rotterdam, 1892-1907), III, 466.

[45] B.P., I, 371; H.M.C., *Portland MSS*, III, 137-38; Tanner MS. 59, fol. 57; C. Te Lintum, *De Merchant Adventurers in de Nederlanden* (The Hague: Martinus Nijhoff, 1905), pp. 173-75.

[46] Middelburg C.R., I, 112 (Dec. 25, 1643), 119.

[47] B.P., I, 371-75; Res. States of Holland, no. 78, pp. 141, 152.

years, although the Republic now prevailed in England, Beaumont retained prayers for the king until ambassador George Downing in 1658 protested. He got an order from the Dutch Council of State to stop the prayers. At this turn, Elizabeth of Bohemia, aunt of Charles II, withdrew from the church.[48]

The Amsterdam English Reformed Church had a strong Royalist, anti-Republican faction. The ministers were Richard Maden, a former Anglican conformist, and William Price, an ardent Presbyterian and hater of Oliver Cromwell. A Republican agent reported them in 1654 as "violent incendiaryes." Price "prayeth and preacheth vehemently." When the first Anglo-Dutch war ended in 1654, Price and Maden were frustrated that Cromwell had survived the war. They had no enthusiasm for the officially sponsored thanksgiving for the peace treaty and gave only grudging thanksgiving. They "rather prayed to incense the people against the protector and the government. And whereas it stood in the states proclamation, there should be thanksgiving for a peace made betwixt them and the protector of England, &c. they translated it, betwixt those of England, who were in possession at present; and constantly pray, that the people may prove magnanimous to maintain their rights, and caste off the yoke of bondage, and to preserve Charles Stuart, and restore him."[49] A core of large merchants (John Webster, Richard Bridgman, Edward Man) supported the preachers' Royalism. However, part of the church was outspokenly Republican and was offended at hearing Royalism from the pulpit. George Hewett, a cobbler, asked for his demission because of the public Royalist prayers.[50]

The most distressing revolutionary event was the execution of King Charles in 1649. An outbreak of violent deeds erupted in the Netherlands and Germany. Inflamed Royalists murdered Isaac Dorislaus, Parliamentary agent, at The Hague in 1649; in the same year Isaac Lee, deputy of the Merchant Adventurers, was kidnapped by Royalists at Hamburg and the preacher of the church, Jeremiah Elborough, was attacked by Royalist assassins. Three armed men leaped on Elborough as he was entering church, Bible under his arm, but by a miracle he escaped without injury.[51] Hewett, the cobbler, at Amsterdam regarded the execution as justice and proposed that now the orphaned royal children could

---

[48] Thurloe, *S.P.*, VII, 246, 257-58; Fred. Oudschans Dentz, *History of the English Church at The Hague, 1586-1929* (Delft: W. D. Meinema, 1929), p. 21.

[49] Thurloe, *S.P.*, I, 118, 514; II, 319, 373-74.

[50] Alice C. Carter, *The English Reformed Church in Amsterdam in the Seventeenth Century* (Amsterdam: Scheltema & Holkema, 1964), p. 97.

[51] *D.N.B.*, s.v. Dorislaus; William E. Lingelbach, "The Merchant Adventurers at Hamburg," *A.H.R.*, 9 (Jan. 1904), 275; Hans Fernow, *Hamburg und England in ersten Jahre der Englischen Republik* (Hamburg: Lütcke & Wulff, 1897), p. 10.

make their own living by honest trades like cobbling.[52] Balmford at The Hague took the execution calmly and "would not name the King in his Church, and what he seemingly prayed for him was indeed more against him."[53] The deputy of the Merchant Adventurers of Rotterdam closed the church temporarily in 1649 for fear of disturbances, having heard that the chaplain intended to pray for the king. Their chaplain in 1649 was Henry Tozer.[54] Some of the English people of Rotterdam openly rejoiced at the news of the king's death, "and, as it is reported, they feasted for that reason." This was reported by Lord Hatton (Christopher Hatton) as happening at the church of the Rotterdam "Brownists." However, because Rotterdam had no Brownist church nor known colony of Brownists at this time, he more likely referred to the Independents. The king's beheading caused a horrible despondency among the Anglican exiles. The new struck one woman dead on first hearing it and put another at death's door. Lord Hatton wrote in March 1649, "This late sad and execrable murther of our blessed master hath soe disordered me that I shall hardly ever recover true quiet of mind."[55] Although momentous news, none of the British churches recorded the execution in the consistory registers.

The Scottish Churches and the Revolution

Two of the churches were distinctly Scottish, the staple church at Veere and the Scots Church at Rotterdam. Three Scottish regiments served in the Netherlands and these had Scottish chaplains. Other than these, the English and Scots were combined into joint English-language churches. All of the *Engelse Kerken* had Scottish members, some of the churches being known occasionally as the "English and Scottish church" in the municipal and Dutch Reformed records. Such was the case at Leiden, Utrecht, and Middelburg, but even here the usual term was "the English church." The first and longest serving president of the English Synod was John Forbes of Scotland. The Delft church, organized in 1636, was served predominantly by Scots from its earliest days; and by the eighteenth century, most of the churches were relying on ministers from Scotland.

The overseas Scots were quickly drawn into the events of the Scottish Revolution. The Covenanters looked to the Scots of the Netherlands for

---

[52] Carter, *English Reformed Church*, p. 97.
[53] Edward Nicholas, *The Nicholas Papers*, ed. George F. Warner, Camden Society, N.S., 40 (1886), 118-19. The letter (Mar. 9, 1649) does not mention Balmford by name but refers to the English minister at The Hague (who was Balmford in 1649).
[54] Ibid., p. 119.
[55] Ibid., p. 118; Hyde, *History of the Rebellion*, p. 322.

recruiting, raising funds, and shipping of supplies.[56] Thomas Cuningham and other Covenant supporters of Veere helped to keep the Scottish army in weapons by shipping over in 1639 "great quantity of armes, ammunition, cannon and other warre-like necessaries."[57] The prominent Scot preachers of the Netherlands, all Presbyterians, threw their support to the Covenanters. Some went to Scotland to subscribe personally to the Covenant.[58] William Spang of Veere, Robert Baillie's cousin, and Alexander Petrie of Rotterdam were Covenant supporters. Baillie gave Spang and the other Scottish preachers the special task of rallying support for Scottish Presbyterianism among Dutch Reformed clergy. When Independency reared itself at the Westminster Assembly, Baillie urged Spang to produce some anti-Independent declarations from the Dutch.[59]

The Scots church of Rotterdam and the Scots church of Veere adopted the Covenant as creedal foundations. The Covenant issue provoked controversy at Veere between Sir Patrick Drummond, the conservator, and the pro-Covenant faction led by Cuningham and Spang. When the Covenanters prevailed, Drummond was deposed and replaced as conservator by Cuningham in 1644; and with Cuningham in control, the church members subscribed to the Solemn League and Covenant on May 29, 1644.[60] The Rotterdam Scots church under the ministry of Petrie took the Covenant of 1638 as almost its very founding act. On page two of the consistory register, October 1, 1643, the church officers "agreed that the covenant or confession of the kirk of Scotland shalbe read from the Pulpit on Sunday, to the end, that all may know it, and after consideration thereof all the members of this congregation who are receved or ar to be receved hereafter at any time shall subscribe it."[61] As loyal Scots, the churches of Veere and Rotterdam observed days of fasting and prayer for the success of Scottish arms and religion.[62]

When the Covenanters won, Episcopalians from Scotland became exiles in the Netherlands. One of the first was John Forbes of Corse, professor of divinity at Kings College Aberdeen. Professor Forbes, unlike his

---

[56] David Stevenson, *The Scottish Revolution 1637-1644: The Triumph of the Covenanters* (Newton Abbot: David & Charles, 1973), pp. 128, 189; Andrew L. Drummond, *The Kirk and the Continent* (Edinburgh: St. Andrew Press, 1956), p. 82.

[57] Thomas Cuningham, *The Journal of Thomas Cuningham of Campvere 1640-1654*, ed. E. J. Courthope, *Publications* of the Scottish History Society, 3rd ser., 11 (1928), preface, p. ix.

[58] Patrick Forbes, *D.N.B.*

[59] Baillie, *Letters*, II, 193; see above chapter 13.

[60] John Davidson and Alexander Gray, *The Scottish Staple at Veere* (London: Longmans, Green, & Co., 1909), p. 291; Cuningham, *Journal*, pp. 40-47.

[61] C.R., I, 2.

[62] Davidson and Gray, *Scottish Staple*, pp. 289-94; Steven, p. 15.

uncle John Forbes of Middelburg and Delft, was a defender of Episcopacy. After being deposed from his professorship for opposing the Covenant, he went into exile 1644-46. He already knew the Netherlands well, having lived with his uncle at Middelburg in 1619 and marrying a Dutch wife, Soete Roosboom. Forbes kept a diary which recorded his Dutch exile; it is almost exclusively composed of notes about sermons heard or sermons preached. He preached at the English churches at Middelburg, Amsterdam, Utrecht, and Delft, but apparently at none of the Scots churches.[63] Veere was his first stop, but Spang, although making arrangements for him to preach at Middelburg, refused to invite him into his own church, a prudence which Baillie approved. "As for Dr. Forbes, you have done very well, in my mind, who hath not given him your pulpitt. As yow desire not to be mistaken by too many, meddle not with him. ... Send him away."[64] Another Episcopalian refugee was David Michael (or Mitchell), deprived rector of St. Giles, Edinburgh. After a brief career as a watchmaker in Rotterdam, he was given a call in 1656 to be minister of the English church at Breda.[65] William Colvill, Presbyterian preacher of Edinburgh, removed to the Netherlands in 1649, having been suspended by the church General Assembly and deported for supporting Hamilton's expedition into England. He settled at Utrecht and in 1651 and 1652 was nominated for various pastoral vacancies, but he never received an official appointment as preacher in the British churches. In 1652 he was called home as principal of Edinburgh University, "but having been carried prisoner to the Castle for praying for Charles II, he was not permitted by Cromwell's Government to take possession of the office, which was declared vacant, 17 January 1653."[66]

During the revolutionary period, stress between English and Scottish patriots arose in several congregations. At Dort a visiting Scottish preacher in 1641, Mr. Jackson, complained to the consistory of humiliation done unto him by Beatrice Lindsey. She had walked out of his sermon saying, "Why should I stay to heare a foole or a mad man preach?" The elders found it impossible to administer a punishment, there being "no two witnesses that did testify the same words to have been used at

---

[63] The Forbes diary is published in his *Opera Omnia* (Amsterdam, 1703), II, 92-265; G. D. Henderson, "John Forbes of Corse in Exile," *Aberdeen University Review*, 17 (Nov. 1929), 25-35; Drummond, *Kirk and the Continent*, pp. 84-91.

[64] Baillie, *Letters*, II, 166.

[65] Acta Classis Breda, II, 321v; *F.E.S.*, I, 70; Bosher, *Restoration Settlement*, p. 291.

[66] *F.E.S.*, I, 134; Middelburg C.R., I, 169; Flushing C.R., June 28, 1651. He was said to have received a year's stipend in consideration of giving up his charge in Holland; however, I find no evidence of his having had a "charge."

the same time."⁶⁷ At Brielle in 1644, where the English and Scots were attempting to form a church, the project failed because of animosities between the two nations.⁶⁸ Breda witnessed a bitter split between English and Scottish troops. The six English captains in 1637 appointed Richard Dell as chaplain, but the Scottish officers shunned him. Dell was a Laudian conformist. The Scots instead chose Patrick Forbes, son of John Forbes of Delft. Because Forbes refused to cooperate with Dell in administering the English liturgy, each preacher formed a congregation for his own countrymen; and according to Dell, such "a rent between the Scots and English ... hath never beene in any Garrison in these landes." The Scots, inspired by Forbes, mightily objected to the public use of English ceremonies in Breda, and some of Forbes's upholders, which also included the radical English of Breda, proclaimed that the Church of England was a "whore." Forbes, who took the Covenant at Glascow in 1638, inflamed the situation by upholding the Covenanters against England and praying them God's blessing.⁶⁹

Another English-Scottish schism occurred at Utrecht in 1647-48. Walter Bowie, a Scot, became minister in 1647 over the objections of the English garrison. The worst fears of the English were fulfilled when Bowie began talking against the king, queen, Parliament, Independents, and army, praying that "God would breake the kings hart and to convert the Queene." He further offended the English by his imperfect Scottish pronunciation, "often times not to be understood." The exasperated English officers schismed from the main congregation for a time in 1647-48.⁷⁰ In the second half of the seventeenth century, Scots gained increasing numerical predominance in several English congregations. When William Spang moved from Véere to Middelburg in 1652, he offended some by referring to the English church as the "British Church" and even "the Scottish Church."⁷¹

The English-Dutch Wars

At mid-century, England and the United Provinces entered a period of intermittent wars (1652-54, 1665-67, and 1672-74). These wars tested the loyalty of the English churches in the Netherlands. In such times, what was due unto Caesar? Who was Caesar? As natives of a country suddenly become the enemy, the English settlers found themselves under suspicion

---

⁶⁷ Dort C.R., no. 5, fols. 22-23.
⁶⁸ Res. Vroedschap Brielle, no. 9, fol. 53v (Sept. 10, 1644). See above chap. 6.
⁶⁹ B.P., I, 272, 290, 293. See above chap. 10.
⁷⁰ B.P., I, 384, 386, 398; Acta Kerkeraad Utrecht, E, fol. 47v. See chapter 8.
⁷¹ John Quick, "Icones Sacrae Anglicanae," I, i, 271.

and abuse. A Rotterdam settler (Judeth Stevens) in July 1652 complained of the persecutions: "The case of all English of this time in Holland is such that none can so much as passe the streets in peace, quarrells so frequently pickt that every English man is *eo nomine*, because English, in dayly hazzard." As an example, she reported about an English merchant of Rotterdam, who had his goods plundered for alleged disrespect to an admiral; his wife was beaten up and robbed; his son, a burger of the city, had to seek protective imprisonment to escape murderous crowds. Finally the family fled.[72] The English churches, as wards of the Dutch state, were expected to rally to the war effort. At crucial points in the wars, the magistrates ordered days of prayer and thanksgiving. Woe to the English preacher who prayed unenthusiastically for Holland's victory. Richard Maden of the Amsterdam English Reformed Church in 1666, during the second Anglo-Dutch War, imprudently prayed for the speedy recovery of London after the Great Fire. He was reported on September 30, 1666, to the States of Holland for his unpatriotism."He prays very heartily for London's prosperity and for her restoration." In the previous Sunday's prayer, Maden had prayed to God Almighty, alluding to London, "to turn her 'ashes into beauty and her sorrow into the oil of joy,' [Isaiah 61:3] by which expression the congregation, mostly English and English-minded, were not only moved to compassion for the enemy but also to hate Mr. Woodward, the co-minister, who was doing his utmost to bring the people to obedience to their lawful government."[73] Maden within the week was suspended from his office, but he was restored a few months later. Fortunately he was able to prove that he had prayed for the success of the Dutch fleet along with his prayers for London.[74]

During the third Anglo-Dutch War, Joseph Hill of Middelburg was deposed from his pulpit at the English church for meddling in politics. In 1673 he published a political book, *The Interest of these United Provinces. Being a Defence of the Zeelanders Choice*, which the States of Zeeland declared to be "false, calumnious, and criminal." Hill rashly raised the question of seeking collaboration with England: Whether if not able to defend themselves, the Dutch should choose "to be under England than France in regard of Religion, Liberty, Estates, and Trade." The States banned the book and expelled Hill from Zeeland.[75] After several years in England, Hill was able to secure in 1678 the pastorate of the Rotterdam

---

[72] Hessels, *E.L.B.A.*, III, 2208-09 (no. 3143).
[73] Res. States of Holland, no. 99, p. 59. Maden's prayer was based on quoting Isaiah 61:3.
[74] Ibid., no. 99, pp. 66-67; Steven, pp. 275-76.
[75] Reported by States of Holland, no. 106, p. 95; Joseph Hill, *The Interest of These United Provinces. Being a Defence of the Zeelanders Choice* (Middelburg, 1673). A Dutch edition was printed at Amsterdam.

English Reformed Church. With a few exceptions, the British preachers avoided Dutch political controversy. Steven commended the non-political tradition of preachers, indeed he rejoiced, that the British clergy "have had the wisdom never to take any active part in the commotions which at different times have distracted this country."[76]

The largest English commentary on the Anglo-Dutch wars is found in the consistory register of the Flushing church during the ministry of Arnold van Laren. He recorded many items about "the sad warrs." He had news about the transfer of troops, the days of prayer; and when the Dutch and English fleets were in battle off the coast, he could hear the guns roaring. He had this description of the Four Days' Battle:

> June 12, 1666: This day being the second day of the fight betwene the two mightie navies of England and these parts, the people of God mett together in two churches and after the reading of divers chapters out of scripture, divers psalmes were sung ... then the minister made a large prayer which being ended he caused an other psalm to be sung and so the church was dismissed with the ordinary blessing.
>
> June 14, 1666: The day, being monday, the English having received a fresh supply under prins Robbert, we heard againe the terrible roaring of the canon, and not knowing how this fight yet fall out, the people came together in al the three churches, it being the second day of Whitsunday, and the ministers prayed most heartily that God would be pleased to give these countries the victory.
>
> June 15, 1666: The following day, not knowing yet what succes there was, we again mett together in two churches. ... About noon the whole fleet (except some that were gone to Holland) came in here with many signes of triumph, whereupon we mett together againe in the afternoon in two churches, to thank the lord for the great blessing bestowed upon these countries, and first was sung psalms 98 then a thanksgiving, after which was sung the 118 psalm from the 29 vers to the end, and so was the congregation again without a sermon dismissed with the ordinary blessing. During this fight the French and the English (except on the lords day) joyned onely with the Dutch in the publick services as their auditors.[77]

As needed, there were days of thanksgiving or prayer for the success of the war. On July 6, 1667, Van Laren recorded news about the Dutch victory at Chatham, "taking and destroying a fort, the kings magazijn, and the principal ships of England, viz. the royal Charles, royal james, the royal oake, loyal London and divers others." Finally for September 7,

---

[76] Steven, p. 276.
[77] Flushing C.R., 1666.

1667, the minister set down the coming of the Peace of Breda, "a day of thanksgiving for the happy peace made between England and these united provinces on the 31 of July last at Breda: blessing the Lord for his undeserved mercy and favour ... that he wil be pleased to make both nations a peculiar people unto him, that he wil be pleased dayly more and more to unite their hearts in a true and unfeigned Christian love, one to another." That night there were bells, canons, and bonfires.[78]

---

[78] Ibid., 1667. Van Laren had reports about all three of the Anglo-Dutch wars.

PART THREE

FROM THE RESTORATION TO THE
GLORIOUS REVOLUTION (1660-1700)

CHAPTER FIFTEEN

AFTER THE RESTORATION: THE CHURCHES OF AMSTERDAM, HAARLEM, LEIDEN, THE HAGUE, DELFT 1660-1700

In 1660 the English Republic came to an end. In a great reversal of fortunes, the Royalist exiles returned home rejoicing, while Regicides, Republicans, and unrepentant Puritans fled to the Continent, many of them to the old haven of the Netherlands. An informer of 1664 reported about English troublemakers at Amsterdam, Arnhem, and Rotterdam ("more fanaticke army men then in any where else").[1] In 1665 came information of "above 160 English officers, fugitives, and disaffected persons, who are meeting this day at Leyden," the ringleaders being Major-General John Desborough, Colonel Edmund Ludlow, Colonel Joseph Bamfield, Colonel Faire, Major Burton, Captain White and other ex-Cromwellians.[2] There was constant noise of "designs," secret armies, and "plots," which the English government, having barely survived the Revolution, took seriously. All the plots and uprisings of England and Scotland had some roots, or at least a strong support, in the Netherlands. The refugee community sustained itself on rumors of hope and return. "They expected a call over."[3] During the Anglo-Dutch wars some of the exiles were sorely tempted to pray for a Dutch victory, imagining "that if Ingland come to lose one other fightt ther captivitie wil be near expired."[4]

All the plots of the 1660s-1670s came to nothing. In the 1680s the exiles pinned their hopes on the political outcome of the Popish Plot—digging "the Plott at the Root." "There are a sort of people the scum of the fanatiques of England and Scotland who live at Amsterdam and Rotterdam." They "give most horrible impressions of our government."[5] Once again nothing happened. In 1683 the exiles buzzed with happy rumors of the king's death, and they would listen to no contrary reports of his good health—"no denyall must be, of the King's death." At Rotterdam "the same report affirmed with joy." Sir William Waller at Amsterdam went about exulting: "Great newes from England ... The

---

[1] S.P. 29, vol. 90, no. 1.
[2] S.P. 29, vol. 124, no. 72.
[3] *Cal. S.P.D.*, 1668-69, p. 387.
[4] S.P. 29, vol. 159, no. 4.
[5] S.P. 84, vol. 216, fols. 52-53, 150.

King is dead, and the Duke of Monmouth is proclaymed King."[6] In 1685 the exiles rallied behind the futile expeditions of Monmouth and Argyle. Finally in 1688, William of Orange led the triumphant return of the Glorious Revolution, and many exiles went with him.

Some of the post-Restoration refugees were preachers whose careers had been wrecked by the restitution of the episcopal Church of England. "Hell seemed to be broke loose," lamented John Quick, one of the dispossessed Puritans of Black Bartholomew's day.[7] "Divers presbiterian ministers are come out of England and Scotland into theise countryes, more I am sure intend it," said Colonel Bamfield in 1663. "Many presbiterians and independents both ministers and others are come into Holland and into theise parts, and dayley more expected."[8] Calamy's *Nonconformist's Memorial* records over twenty-five ejected English ministers going to the Netherlands after the Restoration.[9] A steady stream of Scottish Presbyterians also made the trip over to the Low Countries.[10] As it had been for more than a hundred years, the Netherlands after the Restoration continued to be haven of refuge for British religion.

The existence of the large English-Scottish refugee group motivated the English government to extreme efforts to counteract the rebels. As a result of new treaties enacted since Laudian days, the English ambassadors had at their disposal more effective instruments of coercion. The Treaty of Westminster (1654) contained provisions that rebels designated by either of the two countries were to be banished. Cromwell appealed to this treaty against the Royalists of the 1650s. The Anglo-Dutch Treaty of 1662 provided that any Regicide found in the Netherlands was to be sent to England. Other rebels of either country were to be banished within twenty-eight days of a request from one government to the other. The anti-rebel clauses were reconfirmed by the

---

[6] S.P. 84, vol. 217, fols. 245-46 (Thomas Hughes Diary).

[7] John Quick, "Icones Sacrae Anglicanae," I, ii, 874.

[8] S.P. 84, vol. 167, fols. 211v, 221. On Bamfield, see *Colonel Joseph Bamfield's Apologie* (n.p., 1685).

[9] Calamy, *N.M.* and Matthews, *Cal. R.* Calamy gives the following Dutch exiles as ejected: David Anderson, Lewis Calandrine, Robert Collins, John Durant, Henry Hickman, Joseph Hill, Alexander Hodge, John Howe, Richard Lawrence, Nicholas Lockyer, Samuel Malbon, Nathaniel Mather, Gamaliel Marsden, Matthew Mead, Matthew Newcomen, Humphrey Philips, Matthew Poole, John Quick, John Reyner, Edward Richardson, Edward Riggs, Gilbert Rule, George Thorne, Robert Tory, Thomas Woodcock; and the following as otherwise harassed into immigration, Ichabod Chauncey, John Spademan. Other ejected ministers should be added to the list: Francis Cross, Robert Brinsley, Henry Sampson, Edward Hulse, Abraham Clifford; also dissenters like John Rogers and Henry Danvers. See Geoffrey F. Nuttall, "English Dissenters in the Netherlands 1640-1689," *N.A.K.*, 59 (1978), 37-54.

Treaty of Breda (1667) and the Treaty of Westminster (1674). However, the recovery of English and Scottish exiles was not so easily done as setting down the words in the treaty. All requests for banishment or extradition of English or Scots were dragged out so long by the Dutch that they were seldom effective, "they being used to promise much and performe nothing."[11] In one case the English ambassador, George Downing, went to extraordinary lengths of intimidation, bribery (and kidnapping if necessary) to seize three Regicides at Delft, Barkstead, Okey, and Corbet, and shipping them back to England.[12] In another case, the English ambassador in 1676-77 succeeded in causing the banishment of three Scots, Robert MacWard, John Brown, and Colonel James Wallace, living at Rotterdam.[13] Other than these few cases, the exiles maneuvered cleverly enough to avoid banishment. Sir William Temple, who handled the MacWard-Brown-Wallace affair, described it as "the hardest piece of negociation that I ever yet entered upon here."[14]

The post-Restoration Netherlands British churches flourished and declined with the ebb and flow of British immigration. Only twelve of the churches survived throughout the seventeenth century: the Reformed and Separatist churches of Amsterdam, the English and Scot churches of Rotterdam, Leiden, Delft, The Hague, Dort, Flushing, Middelburg, Veere, and Utrecht. The church at 's-Hertogenbosch disbanded in 1670; Breda in 1672; Bergen-op-Zoom in 1677. Only one was established in the second half of the century, the church at Haarlem. Three trends characterized the churches in the period 1660-1700. First, they were in numerical decline. Second, they show much evidence of perfunctory religion, far different from the intense Puritan spirit prevailing in earlier century. One church, The Hague, went for fifteen years, 1677-92, without recording a single case of spiritual discipline, and another church, the Rotterdam English, ran so uneventfully that the elders abandoned having regular consistory meetings. Third, the churches were

---

[10] Steven, pp. 25-28, 37-42, 53-54. Among the exiled Scots were Robert MacWard, John Brown, John Carstares, John Livingstone, John Nevay, James Simpson, Robert Trail, Robert Fleming, Richard Cameron, and Col. James Wallace.

[11] S.P. 84, vol. 220, fols. 18-19; James Walker, "The English Exiles in Holland during the Reigns of Charles II and James II," *Transactions* of the Royal Historical Society, 4th ser., 30 (1948), 113-15. Herbert H. Rowen, *John de Witt, Grand Pensionary of Holland, 1625-1672* (Princeton: Princeton Univ. Press, 1978), pp. 440, 453-55, 732-33.

[12] Walker, "English Exiles," pp. 113-14; Ralph Catterall, "Sir George Downing and the Regicides," *A.H.R.*, 17 (Jan. 1912), 268-89; John Beresford, *The Godfather of Downing Street: Sir George Downing 1623-1684* (London: Richard Cobden-Sanderson, 1925), pp. 144-45.

[13] Res. States General, no. 3731, pp. 3, 6; Res. States of Holland, no. 109, pp. 296-97, 607-08; no. 110, pp. 6-10; Steven, p. 36.

[14] Steven, p. 44.

steadily assimilated into Dutch society. Although keeping the name of "English Church" or "Scottish Church," the memberships by 1700 became more Dutch than English.

The Amsterdam English Reformed Church

Amsterdam's fame as a world trading city held strong throughout the seventeenth century. An English merchant of Amsterdam boasted that "many English ships doe arrive at this cittie (the Metropoliton of these Provinces) from all partes of the world" (1676).[15] At the Restoration, Amsterdam attracted a large number of the political exiles, and up to 1688 the English community was growing and active. "If the English tumble over so as they now doe, this may be littell London in tyme."[16] With plotters of the determination of Shaftesbury, Ferguson, and Monmouth, Amsterdam churned with political excitement; a "tornace of Malice waxeth hotter and hotter," complained Royalists. "Too many of his Majesty's unnatural subjects, residing and resorting in these partes."[17]

For English nonconformists Amsterdam had long been the home of Puritan churches. No fewer than ten English churches had functioned at Amsterdam in the early century. William Carr, English consul at Amsterdam, in 1680 wrote to Archbishop Sancroft: "This place hath been the Center or nest where all the Poysoned Phanaticall People of England, and other places resort to, either by corospondancye or by making theire Residence heare. In this City it was where first the English Brownist, Puritane, Anabaptist and Presbyterian first began their Plotts." Carr in 1680 reported five English churches. "My lord in this City ar a Considerable number of English, out of which ar composed 5 Phanaticall Churches or meetings, the 1st a Pesbyterian Church governed by 2 Ministers, 4 Elders, and 4 Deacons; secondly a Brownist Church governed by one Minister and the like number of Elders and Deacons which all preach upon occation; thirdly a Anabaptist Church where all ar Ministers; 4th a Quakers Church where men and women Preach, as their Spiret moves them; 5th an Armenian Church which joyne with the other in their Phanaticall Principalls against Church and State." His recommendation was for Archbishop Sancroft to send over an Anglican clergyman to establish a Church of England, thus to "preserve these

---

[15] S.P. 84, vol. 203, fol. 103 (Abraham Kick, 1676).
[16] William Carr, 1682, in F. A. Middlebush, *Dispatches of Thomas Plott (1681-82) and Thomas Chudleigh, (1682-85)* (The Hague: Typ. Zuid-Holl.- en Handelsdrukkerij, 1926), p. 188n.
[17] S.P. 84, vol. 176, fol. 35.

Sonns of the Church who now are constraint to goe to the french or English Prestbeterian Churches."[18]

Of Carr's reported five English churches of 1680 only the first two, the English Reformed and the Brownist, were established English-language churches. The other three were Dutch churches which attracted some English adherents. Mountague in 1695 mentions the same five churches; "we were at all their conventicles, and heard 'em mouth out their Noise and Nonsense."[19] He tried the English Reformed Church but was not spiritually uplifted. "Here is sorry Preaching, a long, dull, tedious Sermon, an hour and three quarters, about two hundred Auditors, and sometimes four of five hundred, all *Presbyterians*." As parts of the religious establishment, the English, French, and German Reformed churches, like the Dutch, were "allow'd the Use of Bells, and their Ministers are paid by the Magistrates." The English Reformed church, founded in 1607, met in the old Beguine chapel, formerly a Catholic church. "It has yet a nunnery adjoyning to it," observed Mountague; "we saw some of the neat Nuns."[20]

The church membership at the highest was about 466 (1649). In spite of the strong influx of exiles into Amsterdam, which helped to swell temporarily the attendance, the formal membership declined. In 1661 the membership was about 350; in 1674 about 265; in 1700 only about 150.[21] The building in the 1650s had become crowded, and so the church appealed to the burgomasters for an enlargement. In 1663 the burgomasters at last approved and paid for remodeling the church and adding twenty-five Dutch feet to the width. On the south wall a special pew was erected for important visitors. In a capital city the special pew would have been for the ambassador; at Amsterdam they had only an occasional consul for mercantile affairs. "The King of *England* has a Consul here, who makes some small Figure, and sits in an eminent Pew in the Church, and has some Respect paid him."[22] The English Reformed Church was a solidly established part of the Amsterdam scene; its membership was composed of respectable English and Scottish citizens of the city. The church sponsored an English Orphan House and School for

---

[18] William Carr to Sancroft, Aug. 20, 1680, Tanner MS. 37, vol. 123. On Carr see K. H. D. Haley, *The First Earl of Shaftesbury* (Oxford: Clarendon Press, 1968), p. 729.

[19] William Mountague, *The Delights of Holland* (London, 1696), pp. 146-48. By conventicles he refers to Armenians, Brownists or Independents, Anabaptists, and Quakers, "not many of the last."

[20] Ibid., p. 144.

[21] Membership lists nos. 84-99; Alice C. Carter, *The English Reformed Church in Amsterdam in the Seventeenth Century* (Amsterdam: Scheltema & Holkema, 1964), p. 116.

[22] Mountague, *Delights of Holland*, p. 144.

English children in its own building on the Looiersgracht, and also owned other properties and endowments.[23]

Preachers who served the church after 1660 were Richard Maden (1647-68), Richard Woodward (1660-99), Alexander Hodge (1669-89), Adriaan Oostrum (1691-92), and Hugo Fitts (1700-41). Maden, an ejected Anglican who turned Presbyterian, was 69 at the Restoration and talked of going home. He told the elders he would stay in Amsterdam only if his burden of work could be lightened and as easy as a ministry in England. He particularly wanted to be relieved of the weekly Wednesday lecture. Although he had not been giving very vigorous ministry, the elders persuaded him to stay and arranged for him to have an assistant lecturer, Mauritius Bohemus, and for a time a *ziekentrooster* (minister or comforter to the sick), Alexander Hodge.[24] Maden created excitement in the church in 1666, during the second Anglo-Dutch war, by praying publicly for London's prosperity after the Great Fire—"well-intentioned, but ill-timed." The burgomasters suspended him for several weeks but then restored and apparently forgave him. When he retired in 1668 at age 77, having served 49 years in the ministry, they voted him the status of preacher emeritus.[25] Maden's son, Richard Maden, became preacher at the English church at Rotterdam; and his daughter Elizabeth married another Netherlands English preacher, Joseph Hill of Middelburg.

The co-pastor, Richard Woodward, served nearly forty years. His background was as much Dutch as English. He was admitted to the ministry by examination of the Classis of Haarlem in 1652 and then served at the Dutch church at Westmaas under the Classis of Dort. He was thoroughly enough Dutch to be able to function in 1670-71 as scribe of the Amsterdam Classis. Although a steady servant of the church, he was not a very dynamic leader and his preaching was tedious.[26] Alexander Hodge, the ejected Puritan vicar of St. Thomas Apostle's, Exeter, after being *ziekentrooster*, took a position for a short term as minister at Delft (1668-69), and then returned to Amsterdam for twenty years.[27] When Hodge died in 1689, a replacement was hard to find. The consistory tried to find a man in England, but the burgomasters made difficulties about their choices. Finally the church called Adriaan Oostrum, minister of the Dutch Austin Friars Church of London. His

---

[23] Carter, *English Reformed Church*, pp. 130-31.
[24] C.R., III, 228-29, 241.
[25] C.R., III, 247-48. On Maden's prayer, see also chap. 14, no. 73.
[26] Acta Classis Haarlem, V, April 16, June 1, 1652; Mountague, *Delights of Holland*, p. 144.
[27] Quick, "Icones," I, i, 258-59; Calamy, *N.M.*, II, 37-38.

English was so poor that even Oostrum "judged himself incapable of Preaching in Inglish." The Austin Friars church released him but the move puzzled them, because Oostrum was "at present ignorant of the English language."[28] There was little regret when Oostrum resigned in 1692, after less than a year's service. The church by this time had diminished in size down to about 150 members, and the burgomasters took the occasion of the 1692 vacancy to abolish the position of second minister, leaving the aged Woodward as sole minister.[29]

The church received an injection of fresh enthusiasm and membership from the influx of Restoration refugees. One of the signs of growth was the enlarging of the church building in 1663. A goodly company of ejected Puritan preachers resided off and on in Amsterdam; Edward Richardson and Joseph Hill preached occasionally in the church in the 1660s and Alexander Hodge was chosen as one of the ministers. Matthew Poole crossed over during the Popish Plot and died at Amsterdam in 1679. A memorial plaque for Poole was erected in the church.[30] The Congregationalist refugees, who were also a considerable number, could be found mainly at the Separatist church. Although the Restoration immigrants had some enlivening effect upon the church, the congregation was not drawn into the refugee intrigues or English plots. The church records do not reveal any political activity in English affairs. One of the deacons, Daniel Le Blon, was heavily involved in financing Monmouth's expedition, but the church itself was not a party.[31]

During the first half of the century, the Begijnhof church had been powerfully shaped by the religious controversies. With Paget as pastor, it had been a combative church, debating issues of Presbyterianism, Congregationalism, Separatism, and Anabaptism. The church after 1660, fundamentally Presbyterian, embraced no controversial issues or great crusades. Relationships with the Dutch Reformed Church were uneventful. All ministers accepted membership in the Classis of Amsterdam without question. Maden in 1662 took charge of a project to translate into English the principal parts of the Dutch Reformed catechism for use in the church, the actual task of translating being entrusted to Bohemus, the Dutch assistant. It is unlikely that Maden, in spite of his long sojourn in the Netherlands, ever developed a good speaking or writing knowledge of the Dutch language.[32]

---

[28] C.R., III, 306-12; Hessels, *E.L.B.A.*, III, 2691-93.
[29] C.R., III, 319; Carter, *English Reformed Church*, pp. 103-04.
[30] C.R., III, 244 (Hill); S.P. 84, vol. 169, fol. 128v (Richardson). Poole's plaque was erected by the York Civic Trust, Poole being a native son of York.
[31] Peter Earle, *Monmouth's Rebels* (New York: St. Martin's Press, 1977), pp. 152-53.
[32] C.R., III, 234; Carter, *English Reformed Church*, p. 99.

The old battles with the Separatists, so furious during Paget's day, were not revived. Although the two churches had no fraternal ties, the bombastic books and manifestoes—the "Arrows" and "Counterpoysons"—ceased flying. Occasional members slipped back and forth between the two congregations. In 1669 John Turner, a former deacon, went over to the Separatists (now called Independents), much displeasing the elders. They admonished him for his disorderly "breaking his covenant, which he had made with our church." After several months of absence, he was suspended; in the meanwhile, Turner joined the other church. However, on the other side, a Baptist from Huntingdon was won over and joined the Begijnhof church in 1669.[33] Another member, Jacob Denys, being "halfe a Brownist, and his wife 3 quarters," revealed Congregationalist tendencies; nevertheless, he was elected a deacon (1670) and three times an elder (1681, 1685, 1691). The Independent Church exuded dynamic ministry through its minister Samuel Malbon whereas the English Reformed Church under Woodward endured tedious leadership. Denys admitted attending some Brownist meetings. Also in 1670 a woman, who transferred from the English Church at Delft to the English Reformed of Amsterdam, began going to the Brownist Independent Church.[34] The tiny Brownist renaissance in the English Church alarmed the Amsterdam Classis and prompted it to send deputies to confer with Denys and the other deacons, "answering very pithily the chief heads of the objections against the reformed churches of these countryes."[35] After 1670 the Brownist-Independent issue dropped out of the church records. In 1701, when the Independent church disbanded, the English Reformed Church received as members at least four of the ex-Independents. The elders resolved that there was no longer any substantial difference between "them and us."[36]

The burgomasters' "silver chains" binding church and state fitted snugly.[37] Slogans like "due power of the church" or "liberty of the church" as related to classis and magistrates, which had been much heard before mid-century, no longer raised debate. The church, having reached a secure situation of financial stability, was firmly linked to the political and religious establishment. The political control that went along with official sponsorship revealed itself at every pastoral election.

---

[33] C.R., III, 254-56, 259. Thomas Marriot joined by baptism "for as much as he saith he was never baptized, his father being an Anabaptist," III, 256.
[34] C.R., III, 260; Delft C.R., no. 102, Feb. 23, Mar. 23, July 27, 1670 (Mrs. Abraham Kick Senior).
[35] C.R., III, 263.
[36] C.R., IV, April 10, 1701. See below, no. 75.
[37] Carter, *English Reformed Church*, p. 41.

The burgomasters exercised a veto over all elections and in several cases dictated the result. In the election of 1660 the burgomasters disapproved the first two pastoral choices of the church (William Cooper and John Skase), thus in effect forcing the election of Woodward.[38] In the election of 1668-69, after Maden's retirement, the burgomasters disallowed the entire first and second nomination lists and laid down a list of their own. They dictated "not to make any further application to England," and to choose "out of such as did reside in these parts." Hodge, one of the dictated nominees, was then elected.[39]

In the election of 1689-90 the burgomasters disallowed the first elected candidate (Thomas Woodcock), raised problems over the second election (John Spademan), and then dictated that the electee must be native Dutch and knowledgeable in both languages, which pushed the church into the reluctant election of Adriaan Oostrum. Oostrum was at least a third or fourth choice; although Dutch, as had been ordered, his great disability was that he could barely speak the English language. When he tried to preach in English, he was a terrible failure; and the English consistory had no solution but to send him back to England for several months of language study. The burgomaster had another solution, that Oostrum simply preach in Dutch until his English improved (most of the congregation being Dutch speaking). Sensible enough, perhaps, but the church officers viewed such an event as the church's final surrender to assimilation in Dutch society. They feared "inconveniences might come upon our church, if for some considerable time Mr. Oostrum should preach among us in Dutch."[40] After more quibbling between the church and burgomasters about Oostrum, the magistrates lost patience and demanded a statement of total submission from the English consistory. The required document was an act "subscribed by the Brethren that they would fully submit themselves with all respect, and obedience to the order, and resolution of the Lords, that they might not see any alteration hereafter." Having fully submitted, the church was allowed to send Oostrum away "to parfecte His English," and in the meanwhile to have John Leask as interim assistant.[41] Not much congregational autonomy was allowed at Amsterdam.

The election of 1699, following Woodward's death, was the ultimate case of a dictated election. The first election was disallowed, and thereafter the burgomasters laid down the following qualification: The

---

[38] C.R., III, 226-27.
[39] C.R., III, 248-49.
[40] C.R., III, 311-15. The church could find only three candidates that met the qualifications, Hugo Fitts of Flushing, Willem Dorvile of Vlaardingen, and Oostrum.
[41] C.R., III, 316.

new preacher must be able to preach in both English and Dutch, be native and resident of the United Provinces, be 32 years old, have served 6 years as minister, and be "peaceable, sound in doctrine, and blameless in his conversation." There was only one man in the entire country who fulfilled these qualifications, Hugo Fitts of Flushing, so the result was a foregone conclusion. Fitts was elected and served for forty years.[42] The church's duty was "to obey the orders, and commands of their Lordships."[43] Although the electoral arrangements were dictatorial, Fitts turned out to be a good choice and pleased the congregation. None of the seventeenth-century ministers after 1660 were men that the church would have chosen in a free election.

The English Reformed Church of 1607 is the oldest continuously existing Netherlands English church. It still meets in its original building in the Begijnhof. Up through Fitts's ministry all the preachers were English, except for one German (Rulice) and one Dutchman (Oostrum). In the eighteenth century the church allied with the Scottish Presbyterian Church and since then has been served by Scottish ministers. The church has double ties, to the Dutch Reformed Church and the Church of Scotland. Doctrinally their ministers were required to be "Calvinist, & a presbyterian, & be willing to subscribe some Articles of the Synod of Dort & preach without Notes."[44] In the church today are displayed flags of Scotland, the Union Jack, the Orange flag, and the American flag, the latter a gift from the Pilgrim Fathers Society of Plymouth, Massachusetts.[45] Because of the disappearance of the Amsterdam and Leiden Separatist churches, American descendants of the Pilgrim Fathers look to the church building as a place of pilgrimage and for displaying plaques and flags. Visitors to Amsterdam will often be told that this was the church of the Pilgrim Fathers. None of the Separatist pilgrims, however, had any direct association with the church.

The Church of England established a church at Amsterdam, Christ Church, in 1698. Their first meeting place was a former secret Augustinian chapel on the Huidenvettersloot (between Oude Zijds Achterburgwal and Gelderskade), close to the Brownist church. In the eighteenth century the church moved to the Groenburgwal, its present loca-

---

[42] C.R., III, 330-31; Carter, *English Reformed Church*, p. 105.
[43] C.R., III, 324.
[44] These were the requirements in 1739; Geoffrey F. Nuttall, "Philip Doddridge and 'the Care of all the Churches', *T.C.H.S.*, 20 (Oct. 1966), 137-38.
[45] J. A. Groen, "De Engelse Hervormde Gemeente," *Ons Amsterdam*, 9 (Jan. 1957), 238-43. Plaques include one to the Pilgrim Fathers by the clergy of the Reformed Church of America (1927), one from the Chicago Congregational Club (1909), another to the Scottish Regiments of 1572-1782.

tion. The English Reformed and Christ Church, Church of England, are the present day English churches of Amsterdam.[46]

The Amsterdam Separatists (Independents)

The second long-established English church was the Ancient Church, whose Amsterdam history reached back to 1596. Its first preachers, Johnson, Ainsworth, and Canne were among the fathers of Separatism. During the English Revolution, after Canne's removal in about 1647, the church nearly expired. Quaker missionaries proselytized at the church and raised so much commotion in the late 1650s that William Ames the Quaker had to be bodily thrown out by the preacher of the church.[47] The church after 1660 was called by various names: "Brownist," the "English Separation," and increasingly the "Independent Church." The Ancient Church, in spite of its strict Separatist tradition, was soon absorbed into post-Restoration English Congregational or Independent dissent. The records of the church are very scanty; even in the seventeenth century, John Quick could not find much in its archives.[48] Some light is thrown on the church's history by two sources, the first, a series of legal notarial documents of business transactions, the second, diplomatic reports from the Netherlands concerning notorious political members of the congregation.

The church until 1662 met in its historic building on the Lange Houtstraat. In 1662 the old church building burnt down. For a short time the congregation moved to a room in a house on the Groenburgwal, and in 1668 to a new church in the Barndesteeg (in a small alley, the Bruinistengang). The Brownists at this time appealed to the Amsterdam burgomasters (through the *kerkmeesters*) for a piece of land for the church building. The city responded with some help, but how much is not known. To receive any subsidy at all was a Separatist first in the Low Countries—otherwise the congregation threatened to migrate to Rotterdam.[49] The legal transactions of selling the Groenburgwal property and erecting a new church have left a few details about the church and its chief members. In 1670 Francis Prince pressed John Ainsworth, Henry

---

[46] J. Loosjes, *History of Christ Church (English Episcopal Church) Amsterdam 1698-1932* (Amsterdam: M. J. Portielje, 1932), pp. 13-35; H. J. M. Roetemeijer, *Review of the History of Christ Church Amsterdam 1698-1971* (Amsterdam: n.p., 1971), p. 3.

[47] William I. Hull, *The Rise of Quakerism in Amsterdam 1655-1665* (Swarthmore: Swarthmore College Monographs on Quaker History, no. 4, 1938), p. 24.

[48] Quick, "Icones," I, i, 258. He could not find their covenant.

[49] H. J. M. Roetemeijer, "De Bruinisten in Amsterdam," *Ons Amsterdam*, 21 (July 1969), 197; H. de la Fontaine Verwey, "De Bruinistenkerk," *Amstelodamum*, 37 (1950), 106-07; H. de la Fontaine Verwey, "Van kerk tot dievenhol, de geschiedenis van de Bruinistenkerk," *Amstelodamum*, 36 (1949), 150-56; H. A. Enno van Gelder, *Getemperde vrijheid* (Groningen: Wolters-Noordhoff, 1972), p. 61.

May, Nathaniel Arnold, and Charles Goodhand, deputies of "the English church named the Brownist Church which meets in the Barndesteeg," for repayment of a loan of 8000 guilders loaned in 1668.[50] Prince was himself probably a member of the church. In 1671 the Brownists ("meeting in the Barndesteeg," John Ainsworth, John Turner, and Jacob Larwood, deputies) sold their Groenburgwal meetinghouse to Portuguese merchant Salvador del Soto for 6800 guilders. The John Turner of the business transaction had only in 1669 come over to the church from the English Reformed Church. The sale was for "a house and grounds lying on the east side of the Groenburgwal consisting of two dwellings where formerly the English assembly was held."[51] Members of the church lived in the Groenburgwal vicinity, some perhaps in dwellings attached to the church.[52] In 1672 the church officers sold some ground with a foundation on it, lying on the north side of the Barndesteeg.[53] The new building was serviceable and utilitarian, "a pretty handsome and convenient Church." Thomas Bowrey, however, thought it very mediocre. "Went to one of the English Churches alias Meeting house, being of the Brownist: a small place meanly sett out; about 200 Persons and most of them seemingly but Ordinary."[54]

The ministry of the church was carried on by ejected English Independent preachers who came to Amsterdam for shelter. By 1663 John Canne, former minister, was back in Amsterdam and had resumed printing Bibles. Whether he resumed the ministry of the church is unknown. He died at Amsterdam in 1667.[55] Samuel Malbon and Richard Lawrence, Congregationalists ejected from Norfolk, apparently served the church during the 1660s. Malbon was "a minister of the church there" about 1663-69 or a little longer. Lawrence was in the Netherlands by 1664.[56] Other Congregationalist preachers who served the church

---

[50] Not. Archive 3610, fol. 254 (Aug. 12, 1670).

[51] Not. Archive 3588, fol. 3 (Jan. 2, 1671); Kwijtscheldingen, no. 57, fol. 28 (May 5, 1671); C.R., III, 254-55.

[52] Not. Archive 1139, fols. 377-80.

[53] Kwijtscheldingen, no. 57, fol. 85v.

[54] Roetemeijer, "Bruinisten," p. 198; Thomas Bowrey, *The Papers of Thomas Bowrey*, Hakluyt Society, 2nd ser., 58 (1925), 37.

[55] Not. Archive 2157, fols. 21-23 (2000 English Bibles in duodecimo printed by Canne were sold at Amsterdam in 1663); Champlin Burrage, "Was John Canne a Baptist? A Study of Contemporary Evidence," *Transactions* of the Baptist Historical Society, 3 (1913), 225.

[56] S.P. 29, vol. 90, no. 1; vol. 91, no. 88; Calamy, *N.M.*, II, 256, III, 15; Matthews, *Cal. R.*, pp. 318-19, 333-34. Neither is named absolutely as being at the Independent church, merely as minister or pastor of a "church" at Amsterdam. The records reveal that they were not at the English Reformed Church; consequently the Independent church was almost certainly their church.

were Robert Ferguson (1679), Matthew Mead (1686), and Thomas Gouge (1685-89). Ferguson ("Ferguson the Plotter"), ejected from Godmersham, Kent served the church during his first trip to the Netherlands. A delegation of the church came out to meet him at Leiden and Haarlem, urging him to stay among them as minister. He wrote to his wife from Amsterdam, October 29, 1679, that he had "service as well as a comfortable provision here." His tenure was short; by 1681 he was already "formerly" minister of Amsterdam, having returned to England where he became a chief designer of the Rye House Plot of 1683. Ferguson was forced to withdraw to the Netherlands at least three times more during the 1680s.[57] Matthew Mead, ejected from Shadwell, Stepney, fled to Holland for a while in the 1660s and again in the 1680s, the second time because of complicity in the Rye House Plot. Scottish student John Erskine heard Mead, "who is a good preacher," at the Amsterdam Independent Church in 1686 and at the Utrecht English Church in 1686 and 1687. In his preaching "he touched a little on Millenary opinions." Mead returned to England in 1687 after the Declaration of Indulgence.[58]

Thomas Gouge, who became minister of the church in 1685, was only twenty-one years of age. Erskine and Edmund Calamy, students of Utrecht University, heard Gouge preach at Amsterdam (1686, 1688). Calamy dined with Gouge in 1688 and found him to be "very great" with John Partridge, the astrologer. Together they had "with great exactness calculated the year, the month, the day, and the very hour, when the city of Rome was to be burnt and destroyed, so as never to be rebuilt any more." When Calamy asked for more details, Gouge declined to name the date but assured Calamy he might well expect to "live to see that time." After the Glorious Revolution, Gouge in 1689 returned home and accepted the ministry of the Congregationalist church at Three Cranes, Thames Street, London.[59] The Ancient Church also had a long tradition of lay preaching to augment the professional preacher. Elders and deacons often functioned as preachers. William Carr's description of the Brownist or Independent church had it governed by one minister, one

---

[57] S.P. 84, vol. 215, fol. 208; Add. MS. 37,981, fol. 68; James Ferguson, *Robert Ferguson the Plotter* (Edinburgh: David Douglas, 1887), pp. 37-38. Congregationalists are not very willing to claim him; see *T.C.H.S.*, 2 (1905-06), 139, "He was a worthless man and it is to the honour of Congregationalists that they early detected and disowned him."

[58] John Erskine, *Journal of the Hon. John Erskine of Carnock. 1683-1687*, ed. Walter Macleod, *Publications* of the Scottish History Society, 14 (1893), 190, 209, 216, 219; *D.N.B.*, s.v. Mead; Calamy, *N.M.*, II, 461-67.

[59] Erskine, *Journal*, p. 190; Edmund Calamy, *An Historical Account of My Own Life*, 2nd ed. (London, 1830), I, 181; Walter Wilson, *The History and Antiquities of Dissenting Churches and Meeting Houses in London* (London, 1808-14), II, 69-72.

elder, and one deacon, "which all preach upon occacion." In 1681 Mr. Prince was reported to be "elder and king, and priest of that church"; and in 1682 Abraham Kick, merchant, was "formerly a preacher of the Independent Church."[60] It is doubtful that the church ever found a permanent replacement for Gouge after his return to England in 1689. In 1701 the church "had been a considerable time, without an ordinarie minister, or administration of the Sacraments."[61]

Great publicity came to the post-Restoration Independent Church because of its close association with the political refugees from England. The Independent Church, the church of "phanatics," was almost the Amsterdam headquarters of the political intriguers. Its preachers were fiery ejected nonconformists, and English exiles found their best hospitality among the Independents. Traitors "by this church ar receved, and assisted."[62] Informants to the English government amassed considerable data on the membership of the church and sent reports about the most rebellious of them. A report of 1681 ("Ye names of his Majesties Phanaticall Subjects in Amsterdam—of the Brownist Church") lists the following members or attenders:

> Mr. Prince (Francis Prince), "Bisshop or Elder of that Church"
> Israel Hayes, Alderman Hayes's son, "kept Sir William Waller at his house"
> Robert Phelps, alias Robert Archer, son of John Phelps, "a pretended judg of our martier King Charles"
> Mr. Haynes, son of Major General Hezekiah Haynes
> John Smith, son of Blagrave of the High Court of Justice
> Thomas Gerard, son of Captain Gerard
> Peter D'Aranda, son of the Huguenot minister
> Thomas Scull, formerly of John Goodhand's church
> Mr. May, a barber, landlord to the Duke of Monmouth on his previous trip to Amsterdam
> Mr. Ellison, son of Colonel Ellison
> Oliver Cromwell, son of Henry Cromwell.[63]

Other Amsterdam Independents thought to be political plotters were Abraham Kick, Louder and Davall (two Fifth Monarchists), and Henry

---

[60] Add. MS. 37,981, fol. 68; Middelbush, *Dispatches*, p. 202; Tanner MS. 37, fol. 123. An older person by the same name (Abraham Kick) was a merchant of Delft and elder of the English church of Delft; he died in 1668. The widow moved to Amsterdam in 1670 and joined the Independent Church, very likely the mother of the Amsterdam Abraham Kick; Delft C.R., no. 102, Feb. 23, Mar. 23, 1670.
[61] E.R.C. Amsterdam, C.R., IV, April 10, 1701.
[62] Add. MS. 37,981, vol. 2v.
[63] S.P. 84, vol. 216, fol. 158; Add. MS. 37,981, fols. 2, 4, 68.

Harrison, son of Thomas Harrison "the traitor." Such people, "the coffy men," could usually be found idling about the Amsterdam coffee houses.[64]

Members of the congregation were involved in every plot and design against Charles II and James II. In 1670 a certain nonconformist English minister of Amsterdam, perhaps Malbon, was propagandizing with anti-Royalist books. "All the Brownists and phanatics flock to his chamber in Amsterdam where he reads his new peaces which will be a sting to the tymes."[65] In October of 1679, at the time Robert Ferguson was minister, the Duke of Monmouth found a great welcome at the church. He lodged at Mr. May's house, "a great enemy of the King's. The chief man who invited him was one Hayes a phanatic." Monmouth was several times at the church, once with a retinue of eighteen followers. William Carr in 1681 nicknamed Monmouth's chief twelve confederates "the Duke of Monmouth's Apostells." Most of the twelve were from the Independent church. They feasted the Duke at a great dinner and promised to raise money for him. Israel Hayes "danced with his sword on before the Duke."[66]

In such an atmosphere religion and politics mixed easily into one brew. The Independents called a prayer and fast day in February 1681 to uphold the Parliament in its "Exclusion" policies. A large number gathered for the fast day, "where was prayers untill 12 at noone and afternoone a sermon and prayers." The preacher, using a text from Daniel, expounded that the time was near that all nations should be converted to true faith and "in all likelihood it would begin first in England, and those people prayed heartyly for the Parliament that must ere stand the test." In 1686 Matthew Mead prayed (with "foaming mouth") that "Babylon might be destroyed in England." Carr promised to counteract the fanatic enterprises "of some of the Brownist Church who too freely talke seditiously of our Kings concernes."[67]

Following the discovery of new plots in 1682-83, fresh waves of emigrés descended on Amsterdam. The Earl of Shaftesbury and Robert Ferguson arrived December 2, 1682; Shaftesbury lodged at the house of Abraham Kick. "While the said Earle was able to goe abroad, he often walked Amsterdam streets, suported on the right wing by Sir William Waler, and on the left, by his Chaplain (Ferguson). His traine were the English and Scotch nonconformists." Shaftesbury died at Amsterdam in January

---

[64] Ibid.
[65] S.P. 84, vol. 186, fol. 77.
[66] S.P. 84, vol. 216, fol. 158; Henry Sidney, *Diary of the Times of Charles the Second* (London, 1843), I, 155, 166-68.
[67] Add. MS. 37,981, fols. 2, 42; Earle, *Monmouth's Rebels*, p. 154.

1683.⁶⁸ John Locke arrived later in 1683. Each failed plot (Rye House, Monmouth's, Argyll's) brought over more exiles or forced the old ones to come running back. King James in 1686 complained anew about rebels entrenching themselves at Amsterdam—Slingsby Bethel, Sir Robert Peyton, Edward Matthews, Dr. Gilbert Burnet—but got little satisfaction from the Dutch.[69] The various refugees found it prudent to secure citizenship at Amsterdam as insurance against deportation. They also found it wise to pass themselves off as religious refugees, "forced to flie for being prosecuted by the bishops."[70] After the successful Glorious Revolution, many of the church members and attenders, including Gouge the pastor, hurried home as quickly as the "Protestant wind" would take them, leaving a big hole in the congregation.

As in years before, Amsterdam after 1660 functioned as a center of nonconformist printing. Steven Swart and Widow Bruyningh, widow of Joseph Bruyningh, were printers and booksellers for the Whiggish nonconformist cause. According to Carr, they were "the printers of all seditious Papers: at whose shops come every post Smiths Domestic, Intelligencer and written papers of seditious lies." At Swart's shop the English and Scots could go and read all the latest news sheets "for a stiver apeace" and then would spread the sedition all around town. Books printed by Swart were sent out from Amsterdam for export to England, shipped over by small ships, "as fast as one is loaded the next lyes on." Swart and Buyningh were not practicing Independents but had close Brownist connections. They sometimes attended the Ancient Church.[71] Swart, a Dutch printer, married Abigail May, the daughter of elder Henry May and Susanna Bruyningh May of the Ancient Church. Members of the family were still in the church. Swart and his family joined the English Reformed Church, where he served as a deacon. Joseph Bruyningh was uncle of Abigail May Swart, being brother of Henry May's wife. After the death of Joseph Bruyningh, his widow and Swart did business together.[72]

The 1690s, following the return of the exiles, saw the serious decline of the church. The last recorded functioning of the Brownist-Independent church was 1698, when Thomas Bowrey visited (200 attenders).[73] Unlike

---

[68] S.P. 84, vol. 217, fol. 245; Louise F. Brown, *The First Earl of Shaftesbury* (New York: D. Appleton-Century, 1933), pp. 301-02; Haley, *Shaftesbury*, pp. 728-32; Earle, *Monmouth's Rebels*, pp. 71-72.

[69] Add. MS. 34,508, fol. 50; S.P. 84, vol. 220, fol. 16; Maurice Ashley, *The Glorious Revolution of 1688* (New York: Charles Scribner's Sons, 1966), p. 76.

[70] Add. MS. 41,811, fol. 121.

[71] Add. MS. 37,981, fol. 2v; S.P. 84, vol. 216, fol. 154.

[72] I. H. van Eeghen, *De Amsterdamse boekhandel 1680-1725* (Amsterdam, 1960-67), IV, 135-38.

[73] Bowrey, *Papers*, p. 37.

the English Reformed Church, which was also small but had a regular subsidy, the Independents were completely responsible for their own financial support. After being without a trained minister for several years, the church in 1701 decided to cease. The building was turned over to the Dutch Reformed deacons "with an explicit understanding that it should never be used but by those of the Reformed religion."[74] The remnant members scattered to other churches. Six applied "earnestly" to the English Reformed Church in 1701-02, and eventually four of the six were admitted as members, the other two being postponed because of scandalous life. The English Reformed consistory made it easy for joining, "seeing there was no difference between them and us in the fundamental articles of our Christian faith, but only about Church Government, and the use of formes." They were merely required to submit to the Reformed doctrine in the matter of government and worship practice and undergo examination of their life and conversation. They came in by transfer of membership, which was in marked contrast to the humiliating recantations exacted from ex-Brownists by John Paget in the old days. In 1703 one was elected deacon.[75] Other members of the disbanded church transferred to the Dutch Reformed Church, at least one being admitted in 1702 on promise of conformity to Reformed doctrine and church government.[76] The old battles no longer mattered much.

The deserted building, after being vacant for several years, was sold for secular purposes. The English Episcopalians, who had established a Church of England, attempted to rent the "shut up" church in 1703 but were turned away. The church building became a warehouse and tenement house, and the neighborhood deteriorated into one of the poorest slums of the city—"the inhabitants of the former Brownist church belong to the lowest sort of people" (*Duister Amsterdam*, 1911).[77] Henry Martyn Dexter, the American historian of Congregationalism, visited the old church building in 1867. He reported, "the building stands with its side to the narrow alley, and its rear abutting upon one of the ever-present canals which reticulate that Venice of the North; and looks like a cross between a church and a model lodging-house." He was deeply moved by the pilgrimage, "there is that there which can make thoughtful men think."[78] The old church building and the Bruinistengang have now

---

[74] Steven, p. 272.

[75] C.R., IV, April 10, 24, Aug. 14, Dec. 11, 1701; Feb. 12, Oct. 15, 29, 1702; Feb. 7, 1703. Admitted members were Lidia May, Nathaniel Haulcie, Elizabeth Cokrie, Marie Ranson. Refused were Thomas Perseval and wife.

[76] Acta Kerkeraad Amsterdam, XVII, 192, 202 (April 20, 27, July 20, 1702). Anna Huijgen was admitted.

[77] Roetemeijer, "Bruinisten," pp. 198-200.

[78] Dexter, *Congregationalism*, I, 355-56.

disappeared. In 1915 the Vereniging Tot Heil des Volks (The Salvation Army) bought up land on the Barndesteeg, including the old Brownist church and alley, and constructed a new building for its charitable work.[79]

Haarlem

Haarlem had a short-lived English church in the 1660s. Rather surprisingly, no English church had developed at Haarlem in the early seventeenth century during the great English church-building age. English inhabitants of the earlier period were compelled to go to the Dutch Reformed church.[80] The new English church was first commissioned by the burgomasters in 1664, and it met in the Orphan Church (Weeskerkje). The only known minister was Dr. Edward Richardson (1664-70), former minister of Delft. During the Revolution he returned to England, but in 1663 he once again fled to Holland, having been implicated in the Yorkshire Conspiracy. As an accused rebel he faced almost daily threats of deportation; consequently he bought Haarlem citizenship in 1664. Richardson lived in the Guldenbergspoort. In the *Haarlemsche Courant* of June 28, 1664, he gave that address and advertised for sale "two sermons preached by him on the inner love and life power."[81] The burgomasters modestly supported Richardson from 1664 to 1669 or 1670. The financial records refer to him as "preacher of the English Church in this city" and the money was paid "as a gratuity for good service and for the progress he is making in the English Church."[82] One of his notable achievements as Haarlem minister was the reconversion of Jan Coughen away from Quakerism. Coughen, "discoursing with him about Religion ... was so influenc'd by his company that he forsook the Quakers and their Society."[83] Richardson resigned to become minister at Leiden. There is no sign of any replacement being employed or that the church continued after his leaving.

---

[79] Roetemeijer, "Bruinisten," p. 201.

[80] Acta Classis Haarlem, III, Oct. 18, 1633 (N.H.A.).

[81] Cornelis de Koning, *Tafereel der stad Haarlem* (Haarlem, 1807), I, 34; Steven, p. 307; F. Allen, *Geschiedenis en beschrijving van Haarlem* (Haarlem: J. J. van Brederode, 1874), I, 37; James Walker, "The Yorkshire Plot, 1663," *The Yorkshire Archeological Journal*, 31 (1933), 348-59.

[82] Rekening van de Thesaurie, no. 1419, fol. 79; no. 1420, fol. 79v; no. 1422, fol. 78 (G.A. Haarlem); G. Scheurweghs, "English Grammars in Dutch and Dutch Grammars in English in the Netherlands before 1800, *English Studies*, 41 (June 1960), 138-39.

[83] Croese, *Historia Quakeriana* (1695), in William I. Hull, *Benjamin Furly and Quakerism in Rotterdam* (Swarthmore: Swarthmore College Monographs in Quaker History, no. 5, 1941), pp. 22-23.

Leiden

In the early seventeenth century, Leiden had two English churches, the English Reformed (1607) and the Separatist (1609). Following the Restoration only the English Reformed Church remained, the Separatists having disbanded soon after John Robinson's death. The English Reformed Church proved more durable because of official subsidies from the city and provincial magistrates. Their building, which was in the Begijnhof, was provided by the city. Hugh Goodyear (1617-61) was succeeded by the following ministers: Matthew Newcomen (1663-69), Edward Richardson (1670-74), Henry Hickman (1674-92), William Carstares (second minister, 1688), Robert Fleming Junior (1692-95), John Milling (1696-1702), and Robert Milling (1702-15).

The Leiden ministers after 1660 were ejected Puritans; the city and church attracted various disaffected English citizens.[84] Leiden University was a haven for dissenter English and Scots, the flood of British nonconformists having caused serious overcrowding of accommodation in the city.[85] Matthew Newcomen, ejected as lecturer from Dedham, Essex, appeared on a list of fourteen fugitives (along with Richardson and Hickman) who were to be ordered home in 1666 for trial and punishment. At the last moment his name was deleted. Newcomen prudently purchased citizenship at Leiden, "here in the land of my Pilgrimage."[86] Joseph Hill and Henry Hickman, ejected ministers without pastorates, lived with Newcomen after coming over. They assisted him with preaching in the church (1664).[87] Newcomen was in charge of organizing a fast day in June 1664 for success of the forces. He set aside one quarter of the day for preaching, one quarter for confession and prayer, and the remainder for private devotions. "Wee shall bee more large in our confessions and prayers and more large in our preaching then on other daies." Newcomen died of plague or "epidemical fever" in 1669.[88]

Richardson (1670-74) transferred from Haarlem to Leiden. He earned the M.D. degree at Leiden University in 1664, and previously had practiced medicine in England; therefore he was known as Doctor Richardson. Because of his involvement in the Yorkshire Conspiracy, he was one of the most wanted "treasonous" rebels but was never taken or deported. Royalists considered him more a "doctor of plotters" than a doctor of

---

[84] S.P. 84, vol. 176, after fol. 90.

[85] Walker, "Exiles," p. 112.

[86] S.P. 29, vol. 162, no. 60, p. 8; Reg. kerk. zaken, no. 2155, fol. 156; *Cal. S.P.D.*, 1665-66, pp. 318, 342; 1666-67, p. 549.

[87] Sermon notes from Hill, Hickman, and Newcomen (Leiden, 1664) are in Sloane MS. 608, fols. 217-29 (B.M.).

[88] Ibid.; Calamy, *N.M.*, II, 196-98.

healing medicines—"a villaine of Villains." At Leiden, if not before, Richardson fell under the influence of Johannes Rothe, the millenarian, pietistic sage of Amsterdam. He also took up grammar and wrote a famous English-Dutch grammar, *Anglo-Belgica, or the English and Netherdutch Academy* (editions at Amsterdam in 1677, 1689, 1698, also in Dutch editions).[89] In spite of his reputation as plotter, Richardson called himself a man of "no party but for that of righteousnes against unrighteousnes, for Jesus Christ against every way of wickednes among whomsoever it is practised." He thought he stood above national loyalties; "I concern not myself in the victories on either side." He could pray as heartily for Holland as for England. His first wife was Dorcas Hering, daughter of Julius Hering of Amsterdam. He resigned the Leiden pastorate in 1674, under Rothe's influence, and he died at Amsterdam about 1677.[90]

Henry Hickman (1674-92) another of the preachers on the 1666 list of fugitives, was ejected from St. Aldate, Oxford and from his fellowship at Magdalen College. John Erskine, a connoisseur of sermons, heard Hickman preach in 1685 on Titus 1:6, "not accused of riot or unruly," but he did not comment on its quality. Another visitor to the church during Hickman's tenure complained that the preaching was done "very slenderly, I thought, considering it was an university."[91] Although Goodyear had eventually become a member of the Classis of Leiden, few if any of his successors were classis members. When Hickman came in 1674, the Dutch urged that he come under the classis "as formerly Mr. Goodyear did and in conformity with other English churches in Holland and Zeeland." However, no action was taken because Hickman could not understand the Dutch language, and it was decided to wait "until Hickman understands Dutch better."[92]

The church gained extra stature in 1688 by being awarded a second minister. This came about because the Prince of Orange wished to do a favor for William Carstares, his Scottish chaplain, and he arranged for it with the States of Holland. The English church of The Hague gained a second minister at the same time. Hickman's new colleague, William Carstares, was a zealous Scottish Covenanter (pseudonym "Mr. Red"). Carstares's office "was founded by the Stadtholder solely on his account." However, Carstares gave short service (February-October

---

[89] S.P. 84, vol. 169, fol. 57; *Cal. S.P.D.*, 1665-66, p. 342; Scheurweghs, "English Grammars," pp. 138, 149-52; Nuttall, "English Dissenters," p. 47.

[90] S.P. 29, vol. 167, no. 159; Calamy, *N.M.*, III, 445-46; Matthews, *Cal. R.*, p. 410.

[91] Erskine, *Journal*, pp. 110-11 (he also heard a Mr. Holmes); Ralph Thoresby, *The Diary of Ralph Thoresby*, ed. Joseph Hunter (London, 1830), I, 19; Matthews, *Cal. R.*, pp. 260-61. Thoresby did not say whether the "slender" preaching was by Hickman or a guest preacher.

[92] Acta Kerkeraad Leiden, no. 006, Feb. 22, May 3, 1675.

1688) and soon went to England accompanying William on the Glorious Revolution.[93] Carstares led the thanksgiving service at Torbay. After the victory, Carstares was rewarded with higher places and was appointed royal chaplain and eventually principal of the University of Edinburgh.[94] When Carstares resigned (by letter), the position of second minister lapsed. The size of the congregation hardly warranted a double ministry. After Hickman's death in 1692, the church secured Robert Fleming Junior (educated at Utrecht and Leiden), son of Robert Fleming of Rotterdam. In 1695 Fleming moved to the Rotterdam Scots Church to succeed to his father's old pulpit.[95] From Fleming onward, the church took on a more Scottish flavor; all the remaining ministers were Scots.

In the eighteenth century the English church withered almost totally away, in conjunction with the decline of the basic textile industry of the city. The city magistrates in 1761 resolved to end the church after the retirement of its present minister, William Mitchell, because "no English students any longer attend Leiden University, nor are there any English families here." Mr. Mitchell, however, long frustrated the magisterial design by surviving in his office for fifty-two years, 1753-1805. The church was totally suppressed in 1807, the year of the church's bicentenary.[96]

The Hague

The English church, which had been offficially established in 1627, by another calculation traced its roots to 1596 (the old garrison church) and thus celebrated its centenary in 1696. The church building in the Noordeinde was used jointly by the English and Germans; however, the English had first claim to it at the most convenient hours. The Germans were restricted to the Sunday mornings before 9:00 a.m., or in late century before 10:00 a.m.[97] The membership had much declined; nevertheless, because of the presence of the English embassy and other English aristocrats, including Mary Stuart, wife of William of Orange (the future King William III), the church had a rather fashionable reputation. There were frequently English visitors, attempting to attach themselves to the

---

[93] Steven, p. 312; A. Ian Dunlop, *William Carstares and the Kirk by Law Established* (Edinburgh: St. Andrew Press, 1967), pp. 53-54.

[94] Andrew L. Drummond, *The Kirk and the Continent* (Edinburgh: St. Andrew Press, 1956), pp. 98-99; *D.N.B.*; Dunlop, *Carstares*, pp. 59-60.

[95] *B.W.P.G.*, III, 58. Some of Fleming's sermons preached at Leiden and Rotterdam, 1692-98, are in the Rawl. MSS at Oxford (E. 47-48).

[96] Frans van Mieris, *Beschryving der stad Leyden* (Leiden, 1762-84), I, 101; Steven, pp. 312-13.

[97] The Hague C.R., no. 68 (1677-1821), Mar. 30, 1697 (P.R.O., RG 33, no. 84).

court of William and Mary. The church kept to a level, noncontroversial religion, Presbyterian in name but with snippets of Anglican practice thrown in. William Mountague visited The Hague in 1695: "Here is an *English* Church, or Chappel rather, for 'tis a small one, very plain and ordinary. The *Germans* preach there early in the morning, then the *English*, who have the *English Liturgy* read to 'em; the Auditors are but few, we counted about Seventy."[98]

The hallmarks of the church were stability and respectability. During the entire period of 1660-1700 two preachers sufficed to serve the church: John Price (1661-76), and Philip Bowie (1676-1715), with David Blair as second or associate minister (1688-89). Hardly a ripple of theological or political agitation surfaced in the church. No discipline cases were publicly handled between 1677 and 1692. The most substantive issue confronting the consistory was finding a reliable reader or *voorlezer*. In 1692 the old reader had to be suspended for drunkenness, another reader was suspended also for drunkenness in 1718, another for the like crime in 1748.[99] Price and Bowie were noncontroversial preachers. Price, son of William Price of Amsterdam, resigned in 1676 to go as a preacher to Guiana, having been commissioned by the States of Holland.[100] Philip Bowie, Phil. D., was also a second generation Netherlands British preacher, being the son of Walter Bowie of Utrecht.[101] The grant of a second ministership in 1688 came through the patronage of William of Orange. Bowie reported to the consistory in 1688 that a certain "Person of Qualitie" (assumed by all to be the Prince of Orange) was making arrangements for a second minister. The States of Holland voted for the additional minister on April 7, 1688, "at the recommendation, it is believed, of the Prince of Orange."[102]

As Bowie's colleague, the church elected David Blair, living at Leiden. Blair was a devoted Scottish Presbyterian, and he hesitated because of scruples over some practices of the Dutch churches. He desired: "Whereas he was Rooted into the Presbyterian Church of Scotland and that among them no minister was bound to observe the festivall days, or use the formes, that therefore he might (if possible) be dispensed of the same." The church and the Dutch officials granted his request. He was required to subscribe to the form of unity (*formelier van eenigheyt*) but other-

---

[98] Mountague, *Delights of Holland*, p. 51.

[99] C.R., no. 68, see 1692, 1718, 1748; M. G. Wildeman, "Bijdragen tot de geschiedenis der Presbyteriaansche Kerk te 's-Gravenhage," *De Navorscher*, 45 (1895), 173, 177.

[100] *F.E.S.*, VII, 538, 545; Jacob de Riemer, *Beschryving van 's Graven-Hage* (Delft, 1730), I, 415.

[101] *F.E.S.*, VII, 545.

[102] C.R., no. 67, fols. 110-18. Steven, p. 308.

wise was exempted from having to preach on Easter, Whitsuntide, Christ's Nativity, and Ascension Day. The senior minister, Bowie, agreed to take Blair's place at preaching on the festival days and for administering the sacraments, where Blair otherwise would have had "to read the formes used in these Churches."[103] The influence of the "Person of Qualitie" (Prince of Orange) made all of these compromises easy to arrange. Nevertheless, Blair served only about eighteen months (June 1688-December 1689) because of his joining the Glorious Revolution. In 1691 he settled at Edinburgh as minister of the Old Kirk or South-East Parish. The Revolution, he told Bowie, "is acknowledged by all to have been the work of God rather then of Man: for, as his Highnesse hath expressed it, God hath done all and we have done nothing."[104]

The consistory register reports several times that the congregation had "exceedingly decreased" (1676) or was "very much decreased" (1693, after the Glorious Revolution).[105] During Price's ministry the number of elders and deacons had to be reduced from four each to two because of decreasing members; however at Bowie's coming, 1676, there was an upturn. "The number of Hearers, and Communicants was exceedingly increased in the first year of his Ministery" and the number of elders and deacons was increased to three each.[106] The church records reveal a small and rather inactive congregation, only 42 baptisms 1677-1700, many of them from Dutch rather than English families. Marriages were more numerous; 106 were performed 1677-1700 (83 of them 1696-1700, most Dutch couples, not members of the church). The Dutch church was displeased and requested Bowie to cease doing marriages in the Dutch language.[107]

Since early century The Hague had a second or even a third English chapel in the houses of the great English families. Before 1660, Elizabeth of Bohemia and Mary, wife of William II, each kept Anglican chaplains. The tradition of an Anglican chaplaincy at The Hague was revived in 1677 with the marriage of Mary, daughter of James of York, to William of Orange. Mary regularly kept an Anglican chaplain (William Lloyd, 1677, George Hooper, 1677-79, Thomas Ken, 1679-80, Jonathan Blagrave, 1681, John Covel, 1681-85, William Stanley, 1685-89). Prince William, no enthusiast of Anglican religion, did his best to lessen her dependence on the chaplains and encourage Presbyterianism. "Shee did

---

[103] C.R., no. 67, fol. 115; Acta Classis Hague, IV, Nov. 1, 1688.
[104] Blair to Bowie, Dec. 24, 1688, F.O. 259, box 1 (P.R.O.).
[105] C.R., no. 68, Dec. 13, 1676, Jan. 5, 1678, Jan. 15, 1693.
[106] C.R., no. 68, Jan. 5, 1678.
[107] C.R., no. 68, Mar. 30, 1697; baptism and marriage register, no. 306 (G.A. The Hague). Acta Kerkeraad, no. 104, fol. 385.

sometimes goe (by Dr. Lloyd's connivance) to the English congregation at the Hague.'' High Anglicans thoroughly disapproved of Mary's association with English Presbyterianism.[108]

When George Hooper became chaplain, he set up a little chapel furnished for Anglican worship in Mary's rooms in Huis ten Bosch. He built an altar on a small platform. "In this station he was directed to regulate the Performance of Divine Service in Her Highness's Chappell, according to the usage of the Church of England." William pounced on these alterations and kicked at the steps on which the altar was elevated. "What was the use of them?" he demanded. Hooper also set Mary to work on a reading program of Hooker and Eusebius to counteract the Reformed atmosphere at The Hague. "Well, Dr. Hooper, you will never be a Bishop," the displeased William told Hooper (nevertheless, the future bishop of Bath and Wells). According to Burnet's *History*, Prince William was favorable to the generalities of the Church of England but wished that some of the ceremonies "were laid aside."[109] Seldom did the chaplains get on well with the Prince. Ken, who replaced Hooper, was "horribly unsatisfied with the Prince, and thinks that he is not kind to his wife." Covel, because of spreading reports of William's rough behavior of his wife, was dismissed and shipped back to England on three hours notice in 1685. Dr. Stanley, however, did good service to the Prince by propagandizing for him among Anglicans in England.[110]

The church prided itself on its close association with the Prince and Princess of Orange. "This church, especially during the Stadtholdership, was always much frequented by the royal family." Pastor Bowie claimed to have influence and "interest at the Court."[111] When the church underwent renovation in 1679-80, special chairs with canopies overhead were erected for Princess Mary—at her own request—and for other members of the Orange family. In 1685, at Charles II's death, the seats were draped over with fine black cloth "by His Highnesses order." The church had a firm sense of decorum and hierarchical rank; and having made seats for the stadtholder's family, the officers erected seats for other dignitaries: magistrates, advocates, and ambassadors, special railed seats

---

[108] Edward Lake, *Diary*, Camden Miscellany, 1 (1847), 26.

[109] William M. Marshall, *George Hooper, 1640-1727, Bishop of Bath and Wells* (Sherborne: Dorset Publishing Co., 1976), pp. 20-25; *D.N.B.* s.v. Hooper; E. H. Plumptre, *The Life of Thomas Ken, D. D. Bishop of Bath and Wells* (London: William Isbister, 1888), I, 141; Herbert M. Luckock, *The Bishops in the Tower* (London, 1887), p. 203; Gilbert Burnet, *History of His Own Times* (London: J. M. Dent, 1906), p. 250.

[110] Plumptre, *Ken*, I, 143; *D.N.B.* s.v. Covel and Stanley; Douglas R. Lacey, *Dissent and Parliamentary Politics in England, 1661-1689* (New Brunswick: Rutgers Univ. Press, 1969), p. 196.

[111] C.R., no. 68, Sept. 2, 1689; Steven, p. 308.

for elders and deacons, and finally seats for former elders and former deacons, each railed in and locked. Splendid green velvet cushions and hangings were installed in the pulpit.[112] From time to time, well-to-do members left bequests for luxurious adornments, among them two silver flagons in 1682 and two silver plates in 1685.[113] Investments and bonds were accumulated. Mary kept up her subsidy to the church after returning to England and William continued the grant after her death. William also provided bread and wine for the communion service. John Spademan of Rotterdam asserted that Mary retained a lifelong "Kindness and Respect with which she treated English Dissenting Ministers."[114] The church's reputation as favored by the family of Orange encouraged membership from prominent people of The Hague (John Bruynesteyn, elder, "physician to his Highnesse the Prince of Orange" and John Jacob Wierts, elder, "one of his Highnesses the Prince of Orange his Councill").[115] However, the church lost membership after "Her Majesty left this place." Queen Mary's death was a deeply-felt loss to the church, and mourning was immediately decreed, her personal chair being covered with purple cloth and the pulpit with black "round about, behinde, over head, and the staires," and not taken down for seventeen months.[116]

Although required by law to be Calvinist and Presbyterian, the church because of its aristocratic and ambassadorial connections, absorbed many Anglican influences. Several of Mary's chaplains preached occasionally in the church and for ten months (1687-88) Gilbert Burnet, while in exile from the wrath of King James II, preached in regular turn with Bowie. Although not a convinced Presbyterian, Burnet was willing to be "an occasional conformist" with Presbyterians because of the crisis of the times.[117] The Prayer Book was used in the 1690s. However, the Dutch preachers became concerned that the church was veering too swiftly toward Episcopalianism, and in 1715 they objected to the election of Robert Milling, chaplain to the Dutchess of Portland, because of his Anglicanism.[118] The controversy over Milling's candidacy caused a

---

[112] C.R., see 1679, 1680, 1681, 1682, April 23, 1695.
[113] C.R., 1682, 1685.
[114] C.R., April 27, Sept. 2, 1689, Sept. 6, 1692. Nuttall, "English Dissenters," pp. 51-52.
[115] C.R., 1684, 1687.
[116] C.R., Jan. 15, 1693, Jan. 7, 1695.
[117] Wildeman, "Bijdrage," pp. 215-16, 223-24; Marshall, *Hooper*, p. 35; Norman Sykes, *The Church of England & Non-Episcopal Churches in the Sixteenth & Seventeenth Centuries* (London: S.P.C.K., 1948), p. 32.
[118] Mountague, *Delights of Holland*, p. 51; "Stukken betreffende het proces tusschen de Classis van 's Gravenhage en den Engelschen Kerkeraad aldaar," no. 83, Classis of The Hague (N.H.A.).

lawsuit by the Hague Classis against the church to block his election, but the English won the case.[119] The church had no regular association with the classis, only as Samuel Balmford used to say, "a linke to the Dutch Classe." The classis gave some supervision to the church; and Bowie became a member in 1676 soon after his arrival at The Hague.[120] The election and installation of Beaumont in 1651, Price in 1661, and Bowie in 1676 took place according to a pattern approved by the classis and burgomasters.[121] The church was pleased to stress its close relationship with great and mighty people (the Prince, the States of Holland, and the burgomasters). The political rulers, the lords of Holland, were "their Souveraigne Lords, Patrons, Protectors, and Benefactors."[122]

In 1696 the church celebrated its centennial with a banquet and jubilee at the Golden Lion Inn, "that the English and Scots had during that time successively served Almighty God in the English language." A survey of the honored office holders at the 1696 jubilee reveals how far along the Dutch influence had come. The "English" officers were: Van der Esch, Le Sage, De Mele, Van Houcken, Lilly, Burghart, Wierts, Van Schaap, Willet, Immerzel, Van der Maa, Anckershouck, Middelbeek, and Smith.[123] In the eighteenth century the church was composed almost exclusively of Dutch except for some members of the English embassy.[124]

The church was closed by royal decree in 1822 and the building was soon demolished. In the final sermon preached at the church, the minister paid tribute to its long orthodox tradition, because "here at least Jesus Christ and his righteousness have been taught for ages. During the long period of nearly 230 years one pastor after another have taught, that the gift of God is eternal life through Jesus Christ our Lord."[125] The present English Church at The Hague, Ary van der Spuyweg, is a Church of England established in 1844.

Delft

The English Reformed Church at Delft, established in 1636 to replace the Merchant Adventurers church, met in the Gasthuis Church. Every Sunday there was a sermon at 9:00 in the morning and another in the

---

[119] Wildeman, "Bijdrage," pp. 215-40; Fred. Oudschans Dentz, *History of the English Church at the Hague, 1586-1929* (Delft: W. D. Meinema, 1929), p. 28.

[120] Knuttel, *Acta Synoden Zuid-Holland*, V, 223.

[121] Acta Classis Hague, III, Jan. 2, Dec. 1, 1652; June 26, 1661; Jan. 18, 1677.

[122] C.R., no. 68, Oct. 7, 1696.

[123] C.R., Sept. 19, 1696.

[124] M. G. Wildeman, "Het doop- en trouw-boek der Engelsche Kerk te 's-Gravenhage," *De Nederlandsche Leeuw*, 11 (1893), 13; C. A. van Sypesteyn, "De voormalige Engelsche Kerk te 's-Gravenhage," *Haagsch Jaarboekje*, 1 (1889), 63.

[125] Alexander B. Mackey, sermon, Feb. 3, 1822 (MS, G.A. Hague).

afternoon at 3:00.[126] The church received a very modest subsidy of 500 guilders per year from the States of Holland, to which the burgomasters "would promise no more" except for providing the church building and sometimes a small housing allowance.[127] The church membership was always small. In 1645 the membership was 27 and in 1668 it had advanced to only 34. Alexander Petrie kept careful membership records; during the period 1668-83 he added 47 persons as communicant members, an average of two or three a year. However, because of the steady toll of members dying or moving away, the total membership never increased. The number of baptisms was small, only about 103 for the entire history of the church (1636-1724).[128]

Ministers of the church after 1660 were: Alexander Petrie (1645-68; 1669-83), Alexander Hodge (1668-69), John Sinclair (1684-87), Thomas Hoog (1689-94), and Wilhelm van Schie (1694-1724). Petrie, Sinclair, and Hoog were Scots, Hodge was an Anglo-Scot (Scottish father, born in England), and Van Schie was Dutch. Delft was Petrie's first official pastorate, and he stayed nearly the rest of his life. The son of Alexander Petrie of Rotterdam, he had his theological examination from the Classis of Schieland in 1644 and preached a few weeks at Brielle. He subscribed to all the Dutch confessions. In 1668 he resigned and announced he was returning to Scotland for a new pastorate; but somehow the plan miscarried, and after a few months he was back at Delft as a private person. During his absence the church called Alexander Hodge (April 1668-January 1669), an ejected Puritan living at Amsterdam. After ten months Hodge received an invitation to become one of the ministers of the English church at Amsterdam, leaving the Delft pulpit open. Petrie, living unemployed at Delft, was very available for the position, and the church reappointed him as pastor. His total pastorate was almost 38 years.[129]

John Sinclair (1684-87), Scottish refugee, received massive opposition from Thomas Chudleigh, English ambassador. The consistory had been somewhat cautious about electing Sinclair because of his rebellious reputation and took him only "with the praeviso that if he were free from

---

[126] *Beschryvinge der stadt Delft* (Delft: Dirck van Bleyswijck, 1667), p. 291. The church building was used jointly by the English and the Dutch Reformed.

[127] C.R., no. 102, fol. 35v (Mar. 16, 1668); Res. burgomasters, III, 532-33 (no. 16, G.A. Delft); States of Holland, no. 4410. A copy of the Delft consistory register is also at New College, Edinburgh.

[128] Baptism register and membership lists, C.R., no. 101 (1643-1723). No records are available for the period 1636-42.

[129] C.R., no. 102, fols. 34-35; Knuttel, *Acta Synoden Zuid-Holland*, II, 446; *F.E.S.*, VII, 543. On his Dutch Reformed subscription, "Stukken betrekkelijk Eng. predikanten te Delft," no. 60 (Kerkeraad of Delft).

all censor or imputatione in Scotland." Chudleigh declared that Sinclair was most unsatisfactory, "accusing the said Mr. Sinklare of enormous crimes tending to discredit him, but no proofe of any particulars at all." Chudleigh by a "very peremptorie and sharp" letter ordered the church to drop Sinclair. By this point Sinclair had been approved by the Delft burgomasters, who refused to back down, and the affair was finally settled by having the town pensionary negotiate directly with the ambassador—"he hath been quiet since in the busines heir." Once in office Sinclair served without controversy.[130] Thomas Hoog (1689-94), another fugitive Scot, was the nephew of John Hoog of Rotterdam. He came to Delft from a position as rector of the Latin school at Goes.[131] The last minister of the church, Wilhelm van Schie (1694-1724) was a Dutchman whose previous ministry had been at the Dutch church at Norwich.[132]

Because the church was small, much of its business was transacted in open congregational meetings. The church also had an old tradition of Congregationalism dating back to the time of Robert Park (1636-41), which highly valued popular participation. The Scottish Presbyterian ministers had no love for democratic decision-making, but the small size of the congregation necessitated having participation from nearly everyone. The consistory elections of 1662 were conducted by calling together all male church members "and after the businesse was debated, by most voices were chosen"; in 1665 the elections were debated in a congregational meeting and "caried by plurality of voices." The reason for this procedure was necessity, "to wit, that by reason of the so small number, it seemed good to call all together to consult."[133] Nevertheless, by the 1680s the democratic process had been diluted, and the officers simply conducted business within the consistory and announced their decisions to the few other persons of the membership.[134]

John Sinclair was the first minister of the church to be a member of the Delft classis. In 1684 he applied for membership, which was granted January 8, 1685, but only on a half-way status. The classis set down nine conditions, which considerably watered down the privileges of his membership: He was not eligible to bring an elder to meetings, the church was not to be included in the classis visitations nor was Sinclair to serve as a classis visitor, and he was exempted from being an examiner of proponents or from serving on classical and synodical commissions.[135]

---

[130] C.R., no. 102, fols. 28-30; Steven, pp. 295-96.
[131] C.R., no. 102, fol. 26v (Aug. 2, 1689); B.W.P.G., IV, 247-48; Steven, pp. 141-42.
[132] C.R., no. 102, fol. 15v; Res. burgomasters, IV, 279-80.
[133] Ibid., fols. 36-37.
[134] Ibid., fol. 30.
[135] Acta Classis Delft, no. 139, fol. 563.

Van Schie in 1723 asked for full membership with full voting power, but he was turned down (by this time the church was almost ready to permanently close its doors, so the timing was bad for Van Schie).[136] Although the Dutch churches in the cities with English churches sought to have supervisory powers over the English churches, seldom did the arrangement work out well; and often, as at Delft, the English were relegated to a marginal kind of participation.

The Delft church kept up an energetic program of worship and discipline, at least into the 1680s. Offenses of adultery, drunkenness, neglecting of sermons, and such like, were dealt with severely. One sinner, Sir Robert Steward, was warned "that at no time hereafter hee shall receive the Sacrament in this congregation untill hee have witnessed his repentance before the Consistorie."[137] The older discipline had been confession before the congregation, but this was seldom practiced in any of the Netherlands English churches in the late seventeenth century. Richard and Magdalene Houghton were suspended from membership in 1670 because of habitual absence from services. Two years later the wife attempted, even "presumed," to come to the table for communion, but the ever-vigilant Petrie "beckoned to her to keep away, and sent the Elder Mr. Jenkins to forbid her comming to this Table." At the next consistory the elders commended Petrie for his quick action.[138] Another discipline case, more political than religious, was Henry Lilburne, a political radical who joined in 1666 and was suspended in 1667. His offenses were (1) that he slighted and reviled the Reformed churches and called the classis "150 asses," (2) that he slandered other church members and attempted to seduce a woman, (3) "that he rails against the late King, and the present King of great Britaine."[139] One of the elders, Abraham Kick, showed Republican tendencies and collaborated with fugitive Regicides after the Restoration, giving several "refuge" in his house. However, he also accepted bribes from George Downing to betray his friends (Barkstead, Okey, and Corbet) and set them up for arrest. Kick's widow and son (the younger Abraham Kick) became Independents at Amsterdam.[140]

During the 1690s the church records begin to show signs of irreparable decline in membership and spiritual vitality. The group was so small that the church had only five baptisms 1690-1700, and the keeping of the con-

---

[136] Ibid., no. 141, fol. 279.
[137] C.R., no. 102, fols. 37-38 (1658). Steward was guilty of adultery but left the province without making his churchly repentance. He promised to pay expenses of the child.
[138] Ibid., fols. 32v-33r.
[139] Ibid., fol. 36.
[140] Catterall, "Downing," pp. 274-88; see above no. 60.

sistory register, especially after Van Schie became minister, was sketchy and indolent. An entire year's report ordinarily contains nothing more than notice of elections, if held, mention of the bimonthly communion ("'t' lords supper celebrated"), and sometimes the addition of the stock phrase, "t' state of t' church cons'd."[141]

The church was embarrassed in 1692 by an unseemly fight between the elders and William McBee, the church reader. The elders criticized him for inept reading and singing, "nor so that he could without great difficulty be understood; besides his frequent erring in singing." Still the elders hoped for some "ammendment." The outraged McBee publicized his side of the story by going to the Dutch Reformed Church, the burgomasters, even the English ambassador at The Hague. He became personally abusive to pastor Hoog, shouting "I am your Enemy ... I need not your friendship, and care not for it." The church abhorred McBee's public commotion—"presumptious madness," they called it—but they had little defense against his gossip. The elders refused to allow the Dutch clergy to meddle in this affair; they declared "that the English consistory did no more depend on the Dutch, then the Dutch did on them." Not until 1701 did McBee make his peace with the church, whereupon he was restored to a half-time reader's position.[142] There are many evidences in the church records of spiritual cooling. In 1690-91 the communion services were cancelled for six months because of gross ignorance of the members, the minister judging "some very unfitt." In 1691 the Thursday evening catechism exercise was ended because of lack of attendance, but a Sunday night catechism sermon was instead scheduled. Five months later the Sunday night sermon was also abolished for poor attendance, the elders concluding that "our people had already begun to weary of catechetick instruction, so that there were some times but 3 or 4, present."[143]

The church closed permanently in 1724 after the death of Van Schie. The last years' existence had already been by sufferance of the burgomasters, who regarded the English church as not very necessary. As early as 1706 they resolved that the church could be suppressed at the next ministerial vacancy but they would allow the present incumbent, Van Schie, to go on. Eighteen years later, when Van Schie died, the burgomasters closed the church because "there were very few members and these few were all acquainted with the Dutch language."[144]

---

[141] C.R., no. 102, fols. 13-14.
[142] Ibid., fols. 26, 20-25, 12.
[143] Ibid., fols. 25-26.
[144] Res. burgomasters, V, 31, 243; *Beschryving der stadt Delft* (Delft: Reinier Boitet, 1729), p. 327.

CHAPTER SIXTEEN

THE POST-RESTORATION CHURCHES AT ROTTERDAM, DORT, MIDDELBURG, FLUSHING, VEERE, AND UTRECHT 1660-1700

Rotterdam had two, sometimes three, English and Scottish churches. The first was the English Reformed Church, founded in 1619, the second was the Scots Church of 1643. The Merchant Adventurers also had a church at Rotterdam (1635-1655). On the unofficial level, Quaker missionaries had been active in Rotterdam since 1655, and a Quaker meeting serving both English and Dutch people took shape. The Quakers met in the house of merchant Benjamin Furly. Northleigh heard William Penn preach an English sermon to the mainly Dutch congregation (1686).[1] In 1700 Anglicans established a Church of England at Rotterdam. The city had great variety in English religion.

Throughout the seventeenth century Rotterdam was a rapidly growing commercial city with a large English and Scottish merchant community. "Little London" it was called. The merchants said: Rotterdam is "where the Trade lies." The whole trade of the nation "bends towards Rotterdam."[2] After the Restoration Rotterdam began drawing political refugees, nearly rivaling Amsterdam as a headquarters of English political "fanatics." For the nonconformist Scots Rotterdam was the safest city of refuge, "where a greater number of banished Scottish ministers resided than at any other town in the Low Countries."[3] Because of the notoriety and zeal of its emigrés, the city seemed to function as "the general azile of all the sectaries, and discontented persons, or to call them their owne appellation, of all that are persecuted." Thus, "Day by day a continual accession of them." Agents reported that "several of the old army live at Rotterdam" and also many nonconformist English preachers (John Reyner, Edward Riggs, Edward Richardson, Nicholas Lockyer). Richardson and Riggs, supported themselves

---

[1] John Northleigh, *Topographical Descriptions* (London, 1702), p. 11; William I. Hull, *Benjamin Furly and Quakerism in Rotterdam* (Swarthmore: Swarthmore College Monographs on Quaker History, no. 5, 1941), p. 30; Hull, *William Penn and the Dutch Quaker Migration to Pennsylvania* (Swarthmore College Monographs on Quaker History, no. 2, 1935), pp. 116-18, 302.

[2] MSS Relative to the Staple and Church of Campvere, no. 9 (Campvere MSS), New College Library, Edinburgh; William Carr, *An Accurate Description of the United Provinces* (London, 1691), p. 7.

[3] Steven, p. 33.

temporarily as medical doctors. Said Richardson: "Providence hath now cast me my lot in these lands, where through mercy I find such imployment as preserves mee, and that with such freedom to my Conscience as England would not affoard mee." Reyner became a "very serious, prudent, and conscientious" merchant, grew prosperous, and died there about 1697.[4]

The Rotterdam English Reformed Church

The English church met in its own building on the Haringvliet (1651). The church had reached its height of prosperity in about 1640, having a membership of 1000. Thereafter the church suffered a setback because of schisms in the congregation and the return of the immigrants to England during the Revolution (1640s). In 1715 the church received a new building paid for by the burgomasters on the old Haringvliet location, a "compact and neat church."[5] The church had 210 baptisms (1660-1700) and 199 marriages.[6] The post-Restoration preachers were: Richard Maden (1660-80), Nathaniel Mather (assisted Maden c. 1663-71), Joseph Hill (1678-1705), John Spademan (1681-98), and Joseph Hill Junior (1699-1717).

The position of second minister (first provided in 1633 but lapsed) was re-established by the States of Holland and city magistrates in 1678, "because our church was greatly increased."[7] Joseph Hill was elected to join Maden. The senior minister, Richard Maden, the son of the Amsterdam minister of the same name, had come to Rotterdam as his first charge. He studied at Utrecht and Leiden University (Richardus Maden Londinensis) and had his theological examination by the Classis of Schieland.[8] Hill, ejected lecturer from All Hallows Barking, London, had previously served at Middelburg but was banned from Zeeland because of his book, *The Interest of These United Provinces* (1673). During the third Anglo-Dutch war he resided in England but returned to Holland, "being altogether dissatisfied with the terms of conformity," on

---

[4] S.P. 84, vol. 167, fol. 240; S.P. 29, vol. 84, no. 65i; vol. 98, no. 56. For Lockyer, S.P. 29, vol. 173, no. 4; for Riggs, S.P. 29, vol. 98, no. 56; for Richardson, S.P. 29, vol. 98, no. 56; vol. 94, no. 112; for Reyner, Calamy, *N.M.*, III, 14 and Browne, *Congregationalism*, p. 594.

[5] Steven, p. 333. A. L. Schenk has included a history of the English church in "Historical and Remarkable Documents" (MS. 1010, Scots church archive).

[6] Baptism and marriage register, no. 356 (archive of the Rotterdam E.R.C., now in the Scots church of Rotterdam).

[7] C.R., no. 342, fols. 2-3; O.S.A. Rotterdam, no. 2726 (G.A. Rotterdam).

[8] Knuttel, *Acta Synoden Zuid-Holland*, IV, 214; Acta Classis Schieland, VI, Mar. 2, 1660 (G.A. Rotterdam); Leiden Univ. *Album*, col. 459; Utrecht Univ. *Album*, p. 41; documents on Maden's calling are in no. 346 of the church archive.

invitation of the Rotterdam church. Hill, who had married Elizabeth Maden, was Maden's brother-in-law. Besides his imprudent political writing, Hill had scholarly accomplishments, among them the editing of a new version of Schrevelius's Greek-Latin Lexicon (1699 edition) and some contributions to Matthew Henry's commentaries.[9] John Quick praised Hill as "a most learned and laborious Pastor." Hill once wrote to Samuel Pepys that he had come to Rotterdam to find a tranquil ministry, "that being tired with the buss of both parties at London, I retired hither, where I live to my owne content in great peace and quietness, above the frownes of fortune, and below the envy of my enemies." One of his Rotterdam sermons, a funeral discourse for Mrs. Mary Reve, was published in 1685. In 1705 Hill became pastor emeritus and died at Rotterdam in 1707.[10]

Spademan, who replaced Maden in 1681, was a late nonconformist. After graduating at Cambridge, he conformed for several years in a pastorate. "Quitting the established church and his living, he went over to *Holland*." In the election of 1680 the elders first offered the position to several well-known English preachers (Richard Baxter, David Clarkson, John Howe, and Henry Newcome), but each refused. Next they considered Ds. Boreman, a Dutchman, Francis Robarts, living at Amsterdam, Dudley Rider, and Spademan. All preached trial sermons but Spademan gave the most satisfaction; he was also Hill's nephew. In 1690 Spademan declined an invitation to the Amsterdam church, but in 1698 he accepted a position in London as co-pastor with John Howe at a Presbyterian church.[11] Although Dutch candidates were at times considered for minister, the church kept strictly to English ministers, being resolved to hold to its Puritan tradition. Boreman in 1680 had been rejected, "having not the idiome of the English tongue." The eldership went on record "that none shall be chosen for Minister of the congregation but he that is a perfect English Man for language."[12]

The church supported a school for the children of English families of the city. The office of schoolmaster was combined with the reader.[13] At the petitioning of a faction of the church, the elders in 1687 added a Sunday evening lecture to supplement the long-established two Sunday ser-

---

[9] *Notulen* van Staten of Zeeland, 1673, p. 146; *B.W.P.G.*, IV, 31; Calamy, *N.M.*, I, 267-69; Steven, p. 319.

[10] Quick, "Icones Sacrae Anglicanae," I, ii, 880; Rawl. MS. A 183, vol. 245 (Bod.); Matthews, *Cal. R.*, pp. 264-65; Joseph Hill, *The Providence of God in Sudden Death* (Rotterdam, 1685).

[11] C.R., no. 342, fols. 8-9; Calamy, *N.M.*, II, 436; Matthews, *Cal. R.*, p. 453; Wilson, *Dissenting Churches*, III, 41-47.

[12] C.R., no. 342, fols. 2, 8, 28.

[13] Ibid., fols. 4, 12, 22.

mons (morning and afternoon) and Wednesday evening sermon. The petitioners desired to have John Shower as special Sunday evening lecturer and agreed to pay for the sermon by voluntary contributions. Shower, a young Presbyterian who had been one of the Exchange Alley Lecturers at London, served as Sunday lecturer 1687-90.[14] His supporters, led by deacon Francis Greenwood, were a grassroots movement in the church seeking a more dynamic spiritual message. Pastor Hill was reluctant to approve another sermon because "there was allready more preaching then they, or the generality of the Congregation frequented; yet if they had an opinion or hoped, that any other could doe their souls good, for his part he was content, that any such minister should have the liberty of the pulpit; but they must take care for his subsistance, and audience."[15] Deacon Greenwood had earlier shown himself to be an innovator by calling for ministerial elections in the entire membership instead of in the closed consistory, but the other officers rejected his elections motion as "unusuall and against the practise of the Dutch Churches here, at this our owne, and that which might breed contests and divisions in the Church."[16] Greenwood's motion would have been in line with the church's original tradition before 1650 but not its recent practice since 1660. Compared to its vigorous early seventeenth-century history, the church in late century slumped into an uneventful existence, which the Greenwood party had tried to counteract with the Shower lectures. By the 1680s the elders felt led to dispense with regular consistory meetings "by reason of the great peace, through Gods blessing amongst us."[17]

None of the ministers had membership or association with the Schieland classis. In 1662 young Richard Maden applied to the classis to become an ordinary member; but after several months of negotiation, they decided against admitting him although allowing him fraternal ties "by form of correspondence." Maden unfavorably impressed the classis brethren by negligence in pressing his case and not presenting proper documents.[18] The English consistory defined the church's position as follows, "that seeing our Church is not under the Classis, but the Lords of this city only, we cannot without their consent grant any demission" of minister (or conduct any other item of great business).[19] Being directly under the burgomasters and having funds from them, the church felt

---

[14] Alexander Gordon, *Freedom after Ejection* (Manchester: Univ. Press, 1917), p. 352; W. Tong, *Some Memoirs of the Life and Death of the Reverend Mr. John Shower* (London: John Clark, 1716), pp. 52-61.
[15] C.R., no. 342, fol. 17.
[16] Ibid., fol. 9.
[17] Ibid., fol. 16.
[18] Acta Classis Schieland, VI, Apr. 17, June 19, Sept. 4, Oct. 2, 1662.
[19] C.R., no. 342, fol. 20 (Aug. 14, 1690).

obliged to follow the directions laid down by the political lords. At the ministerial election of 1680 the magistrates strongly recommended choosing a man "that could speak Dutch." The election of John Spademan was subsequently presented to the magistracy as fulfilling their instructions, Spademan having "lived some years heretofore in this country."[20] Although supposedly restored to Presbyterianism during the 1650s by Thomas Cawton, the Rotterdam church was always the most "Independent" of the Netherlands churches, being often served in the eighteenth century "by clergymen belonging to the Independent connection." In 1816 when the Dutch Reformed Church underwent a general reorganization, the church by royal decree was incorporated for the first time into the classis.[21] The church closed in 1876, and the building has been demolished.

The Rotterdam Scots Church and Covenanters

During the seventeenth century Rotterdam far surpassed Veere as the center of Scottish trade and settlement in the Netherlands. Scottish religious refugees congregated at Rotterdam and made the city the outpost of Presbyterianism-in-exile. The Scots church was the central institution ministering to Scottish spiritual, educational, and material needs. "A Scotsh Church in this place is absolutely needful, the langwage of the place being unknown to our nation," declared the consistory in 1698.[22] The number of Scots at Rotterdam in the 1690s was, at the least, 800 to 1000. The church performed about 770 baptisms (1660-1700) and over 480 marriages. A new church building of 1697 accommodated 900 persons. The Scottish population of Rotterdam was much larger than any other Netherlands city, "yea so far as we know or hear of above what is in any other City in the world outside of Britain.[23] The church organized a Scottish school in 1676, raised funds for poor relief, and sponsored in 1697 a friendly society for sailors known as the Scottish Seamen's Box.[24]

The seventeenth-century ministers of the church were Covenanter Presbyterians, several of them veterans of the anti-episcopal struggles in Scotland. Alexander Petrie, the first minister, had been active in the

---

[20] Ibid., fol. 9.

[21] Steven, pp. 399, 334.

[22] C.R., III, 12 (archive in the Scots church); in addition to Steven's history of the church, A. L. Schenk has done several histories of the church in typescript all in the Scots archive, "Historical and Remarkable Documents" (no. 1010); "The Golden Book of the Scots Church" (no. 1011); "Het tweede bedehuis" (no. 1006).

[23] C.R., III, 22; Steven, pp. 123, 127, 227. For baptism and marriage statistics, see registers no. 47, 957, 958.

[24] Steven, pp. 35, 47, 145.

Covenant movement of the 1640s. John Hoog (1662-89) was an evangelical Presbyterian, "ane old Scots minister who is dissatisfied with the times."[25] The notable growth of the congregation persuaded the magistrates to provide a second minister, a position filled by Robert MacWard (1676-77) and next by Robert Fleming (1677-94), both ejected nonconformists. Later ministers were James Brown (1691-1713), Robert Fleming Junior (1695-98), and Thomas Hoog (1699-1723). The ministerial families founded small dynasties in the Netherlands British churches, Petrie's son serving at Brielle and Delft, Fleming's son at Leiden and Rotterdam, and Thomas Hoog, nephew of old John Hoog, at Delft, Veere, and Rotterdam. Three of Thomas Hoog's sons became Dutch Reformed ministers.[26]

The Scots Church earned an importance far beyond the bounds of the city itself. As the city became the refuge of religious and political dissidents, the church served as the unofficial headquarters of militant Presbyterians. Distant from Episcopal authorities, the church could practice a pure Presbyterian religion and provide safe harbor for the refugees. Rotterdam "afforded an asylum to many who were glad to avoid, by voluntary or constrained exile, the tyrannical and persecuting government of the Stuarts." Within the church and Scot community, a clandestine nucleus year by year planned strategies for supporting the struggle in Scotland. Robert MacWard admonished the church to always keep up its great international mission: "Now you are that congregation of all others wherein he hath set and settled the ornament of his beauty in the same majesty it was settled in the Church of Scotland." The eyes of God and the eyes of Scotland are upon you, he warned, "you are the only congregation belonging to that church set up as a beacon on a mountain."[27]

Among the banished and unemployed Presbyterian ministers at Rotterdam were John Carstares, Robert MacWard, John Brown, John Livingstone, John Nevay, James Simpson, Robert Trail, Richard Cameron, and John Blackader. John Howie's *Scots Worthies* lists over twenty nonconformist Scots who were exiles in the Netherlands.[28] After each unsuc-

---

[25] Ibid., p. 29.

[26] Ibid., pp. 25, 61; *B.W.P.G.*, IV, 247-51. On the various preachers, see *F.E.S.*

[27] Letter to the consistory, Jan. 20, 1678; Steven, pp. 24, 352-53.

[28] John Howie, *The Scots Worthies*, ed. W. H. Carslaw (Edinburgh: Oliphant, Anderson, and Ferries, n.d.). He included the following: John Forbes, Robert Dury, and David Calderwood from the early 17th century; and after 1660 John Nevay, John Livingstone, John Brown, Richard Cameron, Donald Cargil, Walter Smith, Robert MacWard, John Shields, John Nisbet, John Blackader, James Renwick, Thomas Hoog, Robert Fleming, Alexander Fields, Sir Robert Hamilton, William Veitch, John Balfour, Robert Trail. The records of the Scots church of Rotterdam mention the following as participants in some regard: Robert MacWard, John Livingstone, John Nevay, James Simpson, John

cessful uprising in Scotland, new emigrés arrived, soldiers as well as preachers; Colonel James Wallace came after the battle of Pentland, Robert Hamilton after the battle of Bothwell Bridge. The Earl of Argyle came over to Holland rather than accept the Test Act.[29] The church welcomed militant Covenant religion and raised a special fund to support distressed Scots. The refugees, being articulate and zealous, came to places of prominence in the church. Robert MacWard in 1676 was elected associate minister to John Hoog, and Colonel Wallace the same year was elected elder. Many of the ministers were called upon to temporarily fill the pulpit, which guaranteed a fervent quality of sermons. "I did communicat again at M. Hogs meetting house in Roterdame where Mr. Mcquare, Mr. Browne did assist," wrote Sir John Clerk in 1676.[30] When student John Erskine visited the church in 1685 and 1686, in addition to John Hoog and Robert Fleming, he heard sermons from Patrick Verner, James Kirkton, Thomas Forrester, Robert Archibald, and Thomas Hoog. Hoog predicted that Scotland would suffer further religious persecution. "He thought the clouds would be darker, but it would not last." As Argyle's ill-fated expedition was launching, Erskine as one of the volunteers took communion, "considering upon what I might be called to shortly, and not knowing if again I ever might have that blessed opportunity of meeting with Christ."[31] Erskine survived and came dashing back to Holland.

Through the involvement with the refugees, the church kept a strong link with Scottish affairs. Subscribing to the Covenant of 1638 was a requirement for church membership. The consistory in times of great Presbyterian need called special days of prayer and humiliation for Scotland. Nonconforming Scottish students were educated at Dutch universities and on occasions the church performed extraordinary ordinations of young men. MacWard, Brown, and Jacobus Koelman in 1679 ordained Richard Cameron in the church and commissioned him for hazardous service in Scotland: "Behold, all ye beholders, here is the head of a faithful ministers and servant of Jesus Christ, who shall lose the

---

Blackader, John Brown, Rev. Adair, Thomas Hoog, Richard Cameron, Michael Totter, John Chalmers, Thomas Douglas, William Thompson, George Barkley, Robert Trail, James Forrester, John Harvey, John Sinclair, Patrick Verner, Patrick Cowper, Robert Archibald, George Campbell, John Howie, Alexander Hasty, William Berman, William Carstares ("Golden Book").

[29] Ian B. Cowan, *The Scottish Covenanters 1660-1685* (London: Victor Gollancz, 1976), pp. 51, 64, 95, 110.

[30] Sir John Clerk of Penicuik, "Journal, 1676" (Scottish Record Office, G.D. 18/2089).

[31] John Erskine, *Journal of the Hon. John Erskine of Carnock, Publications* of the Scottish History Society, 14 (1893), 109-113; 162-64; Andrew L. Drummond, *The Kirk and the Continent* (Edinburgh: St. Andrew Press, 1956), pp. 105-06.

same for his Master's interest, and it shall be set up before sun and moon, in the view of the world." A year later Cameron was killed in a Covenanter uprising in Scotland and beheaded—his head was put on display at Edinburgh.[32] The Synod of South Holland took a critical view of these irregular Scottish ordinations and ordered a stop to them.[33] The Rotterdam Covenanters, using every available weapon of propaganda, sent forth a barrage of books hateful to Episcopalians but "esteemed as a timely and consoling draught by the Presbyterians." MacWard's *The Poor Man's Cup of Cold Water, Ministered to the Saints and Sufferers for Christ in Scotland* (1678) and Brown's *Apologeticall Relation of the Particular Sufferings* (1665) and his *History of the Indulgence* (1678) made a great noise and drew critical reaction from officials in London and Edinburgh. The two Robert Flemings, father and son, wrote devotional books.[34]

The Covenanter circle at Rotterdam operated in part through a weekly meeting at the home of Andrew Russel, a Scottish merchant and elder of the church. These were "holy convocations" for prayer, preaching, conference, and ofttimes for plotting strategy on Scottish affairs. At the meetings the most recent intelligence was communicated from Scotland concerning the sufferings of the church and state. Attended by ministers and key elders, the Russel meetings carried great weight in the business of the church, many of the crucial decisions being first thrashed out at Russel's house before coming to the consistory as a whole.[35]

The solidarity of the Covenanters was splintered in the 1670s over the issue of indulgences. As in England, King Charles at various times promised indulgence to ejected Scottish Presbyterian ministers, with the result that the Church of Scotland deeply split over whether to acknowledge the indulgence or not. Pastor Fleming offended the anti-indulgents, headed by MacWard and Brown, by speaking favorably of the indulgence proclamation. MacWard and Brown were bitterly against "that wretched indulgence" and attacked Fleming as a turncoat. The United Societies, an anti-indulgent group of west Scotland, censured the Rotterdam Church for permitting indulgents to come to the Lord's Table, and printed an embarrassing pamphlet against the church. The rift in the Rotterdam church was only slowly repaired.[36]

---

[32] Howie, *Scots Worthies*, pp. 423-24; Steven, pp. 66, 73-74.
[33] Knuttel, *Acta Synoden Zuid-Holland*, V, 287-88, 325.
[34] Steven, p. 81.
[35] Ibid., p. 67. John Erskine in 1685 attended the meetings at Russel's house, *Journal*, p. 164.
[36] Robert MacWard, *Earnest Contendings for the Faith* (n.p., 1723), written against Fleming; Steven, pp. 87-94. The United Society's booklet was *The Protestation of the Antipopish, Antiprelatick, Antierastian, true Presbyterian, but poor and persecuted Church of Scotland, against the Scottish Congregation at Rotterdam in Holland* (n.p., 1684).

The Covenanters by their lives and zeal won widespread support from the Dutch churchmen and politicians. The burgomasters of Rotterdam were persuaded to approve the ministerial elections of MacWard and Fleming, two of the ejected ministers, and the town fathers quietly channeled funds to the church for use in supporting the Scottish immigrants of conscience.[37] Many Dutch clergy, habitually anti-Episcopal, were easily won over to the Covenanter point of view. Jacobus Borstius, preacher of Rotterdam, was a friend of banished nonconformists and helped to disseminate Covenanter news around the city. MacWard, Livingstone, Nevay, Trail and Brown had "great fellowship" with him. Borstius also advanced the Scottish cause by translating and publishing several Scottish works into Dutch, among them the *Historie der kerken van Schotland tot het jaar 1667* (Rotterdam, 1668) and books by Rutherford.[38]

Another Dutch confederate was Jacobus Koelman, a Dutch Reformed preacher removed from his charge at Sluis for refusing to conform to the festival days and forms. His nonconformity gave him great credit with the Scots, who had equal scruples over some of the Dutch practices. He often preached to Scottish audiences and took on numerous projects of translating English and Scottish authors into Dutch—"books of the heart" (John Brown, Samuel Rutherford, David Dickson, Hugh Binning, Thomas Hooker, Thomas Goodwin, Richard Baxter). "He was a great lover of the Scots church and people, and was usefull to many of them."[39] At Utrecht Voetius, Nethenus, and Van Mastricht showed favor to Scottish Presbyterians, and Van Mastricht went so far as to praise the discipline of the Church of Scotland as "the purest that has been since the apostles' days."[40]

The fervor of Presbyterian activity at Rotterdam prompted harsh counter-measures from London. The king had no desire to have a Presbyterian "beacon on a mountain" just across the water; consequently he sent the English ambassadors on frequent trips to Rotterdam to gather information and then to The Hague to stir up repressive resolutions in the States General or the States of Holland. In 1670 ambassador William Temple tried unsuccessfully to have MacWard, Nevay, and Trail deported; however, in 1676 Temple succeeded in having Brown, MacWard, and Wallace banished under the anti-rebel clauses of the Treaty of Breda. The Dutch politicians delayed interminably, and when finally pushed into expelling them from the province of Holland (not

---

[37] Steven, p. 34.

[38] Borstius, *Vyftien predicatien* (Utrecht, 1696), p. E3v.

[39] Erskine, *Journal*, p. 184; Drummond, *Kirk*, p. 102; Steven, pp. 72-73; *B.W.P.G.*, V, 102-09. Wilhelm Broes, *De Engelsche Hervormde Kerk, benevens haren invloed op onze Nederlandsche* (Delft: De Wed. J. Allart, 1825), II, 166.

[40] Erskine, *Journal*, p. 184; Steven, p. 33.

from the entire United Provinces), they sub rosa provided each of the Scots with a passport and testimonial of good character. The banishment policies were seldom applied and never enforced effectively. In the case of Brown, MacWard, and Wallace, the first two traveled only as far as Utrecht and soon returned. Wallace traveled to France temporarily but returned to Rotterdam in 1678.[41] Nevertheless, the threat of harassment always hung over the heads of the refugees. When John Erskine visited the city during the Argyle affair, he took care to avoid public notice and at the church "sat in a hid place." He also used an assumed name. One of the refugees at Rotterdam in 1685 had his house searched by the ballie at 11:00 at night. "This did alarm us," said Erskine, "considering the security that was expected at Rotterdam, there being fair promises given for that effect."[42]

In 1683 King Charles stepped up his attacks on the church. He sent a sharp complaint to the Raad-Pensionaris of Holland about the Scots church. In particular, he named John Hoog and Robert Fleming, the ministers, and merchants Andrew Russel and John Fleming as having connections with Scottish rebels. "The Rotterdam preachers permit rebels from Scotland to preach in the Scottish Church. They maintain the Covenant and have excluded from the Holy Communion persons who acknowledge His Majesty's government, and instead admit John Balfour, guilty of the murder of the Bishop of St. Andrews. Finally, the two preachers have also prayed that God Almighty would give his blessing to Dutch arms against those of the King of Great Britain during the last war between the Netherlands and Great Britain." All four of the accused were registered citizens of Rotterdam, and no harm befell them.[43] The amount of English ambassadorial energy spent at Rotterdam gives a strong clue to the effectiveness of the Rotterdam Presbyterians. Temple complained that the Scots, when added to all of his regular business, "keepe me just from having nothing to do."[44] The Scots church to this day is proud of its association with the Covenanters. In 1933 two memorial windows to the Covenanters were installed in the church, one (with John Knox at the center) portrayed MacWard, Brown, Cameron, Wallace, and Rutherford, the other (with William III at the center) had Trail, Livingstone, Petrie, Nevay, and Simpson.[45]

---

[41] Secret Res. States General, no. 3963, Feb. 6, 1677; Res. States General, no. 3731, pp. 3, 6; Res. States of Holland, no. 109, pp. 607-08; no. 110, pp. 6-10; Secret Res. States of Holland, no. 301, fols. 572-74; Steven, pp. 49, 66.

[42] Erskine, *Journal*, pp. 162-66, 171.

[43] Res. States of Holland, no. 116, p. 125 (Apr. 2, 1683).

[44] S.P. 84, vol. 186, fol. 137.

[45] J. Verheul, *De Schotsche gemeente en haar oude kerkgebouw te Rotterdam* (Rotterdam: Stemerding, 1939), pp. 62-64.

Although Rotterdam was the center, colonies of Covenanter Scots lived also at Amsterdam, Utrecht, and Leeuwarden. Following the disastrous Battle at Bothwell Bridge (1679), Scottish refugees gathered at Leeuwarden, Friesland, presided over by Sir Robert Hamilton, the defeated commander and another Hamilton, former captain in the Earl of Dumbarton's regiment. Both Hamiltons married Dutch wives. Hamilton's colony represented the strictest anti-indulgent Scots (the United Societies) for whom Rotterdam was too liberal. They claimed to be the true Presbyterian remnant. Hamilton arranged for James Renwick, who was sent over by the United Societies, to be ordained by the Classis of Groningen—a pure Reformed ordination uncontaminated by Indulgents.[46] The Leeuwarden Scots had a little house church, where Jacobus Koelman preached to them. Koelman, "a very factious man," resided ordinarily at Amsterdam but sometimes at Leeuwarden. "He preaches both here and there in houses." The Leeuwarden Scots said: "The King is an Appostate, that they owe him no obedience nor ever will submit to his government."[47] After the failure of Monmouth's Rebellion, some of his refugee followers (Joseph Tilly and Joseph Hilliard) established an English textile factory at Leeuwarden and promised to make it an English center. Pardons from King James in 1686 lured the Leeuwarden English home.[48]

When William and Mary gained the throne, the situation reversed for the refugee Scots. Large groups of refugees returned to Scotland to enjoy the new regime. The Scots Church of Rotterdam lost its international significance as a bastion of Presbyterianism-in-exile and functioned at the lesser, but more normal, task of serving a local Scottish population in its ordinary religious worship. St. Sebastian's chapel served as the church building from 1658 to 1697; then a new building for the Scots was completed on the Vasteland by Schiedam Dike (Schiedamsevest). The building was dignified but simple, "corresponding with the stern Calvinistic doctrine and sober worship of the Presbyterian church order."[49] This historic Scots building was destroyed by bombing in 1940. After the war, the Scottish church rebuilt on the same location and carries on its ministry.

Dort

Dort had two English churches, the English Reformed Church (1623-1839) and the Merchant Adventurers Church (1655-1700). The

---

[46] Howie, *Scots Worthies*, p. 599; Drummond, *Kirk*, pp. 103-05. Two Hamiltons enrolled at Franeker University in 1678, William and Arthur Hamilton, Franeker Univ. *Album*, p. 222.
[47] S.P. 84, vol. 217, fols. 237-42; vol. 218, fol. 258 (1683-84).
[48] Peter Earle, *Monmouth's Rebels* (New York: St. Martin's Press, 1977), pp. 156-60.
[49] Verheul, *Schotsche kerkgebouw*, p. 61.

English Reformed Church met in the Orphan Hospital (Mariënborn Klooster). The post-Restoration church had long pastorates: Robert Paget (1638-83) and Dr. Samuel Magapolensis (1685-1700), spanning a period of sixty-two years. Paget was highly respected among Netherlands English ministers and received invitations to Utrecht in 1655 and Amsterdam in 1668.[50] Megapolensis came to Dort with experiences in both Holland and America. Growing up in colonial New Amsterdam, where his father was a preacher, he had been educated at Harvard for three years and then had taken a medical degree at Utrecht University. Before Dort, he served the English church of Flushing. Being knowledgeable in both languages, Megapolensis's assigment was to preach in the English church on Sunday mornings and in Dutch in the Augustijn Kerk on Monday evenings.[51]

Like the other Pagets of Amsterdam, Robert Paget was an earnest Presbyterian. He had many connections with Presbyterians in England. His friends wrote to him in 1660-61 with hopeful news about the Restoration. "They have great cause to blesse God for his Majesties gracious concessions, in his indulgent Declaration, that they might wish more, but did not expect so much." However, Paget and his correspondents feared the "remounted Bishops, by reason of their early fierce driving unto formalities and superstitions." In a letter of June 15, 1661, Paget reported the news from England that all the English Presbyterians rallied to the King, for truly "there is none other upon whom the interest of England can bottom it self."[52] His opinions after Black Bartholomew's Day may have been less cheerful.

Paget gained membership in the Classis of Dort in 1646; Magapolensis, his successor, also had membership.[53] English membership, however, was on conditions laid out in 1646 that allowed for little participation. The Dutch church of Dort did not acknowledge the English church as an equal city church of the Ring of Dort.[54] Several times the English minister had to complain of not being valued as a "true member" of the classis. Consequently, in 1703 the church withdrew from the classis.[55]

---

[50] C.R., no. 5, fols. 92-97, 122 (G.A. Dort); N.N.B.W.V, 419-20.

[51] N.N.B.W., III, 839-41; J. L. van Dalen, *Geschiedenis van Dordrecht* (Dort: C. Morks, 1931-33), II, 800; Gerald Francis de Jong, "Dominie Johannes Magapolensis: Minister to New Netherland," *New-York Historical Quarterly*, 52 (Jan. 1968), 31.

[52] Four letters of Paget to Hugh Goodyear (1659, 1661) are in the Goodyear Papers, Weeskamer Archief, no. 1355 (G.A. Leiden). One of his English correspondents was William Barlee.

[53] C.R., no. 5, fols. 50-52; Knuttel, *Acta Synoden Zuid-Holland*, VI, 105.

[54] Acta Classis Dordrecht, VIII, 93; IX, Nov. 7, 1662; XI, Apr. 15-16, 1692 (N.H.A.).

[55] C.R., no. 5, fol. 199.

The late seventeenth-century English and Scottish community shrank to a small group, and the church had little chance to grow or even to hold its own (78 members in 1664). The church had an aging membership. They baptized only 7 babies for the entire period 1661-1700 and had only 12 marriages, none at all being recorded between 1677 and 1702.[56] Reformed worship was faithfully performed but the archives of the church reveal little sign of dynamic spiritual life. The entries in the consistory register during Paget's later ministry and by Megapolensis are perfunctory. In 1682 the church, lacking suitable candidates of its own, "borrowed" a Dutch elder from the Dutch Reformed Church; and in 1686 the burgomasters reduced the reader's salary because of the smallness of the congregation, on condition "if in processe of time the church should florish, his wages should be augmented accordingly."[57] The church by 1700 had many Dutch names and was well on the way to becoming an almost wholly Dutch congregation of a few persons desiring some tie to the English language and culture. The minister in 1700 was Dutch (Megapolensis) and the consistory members were hardly old stock Englishmen (Van Leeuwen, Van der Spoor, Croes, and Voskamp).[58]

The Merchant Adventurers Church, meeting in the guild chapel on Wine Street, was pastored by Dr. Thomas Marshall, Dr. Philip Bowie, Augustine Freezer, and Mr. Whittel. It suffered declining membership as the Adventurers lost ground, their monopoly having been abolished. The two churches combined into a common Reformed church about 1700, thereafter making common use of the Adventurers' Wine Street building. The combined congregation called a conjoint minister, Samuel Masson (1700-42). In 1839 the church closed. The building was demolished in 1840, except for the turret, which was salvaged and installed on top of the Walloon church.[59]

Middelburg

The three British churches of Middelburg, Flushing, and Veere provided worship, baptisms, marriages, poor relief, and national identity for the English and Scots of Zeeland. The churches were mainly composed of the "merchants, masters, and common Sea-men" of a commercial community. However, the greatest days of English population were in the past; the English troops left Flushing in 1616 and the Merchant Adventurers deserted Middelburg in 1621. The main English-Scottish commercial traffic in the late seventeenth century went to Rotterdam and

---

[56] Membership book, no. 38; baptism and marriage register, no. 42 (G.A. Dort).
[57] C.R., no. 5, fols. 143, 153.
[58] Ibid., fol. 185.
[59] Dalen, *Dordrecht*, II, 799-801; on the Merchant Adventurers, see chap. 9.

Amsterdam, and the students went to Leiden and Utrecht. William Mountague touched at Middelburg, Veere, and Flushing before sailing home in 1695. He found them decaying places. At Middelburg "here were formerly some considerable *English Merchants*, but now none, there being but little Trade between them and us."[60]

The English Reformed Church of Middelburg, founded in 1623, had its own building, the Engelse Kerk, behind the Stadhuis. In 1664 the congregation carried out some improvements and redecoration, including new lettering on the walls for the Ten Commandments, Lord's Prayer, and Creed. Membership was small, 47 in 1642, 105 in 1664, 74 in 1679, 41 in 1692. Because of members in trade and sailing, the congregation was mobile, people coming and going to places like Surinam, Genoa, and the East Indies. On the 1642 membership list (47 persons), 6 were under discipline or not in good standing, some having gone away disorderly without attestation to the Indies, others under discipline for odious scandal or wicked opinions.[61] Nine ministers served the post-Restoration church: William Spang (1652-64), David Anderson (1664-66), Joseph Hill (1667-73), Nicolas Shepheard (1674-79), John Quick (1680-81), William Spang Junior (1682-83), Robert Tory (1683-91), John Leask (1692-97), Cornelius Coorne (1698-1724).

Four of the ministers were ejected Puritans (Anderson, Hill, Quick, and Tory). Anderson, ejected from Walton on Thames, Surrey, "fearing because of that wicked Act of Uniformity ... that Popery like a flood would overflow the Land, immediately retired with his family into Zealand."[62] Anderson, having a wife and five small children but no employment, was desperately poor, walking the streets "with a dejected appearance." A kindly Dutch merchant named De Hoste gave the family aid; and after Spang's death, Anderson received the Middelburg pastorate. As an ejected nonconformist, Anderson was accused of disloyalty to England, but the English consistory of Flushing, where he sometimes preached, gave him an attestation for being always discreet and loyal in sermons and prayers. Anderson was famous throughout Middelburg for his prayers which he "animated with very melting affections."[63]

---

[60] William Mountague, *The Delights of Holland* (London, 1696), p. 229; Thomas Mowbray, *The Honour of Kings Vindicated and Asserted* (Middelburg, 1663), a sermon preached at Veere, May 3, 1661, to a "considerable number of Merchants, Masters, and common Sea-men from several places."

[61] Middelburg E.R.C. marriage, baptism, and membership book, no. 27; Middelburg C.R., I, 228 (R.A. Zeeland).

[62] John Quick, "Icones," I, i, 271. For all Middelburg ministers, see *Naamlyst der predikanten, ouderlingen en diakenen* (1770), no. 32.

[63] C.R., I, 230; Flushing C.R., no. 4469, Apr. 26, 1664; Quick, "Icones," I, i, 271-74; Calamy, *N.M.*, III, 307-08; Matthews, *Cal. R.*, p. 11.

Joseph Hill, ejected from a fellowship at Magdalen College, Oxford and the lectureship at All Hallows Barking, London, received his call at Leiden, "then residing as a Travellor and Student in the University of Leyden in Holland."[64] As Middelburg minister he caused a commotion in 1673, in the midst of the third Anglo-Dutch War, by publishing a book, *The Interest of These United Provinces. Being a Defence of the Zeelanders Choice* (also a Dutch edition, *Het tegenwoordige interest der Vereenigde Provincien*). The book tended to undermine the war effort by arguing for alliance rather than belligerence with England: "We may remain a Republick. And That our Compliance with England is the only means for this." The States of Zeeland objected to these opinions and banished him from the province. Although an exile, Hill had no place to go but back to England; the risk was small, however, because King Charles II was well pleased with his book and granted Hill a sinecure rectory worth £80 (which continued to pay *in absentia* until at least 1702).[65] The Flushing church in 1676 invited Hill to return to Zeeland as their minister, but Hill thought returning would not be wise. "He would never come again into Zeeland," he said. Instead he accepted a pastorate at Rotterdam.[66] John Quick (1680-81) was an ejected minister from Brixton, Plympton, Devonshire, and Robert Tory (1683-91) was ejected from St. Mary Magdalene, Bermondsey, Surrey.[67] The remaining Middelburg preachers were less controversial. Nicolas Shepheard Ph.D., who had been Dutch preacher at Cillaarshoek, near Dort, was from an old English family of Rotterdam. William Spang Junior was the son of the earlier Spang. John Leask, former minister of Mohill, Ireland, had served in 1691 as temporary preacher "with good content" at Amsterdam. Cornelius Coorne, Dutchman, was former minister of the Dutch church at Sandwich.[68]

With the Restoration accomplished in England, the church resolved to put all the old political controversies behind. Members had previously been on both sides of the Revolution. In 1663 some disgruntled members accused an elected elder of anti-Royalist, anti-Episcopal opinions. They reported him for saying the king and the Duke of York were Papists, that

---

[64] C.R., II, 23; Calamy, *N.M.*, I, 267-68.

[65] The English edition was printed by Thomas Berry of Middelburg; the Dutch edition was printed at Amsterdam; *Notulen* van Staten van Zeeland (1673), p. 146; Steven, p. 319; Matthews, *Cal. R.*, pp. 264-65; *B.W.P.G.*, IV, 31; Nuttall, "English Dissenters," pp. 48-49.

[66] Flushing C.R., no. 4469, Nov. 10, 1676; Feb. 3, 1667.

[67] Matthews, *Cal. R.*, pp. 401-02, 489; W. W. D. Campbell, "John Quick (1636-1706)," *Journal of the Presbyterian Historical Society of England*, 3 (1924-27), 8-15.

[68] *Naamlyst*, pp. 8-13; E.R.C. Rotterdam C.R., no. 342, Dec. 27, 1679 (on Shepheard); Amsterdam C.R., III, 315 (on Leask).

religion in England was popish, and that the bishops did not preach. He defended himself: "It was notorious that bishops there preached seldom and that too many of the inferior clergie were either profane or ignorant." Because of the emotions raised, it was decided that he was not to be admitted to office.[69] In another incident, a prospective member transferring from London was tested on three criteria, a life without scandal, attestation from a "true reformed church" at London, and that "he had no hand directly or indirectly in any insurrection or plot in England." Middelburg gave little encouragement to political plotters, and few were attracted there. "Here are few English and these not considerable."[70]

True to its Puritan tradition, the church kept up an orderly system of discipline, examination of members, and pre-communion house visitation. David Anderson inscribed the following motto in the consistory register: *Ordo est a Deo, Confusio ab Orco.*[71] The elders and deacons were businessmen who applied businesslike efficiency to the church's resources. An increasing amount of consistorial time was devoted to handling the investments. The "Estate of the Church" in 1669 showed investments in the West India Company (a note at 2%), notes at the Bank van Lening (fl. 2230), a mortgage (fl. 1000) yielding $4^{1}/_{2}\%$, and the proceeds from the sale of the parsonage, a total treasury of 5400 guilders.[72] The practical-minded merchant elders kept careful accounts and laid up churchly treasures.

As guardians of the English-Scottish community, the consistory ministered to both material and spiritual needs. Little sums were doled out from the church treasury but under very stringent conditions—it was no case of whosoever will may come. The church officers lived in fear of unworthy slackers devouring church funds. Only members could receive regular subsidies, and strangers were almost always refused and hurried on elsewhere. An old Englishman who drifted in from 's-Hertogenbosch was denied a pension "in regard he is no member with us." Where possible, poor strangers were advised to return to their last place or sent over to the Dutch church for aid. A needy widow from Maastricht was not welcome; "we advised her to get her selfe admitted a member with the Dutch church, she understanding that language that so she might obtain some reliefe from them." The church funds, the elders lamented, were "so insufficient" for generosity.[73] After minister David Anderson's

---

[69] Middelburg C.R., I, 222-24.
[70] Ibid., I, 227; S.P. 84, vol. 167, fol. 240v.
[71] On the cover of C.R., I.
[72] C.R., II, 19, 85.
[73] Ibid., II, 33, 54, 88-90, 169.

death, leaving several orphans, the church found excuses to avoid taking on their support and handed them over to the Dutch church. Fortunately, the Dutch responded and "became guardians to the five orphans whom he left behind him." One of Anderson's daughters was provided for by Anna Maria van Schurman.[74] Questions of poor relief troubled relations between the English and Dutch churches.

The English church belonged to the Classis of Walcheren. No serious church-classis problems erupted until 1679. Then, when the church attempted to call Mattheus Noper (in 1679-80), preacher of the Dutch church of Norwich, the classis absolutely refused to approve him. The classis brethren accused Noper of inclining toward the "disturbing noveltys of these times" (Cocceianism). During the proceedings the classis referred to the English church as "this miserable Congregation."[75]

As a replacement for the vetoed Noper, the church elected John Quick (1680-81). He was a thoroughly orthodox Calvinist, but with some Congregationalist persuasions in his attitude to the classis and in refusing to use the common "forms" for baptism and communion. Quick subscribed to the required canons and even took brief session in the classis, but beyond that he would not go. Because of his nonconformity in worship, the magistrates cut off his salary, and within the congregation several of the members abstained from the communion until the customary forms would be restored. The Noper-Quick affairs instigated some hot talk at the church about "prejudiced rights" and "usurpeted authority" of the classis. Inducted January 5, 1681, Quick, "their quondam minister" gave up quickly on Middelburg and departed for London by July, 1681. He did not receive his final salary settlement for five years.[76] During his short pastorate Quick aroused the church to his two special concerns, classis and magisterial dictatorship and the growing Scottish influence in the church. Quick had a swift temper, being famously known for "the suddenness and warmth of his temper" which "made him generally the more active, though sometimes it eclips'd his worth, and was his bewailed burden."[77] Quick's Middelburg career was not all wasted, however, since it provided him with the occasion for Dutch historical research which he later incorporated in his "Icones Sacrae Anglicanae." The Walcheren Classis thought the best kind of minister for the English church would be someone more cooperative than Quick, "a man that

---

[74] Ibid., II, 38, 46, 50; Calamy, *N.M.*, III, 308; Quick, I, i, 275.
[75] C.R., II, 109-32; Quick, "Icones," I, i, 276-77.
[76] C.R., II, 130-31, 137-50.
[77] Funeral sermon for Quick, in Daniel Williams, *Practical Discourses on Several Subjects* (London, 1738), II, 129; Quick, "Icones," I, i, 268, 270-71.

was avers to the new church stirring novelties ... a true presbyterian who was avers to the Episcopal grounds and maxims."[78]

Although small, the church survived into the twentieth century, one of the longest-lived Netherlands British congregations. Throughout the late seventeenth century the church lacked sufficient leadership of its own and relied on the Dutch to provide one of the elders, elections being set up for one "English elder" and one "Dutch elder."[79] Several of the ministers were Dutch and the congregation increasingly took the form of a Dutch congregation with English-language services. Mountague in 1695 described the church as "about an hundred Auditors, all *Presbyterians*, and *Dutch*, from *English* and *Scotch* Parents."[80] The churches of Middelburg and Flushing were combined by royal decree in 1815 into a single pastorate although they retained separate meetings and officers in the two cities. Many ministers of the eighteenth and nineteenth centuries were drawn from Scotland. The church closed December 31, 1921.[81]

Flushing

The English church of Flushing had a history similar to Middelburg's with falling membership and increasing Dutch assimilation. There were 55 members in 1677 and no signs of growth thereafter.[82] Established in 1620 to replace an earlier garrison church, the English met in a chapel of the Groote Kerk. Ministers of the last half of the century were Arnold van Laren (1651-76), Samuel Megapolensis (1677-85), Hugo Fitts (1689-1700); Simon van der Pyl served 1700 to 1732.

The Flushing people had little success in attracting native English or Scottish preachers. Van Laren was a Dutch preacher from Veghel, who had previously been minister at a Dutch church in England.[83] After Van Laren's death in 1676, the church searched for an English or Scottish man, going first for Joseph Hill, former Middelburg minister, and then for Philip Bowie of Dort; both "desired to be excused."[84] Finally they secured Dr. Samuel Megapolensis, who the past seven years had served as Dutch preacher at Nieuwe Zijp (Classis of Alkmaar).[85] Hugo Fitts, ap-

---

[78] C.R., II, 197.
[79] Ibid., II, 6, 32, 102.
[80] Mountague, *Delights of Holland*, p. 229.
[81] Steven, pp. 322-23; *F.E.S.*, VII, 547-49; W. S. Unger, *Geschiedenis van Middelburg* (Middelburg: Zeeuwsch Genootschap der Wetenschappen, 1966), p. 57. The church was declared officially closed Jan. 1, 1922 (C.R., Sept. 21, 1921). W. S. Unger, "De voormalige Engelsche kerk te Middelburg," *Buiten*, 17 (May 5, 1923), 213.
[82] Flushing C.R., no. 4469, June 29, 1677.
[83] Ibid., June 28, 1651; Amsterdam C.R., III, 218.
[84] C.R., no. 4469, Nov. 20, 1676, Feb. 3, 1677.
[85] Ibid., Feb. 28, 1677. For Megapolensis's career at Dort, see above, no. 68.

parently of the English Fitts family of Amsterdam, was nearly as much Dutch as English in upbringing. Fitts had been educated at Utrecht (Hugo Fittz Amstelo-Batavus, 1680) and then served Dutch pastorates at the fortress of Retrenchment and at Meliskerk before coming to Flushing.[86] Van der Pyl was Dutch, but had lived at Canby, Essex.[87] During the eighteenth and nineteenth centuries, the church secured ministers from Scotland.

None of the later Flushing preachers were the usual refugee Puritans serving in the Netherlands churches. The preachers had Dutch rather than English links; consequently the congregation on the whole was uninvolved with the English and Scottish Puritan and Covenanter controversies. As a seaport Flushing had first hand news about the wars at sea. Van Laren was an enthusiastic reporter of events of the various Anglo-Dutch and French wars. From their church and homes they could sometimes hear "the roaring canon," whereupon "the more fervent prayers were poured forth to God Almightie ... that He would be pleased to preserve this country their fleet and to give them the victory." (1666). At the Peace of Breda (1667) the town had ringing of bells, canon shots, bonfires, and in the churches prayers of thanksgiving and praise.[88] During the English and French wars of 1672, Van Laren kept records of events on land and sea.

As the English population of Flushing shrank, the Dutch portion of the congregation predominated. The preachers were Dutchmen, and the majority of elders and deacons had Dutch names as well. In the consistory laws of 1681 it was necessary to legislate that the English language be spoken in consistory, a fine of half a stiver being levied for each Dutch word spoken. The officers of the time were named Rickets, Michielss, Gelijnss, Hoefnagel, Cooly, and Donckerts. The minister was ordered to report to the church on Sundays by 9:00 a.m. and 1:30 p.m., a fine of three stivers if more than fifteen minutes late. He was told to limit his sermons to one hour.[89]

When Megapolensis accepted a call to Dort in 1685, the Flushing church almost went defunct. No replacement could be found for four years; meanwhile, for several years (since 1682) the States of Zeeland had been considering a policy of allowing the church to expire.[90] The con-

---

[86] C.R., no. 4469, Oct. 15, 1689; Middelburg C.R., II, 151, 159; Utrecht Univ. *Album*, col. 74; Alice C. Carter, *The English Reformed Church in Amsterdam in the Seventeenth Century* (Scheltema & Holkema, 1964), p. 50.
[87] C.R., no. 4469, Jan. 23, 1700.
[88] Ibid., Aug. 4, 1666, Sept. 7, 1667.
[89] Ibid., June 29, 1677, Feb. 5, 1681.
[90] Ibid., May 20, 1682.

sistory register is a complete blank for the years 1685-89. Then in 1689 the church was revived, and Hugo Fitts accepted the call as minister. During the Megapolensis and Fitts pastorates, the consistory register reveals a languishing, unlively church. Little more than necessary records of elections and communion business were inscribed.

In 1815 the Flushing church was united with the English church of Middelburg but continued to have its separate meeting. The church building burned down in 1911, and for three years the English temporarily used the building of the Doopsgezind Church on Van Dishoeckstraat. On January 4, 1914, the English moved into a building of their own on the Nieuwe Markt. Formal services ceased in 1917, and the church, along with Middelburg, was formally closed by a resolution of September 21, 1921.[91]

Veere

The Scots church of Veere (Campvere) was an appendage of the Scottish Staple Company and directly dependent upon the fortunes of the company. During the course of the seventeenth century the Scottish Staple, and its church, declined rather than flourished.[92] When trade between Scotland and Veere was interrupted because of the Anglo-Dutch wars, the company in 1668 moved to Dort. However the rank-and-file merchants did not approve of the move to Dort; "on account of the Inconvenient Situation of the place our Merchants could not be brought to frequent it as their Staple port."[93] During the confusion the merchants scattered elsewhere, many to Rotterdam; and when the staple was officially re-established at Veere in 1675, it was on a weaker basis than before. The 1675 staple contract was for 21 years and it was renewed in 1697 and regularly thereafter until 1799, when the Batavian Republic totally annulled the Veere privileges. The late seventeenth-century staple and Scottish community of Veere was thoroughly decayed—"our trade could not be brought back to that very staple port where it had so long flourished."[94]

By the coming of Sir Andrew Kennedy as lord conservator in 1689 "there hardly remained the face of a Scots Corporation at the Staple Port, and our trade to it was inconsiderable." Many of the factors preferred a transfer to Rotterdam. Veere, they said, was so shrunken that it had "litle or no Trade nor resort of merchants to it" apart from the

---

[91] N. Veldhuis, archivist of Flushing, to the author, Mar. 19, 1979.

[92] John Davidson and Alexander Gray, *The Scottish Staple at Veere* (London: Longmans, Green, & Co., 1909), pp. 301-36.

[93] "Some Observations upon the Ancient and Modern State of the Scots Staple Trade to the Netherlands," Campvere Documents, no. 2, fols. 9-10.

[94] Ibid., fols. 10-11.

Staple, and was also "a sicklie place" to the detriment of health. Kennedy could not be optimistic about the future—"our Scots staple seems to be quite broke."[95] A slight revival took place in the 1690s. However, the monopolistic policies of the staple were out of step with the times, an anachronism. According to Davidson and Gray, "the later history of the Staple is little more than a history of failure. Contracts were made only to be broken."[96]

The post-Restoration ministers of the church were: Thomas Mowbray (1660-64), Andrew Snype (1664-86), Charles Gordon (1686-91), Thomas Hoog (1694-98), and John Chalmer (1699-1729). The Veere burgomasters according to the staple contract provided the building (a chapel of the Groote Kerk) and the salary for a minister. All ministers were Presbyterians sent out from Scotland by the Convention of Burghs, which exercised the right to elect ministers and remove them. The Convention, said Thomas Mowbray, are "the undoubted and unquestionable Patrons of the *Scots* Church, at the Stapel-Port in *Camp-veer*."[97]

Mowbray, an ex-chaplain with Scottish troops in Prussia, ushered in the Restoration at Veere with a rousing Royalist sermon, "The Honour of Kings Vindicated and Asserted" (May 3, 1661), by which he hoped to prove his "fidelitie, and loyaltie to his Majesty." He denounced Anabaptists as Anarchists and Cromwell as the "Arch-Traitor." Because of unsatisfactory service, he was removed in 1664 by action of the Convention of Burghs and the archbishop of St. Andrews.[98] Andrew Snype (1664-86), M.A. from the University of Glasgow, had Netherlands connections through his wife, Christine, daughter of Alexander Petrie. During Snype's ministry James Kennedy, a Roman Catholic, was named lord conservator (1682-88). To the alarm of the Scottish Presbyterians he attempted to insert Roman Catholic practices into the church and, after Snype's death, to name a Roman Catholic minister; however, this was resisted.[99] While Charles Gordon was minister (1686-91), the church burned and was not repaired until 1699, during which time the congregation moved into the poor house. Gordon also had the ill fortune to be captured by a French warship in 1689 while traveling to Scotland to be married. He was held prisoner for seven months, leaving the church pastorless.[100]

---

[95] Ibid., no. 2, fol. 11; no. 9; Leven and Melville MSS (G.D. 26/13/73, Scottish Record Office).

[96] Davidson and Gray, pp. 211-12.

[97] Mowbray, *Honour of Kings*, dedication; Davidson and Gray, appendix VII.

[98] Davidson and Gray, pp. 302-03; *F.E.S.*, VII, 541-42; Mowbray, *Honour of Kings* (printed by Thomas Berry of Middelburg, 1663), p. 16.

[99] Campvere Documents, no. 2, fol. 11; Davidson and Gray, p. 304.

[100] Davidson and Gray, pp. 304-05; *F.E.S.*, VII, 541; Steven, pp. 291-92.

Thomas Hoog (1694-98) transferred from Delft after many urgings from the Veere merchants. Lord conservator John Hamilton came personally to Delft to press the call, bearing a document of invitation with more than seventy signatures. The need was urgent. The church was destitute of ministry, "there being there about 400 merchants and mariners, that could not understand Dutch sermons."[101] However, four years later, when Hoog received a call to the Scots church of Rotterdam, he swiftly accepted the invitation, much disillusioned about the future of Veere and the unfriendliness of the magistrates and Dutch Reformed ministers. "Arbitrary government and enmity against our nation," he complained. His successor, John Chalmer, had formerly been assistant at the Rotterdam Scots church.[102]

The Veere church had the distinction of being a constituent member of the Church of Scotland. Veere had been incorporated with the General Assembly in 1642 although ministers seldom attended sessions. In addition, the church acknowledged a direct link with the Dutch Reformed Church by joining the Classis of Walcheren in 1669 (during the interval when the staple moved to Dort). Although this double link continued for twenty-four years, the Scots chafed under Dutch Reformed supervision, and in 1686, 1691, and 1693 they complained about Dutch interference in the privileges of the congregation, especially so during the interim between preachers Gordon and Hoog.[103] During the interim the classis brethren stepped in to insure that the church would choose "an orthodox preacher conformable to the order of these churches here in the Netherlands," but the Scots took this as meddling. The lord conservator in 1693 warned the deputies of the classis "that he could not permit the Scot church to be subordinate to the Classis of Walcheren, because such was forbidden by his instructions." At this time (1693) the church of Veere ceased membership in the classis and meanwhile tried to strengthen the old ties with the Church of Scotland.[104] Gordon during his ministry was admitted as a member of the Presbytery of Edinburgh, which practice was carried on by all succeeding ministers of the church; and according to James Yair (minister 1739-84) they were also members of the Synod of Lothian and Tweedale. The Scots minister, paid by Dutch money, "was the only minister of the Church of Scotland who has

---

[101] Delft C.R., no. 102, Sept. 6, 1693; Feb. 12, 1694.
[102] *F.E.S.*, VII, 541-42; Steven, p. 360.
[103] Acta Classis Walcheren, V, 142; William Mair, *A Digest of Laws and Decisions Ecclesiastical and Civil*, 4th ed. (Edinburgh: William Blackwood, 1923), pp. 370-72.
[104] Acta Classis Walcheren, VIII, 336, 358; Mair, *Digest*, pp. 371-72.

his charge in a foreign country." The last representative from the church to attend the General Assembly was in 1797.[105]

The final minister of the church, James Lickly, left Veere November 24, 1799; by then only four merchants remained.[106] A few items of the church records were given to the English church of Middelburg for safekeeping, and this church handled occasional matters of Scottish poor relief. Consequently, the Middelburg church thereafter claimed to have incorporated the remnant of the old Scots church of Veere.[107] In 1894 Arthur Frater, Scottish minister of Middelburg-Flushing, tried to claim Veere's ancient right in the General Assembly of the Church of Scotland, being "the remnant congregation of the Scotch church of Campvere." Appearing before the assembly, Frater told them: "He stood before them a living man—(loud laughter)—representing a living church—(applause)—and not a shadow haunting a heap of ruins." After the laughter died down, the assembly voted against Frater's suit on grounds that the church of Veere was, in fact, totally extinct. Nevertheless, the name "Campvere" had never been removed from the assembly roll; and the assembly voted "that the Church of Campvere remain on the Roll of Assembly." Although extinct, "Campvere" remained on the roll of the Church of Scotland General Assembly until 1929.[108]

Utrecht

Utrecht after the Restoration had the only remaining English church of Utrecht, Gelderland, and Overijssel provinces. The city retained a modest sized English-Scottish community composed of merchants and students. Although the Royalist refugees of the 1650s had departed, their places were taken after 1660 by nonconformist English and Scots (e.g. John Rogers, the Fifth Monarchist). The University of Utrecht was much favored by nonconformists, "free from those shackles that were imposed at home," and the province was attractive for residence, "for we almost phansied our selves in *England*, this being like some of our old Cities."[109] The English Reformed Church, established in 1622, kept a

---

[105] Mair, *Digest*, pp. 371-72 (he said, regarding the supposed membership in the Synod of Lothian and Tweedale, "of this there is no trace."); Campvere Documents, no. 2, fol. 15.

[106] Mair, *Digest*, p. 372.

[107] "Stukken betreffende de Schotsche court en de Schotsche kerk te Veere," (1822), no. 22, Middelburg E.R.C. The majority of records, however, remainded at Veere and were destroyed by fire in 1940.

[108] Newspaper reports in Campvere Documents, May 29, 1894; Mair, *Digest*, pp. 374-75; Drummond, *Kirk*, p. 151.

[109] Mountague, *Delights of Holland*, p. 196; Wilson, *Dissenting Churches*, I, 242. Among the nonconformist students, not mentioned in the text, were: Robert Trail Junior, John Collins, Thomas Collins, Thomas Reynold, Richard Mead, Samuel Mead.

steady membership of 150 to 180 until 1665; thereafter the disturbances of war caused serious disruptions from which the church never fully recovered. The membership was 180 in 1665, 113 in 1670, but only 50 in 1681, 50 in 1690, and down to 40 in 1700.[110] The congregation in 1656 began meeting in a partitioned off section of the Maria Kerk, other portions being used for selling books and lumber.[111] The English church had remarkable ministerial stability. The entire period of 1655-1748 (93 years) was served by two ministers: John Best (1655-1696) and James de la Faye (1696-1748).

During Best's early ministry, up to the French invasion of 1672, the Utrecht church was a typical mid-century English Reformed church, diligent, if somewhat staid, in matters of worship, discipline, and poor relief. The church held quarterly communion, always preceded by preparation sermon, *censura morum* in consistory, and house to house visitation. However, the potency of discipline was waning, some sinners remaining obdurate for years. Several deviant members were defiant against consistorial authority, which the elder took "very ill."[112] After the visitation of December 1664, the elders "understand with grief that the persons kept of the sacrament the last time for their offences had not amended their life so farre that they might be invited and admitted to the sacrament at this time."[113] Then after years of discipline, the cut-off offender sometimes at last submitted. At the rescue of every lost sheep there was rejoicing in the eldership.

As the central institution of British life in Utrecht, the church had a material as well as a spiritual ministry. When the poor, the halt, and the blind came, the officers handed out little sums of poor relief. In 1665, with the congregation at its numerical height and great demands being put upon the fund, the elders resolved to give "somewhat extraordinarily" to the poor members but not a regular pension, "seeing this doth exhaust the purse very much."[114] In 1666 the elders devised a non-monetary help for the poor—a special weekly poor lecture. "The number of the poore and poverty of the same encreasing, and the collections by reason of the bad times growing lesse, the brethren thought on means to supply the wants of the poore, and nothing more convenient occurring as an ordinary weekely lecture." The elders engaged Robert MacWard of

---

[110] Memoriaal van visitaties der kerken, Classis of Utrecht, no. 7, pt. 1 (G.A. Utrecht).

[111] G. G. Calkoen, "De kapittelkerk van St. Marie," pp. 56-57 (MS, 1916-17, G.A. Utrecht); Northleigh, *Topographical Descriptions*, p. 81.

[112] Utrecht C.R., no. 848, Feb. 3, 1662.

[113] Ibid., Dec. 30, 1664.

[114] Ibid., Jan. 2, 1665.

Rotterdam to deliver the lecture for the poor on Wednesday mornings "that so the loving knowledge of God might be furthered and the poore better solaced."[115]

MacWard was a spirited preacher and soon had a following in Utrecht. When pastor Best had to go to Rotterdam for eye treatments, MacWard supplied his place; between times he conducted house meetings at the home of Mr. Simson, "prayers before and after sermon," and at times at the house of Best.[116] MacWard was a zealous Covenanter banned from Scotland, so dyed in the grain a Scottish Presbyterian that he refused to use the customary liturgical forms of the church. Some of the elders complained about MacWard's omitting of the Lord's Prayer, "also some expressions in prayer concerning England." On June 3, 1667, the elders resolved by a plurality "that henceforth no minister shall be admitted to preach in this congregation, that refuseth to say the lords prayer and to use the formes or liturgy in the administration of baptisme, lords supper, confirmation of elders and deacons, and solemnization of marriage, according to the order of the church arrested in this province." The eldership laid down a policy of absolute conformity to Dutch Reformed practice. Best thought they had gone too far "and did dissent from these brethren by protestation judging this resolution to be very prejudiciall to the practise and liberties which the English churches in the Netherlands hitherto enjoyed."[117]

The French War (1672-78), when the French army overran Utrecht province, irreparably disrupted the church and scattered the congregation. French troops occupied and desecrated the Maria Kerk by using it as a barracks and stable. The fleeing English removed their consistory books and communion plate "because the soldiers lodged in our church." There was a break in the services of the church, and the English could not regain possession of their building for three years. The church, greatly reduced in size, had to meet temporarily in a substitute hall, although where is not known. In 1673 one elder was reported dead, and two other elders and one deacon had withdrawn to Holland, and "they are not likely to return during this war."[118] To cause still more confusion, Mr. Tuer the reader at that very time fell into scandalous drunkenness, even while at the reader's desk, being so overcome with drink "that he was not able to perform his duty in the morning before the sermon, but did read so that he cod not be understood and did fail in Singing ... until by reason of the disorder the minister did desire them to seise."[119]

---
[115] Ibid., Feb. 5, 1666.
[116] Ibid., June 1, 1667.
[117] Ibid., Feb. 11, June 3, 1667.
[118] Ibid., July 2, 1672; Mar. 2, 1673; Northleigh, *Topographical Description*, p. 81.
[119] C.R., May 30, 1673.

After the French withdrew, the church regained its building but did not recover to more than about half of its former size. In 1675 the Maria Kerk "being emptied of hay," the congregation moved back in.[120]

The resident church membership had a large Dutch faction. Many of the leading members were English-speaking Dutch people. John Best himself was more Dutch than English. Best was the son of the one-time English Brownist of Amsterdam, William Best. Before being called to Utrecht, he had previously served as minister of the Dutch church at Schermer, and listeners to his sermons were never quite sure if he was English or Dutch. His Dutch was better than his English.[121] In 1656 and 1661 the English church had to resort to borrowing Dutchmen to serve in the consistory because, Best admitted, "they had such difficulty in choosing elders and deacons out of their own nation."[122] By the 1690s the officers were predominantly Dutch (Van der Heyden, Jarman, Van Werkhoven, Koolenkamp, Bijer, Glover, Van Banen, De Jong, Brandes, Boschen).[123] The English and Scottish students at the university did not feel the church met their needs.

During the 1680s, after the Rye House Plot and Monmouth's Rebellion, nonconformist students and political refugees flocked into Utrecht. Edmond Calamy from London (student 1688-91) and John Erskine of Carnock (student 1685-88) have both left journals of student life at Utrecht. Calamy chose Utrecht over private study in England; there "we found a good number of our countrymen, at that time there."[124] Erskine reported that in 1686 twelve English families arrived within a week or two. So large was the concourse of English and Scottish students that there "was a great hindrance to the studies of these who did not keep themselves much retired from company." The Utrecht community was a hotbed of rebellious talk. King James, they said, "when he could not advance his interest by a legall kind of way, he designs by violence to make idolatry and tyranny our lot." The angry students refused to drink the king's health. On ambassador Bevil Skelton's periodic searches about Utrecht, he investigated the English church, looking for evidence of Scottish and English fugitives.[125]

The English church of the 1680s and 1690s, presided over by aged, near-blind Best, offered inadequate ministry to the students. Calamy

---

[120] Ibid., Mar. 6, Oct. 2, 1675.
[121] Edmund Calamy, *An Historical Account of my Own Life*, 2nd ed. (London, 1830), I, 144; Carter, *English Reformed Church*, p. 107.
[122] Acta Kerkeraad Utrecht, F, Apr. 8, 1656; H, Jan. 11, 1661 (G.A. Utrecht).
[123] C.R., 1691-95.
[124] Calamy, *Own Life*, I, 139, 142.
[125] John Erskine, *Journal*, pp. 182, 193, 199, 214.

described John Best as charitably as possible, "a Dutchman who spoke English very brokenly, and though an honest good man, yet a very indifferent preacher. It was no small disadvantage to the English students then at Utrecht, that they were not better entertained on the Lord's day." Erskine found the situation the same, "a blind minister, and truely to me his preaching was very dark, if not blind, and others had told me so before."[126] Best in his old age suffered from infirmity, bad eyes, and palsy; but mercifully for the church, there were many vigorous British preachers available for temporary preaching and these injected some liveliness into the drab church. Among the visiting preachers at the English church were John Nesbet (living under the pseudonym of "White"), Thomas Woodcock, John Howe, Nathaniel Taylor, Matthew Mead, Robert Bragge, Gilbert Burnet, Mr. Cameron, Walter Cross, Mr. Griffeth, and Mr. Peacock. John Best Junior sometimes preached.[127] In 1686 the church opened a regular Wednesday sermon, approved by the burgomasters, filled by John Howe and Matthew Mead.[128] The students were delighted when visitors took Best's place. In search of good preaching, many of the students attended the French church, and there were also numerous house meetings and conventicles for prayer and preaching. Erskine attended small house meetings for students (preaching by David Blair, William Moncrief, George Barclay, Alexander Hastie, John Howe, and John Sinclair).[129]

In 1692 Best became too weak to minister in any fashion. The university felt obliged to intervene because of English students being deprived of ministry at the church. The university senate in 1693 discussed the matter of Best, being "always sick and can no longer perform his duties." A group of seventy to eighty English and Scottish students were being deprived of regular preaching. After consultation among officials of city, church, and university, arrangements were made to hire an assistant (a proponent) to supply the pulpit; the States of Utrecht provided 200 guilders, the burgomasters 100 guilders, and 150 guilders came from Best's salary.[130] James de la Faye, a young Presbyterian from England, took the pulpit in 1694, and after Best's death in 1696, De la Faye succeeded to the pastorate.[131] Mountague visited the church in 1695 and

---

[126] Calamy, *Own Life*, I, 144-45; Erskine, *Journal*, p. 167.
[127] C.R., July, 1692, on Robert Bragge and (Roger?) Griffeth; the remainder are reported by Calamy and Erskine. Calamy also noted other refugee ministers at Utrecht: Thomas Collins, Peter D'Aranda, William Nokes, William Carstares.
[128] Erskine, *Journal*, p. 216; Calamy, *Own Life*, I, 145-46.
[129] Erskine, *Journal*, pp. 168, 172-75.
[130] C.R., July 2, 1692; G. W. Kernkamp, *Acta et Decreta Senatus ... de Utrechtsche Academie* (Utrecht: Kemink en Zoon, 1938-40), II, 128.
[131] C.R., fols. 197-98.

recorded these impressions: "On *Sunday* (in most decent manner) we went to the *English* church, which is a good old Piece of Building; the chancel is let for a Joyners Shop ... the Congregation was small, between one and two hundred, zealous Parson and People, no *English Liturgy* read here, all *Presbyterians.*"[132]

The eighteenth-century church was a tiny gathering. The Dutch classis in 1753 noted sternly that the church had only fourteen members, but the Reverend William Brown argued that smallness was no sign of spiritual weakness. After all, Christ had only twelve apostles and "where two or three are gathered together in my name, there am I in the midst of them." The classis brethren demoted the church from the status of a city church and put it back with the village churches. The indignant Brown took his case all the way to the States of Utrecht and won reinstatement of the church as a city church.[133] The last English Reformed minister terminated his service at Utrecht in 1794, at the time of the French revolutionary invasion. The church was largely inactive from that point, but the official suppression took place by Royal decree in 1841.[134] The present English church of Utrecht, Holy Trinity Church, is an Anglican Church founded in 1876.[135]

The Glorious Revolution

The Netherlands English and Scottish churches during the sixteenth and seventeenth centuries were the outposts of Puritanism in the Low Countries. Many of the ministers and members were refugee Puritans and Covenanters. The churches were vigorous partners in the three-cornered world of international Puritanism (England, Netherlands, and America). Then, the Glorious Revolution of 1688 changed the situation entirely. "The Providence of God opened a new and wonderful Scene in *England*, which had a great Influence upon all the affairs of *Europe.*"[136] The deposing of James II and the accession of William and Mary restored Presbyterianism in Scotland and allowed toleration for dissenters in England. The door was open to return home. Since their foundations in the sixteenth century, the overseas British churches had

---

[132] Mountague, *Delights of Holland*, p. 198.

[133] C.R., fol. 269-300 (1753); Steven, pp. 341-42.

[134] C. H. D. Grimes, *The Early Story of the English Church at Utrecht* (Chambéry, 1930), pp. 37-38.

[135] C. M. Breuning-Williamson, *Holy Trinity Church Utrecht, 1913-1963* (Wageningen, 1963). Some Anglican group functioned at Utrecht before 1876. William Jamieson preached a sermon, "The Establishment of the Reformation in England under Queen Elizabeth" (at "the English Episcopal Church service in the city of Utrecht" Mar. 17, 1858, MS G.A. Utrecht).

[136] Tong, *Memoirs of John Shower*, p. 53.

been the havens for religious and political nonconformists. After 1688 the Netherlands was no longer needed for that function. Although individuals for personal reasons might still retreat into exile, no general policy thereafter drove large groups into forced exile. The refugee population dropped away, leaving the churches numerically smaller and serving local needs. Up to this time, the churches had been in the mainstream of England and Scottish history (the guardians of Puritanism-in-exile); thereafter their mission was much smaller.

The churches wholeheartedly supported William of Orange's expedition to England, public prayers being offered in all the Dutch and English Reformed churches. "The ministers prayed for a north-east wind, by name." Several preachers accompanied William's army (William Carstares, David Blair, Gilbert Burnet, Robert Ferguson). The success of the revolution was evidently "the work of God."[137]

The exodus of the refugees greatly reduced the size of the churches and sped their assimilation into Dutch society. By 1700 the congregations were all diminished, and ever larger proportions of the membership were English-speaking Dutch people rather than recent immigrants or visitors. As the supply of ejected Puritans ceased, the churches faced nearly insurmountable problems in attracting native English preachers. Some Scottish ministers, however, were still to be had although not of the stature of the former banished Covenanters. The Scottish church of Rotterdam complained bitterly in 1698, when one of their ministers, Robert Fleming, was called to a pulpit in London: "Pray consider how difficult if not impossible it would be to get this place sutably supplied at this time, when Scotland has none to spare.[138]

The English church of Rotterdam in 1690 summarized the problems of ministerial recruitment after the Glorious Revolution:

> 1. There being liberty granted by law, for the Presbyterians to preach publiquely now in England: it will be more difficult now to procure one from hence then formerly. Men of parts and ability since this liberty either have or hope for congregations, and a competent subsistence in their own country.
>
> 2. Our salary here is not competent for maintaining those that have families, and have not means of their own: so that it must be a single person in all likelihood that will accept of the place.
>
> 3. It being a time of war, and the seas dangerous, several will be loath to venture themselves in passing, and repassing them to us, to preach on tryal, and from us back againe.

---

[137] Calamy, *Own Life*, I, 151; David Blair letter, Dec. 24, 1688 (F.O. 259, box 1, P.R.O.).
[138] Scots C.R., III, 12.

>   4. Besides the danger of the seas, several will be loath to come over, and preach upon uncertainties of being called: and we cannot call those the congregation hath never heard, upon the bare testimony of others: knowing how easy and usual it is, for men to procure testimonials above their merits.[139]

In order not to be destitute of ministry several of the late seventeenth-century churches turned to English-speaking Dutch ministers for pastoral supply. In the eighteenth century Scots usually filled the pulpits, a surplus apparently being available in Scotland. When Steven wrote his history (1833) "with very few exceptions, all the British Presbyterian congregations in Holland, for upwards of half a century, had been supplied with pastors by the Church of Scotland."[140]

Of the more than thirty English and Scottish Reformed churches of the early seventeenth century, only twelve survived to 1700. Four of the churches survived into the twentieth century: Amsterdam, the Rotterdam Scots church, Flushing (1921), and Middelburg (1921). The Amsterdam English Reformed Church and the Rotterdam Scots Church are alive and ministering actively today.

---

[139] Rotterdam C.R., no. 342, fol. 20.
[140] Steven, p. 402.

CHAPTER SEVENTEEN

EPILOGUE:
THE PURITAN MIND IN ENGLAND, THE NETHERLANDS, AND AMERICA

The theme which runs throughout this book is Puritanism: As it developed and functioned in England, was transported to the Netherlands, and interconnected to America. Although difficult to define, to the satisfaction of all scholars, Puritanism, at the least, means the English Calvinist dissenting movement against established Anglican religion, dedicated to simplifying and purifying the church along Reformed lines. Most Puritans in England before 1660 operated within the larger Church of England, hoping to reform from inside. Their ideological loyalties were mainly to the international Calvinist movement; but fragmentation within the ranks followed in due course.[1] Puritanism was parent to diverse groups of Baptists, Levellers, Diggers, Quakers, and other sects. This broad spectrum of Puritanisms shared the opposition to Anglican prelatical religion but not necessarily one set of doctrinal propositions.

Puritanism spread eastward to the Continent and westward to America among English-speaking people. Unlike areas like Scotland or the Netherlands, where Calvinism quickly became the predominant religion, or France, where the Calvinist Huguenots were a perpetual minority, the Puritanical English Calvinists existed as a movement within the larger structure of the Church of England. English Puritans exerted an influence but seldom held the reins of power. The mainstream Puritans aspired for power—the better to refashion church and society—but except for a few exceptional occasions, the goal eluded them.

The essence of Puritanism was a balanced combination of doctrinal Calvinist theology and intense personal piety. Perry Miller proposed that Puritanism should first of all be viewed as part of a recurring theme in Christian history, exemplified by the piety of St. Augustine. "Inside the shell of its theology and beneath the surface coloring of its political theory, Puritanism was yet another manifestation of a piety to which some men are probably always inclined and which in certain conjunc-

---

[1] William Haller, *The Rise of Puritanism* (Harper Torchbooks, 1957), p. 8. Compare R. T. Kendall, *Calvin and English Calvinism to 1649* (Oxford: Oxford Univ. Press, 1979), p. 212.

tions appeals irresistibly to large numbers of exceptionally vigorous spirits."[2] Puritanism carried forward a venerable Christian tradition. One of the clearest definitions of Puritanism came from within the movement by Doctor William Ames and William Bradshaw in their little treatise, *English Puritanisme* (1605, 1610). Bradshaw composed the main body of the book and Ames did the preface and re-edited the book in 1610. The Ames preface made three assertions about the beliefs and practices of Puritans: (1) They desire a purified church; (2) They strive for personal and public righteousness (meaning, a reform of manners and morals, Sabbath observance, prayers, good conversation, and the shunning of stage plays, swearing, drunkenness, masking, dicing, and all sorts of reveling); (3) Their authority was the Bible. This third point was the most basic. Everything goes back to Scripture. Every part of Puritan doctrinal faith and church discipline "is to be sought from Christ in the word, and out of the sacred papers they make all their book."[3] These convictions prove to be the most common elements of Puritanism wherever in the world it was found.

While earnestly espousing public and personal piety, Puritanism also built strong philosophical foundations. The chief Puritan theoreticians were products of the academy (Cambridge and Oxford in England; Harvard and Yale in America; Leiden, Utrecht, and Franeker in the Netherlands). The favorite Puritan philosopher was Peter Ramus, from whom came the theories of *technometria* and methodical theology; but much they also gained from Aristotle, Plato, the medieval scholastics, and the Renaissance scholars. In studying the Bible or building sermons, Puritans said, "Resolve them logically." The teacher of the Word was to follow a method of resolving, explaining, and applying doctrines to daily uses. These were acts of the logical mind; "Puritan piety was formulated in logic and encased in dialectic; it was vindicated by demonstration and united to knowledge."[4] Nevertheless, the Puritan mind aimed to avoid any lopsidedness of intellectual discourse or mere good works. Both theory and practice must be equally combined. Divinity is both doctrine and living ("the doctrine of living to God"), said Doctor Ames; "There are two parts of Divinity, Faith and Observance."[5] William Perkins

---

[2] Perry Miller, *The New England Mind: The Seventeenth Century* (Cambridge: Harvard Univ. Press, 1963), p. 4.

[3] William Ames preface to *English Puritanisme* (1660 edition). The Ames preface first appeared in the 1610 Latin edition. *English Puritanisme* (n.p., 1605), p. 1.

[4] Perry Miller, *The Puritans*, rev. ed. (Harper Torchbooks, 1963), I, 24; William Ames, *The Substance of Christian Religion* (London, 1659), preface; Miller, *New England Mind*, p. 112.

[5] Ames, *The Marrow of Sacred Divinity* (London, n. d.), chapters 1-2.

preached that the "Body of Scripture is a doctrine sufficient to live well."[6] The Puritan, then, had a double calling: Doctrine and Use.

Thus far, many Puritans of England, Holland, and America were agreed. The issue of church government, however, did not produce one single Puritan position. The Puritan preoccupation with the structure of the church was unique to Reformed religion. The search for perfection of church government powerfully motivated Puritans in their controversies with the hierarchical Church of England, and then created deep divisions within the movement itself. Bishop George Downham, who espoused strong Calvinist doctrines, believed that preoccupation with church government was the "chiefe and principal" Puritan characteristic. "The rest to be but controversies in pretence."[7] Most Elizabethan Puritans assumed that the Word lead unswervingly to a Presbyterian-Reformed system. Ames and Bradshaw in *English Puritanisme* read the Bible differently; they argued that Puritanism should be Congregationalist in its view of the church. "They hould and maintaine that euery Companie, Congregation or Assemblie of men, ordinarilie ioyneing together in the true worship of God, is a true visible church of Christ."[8] Anabaptists like John Smyth believed the rule of Scripture led straight to Anabaptism. Puritans splintered into groups of Presbyterians, Congregationalists, Separatists, Anabaptists, Baptists, Quakers, and many more. Some latter-day Puritans leveled, dug, or ranted. Puritanism is a term broad enough to cover the wide variety of churches and sects emerging out of the anti-Anglican ferment.

In the effort to purify the church and promote piety, Puritans clung tenaciously to the Protestant doctrine of the Scriptures, *Sola Scriptura*. All things must be tested by the Bible, for everything necessary for salvation is contained in Scripture; moreover, the Bible gives infallible directions for every area of life. No aspects of religion were indifferent. The Hooker school of Anglican theologians denounced the Puritans for drawing "all things unto the determination of bare and naked Scripture." Such narrowness would entirely undermine "the estimation and credit of man." The Puritans, Scriptural particularists, dissented from the usual Anglican position that Scripture was authoritative in matters of salvation but not in every detail of religion. Hooker predicted, "Much the church of God shall always need which the Scripture teached not."[9] Puritans trembled at this prelatical imperialism.

---

[6] William Perkins, *Workes* (London, 1612-13), I, 11.

[7] George Downham, *A Sermon Defending the Honourable Function of Bishops* (London, 1608), preface.

[8] *English Puritanisme* (1605), p. 5.

[9] Richard Hooker, *Of the Laws of Ecclesiastical Polity* (Everyman's ed.), II, 7, i; also quoted in William Ames, *Fresh Suit against Human Ceremonies* (n. p., 1633), pt. II, 2.

Although Puritanism prior to 1640 achieved a cohesive, well-defined doctrine of the authority of the Bible, under the impact of war and revolution the Puritan movement showed great capacity for change. The original Puritan vision of a purified church and reformed commonwealth stretched into new forms—Baptists, Levellers, Diggers, Quakers. These new forms of Puritanism drew upon elements in the original Puritan vision but magnified one or another of them (the Holy Spirit, the church of believers, Biblical egalitarianism, social justice, or the millennium). Such a profusion of sects should not have been very surprising. When the Puritan method of rational interpretation was linked with individual judgment (finding various practical or idealistic solutions to problems), Puritanism was on the high road toward factionalism, each party with the Bible.

From 1550 to 1700, the years covered by this book, Puritanism matured. Puritans experienced moments of power under Cromwell in England and in the New England Colonies. However, after the Restoration of 1660, Puritanism in England retreated to the side lines of English life, existing but chastened. Unanticipated problems troubled Puritanism during these 150 years. Puritans discovered that it was easier and more heroic to be a grassroots movement in opposition than to carry the burdens of power. The early periods of Puritanism had a freshness and Spartan simplicity; once in power, compromises had to be made, some of them unpleasantly similar to their old opponents, the prelates and the royalists. Another problem was Puritanism's fragmentation into the multiplicity of churches and sects. From a libertarian viewpoint, multiplicity was a virtue; to the mainline Puritans, it was catastrophe. How could the Bible lead in so many different directions? The Dutch exiles John Smyth and Leonard Busher were the first Puritans to extoll absolute religious freedom for all Christians.[10] This view was the exception. A third development, primarily post Restoration, was the narrowing and hardening of the Puritan vision. The original goal was an energetic, exuberant program of purified church and commonwealth; the victory of public and private righteousness; the smashing of Babylonish wickedness. The later Puritanism in England and the Netherlands sharpened its doctrinal orthodoxy and cultivated the inner life of congregations, but the social vision languished. No longer could Puritans realistically expect, even with the help of God, to refashion society. Puritans became dissenters.

Puritanism in the Netherlands, although sharing in the central Puritan values, had its own role to play. In England Puritanism leavened society

---

[10] Michael R. Watts, *The Dissenters* (Oxford: Clarendon Press, 1978), I, 60.

and made a strong impact on the church and society for many decades. Conversion, piety, and simplicity of worship were the Puritan message. In America Puritan settlers appropriated a wilderness for their own uses and there established a Puritan commonwealth. What had been theoretically formulated in the homeland of England could be put into action in America. The results were not always as expected nor attractive; nevertheless, Puritanism has been one of the most enduring forces in American life. In the Netherlands Puritans, although a potent force among refugee English and Scots, were merely one current among many in a rather pluralistic society. The Dutch Puritan message was practical divinity, the need to go beyond doctrinal purity. Puritans in the Netherlands made a witness to majority Dutch society, but pre-eminently they functioned to preserve the zeal and identity of English-speaking people living abroad. As links in the network of international Puritanism, the Dutch Puritans were in the Puritan vanguard. They forged significant connections with religious and political developments in England and America.

SELECTED BIBLIOGRAPHY

ENGLISH AND SCOTTISH CHURCHES IN THE NETHERLANDS

I. MANUSCRIPTS

Algemeen Rijksarchief, The Hague.
    Res. States General, 1576-1671 (nos. 3095-3282).
    Res. States General, 1671-1700, gedrukte (nos. 3727-3755).
    Secrete Res. States General (no. 3963).
    Liassen Engelandt, States General (nos. 5892, 5897, 5901).
    Res. States of Holland, 1575-1700 (nos. 11-133).
    Secrete Res. States of Holland (no. 301).
    Register van predikanten en kerkelijke zaken, States of Holland (no. 4410).
    Waalsche en Engelsche Gemeenten, Breda (Archief van Nass. Domeinen, 1086).

Amsterdam Gemeente Archief.
    Acta Classis Amsterdam.
    Acta Kerkeraad Amsterdam.
    Acta Synod North Holland.
    Doopsgezinde Archive (Wybrantsz Memoriael A, B).
    "Engelsche Synode, 1622" (Synod, no. 388).
    English Reformed Church Archive: C.R. 1607-present; other documents.
    Notarial Archives.

Arnhem Gemeente Archief.
    Res. Magistraat.
    Acta Kerkeraad Arnhem.

Bergen-op-Zoom Gemeente Archief.
    Acta Kerkeraad Bergen-op-Zoom.

Bodleian Library, Oxford.
    Add. MS. C. 69.
    Barlow MS. 13.
    Rawl. MSS. E. 44-67; A. 183; E. 161.
    Tanner MSS. 37, 52, 65, 68, 93, 216, 220, 395, 458.

Breda Gemeente Archief.
    Acta Kerkeraad Breda.
    Kollektieboek van Diakonie, English Church, 1646-53 (no. 1117).

Brielle Gemeente Archief.
    Res. Vroedschap.

British Museum (British Library), London.
    Add. MSS. 17,677; 18,744; 22,919; 24,023; 29,492; 29,588; 34,507-12; 37,979-92; 41,803-46.
    Boswell Papers, Add. MSS. 6394, 6395.
    Harley MSS. 787, 3783, 6942.
    Sloane MSS. 608, 1465, 3088, 4275.
    "Tracts relating to the English Church at Amsterdam," Add. MS. 24,666.

Delft Gemeente Archief.
    Acta Kerkeraad Delft (in Oude Kerk).
    "Stukken van de Engelse predikanten te Delft" (no. 60).
    "Memorie van lidmaten der Engelse Kerk" (no. 61).
    English Reformed Church Archive: C.R. 1643-1723 (including marriage and baptism register).
    Res. Burgemeesteren.

Doctor Williams's Library, London.
    John Quick, "Icones Sacrae Anglicanae" (MS. 38.34, 35).
    Richard Baxter Letters (MS. 29.1-6).
    MSS. 24.1; 28.2; 28.30; 76.20; 201.23; 201.29.

Dordrecht Gemeente Archief.
    Acta Kerkeraad Dordrecht.
    English Reformed Church Archive: C.R. 1639-1839; other documents.

Gelderland Rijksarchief, Arnhem.
    Acta Classis Nijmegen.
    Acta Classis Over-Veluwe.
    Acta Classis Tiel.
    Acta Synod Gelderland.

Gorinchem Gemeente Archief.
    Acta Kerkeraad Gorinchem.

Haarlem Gemeente Archief.
    Rekening van de Thesaurie.

The Hague Gemeente Archief.
    English baptism and marriage register, 1677-1810 (no. 306).
    Alexander Mackey, sermon, Feb. 3, 1822.
    M. G. Wildeman, "Varia Presbyteriaansche Kerk te 's-Gravenhage." (English Reformed Church Archive is in the P.R.O., London).

Hamburg Staatsarchiv.
    Englisches Kirchenbuch, 1617-1738.

's-Hertogenbosch Gemeente Archief.
    English baptism, marriage, and burial register, 1668-70 (no. 213).
    Res. Stadsregering.

Heusden Hervormde Kerk.
    Acta Classis Gorinchem.
    Acta Kerkeraad Heusden.

Lambeth Palace Library.
    MSS. 1766, 1860.

Leiden Gemeente Archief.
    Acta Kerkeraad Leiden.
    Hugh Goodyear Papers (Weeskamer 1355).
    Hugh Goodyear Sermons (no. 66751).
    Register van Kerkelijke Zaken.
    Res. Burgemeesteren.
    "Stukken betreffende de benoeming van ouderlingen, 1638-60" (Weeskamer 4909).

Merton College Library, Oxford.
  Griffin Higgs Diary.

National Library of Scotland, Edinburgh.
  Wodrow MSS.

Nederlandse Hervormde Kerk Archief, 100 Javastraat, The Hague.
  Acta Classis: Tholen en Bergen-op-Zoom; Breda; Brielle; Delft; Dort; Haarlem; The Hague; Leiden; Zwolle.
  Acta Kerkeraad: The Hague.
  Acta Synod: Overijssel; South Holland (also see Knuttel).
  "Engelse predikanten, 1641" (Synod of South Holland, III, 35, iii, 29).
  Fockema Andreae, S. J. "Aantekeningen betreffende de archieven der Hoogduitse, Engelse en Schotse gemeenten in verband met de Ned. Herv. Kerk" (1952).
  "Stukken betreffende het proces tusschen de Classis van 's Gravenhage en den Engelschen Kerkeraad aldaar, 1716 (Classis of the Hague, no. 83).

New College Library, Edinburgh.
  English Reformed Church of Delft: copy of C.R. 1643-1723 (original at Delft).
  "Documents Relative to the Scottish Colony and Church at Veere."
  William Steven MSS.

Nijmegen Gemeente Archief.
  Acta Kerkeraad Nijmegen (in the church).
  Rekening St. Jansgoederen.
  Res. Raadsignaat.

Noord Brabant Rijksarchief, 's-Hertogenbosch.
  Acta Classis 's-Hertogenbosch.

Public Record Office, London.
  S.P. 14, 16, 18, 29, 83, 84.
  Acts of the Privy Council.
  English Reformed Church of The Hague Archive: C.R. 1627-1822; other documents. (RG 33, nos. 83-84; F.O. 259).

Rotterdam Gemeente Archief.
  Acta Classis Schieland.
  Acta Kerkeraad Rotterdam.
  Res. Vroedschap.

Rotterdam Scots Church.
  English Reformed Church of Rotterdam Archive: C.R. 1668-1877; other documents.
  Scots Church Archive: C.R. 1643-present; other documents.
  A. L. Schenk. "Het tweede bedehuis" (no. 1006).
  ———. "The Golden Book of the Scots Church" (no. 1011).
  ———. "Historical and Remarkable Documents" (no. 1010).

Scottish Record Office, Edinburgh.
  Acts of the General Assembly.
  Douglas MSS.
  Leven and Melville MSS.

Utrecht Gemeente Archief.
  Acta Classis Amersfoort (in classis of Utrecht).

Acta Classis Utrecht.
Acta Kerkeraad Utrecht.
Acta Synod Utrecht.
English Reformed Church Archive: C.R. 1657-1838; other documents.
William Jamieson, sermon, Nov. 17, 1858.
Res. Vroedschap.

Utrecht Rijksarchief.
"Over een geschil tusschen den kerkeraad der Engelsche Gemeente en de Classis van Utrecht" (Griffie van de staten, 364, pt. 231).
Res. States of Utrecht.

Vlissingen Gemeente Archief.
English Reformed Church Archive: C.R. 1620-1917; other documents.

Zeeland Rijksarchief, Middelburg.
Acta Classis Walcheren.
English Reformed Church of Middelburg Archive: C.R. 1623-1921; other documents.
Res. States of Zeeland.

II. PRIMARY SOURCES

Algemeen regelement voor het bestuur der Hervormde Kerk in het Koningrijk der Nederlanden. The Hague, 1816.
Baillie, Robert. *A Dissvasive from the Errours of the Time.* London, 1645.
Best, William. *The Chvrches Plea for her Right.* Amsterdam, 1634.
Bradford, William. "A Dialogue or a sume of a Conference between some younge men borne in New England and sundery ancient men that came out of holland and old England anno dom 1648." *Publications* of the Colonial Society of Massachusetts, 22 (1920), 115-41.
———. *Bradford's History of Plymouth Plantation 1606-1646.* Ed. William T. Davis. 1908; rpt. New York: Barnes & Noble, 1946.
Brereton, Sir William. *Travels in Holland the United Provinces England Scotland and Ireland.* Ed. Edward Hawkins. Chetham Society (1844).
Broughton, Hugh. *Works.* Ed. John Lightfoot. London, 1662.
Browne, Robert and Robert Harrison. *The Writings of Robert Harrison and Robert Browne.* Ed. Albert Peel and Leland H. Carlson. London: George Allen and Unwin, 1953.
Clapham, Henoch. *Theologicall Axioms or Conclvsions: Pvblikly Controverted, Discussed, and Conclvded by That Poore English Congregation in Amstelredam.* n.p., 1597.
Copie van de officieele documenten betreffende de oprichting van de "Schotsche Kerk" te Rotterdam in 1643. Rotterdam: n.p., n.d.
Cuningham, Thomas. *The Journal of Thomas Cuningham of Campvere 1640-1654.* Ed. Elinor Courthope. *Publications* of the Scottish History Society, 3rd ser., 11 (1928).
Davenport, John. *A Apologeticall Reply.* Rotterdam, 1636.
———. *A Ivst Complaint against an Vnivst Doer.* n.p., 1634.
———. *Letters of John Davenport, Puritan Divine.* Ed. Isabel M. Calder. New Haven: Yale Univ. Press, 1937.
Edwards, Thomas. *Antapologia.* London, 1644.
———. *Gangraena.* 3 pts. London, 1646.
[Forbes, Alexander]. *The Anatomy of Independency.* London, 1644.
Goodwin, Thomas, et al. *An Apologeticall Narration.* London, 1644.
Hessels, Joannes H., ed. *Ecclesiae Londino-Batavae Archivum.* 3 vols. Cambridge, 1887.
Hoornbeek, Johannis. *Summa Controversiarum Religionis.* 2nd ed. Utrecht, 1658.

Hornius, Georgius. *Historia Ecclesiastica et Politica.* Leiden, 1665.
Johnson, George. *A Discourse of Some Troubles and Excommunications in the Banished English Church at Amsterdam.* Amsterdam, 1603. See also a modern, critical version by Michael E. Moody, "A Critical Edition of George Johnson's *A Discourse.*" Diss. Claremont 1979.
Knuttel, W. P. C., ed. *Acta der particuliere synoden van Zuid-Holland 1621-1700.* 6 vols. Rijks Geschiedkundige Publicatiën. The Hague: Nijhoff, 1908-16.
Lawne, Christopher, et al. *The Prophane Schisme of the Brownists or Separatists.* n.p., 1612.
Offwood, Stephen. *An Advertisement to Ihon Delecluse, and Henry May the Elder. Heady and Rash Censures Seasonably Reproved.* n.p., [1632].
Paget, John. *An Answer to the unjust complaints of William Best.* Amsterdam, 1635.
———. *An Arrow against the Separation of the Brownists.* Amsterdam, 1618.
———. *A Defence of Chvrch-Government, Exercised in Presbyteriall, Classicall, & Synodall Assemblies.* London, 1641.
Reitsma, J. and S. D. van Veen, eds. *Acta der provinciale en particuliere synoden, gehouden in de noordelijke Nederlanden gedurende de jaren 1572-1620.* 8 vols. Groningen: J. B. Wolters, 1892-99.
T., A. *A Christian Reprofe against Contention,* n.p., 1631.
Wildeman, M. G. *The Eldest Church-book of the English Congregation in The Hague, that came to us, given as a transcript.* The Hague: De Wapenheraut, 1906.
Williams, George H., et al., eds. *Thomas Hooker: Writings in England and Holland, 1626-1633.* Harvard Theological Studies, 28. Cambridge: Harvard Univ. Press, 1975.

III. SECONDARY WORKS

Arber, Edward, ed. *The Story of the Pilgrim Fathers, 1606-1623 A.D.* London: Ward and Downey, 1897.
Commissie voor de Archieven van de Nederlandse Hervormde Kerk. *De archieven van de Nederlandse Hervormde Kerk in korte overzichten.* 2 vols. Leiden: E. J. Brill, 1960-74.
Atkinson, Ernest G. "Records of the English Church at the Hague." *Journal of the Presbyterian Historical Society of England,* 1 (1914-19), 153-55.
Baan, J. van der. "Engelsche gemeente te Bergen-op-Zoom." *Navorscher,* 32 (1882), 77-81.
Bakker, Johannes. *John Smyth, de stichter van het Baptisme.* Wageningen: H. Veenman & Zonen, 1964.
Ball, Bryan W. *A Great Expectation: Eschatological Thought in English Protestantism.* Leiden: E. J. Brill, 1975.
Bangs, Carl O. "The Leiden Pilgrims in American History." *Leids Jaarboekje* (1970), 43-50.
Bartlett, Robert M. *The Pilgrim Way.* Philadelphia: Pilgrim Press Book, 1971.
Beek, J. van. "Archibald Hamilton, een gevluchte Anglicaansche aartsbischop in Nederland." *Nederlandsch Archief voor Kerkgeschiedenis,* N.S., 4 (1907), 148-80.
Bosher, Robert S. *The Making of the Restoration Settlement: The Influence of the Laudians 1649-1661.* London: Dacre, 1951.
Bouwman, Marius. *Voetius over het gezag der synoden.* Amsterdam: S. J. P. Bakker, 1937.
Brachlow, Stephen. "More Light on John Robinson and the Separatist Tradition." *Fides et Historia,* 13 (Fall 1980), 6-22.
Breuning-Williamson, C. M. *Holy Trinity Church Utrecht, 1913-1963.* Wageningen, 1963.
Briels, J. G. C. A. *Zuidnederlandse boekdrukkers en boekverkopers in de Republiek der Verenigde Nederlanden omstreeks 1570-1630.* Nieuwkoop: B. de Graaf, 1974.
Broes, Wilhelm. *De Engelsche Hervormde Kerk, benevens haren invloed op onze Nederlandsche, van den tijd der Hervorming.* 2 vols. Delft: Allart, 1825.
Burger, C. P., Jr. "Een Metselaar-Latinist." *Het Boek,* 20 (1931), 305-10.
Burgess, Walter H. *John Robinson Pastor of the Pilgrim Fathers: A Study of His Life and Times.* London: Williams and Norgate, 1920.

———. *John Smith, the Se-Baptist, Thomas Helwys and the First Baptist Church in England.* London: James Clark, 1911.
Burrage, Champlin. *The Church Covenant Idea: Its Origin and Development.* Philadelphia: American Baptist Publication Society, 1904.
———. *The Early English Dissenters in the Light of Recent Research (1550-1641).* 2 vols. Cambridge: Cambridge Univ. Press, 1912.
———. *The True Story of Robert Browne (1550?-1633) Father of Congregationalism.* Oxford: Oxford Univ. Press, 1906.
———. "Was John Canne a Baptist? A Study of Contemporary Evidence." *Transactions of the Baptist Historical Society*, 3 (1913), 212-46.
Campbell, Douglas. *The Puritan in Holland, England, and America.* 4th ed. New York: Harper & Brothers, 1892.
Carter, Alice C. *The English Reformed Church in Amsterdam in the Seventeenth Century.* Amsterdam: Scheltema & Holkema, 1964.
———. "John Robinson and the Dutch Reformed Church." *Studies in Church History.* Ed. G. J. Cuming, 3 (Leiden: E. J. Brill, 1966), 232-41.
Carter, Harry. "Archbishop Laud and Scandalous Books from Holland." *Studia Bibliographica in Honorem Herman de la Fontaine Verwey.* Ed. S. van der Woude. Amsterdam: Hertzberger, 1967.
Christianson, Paul. *Reformers and Babylon: English Apocalyptic Visions from the Reformation to the Eve of the Civil War.* Toronto: Univ. of Toronto Press, 1978.
Cowan, Ian B. *The Scottish Covenanters 1660-1688.* London: Victor Gollancz, 1976.
Davidson, John and Alexander Gray. *The Scottish Staple at Veere: A Study in the Economic History of Scotland.* London: Longmans, Green, & Co., 1909.
Dentz, Fred. Oudschans. *History of the English Church at the Hague, 1586-1929.* Delft: W. D. Meinema, 1929.
Dexter, Henry Martyn. *The Congregationalism of the Last Three Hundred Years.* New York: Harper & Brothers, 1880.
Dexter, Henry Martyn and Morton Dexter. *The England and Holland of the Pilgrims.* Boston and New York: Houghton, Mifflin and Co., 1906.
Dorsten, J. A. van. *Thomas Basson 1555-1613: English Printer at Leiden.* Leiden: Sir Thomas Browne Institute, 1961.
Dow, Alexander C. *Ministers to the Soldiers of Scotland: A History of the Military Chaplains of Scotland Prior to the War in the Crimea.* Edinburgh: Oliver and Boyd, 1962.
Drummond, Andrew L. *The Kirk and the Continent.* Edinburgh: St. Andrew Press, 1956.
Duker, A. C. *Gisbertus Voetius.* 3 vols. Leiden: E. J. Brill, 1897.
Earle, Peter. *Monmouth's Rebels.* New York: St. Martin's Press, 1977.
Eeghen, I. H. van. *De Amsterdamse boekhandel 1680-1725.* 4 vols. Amsterdam: Publicaties van de Gemeentelijke Archiefdienst, 1960-67.
Eekhof, A. *Three Unknown Documents concerning the Pilgrim Fathers in Holland.* The Hague, 1920.
"Eerste vestiging der Engelsche gemeente te Leiden." *Kronyk van het Historisch Genootschap*, 6 (1850), 98-101.
Evenhuis, R. B. *Ook dat was Amsterdam.* 4 vols. Amsterdam: W. Ten Have, 1965-74.
Fasti Ecclesiae Scoticanae. Ed. Hew Scott. 8 vols. (vol. 7, *The Church of Scotland Overseas*). Edinburgh, 1915-50.
Ford, Worthington C. "Davenport-Paget Controversy." *Proceedings* of the Massachusetts Historical Society, 43 (1909), 45-68.
———. "Letters 1624-1636." *Proceedings* of the Massachusetts Historical Society, 42 (1909), 203-35.
Foster, Stephen. *Notes from the Caroline Underground: Alexander Leighton, the Puritan Triumvirate, and the Laudian Reaction to Nonconformity.* Studies in British History and Culture, vol. 6. Hamden: Archon Books, 1978.
Gelder, H. A. Enno van. *Getemperde vrijheid.* Groningen: Wolters-Noordhoff, 1972.
Greaves, Richard L. "The Tangled Careers of Two Stuart Radicals: Henry and Robert Danvers." *The Baptist Quarterly*, 29 (1981), 32-43.

Grimes, C. H. D. *The Early Story of the English Church at Utrecht*. Chambéry: Imprimeries Réunies, 1930.

Groen, J. A. "De Engelse Hervormde Gemeente." *Ons Amsterdam*, 9 (1957), 238-43.

Grol, H. G. van. "Iets van de oudste geschiedenis der Engelsche Kerk te Vlissingen." *Bijlage bij Jaarverslagen betreffende het archiefwezen en de oudheidkundige verzameling der Gemeente Vlissingen* (1913).

Gustafsson, Berndt. *The Five Dissenting Brethren: A Study of the Dutch Background of Their Independentism*. Lunds Universitets Årsskrift, n.f., 51 (1955).

Hallema, A. "De Engels-Hervormde gemeente te Breda gedurende de 17de eeuw." *De Oranjeboom*, 1 (1948), 70-100.

Hardacre, Paul H. *The Royalists during the Puritan Revolution*. The Hague: Martinus Nijhoff, 1956.

Harris, Rendel and Stephen Jones. *The Pilgrim Press, a Bibliographical & Historical Memorial of the Books Printed at Leyden by the Pilgrim Fathers*. Cambridge: W. Heffer and Sons, 1922.

Hart, Simon. "The Dutch and North America in the First Half of the Seventeenth Century. Some Aspects." *Mededelingen van de Nederlandse Vereniging voor Zeegeschiedenis*, 20 (1970), 5-17.

Henderson, G. D. "John Forbes of Corse in Exile." *Aberdeen University Review*, 17 (1929), 25-35.

Hitzigrath, Heinrich. *Die Kompagnie der Merchants Adventurers und die engelsche Kirchengemeinde in Hamburg 1611-1835*. Hamburg: Johannes Kriebel, 1904.

Hoop Scheffer, J. G. de. "De Brownisten te Amsterdam gedurende den eersten tijd na hunne vestiging, in verband met het ontstaan van de broederschap der Baptisten." *Verslagen & Mededeelingen van de Koninklijke Akademie van Wetenschappen* (1881).

———. *History of the Free Churchmen Called the Brownists, Pilgrim Fathers and Baptists in the Dutch Republic*. Ed. William Griffis. Ithaca: Andrus & Church, 1922.

Horst, Irvin B., *The Radical Brethren: Anabaptism and the English Reformation to 1558*. Nieuwkoop: B. de Graaf, 1972.

Howie, John. *The Scots Worthies*. Edinburgh, 1870.

Hull, William I. *The Rise of Quakerism in Amsterdam 1655-1665*. Swarthmore: Swarthmore College Monographs on Quaker History, 4 (1938).

Hulshoff, A. "Britsche en Amerikaansche studenten op bezoek of voor studie te Utrecht." *Historia*, 12 (1947), 185-90, 229-40.

Jager, H. de. "Engelsche predikanten te Brielle." *De Navorscher*, 43 (1893), 593-603.

Jensen, J. N. Jacobsen. *Reizigers te Amsterdam*. Amsterdam: Genootschap Amstelodamum, 1919.

Jewson, Charles B. "The English Church at Rotterdam and its Norfolk Connections." *Norfolk Archaeology*, 30 (1952), 3-16.

Johnson, A. F. "The Exiled English Church at Amsterdam and Its Press." *The Library*, 5th ser., 5 (1951), 219-42.

———. "J F. Stam, Amsterdam, and English Bibles." *The Library*, 5th ser., 9 (1954), 185-93.

———. "Willem Christiaans, Leyden, and His English Books." *The Library*, 5th ser., 10 (1955), 121-23.

Jones, Rosemary L. "Reformed Church and Civil Authorities in the United Provinces in the Late 16th and Early 17th Centuries, as Reflected in Dutch State and Municipal Archives." *Journal of the Society of Archivists*, 4 (1970), 109-23.

Jonge, C. de. "Franciscus Junius (1545-1602) en de Engelse Separatisten te Amsterdam." *Nederlands Archief voor Kerkgeschiedenis*, 59 (1978), 132-59.

Kannegieter, J. Z. *Geschiedenis van de vroegere Quakergemeenschap te Amsterdam 1656 tot begin negentiende eeuw*. Amsterdam: Scheltema & Holkema, 1971.

Kist, N. C. "John Robinson, predikant der Leidsche Brownisten-Gemeente." *Archief voor Kerkelijke Geschiedenis inzonderheid van Nederland*, 19 (1848), 369-407.

Knox, S. J. *Walter Travers: Paragon of Elizabethan Puritanism*. London: Methuen, 1962.

Lingelbach, W. E. *The Merchant Adventurers of England: Their Laws and Ordinances with*

Other Documents. Translations and Reprints from Original Sources of European History, 2nd ser., 2 (1902).
Lintum, C. te. *De Merchant Adventurers in de Nederlanden.* The Hague: Nijhoff, 1905.
Loosjes, J. *History of Christ Church (English Episcopal Church) Amsterdam 1698-1932.* Amsterdam: M. J. Portielje, 1932.
Meindersma, Wigger. *De Gereformeerde Gemeente te 's-Hertogenbosch 1629-1635.* Zalt-Bommel: H. J. van de Garde, 1909.
Moody, Michael E. "Trials and Travels of a Nonconformist Layman: The Spiritual Odyssey of Stephen Offwood, 1564- ca. 1635." *Church History,* 51 (1982), 157-71.
Naamlyst der predikanten, ouderlingen, en diakenen die Engelsche Gereformeerde Gemeente te Middelburg. Middelburg, 1770.
Nauta, D. *De Nederlandsche Gereformeerden en het Independentisme in de zeventiende eeuwe.* Amsterdam: H. J. Paris, 1936.
Nobbs, Douglas. *Theocracy and Toleration: A Study of the Disputes in Dutch Calvinism from 1600 to 1650.* Cambridge: Cambridge Univ. Press, 1938.
Nuttall, Geoffrey F. "English Dissenters in the Netherlands 1640-1689." *Nederlands Archief voor Kerkgeschiedenis,* 59 (1978), 37-54.
———. *Visible Saints: The Congregational Way 1640-1660.* Oxford: Basil Blackwell, 1957.
Oosterbaan, Dinant P. *Het oude en nieuwe gasthuis te Delft (1252-1795).* Delft, 1954.
Pearson, A. F. Scott. *Thomas Cartwright and Elizabethan Puritanism 1535-1603.* 1925; Rpt. Gloucester, Mass.: Peter Smith, 1966.
Plooij, D. *The Pilgrim Fathers from a Dutch Point of View.* New York: New York Univ. Press, 1932.
Powicke, Fred. J. *Henry Barrow Separatist (1550?-1593) and the Exiled Church of Amsterdam (1593-1622).* London: James Clark, 1900.
Roetemeijer, H. J. M. "De Bruinisten in Amsterdam, op- en neergang van een kerk." *Ons Amsterdam,* 21 (1969), 194-201.
———. *Review of the History of Christ Church Amsterdam 1698-1971.* Amsterdam, 1971.
Roldanus, C. W. "Nederlandsch-Engelsche betrekkingen op den boden van 'Arminianisme'." *Tijdschrift voor Geschiedenis,* 58 (1943), 6-21.
Rostenberg, Leona. *The Minority Press & the English Crown: A Study in Repression, 1558-1625.* Nieuwkoop: B. de Graaf, 1971.
Schelven, A. A. van. "Engelsch Independentisme en Hollandsch Anabaptisme." *Nederlandsch Archief voor Kerkgeschiedenis,* N.S., 17 (1924), 108-26.
"Schotten en Britten te Utrecht." *Maandblad van "Oud-Utrecht,"* 27 (1954), 123-24.
Shaaber, Matthias A. *Check-list of Works of British Authors Printed Abroad, in Languages Other Than English, to 1641.* New York: The Bibliographical Society of America, 1975.
Shipps, Kenneth W. "Lay Patronage of East Anglian Puritan Clerics in Pre-Revolutionary England." Diss. Yale 1971.
Shuffleton, Frank. *Thomas Hooker 1587-1647.* Princeton: Princeton Univ. Press, 1977.
Smedt, Oskar de. *De Engelse natie te Antwerpen in de 16e eeuw (1496-1582).* 2 vols. Antwerp: De Sikkel, 1950-54.
Smith, Dwight C. "Robert Browne, Independent." *Church History,* 6 (1937), 289-349.
Sprunger, Keith L. "Archbishop Laud's Campaign against Puritanism at The Hague." *Church History,* 44 (1975), 308-20.
———. "The Dutch Career of Thomas Hooker." *The New England Quarterly,* 46 (1973), 17-44.
———. "English and Dutch Sabbatarianism and the Development of Puritan Social Theology (1600-1660)." *Church History* (1982), 24-38.
———. "English Puritans and Anabaptists in Early Seventeenth-Century Amsterdam." *Mennonite Quaterly Review,* 46 (1972), 113-28.
———. *The Learned Doctor William Ames: Dutch Backgrounds of English and American Puritanism.* Urbana: Univ. of Illinois Press, 1972.
———. "Other Pilgrims in Leiden: Hugh Goodyear and the English Reformed Church." *Church History,* 41 (1972), 46-60.

Stearns, Raymond P. *Congregationalism in the Dutch Netherlands.* Chicago: The American Society of Church History, 1940.

——. *The Strenuous Puritan: Hugh Peter, 1598-1660.* Urbana: Univ. of Illinois Press, 1954.

Steven, William. *The History of the Scottish Church, Rotterdam.* Edinburgh: Waugh & Innes, 1883.

Stoeffler, F. Ernest. *The Rise of Evangelical Pietism.* Leiden: E. J. Brill, 1965.

Stoye, John W. *English Travellers Abroad 1604-1667.* London: Jonathan Cape, 1952.

Sypesteyn, C. A. van. "De voormalige Engelsche kerk te 's-Gravenhage." *Haagsch Jaarboekje,* 1 (1889), 58-63.

Trevor-Roper, H. R. *Archbishop Laud 1573-1645.* 2nd ed. London: Macmillan, 1963.

Unger, W. S. "De voormalige Engelsche kerk te Middelburg." *Buiten,* 17 (May 5, 1923), 213-14.

Van Alphen's nieuw kerkelijke handboek. Ed. M. W. L. van Alphen.

Veltenaar, Cornelis. *Het kerkelijke leven der Gereformeerden in Den Briel tot 1816.* Amsterdam: A. H. Kruyt, 1915.

Verheul, J. *De Schotsche gemeente en haar oude kerkgebouw te Rotterdam.* Rotterdam: Stemerding, 1939.

Verwey, H. de la Fontaine. "De Bruinistenkerk." *Amstelodamum Maandblad,* 37 (1950), 106-10.

——. "Thomas Basson en het Huis der Liefde." *Het Boek,* 3rd ser., 35 (1961-62), 219-24.

——. "Van kerk tot dievenhol: De geschiedenis van de Bruinistenkerk." *Amstelodamum Maandblad,* 36 (1949), 150-56.

Walker, James. "The English Exiles in Holland during the Reigns of Charles II and James II." *Transactions* of the Royal Historical Society, 4th ser., 30 (1948), 111-25.

Watts, Michael R. *The Dissenters,* vol. I, *From the Reformation to the French Revolution.* Oxford: Clarendon Press, 1978.

White, B. R. *The English Separatist Tradition from the Marian Martyrs to the Pilgrim Fathers.* Oxford: Oxford Univ. Press, 1971.

Wildeman, M. G. "Bijdrage tot de geschiedenis der Presbyteriaansche Kerk te 's-Gravenhage." *De Navorscher,* 45 (1895), 156-84, 215-57.

——. "Het doop- en trouw-boek der Engelsche Kerk te 's-Gravenhage." *De Nederlandsche Leeuw,* 11 (1893), 13-16, 34-37, 43-40, 55-6.

Wilson, J. Dover. "Richard Schilders and the English Puritans." *Transactions* of the Bibliographical Society, 11 (1909-11), 65-134.

Wilson, John F. "Another Look at John Canne." *Church History,* 33 (1964), 34-48.

Wilson, Walter. *The History and Antiquities of Dissenting Churches and Meeting Houses in London, Westminster, and Southwark.* London, 1808-14.

Woude, C. van der. "Amesius' afscheid van Franeker." *Nederlands Archief voor Kerkgeschiedenis,* 52 (1972), 153-77.

Zuck, Lowell. "Reviewing Congregational Origins among Puritans and Separatists in England." *Bulletin of the Congregational Library,* 29 (Winter 1978), 4-13.

(See also items in List of Abbreviations, pp. xii-xiii)

INDEX OF PERSONS

Abbot, George, 355-56
Adair, Rev., 433n
Adams, Thomas, 100-01, 116, 119, 121
Adams, Thomas (author), 359-60
Ainsworth, Henry, 77, 324, 336-41; at Amsterdam, 48-67, 96-97, 99, 101, 359
Aitken, James, 381n
Allen, Benjamin, 312
Allen, Thomas, 168, 285n, 286
Ambrose, Dr., 259
Ames, William (Dr.), 8, 24n, 71, 103, 116, 133, 136, 141, 143, 163, 165, 166, 188, 194, 238-39, 250, 262n, 263, 285n, 297n, 301, 305-06, 308, 309, 314, 318, 319-20, 331, 341, 345, 356, 359, 458; at Franeker University, 188, 193, 202, 359; on covenants, 165, 191, 346-47; at Rotterdam, 165-166
Ames, William, Jr., 172
Ames, William (Quaker), 350-52
Amyraut, Paul, 6n, 168, 214, 216-17, 223, 225, 269, 285n
Anderson, David, 188, 398n, 440, 442-43
Apollonius, Willem, 365-68
Archer, John, 285n, 347; at Arnhem, 169, 226n, 227, 229; and millenarianism, 229-30, 332
Archibald, Robert, 433
Arminius, Jacobus, 47, 54
Argyle, Archibald Campbell, Earl of: Argyle's Rebellion, 398, 433
Arnway, John, 381n
Ask, Edward, 226
Aspinwall, William, 131, 133
Athias, Joseph, 73, 310
Augustine, Saint of Hippo, 457
Avery, Joseph, 258
Avery, Samuel, 237, 244n, 247, 250, 258-59

Bachelor, John, 173, 347
Bachelor, Samuel, 183, 188, 237, 262, 264, 329, 347; at Gorinchem, 275-76; and English Synod, 290, 294-306 *passim*
Backus, Isaac, 77
Baillie, Robert, 69, 78, 89, 173, 180, 209, 210, 231, 343, 347, 385; gathers Presbyterian support in Neth., 365-67
Balcanqual, Walter, 355-56
Bale, John, 14
Balfour, John, 432n, 436

Balmford, Samuel, 112, 296, 301-02, 329, 366, 386; at The Hague, 143-53
Bamfield, Joseph, 397, 398
Bancroft, Richard, 70, 76n
Barkely, Thomas, 163-64, 276, 290, 292-96
Barkley (Barclay), George, 433n, 453
Barrow, Henry (Barrowists), 25, 27, 46, 47, 61
Basson, Govert, 142
Basson, Thomas, 142, 335
Bastwick, John, 73, 126, 310, 311, 313, 315
Batt, Timothy, 279-80, 349
Baxter, Richard, 359, 429, 435
Bayle, Pierre, 4, 44
Bayley, George, 47
Bayly, Lewis, 310, 359
Baynes, Paul, 71, 347, 358-59
Baynham, Theophilus, 379, 386
Beauchamp, John, 64
Beauchamp, Richard, 75, 108
Beaumont, George, 143, 154-56, 173, 248-50, 252, 276-77, 352-53, 384, 386
Bennet, Edward, 243, 258
Bennet, Richard, 64
Berman, William, 433n
Bernard, Richard, 62, 66, 137
Best, John, 214, 220, 450, 452-53
Best, John, Jr., 453
Best, William, 98, 116, 117, 118, 119, 121, 220n, 328-29, 335, 452
Bethel, Slingsby, 412
Birkhead, Christopher, 197, 350
Black, John, 283
Blackader, John, 432n, 433
Blackwell, Francis, 51, 67, 71
Blagrave, Jonathan, 419
Blair, David, 143, 418, 453
Blake, Edmund, 69n, 73
Blancquius, John, 125
Blon, Daniel Le, 403
Bogerman, Johannes, 334
Bohemus, Mauritius, 402, 403
Bolton, Robert, 359
Boreman, Ds., 429
Borselen Family (at Veere), 206, 207
Borstius, Jacobus, 133, 184, 363, 435
Bosher, Robert S., 381
Boswell, Sir William, 4, 17, 18, 20, 38, 74, 76, 104, 115, 144-52, 156, 157, 217, 218, 220, 233, 238-46, 252, 270-

71, 312-16, 352-53, 363, 380, 384; and English Synod, 287, 301-06
Bowie, Philip, 143, 148, 255, 418-20, 439, 444
Bowie, Walter, 214, 219, 225, 275, 391
Bowman, Christopher, 48n, 49, 50
Bowrey, Thomas, 162, 408, 412
Boynton, Sir Matthew, 226
Bradford, William, 25, 135, 136
Bradshaw, Richard, 260
Bradshaw, William, 308, 342, 347
Bragge, Robert, 453
Brewer, Thomas, 126, 141-42
Brewster, William, 134, 135, 137, 141-42, 309
Brereton, Sir William, 43, 69, 98, 132, 145, 182, 184, 323, 327
Bridge, William, 163, 168-73, 270, 285n, 286, 325, 332
Bridgman, Richard, 387
Brightman, Thomas, 332
Brinsley, John, 356
Brinsley, Robert, 398n
Broerss, Joost, 310
Brough, William, 381n
Broughton, Hugh, 23-24, 28, 33, 71, 92, 233, 331, 336
Brown, Edward, 223
Brown, James, 177, 432
Brown, John, 399, 432, 433, 435-36
Brown, William, 224, 454
Browne, Robert, 10, 22, 40; at Middelburg, 29-33
Browne, Robert (of Veere), 208
Browne, Thomas, 155-56, 353, 383-84
Browne, Sir William, 36, 200
Bruyningh, Joseph, 74
Bruyningh, Susanna, 74
Bruyningh, Widow (Mrs. Joseph), 412
Bullen, Daniel, 381n
Bulward, Robert, 59, 100
Burgess, John, 143, 144
Burghley, William Cecil, Lord, 26
Burnet, Gilbert, 412, 420-21, 453, 455
Burrage, Champlin, 68
Burroughes, Jeremiah, 163, 168-72, 230n, 270, 285n, 313, 332, 378
Burton, Henry, 73, 310, 315
Burton, Major, 397
Busher, Leonard, 81, 82, 83, 460
Butler, John, 269, 274
Butler, Thomas, 279, 281

Cade, Thomas, 381n
Calamy, Edmund (1671-1732), 327, 409, 452-53

Calandrine, Lewis, 398n
Calderwood, David, 71, 72, 138, 142, 235, 309, 343, 432n
Cameron, Richard, 399n, 432-33, 434
Campbell, George, 433n
Canin, Isaac, 308
Canne, John, 55, 140, 174, 320, 332, 338-41, 346; at Amsterdam, 68-69, 408; printer, 72-73, 75, 76, 117, 309, 311, 315-16
Cargil, Donald, 432n
Carleton, Sir Dudley, 9, 130, 142, 144, 146, 162, 201, 214, 235, 264, 308, 327, 355-56, 370; and English Synod, 285-300
Carleton, George, 296, 354-56
Carleton, Guy, 381n
Carr, William, 400-01, 409, 411, 412
Carstares, John, 399n, 432
Carstares, William, 126, 415, 416, 433n, 453, 455
Carter, Alice C., 328
Cartwright, Thomas, 29, 38, 40, 132, 142, 319-22; and Merchant Adventurers, 16-23, 30n, 39, 233; against Brownists, 22-23, 32
Casaubon, Isaac, 363
Castellanus, Daniel, 125
Caton, William, 196, 349
Cawton, Thomas, 133, 163, 166, 174-75, 361, 363, 380, 431
Cecil, Edward, Viscount Wimbledon, 213, 262n, 268, 294
Chadwick, Owen, 9
Chalfont, Richard, 382
Chalmer, John, 208, 433n, 447-48
Charke, William, 16n
Charles I, 235-36, 242, 275, 300, 306, 354; execution of, 387-88
Charles II, 156, 255, 272, 380, 382, 420, 434, 436, 441
Chauncey, Ichabod, 398n
Christiaensz, Willem, 75, 142, 311-12, 314-15, 360
Chudleigh, Thomas, 423-24
Clapham, Henoch, 61-62, 78-79
Clare, Andrew, 382
Clark, Alexander, 266, 269, 279
Clark, George, 213-14, 262, 265, 294-95
Clarkson, David, 429
Clayton, George, 47
Clayton, Ralph, 214, 216n, 223
Clerk, Sir John, 433
Clifford, Abraham, 398n
Clifton, Richard, 64, 70, 135
Clyfton, Edward, 100

INDEX OF PERSONS

Clyfton, Mary, 100
Cocceius, Johannes, 362, 443
Cockyn, Robert (alias Leonard Verse), 140, 312
Coke, John, 244
Coke, Roger, 6
Cokrie, Elizabeth, 413n
Cole, William, 14, 15
Collins, Robert, 398n
Collins, Thomas, 453
Collinson, Patrick, 15
Colvill, William, 220-21; 390
Constable, Sir William, 226
Cook, Nicolas, 47
Cooper, William, 145, 154, 278, 279-81, 366, 382, 405
Coorne, Cornelius, 189, 440-41
Corker, Francis, 381n
Cotton, John, 133, 139, 165, 193, 347
Coughen, Jan, 414
Covel, John, 419-20
Coverdale, Miles, 14
Cowper, Patrick, 433n
Crafford, Thomas, 73, 74, 75, 316
Cranmer, William, 253
Craven, Lord William, 144
Creighton, Robert, 220, 381n
Cromwell, John, 154, 277
Cromwell, Oliver, 122, 156, 210, 221, 254, 265, 447
Cromwell, Oliver (son of Henry Cromwell), 410
Cross, Francis, 398n
Cross, Walter, 453
Cruickshank, Charles, 263
Cuningham, Thomas, 209, 210, 389

Daniel, Mr., 312-13
Danvers, Henry, 398n
D'Aranda, Peter, 410, 453
Davenant, John, 355
Davenport, George, 381n
Davenport, John, 131, 146, 147, 149, 191, 202, 285n, 301, 305-06, 310, 318; at Amsterdam, 97, 112-19; at Rotterdam, 163, 166, 167, 172
Davies, Horton, 322
Davison, William, 15, 16, 18, 19, 234
Dawes, Thomas, 58
Dawson, John, 207
Day, Gamaliel, 123, 262, 279, 280n, 283, 296, 299
Dell, Richard, 269-71, 279, 352, 391
Delme, Elie, 278
Denham, Sir John, 379
Denman, Zacharias, 269, 273-74

Dennis, Thomas, 278, 335, 357n
Descartes, René, 4
Desborough, John, 397
Dexter, Henry Martyn, 413
Dibbet, Francis, 184-85, 227
Dibdale, John, 382-83
Dickey, Thomas, 47
Dieu, Daniel de, 36
Dieu, Ludovicus de, 200
Dod, John, 360
Dodd, Randall, 93n
Domcelius, Petrus, 266, 268
Dorislaus, Isaac, 384, 387
Dorvile, Willem, 405n
Douglas, John, 92, 163, 213-14, 222, 335
Douglas, Thomas, 433n
Downham, George, 459
Downing, Sir George, 8, 156, 380, 387, 425
Drake, John, 188-91, 297, 324
Drummond, Sir Patrick, 208, 210, 389
Druw, John, 84
Druw, Joseph, 84
Durant, John, 398n
Dury, John, 155, 250-52, 257-60, 366
Dury, Robert, 93n, 125-26, 134, 199-200, 207, 432n
Dyke, Daniel, 359

Earle, John, 382
Eaton, Samuel, 119-20, 167, 172, 285n, 333, 347
Ecluse, Jean de l', 48, 49, 50, 64, 65, 68, 69, 71, 92, 138, 337
Edmunds, Sir Clement, 354
Edwards, Robert, 251
Edwards, Thomas, 170, 227, 228, 229, 231, 344, 365, 380
Elborough, Jeremiah, 205, 214, 216, 222, 256-60, 297, 352, 387
Elizabeth I, 3, 13, 15, 369
Elizabeth, Queen of Bohemia, 144-45, 151, 154-55, 156, 299, 303, 352, 380, 382
Elliott, Leonard, 18
Ellison, Mr. (son of Col. Ellison), 410
Episcopius, Simon, 334
Erskine, John, 409, 433, 452-53
Evenhuis, R. B., 93
Ewing, Thomas, 208

Faire, Col., 397
Faye, James De La, 214, 450, 453
Fen, Humphrey, 38
Fenner, Dudley, 19, 23, 24n, 233, 319-21
Fenwick, John, 257

Ferrers, Thomas, 26
Ferguson, Robert, 409, 411, 455
Fields, Alexander, 432n
Firsby, Mr., 279
Fitts, Hugo, 201, 204; at Amsterdam, 405n, 406; at Flushing, 444-46
Fitts, Hugo (merchant), 75
Fitts, Mr. (chaplain at Flushing), 36
Fleming, Robert, 177, 432-35, 436
Fleming, Robert, Jr., 126, 177, 323, 415, 417, 432
Fletcher, Thomas, 116, 118
Foot, John, 270, 313
Forbes, Alexander, 343-44, 365, 368
Forbes, James, 344n
Forbes, John, 93n, 102, 116, 125, 143, 157, 164, 183, 199, 207, 233, 267, 269, 275, 329, 334, 343, 432n; minister to Merchant Adventurers, 24, 28, 111-12, 235, 237-47, 250; and English Synod, 164, 183, 205, 222, 240, 290-306 *passim*
Forbes, John (of Corse), 93n, 121, 210, 229, 381n, 389-90
Forbes, Patrick, 93n, 157-58, 160, 262, 269-71, 343, 344n, 391
Ford, Richard, 380
Forme, James, 279-80, 295
Forrester, James, 433n
Forrester, Thomas, 433
Forrett, John, 208, 209
Fortescue, Sir John, 263
Forty, Isaac, 214, 222-23, 225
Fowler, John, 100
Frater, Arthur, 449
Frederick of Bohemia (Winter King), 145
Freezer, Augustine, 255, 439
Frith, John, 14
Fuller, Thomas, 3, 9, 16, 23
Furly, Benjamin, 427

Gataker, Thomas, 361
Gatford, Lionel, 260
Gedney, James, 172
Gerard, Thomas (son of Capt. Gerard), 410
Gerritsz, Lubbert, 82
Gilgate, William, 70
Gillespie, George, 180
Gilpin, Bernard, 14
Gilpin, George, 18, 234
Glover, Samuel, 384
Gomarus, Franciscus, 125, 362
Gooch, Stephen, 172
Goad, Thomas, 355-56
Goodwin, Thomas, 72, 169, 227, 229, 230, 260, 332, 359, 378. and *Sions Glory*, 230, 332
Goodyear, Hugh, 20, 222, 292-94, 304, 320, 329; minister at Leiden, 126-34, 136, 139, 141
Gordon, Charles, 208, 447
Goring, George, Col. 262n
Gouge, Thomas, 409-10
Greenhill, William, 168, 285n, 313
Greenwood, John, 25, 27-28, 46, 48
Greenwood, Mr. (of Amsterdam), 69
Grey, Henry, 92
Gribius, Petrus, 188, 192, 194, 195, 278, 283, 322, 372
Griffeth, Mr., 453
Griffin, Thomas, 260
Grim, Egbert, 132, 297, 304
Grindal, Edmund, 15
Goffe, Stephen, 65, 112, 115, 127, 130, 132, 143, 169, 247, 262-63, 265, 276, 296-97, 303-04, 352-53, 363, 379
Grotius, Hugo, 357, 363-64
Grove, David, 47
Gunter, John, 260

Hales, John, 264, 356
Hall, Joseph, 77, 355
Hamilton, Archibald, 382
Hamilton, John, 448
Hamilton, Sir Robert, 432-33, 437
Hancock, John, 81
Harris, Francis, 279
Harris, George, 347
Harris, Malachi, 155, 214, 218, 225, 352-53, 372, 382
Harrison, Henry, 411
Harrison, Robert, 22, 29-34, 40, 142
Hartly, John, 125
Harvey, John, 433n
Harwood, Edward, Col., 262n, 297
Hassall, John, 143, 144, 145, 163, 262n, 294-95
Hasty, Alexander, 433n, 453
Hatton, Lord Christopher, 388
Hayes, Israel (son of Alderman Hayes), 410, 411
Haynes, Mr. (son of Hezekiah Haynes), 410
Helwys, Thomas, 65, 67, 81, 89, 399
Henrietta Maria: seeks Royalist support in Neth. 379
Herbert, Col., 262
Hering, John, 214, 217, 225
Hering, Julius, 6n, 93, 97, 120, 121, 217, 285n
Hexham, Henry, 158, 159, 161, 267

INDEX OF PERSONS

Heylyn, Peter, 21, 380
Heywood, Richard, 174n
Hickman, Henry, 126, 415-16, 398n
Higgins, John, 351
Higgs, Griffin, 145, 303, 352-53
Hildersam, Arthur, 125, 360
Hill, Francis, 309
Hill, Joseph, 163, 188, 189, 191, 392-93, 398n, 402, 403, 415, 428-30, 444
Hill, Joseph, Jr., 163, 428
Hill, Thomas, 18
Hillen, Francis, 172
Hilliard, Joseph, 437
Hodge, Alexander, 93, 97, 158, 402-03, 405, 423, 398n
Hoffman, Melchior, 80, 82
Hollis, Col., 304
Holmes, Matthew, 23, 24n, 28, 233
Holmes, Nathaniel, 327
Hommius, Festus, 136, 139
Honywood, Michael, 220, 381n
Hoog, John, 177, 432-33, 436
Hoog, Thomas, 158, 177, 423-24, 432-33, 447-48; Hoog family, 432
Hooker, Richard, 459
Hooker, Thomas, 131, 146, 147, 166, 172, 191, 285n, 297, 301, 305-06, 311, 320, 329, 358-59; at Amsterdam, 97, 102-11, 113; at Delft, 111, 237-38
Hooper, George, 419-20
Hoornbeek, Johannes, 141, 165, 367
Hornius, Georgius, 165, 230
Howe, John, 398n, 429, 453
Howell, James, 4, 43, 50, 188
Howell, Roger, 11
Howell, William, 279-82, 294-95
Howie, John, 432
Hughes, Andrew, 268, 294-95
Hughes, Jacobus, 216n
Hulse, Edward, 398n
Hunter, Andrew, 38, 262, 294-95
Hyts, Richard, 265

Joachimi, Albert, 149
Jacob, Henry, 23, 24n, 32, 68, 136, 137, 233, 294n, 320n, 341, 345-46. *See also* Jacobites
James I (VI), 77, 95, 199, 215, 235-36, 290-92, 296, 298, 355, 372
Jansson, Johannes, 75, 309
Jay, George, 381n
Jay, Samuel, 256
Jepson, William, 139
Jermyn, Michael, 145
Jewson, Charles, B., 172
Johnson, Francis, 33, 71, 77-78, 81, 141, 307, 336, 340; at Middelburg, 23-28, 190, 233, 239; at Amsterdam, 46-67, 70
Johnson, George, 34, 48, 49, 55-65 *passim*, 70, 71, 77, 78
Johnson, Israel, 46, 47, 48, 62
Johnson, Jacob, 100
Johnson, Sampson, 145, 151-52, 154, 269, 272-73, 303, 335, 352, 379
Johnson, Thomasine Boys (Mrs. Francis), 63-64
Johnson, William, 381n
Jones, Thomas, 381n
Jones, Mr. (Merchant Adventurer), 253
Jordan, John, 45, 88-89, 94
Joye, George, 14
Junius, Franciscus, 52, 71

Keble, John, 139
Ken, Thomas, 419-20
Kennedy, Sir Andrew, 446
Kennedy, James, 447
Kick, Abraham (of Amsterdam), 410, 411, 425
Kick, Abraham (of Delft), 410n, 425
Kier, Andrew, 269, 273
Killigrew, Henry, 15
Kirkton, James, 433
Knell, Paul, 381n
Knewstub, John, 38
Knyviton, George, 48n, 50
Koelman, Jacobus, 358, 433, 435, 437

Lambert, John, 14
Lambert, John (murderer), 216
Laren, Arnold van, 196, 201, 203, 204, 205, 393-94, 444-45
Laud, William, 11, 144, 286, 313, 356; campaign against Puritanism in Neth., 144-52, 236-37, 241, 244-51, 259, 264-65, 270, 288-89, 297, 300-04, 308, 314-17, 369-71; supporters of in Neth., 154-55, 247, 250, 259-60, 270, 276-77, 279, 303, 352-53, 363-64, 372
Lawne, Christopher, 34, 56, 65, 81, 99-100
Lawrence, Henry, 226-28, 230, 231, 349
Lawrence, Richard, 398n, 408
Leamer, Thomas, 82
Leask, John, 189, 405, 440-41
Laet, Johannes de, 363
Lee, Isaac, 387
Leicester, Robert Dudley, Earl of, 35-39, 213, 234, 369-70
Leighton, Alexander, 73, 126, 214, 216, 223, 285n, 309-10, 317
Leslie, Henry, 381n

Levistone, Col., 216
Lickly, James, 449
Lilburne, Henry, 425
Lilburne, John, 307, 313, 315, 380
Lisle (L'Isle), Robert Sidney, Viscount (1536-1626), 25, 26, 35, 36, 198
Lisle, Robert Sidney, Viscount (1595-1677), 294
Livingstone, John, 399n, 432n
Lloyd, John, 382
Lloyd, William, 419-20
Locke, John, 412
Lockyer, Nicholas, 398n, 427
Loddington, Nicholas, 19
Loe, William, 256-57
Lowen, John, 381n
Ludlow, Edmund, 397
Lushe, John, 47

MacDowell, William, 380
MacDuff, Alexander, 208, 210, 291, 294-95
Mackinzie, John, 279n
MacWard, Robert, 177, 399, 432-33, 434-36, 450-51
Maden, Richard, 93, 121-22, 214, 382-83, 387, 392, 402
Maden, Richard, Jr., 163, 402, 428-30
Mainestone, Willem, 47
Maire, Johannes le, 76, 315-18, 363
Malbon, Samuel, 398n, 404, 408
Maling, Miles, 282, 294-95
Man (Manning), Edward, 108
Maplet, John, 381
Maresius, Samuel, 367
Marsden, Gamaliel, 398n
Marshall, Thomas, 250, 253-55, 363
Martin, Edward, 220, 381n
Martin, Henry, 78, 81, 82
Mary II, Princess of Orange, 417, 419-21, 437, 454
Mary, Princess of Orange (daughter of Charles I), 154-55, 219, 252, 272, 353, 379, 382, 384
Masson, Samuel, 255, 439
Mastricht, Petrus van, 358, 435
Mather, Cotton, 106, 237
Mather, Increase, 345
Mather, Nathaniel, 163, 398n, 428
Matley, Richard, 59n
Matthews, Edward, 412
May, Abigail, 74, 412
May, Henry, 64, 65, 68, 74
May, Henry (supporter of Monmouth), 407-08, 410, 411
May, Lidia, 413n

Mead, Joseph, 331
Mead, Matthew, 398n, 409, 411, 453
Megapolensis, Samuel, 184, 201, 204, 438-39, 444-46
Melville, Andrew, 236, 316
Mercer, Robert, 93n, 351
Mercer, Stanshal, 47
Mewes, Peter, 381n
Michael (Mitchell), David, 269, 273, 383, 390
Michaelson, John, 381n
Miles, Dr., 145
Miller, Perry, 457
Milling, John, 126, 415
Milling, Robert, 148, 415, 421
Milton, John, 257
Misselden, Edward, 11, 18, 45, 258-59, 303-04, 311; against Puritans at Delft, 237-47; memo on Dutch-English affairs, 241-43; a Ramist, 320-21
Mitchell, Thomas, 78, 79
Mitchell, William, 417
Moncrief, William 453
Monmouth, James Scott, Duke of: Rebellion of, 398, 403, 452; supporters at Amsterdam, 398, 410-11
Morgan, Sir Charles, 157, 262, 265, 275, 304, 306
Morgan, Elizabeth Marnix, 157
Morley, George, 145, 154-55, 353, 381-83
Morgan, Louis, 279, 280n
Morgan, Thomas, 281
Morton (Murton), Janneke, 85
Morton, Thomas, 266
Mountague, William, 43, 145, 401, 418, 440, 444
Moryson, Fynes, 12, 35, 123, 157, 187
Mowbray, Thomas, 208, 447
Moxon, James, 158, 313-14
Munter, Jan, 83, 88, 89
Murton, John, 81, 85. *See also* Janneke Morton

Nalton, James, 174, 380
Neal, Daniel, 29
Neile, Richard, 286
Nesbet, John, 432n, 453
Nethenus, Matthias, 133, 358-59, 435
Nevay, John, 399n, 432, 435
Newcome, Henry, 429
Newcomen, Matthew, 126, 398n, 415
Nokes, William, 453
Nolthenius, Georgius, 360
Noper, Mattheus, 443
Norringham, Mr., 262n
Northleigh, John, 368, 427

INDEX OF PERSONS

Norton, John, 365
Nosche, Joacham, 310
Nuttall, Geoffrey F., 137
Nye, Philip, 169, 227, 230, 285n

Offwood, Stephen, 57, 65, 74, 100, 103, 111, 116
Offwood, Susanna, 74
Ogle, Sir John, 92, 213, 262n
Oldsworth, Mr., 246
Oostrum, Adriaan, 93, 402-03, 405
Orange, Prince of, 269, 181, 273; Frederick Hendrik, 219-19; William II, 155; William III, 398, 416, 418, 420-21, 437, 455
Osborne, John, 100, 108
Oswald, John, 182-83, 295, 298
Overton, Richard, 86
Oxford, Robert de Vere, Earl of, 283-84

Paget, John, 131, 133, 137, 143, 146, 147, 166, 202, 262n, 263, 285n, 324, 328; against Separatism, 45, 48, 50, 51, 52, 55, 56, 63, 66, 67, 68, 69, 72, 96-97, 99-100; on Anabaptism, 76-77, 87-89; Minister at Amsterdam, 92-120; and English Synod, 289-94, 303; defender of Presbyterianism, 333, 342-43, 346, 366n
Paget, Robert, 133, 184-86, 342-43, 363, 438-39
Paget, Thomas, 93, 120, 122, 285n, 342-43
Paginham, Philip, 262
Paine, Steven, 266-67, 296-98, 304, 330
Palmer, John, 283
Palmer, Mr., 183
Park, Robert, 158-160, 163-72, 285n, 332, 347, 367
Parker, Robert, 24n, 59, 95, 96n, 97, 116, 136, 263, 282, 344, 367
Parsons, Thomas, 282, 297
Partridge, John, 409
Payne, John, 48, 78
Peacock, Mr., 453
Pedder, Leonard, 78, 81, 82, 89
Penn, William, 350, 427
Penry, John, 46
Pepys, Samuel, 429
Perkins, William, 359, 361, 458
Peter, Hugh, 67, 102, 116, 133, 237-39, 250, 252, 275, 285n, 296,, 298, 301-306, 310, 320, 329, 384; at Rotterdam, 163-67, 172-73
Petrie, Alexander, 176-80, 332-33, 363, 366, 389, 431

Petrie, Alexander, Jr., 158, 161, 177, 181, 423
Peyton, Sir Robert, 412
Phelps, Robert (son of John Phelps), 410
Phillips, John, 202n
Philips, Dirk, 80
Philips, Humphrey, 398n
Pigott, William, 81
Plancius, Petrus, 53, 63
Plater, Richard, 71, 100, 275, 309
Polwheel, Degory, 381n
Polyander, Johannes, 136, 362
Poole, Matthew, 398n, 403
Porterfield, John, 210
Posthumus, N. W., 124
Potts, Lawrence, 23, 24n, 36, 198n
Potts, Thomas, 27, 36-37, 93, 95, 97, 102, 198-200, 292-95
Potts, Thomas, Jr., 201-04, 214, 220
Poulter, Henry, 119, 121
Price, John, 143, 418-19
Price, William, 93, 97, 122, 254, 387
Prickett, Robert, 181
Prince, Francis, 407, 410
Prynne, William, 73, 252, 311-12, 315, 359-60
Pygott, Thomas, 84
Pyl, Simon van der, 204, 444-45

Quarles, John, 244n, 245n
Quick, John, 189, 191-92, 196, 203, 323, 334, 338, 362, 398, 407, 440-41; *Icones* of, 194, 443

Ramus, Peter, 320-21, 458
Ratcliffe, Hugh, 18
Ray, John, 265, 268
Raymond, Thomas, 143
Remington, Robert, 219, 225
Renwick, John, 432n, 437
Reyner, Edward, 231
Reyner, John, 398n, 427-28
Reynolds, John, 141
Richardson, Edward, 126, 158, 160, 415-16, 398n, 403, 414, 427-28
Richardson, Samuel, 260
Rider, Dudley, 429
Ries, Hans de, 82
Riggs, Edward, 398n, 427
Rivetus, Andreas, 362
Robarts, Francis, 429
Robinson, John, 24n, 64, 68, 70, 77-78, 142, 335, 336, 340-41; at Amsterdam, 66-67, 96; at Leiden, 134-40, 341; a semi-Separatist, 137-39, 341
Robinson, Mrs. John, 133, 139, 140-41

Robertson, George, 208
Roe, John, 195, 201-02, 204, 283, 297-98, 374
Rogers, John, 14
Rogers, John (Fifth Monarchist), 398n, 449
Rogers, Peter, 266, 279-81, 294-96
Rothe, Johannes, 416
Rowland, John, 381n
Roy, William, 14
Roystone, Mr., 183
Rule, Gilbert, 398n
Rulice, Johannes, 93, 97, 120
Rushe, Nicholas, 180, 183, 288, 348
Russel, Andrew, 434
Rutherford, Samuel, 435

Saltonstall, Sir Richard, 226
Sampson, Henry, 398n
St. John, Oliver, 154
Sancroft, William, 220, 381n, 400
Saravia, Hadrian, 363-64
Schie, Wilhelm van, 158, 423-26
Schilders, Richard, 20, 28, 31, 39, 308
Schurman, Anna Maria van, 358, 443
Sclaer, Mr., 262, 283, 297, 301-04
Scott, Thomas, 214-16, 222, 263, 285n, 290, 294-96, 352
Scull, Thomas, 410
Seamer, Thomas, 81
Sedgewick, Obadiah, 262n
Sedgwick, Richard, 256, 258
Seroyen, Michael, 37, 180
Settle, Thomas, 70
Sewel, J. W., 351
Sewel, William, 351
Shaftesbury, Anthony Ashley Cooper, Earl of, 411
Shepheard, Nicolas, 188, 440-41
Sheringham, Robert, 155, 353
Shields, John, 432n
Shower, John, 430
Sibbald, Henry, 246, 262, 279, 281, 296-97
Sibbes, Richard, 359
Sidney, Sir Philip, 36
Sidney, Sir Robert. *See* Lisle, Viscount (1563-1626)
Simons, Menno, 77, 80
Simpson, James, 399n, 432
Simpson, Sydrach, 163, 168-73, 285n, 325, 378
Sinclair, John, 158, 423, 433n, 453
Skase, John, 188, 193, 405
Skelton, Bevil, 452
Slade, Allis (Mrs. Matthew), 92n

Slade, Matthew, 50, 54, 63, 65, 67, 91-92, 334, 336
Smith, John (son of High Justice Blagrave), 410
Smith, Ralph, 133
Smith, Walter, 432n
Smyth, John, 58, 62, 65, 67, 70, 324, 339, 460; and English Anabaptist church of Amsterdam, 79-89 *passim*
Smyth, William, 49, 70
Snelling, Robert, 202
Snype, Andrew, 177, 208, 211, 447
Spademan, John, 163, 398n, 405, 421, 428-30
Spang, William, 188-90, 196, 205-06, 208-11, 343, 365-66, 385, 389, 391, 440
Spang, William, Jr., 188-89, 193, 440-41
Spranckhuysen, Dionysius, 158
Stafford, Thomas, 74-75
Stam, Jan Fredericksz, 72-74, 75, 309
Stamp, William, 145, 154-55, 352, 381-82
Stanley, William, 419-20
Staresmore, Sabine, 68, 71, 117, 137, 341
Stell, Hans, 308
Stephenson, James, 380, 381n
Steven, William, 178, 180, 197, 232, 276, 376, 393, 456
Steward, Richard, 381, 382
Stockbridge, Nicholas, 18
Stone, John, 276-77, 383
Stresso, Casper, 93n
Strickland, Walter, 154, 253, 380, 384
Stubbe, Alice, 22, 23
Stubbs, John, 196, 349
Studley, Daniel, 48n, 49, 50, 60, 61, 65
Swart, Steven, 74, 310, 412
Sydserff, George, 208-09
Symmons, Matthew, 310-12, 315
Symonds, Joseph, 163, 168-74, 285n, 349

Taffin, Jean de (Taffinus), 47, 54, 358
Taylor, Henry, 47
Taylor, Nathaniel, 453
Teellinck, Maximiliaan, 194, 201-04, 297
Teellinck, Johannes, 188, 193, 194
Teellinck, Willem, 193, 194, 202, 358-62
Temple, Sir William, 5, 43, 399, 435-36
Thatcher, Humble, 351
Thilenus, Johannes, 194, 362
Thompson, William, 433n
Thoresby, Ralph, 91
Thorndike, Herbert, 220, 381n
Thorne, George, 398n
Thorp, Giles, 64, 68, 71, 75, 142, 309
Throckmorton, Sir John, 37, 197-99
Thysius, Antonius, 362

Tilly, Joseph, 437
Tolwine, Father, 30
Tomson, Laurence, 16
Tory, Robert, 189, 398n, 440-41
Totter, Michael, 433n
Tozer, Henry, 250, 253, 382, 388
Trail, Robert, 399n, 432, 433n, 435
Trasy, John, 117
Travers, Walter, 16-21, 28, 29, 40, 233, 319-20
Trigland, Jacobus, 105
Turner, John, 404, 408
Tuthill, Henry, 314
Tyndale, William, 14

Udemans, G. C., 358

Vane, Sir Henry, 144, 146
Veitch, William, 432n
Vere, Sir Francis, 38
Vere, Sir Horace, 92, 143, 146, 247, 262, 267, 287, 288n, 297
Vere, Lady Mary, 146, 149, 287-88n
Verner, Patrick, 433
Veseler, Joris, 73, 75
Vincent, Mr. (chaplain), 262n
Vincent, John, 184
Volmarius, Jonas, 125
Voetius, Gisbertus, 9, 160, 217, 223, 225, 358-59, 361-62, 366; on English Synod, 306; on Congregationalism, 367-68
Vorstius (Konrad von der Vorst), 334, 355
Vossius, G. J., 115, 363-64
Vossius, Isaac, 363

Walaeus, Antonius, 136, 139, 362
Waldegrave, Robert, 20, 322
Wale, Edward, 168, 171-73, 285n, 286
Wallace, James, 399, 433, 435-36
Waller, Sir William, 397, 410, 411
Walls, George, 260
Walsingham, Sir Francis, 15, 19
Ward, John, 163, 168-73, 270, 285n, 286, 325

Ward, Samuel (Puritan), 216, 218
Ward, Samuel (of Sidney Sussex), 355-56
Warren, Mr., 260
Waters, George, 183, 308
Watson, William, 94n, 108
Watts, Michael, 342
Wedderburn, Alexander, 278
Wedderburn, John, 278
Weld, Thomas, 103
Whately, William, 359, 361
Wheelers (printer), 312
Whetstone, Walter, 268, 294-95
Whitaker, Henry, 94n
Whitaker, Samuel, 100
Whitaker, William, 118
William III, 454-55. *See also* Orange, Prince of
Widdows, Daniel, 269, 275-76, 282, 296-97
Wilford, Thomas, 8
Williams, Sir Roger, 34
Wilson, Mrs. John, 133
Wing, John, 143-44, 201-02, 204, 256-57; and English Synod, 290-99
Winslow, Edward, 137, 139, 141
Winwood, Sir Ralph, 134, 144, 289
Wishart, George, 381n
Witcomb, William, 47
Witt (De Witt family of Dort), 184
Wharton, John, 313
White, Capt., 397
White, John, 239
White, Thomas, 62-63, 70, 92
Whitgift, John, 23
Whittel, Mr., 255, 439
Woodcock, Thomas, 398n, 405, 453
Woodward, Richard, 93, 402-03
Wren, Matthew, 168, 216, 286n, 312, 318
Wright, Robert, 21

Yair, James, 448
Yard, James, 380
Young, Thomas, 256, 257

INDEX OF SUBJECTS AND PLACES

Amboyna massacre, 201
Amersfoort: English church at, 212, 222, 283-84
Amsterdam, 43-45, 380; immigration to, 4, 43-44, 400; English Reformed church at, 6, 91-122, 184, 387, 400-07, 412; Separatists at, 45-76, 99-100, 404, 407-14; Anabaptists at, 66-67, 76-90; churches after the Restoration, 400-01; Christ Church at, 406-07, 413
Anointing with oil, 229
Anabaptists, Anabaptism, 62, 161, 324, 335, 342, 447; at Naarden, 49, 78; at Amsterdam, 66-67, 76-90; relationship to Separatists, 76-78, 85-86, 89; at Rotterdam, 174; at Arnhem, 231; at Nijmegen, 280; development of English Anabaptism in the Neth., 348-49. *See also* Mennonites; Waterlanders
Ancient Church (Amsterdam), 45-76, 336; relationship with Leiden Separatists, 135, 137-38, 341, 407
Anglicanism: Anglican churches in the Neth., 10, 353, 406-07, 454; Anglican practices, 132, 145-46, 149-52, 154-55, 158, 218, 225, 247, 253, 255, 259-60, 270-72, 276-77, 283-84, 304, 352-53, 369, 381-84, 420-21; Dutch aversion to, 302, 363-64, 370, 372-73. *See also* ceremonies; England, Church of; Prayer Book
Antwerp, 14-21
Arianism, 79, 82
Arminianism, 121, 133, 138, 142, 213, 218, 249, 334, 355-57, 401
Arnhem: English church at, 168, 169, 184, 226-32, 331
Assimilation (into Dutch culture), 400, 455
Austin Friars Church (London), 27, 97, 158, 194, 385, 402

Bankruptcy, 99, 192, 247, 326
Baptism, 63, 104, 107, 113-15, 146, 200, 231, 238, 323, 326, 333
Baptists, 81, 348, 404
Bergen-op-Zoom: English church at, 38, 265-68, 304, 376
Bible, 339, 342; printing of, 73, 308-09, 314; Puritan view of, 458-59
Books: Puritan books, 215, 308-10, 319-20, 411; transportation and smuggling of, 310-12; translation into Dutch, 359, 435; Royalist books, 380, 381; Scottish books, 434. *See also* Bible; Printing
Brazil, 193
Breda: English church at, 268-74, 391; Treaty of Breda (1667), 394, 399, 435
Brielle (The Brill), 6, 34, 35, 143, 369; English church at, 35, 37, 180-82, 391
Brownists, 29-34, 45-70, 293-94, 305, 404; at Rotterdam, 162, 174; at Dort, 182. *See also* Separatists
Business ethics, 99, 185, 192, 326-27. *See also* Bankruptcy

Cambridge University, 180-81, 218, 362
Camphere, 282n
Campveere: See Veere
Catechism, 403
Catholics, Catholicism: English Catholics in the Neth., 11; practices introduced at Veere, 447; Anglicanism as popery, 152, 302
Ceremonies, 144, 151, 155, 270, 275, 277; Dutch aversion to, 302, 383, 385
Chaplains (military), 35-36, 143, 199, 213, 262-84, 288-89, 306; controversy between military and civilian people, 219
Cheshire, 92, 119, 285
Church: Puritan definition of, 224, 342
Citizenship (Dutch), 44, 200, 281, 380, 415, 436

Classes and Synods, 17, 325, 343
Cloth Trade, 7, 45, 437. *See also* Merchant Adventurers
Collegiants, 351
Collegium Qualificatum, 195, 203, 371
Confession: public confession, 192, 204, 425
Congregationalism, 172, 325, 459; developments at Amsterdam, 100-21; at Leiden, 131; at The Hague, 146-47; at Delft, 159-61, 424; at Rotterdam, 164-75, 431; in England and America, 172-74, 347; at Middelburg, 191, 196; at Arnhem, 227-31; at Hamburg, 257-58; 260; in the English Synod, 299, 305, 329-30; Non-Separatist Congregationalism, 344-48, 365-68. *See also* Jacobites; Independents; Separatists
Contra-Remonstrants, 138; Puritans and, 335-36. *See also* Dort, Synod of
Covenant (church), 128, 330-33, 345-47; at Middelburg, 25-26, 190; Separatist, 55-56, 338-39; at Amsterdam, 101-02; at Rotterdam, 164-66; at Middelburg, 190-91; at Arnhem, 229, 331; at Delft, 238-39. *See also* Presbyterian "canons."
Covenants (Scottish): Scottish National Covenant, 179, 269, 389, 433; Solemn League and Covenant, 209-10, 386
Covenanters, 177, 209, 273, 378, 388-91, 416, 431-37
Convention of Royal Burghs, 207, 208, 447
Council of State (Dutch), 245, 285, 290, 301, 303, 362
Credentials for ministers, 281, 282, 295, 297

Dedham Classis, 23
Delft: English church at, 6, 157-61, 367, 422-26; Merchant Adventurers at, 111, 236-48; Regicides at, 399
Democracy (church), 59-61, 100, 173, 324, 329, 339-40, 424
Discipline (church), 20, 58-59, 98-99, 128-30, 179, 185-86, 192-93, 204, 221, 326, 425, 442, 450
Dissenting Brethren, 168, 223, 227-28, 334, 347-48, 358
Doesburg: English church at, 282
Dort (Dordrecht): English church at, 182-86, 390-91, 437-39; Merchant Adventurers at, 182-83, 254-56; Scottish Staple at, 182, 446
Dort, Synod of, 138, 182, 296, 334, 355-57, 375
Douai, 23, 287
Dutch Reformed Church: and economics, 5; synods, 17, 39, 234; relationship to Netherlands English churches, 19, 91-95, 127, 130-31, 143, 147-48, 193-94, 221-24, 237, 271-73, 274, 279-83, 337-38, 370, 372-77, 430, 443-44; relationship to Separatists, 30, 33, 46-47, 49, 51-55, 57, 91-92, 135, 138, 139, 339, 404; *Engels gereformeerde gemeente*, 91, 127; English membership in Dutch classes, 92, 94-95, 178, 185-86, 193, 195-96, 202, 204-06, 211, 213, 267, 268, 272-73, 278, 283, 325, 373, 375, 416, 422, 424, 431, 438; relationship to Scottish churches, 178-79, 211; 357; relationship to Puritan movement, 193-94, 357-59; attitude and relationship to Church of England, 158, 195, 302, 354-68, 362-63, 382-83; support of Parliamentary side in English Revolution, 362. *See also* Reformed Church

East Anglia, 286, 347
Elders, 18, 36, 324, 329; power of, 61, 64-65, 173, 340; *jure divino*, 218, 366
Emden, 65, 67, 256
England: connections with the Neth., 3-12; Dutch immigrants in, 3-4; economic relations between England and Neth., 7-8
England, Church of: defended by Puritans, 20, 22-23, 96; condemned by Separatists, 32, 56, 59, 336; 39 Articles, 135, 155; Anglican churches and practices in the Neth., 353, 400-01, 406-07, 419-21, 422, 427, 454; condemned by Puritans, 270; relationship to Dutch Reformed Church, 354-58, 363-64, 383-84; in exile during English Revolution, 380-84. *See also* Anglicanism; ceremonies; Laud, William
English Revolution (1640s-50s), 121-22, 154-56, 203, 220, 252-54, 378-91; and Dutch Reformed Church, 364-68, 385. *See also* Royalists

English Synod, 94-95, 102, 130, 146, 205, 210, 285-306, 369, 370
Erastianism, 196
Excommunication, 54, 56, 59, 63, 340
Exiles: in Netherlands, 285-86, 400, 427-28; return home, 378, 455; ejected English nonconformists, 397-99; Scottish exiles, 399. *See also* Royalists
Extradition, 4-5, 399

Family of Love, 142
Feast Days (Dutch), 233; objected to by Puritans, 206; objected to by Scots, 334, 418
Fifth Monarchists, 69, 332, 410, 449
Flushing (Vlissingen), 3, 6, 34, 187, 369; English church at, 5, 35-37, 197-206, 298, 393, 444-46
Franeker University, 8, 188, 193, 202
Frankfurt, 10, 13
Free Will, 80, 82, 357
Freedom, religious, 460
French (Walloon) Churches, 48, 92, 95, 138, 182, 270-71, 278, 280, 289-90, 298, 337, 370, 377

Geertruidenberg: English church at, 279
Gelderland, Synod of, 280, 374
German Churches, 95, 143-44, 417-18
Glorious Revolution (1688), 409, 412, 417, 419, 454-56
Godliness, Doctrine of, 358-59, 362. *See also* Pietism
Gorinchem: English church at, 275-76
Gouda, 123, 283
Government: connection between churches and Dutch state, 94-95, 97-98, 152, 177-78, 195, 203, 215, 221, 368-72, 385, 402-06, 422, 430-31; financial support of English churches, 123, 157, 177, 189, 203, 205, 215, 262, 265, 269; dictates election of ministers, 405-06. *See also* States General
Grave: English church at, 283

Haarlem: English church at, 414
Hague, The: chaplain at, 37-38, 142-43; English Reformed church at, 142-58, 376, 386-87, 399, 417-22; Church of England (St. John and St. Philip) at, 422
Hamburg, 201, 216; Merchant Adventurers at, 256-61, 387
's-Hertogenbosch, 374; English church at, 277-79
Heusden: English church at, 185, 276-77
High Commission, 16, 18, 19, 59, 125, 149, 216, 317
Holland, States of, 123, 147-48, 162, 371-72
Holy Kiss, 229

Immigration: to the Neth., 3, 4, 5, 6, 7, 286-87; Dutch immigration to England, 3-4; to Amsterdam, 5, 43-44; to Leiden, 124; to Rotterdam, 168; to Arnhem, 226; return to England, 230-31, 378, 455. *See also* Exiles; Scotland
Incarnation: Anabaptist view of, 79, 82-83
Independents, Independency, 165, 185, 331, 332-33, 348, 367, 389, 398, 431; Independent church at Amsterdam, 404, 407-14
Indulgence, Declaration of, 409; Scottish indulgence, 434
Interlopers, 45
Investments (church), 442
Ireland: chaplains in; collections for, 364, 385

Jacobites (Henry Jacob), 294, 299, 305, 330, 343, 345
Jews, 44, 50

Kampen: Separatists at, 47-48, 78

Lancashire, 97, 119, 120, 158, 174
Language: use of English, 402-03, 405, 426, 429, 438, 445, 452; use of Dutch, 224, 431
Laying on of hands, 229
Lecturers, 114, 246, 430
Leeuwarden: English and Scots at, 437
Leiden, 362; English Reformed church at, 5, 123-34, 376, 415-17; chaplain at, 37-38; Separatists at, 134-41
Leiden University, 8, 52, 124, 136, 160, 357, 362-63, 366, 415
Levellers, 86, 460
Liturgy, 20, 146, 193, 238, 253, 267, 299, 322-23
Lord's Table (communion), 98, 144, 153, 185, 191, 221, 229, 238, 323, 450; tokens for, 98, 192, 323-24
London, 76, 78, 153, 174, 285, 347, 429, 430
Lutherans, 38, 253, 256

Maastricht: English church at, 283
Marian Exiles, 4, 9, 10, 13, 14
Marriage: Separatist marriage outside of own church, 57, 58, 59n
Mayflower, 134, 139
Medical doctors, 37, 216, 415, 428
Mennonites, 77, 80, 81-87, 348, 351, 357. *See also* Anabaptists; Waterlanders
Merchant Adventurers, 7, 45, 212, 233-61, 288-89; at Antwerp, 14-21; at Middelburg, 21-29, 187-88; at Rotterdam, 162, 167, 248-54; at Delft, 236-48; economic decline of, 243; at Hamburg, 243, 244, 247, 256-61; 387; at Dort 254-56, 439; and English Revolution, 385-86, 388
Middelburg: Merchant Adventurers at, 16, 21-29; Separatists at, 21-22, 25-28, 187; English Reformed church, 188-97, 386, 439-44, 449
Millenarianism, 177, 229-31, 331-33, 409, 411, 416

Naarden: Separatists at, 48, 78
Newcastle on Tyne, 10, 11, 257
New Drapery, 4, 124
New England, 3, 134, 139, 347; Dutch Congregationalists in, 167, 172
Nijmegen: English church at, 279-81
Nonconformists: English in Neth., 9; ejected nonconformists, 168, 285-87, 398
North Holland, Synod of, 53, 111, 292, 296, 364, 366, 373
Norwich, 10, 29, 31, 70, 76, 79, 168, 172, 215, 285-86, 299, 313, 424, 443
Nonsuch, Treaty of (1585), 34, 299, 369

Obedience to government, 246, 289
Ordination, 16, 21, 97, 127, 164, 168, 252, 270, 298, 300, 325, 433-34
Orphanages, 93, 401
Overijssel, Synod of, 373
Oxford University, 253, 274, 303, 362

Pacifism, 348
Parliament, 229, 231, 252, 253, 379, 384
Pernambuco, 275, 276n
Pietism, 357-59; Puritan piety, 457-58, 461
Pilgrim Fathers, 7; at Amsterdam, 50, 66-67, 96, 406; at Leiden, 124n, 139. *See also* Leiden; Separatists
Pilgrim Press: 23, 50, 141-42, 308
Plots, 433, 442; Popish Plot, 397; Rye House Plot, 409, 452, Yorkshire Conspiracy, 414-15. *See also* Rebellions s.v. Monmouth, Duke of; and Argyle, Earl of

Poor Relief, 179, 192-93, 213, 215, 221, 431, 442-43, 450
Prayer, 57-58, 330, 339; Lord's Prayer, 238
Prayer Book (Anglican), 13, 15, 19, 57, 93, 131-32, 144, 149, 155, 158, 234, 242, 246, 250, 253, 259-60, 270, 275-76, 283-84, 296, 299, 321, 352-53, 369-70, 421. *See also* Anglicanism; England, Church of
Precisionists, 357, 361
Presbyterians, Presbyterianism, 147, 161, 202, 252, 299, 305, 325, 334, 342-44, 365-68, 398, 424, 459; at Antwerp, 16-21; at Middelburg, 22, 28-29; John Paget and Amsterdam Presbyterianism, 92-121 *passim*, 403, 406; at Rotterdam English church, 174-75; at Rotterdam Scottish church, 175-80; at Dort, 185; at Middelburg, 193, 196; at Veere, 209-11; and Merchant Adventurers, 233-35, 239, 251-55, 257-60; Presbyterianism the model of Netherlands English churches, 321-25; Scottish Presbyterianism in exile, 432-37. *See also* Reformed Church
Presbyterian "canons": at Delft, 238-39; at Hamburg, 257-58
Printing: Separatist printing, 25, 28, 70-76; at Middelburg, 28, 30-31; at Amsterdam, 70-76, 412; at Leiden, 141-42; repression and censorship of book trade, 76, 307, 314-17; Puritan printing, 287, 306-18. *See also* Books; Pilgrim Press; Richt-Right Press
Privy Council, 245, 247, 288, 300
Prophesying, 169, 173, 229, 339-40
Puritanism: activities in Neth., 285-318; Puritan nonconformists in Neth., 285, 301; worship practices, 329-30; splintering into factions, 341-42, 459-60; relationship of English-Dutch-American Puritanism, 457-61; essence of, 457-58. *See also* Congregationalism, English Synod; Presbyterianism

Quakers, Quakerism: in Zeeland, 196-97; development in Neth., 349-52, 400, 414, 427; relationship to Mennonites, 351, 459-60

Readers, 215, 418, 426, 451
Rebels, 398-99, 410-12; Scottish, 423-24, 435-36
Reformed Church: English Reformed churches, 91, 319-21; theology and church practices in English churches, 98, 129, 191, 221, 298-99, 319-323, 369; Separatists and, 135, 138; English Synod and, 295-96. *See also* Dutch Reformed Church
Regicides, 398; Barkstead, Okey, and Corbet, 399, 465
Restoration (1660), 397-98, 438, 447, 460; refugees in Neth. after, 398n, 400, 403, 410-12, 427-28
Richt-Right Press, 72, 75, 309
Rotterdam: English churches at, 162-75, 376, 388, 399, 427-31, 455-56; Puritan college at, 166; Scottish church at, 175-80, 431-37; Covenanters at, 432-36
Royalists: emigrés in Neth., 153-56, 181, 220, 253, 272-74, 378-85; raising support in Neth., 379-80

Sabbath, Sabbatarianism, 80, 95-99, 101, 121, 129, 139, 204, 221, 326-29, 359-60, 361
Schools, 93, 162, 201, 215, 401, 429, 431; Puritan college at Rotterdam, 166, 287
Scotland, 31, 32; Scottish settlement and churches in Neth., 183, 189, 388, 406; Scots at Rotterdam, 162, 175-80, 389, 431-37; Scottish Revolution, 175, 179-80, 388-91; Scots at Veere, 176, 206-11, 389-90; Scottish-English antagonism in Neth., 181, 189-90, 213, 219, 224-25, 269-71, 390-91, 451; Scots at Utrecht, 219, 224-26; Scottish exiles, 197-200, 207, 220-21, 273, 363, 399, 424, 427, 431-33; repression of Scottish exiles, 435-36. *See also* Covenants; Covenanters; Soldiers
Scotland, Church of, 343, 406; relationship to church at Veere, 209, 210, 214, 325, 448-49; objections to Dutch liturgy and forms, 334, 418; relationship to Dutch Reformed Church, 357, 435; ministers serving in Neth., 445, 456; and Amsterdam English Reformed Church, 406
Separatists: at Middelburg, 21-22, 29-34; relationship with non-Separatist Puritans, 22, 32, 33, 137; at Amsterdam, 25, 28, 45-76, 95-97, 309, 404, 407-14, and printing,

30-31, 70-76; relationship to Church of England, 56, 59, 136, 336-37; relationship to Netherlands English churches, 56, 91-92, 104; at Leiden, 134-41; theology and practice of, 335-41, 344; and Dutch Reformed Church, 138, 337-40; more moderate position of, 136-139, 341; Semiseparatism, 137, 341
Sermons, 19, 321
Singing (hymns), 58, 229, 257, 321, 342
Socinianism, 151, 156
Soldiers: English soldiers in Neth., 5, 8, 34, 39-40, 182, 262-65; Scottish soldiers, 5, 38, 262-63, 268, 281; military chaplains, 35-36, 143, 213, 262-81; soldier's oath, 198; controversy between civilians and soldiers, 219, 225-26
South Holland, Synod of, 51, 127, 150, 160, 185, 289, 290, 297, 364, 366, 372-73; regulation of English churches by, 374-75
Star Chamber, 313, 314, 317
States General: financial support of English churches, 35, 153, 235, 262, 266, 269, 368; resolutions of, 150, 290, 299-301, 303-04, 370-71; Puritan influence at, 301, 303
Students: English students in Neth., 8, 124, 212; Scottish students, 357, 433. *See also* Franeker University; Leiden University; Utrecht University
Suffolk, 172, 202

Tervere: See Veere
Theater, 163, 360
Tiel: English church at, 283
Toleration: Dutch toleration, 5, 6-7, 44, 66
Travelers: English travelers in Neth., 11

United Societies (Scotland), 434, 437
Usury, 327
Utrecht: chaplain at, 37-38, 213; English Reformed church at, 5, 184, 203, 212-26, 362, 376, 391, 449-54; Holy Trinity Church, 454
Utrecht, Synod of, 222, 283, 373
Utrecht University, 8, 160, 212, 361, 366-67, 449, 452-53

Veere (also Campveere), 246, 283; Scottish church at, 28, 176, 195, 206-11, 446-49; Scottish Staple at, 206, 446-47
Viana, 226

War, 397; First Anglo-Dutch War (1652-54), 392; Second Anglo-Dutch War (1665-67), 274, 392, 402; Third Anglo-Dutch War (1672-74), 392-94, 428, 441; French War (1672-78), 445, 451-52; French Revolutionary Wars, 208, 454
Waterlander Mennonites, 81, 83, 84-86
Wesel: English church at, 283
West India Company (Dutch), 94, 193, 275
Westminster Assembly, 122, 153, 219, 229, 231, 253, 348, 364-66, 386, 389
Women, 164, 173, 324-25, 329, 331, 333-34, 400
Worship, 19, 20, 300, 322; Separatist, 58, 336; Puritan, 329-30
Worship Books: *Booke of the Forme* used by Dutch Puritans, 20, 39, 132, 234, 305, 322, 330; printed by Schilders, 20, 28; other worship books, 193, 267, 322-23

York, Yorkshire, 10, 119, 161, 226, 286, 403n
Yarmouth, 168, 217, 313

Zeeland: "Puritanical" religion of, 193-94; contacts with English Puritan, 194
Zeeland, Synod of, 364, 385
Zutphen: English church at, 281-82
Zwolle: English church at, 283
Zwolse Bible, 212

www.ingramcontent.com/pod-product-compliance
Lightning Source LLC
Chambersburg PA
CBHW080531300426
44111CB00017B/2678